Human Resource Management

KENT *Series in Management*

Barnett/Wilsted, Strategic Management: Concepts and Cases
Barnett/Wilsted, Strategic Management: Text and Concepts
Barnett/Wilsted, Cases for Strategic Management
Berkman/Neider, The Human Relations of Organizations
Carland/Carland, Small Business Management
Crane, Personnel: The Management of Human Resources, Fourth Edition
Davis/Cosenza, Business Research for Decision Making, Second Edition
Dowling/Schuler, International Dimensions of Human Resource Management
Finley, Entrepreneurship
Kirkpatrick, Supervision: A Situational Approach
Mitchell, Human Resource Management: An Economic Approach
Nkomo/Fottler/McAfee, Applications in Personnel/Human Resource Management: Cases, Exercises, and Skill Builders
Plunkett/Attner, Introduction to Management, Third Edition
Punnett, Experiencing International Management
Scarpello/Ledvinka, Personnel/Human Resource Management: Environments and Functions
Singer, Human Resource Management
Starling, The Changing Environment of Business, Third Edition
Steers/Ungson/Mowday, Managing Effective Organizations: An Introduction

KENT *Series in Human Resource Management*

Series Consulting Editor—Richard W. Beatty

Bernardin/Kane, Performance Appraisal, Second Edition
Cascio, Costing Human Resources: The Financial Impact of Behavior
Kavanagh/Gueutal/Tannenbaum, Human Resource Information and Decision Support Systems: Development and Application
Ledvinka/Scarpello, Federal Regulation of Personnel and Human Resource Management, Second Edition
McCaffery, Employee Benefit Programs: A Total Compensation Perspective
Wallace/Fay, Compensation Theory and Practice, Second Edition

Human Resource Management

Marc G. Singer
James Madison University

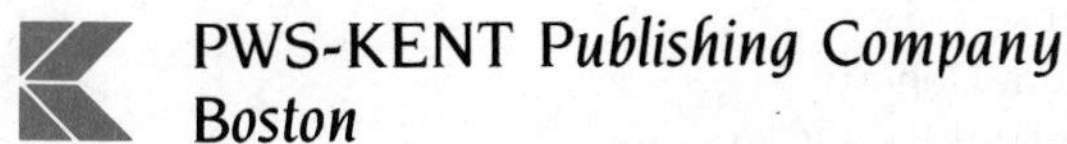

PWS-KENT
Publishing Company

20 Park Plaza
Boston, Massachusetts 02116

PWS-KENT Publishing Company is a division of Wadsworth, inc.

Library of Congress Cataloging-in-Publication Data

Singer, Marc G.
Human resource management / Marc G. Singer.

ISBN 0-534-92179-5
1. Personnel management. I. Title.
HF5549.S59335 1990 89-36567
658.3—dc20 CIP

Printed in the United States of America.
90 91 92 93 94 — 10 9 8 7 6 5 4 3 2 1

Sponsoring Editor Rolf Janke
Editorial Assistant Laura Mosberg
Production Supervisor Elise Kaiser
Manufacturing Coordinator Marcia A. Locke
Composition David E. Seham Associates Inc.
Interior/Cover Design Elise Kaiser
Interior Illustration Debra Doherty
Cover Printer New England Book Components
Text Printer/Binder R. R. Donnelley & Sons Company
Cover Art *Strokes 87-14* by Takeshi Hara, Tokyo, Japan.
A silkscreen print used with the permission of the artist.

For Ellen, Jennifer, and Adam

Preface

The focus of *Human Resource Management* is centered on the individuals most likely to be involved in the broad domain of human resource management. This group includes academicians, researchers, students, personnel professionals, line supervisors, and managers in the field. The principal goal in writing this book is to present readers with an approach that would span the boundaries of their varying educational and experiential backgrounds. If I have successfully accomplished this goal, this text has the potential to be a useful resource for a wide variety of readers.

A textbook is an essential element of human resource management education and training. However, it is not an effective learning device if readers merely absorb the information and are unable to transfer or apply what they have learned to the real world. Traditional human resource textbooks are often encumbered with research studies, and they unwittingly prevent readers from becoming involved in the subject matter. Readers sometimes become so preoccupied with names, dates, and specifics of research that applicable aspects are overlooked, minimized, or obscured. In addition, the elements of theory often appear to highlight idealistic solutions that are difficult, if not impossible, to implement in an actual work situation.

In the response to the dilemma of how to bridge the gap between textbook and real-life experience, academicians have become increasingly more creative. They have introduced experiential exercises into classrooms, relied more heavily on case instruction, utilized audio-visual aids, and created computer simulations. What continues to remain static, however, is the manner in which textbook material is presented.

The present text presents essential, relevant material in a clear, practical, and easy to read manner. The content matter is presented in such a way as to facilitate understanding of both human resource principles and their applications in the workplace. Facts are supported by proven research studies, but detailed research data has purposefully been eliminated. Practical, actual worksite examples are woven throughout the text to enhance the clarity of important topics and concepts. In addition, chapters include objectives, real-life cases based on actual incidents, and discussion questions, which require readers to not only know the facts but also be able to apply them to real workplace situations.

Features of the Book

The text material is divided into distinct parts representing the basic functions performed by human resource managers. The chapter progression follows the standard format of most traditional personnel management textbooks, but no hard and fast rule dictates a particular sequence. Each chapter is presented as a total and separate entity, and the chapters may be interchanged to suit the particular needs of the reader.

Learning aids are incorporated in each chapter to assist readers in mastering relevant material. Chapter objectives are presented in order to alert readers to significant concepts covered by the chapter. Important terms and concepts are defined and highlighted to facilitate identification. These terms are subsequently listed at the end of each chapter in order of their appearance; they are also included in a glossary at the end of the book. Each chapter concludes with a summary of the material, two types of questions for discussion (one form that tests factual knowledge and one that requires the reader to apply the information learned), and a case for analysis.

Two additional learning features have been incorporated into the book to promote reader understanding. Interwoven throughout the text are short vignettes portraying situations that actually occurred at worksites. These examples were chosen to clarify difficult concepts and to facilitate the transfer of theoretical material to the workplace. Additionally, the figures, exhibits, and illustrations appearing in the text were selected because of their broad applicability across populations. Every attempt has been made to secure facsimiles of documents that readers are likely to encounter at the worksite.

Human Resource Management is written to provide a common body of knowledge for readers with diverse perspectives. It accomplishes this task by bridging the gap between textbook and real-life experience through its continuous interweaving of theoretical principles and real world experience. If my purpose is realized, readers will master human resource management principles easily, apply them appropriately, and become contributing members to the field.

Supplementary Material

The publisher can provide the following items to interested instructors:

- an *Instructor's Manual,* which contains chapter outlines, key term definitions, suggested solutions to the end-of-chapter questions and cases, and true/false and multiple-choice questions written by the author.
- a set of acetate *transparencies,* containing important figures and exhibits from the text—available for adopters only.

Acknowledgments

No work of this magnitude can ever be accomplished alone. I am indebted to numerous individuals who contributed their time and expertise to the development of this book.

I would like to thank the following reviewers for their constructive comments throughout the various stages of this project: John Joseph Bunnell, *Broome Community College;* Joseph Culver, *University of Texas at Austin;* William Dickson, *Green River Community College;* Paula S. Funkhouser, *Truckee Meadows Community College, Reno;* Barbara Hastings, *University of South Carolina at Spartanburg;* Mary Lou Kline, *Reading Area Community College;* Jeff Stauffer, *Ventura College;* Fred C. Sutton, *Cuyahoga Community College, Metro Campus;* and Sumner White, *Massachusetts Bay Community College.*

Many chapters would have been incomplete without the concluding cases. I appreciate the time and ingenuity of the following colleagues: Lester R. Bittel, Professor Emeritus, *James Madison University;* O.C. Brenner, *James Madison University;* Sally Coltrin, *University of North Florida;* Barbara Hastings, *University of South Carolina at Spartanburg;* David Holt, *James Madison University;* Charles Pringle, *James Madison University;* Larry Rothman, *National Labor Relations Board;* and W. Lee WanVeer, *Virginia Power Company.*

Special thanks are also due the following individuals who provided information, continual encouragement, and special assistance: Lester Bittel, Professor Emeritus, *James Madison University,* Harold Durrett, *Durrett Enterprises;* Daniel Gallagher, *James Madison University,* Charles Pringle, *James Madison University;* and Sophia Zukrowski, *Woodrow Wilson Rehabilitation Center.*

I am also grateful to the exceptional staff at PWS-KENT Publishing Company who made life more bearable during the course of this project: Rolf A. Janke who provided ongoing encouragement and support; Laura Mosberg who always provided me with the right answers; and Elise Kaiser, the masterful coordinator of the final project.

Lastly, I am indebted to my wife Ellen, who meticulously edited the manuscript, provided ideas for many of the chapters, co-authored the Instructor's Manual, and tolerated me during my many anxious moments.

Marc G. Singer

Contents

Human Resource Management

Part 1

The Human Resource Management Function

Chapter 1

Introduction to Human Resource Management

Objectives

After reading this chapter you should understand:

1. The activities and function of human resource management.
2. The evolution of present-day human resource management.
3. The impact of different historical events on today's human resource function.
4. The method of and reasoning for the creation of human resource departments within organizations.
5. The scope and underlying philosophical approach of this book.

Organizational success depends on the effective blending of machines, money, materials, and human resources in order to achieve both short- and long-term business objectives. Because of the uniqueness, complexity, and diversification of enterprises, specialty fields have evolved to maximize the potential benefits of the various essential ingredients. Financial management attempts to increase organizational efficiency by manipulating available financial resources. Materials management develops methods and techniques to optimize the handling and processing of essential materials. Production management works with manufacturing and develops effective equipment design. Finally, human resource management develops programs to optimize human potential, in order to realize the goals of both the individual and the organization.

Human resource management

Human resource management is a specialty field that attempts to develop programs, policies, and activities to promote the satisfaction of both individual and organizational needs, goals, and objectives.

Human resource management, a relatively new term, emerged during the 1970s. Many people continue to refer to the discipline by its older, more traditional titles, such as personnel management, personnel administration, and industrial relations. Generally, the terms are synonymous and interchangeable, and their usage depends largely on individual preference. There are, however, individuals who maintain that contemporary human resource management is vastly different from the outmoded profession that preceded it.

Historically, personnel management activities were viewed as secondary in importance to almost all other organizational functions. In many instances, personnel departments were staffed by former line supervisors or managers who had outlived their usefulness in their former positions. These personnel administrators were usually untrained and unskilled in human resource activities, and leftover tasks that were unpopular with other employees were relegated to them. Their duties consisted of screening initial job applications, processing health and benefit forms, arranging and coordinating recreational activities, orienting new employees, publishing in-house newsletters, and conducting various employee surveys.

Generally, the duties of both personnel managers and supervisors were attributed little, if any, importance in the scheme of the organization. Today, this state of affairs has drastically changed. Personnel management, once thought of as merely common sense, is currently gaining the attention and recognition it deserves. The managers of organizations are realizing that they cannot afford to make mistakes in the everyday management of their personnel. Employee suits against employers for mistreatment are becoming more frequent, and courts are awarding substantial settlements to workers. Increased competition for talented labor is causing turnover in organizations that are underpaying or mistreating their workforces. In addition, research has demonstrated that there are strong relationships between the overall economic performance of companies and the strength of their human resource management departments.[1]

The changes in the importance of human resource management activities are reflected in the expertise of new employees entering the field, as well as in the compensation these workers earn. It is not unusual to find personnel departments, once scoffed at as second class departments, being headed by highly trained and experienced personnel receiving benefit packages commensurate with those of other top organizational executives. Furthermore, the skill levels and salaries of employees and the overall budget allocations for human resource management departments has greatly increased over the past decade.[2]

The increased importance of human resource management departments has also contributed to their involvement in the mainstream of the organization. Today, human resource managers engage in a wide array of activities previously reserved for others. A discussion of how the personnel management function evolved into its present state, where it fits in the organizational structure, and what activities human resource managers currently engage in, is the focus of this chapter.

The Evolution of Human Resource Management

It is highly feasible that personnel management activities existed as early as prehistoric times. With a little imagination, one can envision Neanderthal supervisors using a crude selection technique in order to determine which tribe members were responsible for hunting and which tribe members were accountable for tending the camp site. Subsequent civilizations undoubtedly continued and expanded these successful personnel-related activities to meet the growing demands of their evolving organizations. Conceivably, Roman personnel directors were responsible for recruiting, selecting, training, and assigning gladiators to their tasks. Even a rudimentary performance appraisal and reward system could be evident, as highly successful employees were promoted to gladiator trainers and rewarded with accolades. Similarly, the consequences associated with poor performance were negative enough to motivate even the most obstinate workers.

Despite the fact that personnel activities span back to ancient times, it was not until the late nineteenth century and early part of the twentieth century that the first formal indications of personnel as a managerial specialty became evident. This time period in history was characterized by the Industrial Revolution and a massive influx of workers into factory positions. At the same time, members of the labor movement in the United States were fighting for recognition, and violent struggles between employers and employees ensued. These overwhelming events caused managers to seek out new and more efficient methods for dealing with workers. The early influences, which began near the end of the nineteenth century and continued into the first part of the twentieth century include: (1) the social welfare movement, (2) the development of scientific management, (3) the application of psychological principles to the field of business and industry, and (4) World War I.

Early Influences—The Turn of the Century (1880–1920)

Prior to the turn of the century, the prevailing view concerning workers was that they existed solely to serve employer needs. Little consideration was given either to overall employee welfare or to individual employee needs. These beliefs were not restricted to managerial personnel; they were also supported by government and judicial philosophies that favored laissez-faire attitudes toward private industry. Workers were simply another element in the production process that was to be obtained and used as cheaply and efficiently as possible.

The social welfare movement

In an attempt to thwart the growth of labor unions in the late 1800s, and in an effort to deal more effectively with their rapidly expanding labor forces, employers began to engage in activities designed to improve the working environment. As an outgrowth of this interest in the well-being of their workforces, many employers hired **social** or **welfare secretaries** to assist workers by making suggestions to improve their working conditions. In fact, the aid they provided went beyond the workplace and extended into the personal lives of employees. The aid included providing employee assistance to obtain housing, medical care, home purchases and improvement, and even making library and recreational facilities available.[3] It is largely from the influence of these welfare secretaries that present-day benefit administration developed.

> **Social or welfare secretaries**
>
> *Social or welfare secretaries were individuals employed by organizations during the early part of the twentieth century for the purpose of assisting workers in improving their work environment and personal lives.*

Scientific management

In addition to promoting the establishment of welfare secretaries, the influx of large numbers of workers in manufacturing environments caused employers to consider new methods to increase efficiency. **Scientific management,** which was popularized by Frederick Taylor and his contemporaries Frank and Lillian Gilbreth in the late 1800s and early 1900s, represented the launching of this management endeavor to optimize productivity. Their approach to management was characterized by the belief that poor performance was the direct result of universally applied managerial techniques and that it did not take into account differences in work situations.[4]

For Taylor and his contemporaries, acquiring efficiency required that tasks be systematically and uniformly analyzed through method study to discover the choice method for performing each job. Utilizing time and motion studies as the principal means of investigation, Taylor developed a set of principles for improving the efficiency of the workplace. Included among these principles are the direct forerunners underlying modern personnel practices. They include:

1. The systematic and uniform collection of task information resulting in a detailed list of task instructions.
2. The recruiting and selecting of the best person to do the job.
3. Pay for performance.
4. Management–union cooperation.

Industrial psychology

Parallel to the development of Taylor's scientific management was psychologist Hugo Munsterberg's pioneering the application of psychological principles to business and industry. The ideas and research of this early psychologist formed the initial foundation for the field of Industrial Psychology and became an integral part of the early body of personnel management knowledge.

Hugo Munsterberg's work is probably most directly linked to early personnel management. Munsterberg's major contributions stem from his work with the Boston Elevated Railway Company in 1913.[5] While attempting to test the discrimination abilities of applicants for the position of motorman, Munsterberg developed a test incorporating a series of cards which the applicant moved by turning a crank. The results of this testing procedure led Munsterberg to conclude that the best method for selecting employees was to first analyze jobs in terms of their physical, mental, and emotional requirements, and subsequently to test applicants' performance of these functions. Hence, the initial importance of statistical validation, specifically predictive validity (which will be discussed in detail in Chapter 5), was realized.

World War I

Despite the early contributions made by Munsterberg, it was not until World War I that the major impact of psychology on personnel management was felt. World War I placed a previously unprecedented demand on the workforce. Not only did the war necessitate an increase in productivity, but also it complicated matters by draining the civilian workforce through military inductions. In order to insure efficient operations, managers began to take greater interest in their employees. In fact, in response to government pressures to promote efficiency, many organizations established their first personnel departments during this time period.[6]

The large number of men inducted into the armed forces also presented placement problems for the military. Decisions concerning officer candidate potential, specialized training, and the suitability of individual soldiers for standard military duties caused the army to commission the development of an intelligence test. This instrument, known as the **Army Alpha** test, was developed by the Committee on the Psychological Examination of Recruits headed by Robert M. Yerkes, and is considered the first group intelligence test.

It was discovered, after successive administrations of the Army Alpha, that low literacy, rather than low intelligence levels, caused significant numbers of recruits to be unable to complete the test items. The response to this problem was the development of the **Army Beta** test, which compensated for the inductee's lack of English literacy skills. Immediately following the war, the Army Beta test was extensively used in industry to test the large influx of new immigrant labor.[7] Thus, the Army Alpha and Beta tests represented the beginning of modern-day group selection testing.

The Roaring Twenties (The 1920s)

The growth of personnel departments, prior to and during World War I, continued into the 1920s. Although involved in other activities, these newly formed departments were established primarily for the purpose of handling employee welfare concerns.

The leading cause of growth in employee welfare programs during the 1920s

Exhibit 1.1

Major HRM Historical Events

1792	First local craft union organized by Philadelphia Shoemakers.
1797	Albert Gallatin introduces first profit-sharing plan into his glassworks factory.
1869	The Knights of Labor is founded in Philadelphia.
1876	American Express establishes first pension plan.
1884	Department of Interior establishes the Bureau of Labor and the Bureau of Labor Statistics.
1886	Taylor starts first experiments leading to Scientific Management.
1890	Term *Mental Test* is coined by James Cattell.
1892	American Psychological Association is founded.
1900	First employment department started at B. F. Goodrich.
1901	Labor Department started at National Cash Register.
1903	Congress creates Department of Commerce and Labor.
1911	*Principles of Scientific Management* published.
1912	Date attributed to first formal personnel department.
1914	First job evaluation plan installed at Commonwealth Edison.
1916	Tuck School of Dartmouth College offers first training program aimed at employment managers.
1917	Army Alpha and Beta created.
	Journal of Applied Psychology is published.
1919	Journal *Personnel Management* is published.
	Journal *Personnel* is published.
	Scott Company, first personnel consultants, is established.
1920	First personnel textbook, *Personnel Administration,* is published by Tead & Metcalf.
1922	*Journal of Personnel Research* is published (now *Personnel Journal*).
	AT & T first uses title "Vice President of Personnel Relations."
1924	Hawthorne study starts.
1926	American Arbitration Association is founded.
1937	Division of Industrial/Organizational Psychology of the American Psychological Association is founded.
	Society of Personnel Administration is founded.

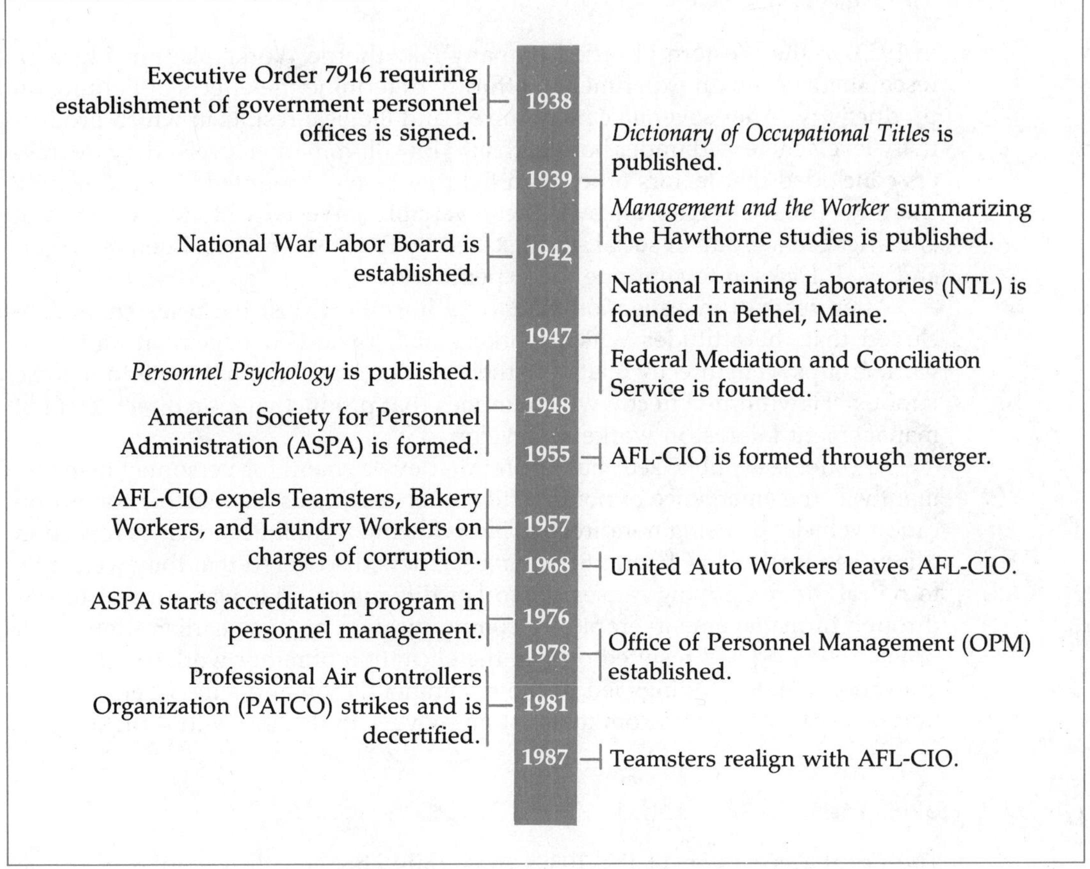

was probably attributable to the overwhelming desire on the part of employers to thwart unionization efforts. In the absence of any specific government legislation, companies engaged in tactics designed to make unions a nonviable alternative. Some organizations offered their workers positive incentives, such as increased benefits, if they refrained from joining unions. Other companies responded by making workers sign "yellow-dog" contracts which stated, as a condition of employment, that the worker would not join a union.[8]

Impeding unions was not the only concern of management during the 1920s. The pre–World War I economic prosperity continued into the early part of the decade. Maximizing productivity in order to capitalize on this business boom was a primary concern of organizations. In an effort to increase productivity, a major research endeavor was undertaken at the Western Electric Company's Hawthorne Works in Chicago. The results of this study led to the development of the **human relations movement** in industry and introduced many of today's personnel activities to organizations.

The Hawthorne studies

In 1923, at the Western Electric Company Hawthorne Works plant in Chicago, researchers began an experimental effort to determine the effects of lighting on productivity. After several years of mixed and illogical results in which productivity levels increased under both high and low illumination levels, the researchers concluded that factors other than lighting levels accounted for productivity changes. In an effort to uncover these variables, Western Electric sought out and engaged a group of social scientists led by Elton Mayo, Fritz Roethlisberger, and W. J. Dickson to continue the experiment.

After years of investigation extending into the 1930s, the researchers concluded that the attitudes which workers had toward management and their work groups were directly related to their productivity.[9] From these findings the famous "Hawthorne Effect," which implies that productivity is a direct result of management interest in workers, developed.

Another less publicized, but important development for personnel management was the emergence of nondirective interviewing as an effective communication vehicle. By using nondirective interviewing techniques, such as reflection (discussed further in Chapter 8), the researchers discovered that they were able to reveal the underlying causes of worker difficulties. This was a major breakthrough in management–employee communication because earlier attempts at problem solving had resulted only in the elicitation of minor worker gripes and grievances. These findings led to the recommendation and subsequent institution of workplace counselors to assist employees in dealing with difficulties.[10]

The Depression Years (The 1930s)[11]

The Great Depression of the 1930s drastically changed the complexity of the personnel function. Previously prosperous organizations were now forced to make drastic cost reductions in order to survive. The expenses associated with the welfare programs and fringe benefits instituted during the past decade were no longer justifiable. Consequently, the benefits, and sometimes the personnel departments responsible for administering these benefits, were eliminated.

As a direct result of the Depression, two laws were passed which greatly influenced the fate of personnel management. The Norris–LaGuardia Act of 1932 limited the use of court injunctions and outlawed yellow-dog contracts. The Wagner Act of 1935 guaranteed workers the right to organize and bargain collectively (these laws are discussed in detail in Chapter 13), providing unions with the impetus needed to mount massive organizing efforts. The result was a drastic increase in the total number of unionized workers in the labor force and an influx of unions into previously nonunionized occupations.

The increase in unionization created a new era for personnel management. Those organizations which had not totally eliminated their personnel departments found themselves reorganizing in an effort to effectively deal with unions. Other companies created personnel departments to handle negotiations and bargaining. Personnel departments, which had previously existed solely for the purpose of administering welfare programs, were now totally immersed in labor–management relations.

If it had not been for the enactment of government legislation favoring unions during the mid 1930s, it is highly conceivable that personnel management would have been almost totally eliminated. Instead, personnel departments revamped and shifted their emphases in an effort to effectively handle the new wave of unionization. From these developments, the industrial relations area of human resource management evolved.

World War II (The 1940s)

The contributions made to personnel management during World War I were precipitated by the necessity to select, place, and train large numbers of recruits. These needs were magnified during the war, as even greater numbers of soldiers required training in a wide variety of technical jobs. In order to effectively utilize the available manpower, the military once again turned to psychologists for assistance. The result was the establishment of the first psychological research unit in the U. S. Army Air Force, and the development of an array of psychological tests designed to identify individual attributes. These tests were later widely used in industry to match candidate characteristics to job requirements.

Military endeavors were not the only influences on personnel management during World War II. As the war escalated, greater numbers of recruits and volunteers entered the armed forces, leaving voids in the labor force. These vacancies in the civilian workforce, particularly in defense factories, were rapidly filled by women and older workers who were eager to contribute to the war effort. Although their enthusiasm was great and their morale was high, many of these new workers had little, if any, factory experience. To develop methods to effectively recruit and train both military and civilian workers, the government created the **War Manpower Commission**.

As a direct result of the commission's efforts, training programs, such as **Job Instruction Training** (JIT), a method still widely used in industry for on-the-job training, were developed. Furthermore, under government funded programs, the first programs designed to educate managers and executives in personnel management and other business related topics were developed and implemented at major colleges and universities across the country.

The impact of labor unions was also carried into the 1940s. Labor unions were heavily involved in efforts to organize the workforce. These organizing efforts often had unsettling effects on the workforce as rival unions vied for representation rights. Realizing that the country could ill afford work stoppages and other disrupting influences on productivity, the government created the National War Labor Board to avert labor disputes.

Wage and salary control programs, initiated by the War Labor Board, have had a lasting impact on present-day personnel programs. With the ability to exercise authority over any employer that had nine or more employees, the board handed down the "Little Steel" formula establishing limits on the amount

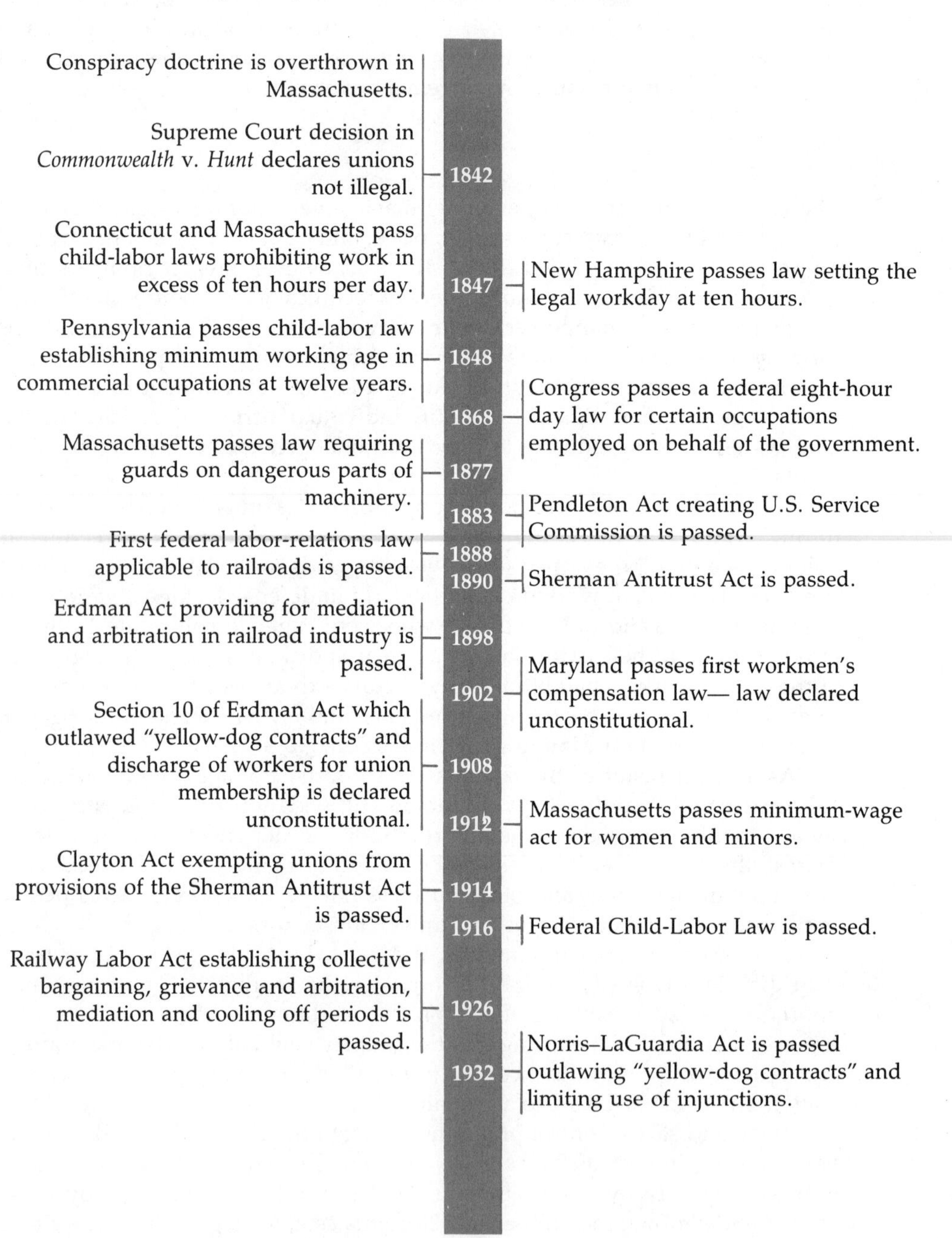

Exhibit 1.2

Major Laws Affecting the Development of HRM

1933 — National Industry Recovery Act (NIRA) giving workers right to organize and collectively bargain is passed.

1933 — Wagner-Payser Act providing for social security is passed.

1936 — Social Security Act is passed.

1936 — National Labor Relations Act (Wagner Act) is passed reaffirming the NIRA and outlining unfair labor practices for employers.

1938 — Fair Labor Standards Act establishing minimum wage provisions and time and one-half pay is passed.

1942 — Stabilization Act authorizing the president to stabilize wages and salaries is passed.

1947 — Labor Management Relations Act (Taft–Hartley) amending the Wagner Act is passed.

1959 — Labor Management Reporting and Disclosure Act (Landrum–Griffin) is passed.

1962 — Executive Order 10988 encouraging unionization of federal employees is signed.

1963 — Manpower Development and Training Act is signed.

1963 — Equal Pay Act is passed.

1964 — Civil Rights Act prohibiting discrimination is passed.

1965 — Executive Order 11246 establishing affirmative action is signed.

1967 — Age Discrimination in Employment Act (ADEA) prohibiting discrimination of persons 40–65 is passed.

1970 — Occupational Safety and Health Act is passed.

1971 — *Griggs* v. *Duke Power* ruling by Supreme Court outlines testing regulations.

1973 — Rehabilitation Act protecting handicapped is passed.

1974 — Employee Retirement Income Security Act (ERISA) is passed.

1974 — Federal Privacy Act is passed.

1974 — Vietnam Veterans Readjustment Assistance Act providing assistance to Vietnam era veterans is passed.

1978 — Pregnancy Discrimination and ADEA amendments to Title VII of Civil Rights Act is passed.

1986 — Consolidated Omnibus Budget Reconciliation Act (COBRA) requiring employers to offer to continue health insurance to terminated employees is passed.

1986 — Immigration Reform and Control Act making employers liable for hiring undocumented aliens is passed.

1988 — Employee Polygraph Protection Act banning the blanket use of lie detector tests in employment situations is passed.

1988 — Plant Closing and Mass Layoff Notification Act requiring employers to give 60 days' notice of mass closings or layoffs is passed.

of salary increases, as well as other benefits, employers were permitted to provide. As a direct result of these actions, unions began to demand, and employers provided, compensation in the form of fringe benefits. Furthermore, since employers did not have to obtain government approval in order to provide raises under a progressive wage increase system, these programs began to develop in large numbers. Present-day compensation programs, which include benefit packages and cost of living adjustments, are direct descendants of these early wage plans.

The Influence of Behavioral Science (The 1950s)

By the end of the 1940s the increasingly widespread acceptance of the human relations movement led to the formation of a new discipline known as behavioral science. This new approach was an outgrowth of a 1949 meeting of scientists who were attempting to determine whether there was sufficient factual information available to formulate a generally acceptable theory of human behavior.[12] This initial conference was followed by additional gatherings of representatives from various fields of study. As a result of these meetings, earlier contributions to the study of human behavior made by psychology, sociology, and anthropology were further supplemented by disciplines such as economics, history, biology, mathematics, and political science. Thus, the **behavioral sciences,** a discipline which combines the social sciences and the biological sciences in an effort to understand human behavior, was created.

A key feature of behavioral science philosophy is that productivity is directly related to workers' individual and group feelings of morale, motivation, and job satisfaction. Studies attempting to demonstrate correlations between satisfied workers and productivity abounded during the 1950s. Many of today's theories on how to lead, motivate, and raise the morale of workers were either developed or influenced by research conducted during this time period. In fact, many current studies in human resource management trace their origins to the principles expounded by early behavioral scientists.

Today, the behavioral sciences continue to impact businesses through the principles formulated by Organizational Behavior (OB) and Organizational Development (OD). The former discipline is concerned with the way in which factors such as supervisory and managerial actions, work groups, and other environmental elements influence employee behavior. Organizational development specialists attempt to manipulate the attitudes, values, and behavioral patterns of individuals and work groups in order to promote greater cooperation among organizational members. The contributions made by these disciplines are readily apparent in Chapters 15 and 16 of this text, which deal with appropriate methods for motivating and communicating with employees.

The Legislative Decades (1960–Present)

Without a doubt, the major impact on human resource management during the past three decades has come from the voluminous amount of government legislation imposed on businesses. Beginning with the Equal Pay Act of 1963 and

Title VII of the Civil Rights Act of 1964 (the various government regulations affecting personnel are the subject of Chapter 2) and extending through the Polygraph Protection Act of 1988, the past three decades have witnessed unprecedented amounts of employment legislation and litigation. The rights of individual employees have become of paramount importance in the legal and legislative arenas. Probably more than any other single factor, the seemingly unending and complex stream of government legislation has caused many organizations to re-evaluate the importance of the personnel function. Today, human resource management activities, which were once thought of as unnecessary and frivolous expenses, are being recognized as important activities that help to determine the ultimate success or failure of organizations.

Human Resource Management's Role Within Organizations

The Responsibility for Human Resource Management

Many people believe that the sole responsibility for personnel functions is and should be borne by human resource management professionals. In part, this is true. Human resource managers are employed by companies to coordinate various personnel-related activities. However, the principal responsibility of effectively utilizing human resources is shared with others. The very nature of their jobs demands that managers, supervisors, and anyone else who has the authority to direct the work of others be involved in human resource activities. In fact, small organizations rarely if ever establish separate personnel departments. All necessary personnel activities are performed directly by line supervisors. They hire and train employees, administer wages and benefits, and are responsible for all other personnel facets of an employee's work life.

Creating human resource departments

A byproduct of organizational expansion is an increasing need for human resource management departments. These departments relieve line supervisors of additional daily administrative duties associated with human resource activities. Routine clerical chores, such as completing time cards and insurance claim forms, as well as complying with the vast amount of government mandated record-keeping requirements, eventually become too cumbersome for supervisors to effectively handle on a daily basis. When the time spent on these personnel assignments detracts from the primary duties of supervisors, organizations add human resource personnel.

Organizations also create personnel departments in order to more effectively coordinate their human resource activities. With the increasing government regulation of businesses, companies cannot afford to make personnel mistakes. It is highly unlikely that line managers can continually stay abreast of the complex government regulations affecting employment, compensation and benefit administration, and safety. Companies are discovering that the addition of human resource specialists is becoming a necessity in order to remain in compliance with the various legal requirements.

Organizational size requirements that determine the justification for distinct personnel departments vary across industries. Financial service firms, such as banks, have more personnel specialists employed per worker than nonbusiness or health care organizations. Smaller firms usually have higher ratios than larger enterprises. Likewise, nonunion companies tend to have higher ratios than unionized environments.[13] As a general rule, the ratio for most organizations appears to be approximately one personnel employee for every one hundred to one hundred fifty workers.[14]

Once the decision to create a separate department has been made, the organization must carefully plan for its implementation. The addition of human resource staff means that the responsibilities for personnel activities will be shared between the line supervisor and the personnel manager. Usually, operations and personnel managers have distinctly different orientations and work motivations.[15] Inevitably, conflict over personnel activities is likely to develop. In order to minimize these potential disputes, it is important for each manager's formal line of authority to be clearly delineated.

Lines of Authority

Authority refers to the legitimate use of power by individuals to make decisions concerning the resources affecting an organization's ultimate goals and objectives. Managers and supervisors are vested with authority to make decisions, to give orders, and to direct the work of employees. Traditionally, two types of formal authority exist in organizations: line authority and staff authority. **Line managers** are vested with the right to make final decisions about a particular phase of the organization's operations. Usually this authority is narrow in scope, and it is exercisable only over the supervisor's immediate subordinates.

Staff managers function in advisory capacities by supplying counsel to other managerial and supervisory personnel. They have no direct authority to direct the work of others, nor can they make final decisions. They serve purely in a support capacity. In most organizations, the primary function of human resource managers is in a staff capacity.

> ***Line and staff managers***
>
> *Line managers have the final decision-making authority over a phase of operations. Staff managers are authorized to assist and counsel line managers in obtaining the organization's objectives.*

In reality, the dichotomy between line and staff authority is often blurred. Human resource managers have line authority over the employees they directly supervise, and they are often invested with an indirect form of power. In many organizations, human resource managers are directly supervised by the CEO or some other high-level executive. By virtue of this reporting relationship, line managers are likely to perceive the personnel manager as having other authority in addition to staff or advisory capacities. Consequently, regardless of the true nature of their authority, suggestions made by these human resource managers are usually implemented.

Line managers also give deference to the recommendations of personnel managers which fall within their recognized areas of expertise. Subjects, such as government rules and regulations, selection and training, safety and benefit administration, and labor relations, are usually considered the domain of human resource specialists. Operations managers are usually more than willing to delegate the authority for and to abide by the suggestions made regarding these activities. Consequently, notwithstanding the fact that the final decision regarding the implementation of human resource programs is ultimately the line manager's, the input provided by the personnel specialist is rarely challenged.

Staffing the human resource function

As previously mentioned, the first formalized personnel activities were conducted by welfare secretaries. In order to be employed in this capacity, individuals had to demonstrate that they had tact, good common sense, and information about labor and industry.[16] Until recently, most organizations, with the exception of unionized companies which realized the importance of labor relations expertise for dealing with unions, still maintained that almost anyone who was personable and had basic clerical skills could function satisfactorily in a personnel role. This belief resulted in the staffing of many personnel departments with longstanding likeable line managers who had outlived their production usefulness.

Today, due in large part to the imposition of extensive government regulations and the realization that the bottom line is directly affected by employment practices, human resource management departments are staffed by people with professional credentials. The specific qualifications of these employees vary from organization to organization and depend largely on whether personnel generalists or specialists are required.

Personnel generalists

Personnel generalists are more likely to be found in smaller organizations. These human resource professionals usually have a broad-based knowledge of all personnel activities and some detailed knowledge of certain human resource areas. Individuals who have entered the personnel field from other corporate disciplines, such as operations or accounting, or specialists who have spent considerable time in small personnel departments, usually develop into generalists.

Personnel specialists

Personnel specialists are usually employed by large organizations with widespread and complex operations. Unlike their generalist counterparts, personnel specialists are narrowly focused and have in-depth expertise in a particular area of personnel administration. Personnel specialists

Exhibit 1.3

Job Description of a Personnel Coordinator

The Lakeside Press
R·R·DONNELLEY & SONS COMPANY

JOB DESCRIPTION

SECTION 1-IDENTIFICATION INFORMATION OD-11

JOB TITLE— Personnel Coordinator
DIVISION— Harrisonburg DATE— November, 1988
DEPARTMENT— Personnel SECTION—
REPORTS TO:
LINE— Personnel Manager
FUNCTIONAL—

SECTION 2-STATEMENT OF PURPOSE

THE PURPOSE OF THIS JOB IS—

Coordinate the recruitment, selection, and placement of hourly and salaried clerical employees. Coordinate the internal placement and promotion of hourly/salaried clerical employees. Coordinate division employee relations, communication, and affirmative action programs.

SECTION 3-RESPONSIBILITIES OF THE JOB

THE ACTION AREAS OF THIS JOB ARE—

1. Recruitment, selection and placement of hourly and clerical employees. 25%
   A. Administer and evaluate current and projected departmental crewing needs.
   B. Recruit prospective employees through continuing contact with the Virginia Employment Commission, local high schools and colleges, employment agencies and employee referrals.
   C. Monitor the divisional applicant log and filing system.
   D. Identify prospective employees who qualify for the Targeted Jobs Tax Credit Program.
   E. Administer and evaluate pre-employment tests.
   F. Conduct screening interviews and coordinate the same between hiring departments.
   G. Prepare wage schedules and assessments for newly hired employees.
   H. Conduct new employee orientation sessions.

2. Internal Placement Coordinator 25%
   A. Administer divisional Job Information Bulletin System.
   B. Administer divisional supplemental application system.
   C. Insure consideration of all qualified employees in the division

Source: Courtesy of R. R. Donnelley & Sons Company, The Lakeside Press.

SECTION 3-RESPONSIBILITIES (CONT'D)

for promotional opportunities.
D. Generate candidate lists for hiring departments.
E. Prepare assessment reports, evaluations and new wage schedules for promoted and transferred employees.
F. Conduct career counseling interviews.
G. Assist departments in evaluating, upgrading and creating positions.

3. Coordinate division employee communications programs and promote public relations. 10%
   A. Serve as editor of the division newsletter.
   B. Coordinate with Corporate Communications in related matters.
   C. Serve as division photographer.
   D. Arrange for annual talks in the division.
   E. Coordinate division campaign for the United Way.
   F. Participate in organizations that promote goodwill between the Company and the community.

4. Facilitate effective employee relations 10%
   A. Provide information and interpretation to employees and Management on questions regarding Company policy.
   B. Counsel employees concerning vocational and personal matters.
   C. Assist in informal and formal grievance procedures.
   D. Insure consideration of minority and other protected groups for transfer and promotion opportunities.

5. Miscellaneous 10%
   A. Assist in professional employment.
   B. Assist in college recruiting efforts.
   C. Assist in administration of suggestion system on an "as needed" basis.
   D. Assist in administration of Task Force.
   E. Special projects as assigned by the Personnel Manager.

6. Coordinate Division Affirmative Action Program 20%
   A. Assist departments in the development of specific Affirmative Action goals.
   B. Recruit minority and other protected groups for consideration for employment. Use appropriate community referral sources for assistance.
   C. Prepare division Affirmative Action and EEO Reports.
   D. Insure consideration of qualified minority and other protected groups for transfer and promotion opportunities.

SUPERVISION/DIRECTION

AVERAGE NUMBER SUPERVISED DIRECTLY— ______
AVERAGE NUMBER SUPERVISED INDIRECTLY— ______
AVERAGE NUMBER SUPERVISED FUNCTIONALLY— ______

SUPERVISION RECEIVED— ____________________

SECTION 4-EMPLOYEE REQUIREMENTS

GENERAL EDUCATIONAL DEVELOPMENT

REASONING DEVELOPMENT— Level 3 - Degree 3

A. Selection of appropriate employees.
B. Promotion and transfer of the most qualified employees.
C. Interpretation of EEO/Affirmative Action regulations and policies.

MATHEMATICAL DEVELOPMENT— Level 2 - Degree 3

A. Project manning requirements in accordance with department budgets.
B. Calculate credit toward apprentice programs and prepare new wage schedules.

LANGUAGE DEVELOPMENT— Level 3 - Degree 3

A. Understand and interpret company policy.
B. Edit division newsletter.

SPECIFIC VOCATIONAL PREPARATION

TYPE AND DEPTH OF KNOWLEDGE— Level 3

SPECIFIC SKILLS AND KNOWLEDGE AREAS—

1. Interviewing skills.
2. Counseling skills.
3. Mathematical Ability.
4. Familiarity with manufacturing process.
5. Written and oral communication
6. skills.

PREVIOUS JOB EXPERIENCE REQUIRED DNA
LICENSE/CERTIFICATION REQUIREMENT DNA
FOREIGN LANGUAGE REQUIREMENT DNA

PHYSICAL REQUIREMENTS

1. VISUAL ACUITY Level 3
2. DEPTH PERCEPTION Applies
3. COLOR PERCEPTION Applies
4. HEARING PERCEPTION Level 3
5. PHYSICAL EXERTION Level 3
6. FINGER DEXTERITY Applies
7. LIMB MOVEMENT DNA
8. HAND-ARM MANIPULATION Applies

JOB CONTEXT

REGULARITY OF WORKING HOURS Regular
DAY-NIGHT SCHEDULE Basic day hours
TRAVEL 2%
OTHER JOB CONTEXT ITEMS— DNA

EQUIPMENT, TOOLS, MACHINERY

(LEVEL 3 AND ABOVE)

ADDITIONAL INFORMATION

THIS SECTION IS FOR THE CONTINUATION OF JOB RESPONSIBILITIES AND/OR THE INCLUSION OF ANY PERTINENT DATA THAT IS FELT TO BRING A CLEARER UNDERSTANDING OF THE JOB.

APPROVALS

PREPARED BY Nanci M. Weaver 11/14/88
APPROVED BY Daniel M. Curley 11/10/88
APPROVED BY R. Johnson 11/11/88

are most commonly found in the areas of government rules and regulations (particularly affirmative action), compensation and benefits, testing, training and development, and industrial relations. Most specialists obtain their in-depth knowledge through extensive academic preparation.

In today's business environment the demand for specialists is at an all time high. Perhaps the major factor contributing to this unprecedented demand for specialists is the continually changing laws in the areas of equal employment opportunity, occupational safety and health, wage and salary administration, and employee rights. The continual attention of knowledgeable personnel specialists is necessary in order to insure that organizations remain in compliance with the complex and ever-changing employment legislation.

The Importance of Human Resource Management

Over the last decade, human resource professionals have greatly increased their involvement in corporate activities. Although they were at one time primarily concerned with recruiting, selecting, training, and benefit administration, personnel departments are now being called upon to assist in corporate planning, organization restructuring, productivity improvement, strategy development, and quality improvement activities.[17] These new and expanded roles indicate the organizational prominence that the human resource function currently enjoys.

The recent recognition of the personnel management function is also reflected in the overall compensation of human resource professionals. In 1987, the average total compensation package for top level human resource professionals exceeded $100,000 for the first time ever. Furthermore, the salaries of middle managers in human resources increased an average of 5.6 percent, compared to an average of 5.2 percent for mid-management functions overall.[18] Entry level employment interviewers, who enter the field with no experience and only a bachelor's degree, can probably expect to receive salaries averaging between $20,000 to $25,000.

As firms continue to implement human resource development programs in the future, the importance of the personnel function will continue. The U.S. Department of Labor estimates that approximately 35,000 new human resource professionals will enter the workforce between 1988 and 1995. However, with the abundant supply of qualified college graduates attempting to enter the field, competition for available positions is projected to be keen. For professionals who have an awareness of the changing human resource emphasis and who design personnel programs to meet organizational objectives, the future looks bright.

The Scope of the Book

The Perspective

In order for readers to achieve the maximum benefit from this text, it is important for them to be familiar with the basic tenets which underlie its foundation. The first tenet is that the ultimate responsibility for effectively utilizing people resides with operations supervisors and managers. Human resource management professionals are employed as resources to assist supervisors and managers in maximizing the potential of their workers. The material in this book is not only intended for personnel professionals, but it also has applicability for line supervisors and managers. Personnel managers may initially screen applicants, but the final hiring decision is usually the supervisor's responsibility. Similarly, personnel professionals may be responsible for the development of wage and salary scales, performance appraisal instruments, disciplinary procedures, and negotiating labor contracts, but it is the supervisor who actually uses these tools on a daily basis.

It has been argued that theoretical answers provide only hypothetical, speculative, and abstract solutions to the complex problems managers face on a daily basis. The elements of theory often appear to highlight idealistic answers to problems which are difficult, if not impossible to implement in an actual situation. On the other hand, the goal of the applied, or practical, approach takes into account the unique features of the situation as well as the realistic constraints of life beyond the research lab. For these reasons, the second tenet of this text is that only research which lends support to practical application of the material should be incorporated.

The Content

The remaining text is divided into five distinct parts representing the basic functions performed by personnel managers. Each part is further subdivided into chapters detailing the principal activities involved in the ongoing process of utilizing human resources. The chapter progression follows the standard format of most personnel management textbooks, but there are no hard and fast rules dictating that sequence. Therefore, each chapter is presented as a total and separate entity. Interchanging their order will not hamper the acquisition or understanding of the material.

Part 2—*planning and selecting personnel* This part deals with the staffing function and includes chapters on the regulatory environment, job analysis, the planning and recruiting of human resources, and the selection of personnel. The issue of government rules and regulations is one which impacts heavily on human resource management, and it is a recurrent theme throughout the book. The initial chapter details the various legislation affecting personnel activities and promotes an understanding of its impact on human resource management.

Part 3—*developing employee potential* Once hired, employees must be trained and provided with feedback about their performance. Counseling and assistance programs should also be available to employees who need these services. Part 3 begins with a chapter on training and developing employees. The next chapter focuses on constructively appraising employee performance in order to promote positive attitudes and increased productivity. The part concludes with a chapter on counseling, disciplining, and terminating employees.

Part 4—*compensation, benefits, and health and safety* The issues of compensation, benefit administration, and health and safety concerns are assuming major importance in organizations. With the elimination of mandatory retirement

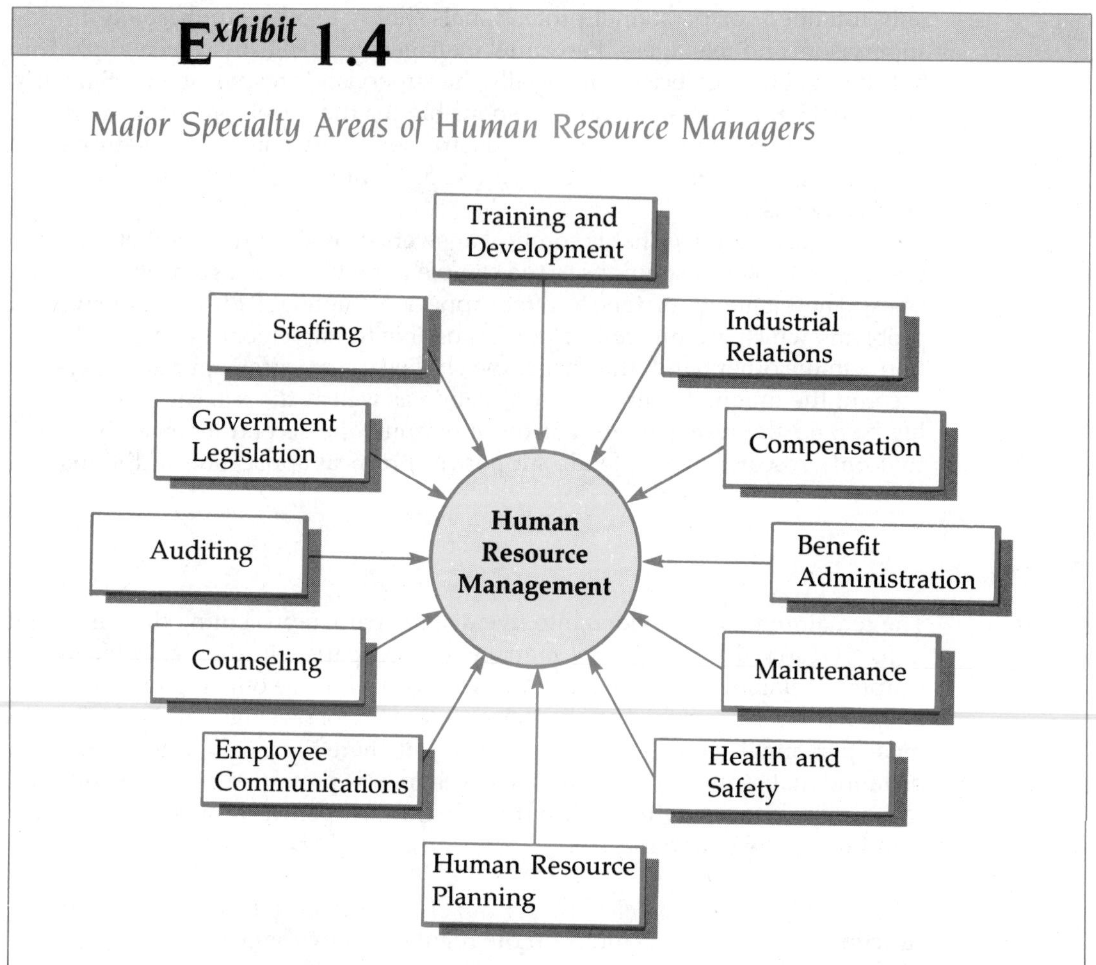

ages, the changing composition of the labor force, and the continual proliferation of government legislation, an unprecedented demand for compensation and benefit specialists has developed. The chapters in this section deal with the establishment of different employee compensation and benefit packages and the ongoing issues concerning health and safety at the workplace.

Part 5—the dynamics of industrial relations Over the last decade, the role of labor–management relations has changed. Union membership has diminished, and labor's overall impact in determining aspects of the work environment has been reduced. Still, unions remain a viable force in industry today. The two chapters in this section detail the history of labor relations, the structural makeup of unions, organizing activities, the collective bargaining process, and the grievance procedure. Both management's and labor's viewpoints are presented in an attempt to provide an unbiased perspective on the labor–management function.

Part 6–effectively utilizing human resources For many people, the subject matter of the first two chapters in this section provides the key ingredients for the effective utilization of human resources. Commonly cited motivation and communication theories, combined with their practical application to the workplace, are the focus of Chapters 15 and 16. The book's concluding chapter identifies several key areas that are predicted to be the focal point of human resource management during the 1990s.

A Final Note

Short vignettes are presented throughout the book in order to enhance and facilitate the understanding of material. The company names and the characters cited are fictitious; the situations, however, are real. The events depicted actually occurred and were either witnessed first hand by the author, or recounted to the author by the supervisors, managers, or workers involved. Similarly, most of the cases presented at the conclusion of the chapters describe situations that really took place.

Summary

Human resource management activities have probably been performed since ancient times. As a formal discipline, however, the roots of human resource management are traceable to the period immediately following the Industrial Revolution. This time period was characterized by a large influx of workers into factory positions and the emergence of the labor movement as a dominant force in the United States, which caused employers to seek new and more efficient techniques for dealing with workers.

Initially, the purpose of human resource activities was to enhance the working environment. In order to accomplish this objective, organizations hired welfare secretaries to assist employees by improving working conditions. These secretaries aided workers in securing adequate housing, medical care, and a wide array of recreational facilities. The influence of these early welfare secretaries is still evident in current benefit programs.

Several additional incidents that took place in the early part of the twentieth century influenced modern-day human resource management. Early studies in the areas of job analysis and testing are responsible for many of today's staffing procedures. Productivity studies, particularly those engaged in at the Hawthorne plant, led to the development of managerial philosophies on how to effectively motivate and communicate with workers. Also, labor–management clashes led to the passage of government legislation which continues to have a significant influence on today's human resource management activities.

The roles of today's human resource managers are vastly different from the roles of those who preceded them. Once viewed as secondary in importance to all other business activities, personnel management now receives greater emphasis and respect in the overall corporate hierarchy. As a result, the present demand for these professionals, as well as the compensation paid to them, is at an all time high. The present trend is projected to continue well into the twenty-first century.

Key Terms to Identify

Human resource management
Social or welfare secretaries
Scientific management
Army Alpha and Beta tests
War Manpower Commission
Job Instruction Training (JIT)
Human relations movement
Behavioral sciences
Line managers
Staff managers
Personnel generalists
Personnel specialists

Questions for Discussion

Do You Know the Facts?

1. What impact did scientific management have on the development of the personnel function within organizations?
2. Discuss the events that transpired during World War I and World War II which impacted on the development of human resource management.
3. Discuss how the human relations school of thought developed. What events led to its being replaced by the behavioral science approach?

Can You Apply the Information Learned?

1. Describe some of the major differences that account for the preference of many people today to refer to the field as human resource management rather than as personnel management.
2. What factors should be considered in determining the reporting relationship of the human resource department within organizations?
3. If you were assigned the responsibility of developing and instituting a human resource department, what factors would you consider in determining whether the department should be staffed by generalists or specialists?

Endnotes and References

1 See N. Basta, "Wanted: Human Resource Pros," *Business Week's Guide to Careers,* Vol. 3, No.1 (1985): 34–37.

2 See data from the Bureau of National Affairs, Inc., (1974–1986) *Bulletin to Management,* Washington, D.C.: Bureau of National Affairs, Inc.

3 See Henry Eilbirt, "The Development of Personnel Management in the United States," *Business History Review,* Vol. 33 (August 1959): 345–364.

4 Although Taylor's work began in the late 1800s in the steel industry, it became highly popularized after the publication of his major work, "The Principles of Scientific Management" in 1911. A concise discussion of these principles can be found in Jay M. Shafritz and Philip H. Whitbeck, *Classics of Organization Theory* (Oak Park, IL: Moore Publishing Company, 1978): 9–23.

5 See Hugo Munsterberg, *Psychology and Industrial Efficiency* (Boston, MA: Houghton Mifflin Company, 1913).

6 See Cyril Ling, *The Management of Personnel Relations: History and Origins* (Homewood, IL: Richard D. Irwin, 1965): 323.

7 See John B. Miner and Mary G. Miner, *Personnel and Industrial Relations,* 4th ed. (New York: Macmillan Publishing Company, 1985): 33.

8 See John B. Miner and Mary G. Miner, *op. cit.,* 34.

9 Detailed results of the Hawthorne studies are reported in F. J. Roethlisberger and W. J. Dickson, *Management and the Worker,* (Cambridge, MA: Harvard University Press, 1939).

10 See Elton Mayo, *The Social Problems of an Industrial Civilization,* (Cambridge, MA: Harvard University Press, 1945).

11 This discussion of the events influencing personnel management during the 1930s and during World War II is based on the treatment of this subject in John B. Miner and Mary G. Miner, *op. cit.,* 35–38.

12 See James G. Miller, "Toward a General Theory for the Behavioral Sciences," *American Psychologist,* Vol. 10 (1955): 513–531.

13 Financial industries have the highest personnel specialist-to-employee ratio with 8 specialists to every 1000 employees. On the other hand, the health care industry has the smallest ratio of 4 specialists to every 1000 employees. See "Personnel Activities Budgets and Staffs 1985–1986," *Bulletin to Management,* ASPA-BNA Survey No. 49, (Washington, D.C.: Bureau of National Affairs, 1986).

14 An ASPA-BNA survey conducted in 1983 found that there were approximately 1.1 human resource management specialists employed for every 100 workers. See "Personnel Activities Budgets and Staffs," *Bulletin to Management,* ASPA-BNA Survey No. 46, (Washington, D.C.: Bureau of National Affairs, 1983). A later finding indicated that the median ratio is 6 specialists for every 1000 employees, or 1 personnel manager per every 167 employees. See "Personnel Activities Budgets and Staffs 1985–1986," *Bulletin to Management,* ASPA-BNA Survey No. 49, (Washington, D.C.: Bureau of National Affairs, 1986).

15 According to some researchers, personnel managers are less assertive, aggressive, and receptive to authority than operating managers. See John Miner and Mary

Miner, "Managerial Characteristics of Personnel Managers," *Industrial Relations*, Vol. 15 (May 1976): 225–234.

16 Early writers in this area maintained that practically any philanthropic or social work background was sufficient to adequately function as a welfare secretary. See Gertrude Beeks, "The New Profession," *National Civic Federation Review*, Vol. 1 (1905): 12.

17 These areas of involvement were identified in a study of ASPA members having the title of vice president who were asked to provide the views of their CEOs. The results are from a sample of 251 companies with half of the companies having more than 1000 employees. See James W. Walker and Gregory Moorhead, "CEOs: What They Want from HRM," *Personnel Administrator*, Vol. 32, No. 12 (1987): 50–59.

18 Statistics are from a 1987 ASPA/Hansen survey and from a study by ECS/The Wyatt Co. For top HRM executives in companies with over 10,000 employees, the average salary was $117,000 while the lowest was $73,100 in companies employing less than 250 employees. See Kirkland Ropp, "HR Management for All It's Worth," *Personnel Administrator*, Vol. 32, No. 9 (1987): 34–40, 120–121.

Part 2

Planning and Selecting Personnel

Chapter 2

The Regulatory Environment

Objectives

After reading this chapter you should understand:

1. The necessity of government regulation of employment.
2. The various laws that impact on human resource management.
3. The meaning of unfair discrimination, and ways of preventing its occurrence.
4. The role of the various government agencies in insuring compliance with employment laws.
5. The way unfair discrimination complaints are legally resolved.
6. The meaning of affirmative action, to whom it applies, and the organization's responsibilities in establishing these programs.
7. The meaning of sexual harassment, how to deal with it, and the organization's responsibility in preventing its occurrence.

Prior to the 1960s, only those employees who were covered by union contracts or who worked for the government were reasonably assured of having specific rights with their employers. All other workers were subject to the absolute power and authority exercised by management. People were hired, fired, disciplined, and promoted for just cause, no cause, or on the whim of employers. These erratic decisions resulted in widespread employment discrimination and caused disproportionate numbers of blacks, Hispanics, and Native Americans to live in poverty. Furthermore, women of all races, except for those engaged in lower paying occupations traditionally viewed as "women's work," were effectively blocked from employment opportunities.[1]

Unfair treatment of minorities was not limited to the workplace. Minority groups were hindered in their attempts to obtain equal educational opportunities, equal housing, public accommodation, and a wide variety of other rights open to majority class members. These blatant social inequities led to the Civil

Rights movement of the 1960s and to the passage of the **Civil Rights Act** of 1964. The Civil Rights Act serves as the cornerstone for all legislation concerning unfair discrimination. **Title VII** of the act (that section dealing with fair employment standards) and its subsequent amendments constitute the major emphasis of this chapter.

Major Employment Laws

The basic purpose of employment laws is to correct the social injustices inflicted upon particular groups. For human resource managers, the focus is on the elimination of employment practices that lead to the discrimination of employees on the basis of sex, religion, race, color, national origin, age, and handicap status. Collectively, these categories constitute the **protected classes.**

Protected classes

The protected classes are those categories of individuals identified by Title VII *and its subsequent amendments as being entitled to protection from discrimination. They include people of minority races, women, the aged, and those with physical disabilities.*

The Equal Pay Act of 1963

The **Equal Pay Act** of 1963 is an amendment to the 1938 Fair Labor Standards Act. It requires employers to pay equal wages to men and women engaged in jobs that require equal skill, effort, and responsibility, and that are performed under similar working conditions. The only exceptions to this law are employees who are paid differential wages based on a bona fide seniority system, a merit system, or a pay plan which takes into consideration the quantity and quality of output, such as incentive systems.

The Civil Rights Act of 1964, *as Amended by the* Equal Employment Opportunity Act of 1972 (EEO)

The Civil Rights Act of 1964 (specifically Title VII), as amended by the **Equal Employment Opportunity Act** of 1972, forbids discrimination in all areas of employer–employee relations including: hiring, terms or conditions of employment, union membership and representation, and the provision of referral services. It applies to almost all employers, labor unions, and employment agencies engaged in any industry affecting commerce, and having fifteen or more employees for at least twenty calendar weeks in the year a charge is filed, or the year preceding the filing of a charge. In addition, any agency, such as an em-

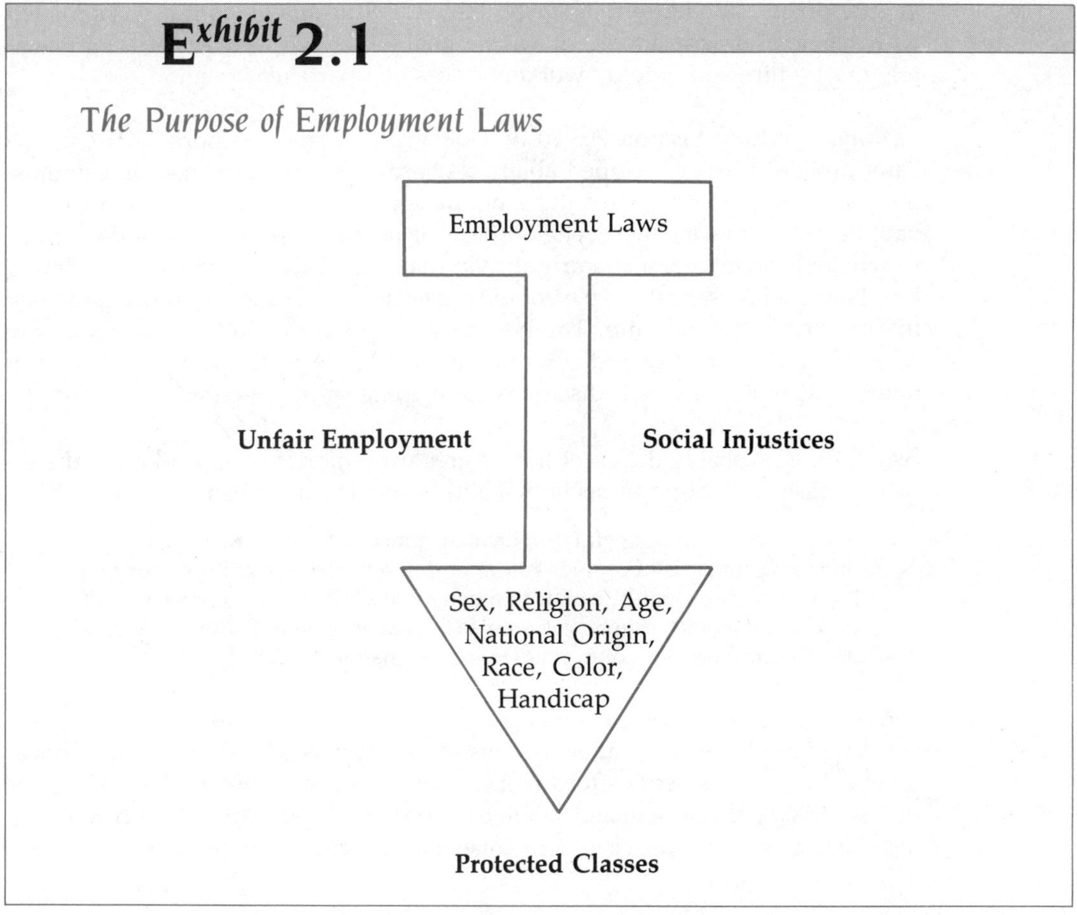

ployment agency, which regularly refers workers to employers covered by the law, is included. Examples of those specifically excluded from the provisions of the law include: tax-exempt private clubs, religious organizations discriminating on the basis of religious preference, United States government-owned corporations, such as the U.S. Employment Service, and corporations connected with Indian reservations.

In addition to listing unfair employment practices, Title VII enumerates several employment practices that are exempt from enforcement. These include the bona fide occupational qualification (BFOQ) exception, the testing exception, and the seniority exception.

Bona fide occupational qualification (BFOQ) Section 703(e) of Title VII allows employers to discriminate on the basis of religion, sex, or national origin in those cases where it can be demonstrated that there is a "bona fide occupational qualification reasonably necessary to the normal operation of that particular business or enterprise." In addition, it is acceptable for educational institutions affiliated with religious organizations, or whose goal is the propagation of a particular religion, to hire and employ workers solely of a particular religion.

Testing Within Section 703(h) of Title VII, Congress authorized the use of "any professionally developed ability test provided that such test, its administration or action upon the results is not designed, intended or used to discriminate because of race, color, religion, sex, or national origin." The judgment as to whether or not a test unfairly discriminates is based on its job relatedness. Employers who use tests as part of their selection procedures must demonstrate the validity of the measure. The two most common methods of validation are criterion-related validity and content validity. These methods are discussed in depth in Chapter 5, which discusses developing selection criteria.

Seniority Probably the exception of greatest importance to workers is the seniority exception found in Section 703(h) of the act. It states that:

> it shall not be an unlawful employment practice for an employer to apply different standards of compensation, or different terms, conditions, or privileges of employment pursuant to a bona fide seniority or merit system . . . provided that such differences are not the result of an intention to discriminate because of race, color, religion, sex, or national origin.[2]

Seniority implies that workers who have extended service with the company are entitled to a priority over other workers for available jobs and other fringe benefits. Seniority agreements afford workers with a measure of job security, so it is not surprising that organized labor has continually sought and succeeded in negotiating seniority provisions in collective bargaining agreements.

The Age Discrimination in Employment Act of 1967 (ADEA)

The **Age Discrimination in Employment Act** of 1967, amended in 1978, makes it illegal for employers to discriminate against employees or job applicants on the basis of age when the individuals are over forty years of age. The law is applicable to any employer that has twenty or more workers for twenty or more calendar weeks in the current or preceding year who is engaged in an industry affecting commerce. In addition, labor organizations having twenty-five or more members, and United States citizens working for United States-controlled corporations in foreign countries are covered by the provisions of the ADEA.

The Rehabilitation Act of 1973

The **Rehabilitation Act** of 1973 requires all contractors and subcontractors receiving federal funds in excess of $2,500 to refrain from discrimination and to engage in affirmative action to hire and advance qualified handicapped persons. According to definition, a handicapped person is an individual who has a physical or mental impairment which substantially limits one or more major life activities, who has a history of impairment, or who is regarded by others as having such an impairment. Major life activities have been interpreted by the Department of Labor to include:

1. Communication, ambulation, self-care, transportation and employment.
2. Retardation and emotional disorders.
3. Certain illnesses, such as diabetes, heart disease, epilepsy, and cancer.
4. Alcoholism and drug dependency, except when the dependency interferes with job performance or serves as a serious threat to the health and safety of others.
5. Communicable diseases, such as tuberculosis.[3]

The Vietnam Veterans Readjustment Act of 1974

The **Vietnam Veterans Readjustment Act** of 1974 provides that employers holding contracts with the federal government in excess of $10,000 must actively take affirmative action to employ qualified disabled veterans and veterans of the Vietnam era. Veterans qualifying under the act are those who:

1. Have been released from service within 48 months of the alleged discriminatory act.
2. Have served 180 days on active duty, some part of which must have been between August 5, 1964 and May 7, 1975.
3. Have not received a dishonorable discharge.
4. Have a disability of 30 percent or more.
5. Receive a discharge or release from the service due to a disability incurred or aggravated in the line of duty.

Defining Discrimination Under Title VII

When Congress passed the Civil Rights Act of 1964, it neglected to clearly define the term *discriminate.* As a result, the courts have identified two legal theories by which a plaintiff may prove a case of unlawful employment discrimination. The first theory is the common sense notion that Congress obviously intended the act to eliminate intentional employment discrimination on the basis of race, color, religion, sex, and national origin. This theory is known as **disparate treatment discrimination.** In this type of case, proving an employer's intent or motive to discriminate is crucial.

> **Disparate treatment discrimination**
>
> *Disparate treatment exists when it is demonstrated that an employer based an employment decision on race, color, religion, sex, or national origin.*

The second theory by which discrimination is demonstrated is the **disparate impact discrimination** theory. Unlike disparate treatment, where the plaintiff's contention revolves around the intention of the employer to discriminate, a litigant showing disparate impact is concerned with the ultimate result of the employment practice, and not the intent. In these cases, aggrieved persons attempt to demonstrate that an employer's surfacely neutral employment practice, such as an employment test, which makes no reference to a protected class and is neutrally applied, does in fact adversely affect one of the five prohibited classifications. If the plaintiff succeeds in proving an allegation and the employer cannot justify the employment practice by showing its job relatedness, disparate impact exists.

Disparate impact discrimination

Disparate impact exists when it is demonstrated that a facially neutral employment practice does in fact adversely affect one of the five protected classes under Title VII.

Demonstrating Disparate Impact

The typical discrimination suit begins with an allegation by an individual that he or she is being discriminated against unfairly as the result of an employment practice. At this point, the burden of proof rests with the litigant to demonstrate either a per se violation or a prima facie violation. If it can be demonstrated that an outright discriminatory action was directed against one of the protected classes, such as openly maintaining a policy of not hiring women for managerial positions, it is called a **per se violation.** More commonly, however, discrimination occurs because employers use ostensibly neutral selection techniques, which in actuality adversely affect a protected class. If the plaintiff succeeds in demonstrating that the questionable employment practice has an adverse impact on members of a protected class, then a **prima facie violation** has been committed.

Per se and prima facie violations

A per se violation occurs when an employer uses an employment practice which overtly discriminates against one of the protected groupings. A prima facie violation occurs when it is demonstrated that ostensibly neutral employment practices have the effect of adversely impacting a protected class.

Once adverse impact has been demonstrated by a prima facie case, the burden of proof shifts to the employer. Employers must now demonstrate that the employment practice being used is job related, or is being used because of business necessity. This "shifting burden of proof" model is applicable in most discrimination cases.

The key to demonstrating prima facie violations is proving the existence of adverse impact. In order to accomplish this, plaintiffs are required to provide evidence which demonstrates that protected class members are in unfavorable employment positions relative to majority class members; for example, a significantly greater percentage of blacks than whites are being rejected for a position. Usually, proof of disparate impact is accomplished in one of three ways. Plaintiffs use: (1) rejection rate data, (2) population comparisons, or (3) evidence of restrictive policies against individual protected group members.

Rejection rate data In order to prove a prima facie case based on rejection rate data, plaintiffs are required to demonstrate statistically that separate pass/fail rates exist for different classes of applicants. The rule of thumb for determining adverse impact has been established in the EEO's Uniform Guidelines on Employee Selection Procedures (1978), as the **four-fifths (4/5) rule.**

Four-fifths (4/5) rule

The four-fifths rule is the ratio identified in the Uniform Guidelines on Employee Selection Procedures to be used in determining whether or not adverse impact exists.

The four-fifths rule requires that the number of minority group members employed divided by the total number of minority group applicants be compared with the number of majority group members hired divided by the number of majority group member applicants. If the ratio of any group is less than 80 percent (4/5) of the most favored group, then adverse impact is demonstrated. For example, suppose an employer has a total applicant pool of 300 candidates, of which 35 blacks and 65 whites are chosen. Further suppose that of these 300 applicants 137 were white and 163 were black. The formula to determine if adverse impact exists would be:

$$\frac{\text{Number of minority applicants chosen}}{\text{Number of minority applicants}} : \frac{\text{Number of majority applicants chosen}}{\text{Number of majority applicants}}$$

or

$$\frac{35}{163} \text{ compared to } \frac{65}{137}$$

This formula shows that 21 percent of blacks were hired and 47 percent of whites were hired. The resulting ratio is thus (21 percent/47 percent). Consequently, adverse impact has been demonstrated.

Another, perhaps easier, way to view the four-fifths rule is to calculate the

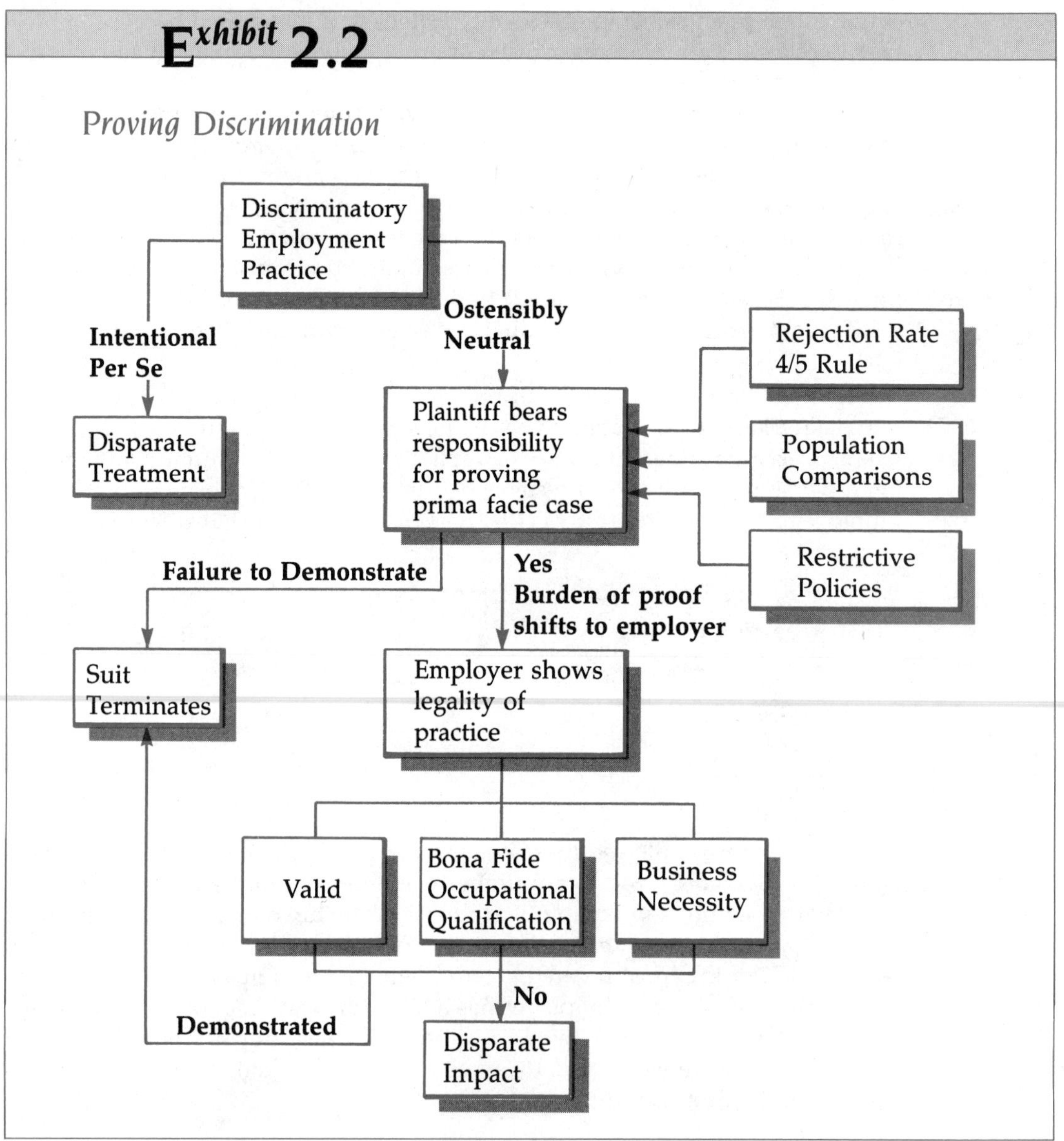

percentage of minority group members needed to avoid discrimination. For example, in the preceding case, because 47 percent of the majority group applicants were hired, exact parity would be the hiring of 77 blacks (163 × .47). Exact parity is not required (only 80 percent is), so avoiding adverse impact would require that 62 black applicants be employed (77 × .80).

Population comparisons Another method by which plaintiffs may demonstrate a prima facie case is to statistically demonstrate that the number of protected group members in the employer's workforce is significantly less than that of the surrounding population. Population statistics are especially important to employers using in-house recruiting methods. Sometimes the tendency to rely on present employee referrals for applicants results in adverse impact.

Restrictive policies The preceding two methods for demonstrating prima facie cases rely on group or class action data. Sometimes, however, only one member of a protected class brings suit, or there are not enough members (total sample) of either the majority or minority classes to statistically demonstrate adverse impact. In these cases the Supreme Court established procedural guidelines for individuals to follow in demonstrating a prima facie case. The steps include:

1. Demonstrating that the discriminated individual is a member of a minority group.
2. Establishing that the plaintiff was qualified and applied for a position for which the employer was seeking candidates.
3. Providing evidence that the plaintiff was rejected despite being qualified.
4. Showing that the employer still sought to fill the position with candidates of the plaintiff's qualifications.

Judicial Interpretations Affecting Discrimination

Since the early 1970s, there have been many court interpretations and applications of the Civil Rights Act of 1964. These cases have established the guidelines human resource managers follow in implementing employment practices. Understandably, a comprehensive discussion of each court case is beyond the scope of this book. For this reason, only those judgments which established major Equal Employment Opportunity precedents will be discussed.

Griggs v. *Duke Power Company*[4]

Griggs v. *Duke Power Company* was the first landmark case decided under Title VII. The case centered around the contention of thirteen black employees that recently enacted selection requirements to work in Duke Power Company's operations units were arbitrary and not job related, and that they screened out significantly more black than white applicants. The selection requirements contested included the registering of satisfactory scores on two professionally prepared aptitude tests and the completion of a high school education. Furthermore, since the job requirements were not retroactive, they did not apply to currently employed workers in the operations units.

Initially, both a lower district court and an appellate court ruled in favor of the company on the grounds that there was no evidence of discriminatory intent. The Supreme Court, however, reversed the lower courts' decisions. It maintained that lack of intent was not a sufficient defense because of the fact that the established requirements were not proven to be job related. In addition, the court ruled that these requirements tended to screen out a greater proportion of black applicants. In deciding in favor of the litigants, the court, rather than prohibiting tests or other selection measures, acknowledged the acceptability of these instruments as long as they were proven to be job related. As Justice Burger wrote for the Court,

> . . . good intent or absence of discriminatory intent does not redeem employment procedures or testing mechanisms that operate as "built-in headwinds" for minority groups and are unrelated to measuring job capability. . . . What Congress has commanded is that any test used must measure the person for the job and not the person in the abstract.

Several important precedents were established by *Griggs* v. *Duke Power Company*. First, under disparate impact, an employer's discriminatory intent is irrelevant. Second, the initial burden of proof in adverse impact cases rests with the litigant. Finally, once adverse impact has been demonstrated, the burden of proof shifts to the defendant who is responsible for verifying the job relatedness of the selection measure.

More recently, the Supreme Court changed part of its decision in *Griggs* v. *Duke Power*. Whereas previously employers had to demonstrate the job relatedness of the selection measure, the courts have shifted the burden of proof to workers who have to now show that the challenged employment practices are not necessary.[4a]

Albemarle Paper Company v. Moody[5]

The case of *Albemarle Paper Company* v. *Moody* strengthened the Court's ruling in the Griggs case. In 1966 four black employees filed a class action suit alleging that Albemarle Paper Company engaged in discriminatory hiring practices by requiring applicants to obtain satisfactory scores on three professionally developed tests. None of these tests had been validated, and passing scores were determined by using national norms.

Attempting to demonstrate the job relatedness of their measures, Albemarle Paper Company hastily conducted validation studies of their tests immediately prior to their trial date. The Court termed the results of the validation studies "an odd patchwork of results," and criticized the company for failing to follow the methodology outlined in the EEOC Guidelines for conducting validation studies. The use of subjective criteria, an inadequate sample, and the fact that validation for lower level jobs was conducted on upper level positions were cited by the Court as the major criticisms.

Two rulings from the Albemarle case impact on human resource management. First, the Court reaffirmed the fact that the EEOC Guidelines are afforded "great deference." Second, in ruling in favor of the litigants, the Court awarded back pay as a penalty for the employer's violation of Title VII. Consequently, a precedent was established for awarding back pay to victims of employment discrimination regardless of the employer's intentions.

Connecticut v. *Teal*[6]

The preceding two cases were litigated on the basis of class action suits which demonstrated that a significantly larger proportion of minority members were excluded from employment opportunities because of the total selection process. In *Connecticut* v. *Teal* a complaint was made by employees of the Department of Income Maintenance of the State of Connecticut against a specific portion of a total selection process. The basis for the complaint was that the initial step in a multi-step selection process for promotion to Welfare Eligibility Supervisor involved passing a written examination which adversely discriminated against blacks. In defense of its process, the defendant countered that although the test adversely affected blacks, the selection procedure, in total, did not result in discrimination against blacks. In fact, it was demonstrated that the selection procedure resulted in a greater percentage of black applicants being promoted.

In its ruling, the Court denounced this "bottom-line" approach as unsatisfactory. In writing for the Court, Justice Brennan stated,

> . . . an employer's treatment of other members of the plaintiffs' group can be of little comfort to the victims of . . . discrimination. Title VII does not permit the victim of a facially discriminatory policy to be told that he has not been wronged because other persons of his or her race or sex were hired. . . . Every individual employee is protected against both discriminatory treatment and against practices that are fair in form, but discriminatory in operation.

The decision in *Connecticut* v. *Teal* is evident. Regardless of the overall impact of the entire selection process, human resource managers must make certain that each and every stage of the process is free from bias. If a step demonstrates adverse impact, it must be confirmed as job related, or be eliminated from the process.

Washington v. *Davis*[7]

Washington v. *Davis* was decided at approximately the same time as the *Albemarle* v. *Moody* case. The ruling in the *Washington* v. *Davis* case is critical to human resource managers because it allows the use of selection devices (tests in particular), despite their having adverse impact, as long as they are shown to be job related. The case of *Washington* v. *Davis* began after a group of blacks brought a class action suit against the Washington, D.C. police department. In the suit the plaintiffs claimed that a verbal skills test being used by the police department for selection was discriminatory since the failure rate of blacks was four times greater than that of whites. The police department countered that there was statistical evidence to show a relationship between scores on the test and performance at the police academy.

Initially, a lower court ruled in favor of the police department. However, the Court of Appeals overturned this ruling on the grounds that success in a training program is not sufficient proof of job relatedness. When the case was presented before the Supreme Court, however, the original decision was upheld on the grounds that performance in a training program, the contents of which can be demonstrated to be job related, is a sufficient criterion for demonstrating job relatedness.

The importance of *Washington* v. *Davis* is twofold. First, the Court's ruling establishes performance in a training program as an accurate measure of job performance if it can be demonstrated to be job related. Second, and perhaps more importantly, the Court upheld the use of proven job-related tests despite the fact that adverse impact exists.

International Brotherhood of Teamsters v. *United States*[8]

The case of *Teamsters* v. *United States* clarified the use of a bona fide seniority system as an exception to Title VII. The question of a seniority systems application arose when the government questioned employment practices engaged in by an employer and a union. The employer, a common carrier, was accused of practicing discrimination against minorities when hiring line drivers. This claim arose from the fact that the employer hired blacks and people with Spanish surnames only for lower paying, less desirable jobs, and discriminated against them thereafter for promotions and transfers as well. The government further claimed that this violation of Title VII was being perpetuated by the seniority system negotiated between the employer and the union. Since seniority was determined by length of service in a particular job, any employee who had previously been discriminated against and who subsequently transferred to a higher level job forfeited all his or her accumulated seniority in the lower level position. Consequently, the employee would receive fewer benefits than contemporaries who had not been discriminated against initially.

After reviewing the allegations, the Court ruled that although the employer discriminated before and after the initiation of Title VII and was guilty of unlawful discrimination, the seniority system was protected by Section 703(h) of the act. In so ruling Justice Stewart wrote for the Court,

> . . . although a seniority system inevitably tends to perpetuate the effects of pre-Act discrimination in such cases, the congressional judgment was that Title VII should not outlaw the use of existing seniority lists and thereby destroy or water down the vested seniority rights of employees simply because their employer had engaged in discrimination prior to the passage of the Act.
>
> To be sure, Section 703(h) does not immunize all seniority systems. It refers only to "bona fide" systems, and a proviso requires that any differences in treatment not be "the result of an intention to discriminate because of race . . . or national origin. . . ."

Diaz v. *Pan American World Airways, Inc.*[9]

The celebrated case of *Diaz* v. *Pan American* involved the issue of whether or not the refusal of airlines to hire males for flight cabin attendant positions violated Title VII. Pan American, the defendant, did not dispute the facts, but claimed that the policy requiring flight attendants to be female was justifiable on the basis that it was a **bona fide occupational qualification** (BFOQ).

The decision of the U.S Court of Appeals in the Diaz case established the basis by which BFOQ is interpreted and applied. Although Pan American demonstrated that females supposedly performed the job better, Justice Tuttle wrote for the Court,

> . . . while we recognize that the public's expectation of finding one sex in a particular role may cause some initial difficulty, it would be totally anomalous if we were to allow the preferences and prejudices of the customers to determine whether the sex discrimination was valid. Indeed, it was, to a large extent, these very prejudices the Act was meant to overcome. Thus, we feel that customer preference may be taken into account only when it is based on the company's inability to perform the primary function or service it offers.

As a result of the Diaz case, male flight attendants, a rarity at the time, are now commonplace. As a result of the court's ruling, sex as a BFOQ is rarely used. In fact, because there has never been a demonstrated BFOQ for either race or color, BFOQ as an exception is usually recognized only in cases of age discrimination. For example, upper age limits are imposed on admission to training programs for police and fire fighting personnel.

Regents of the University of California v. *Bakke*[10]

The Bakke case, as it is most commonly referred to, is probably the most famous reverse discrimination case. Alan Bakke, a white male, applied for and was denied admission to the University of California at Davis medical school. Bakke filed a discrimination suit charging that the university had discriminated against him by reserving a number of openings for disadvantaged applicants who were members of racial minority groups. The requirements for admission into medical school for these special slots were substantially lower than the criteria required under normal admission procedures. Consequently, students of these specified races who were less qualified than Bakke were admitted, while he was rejected.

Although the Court ruled in favor of Bakke, it upheld the right of organizations to institute affirmative action programs as long as they consider candidates on an individual basis and do not specify rigid quotas. The Davis quota system, however, was ruled unacceptable under the Fourteenth Amendment because it denied admission to Bakke solely on racial grounds.

United Steel Workers of America and Kaiser Aluminum & Chemical Corporation v. *Weber*[11]

The case of *United Steel Workers of America and Kaiser Aluminum & Chemical Corp.* v. *Weber* is probably one of the most significant EEO cases to be decided by the courts. The suit resulted when the United Steel Workers and Kaiser entered into a collective bargaining agreement which included an affirmative action plan designed to eliminate racial imbalances in their craftwork forces. The plan called for equalizing the imbalance by reserving 50 percent of the openings in the in-house training programs for blacks, until such time as the percentage of black craftworkers equaled the percentage of blacks in the local labor market. After the first year of the agreement's implementation, seven black and six white craft trainees were chosen for the training program. Weber, one of the rejected white applicants, subsequently filed a class action suit claiming discrimination. His contention was that the affirmative action program had the effect of rejecting more qualified senior white applicants in favor of less qualified junior black employees. Weber's contention was supported by the District Court, and upheld by the Court of Appeals. The Supreme Court, however, in a landmark decision, reversed the judgments.

In ruling against Weber, the Supreme Court maintained that Title VII allows for private, voluntary, race-conscious affirmative action plans. It appears evi-

Exhibit 2.3

Major Court Case Implications

Case	Finding
Griggs v. *Duke Power* 1971	1. Lack of discriminatory intent is not sufficient. 2. Test must measure person for job, not person in abstract. 3. Initial burden of proof is litigant's after which it shifts to defendant.
Albemarle v. *Moody* 1975	1. EEOC guidelines afforded "Great Deference." 2. Back pay awarded to victim irrespective of intent.
Connecticut v. *Teal* 1982	1. Bottom-line approach is unsatisfactory. Each step of process must be free from bias.
Washington v. *Davis* 1976	1. Tests may be used despite adverse impact if shown to be job related. 2. Performance in training program is acceptable as measure of job performance if job related.
Teamsters v. *U.S.* 1977	1. Bona fide seniority system is acceptable for discrimination.
Diaz v. *Pan American* 1971	1. Established basis for BFOQ.
Bakke v. *Univ. of California* 1978	1. Affirmative action programs upheld when candidates are considered individually, and there are no rigid quotas.
Weber v. *United Steel Workers and Kaiser Aluminum* 1979	1. Voluntary Affirmative Action programs to correct racial imbalances are legal.

dent from this ruling that when an affirmative action program is voluntarily entered into between a union and an employer, and when the objective of such an agreement is the correction of a racial imbalance and racial differences are given equal quotas, the program is legal.[12]

Although the Supreme Court chose not to define in detail the boundary between permissible and impermissible affirmative action plans, the following guidelines for permissible plans may be implied from the Weber case. These include:

1. Affirmative action plans must be in connection with a "plan."
2. Self-analyses must be conducted to determine where racial imbalances exist. Thereafter, affirmative action plans must be remedial to open previously closed occupations.
3. Plans must be voluntary.
4. Any affirmative action plans implemented must not trammel the interests of whites.
5. Plans must be temporary.[13]

Affirmative Action

As the term implies, **affirmative action** requires that employers take positive steps to ensure that women, minorities, handicapped persons, and any other protected classes are afforded equal employment opportunities. Affirmative action programs are usually established to rectify past discriminatory practices which are responsible for present employment imbalances. These programs may be voluntarily undertaken by employers, or they may be involuntary (court ordered).

Affirmative action

Affirmative action involves an employer's engagement in positive, results-oriented methods designed to overcome past discriminatory practices by actively seeking to hire and promote women, minorities, handicapped persons, and other protected class members.

Since its inception, affirmative action has had differing interpretations. One noted researcher, James Ledvinka, identifies four definitions which have emerged over the years. These include:

1. **The recruitment of underrepresented groups** Actively attempting to attract employees from groups which are underrepresented in the employer's workforce.

2. **The changing of management attitudes** Making concerted efforts to eliminate any conscious or unconscious prejudices the employer's managers may have against underrepresented groups in the workforce.
3. **The removal of discriminatory obstacles** Identifying employment practices which may be hampering underrepresented groups, and replacing these practices with ones that do not negatively impact on these individuals.
4. **The provision of preferential treatment** Establishing hiring and staffing policies which afford preferential treatment to those underrepresented in the employer's workforce.[14]

Of the preceding definitions, the giving of preferential treatment to underrepresented groups has generated the most controversy and subsequent litigation. Regardless of whether the affirmative action program is court ordered or voluntarily applied, its legal application remains complex. Courts may order preferential treatment to overcome past discriminatory practices, but they cannot order such programs for the following reasons: (1) to correct workforce imbalances which may exist, (2) to override bona fide seniority systems, or (3) to use racial preferences in determining layoffs. Similarly, as demonstrated in the previously cited Bakke case, certain voluntarily instituted programs of preferential treatment are acceptable while others are unlawful. For example, in the 1976 case of *McDonald* v. *Santa Fe Trail Transportation Co.*,[15] the Supreme Court ruled that the firing of two white employees for thievery violated Title VII because the company failed to fire a black employee who was caught stealing with them.

Implementing Affirmative Action Plans

There are several types of employers who need affirmative action plans. Under Executive Orders 11246 and 11375, all employers who have government contracts in excess of $50,000 and who employ fifty or more employees are required to develop and implement written affirmative action plans. Failure to develop and implement affirmative action programs may result in employers being disqualified for receiving contracts, having the receipt of contracts delayed, or having to forfeit existing contracts.

In addition to government contractors, there are other employers who are subject to developing and implementing affirmative action plans. First, many states extend affirmative action requirements to cover all state agencies, including universities, government bureaus, and state contractors and subcontractors. Second, employers who have violated Title VII may be required to institute plans either as part of a conciliation agreement or because it is court ordered. Finally, unions are subject to the same requirements as employers, and may have affirmative action programs invoked on them if discriminatory practices are discovered.

It is apparent from the complexity of the rulings regarding affirmative action that the legality of these programs is situation specific. Those employers imple-

Exhibit 2.4

Establishing an Effective Affirmative Action Program

- Establish a company statement of policy.
- Determine the most effective ways to communicate the policies.
- Assign EEO/AA responsibilities to appropriate personnel.
- Conduct utilization and workforce analyses.
- Establish goals and timetables.
- Set-up procedures for monitoring and reviewing the program.
- Identify any problem areas needing correction.
- Train personnel and establish implementation procedures.
- Prepare documentation and reports for submission to EEO.

menting programs would probably be best advised to follow the guidelines put forth by the Equal Employment Opportunity Commission. These include:

1. Establishing a strong company policy and commitment.
2. Assigning responsibility and authority for the program to executives.
3. Analyzing areas where minorities are being underutilized.
4. Setting behavioral goals for rectifying the underutilization of minorities.
5. Involving all managers and supervisors in the achievement of the affirmative action goals.
6. Reviewing job descriptions for accuracy.
7. Recruiting females and minorities who demonstrate the potential for filling selected positions.
8. Reviewing employment procedures for discriminatory impact.
9. Concentrating on placement of females and minorities into promotion tracks previously unavailable to them.
10. Establishing monitoring systems, and periodically measuring the program's progress.[16]

Enforcing Equal Employment Legislation

The Equal Employment Opportunity Commission

The administration of Equal Employment Opportunity laws rests with the **Equal Employment Opportunity Commission** (EEOC). The agency was created by the Civil Rights Act of 1964 and amended by the EEO act of 1972. It is composed of five presidentially appointed commissioners and a General Counsel, who are empowered to issue and monitor compliance with employment guidelines, and to investigate and conciliate any grievances alleging unfair discrimination based on any of the enumerated protected classes. Furthermore, the 1972 amendments to Title VII authorized the EEOC to:

1. Litigate court actions on behalf of aggrieved parties when attempts at conciliation fail.
2. Bring class action suits.
3. Initiate and litigate allegations of a "pattern of practice" of discrimination (sometimes called systematic discrimination).

Filing Discrimination Charges

Charges of discrimination may be filed with the EEOC by any aggrieved individual, his or her representative, or any of the five EEOC commissioners. The time period for filing charges is 180 days, but this period is extended to 300 days when charges must first be filed with local or state agencies. If the EEOC determines that there is sufficient evidence to indicate that the alleged discrimination did in fact occur, it attempts to work out a mutually agreeable solution between the parties. Should this attempt at conciliation fail, the EEOC may elect to file suit in Federal District Court, or issue a right-to-sue letter, allowing the aggrieved party the right to pursue the case in court. At this point, the complainant has 90 days either to bring suit or to forfeit his or her rights under the act.

The Office of Federal Contract Compliance Programs (OFCCP)

The **Office of Federal Contract Compliance** (OFCCP) was created in 1978 and is headquartered in Washington, D.C. The OFCCP is responsible for:

1. Administering Executive Order 11246, which forms the basis for affirmative action compliance programs.
2. Ensuring that contracting employers make reasonable accommodation for employment of the handicapped.
3. Ensuring that contracting employers provide job opportunities for both disabled veterans and veterans of the Vietnam War.

The OFCCP becomes involved with a government contractor in one of three ways.[17] First, any contractor who bids for and is awarded a government contract of $1 million or more will automatically be subject to a pre-award compliance review. This review takes place within thirty days after the OFCCP is notified by the awarding agency, and no contract may officially be awarded until the OFCCP declares the contractor awardable or nonawardable.

Second, the OFCCP conducts inquiries whenever complaints are filed by employees or applicants. These complaint investigations are the result of discrimination charges and must be filed within 180 days of the alleged act. Usu-

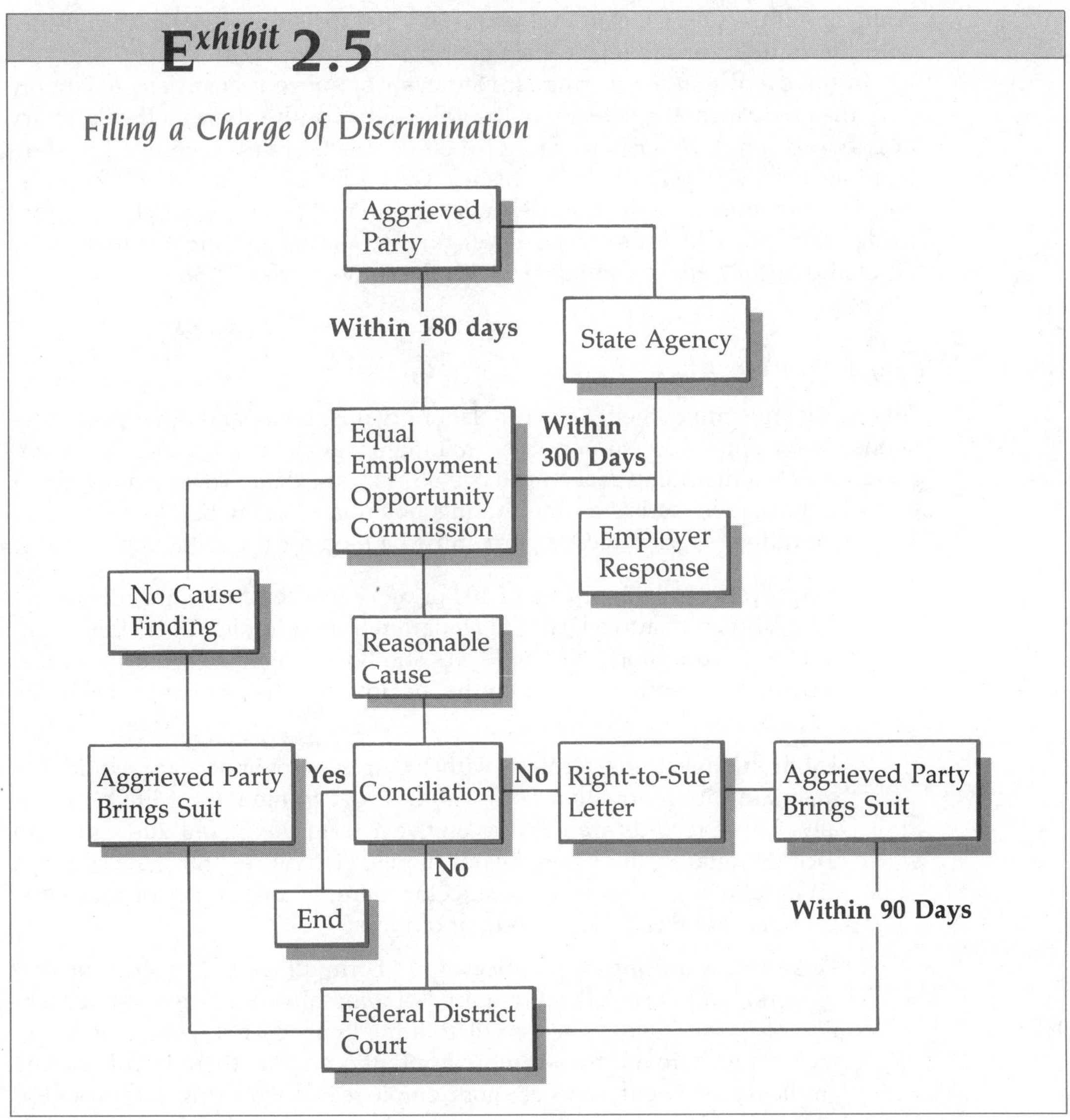

Exhibit 2.5

Filing a Charge of Discrimination

ally, the OFCCP handles only class action suits and refers individual cases to the Equal Employment Opportunity Commission. In practice, however, any complaint to the OFCCP usually triggers reviews by both the OFCCP and the EEOC.

Last, the OFCCP periodically conducts regular compliance reviews of selected employers. These reviews usually begin with the OFCCP's request for copies of the employer's affirmative action plan, its workforce analysis, and any other supporting documents. These documents are then subjected to a desk audit, and if the OFCCP is not fully satisfied that the employer is in compliance with the statute, on-site reviews are conducted.

In the event that a government contractor or subcontractor fails to comply with the guidelines, the Director of the OFCCP has authority from the Secretary of Labor to cancel or suspend any of their contracts. Furthermore, all government agencies are periodically furnished with a list of the names of these debarred contractors, and the agencies must refrain from entering into further contracts with them. In order to regain eligibility, contractors must convince the OFCCP that they are in compliance with Executive Order 11246.

Record-keeping Requirements

All employers, employment agencies, labor organizations, and other people responsible for apprenticeship or other training programs subject to Title VII are required to maintain and make available all relevant data. The documentation of this information assists in monitoring potentially unlawful discrimination acts. In addition, specific EEO reports must be filed for the following:[18]

1. **Employers** All employers of 100 or more workers, who are covered by Title VII or Executive Order 11246, are required to file Report EEO-1 annually. Furthermore, all employers should maintain relevant personnel records for a period of six months, or until the disposition of personnel actions, whichever is later.
2. **Labor organizations** Unions with 100 or more members are required to maintain the information necessary in order to file Report EEO-3 annually. These records are kept for one year from the EEO-3 due date, and include data on the labor organization's: (1) policies, (2) practices, and (3) employees, in terms of race, color, national origin, sex of members, persons referred for jobs, and apprentices.
3. **Persons controlling apprenticeships** Form EEO-2E (required of employers), and Form EEO-2 (required of joint labor–management apprenticeship committees) must be filed annually if the following criteria are met: (1) if there are five or more apprentices, (2) if there is at least one employer of twenty-five or more employees sponsoring the program, and (3) if at least one local union operating a hiring hall or having twenty-five or more members sponsors the program.

In addition to filing requirements, employers are required by law to post in a conspicuous place a notice, jointly issued by the EEO and the OFCCP,[19] which summarizes the law and information on how complaints may be filed. Willful violation of the posting requirement may result in a fine of not more than $100 being levied against the employer. Furthermore, failure to post notices may result in an acceptable excuse for the untimely filing of charges by the aggrieved parties.

Exhibit 2.6

Equal Employment Opportunity is...

THE LAW

Private Employment, State and Local Government, Educational Institutions

Race, Color, Religion, Sex, National Origin
Title VII of the Civil Rights Act of 1964, as amended, prohibits discrimination in hiring, promotion, discharge, pay, fringe benefits, and other aspects of employment, on the basis of race, color, religion, sex or national origin.

Applicants to and employees of most private employers, State and local governments and public or private educational institutions are protected. Employment agencies, labor unions and apprenticeship programs also are covered.

Age
The Age Discrimination in Employment Act of 1967, as amended, prohibits age discrimination and protects applicants and employees aged 40-70 from discrimination in hiring, promotion, discharge, pay, fringe benefits and other aspects of employment. The law covers most private employers, State and local governments, educational institutions, employment agencies and labor organizations.

Sex (wages)
In addition to the sex discrimination prohibited by Title VII of the Civil Rights Act (see above) The Equal Pay Act of 1963, as amended, prohibits sex discrimination in payment of wages to women and men performing substantially equal work in the same establishment. The law covers most private employers, State and local governments and educational institutions. Labor organizations cannot cause employers to violate the law. Many employers not covered by Title VII, because of size, are covered by the Equal Pay Act.

If you believe that you have been discriminated against under any of the above laws, you should immediately contact:

The U.S. Equal Employment Opportunity Commission
2401 E Street, N.W.
Washington, D.C. 20507
or an EEOC field office by calling toll free 800-USA-EEOC. (For the hearing impaired, EEOC's TDD number is 202-634-7057.)

Employers holding Federal contracts or subcontracts

Race, Color, Religion, Sex, National Origin
Executive Order 11246, as amended, prohibits job discrimination on the basis of race, color, religion, sex or national origin, and requires affirmative action to ensure equality of opportunity in all aspects of employment.

Handicap
Section 503 of the Rehabilitation Act of 1973, as amended, prohibits job discrimination because of handicap and requires affirmative action to employ and advance in employment qualified handicapped individuals who, with reasonable accommodation, can perform the functions of a job.

Vietnam Era and Disabled Veterans
Section 402 of the Vietnam Era Veterans Readjustment Assistance Act of 1974 prohibits job discrimination and requires affirmative action to employ and advance in employment qualified Vietnam era veterans and qualified disabled veterans.

Applicants to and employees of companies with a Federal government contract or subcontract are protected under the authorities above. Any person who believes a contractor has violated its nondiscrimination or affirmative action obligations under Executive Order 11246, as amended, Section 503 of the Rehabilitation Act or Section 402 of the Vietnam Era Veterans Readjustment Assistance Act should contact immediately:

The Office of Federal Contract Compliance Programs (OFCCP)
Employment Standards Administration
U.S. Department of Labor
200 Constitution Avenue, N.W.
Washington, D.C. 20210
or an OFCCP regional or area office, listed in most telephone directories under U.S. Government, Department of Labor.

Programs or activities receiving Federal financial assistance

Handicap
Section 504 of the Rehabilitation Act of 1973, as amended, prohibits employment discrimination on the basis of handicap in any program or activity which receives Federal financial assistance. Discrimination is prohibited in all aspects of employment against handicapped persons who, with reasonable accommodation, can perform the essential functions of a job.

Race, Color, National Origin
In addition to the protection of Title VII of the Civil Rights Act of 1964, Title VI of the Civil Rights Act prohibits discrimination on the basis of race, color or national origin in programs or activities receiving Federal financial assistance. Employment discrimination is covered by Title VI if the primary objective of the financial assistance is provision of employment, or where employment discrimination causes or may cause discrimination in providing services under such programs.

If you believe you have been discriminated against in a program which receives Federal assistance, you should immediately contact the Federal agency providing such assistance.

Don't Forget...

Equal Employment Opportunity is the Law!

GPO 920-752

Exhibit 2.7

Joint Reporting Committee

- Equal Employment Opportunity Commission
- Office of Federal Contract Compliance Programs (Labor)

EQUAL EMPLOYMENT OPPORTUNITY
EMPLOYER INFORMATION REPORT EEO–1

Standard Form 100
(Rev. 5–84)
O.M.B. No. 3046–0007
EXPIRES 3/31/85
100–211

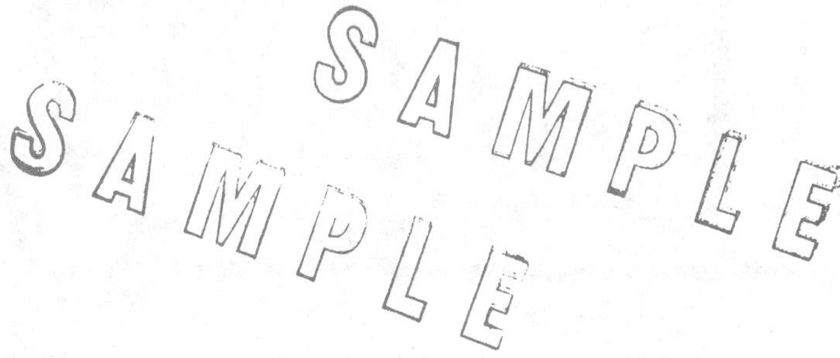

Section A—TYPE OF REPORT
Refer to instructions for number and types of reports to be filed.

1. Indicate by marking in the appropriate box the type of reporting unit for which this copy of the form is submitted (MARK ONLY ONE BOX).

(1) ☐ Single-establishment Employer Report

Multi-establishment Employer:
(2) ☐ Consolidated Report (Required)
(3) ☐ Headquarters Unit Report (Required)
(4) ☐ Individual Establishment Report (submit one for each establishment with 50 or more employees)
(5) ☐ Special Report

2. Total number of reports being filed by this Company (Answer on Consolidated Report only) ________

Section B—COMPANY IDENTIFICATION *(To be answered by all employers)* — OFFICE USE ONLY

1. Parent Company
   a. Name of parent company (owns or controls establishment in item 2) omit if same as label — a.

Name of receiving office				Address (Number and street)	b.
City or town	County	State	ZIP code	b. Employer Identification No.	

2. Establishment for which this report is filed. (Omit if same as label) — OFFICE USE ONLY
   a. Name of establishment — c.

Address (Number and street)	City or Town	County	State	ZIP code	d.
b. Employer Identification No.		(Omit if same as label)			e.

Section C—EMPLOYERS WHO ARE REQUIRED TO FILE *(To be answered by all employers)*

☐ Yes ☐ No 1. Does the entire company have at least 100 employees in the payroll period for which you are reporting?

☐ Yes ☐ No 2. Is your company affiliated through common ownership and/or centralized management with other entities in an enterprise with a total employment of 100 or more?

☐ Yes ☐ No 3. Does the company or any of its establishments (a) have 50 or more employees AND (b) is not exempt as provided by 41 CFR 60–1.5, AND either (1) is a prime government contractor or first-tier subcontractor, and has a contract, subcontract, or purchase order amounting to $50,000 or more, or (2) serves as a depository of Government funds in any amount or is a financial institution which is an issuing and paying agent for U.S. Savings Bonds and Savings Notes?

If the response to question C–3 is yes, please enter your Dun and Bradstreet identification number (if you have one): ☐☐☐☐☐☐☐☐☐

☐ Yes ☐ No 4. Does the company receive financial assistance from the Small Business Administration (SBA)?

NOTE: If the answer is yes to questions 1, 2, or 3, complete the entire form, otherwise skip to Section G.

NSN 7540–00–180–6384

SF 100 Page 2

Section D—EMPLOYMENT DATA

Employment at this establishment—Report all permanent full-time or part-time employees including apprentices and on-the-job trainees unless specifically excluded as set forth in the instructions. Enter the appropriate figures on all lines and in all columns. Blank spaces will be considered as zeros.

JOB CATEGORIES		NUMBER OF EMPLOYEES										
			MALE					FEMALE				
		OVERALL TOTALS (SUM OF COL. B THRU K) A	WHITE (NOT OF HISPANIC ORIGIN) B	BLACK (NOT OF HISPANIC ORIGIN) C	HISPANIC D	ASIAN OR PACIFIC ISLANDER E	AMERICAN INDIAN OR ALASKAN NATIVE F	WHITE (NOT OF HISPANIC ORIGIN) G	BLACK (NOT OF HISPANIC ORIGIN) H	HISPANIC I	ASIAN OR PACIFIC ISLANDER J	AMERICAN INDIAN OR ALASKAN NATIVE K
Officials and Managers	1											
Professionals	2											
Technicians	3											
Sales Workers	4											
Office and Clerical	5											
Craft Workers (Skilled)	6											
Operatives (Semi-Skilled)	7											
Laborers (Unskilled)	8											
Service Workers	9											
TOTAL	10											
Total employment reported in previous EEO-1 report	11											
(The trainees below should also be included in the figures for the appropriate occupational categories above)												
Formal On-the-job trainees: White collar	12											
Formal On-the-job trainees: Production	13											

NOTE: Omit questions 1 and 2 on the Consolidated Report.

1. Date(s) of payroll period used:

2. Does this establishment employ apprentices?
1 ☐ Yes 2 ☐ No

Section E—ESTABLISHMENT INFORMATION *(Omit on the Consolidated Report)*

1. Is the location of the establishment the same as that reported last year?
1 ☐ Yes 2 ☐ No 3 ☐ No report last year

2. Is the major business activity at this establishment the same as that reported last year?
1 ☐ Yes 2 ☐ No 3 ☐ No report last year

OFFICE USE ONLY

3. What is the major activity of this establishment? (Be specific, i.e., manufacturing steel castings, retail grocer, wholesale plumbing supplies, title insurance, etc. Include the specific type of product or type of service provided, as well as the principal business or industrial activity.)

Section F—REMARKS

Use this item to give any identification data appearing on last report which differs from that given above, explain major changes in composition or reporting units and other pertinent information.

SAMPLE

Section G—CERTIFICATION *(See Instructions G)*

Check one
1 ☐ All reports are accurate and were prepared in accordance with the instructions (check on consolidated only)
2 ☐ This report is accurate and was prepared in accordance with the instructions.

Name of Certifying Official	Title	Signature	Date

Name of person to contact regarding this report (Type or print)	Address (Number and street)				
Title	City and State	ZIP code	Telephone Area Code	Number	Extension

All reports and information obtained from individual reports will be kept confidential as required by Section 709(e) of Title VII

WILLFULLY FALSE STATEMENTS ON THIS REPORT ARE PUNISHABLE BY LAW, U.S. CODE, TITLE 18, SECTION 1001

Exhibit 2.8

Union Reporting Program
Washington, DC 20507

EQUAL EMPLOYMENT OPPORTUNITY LOCAL UNION REPORT (EEO-3)

Approved by OMB
No 3046-0006
Expires 5/31/91

SAMPLE

Part A. LOCAL UNION IDENTIFICATION

1. Full name of local union for which this report is filed. (Include local number, if any.)

2. Mailing address.

a. Where official mail should be sent to the union.

Number and street

City

County

State

Zip Code

b. Union office, if different from 2a.

Number and street

City

County

State Zip Code

3. Indicate type of local union report by a check in applicable box:

a. ☐ Report filed by local union in its own behalf
b. ☐ Other (explain)

4a. Are you affiliated with or chartered by a national or international union or national federation? Yes ☐ No ☐

b. If "Yes" to item 4a, give name and address of such national or international organization.

5. Are you affiliated with the AFL-CIO? Yes ☐ No ☐

Part B. LOCAL UNION PRACTICES

1. To the best of your knowledge, does your membership include any:

	Yes	No
a. Blacks (Non-Hispanic)?	☐	☐
b. Hispanics?	☐	☐
c. Women?	☐	☐

2. If "No" to any items 1a, 1b, or 1c, is this because the group or groups not represented:

	(CHECK ALL APPLICABLE BOXES)		
	BLACK NON-HISPANIC 1 (a)	HISPANIC 1 (b)	WOMEN 1 (c)
a. Are not in the local community?			
b. Are not in the bargaining unit?			
c. Are excluded by provision in constitution or bylaws?			
d. Have not applied for membership?			
e. Have applied, but did not have a sponsor?			
f. Have applied, but did not meet qualifications other than sponsorship?			

g. Other reason(s) (Explain)

3. To the best of your knowledge, has your international union chartered a separate local within the same work and/or area jurisdiction which consists only of:

	Yes	No
a. Persons of the same race/ethnic identity	☐	☐
b. Persons of the same sex?	☐	☐

Part C. LOCAL UNIONS REQUIRED TO FILE

	Yes	No
1. Has the local union had 100 or more members at any time since December 31 of the preceding year?	☐	☐
2. Does the local union, or any unit, division, or agent of the local union, or any labor organization which performs, within a specific jurisdiction, the functions ordinarily performed by a local union, whether or not it is so designated:		
a. Operate a hiring hall or hiring office?	☐	☐
b. Have an arrangement under which one or more employers are required to consider or hire persons referred by the local union or an agent of the local union?	☐	☐
c. Have 10 percent or more of its members employed by employers which customarily and regularly look to the union, or any agent of the union, for employees to be hired on a casual or temporary basis, for a specified period of time, or for the duration of a specified job?	☐	☐

The union must complete the entire report if it answered "YES" to Item 1, *AND* the answer is "YES" to any of the three questions in Item 2.

The union is not required to complete the entire report if it answered "NO" to Item 1, *OR* "NO" to all three questions in Item 2. If that is the case, the union must complete Parts A, B, C and E and return this form to the specified address.

EEOC FORM 274, JUN 88 PREVIOUS EDITIONS ARE OBSOLETE

EEOC ORIGINAL

PAGE 1

Part D. REMARKS

Part E. IDENTIFICATION AND SIGNATURE

To the best of my knowledge and belief, the information contained in this report is true and complete. It is further certified that to the extent any data in Schedule I, Items 1 or 2, are based on self-identification by individuals, this information was gathered only after they were advised of its confidential nature and purposes.

1. Type or print name, title, address and telephone number for union business of designated representative

Name ____

Title ____

Work address ____

Telephone number (including area code) ____

2. Signature of designated representative | 3 Date

"Whoever, in any matter within the jurisdiction of any department or agency of the United States knowingly and willfully falsifies, conceals, or covers up by any trick, scheme, or device a material fact, or makes any false, fictitious or fraudulent statements or representations, or makes or uses any false writing or document knowing the same to contain any false, fictitious or fraudulent statement or entry, shall be fined not more than $10,000 or imprisoned not more than 5 years, or both." Title 18, Section 1001, United States Code.

SCHEDULE I—LOCAL UNION REPORT (EEO—3)

MEMBERSHIP, APPLICANT and REFERRAL INFORMATION

1. Method of identification

How was information as to race/ethnic identification and sex in Item 2 below obtained?

This information may be obtained by visual survey, from records made after employment, from personal knowledge or by self-identification. The self-identification method may be used subject to the conditions set forth in the instructions. No State law prohibiting the self-identification method applies, since the Equal Employment Opportunity Commission's regulations supersede such laws.

	Check all applicable boxes
a. Existing Record	
b. Visual Survey	
c. Tally from Personal Knowledge	
d. Self-Identification	
e. Other (Specify)	

2. Statistics

	TOTAL	MALE					FEMALE				
		NON-HISPANIC ORIGIN		HISPANIC	ASIAN OR PACIFIC ISLANDER	AMERICAN INDIAN OR ALASKAN NATIVE	NON-HISPANIC ORIGIN		HISPANIC	ASIAN OR PACIFIC ISLANDER	AMERICAN INDIAN OR ALASKAN NATIVE
	(COLUMNS B-K)	WHITE	BLACK				WHITE	BLACK			
	A	B	C	D	E	F	G	H	I	J	K
a. MEMBERSHIP IN REFERRAL UNIT											
(1) MEMBERS											
(2) APPLICANTS FOR MEMBERSHIP DURING THE PAST YEAR											
b. REFERRALS DURING 2-MONTH PERIOD											
(1) NUMBER OF PERSONS REFERRED											
(2) NUMBER OF REFERRALS											
(3) APPLICANTS FOR REFERRAL											

3. Period Used For Referral Date

You should obtain the figures reported in Item 2 "Statistics" using any 2-month period between August 1 ... November

Dates of 2-month Period ____

EEOC FORM 274, JUN 88 PREVIOUS EDITIONS ARE OBSOLETE

EEOC ORIGINAL

Page

Selected Equal Employment Opportunity Issues

Initially, the passage of the Civil Rights Act of 1964 was motivated by a desire to eradicate racial discrimination. Other issues, such as women's rights, age discrimination, and handicap discrimination, were either not taken seriously or were added to the act as amendments. This fact is obvious since most of the early litigation and precedent setting court rulings focused on issues of racial discrimination. In the past two decades, however, there has been a change in both society's attitudes and the issues raised in the courtroom. The emphasis appears to have shifted from racial discrimination to sexual harassment, the rights of the aged, the employment of the handicapped, and religious accommodation. These are issues that today's human resource managers face on a daily basis.

Sexual Harassment

Unfortunately, unwanted sexual advances on the job are a common problem. It occurs so frequently that one researcher indicated that 70 percent of the females sampled reported being sexually harassed.[20] Some of the sexual harassments are directly related to terms or conditions of employment, while other cases involve joking or abusive comments that are particularly aimed at women who enter traditional male jobs or departments.

Sexual harassment

Unwelcome sexual advances, requests for sexual favors, and other verbal or physical conduct of a sexual nature constitute sexual harassment when (1) submission to such conduct is made either explicitly or implicitly a term or condition of an individual's employment, (2) submission to or rejection of such conduct by an individual is used as the basis for employment decisions affecting that individual, or (3) such conduct has the purpose or effect of unreasonably interfering with an individual's work performance or creating an intimidating, hostile, or offensive working environment.[21]

Legally, **sexual harassment** is sometimes difficult to determine because it often involves perception and consent or acquiescence. Actions or innuendos which are perceived by one individual as harassment may be viewed as innocent behavior by another. Similarly, any element of acquiescence causes the behavior to be normal social interaction between members of opposite sexes. Only when the sexual advance is refused does it begin to take on the quality of sexual harassment.

In addition to consent, courts consider two other elements when determining whether or not sexual harassment has occurred. First, the courts consider the employer's knowledge of the harassment. Did the employer know, or should the employer have been reasonably expected to know, about the alleged incident? Second, sexual harassment is contingent upon the link between the sexual activity and the employment situation. If there are no employment consequences contingent on the advance, or if the employment environment is not affected by the advance, then the likelihood of the court ruling that sexual harassment occurred is nil. The landmark case outlining the liability for sexual harassment is the case of *Meritor Savings Bank* v. *Mechelle Vinson.*

Meritor Savings Bank v. *Mechelle Vinson*[22]

The case of *Meritor Savings Bank* v. *Mechelle Vinson* affirmed the fact that sexual harassment may exist even when it is not directly linked to retaining a job or getting a promotion. In 1974, Mechelle Vinson applied for and was hired for a teller trainee position at Meritor Savings Bank. Over the next four years Ms. Vinson was subsequently promoted to teller, head teller, and assistant branch manager. All parties concerned agreed that her advancement occurred solely on the basis of merit. In September of 1978, Vinson notified her supervisor, Sidney Taylor, that she was taking an indefinite period of sick leave. The bank subsequently dismissed her on November 1, 1978, for excessive use of her sick leave benefit.

Shortly thereafter, Mechelle Vinson sued the bank on the grounds of sexual harassment. Vinson's contention was that during her four years at the bank she had been subjected to constant sexual harassment by Sidney Taylor, her supervisor. According to Vinson, Taylor had made repeated demands on her for sexual favors, and, out of fear of losing her job, she had had sexual relations with Taylor forty or fifty times over the four-year period. Taylor denied the accusations and maintained that the suit was filed as a result of a business-related dispute between him and Ms. Vinson. The bank also denied the allegations, claiming that if any sexual harassment had been engaged in by Taylor, it was completely unknown and unsanctioned.

In ruling on *Meritor* v. *Vinson,* the Court did not determine the truth or falsity of Ms. Vinson's claim. It did, however, set precedent by affirming that sexual harassment clearly falls under the auspices of Title VII, and employment discrimination may occur irrespective of the fact that no economic loss is imposed on the aggrieved person. The Court went on to conclude that in order to find sexual harassment there must be three key ingredients. First, the advance must be unwelcome. Second, the employer must have knowledge, either actual or imputed, of the advance. Last, some employment opportunity must be contingent on the fulfillment of the sexual favor, or a hostile environment must be created.

It is important to note that sexual harassment is not reserved solely for females attempting to fend off unwanted advances directed at them by males. Males can be the subject of unwanted advances made by females, and both sexes may complain of advances made by members of the same sex. Most of the litigation brought to date, however, involves the sexual harassment of women by men.

Exhibit 2.9

A Sexual Harassment Statement

Unwelcome sexual advances, requests for sexual favors, and any other verbal or physical conduct of a sexual nature which causes the discomfort of any worker will not be tolerated. Any employee who feels that they are or have been the subject of such behavior should attempt to have it stopped immediately by informing the offender. In the event the behavior continues, a supervisor or the personnel department should be notified. Offenders are subject to disciplinary procedures.

Preventing harassment—the employer's responsibility[23]

The EEOC guidelines specifically indicate that the best approach for eliminating harassment is to prevent its occurrence in the first place. Employers are not only held responsible for their own actions and the actions of their supervisors, but they are also held responsible for the actions of their employees about which they "should have known." Court rulings have stated that in situations in which employers know of the harassment and take no action to correct the situation, they are also held liable. On the other hand, when employers develop procedures and policies to prevent sexual harassment, and demonstrate good faith efforts to eliminate its occurrence, courts usually find no liability, even though harassment occurs.[24] The EEOC, in conjunction with the courts, recommends the following guidelines for preventing sexual harassment:[25]

1. A specific policy against sexual harassment should be developed and communicated to all levels of employees.
2. A strong statement indicating management disapproval of sexual harassment should be issued.
3. Training sessions for managers on what constitutes sexual harassment should be implemented.
4. Employees should be informed of their rights to be free of sexual harassment, and of the complaint procedures available to them should these rights be violated.
5. A grievance procedure should be implemented and enforced.
6. Those found guilty of violating the policies should be disciplined.

Age Discrimination

Prior to 1978, the solution to the problem of what to do with older, marginal workers was relatively simple. If compulsory retirement at age sixty-five failed to alleviate the problem, demotions or discharges were available to make room for younger, more talented employees. With the passage of the Age Discrimination in Employment Act of 1978 (ADEA), Congress created a whole new outlook on employment of the aged.

The ADEA affects all employment decisions involving workers over forty years of age. No longer can employers solve their problems with the older worker by termination or retirement. Now, ways must be sought that provide opportunities for gainful employment of the aged until such time as it can be demonstrated that they are incapable of satisfactorily performing their job duties. Consequently, age itself is not a sufficient criterion for employment decisions. However, when discharge is for just cause and is unrelated to an employee's age, the termination is justifiable.

The effect of the ADEA on human resource managers[26]

The ADEA has brought forth an abundance of litigation in the 1980s. These problems are compounded by the undeniable fact that the average age of the population and the workforce is increasing. These factors are creating a unique set of problems which human resource managers must learn to deal with effectively. These include:

1. The existence of a more senior, and consequently more expensive, workforce.
2. A reduction in the amount of promotional opportunities available for young, talented workers, which may have the effect of stifling employees and increasing turnover.
3. The creation of the need for the development of validated performance appraisals to justify discharges of inefficient workers.

It is important to note at this point that the employment of older workers may also provide distinct benefits to organizations. The wisdom and experience brought to the environment by many of these workers is irreplaceable. Furthermore, older workers are less likely to turn over, have a greater appreciation of safety matters, and demonstrate increased intelligence levels as they approach retirement age.[27]

Employing Handicapped Workers

Contrary to popular belief, there is no federal law comparable to Title VII that prohibits employment discrimination against handicapped individuals by private employers. The Rehabilitation Act of 1973 serves to promote the employment of handicapped individuals by requiring employers with government contracts in excess of $2,500 to establish affirmative action programs for the handicapped. The statute defines handicapped people as those who have "a physical or mental impairment which substantially limits one or more of such person's major life activities and has a record of such an impairment, or is regarded as having such an impairment."[28] Major life activities are defined by the

Department of Labor and include, among others: communication, ambulation, self-care, transportation, retardation, emotional disorders, diabetes, heart disease, epilepsy, cancer, and certain communicable diseases, such as tuberculosis. Alcoholism and drug dependency are also considered handicaps, provided the dependency does not prevent the employee from satisfactorily completing his or her job duties or pose a threat to the property or safety of others.

The statute requires employers to make **reasonable accommodation** in the employment of the handicapped. Just how much effort constitutes reasonable accommodation is a matter of interpretation. Certainly, the elimination of unnecessary job requirements, the active recruitment of handicapped people for jobs they are qualified for, and minor modifications to the work environment, such as ramps, constitute efforts to employ the handicapped. Some employers even develop special training programs and modify existing job requirements to promote the employment of the handicapped.[29] However, eliminating bona fide job requirements, tolerating poor performance, or placing the handicapped person in a job that may endanger the safety of others is not required.

Adequate performance of job responsibilities is probably not the biggest hurdle facing the handicapped. Rather, handicapped people are continually faced with myths and stereotypes regarding their inability to satisfactorily perform jobs. These attitudes, coupled with the fact that Title VII does not specifically protect the handicapped, make it considerably more difficult for handicapped individuals to obtain meaningful employment opportunities. Hopefully, as more and more handicapped individuals demonstrate job success, and as stereotypes are dispelled, greater numbers of employment opportunities will be made available to them.

Religious Accommodation

To date, most of the emphasis in religious accommodation has centered around hours of work and working conditions. Title VII requires employers to make reasonable efforts to accommodate the religious beliefs of employees. It does not require them to allow complete religious freedom to the extent that it interferes with the normal conduct of their business.

The issue of reasonable religious accommodation was considered in the case of *Trans World Airlines, Inc.* v. *Hardison*.[30] The case developed after Hardison, a senior employee with TWA, began studying the religion of the Worldwide Church of God. Since members of this religion are prohibited from working from sundown Friday until sundown Saturday, Hardison, a senior employee, was granted a shift change to accommodate his religious beliefs. Subsequently, Hardison bid for and received a transfer to another job for which he no longer had seniority benefits. Refusing to violate its seniority provisions, the union declined to allow Hardison to take Saturdays off. Furthermore, a request to allow Hardison to work only four days was declined by the company on the grounds that Hardison's job was essential and could not be filled without undue hardship to the company or other employees. After he refused to work on Saturdays, Hardison was subsequently fired.

The Supreme Court upheld the discharge of Hardison on the grounds that reasonable accommodation was made, and that any additional accommodation would incur an undue hardship on the employer. Specifically, the Court maintained that employers:

1. Need not violate seniority rules of a valid collective bargaining agreement.
2. Are under no obligation to accommodate religious beliefs of one employee by imposing undue hardships on other nonreligious employees.
3. Are not required to incur more than de minimis costs in accommodating the religious beliefs of their employees.

A Final Note

With the enactment of the Civil Rights Act of 1964, a new era in human resource management began. For many managers, the manner in which they previously hired and promoted employees underwent drastic modification. Previously used procedures were scrutinized, and scientific methods were subsequently applied to the development of methods that would accomplish the purposes without illegally discriminating against anyone.

In many organizations, the changes necessary to bring existing employment procedures into legal compliance brought new problems as well. Managers were uncertain of the regulations and unsophisticated in the statistical techniques necessary to validate instruments, and they viewed government regulation as an intrusion into their rights to manage. Rather than apply uncertain standards and techniques to their procedures, managers abandoned the techniques altogether. The logic was simple: Tests cannot possibly discriminate unfairly if they are not used. As a result, selection instruments, such as tests, which were once used in abundance, were totally abandoned by many organizations.

Today's human resource manager must be aware of the everchanging rules and regulations governing employment. However, these statutes should not be the sole criterion for determining employment practices. Confronted with the fear of litigation, some managers immediately offer employment opportunities to protected class members, whether or not they are qualified for the position. This practice is illogical. The laws do not require the employment or promotion of unqualified protected class members at the expense of either qualified majority members or the organization's goals. Equal employment opportunity laws are designed to eliminate unfair discrimination against qualified protected group members. Those organizations that employ proper methods in determining their job requirements, that take care in the development of their selection and promotion instruments, and that train their managers in the proper use of these tools will invariably have legal employment procedures resulting in a qualified workforce.

Summary

In the past, employers utilized whatever criteria they wished when making employment decisions. Workers were hired, fired, promoted, demoted, and transferred at the whim of managers. This state of affairs was drastically altered in 1964 with the passage of Title VII of the Civil Rights Act. This law, and its subsequent amendments, requires employers to refrain from using any employment criteria which has the effect of unfairly discriminating against minorities, women, the aged, and people with handicaps.

Almost immediately after its passage, Title VII generated controversy and confusion. Uncertainty as to the definition of *discrimination*, when it occurred, who was covered, and how the act was to be enforced was widespread. Litigation was abundant, and the first two decades after the statute's passage brought many amendments and judicial interpretations of the act. In fact, to this day, courts are continually faced with a stream of new cases requiring clarification of the statute.

These continually changing government regulations add new dimensions to the jobs of human resource managers. Not only must they familiarize themselves with the laws presently applicable, but they must also continually monitor and review the constant and complex changes that occur. In addition, human resource managers are responsible for: the collection of data, record-keeping, the timely filing of government reports, and the monitoring and training of other management members in order to insure compliance.

Key Terms to Identify

Civil Rights Act
Title VII
Protected classes
Equal Pay Act
Equal Employment Opportunity
Age Discrimination in Employment Act (ADEA)
Rehabilitation Act
Vietnam Veterans Readjustment Act
Disparate treatment discrimination
Disparate impact discrimination
Per se violation
Prima facie violation
Four-fifths Rule
Griggs v. *Duke Power Co.*
Albemarle Paper Company v. *Moody*
Connecticut v. *Teal*
Washington v. *Davis*
Teamsters v. *United States*
Diaz v. *Pan American World Airways*
The Bakke case
Bona Fide Occupational Qualification (BFOQ)
United Steel Workers and Kaiser Aluminum v. *Weber*
Affirmative action
Equal Employment Opportunity Commission (EEOC)
Office of Federal Contract Compliance (OFCCP)
Sexual harassment
Reasonable accommodation

Questions for Discussion

Do You Know the Facts?

1. How did the passage of the Civil Rights Act of 1964 alleviate the major employment problems previously faced by racial minority group members?
2. How do people claiming unfair discrimination prove the validity of their case?
3. Discuss how the early EEO court cases clarified the definition of *discrimination*.
4. Discuss the different jurisdictional powers exercised by the EEOC and the OFCCP. Which of these agencies appears to have greater authority, and why?

Can You Apply the Information Learned?

1. What policies and procedures would you institute within your organization to insure that your managers select and promote employees within the boundaries of the law?
2. What type of training sessions would you recommend in order to educate your managers about the relevant government rules and regulations?
3. What policies and procedures would you implement to guarantee an environment free of sexual harassment?
4. It has been said that "by their nature, properly devised selection procedures can only be legal." Do you agree or disagree with this statement, and why?

A Case of the Wrong Persuasion

It seemed like any other summer day. The outside temperature was in the 90s, and the factory felt like an oven. Juan Gonzales had arrived for work late that day, but he thought that Greg, the assistant supervisor, fully understood the problem he had with his car. Sure, he had been late three times this month, but after all Juan's car certainly wasn't the only car to have overheated during the heat wave. In fact, just the other day, Juan had heard that Jamie Phillips, a second-shift co-worker who had an abominable tardiness record, was excused for the very same reason. Thinking nothing more of it, Juan began to operate his machine.

Shortly thereafter, Juan saw Tom, the new supervisor, approaching in a rage. Without even a word of greeting he looked at Juan and said, "You're fired." "But why?" Juan said. "Why?" screamed Tom. "Because you were late! It's the fourth time this month, and I'm tired of your excuses. Pack up your tools and get out of here immediately." With that, Tom turned and stormed off.

Initially, Juan was shocked. He reasoned that it must be the heat. He had been working at the factory for eight years. Something like this couldn't possibly be happening. Certainly Greg would explain, and Tom would return and say it was all a big mistake. But Tom never came back.

That evening Juan was visited at home by a group of his co-workers. Word of Juan's dismissal had circulated throughout the plant like wildfire. The workers wanted to encourage Juan to take action. Rumors had been circulating that Tom had made some very derogatory comments concerning having to work with people of Juan's "persuasion," and they were certain that was the underlying reason for his dismissal. In fact, since Jamie Phillips had a tardiness record that was worse than Juan's, and he didn't even receive so much as a verbal reprimand, the workers were convinced that Tom's actions were illegal.

Juan was confused. Sure, Jamie Phillips had a poorer tardiness record, and even a worse performance appraisal, but Jamie worked on the second shift. His supervisor was Pete Milligan. Obviously if Jamie worked for Tom and had not been reprimanded, Juan might have a case. But do the actions of one supervisor impact on the actions of another supervisor? There was only one way to find out. Juan filed charges of discrimination the very next day.

Questions for Discussion

1. Do you think Tom was justified in firing Juan? Why or why not?
2. What arguments do you think Juan's attorney will make in order to demonstrate the existence of unfair discrimination? What do you think the company's defense will be?
3. Do you think the court will rule in favor of Juan? Why or why not?

Endnotes and References

1 Patrick J. Cihon and James O. Castagnera, *Labor and Employment Law* (Boston, MA: PWS-KENT Publishing Company, 1988): 299.

2 The Civil Rights Act of 1964 as amended by the Equal Employment Opportunity Act of 1972. 78 Stat. 253 (1964), as amended by Pub.L. 92–261 (1972); 42 U.S.C. Sections 2000e et seq. (1970).

3 Vida G. Scarpello and James Ledvinka, *Personnel/Human Resource Management* (Boston, MA: PWS-KENT Publishing Company, 1988), 142.

4 Supreme Court of the United States 401 U.S. 424 (1971).

4a See the June 5, 1989 opinion written by Justice White in *Ward's Cove Packing* v. *Atonio.*

5 Supreme Court of the United States 422 U.S. 405 (1975).

6 Supreme Court of the United States 457 U.S. 440 (1982).

7 Supreme Court of the United States 426 U.S. 229 (1976).

8 Supreme Court of the United States 431 U.S. 324 (1977).

9 United States Court of Appeals, Fifth Circuit, 442 F.2d 385 (1971).

10 Supreme Court of the United States 438 U.S. 265 (1978).

11 Supreme Court of the United States 443 U.S. 193 (1979).

12 Kenneth L. Sovereign, *Personnel Law* (Reston, VA: Reston Publishing Company, Inc., 1984): 85.

13 David P. Twomey, *Equal Employment Opportunity Law*, 2nd ed. (Cincinnati, OH: South-Western Publishing Company, 1990): 71–72.

14 James Ledvinka, *Federal Regulation of Personnel and Human Resource Management* (Boston, MA: PWS-KENT Publishing Company, 1982): 118–119.

15 Supreme Court of the United States 427 U.S. 273 (1976).

16 Richard Peres, *Preventing Discrimination Complaints: A Guide for Supervisors* (New York: McGraw-Hill Book Co., 1979): 24–25.

17 Kenneth J. McCulloch, *Selecting Employees Safely Under the Law* (Englewood Cliffs, NJ: Prentice-Hall, Inc., 1981): 245–247.

18 For further information, see *1989 Guidebook to Fair Employment Practices* (Chicago, IL: Commerce Clearing House, Inc., 1989): 135–145.

19 Copies of the joint EEO-OFCCP poster may be obtained by writing either the EEOC or the OFCCP.

20 Robert H. Faley, "Sexual Harassment: Critical Review of Legal Cases with General Principles and Preventive Measures," *Personnel Psychology*, Vol. 35, No. 3 (1982): 583–600.

21 EEOC, Guidelines on Sex Discrimination because of Sex, 29 C.F.R. 1604.11(a).

22 54 U.S.L.W. 4703 (Supreme Court of The United States, 1986).

23 For a discussion on dealing with harassment at the workplace, including the rights of the alleged harasser as well as the harassee, see David S. Bradshaw, "Sexual Harassment: Confronting the Troublesome Issues," *Personnel Administrator*, Vol. 32, No. 1 (January 1987): 51–53.

24 See Kenneth L. Sovereign, *op. cit.*, 143–149.

25 Vida G. Scarpello and James Ledvinka, *op. cit.*, 139.

26 On January 1, 1987, H.R. 4154, amending ADEA took effect. This law eliminated mandatory retirement for employees over age 70. Currently, ADEA protects any individual over the age of 40. For expanded discussion of the impacts of H.R. 4154 for human resource managers, see Stephen J. Cabot, "Living with the New Amendments to the Age Discrimination in Employment Act," *Personnel Administrator*, Vol. 32, No. 1 (January 1987): 53–54.

27 Paul R. Baltes and K. Warner Schaie, "Aging and the IQ: The Myth of the Twilight Years," *Psychology Today* (March, 1974): 35–40.

28 The Rehabilitation Act of 1973, Section 7, 29 USC, 706(6).

29 Pati C. Gopal, "Countdown on Hiring the Handicapped," *Personnel Journal*, Vol. 57 (March 1978): 144–153.

30 The Supreme Court of the United States, 432 U.S. 63 (1977).

Chapter 3

Job Analysis and Design

Objectives

After reading this chapter you should understand:

1. The importance of conducting job analyses.
2. The way job analyses are used within organizations.
3. Who conducts analyses and the preliminary steps in conducting job analyses.
4. Both the generalized and the specific methods for collecting job analysis data, as well as the pros and cons of the various methods.
5. The differences among job analyses, job descriptions, and job specifications.
6. The various methods for designing jobs.
7. The importance of work scheduling; you should be able to determine the most effective schedule for use.

The purpose of a **job analysis** is to collect information about what is done on the job, why the job is done, and how the job relates to the overall objectives of the organization. A completed job analysis provides the information necessary to understand the characteristics and behaviors needed to satisfactorily complete the job. Additionally, comprehensively conducted analyses are used for personnel selection by providing information necessary to accurately match employee characteristics to job requirements.

Job analysis

Job analysis is a process undertaken to determine which characteristics are necessary for satisfactory job performance, and to analyze the environmental conditions in which the job is performed.

Completed job analyses are rarely, if ever, used in their entirety.[1] More often, information contained in analyses is extracted in the form of either **job descriptions** or **job specifications.**

> ***Job descriptions and job specifications***
>
> *Job descriptions consist of information extracted from analyses which contain the tasks, behaviors, responsibilities, and activities necessary for the completion of the job. Job specifications are usually used for selection purposes; they summarize the human characteristics, such as knowledge, skills, training, and experiences necessary for satisfactory job completion.*

Typical Uses of a Job Analysis

Over the past decade, the importance of job analyses has been brought to the forefront specifically for their use in complying with the government rules and regulations established under Title VII. Prior to this time period approximately 60 percent of companies surveyed indicated that they did not use job analyses.[2]

Although many organizations started using job analyses principally to satisfy Equal Employment Opportunity rules and regulations, human resource managers have discovered additional benefits in conducting analyses. In most organizations job analyses are used for: selection, training, job evaluation, performance appraisal, health and safety, time and motion studies, and adherence to government rules and regulations.

Selection The most widely used purpose for job analysis is probably the establishment of selection criteria. Selection requires that the characteristics of applicants be identified and subsequently matched to the job requirements. A job analysis provides two major benefits for selection. First, it identifies both the characteristics of the job and the human characteristics necessary for satisfactory performance. Second, it aids in identifying shortcomings in already existing selection procedures. Consider the following case of a sanitation department which failed to conduct job analyses prior to establishing selection criteria.

> A sanitation department of a small city was experiencing a drastic decrease in productivity. Specifically, the trash collectors were unable to complete their assigned routes within the time period allotted by the industrial engineers. Seeking to discover the reasons for this problem, the city engaged a management consultant. Armed with pencils, paper, a stopwatch, and a helmet, the consultant mounted

the truck to observe the process. After a relatively brief period of time, the consultant discovered the problem. Although the collectors began their tasks in earnest, they soon became fatigued and were unable to maintain the desired pace. Questioning the selection procedure, the consultant was surprised to discover that the only requirement for the position was a passing grade on a written examination consisting of math and English sections. At no time was strength considered to be a major selection factor. Upon completion of the job analysis, a validated strength test was instituted and administered to all applicants as part of the selection procedure. Productivity increased as a direct result of matching job performance criteria and selection criteria.

Conducting a job analysis does not necessarily guarantee adequate selection procedures. Without it, however, the likelihood of creating relevant criteria is left to chance.

Training Once selected, employees are usually given orientation training by the organization. For many employees this training consists solely of information about company policies and procedures. Some employees, however, receive comprehensive on-the-job skills training. While these programs are discussed in detail in Chapter 6, common sense dictates that the method of training depend on the material to be taught. Similar to selection, job analysis provides two benefits for training. First, it identifies the task duties in which employees need training, and second, it aids in identifying existing inadequate training methods.

Job evaluation One of the most perplexing problems facing managers is the assignment of a proper wage to a particular job. To aid in this task, they employ a process known as **job evaluation,** in which each job's monetary worth is determined.

Job evaluation

Job evaluation is the process of ascertaining how much each job is worth to the organization, comparing the jobs to one another, and then assigning each job a monetary value.

The successful determination of the relative worth of each job within an organization requires that the jobs be analyzed with respect to certain similar characteristics. Job analyses contain the information needed for this comparison. For example, suppose that an organization is attempting to determine the salary of a newly created driver-salesperson position as compared to an existing route-delivery-person position. By comparing the job analyses of the two positions, the company can determine how many duties are encompassed in the newly created position and which ones are unique to the position. A pay range can subsequently be developed to provide workers with adequate compensation for the additional duties required.

Performance appraisal Most organizations require that all supervisors appraise the performance of their subordinates at least once a year.

For performance appraisals to be successful, two requirements should be met. First, both subordinates and supervisors must understand the job's requirements. Second, performance appraisals need to be validated against job analyses. This means that appraisal instruments are created and tested to make certain that they truly measure those behaviors necessary for satisfactory job performance. The logical first step in familiarizing employees with job requirements and creating valid instruments is job analysis.

Health and safety In some organizations there are jobs which expose workers to hazards. Mine workers, x-ray technologists, and a host of other similar occupations require performance under potentially hazardous conditions. Conducting a thorough job analysis often leads to the discovery of unnecessary exposure to certain dangers. Once discovered, safety procedures may be instituted which lead to greater profits through the decrease in accident rates and the resulting increase in productivity. For example, a job analysis of a retread-tire-casing inspector's job at a major retreading facility indicated that employees inspecting used tire casings have to spread the tire, insert their head into the rim area, and use a small grinder to smooth out any previously patched nail hole repairs. When the noise level within the casing was measured, it was discovered that, due to a chamber effect, the decibel level to which workers were exposed exceeded the acceptable limits for safety proposed by the Occupational Health and Safety Administration. As a result of the job analysis, all casing inspectors were issued earplugs, and were required to wear them during the grinding operation.

Time and motion studies Since the onset of specialization, companies have sought to increase productivity while maintaining quality. In an effort to accomplish this task, they have turned to experts in engineering and efficiency. One of the primary tools employed by these experts is time and motion studies.

Time and motion studies

Determining the best way to accomplish a job by observing the tasks involved and the amount of time necessary to complete each task.

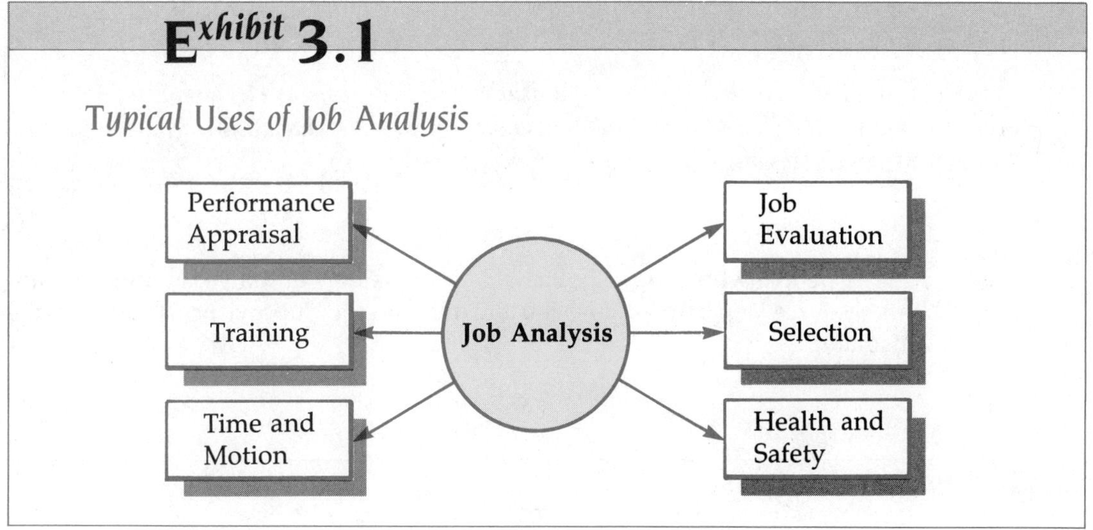

Exhibit 3.1

Typical Uses of Job Analysis

As a preliminary to time and motion studies, job analyses are performed to ascertain the tasks to be studied. For example, analyzing a plumber's job may indicate that a major part of the job is spent slipping threaded nuts onto pieces of pipe having flanges on one end, placing other threaded pieces of pipe into the nuts, and tightening these nuts with a pipe wrench. In an effort to increase the plumber's speed, different techniques for connecting the two pieces of pipe may be developed to save the amount of time and motion necessary during the operation.

Equal employment opportunity For many organizations, the rules and regulations established by the Equal Employment Opportunity Commission over the past two decades has provided an added incentive for conducting job analyses. When faced with a charge of discrimination, companies must demonstrate that their tools (such as tests or performance reviews) are valid, that there is a BFOQ (bona fide occupational qualification), or that a business necessity exists which accounts for the discriminatory practice. It is the job analysis which provides support for these rationales.

Who Conducts Job Analyses?

Upper management, with the assistance of human resource departments, selects individuals to conduct job analyses. Many indirect methods (such as tape recorders, automated counters, and VCR equipment) are used to collect job analysis information without the direct involvement of people. However, most of the time people perform job analyses and are known as **job analysts.**[3]

> ***Job analyst***
>
> *The individual, designated by the organization, who is responsible for collecting the job information. This individual is usually an outside consultant, a current worker, or a supervisor.*

The people who serve as job analysts are usually employees within the human resource department, the job incumbent, the supervisor, or an external consultant.

Conducting the Analysis

There are occasions when the job analyst is totally unfamiliar with the job characteristics or the environment in which the job is being performed. This is particularly true in cases of analysts from human resource departments. These positions, which require writing and interviewing skills, are traditionally filled by new college graduates who have little on-the-job experience. Consider the following hypothetical case:

> Adam, who just received his bachelor's degree in business with a concentration in human resource management, has obtained a position as a job analyst for a large poultry processing plant. After his initial orientation and tour of the facilities, he is wished well and brought to his office. After greeting his co-workers, he enters his office for his first day of work.
>
> Totally enamored with his office and his good fortune in finding such a relevant job, he spends his first hour congratulating himself and swiveling in his chair. Finally, he chances to glance at his desk, locates his in-basket, removes the top memo, and gasps in amazement. The memo reads, "Urgent! Must have qualified Chicken Sexer by next week." The memo is signed Jennifer Pinchek, DVM. At first Adam laughs. It is obviously a welcome-to-the-job joke. Who cares what gender a chicken is? After questioning some people, however, Adam quickly ascertains that it is a true bona fide position. Where to begin? College forgot to teach him about chickens!

The preceding case appears, despite its absurdity, to illustrate a phenomenon often encountered by analysts. Not only does the analyst sometimes lack general knowledge of the job or the environment in which it is performed, but also the analyst is sometimes unaware of or unfamiliar with the existence of

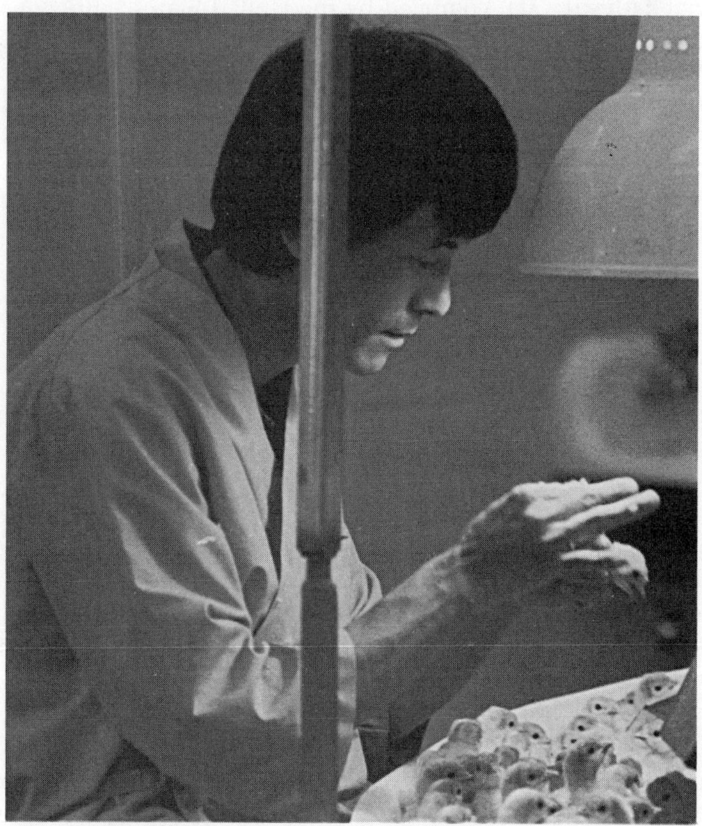

At the Cuddy-Rocco Hatchery each newly hatched chick is examined to determine its sex. Photo courtesy of Rocco, Inc., Harrisonburg, VA.

certain job categories. It is easy to understand how this lack of information could present a problem to a new employee like Adam, but would it really be a problem for an experienced analyst? The answer is yes. Technological advances, expansions, and mergers all create new job dimensions. The job analyst must be prepared to deal continuously with new situations.

Initial Steps

There are several sources of information a job analyst may consult with prior to formally beginning a job analysis. These are: *The Dictionary of Occupational Titles*, previously conducted analyses, and peers and colleagues within the field.

The Dictionary of Occupational Titles (DOT) The **Dictionary of Occupational Titles** (DOT), compiled by the United States Employment Service, contains broad, general descriptions of about 25,000 jobs.[4] Each job is given a code number consisting of nine numerals, which is referred to as the DOT Occupational Code. The first three numbers indicate the occupational categories and subcategories, the middle three digits indicate the worker functions (as derived from the Functional Job Analysis technique discussed later in this chapter), and the last three digits distinguish among jobs classified with the same first six digits.

Consultation of similar analyses Depending upon the occupation or industry being examined, analysts may obtain copies of previously completed job analyses. One source of these publications is the Department of Labor. Another source of information available to analysts is professional associations in the field. Many companies have already conducted analyses on similar jobs, and are willing to share their results with other organizations.

Consultation with peers and colleagues During the initial phase of job analyses, managers tend to often overlook a crucial resource area: their peers and colleagues. When the occasion for analyzing an unfamiliar job arises, contacting a colleague employed in the same occupational field may prove invaluable. In many cases, the colleague has either performed a similar analysis, or he or she will be aware of additional sources of information.

Avoiding the full job analysis

Regardless of whether analysts use the Dictionary of Occupational Titles, consultation with peers and colleagues, or already published analyses, they must carefully consider the comprehensiveness of the material obtained. Rarely, if

Exhibit 3.2

DOT Description for Chick Sexer

411.687-014 Chick Sexer (agric.)
Examines chick genitalia to determine their sex: turns back skin fold of external cloacal opening or inserts illuminating viewer into cloaca to observe genitals. Places chicks into boxes according to sex. May mark content data on boxes of segregated chicks.

Source: *The Dictionary of Occupational Titles, 4th ed.* U.S. Employment Service (Washington, D.C.: U.S. Government Printing Office, 1977): 278.

ever, is the information gathered sufficient to totally forego the conduction of a thorough job analysis. Each environment is different, and each job is specific to its particular environment. Although job titles may be identical, the specific duties in different organizations vary greatly. For example, in a bank, the title *Administrative Assistant* may refer to an executive secretary, while an Administrative Assistant in the White House may be a Presidential advisor. In fact, the identical title within the same occupational field may have different connotations. (A Senior Vice-President in a bank could either be subordinate or superior to a First Vice-President, depending upon the particular bank.) Remember, the initial steps outlined are solely for the purpose of familiarizing the analyst with the general job characteristics. They are no substitutes for actually conducting a job analysis.

Collecting Data: Typical Methods

There are four basic methods of collecting data: observation, interviews, questionnaires, and diaries.

Observation If carried out correctly, observation is a simple, convenient, and inexpensive method for collecting job data. It requires that workers be observed, and records be kept detailing their job behaviors. During observations, certain precautions should be taken. First, analysts must strive to obtain normality. Analysts must observe average workers during average conditions. Second, the analyst must be careful to be unobtrusive. Third, the analyst must make note of the specific job requirements, and not the behaviors specific to particular workers. For example, an analyst observing a baseball game should note that a pitcher is required to throw a baseball to a batter with either hand, not that it should be thrown with the left hand because they happen to be observing a left-handed pitcher. Last, analysts must be certain that they obtain an adequate sample for generalization.[5] The result of not adhering to these guidelines can be seen in the following case.

> Ellen, a freelance job analyst, was contacted by the Post Office to conduct an analysis of the job of letter sorter. Unfamiliar with the job characteristics, Ellen consulted the DOT and spoke with a colleague. Having completed this initial analysis, she entered the Post Office on December 11 to begin observing. After three days of observing the letter sorters and recording job data, Ellen concluded her analysis and presented her findings to the supervisor. Her analysis detailed the amount of letters sorted per hour and the methods by which this sorting was accomplished. After reading the report, the postal supervisor summoned Ellen to his office for a conference. Something was amiss. It appeared that the number of letters which needed to be sorted was approximately four times the amount the supervisor had imagined. How could the supervisor have been so naive? Was this analysis long overdue?

The preceding case illustrates the problems encountered when observation is conducted during atypical times. What Ellen had inadvertently done was to observe the postal workers during the holiday season. As a result, she was unable to generalize her results to post office workers during a typical time period.

Interviews Interviews are the most common, yet most difficult of the data collection methods. The interview method consists of asking questions to both incumbents and supervisors in either an individual or a group setting. The philosophy behind the use of interviews is that job incumbents are the most familiar with the job and can supplement the information obtained through observation. Workers know the specific duties of the job, and supervisors know the job's relationship to the rest of the organization.

Caution must be used when utilizing the interview method. The interviewer must be trained in proper interviewing techniques. Furthermore, since there are

Exhibit 3.3

Guidelines for Conducting Job Analysis Interviews

1. Put the worker at ease, establish rapport.
2. Make the purpose of the interview clear.
3. Encourage the worker to talk through empathy.
4. Help the worker to think and talk according to the logical sequence of the duties performed.
5. Ask the worker only one question at a time.
6. Phrase questions carefully so that the answers will be more than just "yes" or "no."
7. Avoid asking leading questions.
8. Secure specific and complete information pertaining to work performed and worker traits.
9. Conduct the interview in plain, easy language.
10. Consider the relationship of the present job to other jobs in the department.
11. Control the time and subject matter of the interview.
12. Be patient and considerate of the worker.
13. Summarize the information obtained before closing the interview.
14. Close the interview promptly.

Source: *Handbook for Analyzing Jobs.* U.S. Department of Labor, Manpower Administration (Washington, D.C.: U.S. Government Printing Office, 1972): 12–13.

various interviewing styles and approaches, care must be taken to insure that the method used provides the necessary information for the analysis.

Although the interview method provides opportunities to obtain information sometimes unavailable through other methods, it has limitations. First, it is time consuming, and as a result, costly. Second, it relies heavily on the analyst's interviewing skills, and if important information is overlooked, there are legal requirements which may be unmet. Last, if seen as an opportunity to improve their positions, such as to increase their wages, workers may exaggerate their job duties to add greater importance to their positions.[6]

Questionnaires Questionnaires are one of the most economical methods of collecting data, and they have been used extensively. They allow analysts to survey large populations of both workers and supervisors, they enable participants to complete the survey at their leisure, and they provide for a systematic accumulation of data. They do, however, have shortcomings. Designing questionnaires is not a simple task, and caution must be taken so that the respondent does not misinterpret the questions. Additionally, it is difficult to motivate the participants to complete the questionnaires truthfully and to return them.

Diaries This method consists of incumbents completing daily diaries or logs of all their work activities over a period of time. The advantages of using diaries

Exhibit 3.4

Job Analysis Interview Dos and Don'ts

1. Don't take issue with a worker's statements.
2. Don't show partiality to grievances or conflicts.
3. Don't show interest in the job's wages.
4. Be polite and courteous.
5. Treat the worker as an equal.
6. Don't be biased by your own likes and dislikes.
7. Don't suggest changes or improvements in the work situation. Be impersonal.
8. Get the supervisor's permission before talking with the worker.
9. Verify job data with the supervisor.
10. Verify the completed analysis with the appropriate official.

Source: *Handbook for Analyzing Jobs.* U.S. Department of Labor, Manpower Administration (Washington, D.C.: U.S. Government Printing Office, 1972): 13.

include: cost effectiveness, comprehensiveness regarding the duties conducted and time spent on each duty, and the personal gratification workers get from completing the diaries. The disadvantages of diaries are: the time necessary to complete them (which sometimes is prohibitive for assembly line or other jobs); the short time period (typically one to two weeks) in which information is usually gathered; and the fact that employees sometimes attempt to bias the listings to add complexity to their jobs (similar to interviews). Furthermore, many employees are either not able to, or are reluctant to, complete the diaries or logs.[7]

Collecting Data: Special Methods

The previously mentioned methods of data collection require analysts to adapt techniques to specific jobs. To use interviews and questionnaires, the analyst must develop the questions and format to suit each particular job in question. Observation and diaries are open ended and have no preset structure. There are, however, specific techniques which have been developed that provide structure and quantitative procedures for determining what job duties are being completed. Two of these methods are the Functional Job Analysis (FJA), and the Position Analysis Questionnaire (PAQ).

Functional job analysis[8]

The Department of Labor (DOL) methodology For approximately fifty years, the U.S. Department of Labor has been involved in developing a job analysis procedure to provide standardization for rating and comparing different jobs. The outcome of this research is a job analysis procedure called **Functional Job Analysis,** which concentrates on two major categories of information: a) work performed and b) worker traits.

At the core of the DOL method is a description of what the worker does in relation to *data, people,* and *things.* This relationship is expressed in a hierarchical arrangement of twenty-four worker functions, with each function being assigned a corresponding number. These three numbers (one for data, one for people, and one for things), make up the middle three numbers in the *Dictionary of Occupational Titles* code. In the previous example of a chick sexer, the DOT code is 411.687-014. The 6 represents the data rating, and indicates that the job involves "comparing." The 8 represents the "people" function, and indicates that the job involves taking instructions and helping. Lastly, the 7 represents the classification according to "things," and indicates that the job of chick sexer involves handling. As a general rule, the lower the number the higher the level, and higher levels typically include or involve all the functions below them.

In addition to data, people, and things (classified under the category of worker functions), the DOL procedure gathers information regarding

1. Work fields.
2. Materials, products, subject matter, and services.

3. Training time.
4. Aptitudes.
5. Temperaments.
6. Interests.
7. Physical demands and working conditions.

The information collected is subsequently recorded on a form called a *Job Analysis Schedule.*

Advantages and disadvantages of Functional Job Analysis (FJA) As a job analysis technique, FJA clearly provides for a systematic and uniform method of collecting data.[9] Additionally, much research has been conducted through the Department of Labor, and the technique has been demonstrated to provide reliable data. The negative aspects of the procedure revolve around the training time necessary to apply FJA effectively and the time and costs involved. Additionally, since the technique requires extensive judgments and evaluations on the part of analysts, the information obtained could be misleading.[10]

Exhibit 3.5

Worker Functions Relating to Data, People, and Things

Data	People	Things
0 Synthesizing	0 Mentoring	0 Setting Up
1 Coordinating	1 Negotiating	1 Precision Working
2 Analyzing	2 Instructing	2 Operating Controlling
3 Compiling	3 Supervising	3 Driving-Operating
4 Computing	4 Diverting	4 Manipulating
5 Copying	5 Persuading	5 Tending
6 Comparing	6 Speaking-Signaling	6 Feeding–Offbearing
	7 Serving	7 Handling
	8 Taking Instructions–Helping	

Source: *Handbook for Analyzing Jobs.* U.S. Department of Labor, Manpower Administration (Washington, D.C.: U.S. Government Printing Office, 1972): 5.

Exhibit 3.6

Job Analysis Schedule

OMB 44-R0722

U.S. Department of Labor
Manpower Administration

Estab. & Sched. No. ____________

JOB ANALYSIS SCHEDULE

1. Estab. Job Title ____________
2. Ind. Assign. ____________
3. SIC Code(s) and Title(s) ____________

Code ____ DOT Title ____

WTA Group ____ Ind. Desig. ____

4. JOB SUMMARY:

5. WORK PERFORMED RATINGS:

	D	P	T
Worker Functions	Data	People	Things

Work Field ____________
M.P.S.M.S. ____________

6. WORKER TRAITS RATINGS:

GED 1 2 3 4 5 6
SVP 1 2 3 4 5 6 7 8 9
Aptitudes G__V___ N___ S___ P___ Q___ K___ F___ M___ E___ C___
Temperaments D F I J M P R S T V
Interests 1a 1b 2a 2b 3a 3b 4a 4b 5a 5b
Phys. Demands S L M H V 2 3 4 5 6
Environ. Cond. I O B 2 3 4 5 6 7

Source: Handbook for Analyzing Jobs. U.S. Department of Labor, Manpower Administration (Washington, D.C.: U.S. Government Printing Office, 1972): 33–36.

7. General Education

a. Elementary ________ High School ________ Courses ____________________

b. College ________ Courses ____________________

____

8. Vocational Preparation

a. College ________ Courses ____________________

____

b. Vocational Education ________ Courses ____________________

____

c. Apprenticeship ____________________

d. Inplant Training ____________________

e. On-the-Job Training ____________________

f. Performance on Other Jobs ____________________

____

9. Experience ____________________

10. Orientation ____________________

11. Licenses, etc. ____________________

12. Relation to Other Jobs and Workers

Promotion: From ____________________ To ____________________

Transfers: From ____________________ To ____________________

Supervision Received ____________________

Supervision Given ____________________

____

13. Machines, Tools, Equipment, and Work Aids

14. Materials and Products

---

15. Description of Tasks

---

16. Definition of Terms

17. General Comments

---

18. Analyst ______________ Date ________ Editor ________ Date ________

Reviewed By ______________ Title, Org. ______________

National Office Reviewer ______________

Position Analysis Questionnaire

The **Position Analysis Questionnaire** (PAQ)[11] is a structured questionnaire developed to quantitatively sample "worker-oriented" job elements. It consists of 194 items divided into six sections:

1. Information input.
2. Mental processes.
3. Work output.
4. Relationships with other persons.
5. Job context.
6. Other job characteristics.

Of the 194 items, 187 are concerned with work activities, while the remaining 7 deal with compensation factors. Using the PAQ requires a job analyst to consider job behaviors and indicate, for each of the PAQ items, the degree to which the element is an important part of the job. For each element, the analyst records a score between 1 (very minor) and 5 (extreme) or N (does not apply).

Advantages and disadvantages of the PAQ Like every other job analysis technique, the PAQ has several advantages and disadvantages. The major advantages of the PAQ center on the fact that it is both quantifiable and standardized. This technique provides for the collection of similar quantifiable data across different jobs, allowing comparisons among jobs to be made. Once these analyses have been completed, the information gathered may be used for many decisions, such as the salary of each job relative to the salary of every other job.

Over the past twenty years, the PAQ has been researched more extensively than any other job analysis method. As a result, there have been problems raised, such as the reading level required to complete the PAQ. This reading level, which is between high school and college,[12] limits the type of people who could successfully use the PAQ. In addition, the PAQ does not concern itself with tasks, but rather with basic work behaviors, so finite differences among jobs cannot be ascertained. As a result, jobs may be entirely different, but show profound similarities because of similar characteristics. For example, although they are obviously quite different, research demonstrated that the jobs of police officers and housewives have very common job profiles.[13] As a result, sometimes the PAQ does not provide the essential information needed for creating job descriptions.

Job Descriptions and Job Specifications

Job Descriptions

As defined earlier in this chapter, a job description is that portion of the job analysis which typically contains the tasks involved in the completion of the job, along with the various behaviors or activities involved in the completion of these

Exhibit 3.7

A Page from the Position Analysis Questionnaire

RELATIONSHIPS WITH OTHER PERSONS

4 RELATIONSHIPS WITH OTHER PERSONS

This section deals with different aspects of interaction between people involved in various kinds of work.

Code	*Importance to This Job (I)*
N	Does not apply
1	Very minor
2	Low
3	Average
4	High
5	Extreme

4.1 Communications

Rate the following in terms of how *important* the activity is to the completion of the job. Some jobs may involve several or all of the items in this section.

4.1.1 Oral (communicating by speaking)

99 I Advising (dealing with individuals in order to counsel and/or guide them with regard to problems that may be resolved by legal, financial, scientific, technical, clinical, spiritual, and/or other professional principles)

100 I Negotiating (dealing with others in order to reach an agreement or solution, for example, labor bargaining, diplomatic relations, etc.)

101 I Persuading (dealing with others in order to influence them toward some action or point of view, for example, selling, political campaigning, etc.)

102 I Instructing (the teaching of knowledge or skills, in either an informal or a formal manner, to others, for example a public school teacher, a machinist teaching an apprentice, etc.)

103 I Interviewing (conducting interviews directed toward some specific objective, for example, interviewing job applicants, census taking, etc.)

104 I Routine information exchange: job related (the giving and/or receiving of *job-related* information of a routine nature, for example, ticket agent, taxicab dispatcher, receptionist, etc.)

105 I Nonroutine information exchange (the giving and/or receiving of *job-related* information of a nonroutine or unusual nature, for example, professional committee meetings, engineers discussing new product design, etc.)

106 I Public speaking (making speeches or formal presentations before relatively large audiences, for example, political addresses, radio/TV broadcasting, delivering a sermon, etc.)

4.1.2 Written (communicating by written/printed material)

107 I Writing (for example, writing or dictating letters, reports, etc., writing copy for ads, writing newspaper articles, etc.; do *not* include transcribing activities described in item 43, but only activities in which the incumbent creates the written material)

4.1.3 Other Comunications

108 I Signaling (communicating by some type of signal, for example, hand signals, semaphore, whistles, horns, bells, lights, etc.)

109 I Code communications (telegraph, cryptography, etc.)

Source: E. J. McCormick, P. R. Jeanneret, and R. C. Mecham, *Position Analysis Questionnaire.* (West Lafayette, IN: Purdue Research Foundation, 1969): 16. Reprinted with permission.

tasks. Within any given organization, job descriptions typically follow the same format. Across organizations, however, there are many different formats which are usable and acceptable. Regardless of the style used, job descriptions usually contain three sections: the identification section, the definition section, and the description section.

Job identification section Within this section, jobs are given various labels to distinguish them from one another. While some companies utilize numbers, such as a DOT number or department number, others categorize by title, job location, or unit name. Regardless of how the classification is made, care must be taken to make certain that the jobs are easily distinguishable. Titles which utilize the same name but add I, II, or III at the end should be avoided for the sake of clarity[14] (such as Teacher Assistant I, Teacher Assistant II). Furthermore, care must be taken to avoid titles which would give the impression that the job is capable of being completed by one sex or the other. For example, the titles chairman, leadman, and doorman appear to indicate that the position requires a male. More appropriate terminology would be chairperson, leader or crew leader, and door attendant.

Job definition section The information contained in this section discusses the overall purpose of the job. It tells what the worker does, why the job is being completed, and its overall relationship to other jobs and the organization's goals. This section is written in narrative form, and contains the information necessary to determine what constitutes satisfactory and unsatisfactory work performance.

Job description section The job description section includes information regarding the responsibilities inherent in the job; this includes the extent of the employee's supervisory and non-supervisory responsibilities, how closely the employee is supervised, the type of job knowledge that is necessary, and a listing of the major duties. Additionally, if the job involves the use of tools, materials, or equipment, this fact would be listed in the job description section.

Job Specification

As defined in the early part of the chapter, a job specification summarizes the human characteristics necessary for satisfactory job completion. The job specification aids the human resource department in the selection process by determining the type of employee to be recruited, and eventually selected, for the position. It includes factors such as the amount of training, education, and experience necessary for satisfactory job completion. It serves as a basis for determining what traits should be differentiated by selection tools such as tests. Finally, job specifications usually include data regarding physical requirements, mental demands, working conditions, and any other human traits which would determine the success or failure of job incumbents.

Exhibit 3.8

Sample Position Description

Standard Position Descriptions	*Chapter C*
Occupational Code 2315-13 *Craft-Clerk*	*Standard Position 2-633*

U.S. POSTAL SERVICE

Title: Distribution Clerk-Machine, MPLSM — Salary Level: PS–6
Key Position Reference No. 16

BASIC FUNCTION: Operates an electro mechanical machine in the distribution of letter sized mail requiring the knowledge and application of (1) two approved schemes, or (2) city primary or secondary schemes, or (3) memory items used for holdouts or non ZIP Coded mail, or (4) machine schemes consisting of the distribution by any direct and alphabetical or geographical grouping or read the ZIP Code in each letter as it is positioned. Must be able to demonstrate, in examination, operation of the machine requiring an accuracy rate of 98% and sorting speeds as follows:

Distribution	Machine Speed Letters per Minute
Outgoing Primary	60
Outgoing Secondary (ZIP Code)	60
Outgoing Secondary State (Scheme Knowledge)	55
Incoming Primary (ZIP Code)	60
Incoming Primary (Scheme Knowledge)	55
Incoming City Secondary (Scheme Knowledge)	50
Box Mail	60

DUTIES AND RESPONSIBILITIES

A. Reads address of each piece of mail as it is positioned by machine; depresses proper combination of keys to enable machine to divert each letter to the proper bin. This requires a high degree of manual and visual coordination and close visual attention for sustained periods.

B. Serves for a portion of time, on a rotation basis, as a loader or sweeper-tyer, or culling mail to remove that which is nonmachinable; loading consoles; removing mail from distribution boxes in back of machine; verifying sorted mail for accuracy of sorting; and tying mail in bundles, traying and/or dispatching as may be required.

C. May be required to qualify on one or more distribution schemes where essential to the assignment and may also be required to perform manual distribution.

ORGANIZATIONAL RELATIONSHIPS: Reports to a designated supervisor.

Source: U.S. Government Standard Position Descriptions, Washington, D.C., U.S. Government Printing Office.

Job Design

The way jobs are designed has a significant impact on both employees and organizations. Poorly designed jobs often result in boredom and a subsequent aftermath of increased turnover, reduced motivation, low levels of job satisfaction, less than optimal productivity, and an increase in organizational costs. Many of these negative consequences could be avoided or minimized through the proper identification of significant job components. The job design process emphasizes the design or redesign of jobs to incorporate factors which lead to the fulfillment of both employee and organizational objectives.

Job design

Job design involves the integration of significant job components and worker characteristics to create positions which lead to the need fulfillment of both workers and employers.

Techniques for Designing Jobs

Basically, there are four techniques used in the design of jobs. These include: job simplification, job enlargement, job enrichment, and job rotation.

Job simplification Simplification of work requires that jobs be broken down into their smallest units and then analyzed. Each resulting subunit typically consists of relatively few operations. These subunits are then assigned to workers as their total job.

There appear to be two major advantages in using **job simplification.** First, since the jobs require very little training, they can be completed by less costly unskilled labor. Second, job speed increases because each worker is performing only a small portion of a previously large job, and thus is able to master a smaller, less complicated job unit.

On the negative side, job simplification results in workers experiencing boredom, frustration, alienation, lack of motivation, and low job satisfaction. This in turn leads to lower productivity and increased costs.

Job simplification

Job simplification is a design method whereby jobs are divided into smaller components and subsequently assigned to workers as whole jobs.

Job enlargement Unlike job simplification, **job enlargement** broadens the scope of a worker's job by adding further tasks horizontally. Rather than completing one meaningless portion of a job, workers now complete the entire job.

Proponents contend that job enlargement reduces boredom, expands feelings of responsibility and meaningfulness, and increases job satisfaction. Critics, however, maintain that there is little evidence that motivation is increased. Instead, more tasks are added, usually without any additional compensation, which results in lower overall motivation, and consequently, lower productivity.[15]

Job enlargement

Job enlargement involves the addition to or expansion of worker tasks until the job becomes an entire meaningful operation.

Job enrichment While job enlargement expands the horizontal tasks of a worker, job enrichment increases the vertical score of jobs by adding responsibility.[16] For example, a worker who previously only loaded boxes for delivery into a trailer may be given the responsibility of verifying that the customer order is correct. Through job enrichment, autonomy, responsibility, and control become part of a worker's job. This in turn leads to greater feelings of satisfaction, higher motivation, and increased productivity.

Job enrichment

Job enrichment involves the vertical expansion of jobs by increasing the amount of worker responsibilities associated with the positions.

Job rotation Job rotation is often used in order to alleviate the ill effects of boredom and frustration experienced by workers performing simple jobs. Under a rotation plan, employees periodically switch jobs. For example, automobile assembly line workers may spend six weeks placing fenders on cars and then spend the next six weeks installing seats. Theoretically, this type of program alleviates boredom and makes tedious jobs easier to staff. Realistically, however, advocates contend that switching people from one boring job to another boring job probably does little to alleviate monotony.[17]

Job rotation

Job rotation involves the switching of workers on designated dates among several different simplified jobs.

Theories and Approaches to Designing Jobs

Scientific Management

Over the years, different methods for designing and redesigning jobs developed. One of the earliest attempts at job design was Frederick Taylor's industrial engineering approach.[18] Taylor maintained that jobs should be designed on the basis of the division of labor. Each job was analyzed by time and motion to determine the most effective and fastest method to complete each job. The result was a division of jobs into their smallest components. Individual workers were then assigned to each of these tasks.

Scientific management resulted in a set of principles by which jobs should be designed. They include:

1. The standardization of jobs into the single best way by which they can be performed.
2. The training of workers in the single best way to perform the job.
3. The specialization of labor leading to expertise in small narrow jobs.
4. The systematic and specific determination of job descriptions for each job.

A major shortcoming of the scientific management approach is its potential for neglecting workers. Supervisors employing these principles tend to become task masters, driven by efficiency standards often at the expense of the workers' physical and psychological needs. This results in a frustrated, dissatisfied workforce, which reacts by performing at minimal standards.[19]

The Human Relations Approach

The human relations theory arose almost as a direct result of the harshness imposed by supervisors who excessively used scientific management principles. An outgrowth of the famous Hawthorne Studies conducted during the 1920s,[20] the human relations approach de-emphasizes the technical components of a job and concerns itself with the impact of employee social needs on productivity.

Originally the goals of the Hawthorne investigators were to identify elements of the work environment which fostered productivity. Surprisingly, the investigators discovered that the greatest impact on productivity levels was the social interaction patterns of the workers rather than environmental conditions like lighting. These findings led to principles advocating the design of jobs which lead to social need gratification for workers, including the use of nonauthoritarian leadership styles by supervisors and the fostering of effective work groups.

Job Characteristics Theory

A more recent approach to job design is the **job characteristics theory.**[21] This theory stresses the intrinsic aspects of jobs and maintains that workers will be satisfied if they view their jobs as meaningful, if they are given adequate responsibility, and if they receive feedback regarding their performance. This goal is accomplished by focusing on five specific job characteristics when designing jobs. These include:

1. **Skill variety** The degree to which the job requires that workers use a variety of different activities, talents, and skills in order to successfully complete the job requirements.
2. **Task identity** The degree to which the job allows workers to complete whole tasks from start to finish, rather than disjointed portions of the job.
3. **Task significance** The degree to which the job significantly impacts the lives of others both within and outside the workplace.
4. **Autonomy** The degree to which the job allows workers freedom in the planning and scheduling, and the methods used to complete the job.
5. **Feedback** The degree to which the job itself provides workers with clear, direct, and understandable knowledge of their performance.

All of the job characteristic dimensions impact psychologically on workers. The first three dimensions affect whether or not workers view their jobs as meaningful. Autonomy determines the extent of responsibility workers feel. Feedback allows for feelings of satisfaction for a job well done by providing knowledge of results.

Ironically, the main feature of the job characteristics design method—its intrinsic psychological motivation—may be its biggest drawback. Supervisors attempting to apply these principles may discover that for many employees these psychological states are unimportant. In fact, research to date indicates that some employees respond exceedingly well to jobs redesigned according to job characteristic dimensions, whereas for others, it has no discernible impact.[22]

Sociotechnical Systems Approach

The theories of job design discussed to this point are all concerned with designing individual jobs. The approach taken by the sociotechnical systems method is the design of work systems that foster a meshing of the technical and social aspects of jobs. In order to create jobs which have this supportive relationship, work teams, not individual jobs, must be studied.[23] Jobs in the traditional sense are nonexistent, and instead, each worker plays an assigned role in accomplishing the group's objectives.

Redesigning work through sociotechnical systems methods requires the combined efforts of employees, supervisors, and union representatives in analyzing significant job operations. Jobs are not necessarily designed to be intrinsically motivating; rather, they are designed so that the work is accomplished. As in scientific management, a supervisor's goal is to insure that the organization's objectives are met. However, this is accomplished by concentrating only on critical job aspects, by forming work teams consisting of members who have the necessary qualifications to accomplish the tasks, and by allowing work groups the autonomy to manage their own work process.

Work Scheduling

Another aspect of job design which has received considerable attention during the last several decades is the scheduling of work hours. The increase in the workforce of dual-career couples with children, and the increased realization by employers that production needs may be better served by varied schedules, have probably been largely responsible for the shift in workweek scheduling. Workers in the United States previously accepted the eight-hour, five-day workweek as standard; however, today's workers are presented with various working options. These include: (1) part-time employment, (2) compressed workweeks, and (3) flexitime.

Part-time Employment

Part-time employment opportunities are popular among certain segments of the population. Students, mothers, retired persons, and moonlighters are particularly predisposed to seeking part-time work. In addition, retailers and service industries, such as fast food restaurants, use part-time employees extensively. In order to accommodate the different needs faced by both employers and workers, several types of part-time employment programs are in use. These include:

1. **Permanent part-time** Workers who are expected to work in a part-time capacity over an extended period of time.
2. **Temporary employees** Workers who are hired for a short period because the job is not expected to last, such as for a special project.
3. **Job sharing** Two or more workers who are employed in a **job sharing** situation together fill the position of one full-time worker.

Part-time employment provides benefits both to employers and to society. Employers find that the use of part-time employees allows for greater flexibility in scheduling, more accurate matching of the workforce to the workload, and substantial cost savings because part-time workers usually receive no voluntary benefits. Society benefits because involuntary unemployment, and consequently the draw on social welfare benefits, are reduced by providing opportunities to workers who would otherwise be unable to obtain employment.[24]

The major disadvantage to part-time employment is felt by employers in increased costs and union opposition. Benefits mandated by the government, such as unemployment compensation and social security, must be paid for each worker regardless of his or her working status. Consequently, several part-time employees fulfilling the job of one full-time worker may be more costly in benefit administration. Finally, unions sometimes object to the use of part-time employees because it reduces the job opportunities available for their members.[25]

Compressed Workweek

The **compressed workweek** requires employees to complete a full week's work in less than five days. The most common examples of this type of workweek are:

1. The four-day workweek—ten hours per day.
2. The three-day workweek—twelve hours per day.
3. The four and one-half day workweek—nine hours for four days, and four hours on the fifth day.
4. The "5/4-9" workweek plan—nine hours per day for five days during the first week, followed by a week of nine hours for four days.[25a]

There are several advantages to the compressed workweek. First, employers find overhead costs may be reduced by operating their plants less days. Aside from the obvious savings in costs associated with lighting, heating, and cooling, repairs and depreciation decrease because machinery is not started and stopped as often. Employees, particularly young single workers, find that extra time off allows for increased social activities.

Compressed workweeks have several disadvantages. First, organizations which operate five days per week may find it difficult to schedule productivity over a shorter period of time. Second, compressing the workweek for some jobs may lead to decreased productivity by increasing fatigue. For example, a construction worker will probably be able to swing a sledge hammer more effectively eight hours a day for five days than twelve hours a day for three days. Finally, there are government rules and regulations regarding overtime pay which may add excessive costs to the employer.[26]

Flexitime

Flexitime is probably the most popular type of work scheduling program. During the 1980s, the amount of companies using flexitime doubled from the 1970s, with the overall growth approximating 1.5 percent per year.[27] Under a flexitime system, employees work a fixed period of hours, but have a degree of freedom in setting their own starting and stopping times. In setting these times, employees are given wide latitude provided they incorporate a "core" group of hours in their schedules. Suppose, for example, the organization requires all employees to be present between the time periods of 8:30 AM to 11:30 AM, and 2:00 PM until 3:30 PM. Some employees may choose to work 7:30 AM until 3:30 PM, while others might choose an 8:00 AM until 4:00 PM shift. As long as the times selected incorporate the core hours, the shift is acceptable.[28]

Flexitime

Flexitime is an alternative work scheduling procedure which allows workers the freedom to choose their own working schedules provided that they work a fixed number of hours.

There are several types of flexitime schedules which vary according to the amount of scheduling flexibility that is allowed.[29] These include:

1. **Flexitour** Workers choose starting and stopping times, which must be adhered to for a set period of time, from among lists provided by the organization.
2. **Gliding time** Workers may vary their starting and finishing times daily, but must work a set number of hours per day.
3. **Variable working hours** Workers are free to choose hours irrespective of core time, provided they contract a set number of hours with their supervisors.
4. **Maxiflex** Workers have the freedom to vary their hours daily irrespective of core times. Maxiflex is similar to a compressed workweek.
5. **Flexiplace** Workers may work part of the time outside of the workplace, such as at home.

Like other alternative work scheduling systems, flexitime has both benefits and disadvantages. Workers find that the flexibility afforded them under flexitime systems increases the amount of time they can spend together with their families, it allows the scheduling of work hours to avoid commuting difficulties, and it provides feelings of control over the working environment. For employers, flexitime provides ease of scheduling, reduced overtime costs, higher productivity because of increases in morale, and it is a recruiting tool.

For employees, there seem to be few, if any, disadvantages to flexitime systems. Employers, however, sometimes find that overhead costs caused by the variation in hours increases, unions object to the decrease in overtime pay attributable to certain flexitime programs (such as maxiflex), and many supervisors experience difficulty in managing a flexitime workforce.[30]

Summary

This chapter reviewed the many benefits of job analyses and job design for an organization. These included: identifying selection, placement, and training criteria; developing performance evaluation standards and wage differentials; discovering health and safety problems; designing effective productivity methods; and complying with legal guidelines.

Within companies many individuals serve as job analysts, and many methods are used to collect job analysis information. Some of the generalized methods include observations, questionnaires, diaries, and interviews. More specific procedures include Functional Job Analysis and the Position Analysis Questionnaire.

As a direct result of job analysis, job descriptions and job specifications are accumulated. The former lists the tasks involved in completion of the job, while the latter is concerned with the human elements necessary for satisfactory job completion. The value of job analysis, descriptions, and specifications will become even more evident in later chapters.

Finally, the information gathered from job analyses provides data useful in the design or redesign of jobs. By analyzing and dividing jobs into their relevant components, organizations may enhance the productivity capabilities of their workforce by designing more efficient operations. This is accomplished by restructuring the work environment, enhancing the meaningfulness of the task, or using alternative work scheduling.

Key Terms to Identify

Job analysis
Job description
Job specification
Job evaluation
Performance appraisal
Time and motion studies
Job analyst
Dictionary of Occupational Titles (DOT)
Functional Job Analysis
Position Analysis Questionnaire (PAQ)
Job design
Job simplification
Job enlargement
Job enrichment
Job rotation
Job characteristics theory
Job sharing
Compressed workweek
Flexitime
Flexitour
Gliding time
Maxiflex
Flexiplace

Questions for Discussion

Do You Know the Facts?

1. What are the differences among job analyses, job descriptions, and job specifications?
2. Discuss the numerous ways job analyses are used by human resource personnel.
3. What are the four basic methods of collecting job analysis data?
4. What are the advantages and disadvantages of the FJA and the PAQ methods of collecting job analysis data? How do these methods differ from the basic methods of collection?
5. Discuss the differences in the various theories of job design.

Can You Apply the Information Learned?

1. How would you convince a company that conducting job analyses are a necessary prerequisite to other human resource functions?
2. What advantages and disadvantages are there to using outside consultants as job analysts?

3. Would a job analyst use the same method(s) of collecting data for the positions of machinist, salesperson, and distribution manager? Why or why not?
4. What factors are important in determining the most effective work scheduling system in a retailing environment? What are some of the variables to consider in a manufacturing environment?

Still Doing It the Old Fashioned Way

Stoneham National Bank was having difficulty. For years they had been processing checks the same way. Each check arrived at the bank, was encoded in the proof machine, read through the computer, and hand filed into each customer's account. Once a month statements were run, and customers were mailed copies of these statements together with their cancelled checks. Until recently, the system seemed to operate flawlessly. Lately, however, customers were complaining of inaccurate statements, missing cancelled checks, and untimely return of their information. After fruitlessly spending three months trying to discover the source of the problems, the bank decided to hire a consultant.

Jason Chew owned and operated a consulting firm in California. Over the years, Jason had worked primarily with financial institutions on local, national, and international levels. He was noted for being efficient and thorough. It was Jason's firm that the bank contacted for help.

Immediately after his arrival at the bank, Jason was taken on a tour by Carl Upman, senior vice-president for operations. Jason was highly impressed with the bank's operations until he saw the filing room system. It was almost unbelievable. The bank's operations were totally modernized, employing the latest computer technology, but they still used an antiquated check filing system developed in 1905. For eight hours a day, four employees in the customer service area placed cancelled checks into rotary trays containing customer accounts. It was a simple, uncomplicated procedure, but, as Jason quickly ascertained, the system was complicated by the fact that the employees had other duties as well. The phone constantly rang, customers continually approached the counter for assistance, and the general atmosphere appeared to be one of turmoil. Filing checks was secondary to all these other activities.

Jason realized that there had to be a better way. There was no question about the fact that check filing was boring, inconvenient, monotonous, and had to be completed on a daily basis. But did it have to be done using the present system? There was only one way to find out. Jason conducted a thorough job analysis of the position.

Today the bank is totally computerized. Cancelled checks are no longer returned to the customer. Until they changed their system, however, the bank employed Jason's redesigned check filing system. It was really quite simple. The bank hired eight college students who worked in teams of four. The students filed checks in the evenings, when the bank was closed. They controlled their own schedules and were paid for four hours each, regardless of the amount of time it took them to complete the task. The bank's only requirement was that sometime between closing and the next morning, all the checks were filed correctly. The result of the new system was a decrease in customer complaints and an increase in employee job satisfaction.

Questions for Discussion

1. Why do you think the bank was still using an antiquated check filing procedure?
2. Why would Jason's system be any less boring, monotonous, and inconvenient than the original system?
3. Do you think Jason's flexitime system is cost effective? Why or why not?

Endnotes and References

1 J. J. Jones and Thomas DeCotiis, "Job Analysis: National Survey Findings," *Personnel Journal*, Vol. 48 (October 1969): 805–809.

2 Wayne Cascio, *Applied Psychology in Personnel Management* (Reston, VA: Reston Publishing Co., 1982): 59.

3 For extended discussion on selecting job analysts, see Robert D. Gatewood and Hubert S. Feild, *Human Resource Selection* (Chicago, IL: The Dryden Press, 1987): 183–188.

4 U.S. Department of Labor, *Dictionary of Occupational Titles*, 4th ed. (Washington, D.C.: U.S. Government Printing Office, 1977).

5 Summarized from Laurence Siegel and Irving M. Lane, *Psychology in Industrial Organizations* (Homewood, IL: Richard D. Irwin, Inc., 1974): 101–102. For a comprehensive, step-by-step method of conducting observations and interviews, see *Handbook for Analyzing Jobs*, U.S. Department of Labor, Manpower Administration (Washington, D.C.: U.S. Government Printing Office, 1972).

6 Wayne Cascio, *op. cit.*, 59.

7 For expanded discussion, see S. E. Bemis, A. H. Belensky, and D. A. Soder, "Job Analysis: An Effective Management Tool." Washington, D.C.: Bureau of National Affairs, 1983.

8 Sidney A. Fine and Wretha W. Wiley, *An Introduction to Functional Job Analysis: A Scaling of Selected Tasks from the Social Welfare Field* (Methods for Manpower Analysis No. 4) (Kalamazoo, MI: W. E. Upjohn Institute for Employee Research, 1973).

9 Sidney A. Fine, A. M. Holt, and M. F. Hutchinson, *Functional Job Analysis: How to Standardize Task Statements* (Kalamazoo, MI: W. E. Upjohn Institute for Employment Research, 1974).

10 Robert Gatewood and Hubert S. Feild, *op. cit.*, 241.

11 Ernest J. McCormick, Paul R. Jeanneret, and Robert C. Mecham, "A Study of Job Characteristics and Job Dimensions as Based on the Position Analysis Questionnaire (PAQ)," *Journal of Applied Psychology*, Vol. 56, No. 4 (1972): 347–368.

12 R. A. Ash and S. L. Edgell, "A Note on the Readability of the PAQ," *Journal of Applied Psychology* Vol. 60 (1975) 765–766. Also see Wayne Cascio, *op. cit.*, 62.

13 R. D. Arvey and M. E. Begalla, "Analyzing the Homemaker Job Using the PAQ," *Journal of Applied Psychology*, Vol. 60 (1975): 513–517.

14 See BNA Policy and Practice Series-Compensation (Washington, D.C.: Bureau of National Affairs, Inc., 1979): 317–334.

15 S. W. Kozlowski and B. M. Hults, "Joint Moderation of the Relation between Task Complexity and Job Performance for Engineers," *Journal of Applied Psychology*, Vol. 71 (1986): 196–202.

16 Frederick Herzberg is generally credited with popularizing the concept of job enrichment. See "One More Time: How Do You Motivate Employees?" *Harvard Business Review*, Vol. 46, No. 2 (Jan.–Feb. 1968): 53–62.

17 Robert L. Mathis and John H. Jackson, *Personnel: Human Resource Management*, 4th ed. (St. Paul, MN: West Publishing Company, 1985): 153.

18 Frederick Taylor, *The Principles of Scientific Management* (New York: Harper & Row, 1911).

19 Edwin A. Locke, "The Ideas of Frederick W. Taylor: An Evaluation," *Academy of Management Review*, Vol. 7, No. 1 (1982): 14–24.

20 See: Elton Mayo, *The Human Problems of an Industrial Civilization* (New York: Macmillan Publishing Company, 1933).

21 J. Richard Hackman and G. R. Oldham, *Work Redesign* (Reading, MA: Addison-Wesley Publishing Company, 1980).

22 Vida G. Scarpello and James Ledvinka, *Personnel/Human Resource Management* (Boston, MA: PWS-KENT Publishing Company, 1988): 205.

23 A. Cherns, "The Principles of Sociotechnical Design," *Human Relations*, Vol. 29 (1976): 783–792.

24 Jerome W. Rosow and Robert Zager, *New Work Schedules for a Changing Society* (Scarsdale, NY: Work In America Institute, 1981).

25 Stanley D. Nolen, *New Work Schedules in Practice* (New York: Van Nostrand/Work in America Institute Series, 1982).

25a Vida G. Scarpello and James Ledvinka, *op. cit.*, p. 200.

26 Rosow and Zager, *op. cit.* Also see Scarpello and Ledvinka, *op. cit.*

27 Edward G. Thomas, "Workers Who Set Their Own Time Clocks," *Business and Society Review* (Spring 1987): 49–51.

28 The most prevalent core time is 9:00 AM to 3:00 PM, followed by 9:00 to 4:00. For a discussion on flexitime scheduling and jobsharing, see Edward G. Thomas, *op. cit.*

29 For expanded discussion on the various flexitime schedules, see Jerome W. Rosow and Robert Zager, *op. cit.*

30 Rosow and Zager, *op. cit.* Also see Scarpello and Ledvinka, *op. cit.*

Chapter 4

Human Resource Planning and Recruiting

Objectives

After reading this chapter you should understand:

1. Human resource planning and the way it interacts with other organizational planning functions.
2. The reason human resource forecasting is essential for organizations.
3. The different recruiting techniques and their ultimate effectiveness in achieving their purposes.
4. The way organizations utilize various sources to fill job vacancies.
5. The legal ramifications underlying recruitment activities.

In order to grow and prosper, organizations must continually maintain an adequate supply of human resources. As job vacancies increase, either by attrition or by the addition of new positions, the acquisition of new employees becomes increasingly more important. Adequately staffing organizations with qualified employees is a complex process. Jobs must be analyzed, potential employees must be identified and encouraged to apply for positions, and selection must take place among prospective employees. The processing of unqualified personnel is an expensive and time-consuming task, and organizations must endeavor to establish efficient and cost-effective selection procedures to identify the best qualified applicants. Effective programs begin with human resource planning and forecasting, move through recruitment, and terminate with the selection of qualified personnel. This chapter deals with the planning, forecasting, and recruiting of human resources.

Human Resource Planning

Good planning is an important element of successful management. Planning to meet the future skill needs of the organization is the primary reason for human resource planning.[1] Much of this planning is strategic in nature; it addresses the major objectives of the organization and the necessary procedures to follow in order to accomplish these goals. Resources, market conditions, technological changes, product development, and capital requirements all receive considerable attention in the **strategic planning** process.

Unfortunately, human resources are rarely an important component of strategic planning sessions, particularly long-range planning sessions. At best, people planning is a yearly process which assumes the role of allocating moneys for training and recruitment. Perhaps one reason for this lack of effort in planning can be explained by the fact that it is difficult to anticipate precisely how much the various human resource programs will cost in terms of dollars and cents.[2] As one author states, "The financial executive comes to the table with clear dollar outcomes of tax strategies . . . however, when the human resource executive comes to the table, he/she too often describes abstract concepts (e.g. development of people) or lists pure cost items (e.g. benefit costs)."[3]

Many executives view human resource planning as necessary only if maintaining the quantity of workers fosters the accomplishment of the goals and objectives of the business. Consequently, the development of human resource needs is secondary to the development of business strategies. The fact that these human resources may also affect business plans is generally ignored.[4] As long as there appear to be sufficient numbers of personnel available to satisfy the requirements for scheduled operations, human resource planning is rarely detailed or extensive. However, the linking of business and human resource planning is necessary in order to ensure future success.

> **Strategic planning**
>
> *Strategic planning is the process of developing long-term organizational objectives and deciding on the methods and processes by which these goals will be reached.*

Meshing human resource planning and strategic business planning is not easy. To best accomplish this linking process, James Walker recommends a five-step approach. This includes:

1. Defining the corporate philosophy—What is the purpose of the business?
2. Scanning the environmental conditions—What threats and opportunities are present?

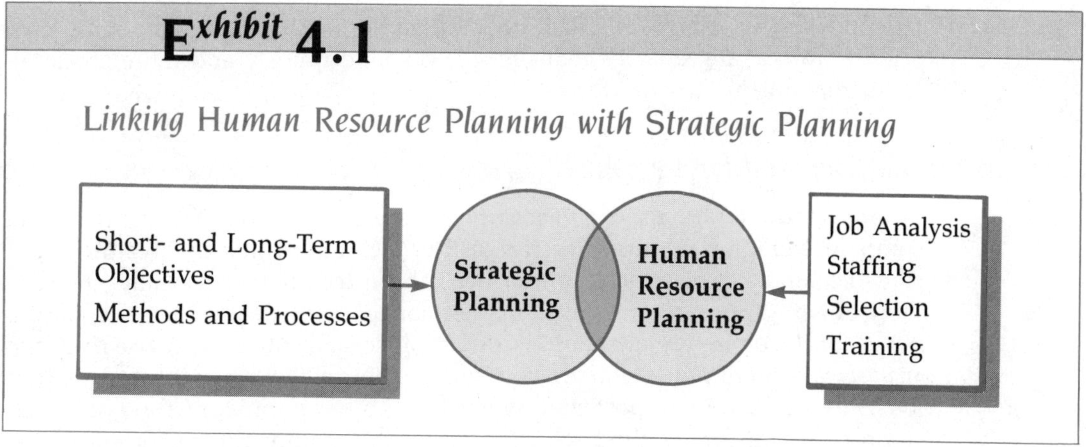

3. Evaluating the corporation's strengths and weaknesses—What may aid or limit future behaviors?
4. Developing objectives and goals—What return is expected, and when?
5. Developing strategies—What courses of action are best followed to achieve the corporate objectives?[5]

Once the decision and commitment to planning have been made, organizations are ready to embark on forecasting human resource needs. This process of analyzing the current status of human resources and predicting future staffing needs is central to the planning process.[6]

Forecasting Human Resource Needs

The Purpose of Forecasting

The goals underlying forecasting are simple. Organizations attempt to translate the broad, generalized needs developed during planning stages into qualitative and quantitative requirements. After determining the number and nature of the jobs (demand) and the personnel (supply) which will be needed in the future, companies are in a position to allocate the necessary resources to human resource activities. These activities include: recruitment, selection, training, job development, promotions and transfers, and any other activities which are necessary to further the strategic plans of the organization.

Ideally, organizations hope that their internal supply of personnel will meet all future position demands. Realistically, this is seldom the case. Companies find themselves either overstaffed, which necessitates the creation of programs designed to decrease the workforce, or understaffed, which necessitates the hiring of additional personnel. Effective use of staffing strategies requires managers to be informed of the available talent in their organizations, as well as the personnel likely to be available in the marketplace. Although it is not a precise science, forecasting enables managers to respond quickly and more efficiently to fluctuations in the workforce.

Forecasting the Demand for Personnel

Several methods are used to accomplish human resource forecasting. Some companies employ **quantitative forecasting** techniques that involve the use of statistical and mathematical approaches. These techniques typically involve a "top down" approach in which upper management determines the staffing needs for the entire organization. For example, organizations may use *time series analysis,* a form of regression analysis which attempts to forecast future staffing job levels by examining past staffing levels. Another popular method of human resource forecasting is the prediction of the types and number of employees needed by estimating either future productivity or future sales.

It would be natural to assume that quantitative techniques would be widely used because they are objective. In fact, **qualitative forecasting** techniques, which assess human resources by subjective methods of sampling supervisory and managerial staff, are more commonly used. These "bottom up" approaches request input from unit managers regarding their judgments about the staffing needs of their particular units.

The choice of an appropriate forecasting method is determined by specific factors within individual organizations. Objective forecasting is advocated by the bulk of writers on human resource planning. However, most practitioners seem to ignore the advice given by experts, preferring less sophisticated subjective measures.[7] This is probably because of the fact that most human resource information systems lack the sophistication necessary to use more complex techniques. As a general rule, objective forecasting would probably be preferable unless:

1. Within the organization there is a lack of skilled individuals who are able to use sophisticated techniques.
2. The organization's computer capabilities are inadequate for the process.
3. The data base is insufficient.
4. There is no established objective method for the desired forecasting.
5. The available forecasting technique is inadequate for predicting over the desired time period.[8]

Quantitative and qualitative forecasting

Quantitative forecasting involves the use of mathematical and statistical techniques to forecast human resource needs. Qualitative forecasting relies heavily on the subjective judgments of individuals regarded as experts—usually the unit managers.

Forecasting the Supply of Personnel and Inventorying Current Personnel

A forecast of the numbers and types of employees necessary to staff future positions begins with an inventory of present personnel and their current skills. Through the planning process and analyses of position requirements, future organizational needs are developed. By assessing the skills of current personnel and matching them to the job requirements, strategies for filling future positions may be developed. For example, suppose the planning process indicates that four supervisory positions will be available in the next five years because of retirement. If an assessment of present personnel indicates a lack of supervisory skills, then the organization may consider either training current employees or recruiting external talent. On the other hand, if there are available internal personnel to staff these positions, the company may need to plan replacements for those employees who will be promoted.

Skills inventories

The first step in predicting future requirements is to assess current in-house talents. One of the oldest and most common methods by which organizations stay apprised of their personnel talents is through the use of **skills inventories.**[9] Typically, skills inventories include the names of employees, together with a listing of their skills, training, and related experiences. Skills inventories were once manually maintained, and they have become more popular with the increased use of computers. Now, managers have readily accessible information about each employee which aids them in choosing the most capable candidate for promotions or transfers.

> **Skills inventories**
>
> *Skills inventories are current listings of each employee's skills, abilities, capabilities, qualifications, talents, educational level, and training.*

The use of skills inventories requires that organizations determine the type of information to be collected, design instruments to gather the data, and decide on the most appropriate method to sample workers. As a general guideline, Thomas Patten suggests seven categories of information to be included on skills inventories. These are:

1. **Personal data** age, sex, and other personal information.
2. **Skills** experience, education, and training.
3. **Special qualifications** professional memberships and associations, awards, and achievements.
4. **Salary and job history** current and past salaries, raises, and previous jobs held.

5. **Company data** personnel data, for example, benefits and seniority.
6. **Capacity of the individual** relevant test scores and health data.
7. **Any special individual preferences** type of job preferred and preferred geographic living area.[10]

In order to be successful, skills inventories must be supported by upper management, they must be viewed as meaningful by workers, and they must be monitored and updated periodically. Most importantly, they must consist of critical job-related information. Additionally, they should supplement the knowledge of employees' current skills with assessments of their potential.[11] Systems which do not provide sufficient information for making decisions or which are viewed as whimsical by personnel will soon become ignored as just another useless record-keeping chore.

Management inventories

As the name implies, **management inventories** are designed specifically to assess the skills of supervisory and managerial personnel. In addition to including data similar to that found on skills inventories, management inventories contain information on an individual's past successes and failures, his or her strengths and weaknesses, and his or her potential for moving into higher managerial positions.

Exhibit 4.2

Items for Inclusion on Skills Inventories

Personal data	Skills/Training	Company data
Birthdate	Specific skills	Date of employment
Address	Seminars attended	Initial salary
Social Security Number	Degrees obtained	Promotions/transfers
Citizenship	Certificates	Current salary
Dependents	Licenses	Date of last raise
Marital status	Interests	Promotability rating
Educational level	Languages spoken	Previous jobs held
Handicap status	Specializations	Date of last appraisal
Medical status	Testing results	Attendance record
Military status		
Hobbies/interests		
Geographic preferences		
Outside organizations		

Management inventories

Management inventories are skills inventories for managerial personnel which also include data concerning the employee's past successes and failures, his or her strengths and weaknesses, and his or her potential for advancement.

Replacement charts

The information from skills inventories can serve as data for **replacement charts.** These charts pictorially represent the incumbents in supervisory and managerial positions and their potential replacements. Unlike skills inventories, replacement charts do not incorporate information on all employees. Rather, they concentrate only on those workers who are most likely to be promoted.

Replacement charts

Replacement charts are visual displays of the positions in an organization, the incumbents, and their potential replacements.

Replacement charts have the advantage of providing management with a quick inventory of positions in the organization. Skills inventories reveal worker potential, and replacement charts identify the specific jobs employees are likely to fill. With this information, organizations can focus on areas of greatest need. For example, jobs for which there are no backup personnel may require greater immediate attention than those for which there are several potentially promotable employees. Similarly, an analysis of replacement charts may reveal a potential turnover problem when it appears unlikely that suitable positions will become available for promotable employees.

The Recruitment Process

Ideally, effective **recruitment** ensures that a pool of potentially qualified candidates exists for every position in the organization. When positions become vacant, organizations attempt to fill them from a pool of available candidates. To accomplish this goal, organizations must conduct comprehensive job analyses,[12] identify sources of potential candidates, and decide on the most appropriate recruitment methods to use.

Exhibit 4.3

Replacement Chart of Executive Personnel

Pauline Fine
Plant Manager
Next Promotion—Retirement

Joe Gambit P/4
Production Superintendent
Next Promotion—Plant Manager

Hank Smith NP/2
Production Manager
Next Promotion—Production Superintendent

Jean James P/4
Finishing Supervisor
Next Promotion—Production Manager

Peter Jones ND/4
Engineering Manager
Next Promotion—Plant Manager

Henry Slope ND/3
Design Manager
Next Promotion—Engineering Manager

Ethel Partridge P/4
Quality Control Manager
Next Promotion—Engineering Manager

Performance Appraisal Codes
P = Promotable NP = Not Promotable ND = Needs Development
1—Poor 2—Below Average 3—Average 4—Good 5—Excellent

Recruitment

Recruitment is the process of actively identifying potentially qualified employees and encouraging them to apply for positions in the organization.

Recruitment Sources

Recruits are obtained from a variety of sources. These sources are divided into two categories: (1) sources internal to the organization and (2) sources external to the organization.

Internal sources

Current employees Employees already working for organizations provide an abundance of recruiting opportunities. Current employees may fill vacancies through promotions, advancements, or transfers. In addition, they serve as a referral service by which potential candidates may be discovered.

In order to maximize the use of current employees, organizations must adequately communicate vacancies and maintain a comprehensive skills inventory on each worker. To apprise workers of available position openings, many organizations use **job posting** and **job bidding** systems. Current job vacancies are announced by postings on bulletin boards or listings in the company newsletter. Usually, the listing includes the job duties, responsibilities, qualifications necessary, salary level, and any other pertinent job information. Qualified employees are then encouraged to either submit formal applications for the position or to sign a list, as in job bidding, indicating their interest in being considered for the position.

Job posting and job bidding

Job posting involves the dissemination of information about available position vacancies by posting the listing on bulletin boards or in employee newsletters. Job bidding occurs when employees sign a list to indicate their interest in being considered as a candidate for an announced position.

Job posting has both advantages and disadvantages for the organization. On the positive side, job posting enables the organization to identify qualified employees who may otherwise be ignored. Supervisors often are unaware of or are unable to identify the qualifications and interests of their current employees. As a result, many talented workers are neglected. Through a posting and bidding system, these employees have an opportunity to apply for positions for which they would otherwise be overlooked. Thus, employee development is enhanced and recruiting costs are reduced.[13]

Job posting also has a negative side. Paperwork is increased because of the necessity of seriously considering each and every job bidder. All internal applicants who are not selected must be apprised of the reasons for their rejection and counseled on how they may improve their credentials to qualify for future job openings. Finally, in the absence of a policy restricting the number of times

Exhibit 4.4

A Job Posting for an Administrative Sales Coordinator

Job Title: Administrative Coordinator

Division: Sales and Marketing

Reports to: Vice-President of Sales

Job Grade: Class V

Description of Duties: Assists the vice-president for sales in the administration of the various sales department functions. Major duties include:

1. Setting up computer pricing.
2. Calculating mark-ups.
3. Monitoring price accuracy and price reduction listings.
4. Monitoring hand tickets.
5. Updating policies and procedures.
6. Establishing policy and procedure compliance review.
7. Relieving telephone sales personnel when necessary.
8. Serving as customer liaison for complaints.

Qualifications: Knowledge of company policies and procedures. Ability to operate calculator, telephone, microcomputer, and typewriter. Class IV Chauffeur license (tractor-trailer) required.

Hours of Work: 8–5 Monday through Friday. Occasional Saturdays and evenings.

ALL INTERESTED EMPLOYEES ARE ENCOURAGED TO CONTACT PERSONNEL. CLOSING DATE FOR APPLICATION MATERIALS IS MARCH 14.

an employee may change positions within a specified period, job posting may cause instability in organizations through continual employee movement from job to job.[14]

Using skills inventories The impact of recruiting from within organizations is increased dramatically for those businesses which maintain current computerized skills inventories on their employees. As mentioned earlier, skills inventories include information concerning employee qualifications, skills, talents, and training programs attended. These listings should be updated periodically to reflect the current levels of all workers. Not only is this information of considerable aid in the selection of job bidders, but also its availability allows the organization to search out qualified current employees who do not respond to the job posting. In fact, some human resource managers scan current employee credentials routinely whenever a job vacancy occurs. Any employees whose credentials appear to qualify them for the position are subsequently personally invited to submit applications for the vacancy.

Employees as referral sources Many organizations rely on current employee referrals to fill job vacancies. The advantages of this recruitment technique are two-fold. First, current employees tend to be highly selective when referring potential candidates because the quality of the applicant's work will ultimately reflect on them. Consequently, applicants referred by current employees have undergone prescreening prior to their recommendation. Second, because the candidates recruited through employee referrals are usually acquaintances, they tend to have more realistic views of the organization, its policies and procedures, and what is expected of them as workers.[15]

Using employee referrals as a sole recruiting source may have legal repercussions. In the case of *EEOC* v. *Detroit Edison Company* (1975),[16] the court ruled that relying on referrals from a predominantly white employee base, rather than seeking recruits in the marketplace, may be discriminatory. The logic behind this ruling is that past discrimination tends to be perpetuated because majority members invariably recommend their acquaintances, the bulk of whom tend to be from majority classes. Consequently, organizations would be well advised to avoid using employee referrals as a sole recruiting source unless their current workforce is racially and culturally balanced.

Transfers and promotions A common way in which many organizations fill vacancies is through transfers or promotions. Sometimes current employees may have skills and talents which would best benefit the organization if they were used elsewhere. For example, Babe Ruth originally began his baseball career as a pitcher. Although highly successful in this capacity, the team management realized that Ruth's skill as a hitter would provide greater benefits to the organization. Ruth was thus transferred to the outfield so that he could play daily.

Many organizations have a policy of *promoting-from-within.* Instituting this policy obligates the organization to search internally for qualified personnel before recruiting externally. Filling positions in this manner rewards workers both for their effort in training for new positions and for their devotion to the organization in general. Additionally, qualified internal personnel usually require less training because they already are familiar with the organization.

There are several disadvantages to strictly adhering to policies of promotion-from-within. First, by limiting the selection procedure to internal candidates, more highly qualified personnel from other sources may be overlooked. Second, filling a position internally creates another job opening, that of the promoted employee. Third, promoting from within requires additional training. Instead of training just one employee, two must be trained: the promoted worker needs to be trained for the new assignment, and the replacement must also be trained. Last, care must be taken to avoid the tendency to promote people to their level of incompetence. Rather than improving the workforce through the promotion, the organization may weaken its existing status. Consider the following case:

> An opening for a production line foreperson developed in the "Stomp-It-Out" metal works factory. Adhering to their policy of strictly promoting from within, the company selected Alice, the top drill press operator, to fill the position. Eager and excited, Alice, undaunted by the fact that she had never had any management training, began her new assignment with enthusiasm. Shortly thereafter, the company realized they had made a gross error. Although highly qualified and talented as a machinist, Alice seemed to have little, if any, people skills. All efforts at training, including countless dollars spent on sending her to seminars, proved fruitless. She just did not appear to have managerial talents. The company was in a dilemma! Demotion was out of the question. All previously demoted supervisors caused excessive morale problems which drastically curtailed productivity. There appeared to be only one solution. With a month's severance pay, Alice was released. The end result: the company fired its best machinist!

External sources

Organizations have a variety of external recruitment resources. Among the most common are: walk-ins, advertisements, employment agencies, and school or college campus recruiting.

Walk-ins Job applicants who appear at personnel offices without appointments are considered walk-in applicants. Large, well-known organizations are likely to have a substantial number of walk-in applicants, particularly in tight labor markets. These walk-ins, who are predominantly blue-collar and clerical workers,[17] are usually unaware of specific job openings, and the likelihood of their credentials immediately matching a vacant position is remote. However, applications are usually retained on file for future openings for which the candidates may be qualified.

Although the quality of applicants received through walk-ins is usually lower than that obtained through other recruiting techniques, proper and courteous handling of these applicants affords benefits to organizations. Not only are walk-ins an inexpensive source of recruits, but also they help enhance the company's image when they inform their friends, relatives, and acquaintances about the favorable treatment they received. Similarly, mistreatment of these applicants may result in damaging public relations for the organization.[18]

Advertisements A common method of recruitment is to invite applications for positions through mass media publications. Help wanted ads, which are circulated in local and national newspapers, professional publications, and on radio or television, usually provide an abundance of applicants. These advertisements usually list the job duties and responsibilities along with the candidate requirements necessary for successful job performance.

In addition to listing job information, advertisements also detail the method by which qualified candidates may apply for the position. Usually, this procedure involves submitting a resume and other pertinent information through the mail directly to the company or to a post office box number. Applicants whose credentials appear to satisfy the job requirements are given further consideration. All other candidates are sent courteous rejection letters which thank them for their interest in the position. As a common practice, many organizations retain these rejected applications on file for a one-year period in the event that a suitable job opens.

The correct preparation of media advertisements is crucial to the success of the recruiting effort. Good advertising can be the most effective recruitment technique.[19] Consideration must be given to the target group for which the ad is designed, as well as the cost of the ad. It may be necessary to place high-cost advertisements in technical journals for specialists, but it may be imprudent to spend excessive amounts of resources on recruiting a part-time seasonal retail clerk for a local department store.

In addition to making sure they are designed for appeal and effectiveness, advertisements must be further examined to insure that they are within the boundaries of the law. Federal and state Equal Employment Opportunity laws prohibit advertisement references to sex, race, color, religion, national origin, and handicap, unless they are job related. Furthermore, affirmative action employers, who actively seek the recruitment of minorities, are obligated to advertise in mass media which reach a large portion of minorities. For example, along

Exhibit 4.5

Want Ads for Human Resource Personnel

Personnel Recruiter $40,000

We are offering a substantial challenge for a talented self-starter to become a part of our ambitious and successful team. The special person we seek is successful and has a proven track record, but has reached a point where more personal as well as financial rewards are desired. Base salary + commissions + benefits. Send resume to:
P.O. Box 888
Washington, D.C. 11111

Personnel Representative Staff Assistant

Career start for college grad seeking professional challenge and advancement opportunity. Our firm has experienced over 10 years of continuing expansion and is ranked as one of the fastest growing in our industry. As a member of our professional team you will assist with a variety of employment activities including: recruitment, interviewing, orientation, community relations, and employee training. Additional duties include front desk reception and special project tasks. Comprehensive salary and compensation package. To apply call: 888/762-4834.

with other position advertisements, letters announcing college faculty positions are specifically sent to predominantly black institutions of higher learning in an attempt to attract qualified minority candidates.

Employment agencies Two types of employment agencies are commonly used in the recruiting process. These are: private and public agencies.

Private employment agencies are used frequently by employers, particularly when they are seeking executive-level personnel. Sometimes referred to as *headhunters,* these agencies either serve applicants or they are hired specifically by organizations. Agencies retained by employers are referred to as *search firms;* they are well versed in specific company needs, and they are usually paid a fee whether or not they fill the position. On the other hand, private employment agencies represent the applicant; they refer him or her to organizations, and they are paid a percentage of the candidate's initial yearly salary (approximately 30–35 percent in the case of higher level management positions)[20] after the candidate is employed.

In spite of what appears on the surface to be a substantial fee, private employment agencies have the potential to save organizations time and money. By prescreening applicants carefully and referring only those qualified, agencies can play a substantial role in the recruitment process. However, many employers express disappointment with agencies. The main reason for the dissatisfaction appears to be the inability of employers to establish effective working relationships with the agencies. In order to facilitate this process, employers should avoid the tendency to engage many agencies and should choose a few select organizations with which to work. Second, specific counselors within each agency should be identified and familiarized with the organization's needs. Finally, if these counselors leave their positions to go to another agency, the organization should likewise switch agencies.[21]

The predominant *public employment agency* is the United States Employment Service (USES) and its affiliated state agencies. Originally established to handle unemployment compensation claims and to find jobs for the unemployed, these agencies now provide a number of services, including the maintenance of a nationally linked job and applicant computer base. There is no fee to use the service, and employers find that these agencies usually provide a ready supply of blue-collar workers.

Even though services are free, many employers refrain from using the USES. One reason for this refusal is the belief that the obligatory legal mandate placed on the agency obstructs the selection process. Because the USES is required to try and place all candidates seeking employment and because the agency's continual funding is based on the number of placements (not necessarily successful placements), little, if any, prescreening or active seeking of appropriate candidates takes place. Furthermore, many candidates referred by the USES are unemployment compensation candidates who are required to seek active employment in order to maintain their unemployment compensation status. As a result, many employers contend that the level of job interest of these candidates is significantly lower than that demonstrated by applicants gleaned from other sources.[22]

School and College Campus Recruiting

School recruiting

Many organizations find that educational institutions offer a good selection of candidates for entry-level or management trainee positions. Guidance and vocational counselors in high schools, vocational and trade schools, and business schools are continually seeking placement opportunities for their graduates. Organizations that establish good working relationships with these personnel often find that the quality of the candidates referred exceeds that of recruits from other sources.

In an effort to generate interest among potential candidates, organizations employ a variety of techniques. Plant tours, career day symposiums, cooperative work-study programs, printed literature, and volunteering their employees to serve as guest speakers are among the most common methods used to disseminate information to prospective candidates. Most organizations find that these methods not only have the potential for creating genuine interest in potential applicants, but also they benefit the organization by enhancing the company's public image.

College campus recruiting

Recruiting on college campuses is an increasingly popular method for obtaining large applicant pools. Most colleges and universities, including junior and community colleges, four-year bachelor's degree institutions, and graduate schools, establish career planning and placement centers on campus which serve as both a training ground for the student and as a quasi-clearinghouse for the employer. The initial employer contacts and the establishment of on-campus recruiting activities is usually coordinated through the placement office.

There are both advantages and disadvantages to campus recruiting. The most obvious benefit is the substantial number of potentially qualified applicants available from which to choose. On the negative side, however, is the fact that many of the applicants have unrealistic job expectations, or they are involved in the process merely for the interviewing "experience." As a result, a substantial number of applicants recruited from college campuses may experience low morale and high turnover during their first five years of employment.[23]

Most college recruiting is conducted in a set fashion. Contact between organizations and the campus placement center usually results in time slots being chosen for on-campus interviewing. The placement center disseminates scheduling information through various sources to the student body, and interested student applicants sign up for interview times. In some instances, company recruiters ask for copies of student files prior to scheduling particular interviews in order to prescreen applicants. These files usually consist of placement applications completed by the students, copies of reference letters, and any other pertinent information supplied by the applicants. Other recruiters specify only the total number of applicants they wish to interview, and leave the task of prescreening to the placement center.

Candidates are usually given printed literature about organizations they are

Exhibit 4.6

Fifteen Knockout Factors (Reasons why candidates receive rejections)

1. Lack of proper career planning—purposes and goals ill defined—needs direction.
2. Lack of knowledge of field specialization—not well qualified—lacks depth.
3. Inability to express thoughts clearly and concisely—rambles.
4. Insufficient evidence of achievement or capacity to excite action in others.
5. Not prepared for interview—no research on company—no presentation.
6. No real interest in the ogranization or the industry—merely shopping around.
7. Narrow location interest—unwilling to relocate later—inflexible.
8. Little interest and enthusiasm—indifferent—bland personality.
9. Overbearing—overaggressive—conceited—cocky—aloof—assuming.
10. Interested only in best dollar offer—too money-conscious.
11. Asks no or poor questions about the job—little depth and meaning to questions.
12. Unwilling to start at the bottom—expects too much too soon—unrealistic.
13. Makes excuses—evasiveness—hedges on unfavorable factors in record.
14. No confidence and poise—fails to look interviewer in the eye—immature.
15. Poor personal appearance—sloppy dress—lacks sophistication.

Source: C. Randall Powell, *Career Planning Today* (Dubuque, IA: Kendall/Hunt Publishing Company, 1981): 241. Reprinted with permission.

interested in, and they are scheduled for an interview time. Typically, these interviews are between fifteen and thirty minutes long, and they serve as preliminary screening techniques. After the initial interviews and usually before leaving campus, those candidates selected are invited for a second interview at the workplace. At this point, they usually enter the full selection process.

Increasing the effectiveness of campus recruiting

There are several ways in which an organization can increase the campus recruitment process. These include:

1. Careful selection of sites.
2. Training of recruiters.
3. Prescreening.
4. Establishing rapport with college personnel.

Selection of sites Organizations usually develop recruiting quotas for the year. These quotas are determined by sampling the various department managers for input on the amount and types of jobs likely to be open in the future. Based on this data, recruiting efforts are aimed at graduates in specific fields, such as accounting and engineering, and the number of campus visits necessary is calculated.

The decision of which campuses to visit is based on several criteria. First, consideration is given to the majors offered by the institution, as well as the school's reputation. Second, the location of the institution in relation to the work site is considered. Not only is it more expensive to recruit at campuses which are not located near the work site, but also graduates of universities in one region, such as Texas, usually do not want to relocate to another locale, such as Connecticut. Last, records of past successes, measured by the amount of job offers tendered and accepted, are considered.[24] It is unwise to continue recruiting at campuses where interviews have not resulted in job offers, or where the acceptance rate is low. When this information is supplemented with performance data about the graduates employed, it will provide a base for determining which institutions are likely to provide the best candidates.[25]

Training of recruiters Campus recruiting is a difficult task. Recruiters must interview a large number of candidates with similar credentials in an abbreviated period of time, and then identify the most qualified applicants. To complicate matters further, many students provide little, if any, previous practical job experience on which recruiters may base their decisions. All too frequently, the ultimate decision of which candidates to invite for second interviews may be based on subjective, non-job-related information.

Recruiter training is a two-fold process. Not only do recruiters serve as preliminary job selectors, but also they serve as an arm of the public relations department by providing company information and creating good will.[26] They must be familiar with the duties of all of the jobs for which they are recruiting. This allows them to distinguish among candidates and to provide answers to applicant inquiries. They must be well versed in selection techniques, particularly interviewing, listening skills, and information gathering. In addition, they need to be trained in how to project a favorable company impression, even to those candidates who are not selected. In summary, recruiter training should focus on evaluating and providing information, selling the organization, and establishing goodwill.[27]

Prescreening Many campus placement services schedule interviews for applicants on a first-come-first-served basis. Any students registered with the placement service who indicate an interest in having an interview are scheduled as long as there are times available. After all available time slots are occupied, the position is closed for further inquiries. As a result, the applicants whom recruiters encounter may be those who responded rapidly to the announcement, or who were able to fit the interview slots available into their class schedules. There is no guarantee that the candidates selected for interviews are those most suited for the positions.

To increase the likelihood of interviewing more qualified candidates, many recruiters are prescreening student applications prior to scheduling interviews. This includes prior screening of interested students' placement credentials, obtaining professors' opinions of these students, and gathering any other background information available. After this prescreening process, campus interviews are scheduled with the chosen students.

Establishing rapport with personnel Aside from establishing a working relationship with career planning and placement personnel, many recruiters find it advantageous to establish rapport with college professors. Through this association, opportunities arise which enable the organization to disseminate information about the company through guest lecture appearances and by sponsoring field trips to the work site. In addition, practicums, internships, cooperative study programs, and direct referrals of students are facilitated.

A word of caution

A major part of a recruiter's job is to inform candidates of what they can realistically hope to expect from both the organization and their job. This Realistic Job Preview (RJP)[28] can aid both the candidate and the organization in matching the needs of the employer with the qualifications of the applicant. Too many recruiters give exaggerated views of the organization, rather than truthful representations. Furthermore, they assume that all college graduates have the necessary skills to perform satisfactorily in most entry-level jobs. Unfortunately, the skills and knowledge learned at school are not necessarily those needed on the job.[29] The result can be low job satisfaction and high turnover.

Recruitment and the Law

Title VII of the Civil Rights Act prohibits employers from discriminating against protected classes in their recruitment practices. More specifically, employers are prohibited from placing advertisements or job notices which indicate preferences, limitations, specifications, or discriminations, based on one of the protected classes, unless a clear, bona fide occupational qualification can be demonstrated.

In the past, the most common violations were in advertisements which indicated preferences for either sex or age. Advertisements which include words such as "salesman," "foreman," and "repairman" have been found to be discriminatory on the basis of sex. For this reason, most advertisements use either neutral language, which implies no particular sex, such as accountant, carpenter, and cashier, or alternative language. Examples of alternative language include words such as salesperson, foreperson, chairperson, or repairer.

Advertisements which state a preference or limitation based on age are also discriminatory, if they have the impact of discriminating against the protected age group (over forty years old). For example, advertisements which request

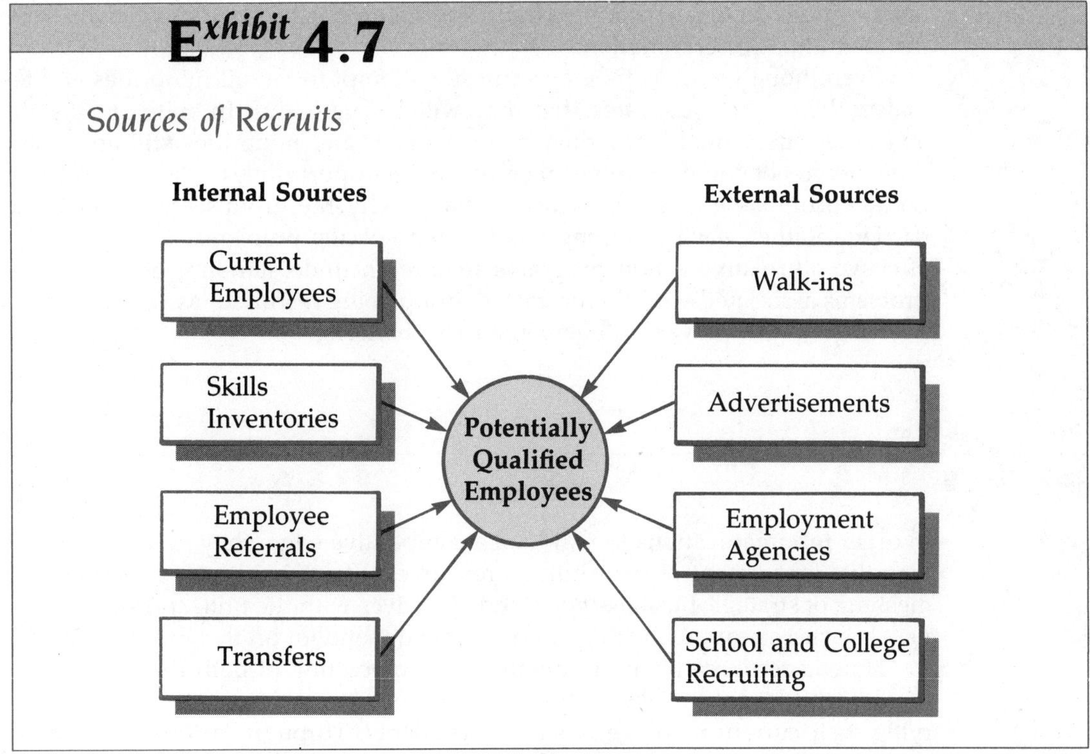

"recent college graduates," or stipulate a certain age bracket, such as ages forty-five to fifty-five, would be considered illegal.

Aside from specifically violating Title VII through direct use of illegal advertising, employers may inadvertently violate the law if it can be demonstrated that the overall effect of their recruiting procedures is the general exclusion of minorities. Using word-of-mouth recruiting methods, such as employee referrals, or advertising in publications read predominantly by majority group members, effectively eliminates groups of minority applicants who are never exposed to the job vacancies.

Affirmative Action Programs

To guarantee equal employment opportunities for minority groups, many employers voluntarily engage in affirmative action programs. These programs (discussed earlier in Chapter 2), which are required of many employers who engage in business with the federal government and employers who have been ordered by the court to rectify past discriminatory practices, are designed to promote the hiring, training, and promotion of minority group members. An affirmative action program involves a concentrated recruitment effort to attract qualified minority group members to the organization. Through its implementation, many organizations have successfully eliminated many practices which inadvertently fostered unfair discrimination.

Even though employers may earnestly attempt to recruit minorities and females, there is no guarantee that they will be successful. In spite of Title VII and other substantial legislation, many females and minorities still encounter difficulty in obtaining meaningful employment opportunities. There is probably no all-encompassing reason which explains why the groups encounter these barriers. Rather, each grouping has its own specific problems. Consequently, effective affirmative action programs require an understanding of the unique problems associated with the protected group being recruited, as well as an earnest effort by employers to overcome these barriers.

Summary

In order for organizations to maintain a competitive edge, they must effectively plan the deployment of their human resources. Effective planning requires the meshing of strategic business goals and objectives with the utilization of personnel. The success of the overall plan is highly dependent on this linking process.

Human resource planning involves the forecasting of both the supply and the demand for future labor. Most organizations begin this process by inventorying their current employees' skills and talents. Through various techniques, such as skills inventories and replacement charts, companies determine the potential for filling future job vacancies with current in-house personnel. Once this assessment has been made, adequate programs to fill the remaining vacancies externally may be developed.

Recruitment for job vacancies occurs in many ways. Some companies use internal sources, such as job bidding and job posting. Other organizations rely totally on external recruiting methods, such as advertisements and employment agency referrals. Still others combine both internal and external methods to accomplish their purpose. Regardless of which methods are employed, however, the goal remains the same—to identify and attract the most qualified applicants.

Key Terms to Identify

Strategic planning
Quantitative forecasting
Qualitative forecasting
Skills inventories
Management inventories
Replacement charts
Recruitment
Job posting
Job bidding

Questions for Discussion

Do You Know the Facts?

1. What steps may be used to assure a linking of strategic business planning with human resource planning?
2. Describe how organizations should collect and use information from skills inventories.
3. What are some of the advantages and disadvantages of job posting and job bidding systems?
4. Why is school and campus recruiting a popular method? Discuss its advantages and disadvantages.

Can You Apply the Information Learned?

1. What arguments would you use to convince an executive board that resources should be expended in planning for human resources?
2. What information would you consider in determining whether recruiting should be done internally, externally, or both?
3. What advice would you give prospective recruits before their initial interview at a placement center?
4. What methods would you use in order to establish rapport with college placement center personnel? Would you use different techniques to build relationships with professors? Why or why not?

The Reluctant Recruits

One morning, Sharon Myele, a professor of human resource management at a small rural college, found a note in her mailbox. The memorandum was from her department head, Chuck Ruffles, and requested that Sharon stop by his office for a moment to discuss a potentially exciting opportunity that had come up for a student. Since her class met in less than five minutes, Sharon jotted down a brief message to Chuck indicating that, if convenient, she would stop by to see him sometime between 10:00 and 11:00 AM. She then proceeded to meet her class.

Later that morning, Sharon stopped by to see Chuck. After exchanging morning greetings, Chuck informed Sharon that he believed he had an exciting job opportunity for a management student. It seemed that Ben Jinckson, the personnel manager at a local metal working factory, had called Chuck the previous afternoon, desperately seeking potential applicants for an assistant personnel manager's position which had recently been created. Chuck further explained that Ben indicated that although the position was in the personnel department, any student who had a business degree, regardless of major, and one year's experience would be acceptable. Chuck thought that it sounded like a wonderful opportunity for one of Sharon's students, and he wondered if she knew of any recent graduates who might be interested in the position.

Sharon was astonished. She could hardly believe her ears. How could Chuck possibly view this as an exceptional opportunity for a student, yet alone one of her highly trained human resource management students? Having been a member of the community for almost twenty years, she was intimately familiar with the company in question. Although it was originally a well-run subsidiary of a Fortune 500 company, it had steadily deteriorated over the past ten years. The personnel department, once a shining example of progressive management, had experienced constant turnover during the last five years. Furthermore, Sharon questioned Ben Jinckson's ability as a personnel manager. Although not totally familiar with his credentials, she did know that he was twenty-six years old and that he had received a degree in history from a small private college. He certainly did not appear to be the type of personnel director that could serve as a mentor for her students.

Chuck, however, was not interested in listening to logic. Recently, there had been emphasis placed on building better rapport with the community, and this appeared to be a golden opportunity. After another hour of discussion, Sharon finally agreed to pass the information along to two of her students who were still residing in the area. Within a week, both students applied for the position.

The following months' events were classic. Both students interviewed for the position. Neither received the job offer. In fact, the position was given to an internal candidate whom Chuck is convinced had been chosen before Ben ever called. Sharon's students were offered low-level supervisory positions on the graveyard shift. The company lost a source of recruits since Chuck refuses to recommend any students for employment there. And, to this day, Chuck still must endure the "I told you so" in Sharon's eyes.

Questions for Discussion

1. Why was Sharon disenchanted with the potential employment opportunity for her students?
2. Do you think Ben's recruiting method was typical or atypical of the norm? Why or why not?
3. If you were Ben, how would you have attempted to recruit Sharon's students?

Endnotes and References

1 Charles R. Greer and Daniel Armstrong, "Human Resource Forecasting and Planning: A State-of-the-Art Investigation," *Human Resource Planning*, Vol. 3, No. 2 (1980): 67–78.

2 Lee Dyer, "Human Resource Planning." In *Personnel Management*, edited by Kendrith M. Rowland and Gerald R. Ferris. (Boston, MA: Allyn and Bacon, 1982): 52–78.

3 George G. Gordon, "Getting in Step," *Personnel Administrator*, Vol. 32, No. 4 (April 1987): 45–48, 134.

4 Elmer H. Burack, *Strategies for Manpower Planning and Programming* (Morristown, NJ: General Learning Press, 1972) and Morton S. Ettlestein, "Integrating the Manpower Factor into Planning, Programming, Budgeting," *Public Personnel Review*, Vol. 31, No. 1 (1970): 51–54.

5 James W. Walker, *Human Resource Planning* (New York: McGraw-Hill Book Company, 1980), 79.

6 For a discussion on strategies for meshing human resource planning with overall organizational planning, see John A. Hooper, Ralph F. Catalanello, and Patrick L. Murray, "Shoring Up the Weakest Link," *Personnel Administrator*, Vol. 32, No. 4 (April 1987): 49–55, 134.

7 Forecasting is often based on subjective judgments made by knowledgeable observers. See Robert D. Gatewood and Elizabeth J. Gatewood, "The Use of Expert Data in Human Resource Planning: Guidelines from Strategic Planning," *Human Resource Planning*, Vol. 2 (1983): 83–94.

8 Vida G. Scarpello and James Ledvinka, *Personnel/Human Resource Management* (Boston, MA: PWS-KENT Publishing Company, 1988), 236.

9 For extended coverage of skills inventories, see S. M. Bailes, "Fundamental Aspects of Establishing a Skills Inventory," *Personnel Journal*, Vol. 41, No. 5 (1961): 226–230, and David J. Thomsen, "Keeping Track of Managers in a Large Corporation," *Personnel*, Vol. 53, No. 6 (1976): 23–30.

10 Thomas H. Patten, *Manpower Planning and the Development of Human Resources* (New York: John Wiley and Sons, 1971), 243.

11 See Paul Sheibar, "A Simple Selection System Called 'Jobmatch'," *Personnel Journal*, Vol. 58 (1979): 26–29, 53.

12 See Hal A. Acuff, "Quality Control in Employee Selection," *Personnel Journal*, Vol. 60, No. 7 (1981): 562–565.

13 Dave R. Dahl and Patrick R. Pinto, "Job Posting: An Industry Survey," *Personnel Journal*, Vol. 56 (1977): 40–42.

14 Ibid.

15 William H. Holley and Kenneth M. Jennings, *Personnel/Human Resource Management* (Chicago, IL: The Dryden Press, 1987), 176.

16 *EEOC* v. *Detroit Edison Company*, U.S. Court of Appeals, Sixth Circuit (Cincinnati), 515 F.2d. 301 (1975).

17 From a survey by the Bureau of National Affairs, "Recruiting Policies and Practices," Survey No. 126, *Personnel Policies Forum,* 1979.

18 Donn L. Dennis, "Are Recruitment Efforts Designed to Fail?" *Personnel Journal,* Vol. 63 (September 1984): 60–67.

19 John P. Bucalo, "Good Advertising Can Be More Effective than Other Recruitment Tools," *Personnel Administrator,* Vol. 28 (November 1983): 73–79.

20 Alix M. Freedman, "When the Headhunter Phones: Listen, Ask Questions, But Don't Reveal Much," *The Wall Street Journal* (February 2, 1985): 31.

21 Erwin S. Stanton, *Successful Personnel Recruiting and Selection* (New York: AMACOM, A Division of the American Management Association, 1977).

22 Vida G. Scarpello and James Ledvinka, *Personnel/Human Resource Management* (Boston, MA: PWS-KENT Publishing Company, 1988), 276.

23 Charles A. O'Reilly III and David F. Caldwell, "The Commitment and Job Tenure of New Employees: Some Evidence of Post Decisional Justification," *Administrative Science Quarterly,* Vol. 26 (December 1981): 597–616. Also see B. Scanlon, "Some Further Views on Changes in Hiring Practices: The Last Decade," *Personnel Journal,* Vol. 59 (June 1980): 480.

24 In general, many organizations use past successes to determine the effectiveness of recruiting practices. See Rick Stoops, "Recruitment Strategy," *Personnel Journal,* Vol. 61 (February 1982): 102.

25 For a discussion on how organizations target institutions, disseminate recruiting information, select and train their recruiters, and evaluate their recruiting efforts, see John Boudreau and Sara Rynes, "Giving It the Old College Try," *Personnel Administrator,* Vol. 32 (March 1987): 78–85.

26 How recruiters treat applicants can greatly influence the perception the candidate has of the company. See Sara L. Rynes, Herbert G. Heneman III, and Donald P. Schwab, "Individual Reactions to Organizational Recruiting," *Personnel Psychology,* Vol. 33, No. 3 (1980): 529–542.

27 Robert P. Seidel and Gary N. Powell, "On the Campus: Matching Graduates with Jobs," *Personnel,* Vol. 60 (July–August 1983): 66–67.

28 For extended coverage of RJP see the following publications by John P. Wanous. "A Job Preview Makes Recruiting More Effective," *Harvard Business Review* (1975): 16, 166, 168; "Tell It Like It Is at Realistic Job Previews," *Personnel,* Vol. 52 (1975): 51; and *Organizational Entry* (Reading, MA: Addison-Wesley Publishing Company, 1980).

29 Gary L. Benson, "On the Campus: How Well Do Business Schools Prepare Graduates for the Business World?" *Personnel,* Vol. 60 (July–August 1983): 61–65.

Chapter 5

The Selection Process

Objectives

After reading this chapter you should understand:

1. The importance of performing preliminary selection analyses.
2. The concept of reliability.
3. The concept of validity and its importance for selection.
4. The various types of validity and how they are obtained.
5. The various steps organizations use in selecting applicants.
6. The differences among application blanks, weighted application blanks, and biographical interest blanks, and their advantages and disadvantages.
7. The different types of test formats and the use of testing within the selection process.
8. The advantages and disadvantages of using reference information.
9. The different types of interview formats, the type of information sought through interviews, the different questioning techniques, and the major interviewing pitfalls.
10. The way information gathered from the various selection techniques is analyzed to make selection decisions.
11. The impact of equal employment opportunity on the use of selection tools.

The adequate selection of human resources within an organization is one of management's most important tasks. Choosing the right person for a job is beneficial to an organization, whereas inadequate selection generates lost time, aggravation, and excessive costs. The methods used for selection, who selects employees, how information is used, and the legal ramifications of selection all contribute to whether or not the selection process is effective. This chapter focuses on how to maximize the selection procedures available within the existing legal boundaries.

> ***Selection***
>
> *The selection process identifies and matches job applicant qualifications to position requirements in order to choose the most competent candidate.*

The Responsibility for Selection

Within many organizations selection is either the sole responsibility of the human resource department or it is an obligation shared with line managers. In small companies the absence of a formal personnel department relegates the total responsibility for selection to the supervisor, while in larger companies the entire responsibility for selection is delegated to specialists called employment managers. Because the diversification of functions varies from organization to organization, the natural question arises: Who should be ultimately responsible for the selection process?

As positions within companies become more complex, as organizations expand, and as managers and supervisors become better trained, they begin to take a more active role in the selection process. Although various organizational settings may justify different procedures, individuals are becoming aware of the fact that the ultimate responsibility for selection rests with the supervisor.

Rather than being the primary agents in the selection process, human resource personnel are serving in advisory capacities. They conduct training programs in effective selection procedures and in government rules and regulations. In addition, they serve as principal job agents when conducting job analyses, they act as liaisons to communities, and they provide additional assistance as needed. Sometimes the human resource department is responsible for the entire selection process from beginning to end; however, the final selection decision should be the ultimate responsibility of the person directly accountable for the position, the supervisor.

Initial Considerations

The ultimate success of a selection program rests on the amount of planning conducted during the early stages of the process. These initial considerations center around the job analysis, the available pool of candidates, the reliability and validity of the selection techniques, and the prevailing government rules and regulations. When human resource departments adequately do their homework, the selection process results in qualified employees who ultimately make significant contributions to the organization. However, if the selection process is conducted hastily in reaction to a crisis, the end result is typically negative for both employees and the organization.

Job Analysis

As defined in Chapter 3, job analysis is a process undertaken to determine which characteristics are necessary for satisfactory job performance, and to analyze the environmental conditions in which the job is performed. Once completed, a job analysis leads to a job description and a job specification. The job specification, which lists the human elements needed for satisfactory job performance, is primarily used for selection.

Job analyses, and the resulting job specifications, enhance the selection procedure. Realistically, however, many companies scramble to accumulate some criteria in order to develop selection procedures. The resulting criteria are usually subjective in nature, reflecting broad generalities provided by supervisors. They are seldom comprehensive, and they typically omit essential details. Rarely, if ever, will these types of analyses provide sufficient information to make fine discriminations among candidates. On the other hand, when job analyses, and the resulting job specifications, are conducted as a routine human resource function, they yield invaluable information. The job specification typically indicates the necessary requirements in the areas of experience and training, education, KSAs (knowledge, skills, and abilities), and other general requirements. Based on these criteria, appropriate selection tools are developed which enable distinctions to be drawn among the candidates.

The Available Candidate Pool

In many instances, the selection decision is determined not only by the nature of the job to be filled, but also by the available labor force. If it is an unskilled position with unpleasant working conditions and few applicants, any candidate who walks through the door is likely to be hired immediately. For example, suppose you have a position for a third-shift truck tire retread mold person. This position requires that extremely heavy weights be handled in an environment which is filled with tire dust and extreme heat, between the hours of 12 AM and 8 AM. The likelihood of having a large applicant pool is nil. In this instance, selection requires merely ascertaining if the candidate is likely to return the following day. On the other hand, the selection of a college professor from hundreds of applicants requires a much more sophisticated process. To determine the available labor force, human resource managers use the **selection ratio.**

Selection ratio

The selection ratio is the proportion of candidates who are hired in relation to the amount of candidates in the available applicant pool. It is typically expressed as:

$$\text{Selection Ratio} = \frac{\text{Number of Candidates Hired}}{\text{Number of Candidates Available}}$$

When the selection ratio is large, approaching 1.0, a firm does not need sophisticated selection procedures. This was demonstrated in the case of the retread mold worker where the company was forced to hire any available candidate. When the selection ratio is low, decreasing toward 0.00, the selection procedure requires greater sophistication and finer discriminatory tools. In general, organizations are at an advantage when they have lower selection ratios. Although more sophisticated instruments are required, they retain the luxury of large applicant pools.

Reliability and Validity

The goal of a selection technique is to discriminate between job candidates who can successfully complete the job requirements and those who cannot. Therefore, it is imperative that selection instruments be reliable (consistent and dependable over time) and valid (accurate measurements). In order to effectively accomplish this task, selection tools are developed to identify and predict the capabilities of applicants. A selection tool is referred to as a **predictor,** and what it measures (job performance) is a **criterion.**

Predictor and criterion

A predictor is a measure, such as a test or an interview, and a criterion is a standard to be accomplished (average or satisfactory job performance).

Reliability

In order to have confidence in a selection measure, the measure must provide consistent results over time. This measure of consistency is referred to as **reliability.** The present discussion will focus on the use of tests. It is important to note, however, that all selection instruments require a degree of consistency.

Reliability

Reliability refers to the degree to which instruments consistently measure what they intend to measure.

Depending on the use and nature of a particular selection technique, reliability may be concerned with any of the following:

1. Consistency over time.
2. Consistency between two equivalent forms of the same measure.
3. Whether or not the measure is internally consistent.

It is important to note at this point that there are occasions when a test is reliable, but it consistently measures the wrong thing. Consider the following example:

> The Failanexam Company created a test to measure mathematical ability. Rather than use purely numerical examples, they created a test which incorporated story problems (If we have two apples and buy three pears, how many fruits do we have?). After validating their instrument, they administered it to non-English-speaking job applicants. All of the applicants failed. As a result, they concluded that the applicants had poor mathematical ability and would perform unsatisfactorily on the job. In fact, they knew for certain that their conclusion was correct because no matter how many times they administered the examination to these applicants, they failed to pass. The applicants were rejected and the company continued to search for more worthy candidates.

Apparently, the preceding test had reliability, for it consistently indicated that the candidates were unable to pass. Unfortunately, while the test was designed to demonstrate mathematical ability, it appears that it was also measuring reading ability. It was indeed reliable, but it consistently measured the wrong thing. In order to be effective, selection devices must not only be reliable, but also valid as well.

Validity

As the preceding case demonstrates, having the reliability of a measure is not sufficient by itself. In fact, it has been widely noted that a test can be consistent without measuring the right areas. To ascertain how well predictors identify characteristics necessary for successful job performance, a statistical technique measuring **validity** is used.

> **Validity**
>
> *Validity is the degree to which an evaluation technique truly measures what it is supposed to measure.*

This definition of validity is simple and standard, but somewhat misleading. Historically, people have inferred from this definition that the instrument, method, or technique itself is valid. However, "validity refers to the appropriateness of inferences from test scores or other forms of assessment."[1] What is important to understand from this definition is that the predictor itself is not valid. Instead, the conclusions drawn from predictors are either valid or invalid. Suppose, for example, that a supervisor concludes that a score of 72 on an English and math examination determines success in a job that requires reading and adding ability. Basically, the supervisor is contending that a score of 72 or greater implies success, while a score of 71 or below suggests failure. In this case we are not validating the test per se, but rather the inferences regarding success based on test performance.

Traditionally, validity has been applied to tests. As the preceding definition from the American Psychological Association indicates, it is also applicable to other forms of assessment. Application blanks, interviews, and any other measures developed for the purpose of discriminating between applicants are also the focus of selection validation. In these instances, the intention of validation is to determine the extent of the relationship between a predictor and a criterion.

Types of validity

Many different validation strategies have evolved over the years. For the present discussion the focus will be on the two types of validity strategies most commonly used in selection. These are: criterion-related validity (predictive and concurrent), and content validity.[2]

Criterion-related validity **Criterion-related validity** is subdivided into two types: predictive and concurrent. These validity strategies differ with regard to the time period in which the predictor and criterion data are accumulated.

> **Criterion-related validity**
>
> ***Criterion-related validity statistically examines and draws inferences about the relationship between a predictor and a criterion.***

Predictive validity To best understand the concept of predictive validity, which is also referred to as the "future-employee method," let us recap the purpose of validation. The validation of a measure (test) is an attempt to draw inferences regarding the relationship between performance on a predictor (the test) and a criterion (job success). Once validated, the test is administered to job applicants. Those candidates whose test scores indicate their likelihood of job success is minimal are screened out, and those individuals whose test scores indicate probable job success are screened in. To accomplish this purpose, it must be demonstrated that scores on the test are indeed indicative of job success.

Predictive validity

A criterion-related validity in which the predictor and criterion data are collected during different time periods.

When a predictive validation strategy is used, the test is administered to all job applicants. These invalidated scores are not used as part of the selection procedure. An applicant is hired based on previously established methods, and over a period of time, data is collected concerning performance on the job (typically in the form of performance reviews). Subsequently, the test scores are compared to the evaluations of the worker's job performance. The validity of the inference which can now be drawn from the predictor (the test) is determined by the strength of the relationship between the test and job success. Suppose, for example, that a test for managerial ability has been created. To validate the test, it is first administered to applicants for the position. The test has not been previously validated, so it is not currently used for selection; thus, decisions regarding hiring are made through other established techniques. Performance data is subsequently collected for those hired over an extended period of time (usually three to five years), and is correlated with the test scores. If a strong degree of correlation is demonstrated between the test scores and the performance appraisals, the test is used for the selection process.

Concurrent validity **Concurrent validity,** which is sometimes referred to as the "present-employee method" of validation, has the same basic goal as predictive validity. Validation of the instrument allows for inferences to be drawn regarding eventual job success or failure. The major difference between the two methods is the time at which the predictor and criterion data are collected. Unlike predictive validity, where the predictor is administered at an earlier point in time and criterion data are gathered later, concurrent validity requires that both the predictor and criterion data be collected at the same point in time. For example, suppose a test to demonstrate success as a computer repairperson needs to be validated. First, a job analysis would be conducted to determine the important characteristics necessary for job success. Second, a test would be created to measure these characteristics. Third, the test would be administered to currently employed technicians, and data concerning their performance (that is, a performance appraisal) would be collected. Finally, a statistical comparison would be made to determine the relationship between the predictor (test) and the criterion (job performance). Once again, the strength of the relationship between the predictor and the criterion determines the validity of the inferences.

Exhibit 5.1

Comparison of Predictive and Concurrent Validity

Predictive validity	Concurrent validity
1. The study requires either a large organization or a period of expansion to obtain a large enough sample.	1. The subjects are already employed, so the degree of motivation to perform well may be lower.
2. The data are collected over a period of time, so applicants must remain with the company long enough to collect criterion data.	2. The results of job incumbents may be a function of knowledge, skills, and abilities learned on the job, rather than potential.
3. The study is longitudinal, so the company must have enough other valid selection tools to hire individuals during the period in which data are being collected.	3. The applicants that have remained may not be a representative sample, but rather the best of those who originally applied.
4. This form of validity indicates what will happen based on training, experience, and other factors over time.	4. This form of validity indicates the present conditions of already trained individuals.

Concurrent validity

Concurrent validity is a type of criterion-related validity in which both predictor and criterion data are gathered at the same point in time.

Content validity Criterion-related validity relies, to a large extent, on statistical measures to determine the relationship between the predictor and the criterion. When quantitative measures are inappropriate, such as when an attempt is being made to sample KSAs (knowledge, skills, and abilities) necessary for satisfactory job performance, **content validity** is employed.

Content validity

A validation strategy used to determine if a measure assesses an entire content area.

Exhibit 5.2

Steps in Using the Validation Strategies

Predictive validity	Concurrent validity	Content validity
1. Identify characteristics of job via job analysis.	1. Identify characteristics of job via job analysis.	1. Identify characteristics of job via job analysis.
2. Develop test.	2. Develop test.	2. Develop test.
3. Administer test to applicants.	3. Administer test and collect performance data of job incumbents.	3. Present test to experts and verify content.
4. Select applicants using previously validated tools.	4. Correlate test to performance data.	4. Add or delete content based on experts' opinions.
5. Hire applicants and collect performance data over time.		5. Verify modified test with job incumbents.
6. Correlate test to performance data over time.		

To obtain a measure of content validity, the judgments of experts are relied upon rather than quantifiable methods. This validation process normally involves three steps. First, a job analysis is conducted to identify the tasks, skills, and abilities necessary for job success. Second, the measure for sampling these characteristics is developed. Finally, experts (the job incumbents) evaluate the items and agree upon the measures that sample the job adequately.[3] To best understand content validity, consider the following example:

> After enrolling in a class in Human Resource Management, Elsa, Paul, and Bernie discover that their grades for the semester will be based solely on a final examination consisting of material taken from a 600-page textbook. Exemplifying the typical procrastinators, Paul and Bernie wait for the last minute to begin the cramming process, while Elsa studies throughout the semester. As a result, Elsa reads all 600 pages, and she retains 70 percent of the material. Bernie, on the other hand, reads pages 1 to 300, but retains 90 percent of the material. Paul, guessing that the examination will only be on the last half of the book, reads pages 301 to 600, and retains 85 percent of the material. The day of the examination arrives, and the three students take the test. How they perform on the test, and their ultimate grade, will depend on the content validity of the test. If the questions are

drawn solely from pages 1 to 300, then Bernie will score the highest. If the items are predominantly from pages 301 to 600, then Paul will obtain the highest score. If, however, the test is content validated, sampling representatively from the entire book, then Elsa will obtain the highest score.

The preceding case demonstrates the ill effects of excluding content validity in test construction. In the first two instances, the performance of Paul and Bernie is a function of chance rather than knowledge. If this had been an employment situation, Bernie would have been hired in the first instance, while Paul would have been hired in the second case. In reality, however, the most knowledgeable student is Elsa, who would have proven to be the best employee.

Using Reliability and Validity Coefficients

Reliability and validity coefficients are reported as a coefficient between 0.00 (indicating no validity or reliability) and 1.0 (indicating perfect reliability or validity). The natural question which arises is: How close to 1.0 must the coefficient be for use? In general, the higher the coefficients the better. In practice, reliability coefficients above .70 are acceptable although there are some frequently used tests which have reliabilities reported in the .50 range.[4] Validity coefficients, on the other hand, are typically lower, falling between .30 and .45.[5]

After developing selection criteria, organizations begin candidate assessments. Some organizations use formal processes involving lengthy procedures through which candidates progress. For other businesses, hiring is an informal process which may involve only a single interview. The smaller the organization, the more likely it is that the selection decision will be made quickly and informally. Regardless of the formality involved, however, all selection processes share certain similarities. First, they all involve a series of steps or hurdles through which applicants must pass. Second, all processes use some combination of techniques designed to gather information from candidates. These include: application blanks, employment tests, reference checks, interviews, and physical examinations.

Selection Steps

Most hiring decisions are made after applicants satisfactorily progress through a series of stages. Very few organizations offer employment to applicants if they complete only one phase of the selection process. On the other hand, however, there are selection programs which reject applicants before they have the opportunity to complete the entire process. Whether an applicant progresses through all the stages before being rejected or whether he or she is terminated at an earlier phase is determined by the job requirements. Depending on the particular situation, organizations use the multiple hurdles strategy, the compensatory strategy, or the mixed strategy.

Multiple Hurdles Strategy

The **multiple hurdles strategy** rejects applicants if they fail to satisfactorily complete any stage of the selection process. For example, some colleges' admission requirements may consist of minimum SAT scores of 900 and a 3.0 high school GPA. Applicants failing to achieve a score of 900 or greater on the SAT are automatically rejected from further admission considerations regardless of their GPAs. Similarly, prospective students whose GPAs are below 3.0 are excluded from consideration regardless of their SAT scores. The use of this process is based on the supposition that certain skills are necessary for satisfactory job performance, and that their absence cannot be compensated for by other abilities. When using this tactic, each step of the selection process must be valid, regardless of whether or not the entire selection procedure is discriminatory. Failure to prove the job relatedness of any stage may result in illegal discrimination.[6]

Compensatory Strategy

When companies determine that positions can be satisfactorily performed using various combinations of abilities, the **compensatory strategy** is used. All applicants proceed through the entire selection process before being rejected or hired. The assumption underlying this process is that candidates' strengths may compensate for their weaknesses. For example, a candidate for a receptionist/secretarial position who demonstrates outstanding verbal communication skills may be selected despite the fact that he or she does poorly on a dictation test.

Mixed Strategy

When certain characteristics are necessary, but not sufficient, for minimum job success, the **mixed strategy** is used. Suppose, for example, that a height of 6′ 10″ is a prerequisite for playing the center position on a basketball team. Every applicant who does not meet this requirement is automatically rejected. Candidates who meet the height requirement, however, are not immediately employed, but are required to demonstrate additional basketball skills. They continue through the other selection steps. Once again, to avoid potential discrimination charges, care must be taken to show the job relatedness of each stage in the process.

Selection Techniques

Application Blanks

The use of **application blanks** is probably the oldest and most widespread selection procedure.[7] The items used on application blanks vary from organization to organization, but are all based on the same premise: what an individual will do in the future can be predicted by what he or she has done in the past. Consequently, application blanks seek information from candidates concerning their previous educational background, past employment history, work references, and personal data.

> ***Application blanks***
>
> *Application blanks are written forms completed by job candidates detailing their educational background, previous work history, past references, and certain personal data.*

For most firms, application blanks are the initial screening tool. In an effort to make greater use of these forms, companies have tended to add vast amounts of items. Before adding items to application forms, several factors should be considered. First, excessively lengthy and complex forms discourage completion by potential applicants. Second, any additional items must be job related. Finally, all questions must adhere to the guidelines dictated by Equal Employment Opportunity laws. Basically, any question which can be construed as discriminating against a protected class must be shown to be job related, or it must be eliminated from the application form.

Initial applicant screening occurs after all potential candidates have completed their application blanks. In many cases, the determination of which candidates are screened in and out is accomplished subjectively. Two types of application forms which change this subjective evaluation to objective, quantifiable measures are weighted application blanks (WAB) and biographical information blanks (BIB).

Weighted Application Blanks (WAB)

The method for creating **weighted application blanks** is similar to the procedure used for validating other selection tools. The application blank is the predictor, and job performance is the criterion. Incumbents are grouped into the categories of high and low performers, or high, middle, and low performers. Next, the application blanks which the incumbents completed as candidates are retrieved and compared to their subsequent job performance. Those items which exhibit strong relationships to job performance are given high scores, while those items which demonstrate minimal relationships to performance are given low scores. The total score of each applicant is derived by summing the weights of the individual item responses. The resulting scores are then used in the selection decision. If the content and the weights assigned are based on the job analysis, WABs are highly valid predictors of job success.[8]

Exhibit 5.3

Application for Federal Employment—SF 171

Form Approved:
OMB No. 3206-0012

Read the instructions before you complete this application. ***Type or print clearly in dark ink.***

GENERAL INFORMATION

1 What kind of job are you applying for? *Give title and announcement number (if any)*

2 If the announcement lists several job titles, which jobs are you applying for?

3 Social Security Number

4 Birth date *(Month, Day, Year)*

5 Name *(Last, First, Middle)*

Street address or RFD number *(include apartment number, if any)*

City | State | ZIP Code

6 Other names ever used

7 Sex *(for statistical use)* ☐ Male ☐ Female

8 Home Phone — Area Code | Number

9 Work Phone — Area Code | Number | Ext.

10 Were you ever employed as a civilian by the Federal Government? If **"NO"**, go to **11**. If **"YES"**, mark each type of job you held with an **"X"**.
☐ Temporary ☐ Career-Conditional ☐ Career ☐ Excepted
What is your highest grade, classification series and job title?

Dates at highest grade: FROM TO

11 Do you have any applications for Federal employment on file with the U.S. Office of Personnel Management? If **"NO"**, mark here ☐ and go to **12**. If **"YES"**, write below and continue in **47** the information for each application: (a) the name of the office that has your application; (b) the title of the job; (c) the date of your Notice of Results; and (d) your rating.

DO NOT WRITE IN THIS AREA

FOR USE OF EXAMINING OFFICE ONLY

Material ☐ Submitted ☐ Returned

Entered register:

Notations:

Form reviewed:
Form approved:

ANNOUNCEMENT NO.

APPLICATION NO.

Option	Grade	Earned Rating	Preference	Aug. Rating
			☐ 5 Points (Tent.)	
			☐ 10 Pts. (30%) Or More Comp. Dis.	
			☐ 10 Pts. Less Than 30% Comp. Dis.	
			☐ Other 10 Points	
			☐ Disallowed	

Initials and Date

☐ Being Investigated

FOR USE OF APPOINTING OFFICER ONLY

Preference has been verified through proof that the separation was under honorable conditions, and other proof as required.

☐ 5-Point ☐ 10-Point—*30% or More Compensable Disability* ☐ 10-Point—*Less Than 30% Compensable Disability* ☐ 10-Point—*Other*

Signature and Title

Agency | Date

AVAILABILITY

12 When can you start work? *(Month and Year)*

13 What is the **lowest** pay you will accept?
Pay $________ per ________ **OR** Grade ____

14 Are you willing to work:	YES	NO
A. In the Washington, D.C., metropolitan area?		
B. Outside the 50 United States?		
C. Any place in the United States?		
D. Only in *(list the location[s])*		

15 Are you willing to work:	YES	NO
A. 40 hours per week (full-time)?		
B. 25-32 hours per week (part-time)?		
C. 17-24 hours per week (part-time)?		
D. 16 or fewer hours per week (part-time)?		
E. In an intermittent job (on-call/seasonal)?		
F. Weekends, shifts, or rotating shifts?		

16 Are you willing to take a temporary job lasting:	YES	NO
A. 5 to 12 months (sometimes longer)?		
B. 1 to 4 months?		
C. Less than 1 month?		

17 Are you willing to travel away from home for:	YES	NO
A. 1 to 5 nights each month?		
B. 6 to 10 nights each month?		
C. 11 or more nights each month?		

MILITARY SERVICE AND VETERAN PREFERENCE

	YES	NO
18 Have you served on active duty in the United States Military Service? *If your only active duty was training in the Reserves or National Guard, answer "NO".* If **"NO"**, go to **22**.		
19 Were you honorably discharged from the military service? *If your discharge was changed to "honorable" or "general" by a Discharge Review Board, answer "YES". If you received a clemency discharge, answer "NO".* If **"NO"**, explain in **47**.		
20 Did you or will you retire at or above the rank of major or lieutenant commander?		

21 List the dates, branch, and serial number for all active duty service.

FROM	TO	BRANCH OF SERVICE	SERIAL NUMBER

22 Place an **"X"** in the box next to your Veteran Preference claim. Mark only **one** box. *See the instructions for eligibility information.*

1 NO PREFERENCE

2 5-POINT PREFERENCE—You must show proof when you are hired.

10-POINT PREFERENCE—**If you claim 10-point preference, you must complete a Standard Form 15, which is available at any Federal Job Information Center. ATTACH THE COMPLETED SF 15 TO THIS APPLICATION, TOGETHER WITH THE PROOF REQUESTED IN THE SF 15.**

3 Non-compensably disabled or Purple Heart recipient.

4 Compensably disabled (less than 30%).

5 Spouse, widow(er), or mother.

6 Compensably disabled (30% or more).

THE FEDERAL GOVERNMENT IS AN EQUAL OPPORTUNITY EMPLOYER

Standard Form 171 (Rev. 2/84)
Office of Personnel Management
FPM Chapter 295

> **Weighted application blanks**
>
> *Weighted application blanks are written forms completed by candidates in which each item is weighted and scored based on its importance as a determinant of job success.*

Biographical Information Blanks (BIB)

In order to use **biographical information blanks,** all items on the form must be compared with job criteria. Those items which prove to be good predictors of job success are then scored appropriately. Similar to the WAB, each individual applicant receives a score, which is then used in the selection decision.

> **Biographical information blanks**
>
> *Biographical information blanks are extensive multiple-choice forms which elicit information from applicants regarding factual material, attitudes, early life experiences, and social values.*

Certain differences and similarities between the WAB and the BIB should be considered when choosing one or the other. The major differences between the two techniques are the length of the forms and the types of data obtained. The WAB is typically much shorter, consisting of between ten and twenty questions, and it elicits factual, verifiable data. The BIB, on the other hand, may consist of more than one hundred questions, the answers to which may be unverifiable. The similarities between the WAB and the BIB center around validity and the legal requirements involved in their use. Both forms have demonstrated validity when used objectively,[9] and both need to conform to Equal Employment Opportunity guidelines. Firms which fail to perform validity studies on either of these techniques will risk the possibility of illegal discrimination suits.

Employment Tests

Over the years, the use of **employment tests** has been the subject of much controversy. Employment tests were widely used in the 1950s and 1960s, but their use diminished in the 1970s. The main reason for this decline appears to be the rising number of court cases and resulting EEO guidelines enacted regarding the use of tests in industry;[10] an example is *Griggs* v. *Duke Power Company* (1971). Nevertheless, tests still remain one of the most objective techniques for measuring human characteristics, and their benefits should not be overlooked.[11]

> **Employment tests**
>
> ***Employment tests are objective and standardized measures designed to obtain information from individuals concerning the specific characteristics, interests, knowledge, abilities, or behaviors they possess.***

Obtaining Information about Tests

The most effective test is one which a company specifically designs for a particular situation. The cost of creating tests, however, makes it prohibitive for many companies to have them custom designed. The option available for these companies is to use previously developed standardized tests. To determine which test is appropriate for a particular situation, companies gather information from published journal articles, individual test manuals, **Tests in Print III,** or the **Mental Measurement Yearbooks.** Collectively, these four publications provide information regarding the various tests' developers, their purposes, costs, availability, and reliability and validity, as well as critical analyses of their use. Prudent analysis of the information allows companies to select an appropriate instrument for use.

Types of Tests

Tests are classified either by their design or by their content. The *design* of a test determines how it is administered. The *content* of a test refers to what a test measures, and it determines when a particular test is most appropriate for use.[12]

Test Design

Speed and power tests A **speed test** is constructed with an abundance of easy items. These items are so easy that candidates can usually get them all correct. There is a time limit, however, and this prohibits anyone from completing the entire test. Individuals' scores are a function of the amount of items correctly answered within the allotted time period. **Power tests,** on the other hand, are designed to sample knowledge, and scores are determined by the total number of items answered correctly. Theoretically, individuals who do not know the correct responses will not increase their score even with unlimited time.

Individual and group tests Individual tests are administered to one person at a time, while group tests are administered to several people simultaneously. Group testing is the predominant method used, unless there is a specific reason for single administration (such as personality test designed only for individual administration).

Paper-and-pencil and performance tests **Paper-and-pencil** tests involve written responses to test items which are usually presented in either multiple-choice or essay formats. **Performance tests** require the manipulation of objects or equipment. Individuals' scores on performance tests are a function of how well they manipulate the objects. By far, the most common form of testing in industry is paper-and-pencil tests.

Test content

In addition to categorizing tests according to their design, tests are also classified according to their content area. For selection purposes, the tests predominantly used measure ability, personality, and work samples.

Ability tests

Ability tests are probably one of the earliest forms of testing used within the field of personnel. They are principally paper-and-pencil inventories, and are designed for group administration. Included within this category are tests which measure intelligence (I.Q. tests), ability and aptitude (mechanical, clerical, and sensory tests), and Multiple Aptitude Batteries (which measure a wide array of abilities and aptitudes).

Ability tests

Ability tests are standardized, objective, paper-and-pencil inventories designed to assess learning potential by measuring existing abilities and aptitudes.

Personality tests

Of all the tests used for selection, **personality tests** have probably generated the most scrutiny and controversy. The definition of personality, methods of measuring personality factors, and the relationship between personality factors and actual job criteria have been the subject of much discussion and research. In addition, there is some question about whether applicants answer the items truthfully, or whether they try to respond in a socially acceptable manner. Regardless of these criticisms, many people still view personality as an important component of job success.[13] As a result, when job analyses indicate that job success is influenced strongly by personality variables, personality tests are used. For example, success as a salesperson may be influenced by certain personality characteristics.

Personality tests

Personality tests are measures that assess the underlying psychological constructs which determine how individuals will behaviorally respond to social situations.

Work sample tests

Work sample tests are designed to measure candidates' existing job skills by having them actually complete tasks on-the-job. Together with ability tests, work sample tests appear to be the best predictors of job success for entry-level positions.[14] Although the most common form of this testing is motor skill assessment, work sample tests can also be used to ascertain other required job skills. For example, requiring secretarial candidates to take typing tests is an example of a motor skill assessment. Similarly, when applicants for the position of interpreter are required to pass a language examination, they are also being assessed by a work sample test.

> ***Work sample tests***
>
> *Measures designed to sample existing job skills by requiring the completion of actual job tasks.*

When compared to measures designed to predict potential work performance, it appears that work sample tests demonstrate greater degrees of reliability and validity. Of course, the relevance of the test depends to a large extent on how well the job analysis identifies appropriate tasks for sampling.

Testing and the Law

According to the Uniform Guidelines on Selection Procedures, a test is considered a selection procedure, defined as "any measure, combination of measures, or procedure used as a basis for any employment decision."[15] As a result, the rules and regulations which apply to testing are universal for all selection procedures and vice versa. Without delving into the specifics of these regulations it should suffice to mention that the primary task facing management is the validation of the test. All selection procedures must demonstrate a strong degree of job relatedness, and tests are no exception. In addition, whether or not the employer meant to unfairly discriminate is legally unimportant. If the employer in fact discriminated, it must demonstrate the validity of the measure.

In general, the category of tests which has proven to be the subject of the least amount of legal action has been work sample tests. Psychological tests involving the measurement of personality, intelligence, and aptitude have generated much litigation. Confronted with legal action, the organization is faced with the burden of demonstrating job relatedness. Prior planning, including job analysis and validation, eases the ordeal and provides for more useful selection tools.

A word of caution

Prior to administering tests to applicants, evaluators should determine if the candidate has ever had experience with the particular instrument being used. For many tests, particularly speed tests, the validity may be affected if subjects

Exhibit 5.4

Some Tests Used in Selection

Test name	Test purpose	Test type
General Clerical Ability Test	Applicants for clerical positions	Clerical
APT Manual Dexterity Test	Auto and truck mechanics' helpers	Manual dexterity
Primary Mechanical Ability Test	Applicants for positions requiring mechanical ability	Mechanical ability
Computer Programmer Aptitude Battery	Applicants for training or employment in computer programming fields	Computer programming aptitude
Sales Attitude Checklist	Applicants for sales positions	Sales aptitude
Electrical Sophistication Test	Applicants for electrical positions	Skilled trades
Leadership Evaluation and Development Scale	Prospective supervisors	Supervisor aptitude
PSI Basic Skills Test for Business, Industry, and Government	Applicants in general	Achievement
Wonderlic Personnel Test	Applicants in general	Intelligence
Minnesota Multiphasic Personality Inventory (MMPI)	Applicants in general	Personality

have prior knowledge regarding the test's contents. Consider the following case.

> Joseph and his wife Sue were both psychology graduate students at a large midwestern university. To pass the time during the evening hours, they amused themselves by competing against each other with different forms of a timed clerical aptitude test. Several months later, Sue decided to seek employment. Upon registering at the local employment bureau, she was handed a clerical aptitude test and instructed to complete as many of the 100 items as she could before time elapsed. Can you imagine the shocked look on the examiner's face when Sue returned a perfect paper three minutes before time had elapsed? Can you envision the reaction when Sue proceeded to

> duplicate the feat with a second form of the test? Future employment certainly was no problem. The employment agency offered her a job on the spot.

Sue's performance was a function of being test wise. When using standardized tests, there is always the possibility that applicants have had previous experience with the instrument.

Reference Checks

If individuals' past behaviors can truly represent future performance, then the importance of **reference checks** is undeniable. In fact, most organizations require that applicants provide reference information in conjunction with their application materials.[16] These data consist of names and addresses of people to contact, or they are in the form of letters of recommendation. The value of the information ultimately obtained is dependent on the methods used to gather the data.

> **Reference check**
>
> *A reference check is a process undertaken to gather information about an applicant's past work history, educational background, and social behaviors, from people with whom the applicant has previously been associated.*

Methods Used to Collect Data

The methods used to collect reference data are fairly standardized, and include the use of telephone inquiries, written recommendations, and personal interviews.

Telephone inquiries The telephone provides the simplest and fastest way to obtain information about candidates. Most application blanks request that applicants list their previous places of employment and the names of their immediate supervisors. The names, addresses, and phone numbers of personal references must also be furnished. Contacting any of these sources provides information about candidates.

Although the telephone is used extensively to obtain information about candidates, it does present problems. Many people are reluctant to make information available to people whom they do not know. Realistically, there is no way to immediately verify the person on the other end of the line. To overcome this problem, companies would be well advised to have applicants inform their references to expect calls from specific prospective employers.

Written recommendations Written recommendations include letters or forms requested by candidates or solicited by companies. These documents request that references provide subjective information regarding the candidate's strengths and weaknesses in those areas judged to be job related. Additionally, most forms include a statement for the applicant to complete in which they either do or do not waive their rights under the Privacy Act to view the document.

There are two problems associated with written recommendations. First, many recommenders view the completion of these letters as a nuisance. They spend minimal time evaluating the applicant, and in many instances they fail to return the forms promptly. Second, if applicants do not waive their rights to view the documents, many references will either disclose minimal information or completely refuse to respond. In spite of these problems, however, many employers have still required applicants to submit letters of recommendation or reference letters.[17]

Personal interviews The most comprehensive method of gathering information about individuals is through personal interviews. Used extensively in background investigations, references are contacted face-to-face and queried regarding candidates. Generally, the investigators have specific information to gather, but they are free to delve into other subject areas.

When the use of personal interviews is contemplated, several factors must be considered. The process is expensive, time consuming, and the investigators must be well trained. As a result, personal interviews are typically limited to situations which involve the selection of higher level positions.

The Value of Reference Information

During the past decade, the subject of what information to disclose concerning applicants has become of paramount importance. The passage of the Privacy Act of 1974 and subsequent state privacy laws has caused many employers to become guarded regarding the information which they will disclose. Legally, the records which employers maintain on workers are the property of the employer and may be used at their discretion. Practically, however, there is a multitude of laws protecting workers' rights of privacy, and most employers are leery of being sued.[18] As a result, more and more employers are providing only objective, behavioral data, such as job title and dates of employment.[19]

As employers become more cautious about releasing information, it is increasingly more important to critically evaluate the data gathered. If the present trend continues, reference checking may become a mere formality, placing a greater burden for selection on other methods.

Employment Interviews

Employment interviews are currently the most widely used selection techniques in industry.[20] Regardless of the nature of the business, the position involved, and the other selection procedures employed, employers usually like to have a

Exhibit 5.5

Sample of a Reference Check Form

Reference Check Form

Applicant Name ____________________

Company Contacted ____________________ Date ____________________

Person Contacted ____________________ Title ____________________

1. Dates of Employment From: ____________ To: ____________
2. Positions and Duties Held ____________________
3. Attendance Record Poor Below Average Average Good
4. Reasons for Termination Discharged Resigned
5. Job Performance Rating Poor Below Average Average Good
6. Friendliness Distant Approachable Warm
7. Attitude Uncooperative Cooperative
8. Knowledge of Field Poor Below Average Average Good
9. Strengths and Weaknesses ____________________
10. Any Additional Information Obtained ____________________

____

Signature of Person Conducting Reference Check ____________________ close-up preview of prospective employees. Some organizations use interviewing as one step in the selection process, while other companies rely on it as the sole criterion for hiring. No matter which method is used, it is important to note that the success of the interview depends largely on the skill of the interviewer rather than on the design of the instrument.

The making of good selection decisions through the interviewing process is a dilemma for industry. Some researchers have determined that interviewing reliability is low.[21] Other research maintains that there is not as much pessimism today regarding the validity of interviewing as there was in the past.[22] The reason for the diversity in findings is caused by several external factors which impact on interviewing validity. To increase the validity and ultimate effectiveness of interviewing requires that these factors be controlled. When used correctly, interviewing can be an effective predictor in the selection process; when conducted haphazardly, it can have great potential for disaster.

Employment interviewing

Employment interviewing is a verbal exchange between an employer and a prospective employee for the purpose of obtaining information about the applicant's job capabilities, and providing the applicant with knowledge about the organization.

Maximizing interviewing effectiveness requires that both candidates and employers obtain the information which they seek. In many situations the interview is the culmination of the selection process. At this point in time, the employer must decide whether or not to tender an offer of employment, and the applicant must decide whether or not to accept it. The style of the interview, the information exchanged, and the skill of the interviewer are all important variables in determining the success of the employment interview.

Types of Interviews

There are several different formats under which interviewers operate. Depending upon the particular interviewing structure established, the interviewer will either have a large amount of latitude for questioning or be required to follow a prescribed formula. Regardless of the structure used, however, the information gathered must allow for comparisons to be made among candidates.

Structured or patterned interview The **structured or patterned interview** offers the least amount of interviewer latitude. Forms are developed which provide interviews with a planned format for questioning candidates. Interviewers are trained in questioning and recording responses. Using a structured or patterned format results in answers which are uniform in nature, but usually narrow in scope. The major drawback of this technique is that it limits the flexibility

Exhibit 5.6

Sample Patterned Interview Questions

Communication skills

Question: What experiences have you had in the preparation of verbal and written materials?

Probe: Give examples of your verbal presentations.

Emotional maturity

Question: Relate a work experience in which you had to deal with the public.

Probe: How did you deal with irate customers?

Decision making

Question: What techniques do you use to analyze data and reach conclusions?

Probe: What is the first action you take?

Work experience

Question: What aspect of your work history is relevant to the job for which you are applying?

Probe: What environmental conditions caused you satisfaction or dissatisfaction in your last job?

Source: Tressie W. Muldrow, *Developing and Conducting Interviews: Some General Guidance* (Washington, D.C.: U.S. Office of Personnel Management, Office of Examination Development, July 1987).

of interviewers and thus it may result in a loss of information crucial to the selection decision. Generally, however, structured interviews provide more reliable and valid data than unstructured interviews.[23]

Unstructured or nondirective interview The **unstructured or nondirective interview** provides the greatest amount of interviewer liberty. There are no established questions or areas to cover. Interviewers adjust to each situation, using their own discretion and skills to probe areas they consider important. The relevance of information gathered by this method is a direct function of the skills of the interviewer. Highly trained interviewers will provide useful data, while untrained interviewers will contribute data which is disjointed, not job related, and disconnected to the purpose at hand. Furthermore, care must be exercised when comparing applicants for whom totally different information was accumulated.

Semistructured or mixed interview The **semistructured or mixed interview** provides an eclectic approach to interviewing. Certain questions that will be asked of all applicants are prepared in advance. However, the interviewer is permitted to digress into other areas. When properly conducted, this form of interviewing supplies basic information on which to compare candidates, as well as additional data within specific areas the interviewer deems noteworthy. Once again, the success of this type of interview relies on the training and degree of skill possessed by the interviewer.

Panel, board, or group interview On certain occasions, organizations deem it beneficial to involve a candidate in a **panel, board, or group interview** setting. Usually, the applicant is interviewed by from three to five people using a patterned or structured format. A group evaluation is arrived at through group discussion or by averaging the group members' estimates. In general, the benefits derived from group interviewing are not substantial enough to justify the extra costs involved. As a result, it is usually reserved for upper level positions.

Stress interview Originally used during World War II, the **stress interview** was designed to assess candidates' current behavior as opposed to their past actions. Rather than seeking information, interviewers are attempting to elicit emotional reactions to situations. They contradict, belittle, and chastise the candidates for the sole purpose of observing their behavior. Appropriate only for highly stressful situations, such as espionage work, stress interviews offer few other benefits. They establish a hostile feeling in the candidates, which is especially manifested in those applicants who are rejected. Companies which interview large numbers of candidates run the risk of establishing a poor company image. As a result, very few organizations use stress interviews.

Information Sought Through Interviews

Most employment interviews last between fifteen and thirty minutes. The amount of information obtained during an interview is a direct function of the interviewer's ability to gather information within the allotted time period. It is important for interviewers to spend as much of the available time as they can on appropriate details, and to avoid irrelevant areas. Material is considered inappropriate for employment interviews when it is either not job related or it is information which may be obtained through other sources.

There are many ways to accumulate information about individuals. **Public information** consists of facts about individuals which can be readily obtained by anyone. Details about a candidate's educational background, employment history, and the nature of past work experiences are examples of information in the public domain. If any of this information is deemed important for selection, it is best ascertained through application blanks or background investigations. Interviews should focus on the area of private information.

Private information consists of personal knowledge individuals choose to keep secret from others, knowledge which is sometimes unconscious, or knowledge which is shared with someone who is perceived as having credibility. The first two categories are concerned with information which is inappropriate for employment interviews. The goal of interviewers is to achieve credibility and to elicit job-related information from candidates. In order for interviewers to be successful, they must project to candidates that their inquiries are based on legitimate business needs. Most people would feel uncomfortable providing friends with salary information. However, when applying for a loan, the same individuals comfortably reveal their entire financial histories to perfect strangers. The trained, experienced interviewer, who is a stranger with credibility, will be able to consistently and reliably obtain appropriate, valid, job-related information from job applicants.

Using the Interview

Employment interviewing is a complex form of communication. Although many individuals conduct interviews, very few people are good interviewers. Interviewing entails more than just meeting candidates, asking questions, and making decisions. Effective interviewers prepare for interviews well in advance and use specific techniques designed to foster productive communication.

Preparing—doing homework

How interviewers prepare for interviews is as important as how they conduct them. Adequate preparation includes:

1. Reviewing all available information about candidates.
2. Allotting sufficient time to conduct interviews.
3. Controlling for interruptions (for example, holding telephone calls).
4. Knowing about the job, by reviewing job analyses or job specifications.
5. Arranging for quiet and pleasant surroundings.

Establishing rapport

Job candidates approach employment interviews with anxiety and apprehension. In order to obtain credibility and to relieve an applicant's tension, the initial task for an interviewer is to create a comfortable environment for the interviewee. The process of putting candidates at ease is referred to as establishing **rapport.** In situations where rapport is not secured, a minimal amount of information will be obtained. Confirming rapport early in the interview contributes significantly to the fostering of effective communication.

Some interviewing approaches

In order to elicit relevant information from candidates, interviewers rely on several proven communication techniques. By themselves, these methods are inadequate substitutes for lack of preparation or failure to establish rapport. Rather, their effectiveness is contingent on whether interviewers have done their homework. When conditions are favorable, using these techniques will prove valuable.

Direct interviewing approach The **direct interviewing approach** utilizes questions which require applicants to respond with a statement of fact or a yes or no answer. Using direct questions rarely generates lengthy responses. Instead, candidates answer succinctly, offering little or no additional information. Interviewers usually employ direct questions when they know precisely what they are looking for, or when they are probing into specific areas. Overuse of direct questions results in perceptive interviewees providing interviewers with "canned" responses which they believe are expected of them.

Non-directive interviewing approach When direct, simple answers are insufficient, and elaborate answers are sought by the interviewer, the **non-directive interviewing approach** is used. Non-directive approaches emphasize a more personal involvement of the interviewee in the process as well as the content area of the interview. Interviewers permit interviewees to control the interview flow by subtly leading them into appropriate areas. It is important to note, however, that despite the easygoing nature of this style, the interviewer ultimately remains in command of the situation. Effective use of the non-directive approach requires strong interviewing skills, particularly in the areas of listening and nonverbal communication.

Eclectic interviewing approach The predominant interviewing approach used in industry is the **eclectic interviewing approach,** which combines features of both direct and non-directive techniques. Experienced and novice interviewers alike will find that a combination approach provides a degree of flexibility otherwise unavailable to them. Direct questions are used to discover facts, and non-directive questions are used to probe more deeply.

Common Interviewing Pitfalls

Even skilled interviewers are prone to certain interviewing pitfalls. They commit inherent interviewing errors because of underlying biases. Trained interviewers learn to recognize the existence of these influences and to make accommodations for them. The most prevalent faults are the halo effect and prejudging.

Halo effect When candidates are viewed as unacceptable because their hair is too long or the interviewer finds their dress distasteful, they are being rejected because of the **halo effect** rather than an inability to perform the job well. The halo effect is the most common interviewer error, and it is potentially the most legally damaging. Allowing inherent prejudices to bias decisions has legal implications when these tendencies cause unfair discrimination against protected classes.

Halo effect

The halo effect is the tendency to make a total assessment of an individual based on observing only one favorable or unfavorable trait.

Prejudging The formation of opinions about candidates prior to interviewing them or before the interview process is concluded are classic examples of **prejudging.** Selection can be viewed as a process of gathering information about individuals, formulating educated guesses, and attempting to verify these hypotheses in order to make a decision. Each step in the selection procedure contributes new and additional information. Prejudging candidates is tantamount to making decisions without having all the facts.

Prejudging

Prejudging is the tendency to draw conclusions concerning candidates before all the available information has been collected.

Exhibit 5.7

Some Potentially Illegal Pre-employment Inquiries

Avoid asking	Suggested alternative
When were you born?	Are you over 18 years of age?
Of what country are you a citizen?	Are you a U.S. citizen or legally allowed to work in the U.S.?
Do you have any disabilities?	Do you have any physical or mental disabilities which would interfere with your ability to perform the job for which you have applied?
What is your native language?	What languages do you speak and/or write fluently?
What is your height and weight?	Almost never permitted unless job relevance is proven.
Have you ever been arrested?	Have you ever been convicted of a felony? If yes, please give details.
What is your race?	Almost never permitted.
Are you a high school graduate?	What is the highest grade you have completed?
What type of discharge did you receive from the armed forces?	Detail your military experience and training.
Have you ever used an alias or another name?	Is there any other name needed in order to check your records?
What is your religion?	Illegal unless job relevance is demonstrated.

Interviewing and the Law

The legal requirements for using other selection instruments are the same for interviews as well. If challenged, companies must demonstrate the validity of the interviewing technique. In light of past research, this is not an easy task. Interviews involve a large degree of subjectivity and are notorious for demonstrating low validity.[24] To minimize the potential for unfair discrimination suits, interviewers would be well advised to comply with certain guidelines. First, interviewers must avoid discussing issues which cannot be proven to be job related. Questions posed to female candidates concerning family matters, child-care arrangements, marital status, and travel arrangements might be construed as sexist unless job relatedness can be demonstrated. Second, interviewers must be aware of their own prejudices and control for them. Litigation rarely occurs when all candidates are treated fairly and equally.

Physical Examinations

When applicants have successfully completed all phases of the selection procedure, many companies require them to have a physical examination prior to employment. The purpose of this examination is to determine if candidates have any physical characteristics which may limit their ability to satisfactorily perform the job. Although costly, the popularity of physical examinations has grown tremendously because of the widespread public concern over drug use and Acquired Immune Deficiency Syndrome (AIDS). Realistically, however, it has not been demonstrated that the use of physical examinations for predicting future physical problems is valid.[25]

Using Polygraphs

Over the years, many employers have used polygraphs or lie detectors as a means for identifying and eliminating dishonest job candidates. Proponents of this device have contended that lie detectors are an excellent, objective method for determining crucial information that is otherwise unobtainable. Critics of this method counter that the questions used, particularly those delving into the personal lives of the applicants, infringe on the individual's rights to privacy.

Regardless of the views taken, as of December 27, 1988, the Employee Polygraph Protection Act of 1988 prohibited the use of polygraphs in about 85 percent of the employment situations in which they had been previously used. This law impacted most notably in the twenty-eight states which previously had no statutes of their own affecting the use of polygraphs.[26] The only exceptions to the statute are federal, state, and local governments and firms doing sensitive work under contract to the Department of Defense, the FBI, or the CIA.

Exhibit 5.8

U.S. DEPARTMENT OF LABOR

EMPLOYMENT STANDARDS ADMINISTRATION

Wage and Hour Division
Washington, D.C. 20210

NOTICE

EMPLOYEE POLYGRAPH PROTECTION ACT

The Employee Polygraph Protection Act prohibits most private employers from using lie detector tests either for pre-employment screening or during the course of employment.

PROHIBITIONS

Employers are generally prohibited from requiring or requesting any employee or job applicant to take a lie detector test, and from discharging, disciplining, or discriminating against an employee or prospective employee for refusing to take a test or for exercising other rights under the Act.

EXEMPTIONS*

Federal, State and local governments are not affected by the law. Also, the law does not apply to tests given by the Federal Government to certain private individuals engaged in national security-related activities.

The Act permits *polygraph* (a kind of lie detector) tests to be administered in the private sector, subject to restrictions, to certain prospective employees of security service firms (armored car, alarm, and guard), and of pharmaceutical manufacturers, distributors and dispensers.

The Act also permits polygraph testing, subject to restrictions, of certain employees of private firms who are reasonably suspected of involvement in a workplace incident (theft, embezzlement, etc.) that resulted in economic loss to the employer.

EXAMINEE RIGHTS

Where polygraph tests are permitted, they are subject to numerous strict standards concerning the conduct and length of the test. Examinees have a number of specific rights, including the right to a written notice before testing, the right to refuse or discontinue a test, and the right not to have test results disclosed to unauthorized persons.

ENFORCEMENT

The Secretary of Labor may bring court actions to restrain violations and assess civil penalties up to $10,000 against violators. Employees or job applicants may also bring their own court actions.

ADDITIONAL INFORMATION

Additional information may be obtained, and complaints of violations may be filed, at local offices of the Wage and Hour Division, which are listed in the telephone directory under U.S. Government, Department of Labor, Employment Standards Administration.

THE LAW REQUIRES EMPLOYERS TO DISPLAY THIS POSTER WHERE EMPLOYEES AND JOB APPLICANTS CAN READILY SEE IT.

**The law does not preempt any provision of any State or local law or any collective bargaining agreement which is more restrictive with respect to lie detector tests.*

U.S. DEPARTMENT OF LABOR
EMPLOYMENT STANDARDS ADMINISTRATION
Wage and Hour Division
Washington, D.C. 20210

WH Publication 1462
September 1988

Under the new restrictions, employees are protected from dismissal, discipline, or discrimination solely on the basis of their refusal to submit to polygraph examinations. Employers can request workers to take lie detector tests if the employees have had access to missing or damaged material and if the employer documents, in a written statement, their suspicion that the particular worker being tested was involved in the theft. If this law remains unchanged, employers will be forced to develop new methods to ascertain any needed honesty information.[27]

Evaluating Candidates

After all available candidate data has been collected, organizations must decide who is capable of performing the job and who wants to perform the job over a sustained period of time. Candidates who have skill but are lacking in desire usually do not perform well. Transient candidates who possess both skill and desire add excessive costs particularly in the areas of training and re-hiring.

Cut-off scores are used to determine which candidates have job skill. Minimal acceptable levels of performance are established for each predictor, or all the predictors combined, and candidates who fall below this level are rejected. For example, some colleges have minimum admission scores required on the SAT, and others require a minimum combination score of SAT and high school grade point average. Cut-off scores are simple to use, but are usually established by trial and error. In addition, their value diminishes when there are small numbers of candidates (high selection ratio).

Cut-off scores

Cut-off scores are minimal acceptable performance levels for predictors which candidates must obtain before being considered further.

Having the capabilities for a job does not automatically guarantee that the candidate will do the job well, nor that the candidate will sustain the work effort over an extended period of time. Motivation, interests, and other personality factors directly impact on these aspects of work performance. Evaluation of these factors is accomplished through data gathered by tests and interviews.

Successful evaluation results when the needs of the candidates selected match those of the organization. Optimally, employment decisions are two-fold processes. Companies decide whether applicants fit in with their overall objectives, and candidates decide if the job will satisfy their particular needs. Practically, however, the major burden for the decision is usually on the organization. Long-range planning is not a process engaged in by most applicants (especially those currently unemployed). Rather, they accept positions without much forethought, provided they satisfy immediate material needs.

To be successful at selection requires that organizations evaluate not only whether the candidate will suit the needs of the company, but also whether the company will meet the aspirations of the candidate.

Usefulness of Techniques

Having reliable and valid instruments and adhering to government rules and regulations do not guarantee errorless selection. Some candidates who are hired will prove unsatisfactory, and other candidates who should have been hired will be rejected regardless of whether or not instruments are valid, reliable, and legal. Analyses should be conducted to determine the effectiveness and costs of the various selection techniques.

Four possible outcomes result from every selection decision:

1. Those who should be hired are hired (**true positive**).
2. Those who should not be hired are rejected (**true negative**).
3. Those who should not be hired are hired (**false positive**).
4. Those who should be hired are rejected. (**false negative**).

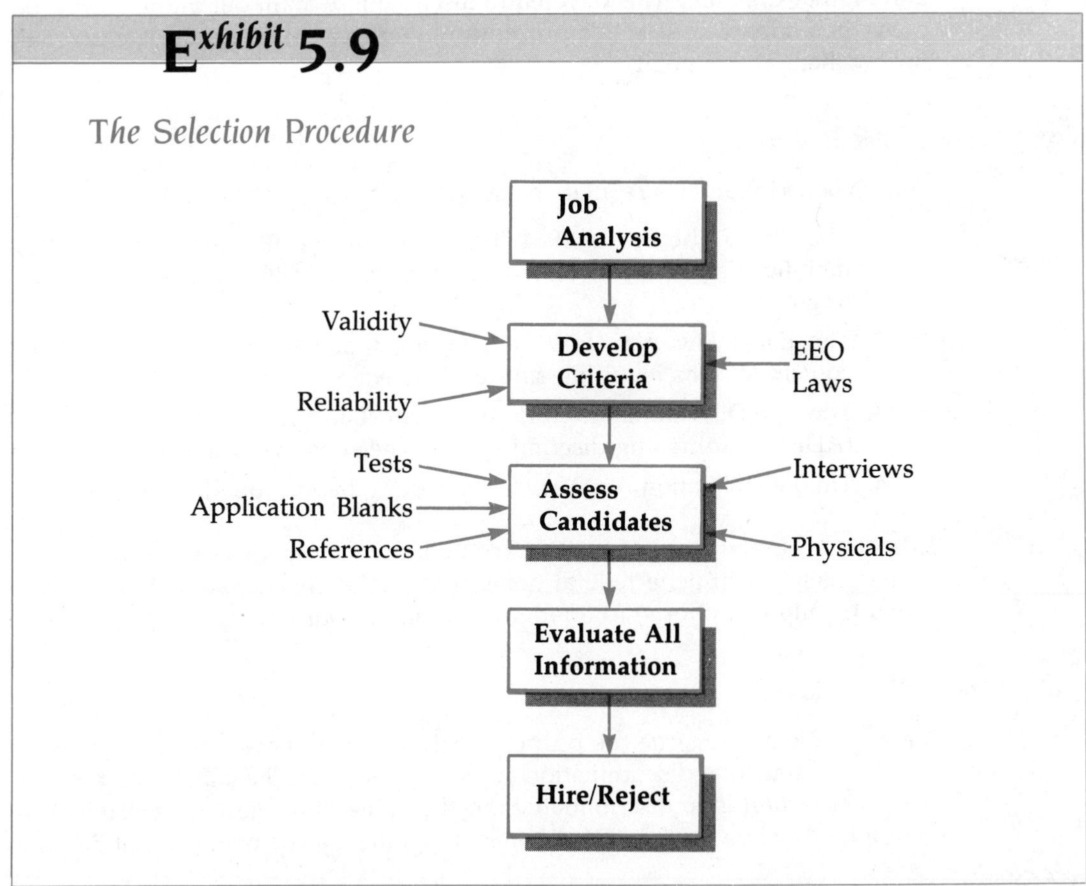

Exhibit 5.9

The Selection Procedure

Highly effective techniques maximize decisions in the first two categories and minimize decisions in the latter two categories.

When contemplating the value and costs of specific techniques, users should consider the particular situation. If there is an abundance of workers available for easily trained low-level positions, then the costs associated with decisions falling into the third and fourth categories are minimal. On the other hand, if the selection procedure is being designed to fill high-level positions and the costs associated with hiring the wrong person are high, every attempt should be made to minimize the errors associated with the latter categories. Needless to say, the goal of all users is to have legally valid and reliable instruments which are cost-effective measures of human potential.

Equal Employment Opportunity Rules and Regulations

Over the past twenty-five years, the complex set of rules and regulations imposed by the Equal Employment Opportunity laws has had a major impact on human resource management. These laws are so detailed, diversified, and important that Chapter 2 was devoted to discussing them in depth. However, because their impact on selection procedures is so great, it is appropriate to briefly review them at this point.

The Major Selection Laws

Four major federal laws regulate equal selection rights. These are:

1. The Civil Rights Act of 1964 (Title VII), and the 1972 amendments, prohibiting discrimination based on race, color, religion, sex, or national origin.
2. The Equal Pay Act of 1963, requiring that men and women be paid equally for jobs requiring substantially equal work.
3. The Age Discrimination in Employment Act of 1967 as amended in 1978 (ADEA), prohibiting discrimination of persons over forty years of age.
4. The Rehabilitation Act of 1973, protecting handicapped workers.

In addition, Executive Order 11246 requires that contractors or subcontractors doing business with the federal government take affirmative action (concentrated recruitment efforts) to offer employment opportunities to minorities.

The Purpose of the Laws

Many people misconstrue the purpose of the selection laws. The laws, as written, do not state that discrimination among applicants is illegal. In fact, the purpose of selection is to discriminate, and the value of a selection instrument is determined by how well it discriminates. What the law maintains is that discrimination among job candidates should be done solely on job-related factors. If, however, an applicant is eliminated merely because he or she belongs to one of the protected groups, and the company cannot justify this rejection based on legitimate legal reasons, then the company is in violation of the law.

Hiring Applicants Legally

To avoid violation of the laws affecting selection, and more importantly to choose the appropriate candidate, care must be taken to make selections based only on job-related criteria. If an organization is confronted with a charge of illegal discrimination, it will have to demonstrate that the hiring decision was based either on justifiable job-related reasons or on a legally acceptable exception to the law. Basically, the company will have to show that:

1. The selection instruments are valid.
2. There is a bona fide occupational qualification (BFOQ).
3. A valid seniority system exists which allows for the discrimination.

Exhibit 5.10

Major EEO Laws Affecting the Selection Process

Law	Year	Provision
Equal Pay Act	1963	Prohibits the payment of different wages based on sex for the performance of similar work under similar conditions.
Civil Rights Act Amended (Title VII)	1964	Prohibits job discrimination on the basis of sex, race, color, religion, or national origin.
Age Discrimination in Employment Act	1967	Prohibits discrimination against persons over the age of 40.
Amended	1978	
Executive Order 11246 Amended by: Executive Order 11375	1965 1968	Prohibits discrimination based on race, creed, color, or national origin by contractors doing business with the federal government.
Rehabilitation Act	1973	Prohibits discrimination against handicapped individuals and requires employers to make reasonable accommodations.

Exhibit 5.11

Selected Court Cases Involving Major Selection Techniques

Technique	Case	Finding
Application blanks	*United States* v. *Inspiration Consolidated Copper Co.* (1973)	Application blanks having adverse impact upon the hiring process are unfairly discriminatory.
Reference checks	*Cort* v. *Bristol-Myers* (1982)	Employee records are the property of employers to be used at their discretion.
Interviews	*United States* v. *Hazelwood School District* (1976)	Struck down the use of interviews for hiring of teachers.
Testing	*Griggs* v. *Duke Power Co.* (1971)	Employment testing and educational requirements must be job-related in order to be used.
Physical requirements	*Dothard* v. *Rawlinson* (1977)	Height and weight requirements must be shown to be job-related, especially if they exclude significant amounts of minorities.

Validity As mentioned earlier, validity indicates that an instrument measures what it is supposed to measure. For selection purposes, the instrument measures job performance. If the tools used for selection are valid, then they identify those candidates who will successfully complete the job requirements. Legally, discrimination may now occur because it is on the basis of projected job performance, rather than on unrelated factors.

BFOQ Within the law (Section 703e) it is stipulated that businesses may discriminate solely on the basis of sex, religion, or national origin if they can demonstrate that these classes constitute a bona fide occupational qualification which is necessary for the operation of the business. For example, sex is a bona fide occupational qualification for the hiring of rest room attendants. When using BFOQ as a defense against discrimination charges, the burden of proof is on the employer to show that there is a legitimate business necessity for this action. To date, there are no court rulings which provide for an acceptable BFOQ for either color or race.

Seniority The preceding exceptions protect new employees' rights to employment opportunities. The third exception to the rules, seniority, has significant importance for existing workers. This exception to the law (Section 703h) stipulates that when a bona fide seniority system exists and the intention of the system is not to illegally discriminate, then length of service may be used in selection decisions. Workers who have extended service are provided with a priority over new hires for available positions. This has the effect of providing security to workers, and as a result, it has been endorsed vigorously by many labor organizations.

Summary

The adequate selection of human resources within organizations relies primarily on the planning and use of selection techniques. Companies determine job criteria, develop legally valid and reliable instruments, and decide how candidates are to progress through the various selection stages. Once these initial considerations are completed, evaluation of candidates begins.

The evaluation process requires that candidates progress through a series of measures, each of which is designed to assess different job-related attributes. Some of the instruments used are designed to collect objective factual data, while others provide subjective information. The final evaluation considers all these factors in determining the most appropriate candidate.

The selection methods and the combinations of methods used are industry specific. Deciding on the most appropriate methods to use for individual circumstances requires an analysis of the labor market, an understanding of error frequency, and a knowledge of the relative costs involved in using specific techniques.

Key Terms to Identify

Selection ratio
Predictor
Criterion
Reliability
Validity
Criterion-related validity
Predictive validity
Concurrent validity
Content validity
Multiple hurdles strategy
Compensatory strategy
Mixed strategy
Application blanks
Weighted application blanks (WABs)
Biographical information blanks (BIBs)
Employment tests
Tests in Print III
Mental Measurement Yearbooks
Speed and power tests
Paper-and-pencil tests
Performance tests
Ability tests
Personality tests

Work sample tests
Reference checks
Employment interviews
Structured or patterned interview
Unstructured or nondirective interview
Semistructured or mixed interview
Panel, board, or group interview
Stress interview
Public and private information
Rapport
Direct interviewing approach
Non-directive interviewing approach
Eclectic interviewing approach
Halo effect
Prejudging
Cut-off scores
True positive
True negative
False positive
False negative

Questions for Discussion

Do You Know the Facts?

1. Describe the stages involved in developing a sound selection program.
2. Discuss the differences between predictive and concurrent validity.
3. Differentiate among the application blank, the weighted application blank, and the biographical interest blank. How is each used in the selection process?
4. What are the three basic test designs? How are tests differentiated with regard to content area?
5. What are the advantages and disadvantages of using reference information when making selection decisions?
6. Discuss the various interviewing formats and the approaches interviewers use to elicit information from applicants.
7. Why is a successful interview dependent on the skill of the interviewer? What pitfalls must even an experienced interviewer be aware of?

Can You Apply the Information Learned?

1. How do reliability and validity assist managers in identifying and predicting the capabilities of job applicants?
2. How would the specific needs of small and large companies be addressed in formulating selection plans?
3. Discuss the implications for selection of the statement, "A test can be reliable without being valid, but a test cannot be valid without being reliable."
4. What arguments would you use to convince upper management that the selection techniques which have been in use for decades must be validated?

5. Discuss the strategies organizations use to make selection decisions. Under what circumstances would each strategy be used? What would be the underlying reason for the use of each strategy?
6. What are the problems facing industry today regarding the use of employment tests?
7. How can employment tests be used and misused by human resource managers?
8. Why is the interviewing of candidates a dilemma for industry?

It Just Doesn't Feel Right

Roger Pintakes was troubled. He thought that he had covered all the bases, but the decision still haunts him. It just doesn't feel right!

It all started two months ago when Roger, senior vice-president for a large bank holding company, received a call from Paul Bangstrom, the bank's president. It seemed that the board of directors had approved a plan which would change the way in which the bank had operated for the past thirty years. "Customer oriented," Paul had said. "A return to the old days when people received personal treatment. When someone cared! And we're going to start by creating a new position, a vice-president for marketing who can get the word out." That was Roger's job. As senior vice-president he was in charge of all of the bank's operations, one of which was the human resource management department. Paul wanted a new person. "New blood," he had said. "Someone who wasn't bogged down in the thinking of the past thirty years."

Roger wasn't certain that the bank needed a new vice-president for marketing. True, Joann Jessup, the current marketing director, had been with the bank for fifteen years and was no public relations person, but she was exceptionally competent, people liked her, and business was good. Maybe all that was necessary was to talk with Joann and have her shift her emphasis to external programs. After all, nobody had ever wanted her to be externally involved before. The bank could even promote her to the new vice-president position. She would be the first woman in the bank's history to hold a vice-president's title. That would certainly create good public relations for the bank.

Initially, Paul would hear nothing of it. He wanted a new person. "Joann can't do it! There are better people out there. People with better skills!" he bellowed. Finally, he compromised. The position would be announced internally, and Joann would be included with all the other applicants. If she were picked, Paul would accept it.

Roger knew he had to be careful. The selection procedure had to be perfect. He couldn't afford to allow bias to enter into it. If Joann were picked, it had to be totally unquestionable. He decided to call his friend Adam at the local college for some advice.

Adam Vinikus was Associate Professor of Personnel and Industrial Relations at the local college; he was also a partner in a local consulting firm which specialized in selection and placement. After Roger explained the situation, Adam readily consented to set up a selection procedure for choosing a marketing vice-president.

Approximately two weeks later, the procedure was established. Following a comprehensive job analysis, it was decided to solicit applications and screen these down to the top five candidates, who, after a background check, would be administered a paper-and-pencil personality inventory and interviewed. The bank then began to advertise both internally and externally. At the same time, without telling Roger, Paul was doing his own recruiting.

As applications began to arrive, a committee was established for initial screening purposes. In total, forty-three candidates submitted credentials, and the committee began the screening process.

Shortly thereafter, the five candidates were chosen, their backgrounds were investigated, and they were invited to the bank for the testing and interviewing phase. Joann was among the five, as were two candidates whom Paul had recruited.

The tests were administered, and the interviews were conducted. Sam Grabelson, a close friend of Paul's nephew, was chosen as the new vice-president of marketing. It was a hard decision, but the committee felt that he performed better than Joann at the interview. They couldn't quite explain why; it was just a gut feeling.

For Roger, it just doesn't feel right!

Questions for Discussion

1. Why is Roger troubled about the selection decision?
2. Were the procedures established for the selection of the marketing vice-president sound? Should anything have been done differently?
3. If you were given the responsibility of filling the vice-president's position, what methods would you have used? Why?

Appendix: Reliability and Validity Measures

Determining Reliability

There are three major methods used to ascertain the reliability of a measure: The test-retest method, the parallel or equivalent forms method, and the measure of internal consistency.

Test-retest reliability

The test-retest format is the simplest method to determine reliability. The same instrument is administered on two separate occasions to the same group of individuals and the scores are compared to each other. Reliability exists if there is minimal fluctuation of an individual's scores from one test administration to the other. On the other hand, a test is unreliable if an individual's scores vary significantly between test administrations.

> **Test-retest reliability**
>
> *Test-retest reliability involves administering a single instrument to the same group of people on separate occasions and comparing the scores.*

The major problems associated with the test-retest method center around the time period between test administrations. People do not live in a vacuum, and much can happen during this time. Individuals can learn additional information, remember items from the first administration, and have changes in their moods. Furthermore, removing workers from their jobs on two separate occasions may make the cost of determining reliability prohibitive.

Parallel or equivalent forms reliability

Parallel or equivalent forms reliability overcomes some of the problems associated with the administration of the same test on two separate occasions. In this instance, two forms of the same test are created to measure the same content area. The tests are administered to the same group of people, either at the same time or on different occasions, and each person's score on the first test is compared to his or her score on the second test. Reliability exists if those who score high on the first test also score high on the second test. If the scores are inconsistent, then the tests would probably be unreliable. An example of a test which demonstrates parallel forms reliability is the SAT. A student taking the SAT in December and repeating the examination in February would be given two parallel forms of the same test. If there is a high degree of reliability between the forms, the student's score will not vary significantly from test to test. In fact, students taking the SAT on two separate occasions usually have a variance in scores of only 50 points.

> **Parallel or equivalent forms reliability**
>
> *Parallel or equivalent forms reliability involves the administration of two comparable tests to the same group of people, and subsequently comparing their scores.*

Parallel or equivalent forms reliability is probably used less frequently than other forms of reliability. It is difficult to develop one good measure, yet alone two. As a result, the use of this form of reliability is limited to situations where it is necessary to have two separate instruments, and where cost of development is not a major factor.

Internal consistency reliability

Internal consistency reliability is used when attempts are being made to determine the homogeneity of test items. If the items are homogenous, they measure the same content. If, on the other hand, the items measure a diverse content area, the test is heterogenous. When an attempt is being made to measure a single trait or ability, high internal consistency is sought. When multiple traits or abilities are being measured, however, the test should be low in internal consistency, demonstrating heterogeneity. For example, an achievement test in a particular subject area would be expected to demonstrate high internal consistency, while an aptitude test might be expected to demonstrate low internal consistency. It is important to note that for heterogenous purposes, test-retest and parallel forms or equivalent forms reliability should indicate high reliability over time.

Internal consistency reliability

Internal consistency reliability involves subdividing a test and treating each part as a separate test.

Internal consistency reliability computations involve the use of either the split-half or the inter-item method. The split-half method involves dividing the test into two equal halves, usually odd and even items, and comparing each individual's scores on one half of the test to his or her scores on the other half of the test. Since the reliability coefficient obtained is really for half a test, it must be translated by means of a statistical procedure such as the Spearman-Brown Formula (see Exhibit A.1).

The computation of inter-item reliability requires that each question within the test be treated individually. Instead of comparing two test halves, each item is intercorrelated to each other item. In essence, each item becomes its own test. Once again, the resulting reliability coefficients must be translated by means of a statistical procedure. For inter-item reliability, a reliability coefficient for the entire test can be obtained by using a statistical formula such as Kuder-Richardson 20 (KR20) (see Exhibit A.1).

Exhibit A.1

Formulas for Determining Internal Consistency Reliability

Spearman-Brown Formula

$$r = \frac{2r_{11}}{1 + r_{11}}$$

r = reliability for whole test
r_{11} = reliability obtained for the half tests

Assuming reliability between the two tests was .83, then:

$$r = \frac{2\,(.83)}{1 + .83} = \frac{1.66}{1.83} = .91$$

Kuder-Richardson 20 (KR20)

$$r_{xx} = \frac{n}{n - 1}\left(\frac{1 - \Sigma pq}{\sigma_x^{\,2}}\right)$$

n = the number of items in the test
p = the proportion of correct responses to a given item
q = the proportion of incorrect responses to each item
$\sigma_x^{\,2}$ = the total test variance

When computing KR20, the major computational task is obtaining p and q. This requires that for each question, the proportion of subjects passing be multiplied by the proportion of subjects failing and then summed over all test items. After obtaining this number, it is a simple matter to compute the other factors.

Split-half and inter-item reliability

Split-half reliability involves dividing the test into two halves and treating each half as a separate test. Inter-item reliability considers each question as a separate test. In both cases the subdivisions are compared to each other.

Exhibit A.2

Using the Three Forms of Reliability

Procedure	Test-Retest	Parallel or equivalent forms	Internal consistency
1. Conduct job analyses	√	√	√
2. Develop one (1) test to measure content area	√		√
3. Develop two (2) tests to measure content area		√	
4. Obtain representative sample	√	√	√
5. Administer test on one (1) occasion		√	√
6. Administer test on two (2) occasions	√		
7. Compare each individual's scores on the tests	√	√	
8. Divide test into parts, and compare each individual's scores on each part			√

Construct Validity

Criterion-related validity and content validity demonstrate a relationship between a predictor and a criterion. This relationship is drawn by comparing the results of the selection instrument (the predictor) to the job performance (demonstrated by performance appraisal). In many cases, however, the behavior which is demonstrated, or the potential to perform the behavior, is determined by an underlying characteristic or trait, called a *construct.* To determine whether the predictor is measuring the underlying characteristic or trait, **construct validity** is employed.

Construct validity

Construct validity is a validation technique used to determine if a predictor measures the underlying characteristic or trait responsible for the behavior.

In many instances, the ability to perform a job well is a function of whether or not the individual possesses certain underlying characteristics or traits. For example, success in an advertising position may be dependent on the degree of creativity an individual possesses. The term "creativity" is the underlying characteristic or construct which we are attempting to measure. A measure that has construct validity will discriminate between individuals who possess the level of creativity necessary for satisfactory job performance and those who do not. Construct validity is used most often to demonstrate the validity of tests measuring psychological constructs.

Synthetic Validity

One of the major problems in using criterion-related validation methods is that they require a relatively large sample size in order to be effective. Except for low-level, line type jobs, most companies do not have sufficient numbers of employees in a given job to conduct statistically sound criterion-related validation studies. The options available to these organizations are to use the instruments without validating them, to select employees based on subjective judgments, or to select without any tools. If the organization wishes to validate tests, but is lacking sufficient sample sizes, synthetic validity can be used.[28]

> **Synthetic validity**
>
> ***Synthetic validity involves identifying jobs with common elements and validating selection tools for these common dimensions.***

While the previously discussed validation strategies required adequate samples of individuals performing the same total jobs, synthetic validity provides an alternative to small sample sizes. After comprehensive job analyses have been completed, jobs with common dimensions can be identified. Regardless of job titles, different job incumbents can now be considered as one group for validating these specific dimensions. For each employee a predictor score and a measure of performance on the common job dimension is obtained. Subsequently, the degree of relationship between the predictor and the criterion (job dimension) is determined. Suppose, for example, that a test for identifying numerical aptitude is to be validated. After identifying the job incumbents, it is discovered that there is an insufficient number of current employees in any one position to provide an adequate sample. By reviewing the job analyses, however, it is discovered that although there are not enough employees in any one position, the positions of marketing assistant, public relations clerk, and bookkeeper all involve dealing with numbers. Using a synthetic validation strategy, the three different positions (bookkeeper, marketing assistant, and public relations clerk) can be combined into one sample, and the test can be validated for numerical aptitude. Of course, the relevance of the validity obtained relies to a large extent on the completion of solid job analyses to identify common job dimensions. Exhibit A.3 demonstrates how a grid can be used to combine common job dimensions for the purpose of synthetic validity.

Exhibit A.3

Using a Grid for Synthetic Validity

Job title	Sample size	Using numbers	Using profit and loss reports	Public contacts
Public Relations Clerk	14	Yes	No	Yes
Bookkeeper	27	Yes	Yes	No
Marketing Assistant	9	Yes	Yes	Yes

For the job dimension of *Using numbers,* the sample size is:

Public Relations Clerk + Bookkeeper + Marketing Assistant = 50.

For the job dimension of *Using profit and loss reports,* the sample size is:

Bookkeeper + Marketing Assistant = 36.

For the job dimension of *Public contacts,* the sample size is:

Public Relations Clerk + Marketing Assistant = 23.

Endnotes and References

1 *Standards for Educational and Psychological Tests* (Washington, D.C.: American Psychological Association, Inc., 1974): 25.

2 These are the principal types of validity used by the EEOC. See Robert D. Gatewood and Lyle F. Schoenfeldt, "Content Validity and the EEOC: A Useful Alternative for Selection," *Personnel Journal,* Vol. 56 (October 1977): 520–524.

3 Richard D. Arvey, *Fairness in Selecting Employees* (Reading, MA: Addison-Wesley Publishing Company, 1979): 34.

4 Paul M. Muchinsky, *Psychology Applied to Work,* 2nd ed. (Chicago, IL: The Dorsey Press, 1987): 195.

5 Laurence Siegel and Irving M. Lane, *Personnel and Organizational Psychology,* 2nd ed. (Homewood, IL: Richard D. Irwin, Inc. 1987): 74.

6 See the discussion of *Connecticut* v. *Teal* (Supreme Court 457 U.S. 440, 1982) in Chapter 2.

7 Wayne F. Cascio, "Accuracy of Verifiable Biographical Information Blank Responses," *Journal of Applied Psychology,* Vol. 60, No. 6 (December 1975): 767–769.

8 Larry A. Pace and Lyle F. Schoenfeldt, "Legal Concerns in the Use of Weighted Applications," *Personnel Psychology,* Vol. 30, No. 2 (Summer 1977): 159–166.

9 Richard R. Reilly and Georgia T. Chao, "Validity and Fairness of Some Alternative Employee Selection Procedures," *Personnel Psychology,* Vol. 35, No. 1 (Spring 1982): 1–62.

10 See *The Wall Street Journal,* Sept 5, 1975, 1.

11 Today, the use of tests has once again increased. This renewed interest is caused, in large part, by the U.S. Employment Service's use of validity generalization on ability tests. For further information on the benefits of validity generalization to organizations, see Robert M. Madigan, K. Dow Scott, Diana L. Deadrick, and Jil A. Stoddard, "Employment Testing: The U.S. Job Service is Spearheading a Revolution," *Personnel Administrator* (September 1986): 102–112.

12 For extended information on test design and content, refer to any industrial psychology or testing design textbook. See, for example, Laurence Siegel and Irving M. Lane, *op. cit.,* 184–201.

13 Walter Mischel, *Introduction to Personality* (New York: CBS College Publishing, 1981): 2.

14 John E. Hunter and Ronda F. Hunter, "Validity and Utility of Alternative Predictors of Job Performance," *Psychological Bulletin,* Vol. 96 (July 1984): 72–98.

15 Section 1607.16Q Definitions. *Uniform Guidelines on Employee Selection Procedures (1978);* 43 FR (August 25, 1978).

16 Edward L. Levine and Stephen M. Rudolph, *Reference Checking for Personnel Selection: The State of the Art.* (Berea, OH: American Society of Personnel Administrators, 1977): 5.

17 Carole Sewell, "Pre-employment Investigations: The Key to Security in Hiring," *Personnel Journal,* Vol. 60 (May 1981): 376–379.

18 Employers who have been sued for invasion of privacy in the past are usually afraid to provide reference data. See Kenneth L. Sovereign, *Personnel Law* (Reston, VA: Reston Publishing Company, 1990): 156–160. Also see John D. Rice, "Privacy Legislation: Its Effects on Pre-employment Reference Checking," *Personnel Administrator,* Vol. 23 (February 1978): 46–51.

19 Ibid.

20 The Bureau of National Affairs, *ASPA-BNA Survey No. 45. Employee Selection Procedures* (Washington, D.C.: Bureau of National Affairs, May 5, 1983), 2. Also see Arthur Bragg, "Recruiting's Finest Hour: The Interview," *Sales and Marketing Management,* Vol. 127 (August 1981): 58–60.

21 Richard R. Reilly and Georgia T. Chao, *op. cit.,* 1–62.

22 Richard D. Arvey and James E. Campion, "The Employment Interview: A Summary and Review of Recent Research," *Personnel Psychology,* Vol. 35 (1982): 281–322.

23 Ibid.

24 For extended discussion on whether or not interviews are reliable sources of data see David H. Tucker and Patricia M. Rowe, "Relationship Between Expectancy, Causal Attribution, and Final Hiring Decisions in the Employment Interview," *Journal of Applied Psychology,* Vol. 64 (February 1979): 27–34.

25 Mitchell S. Novitt, "Physical Examinations and Company Liability: A Legal Update," *Personnel Journal,* Vol. 61 (January 1982): 47–53.

26 The twenty-eight states where the new polygraph laws have the greatest impact include: Alabama, Arizona, Arkansas, Colorado, Florida, Georgia, Illinois, Indiana, Kansas, Kentucky, Louisiana, Mississippi, Missouri, Nevada, New Hampshire, New Mexico, New York, North Carolina, North Dakota, Ohio, Oklahoma, South Carolina, South Dakota, Tennessee, Texas, Utah, Virginia, and Wyoming. Of the remaining states, either the state or the federal statute takes precedence, whichever is the more restrictive.

27 For an excellent discussion on using both polygraphs and physical examinations for employment situations, see Anne E. Libbin, Susan R. Mendelsohn, and Dennis P. Duffy, "Employee Medical and Honesty Testing," *Personnel*, Vol. 65 (November 1988): 38–48.

28 Robert D. Gatewood and Hubert S. Feild, *Human Resource Selection* (New York: Dryden Press, 1987): 162–164.

Part 3

Developing Employee Potential

Chapter 6

Training and Development of Personnel

Objectives

After reading this chapter you should understand:

1. The reasons for conducting training.
2. The ways organizations determine their training needs.
3. The learning principles which are important in the design of training programs.
4. The difference between on-the-job and off-the-job training methods.
5. The different training programs and their advantages and disadvantages.
6. The importance of career development, and its organizational impact.
7. The process for evaluating training programs.

The **training** of employees is analogous to the maintaining of machinery. In order to operate at peak efficiency, machines usually require an initial adjustment period, followed by regular servicing. To maximize individual productivity, employees are first oriented to the work environment, and then periodically provided with additional training.

Training

Training entails the use of prepared programs which reinforce employees' existing competencies or facilitate the acquisition of new knowledge, skills, and abilities in the interest of improving job performance.

Both large and small organizations allocate significant resources for training and developing human resources. Some employees receive only orientation training, while other workers are exposed to extensive supervisory and managerial seminars. Programs range from informal in-house training conducted by supervisors, to elaborate symposiums in plush hotels conducted by highly trained professionals. For some companies, training is an ongoing activity, and entire staffs are devoted to this effort. Virtually all employees are exposed to some form of training during their tenure.

The fact that so much effort and money are expended for training gives rise to three questions. First, what is the rationale for training? Second, what is the most appropriate way for organizations to accomplish training objectives? And third, how are the effects of training measured? The answers to these questions are the focus of this chapter.

The Rationale for Training

The principle of potentiality The ultimate success of organizations depends on the abilities of employees to successfully complete their present duties and to adapt to new situations. When candidates are selected for positions or incumbents are assigned new duties, the decision is based on their potential for success. The term *potential* implies capability of future performance, given adequate development. Few, if any, individuals have the capacity to perform at peak level their first day on a new job. Even those rare few who have had extensive experience require adjustment periods. In order to capitalize on employee potential, training programs strive to identify, develop, and direct capabilities into appropriate channels.

In addition to the principle of potentiality, three supplementary factors also contribute to the training process. These include: the uniqueness of the situation, job changes, and government rules and regulations.

The uniqueness of the situation Businesses have discovered that employees have smoother transitions when some form of initial training is used. Work environments are varied and unique, and even highly experienced workers find new jobs challenging at the onset. Even if a worker is familiar with a particular machine, this does not guarantee that he or she will be able to operate a similar piece of equipment. Machines are modified or re-tooled to fit individual situations and some machines are industry specific. In addition, organizations have their own policies and procedures, and they often use different methods to perform similar jobs.

Job changes Very few static organizations exist today. To be competitive, companies are constantly updating and changing equipment, methods, policies, and procedures. Individuals change jobs frequently and for many reasons. Promotions and advancements are welcome changes, but they typically involve learning and using new skills. Technological advances make existing equipment obsolete, requiring additional training for employees. This rapid growth brings an influx of new workers to the organization. In order to maintain a competitive edge, the skills and abilities of the workforce must be constantly updated.

Government rules and regulations The ever-increasing pressure by the government to advance minorities in the workforce has caused companies to develop extensive skills training programs for these groups. These programs have grown rapidly over the past two decades, especially because of government funded programs established to subsidize them.[1] In addition, training programs in safety practices are mandated by the government for workers involved in certain jobs identified by the Occupational Safety and Health Commission (OSHA).

The Training Process

Assessing Training Needs

In light of the substantial emphasis placed on training, it would seem likely that most companies would have developed extensive methods to identify training needs. Surprisingly, however, many companies conduct training in a haphazard manner. Some organizations immediately assume that a decrease in productivity is a direct result of poorly trained employees. Many companies are sold on programs that promise miraculous results based on material taught in a seminar. Vast amounts of training dollars are spent on the "Fad of the Year" program. The resources wasted on needless programs may have backfiring effects on organizations. The dollars companies squander on inappropriate training are now no longer available for use in required areas. Workers become frustrated attending useless programs, and they become resistant to future training efforts. In order to be effective and worthwhile, training must concentrate on organizational and individual needs. Consider the following case.

> One Wednesday afternoon, executives from the Canit Vegetable Company met with a consultant to discuss a potential training program. They were prepared to engage the consultant to train first-line supervisors in the art of selection interviewing. When queried about the reason for the company's emphasis on selection interviewing, the personnel director responded, "We believe that our high turnover rate is caused by a deficiency in supervisory interviewing skills." The consultant's preliminary analysis revealed that the company had never conducted job analyses, and it had no standard selection procedures. The hiring process consisted solely of single interviews with applicants that were conducted by immediate supervisors. Surprisingly, it turned out that the supervisors' interviewing skills were not

the problem at all. Rather, it was discovered that in order to reduce the turnover rate, the selection system needed revamping. As a result of the meeting, the personnel department participated in a three-day session on personnel selection.

Before undertaking training ventures, companies are obliged to undergo deliberate investigations of certain crucial elements. Training requires that analysis be continual, that it interface with other organizational areas, and that it incorporate the use of organizational, task, and person analyses.[2]

Organizational analysis **Organizational analysis** is a continuous process of gathering information and reviewing it to determine training needs. Although many departments contribute data, the majority of the information is gathered from the human resource area. Information regarding employee skills and demographic information is compiled as well. This fragmentary information, coupled with general statistics (such as typical retirement age and average age of mortality), often provides clues to training needs. For example, the existence of an aging managerial workforce alerts companies to the fact that successors may be needed in the near future. With this knowledge, companies may begin training eventual replacements.

Combining all relevant factors enables businesses to gain an understanding of the organization's total well-being. Realistically, however, continual follow-up and follow-through in these areas are complex, time-consuming tasks which are engaged in by relatively few organizations. The decisions regarding training needs usually rely more on task and person analyses.

Task analysis Every job consists of several different tasks. To determine what these various tasks are requires the use of a **task analysis.**

Task analysis

Task analysis is a process undertaken to determine the knowledge, skills, and abilities (KSAs) necessary to complete the various tasks involved in a total job.

Adequate job performance usually hinges on workers being able to perform many tasks. The identification of the tasks required to complete a job provides trainers with comprehensive lists of KSAs necessary for job performance. Because employees differ in individual strengths and weaknesses, the particular KSA training emphasis should be determined through the use of person analysis.

Person analysis When conducting job and task analyses, job agents are warned that they should analyze only the jobs, and not the employees perform-

Exhibit 6.1

A Management Needs Assessment

DIRECTIONS: The following questions concern the extent to which specific skill areas are needed within the company. Please indicate your evaluation on a 1–5 scale (1 indicating no need, 5 indicating extreme need) as to the level for which you feel training in the specific area is needed to increase the skill level of the organization's managerial personnel.

1.	The development of long-range plans.	1	2	3	4	5
2.	The development of short-range plans.	1	2	3	4	5
3.	The development of objectives/goals.	1	2	3	4	5
4.	The ability to delegate.	1	2	3	4	5
5.	The ability to manage time effectively.	1	2	3	4	5
6.	The ability to solve problems.	1	2	3	4	5
7.	The ability to consistently enforce company policies and procedures.	1	2	3	4	5
8.	The ability to adhere to legal employment guidelines.	1	2	3	4	5
9.	The ability to conduct performance appraisals.	1	2	3	4	5
10.	The ability to build an effective work group (team spirit).	1	2	3	4	5
11.	The ability to counsel and coach.	1	2	3	4	5
12.	The ability to train.	1	2	3	4	5
13.	The ability to motivate others.	1	2	3	4	5
14.	The ability to hold effective meetings.	1	2	3	4	5
15.	The ability to manage conflict and stress.	1	2	3	4	5
16.	The ability to communicate effectively.	1	2	3	4	5
17.	The ability to promote the company in the community.	1	2	3	4	5
18.	The ability to communicate effectively through memos, letters, and reports.	1	2	3	4	5

Please indicate in the space below, or on the reverse, any other needs which you feel should be the focus of a training session.

ing the job. **Person analysis** concentrates on identifying the strengths and weaknesses specific to individual workers. This process is facilitated by the use of worker performance reviews (discussed in detail in the next chapter) and other custom-designed techniques for gathering information. Based on the information gathered, training can be tailored to improve the shortcomings of individual workers.

Designing Training Programs

Training programs may be designed as soon as training analyses are completed. The process involves determining the most appropriate formats to employ, selecting trainers, and deciding on methods for final program evaluations. In order to make prudent training judgments, an understanding of learning principles is essential.

Principles of Learning

Motivation The effectiveness of any training program is largely dependent on whether or not people have a **motivation** to learn. Some trainees begin instruction with a predisposed desire to learn, while others require more external motivation. For example, some teachers attend graduate programs because of an internal desire to enhance their teaching effectiveness. Others attend only because the state requirements mandate a certain number of post-baccalaureate credits in order to maintain their teaching credential. Materials and training sessions should ideally be designed to emphasize skill acquisition in an interesting and motivating atmosphere. If motivation is not sustained, little, if any, learning will take place.

Feedback Individuals learn more rapidly when they are provided with **feedback**—negative as well as positive—about their performance. A knowledge of results strengthens desired behaviors, which are subsequently repeated, and eliminates inappropriate responses. Suppose, for example, several individuals are learning to play basketball. After each shot, the trainees will probably modify their shooting based on whether or not the ball successfully went through the hoop. With sufficient practice, their proficiency will improve. If, on the other hand, the trainees are blindfolded so that information regarding their performance is eliminated, the likelihood of improvement is nil. When trainees are provided with the results of their actions, they learn to adjust their responses accordingly. Lack of feedback generates uncertainty, frustration, and a decrease in motivation.

Reinforcement The principle of **reinforcement** maintains that the likelihood of a behavior being repeated is dependent on its consequences. Rewarded actions will be repeated, while efforts which are punished or unrewarded will be eliminated. For example, a new studying method which requires more effort than any method used previously will probably be repeated if it results in an "A" on the examination. On the other hand, should it result in either an "F" or a grade similar to that obtained through less strenuous methods, the likelihood of it being repeated is nil. The effective use of reinforcement for training requires that rewards be administered as soon as possible after the desired behavior is performed. It is also important to note that rewards are particular to individuals. Skilled trainers, therefore, must use various reinforcers in an attempt to satisfy the diverse needs of numerous trainees.

Transfer of training The ultimate goal of training is to improve performance on the job. As a result of **transfer of training,** several things can happen. First, **positive transfer** may take place, which is the result for which trainers strive. Positive transfer occurs when the information learned in the training sessions directly transfers to the work environment, resulting in improved performance. The use of simulators to train pilots or nuclear reactor workers is a common way in which positive transfer is promoted. **Negative transfer** ensues when the material learned in the training sessions interferes with job performance; an example would be training individuals in a particular word processing program such as "Framework" and subsequently placing them in an office where "Wordperfect" is used. Finally, **no transfer** occurs when training has neither a positive nor a negative effect on performance. To promote positive transfer, trainers strive to develop programs which teach the KSAs necessary for actual job performance.[3]

Meaningfulness of the material Without a doubt, one of the major considerations in attaining motivation and positive transfer is the meaningfulness of the material to the trainees. Even when the trainer presents relevant KSA material, little learning occurs unless the trainees find relevance in the subject matter as well. All too often, comments such as "this material has no relevance for the real world" or "theory belongs in the classroom" confirm either the inability of the trainer or the ineffectiveness of the materials to demonstrate the applicability of the learning sessions to the actual job situation.

Repetition Learning is enhanced when trainees are provided ample opportunity to repeat the tasks. For maximum benefit, practice sessions should be distributed over time.[4] Realistically, however, spaced practice sessions involve costs which many companies find excessive. As a result, practice sessions are usually massed together.

Environmental considerations Environmental factors play an important role in learning. It is logical that workers who are exposed to training in comfortable environments with adequate, well spaced rest periods are more likely to learn than employees whose training conditions are less than ideal. The length of training periods and the amount of material presented for integration at a single session are also important considerations. Sometimes referred to as "creature comforts," environmental factors are often viewed as unnecessary expenses. Occasionally, however, overlooking environmental considerations may negate the positive effects of a well-planned training program.

Behavioral objectives The final step in designing a training program is to establish **behavioral objectives.** The development of training curricula and the

Exhibit 6.2

The Extent to Which Training Techniques Utilize Certain Principles of Learning

	Motivation: ***Active participation of learner***	**Reinforcement:** ***Feedback of knowledge of results***	**Stimulus:** ***Meaningful organization of materials***	**Responses:** ***Practice and repetition***	**Stimulus-response:** ***Conditions most favorable for transfer***
On-the-Job Techniques					
Job-instruction training	Yes	Sometimes	Yes	Yes	Yes
Apprentice training	Yes	Sometimes	?	Sometimes	Yes
Internships and assistantships	Yes	Sometimes	?	Sometimes	Yes
Job rotation	Yes	No	?	Sometimes	Yes
Junior board	Yes	Sometimes	Sometimes	Sometimes	Yes
Coaching	Yes	Yes	Sometimes	Sometimes	Yes
Off-the-Job Techniques					
Vestibule	Yes	Sometimes	Yes	Yes	Sometimes
Lecture	No	No	Yes	No	No
Special study	Yes	No	Yes	?	No
Films	No	No	Yes	No	No
Television	No	No	Yes	No	No
Conference or discussion	Yes	Sometimes	Sometimes	Sometimes	No
Case study	Yes	Sometimes	Sometimes	Sometimes	Sometimes
Role playing	Yes	Sometimes	No	Sometimes	Sometimes
Simulation	Yes	Sometimes	Sometimes	Sometimes	Sometimes
Programmed instruction	Yes	Yes	Yes	Yes	No
Laboratory training	Yes	Yes	No	Yes	Sometimes
Programmed group exercises	Yes	Yes	Yes	Sometimes	Sometimes

Source: Bernard M. Bass and James A. Vaughan, *Training in Industry: The Management of Learning* (Belmont, CA: Wadsworth Publishing Company, 1966): 131. Reprinted with permission.

subsequent evaluations necessitate that concrete, observable outcomes be stated as succinctly as possible. The obtainment of these outcomes is the ultimate goal of training.

Training Methods

Training methods are usually categorized by the location of the instruction. On-the-job training is conducted when workers are taught relevant knowledge, skills, and abilities at the actual workplace. Off-the-job training, on the other hand, requires that trainees learn at a location other than the real job site.

On-the-Job Training

Undeniably, **on-the-job training** is the most common method of training used in business.[5] In its simplest form, on-the-job training requires that supervisors instruct employees in proper work methods directly at their work stations. When conducted in this manner, on-the-job training has several major advantages. First, it is cost efficient. Workers actually produce while they learn. Second, it enhances motivation and promotes feedback. Actually being on the job creates an eagerness in workers to perform, and they receive immediate results for their actions. Last, problems associated with transfer of training are minimized. When employees learn in the actual work environment, the skills learned are eventually used.

Although on-the-job training is cost efficient and easily administered, it does pose some problems. When trainees are using equipment for learning purposes, productivity is diminished. Experienced workers cannot use the machinery while it is being used for training. Furthermore, because training is conducted with the equipment paced at the normal production speed, trainees are more likely to damage equipment, waste materials, and have significantly higher accident rates.[6]

Another major disadvantage of on-the-job training centers around the trainer. In the majority of cases, particularly when line workers are being trained, the instructors are either supervisors or experienced production workers. In either case, the trainer may not have the teaching abilities, interest, or time necessary to spend training workers. These conditions could produce anxious, frustrated employees who, through no fault of their own, are incapable of performing satisfactorily.

Orientation training

Regardless of the total training time to which workers are exposed in their job tenures, they all receive some form of **orientation training.** Orientation training is sometimes referred to as "indoctrination" or "induction" training, and it is conducted primarily by human resource personnel. Each employee is usually taken on a formal tour of the facilities, introduced to key personnel, and informed about company benefits, policies, and procedures. In addition, many companies require that employees sign and return a form indicating that they have read and understood the policies and procedures in the employee handbooks.

Orientation plays a vital role in insuring new employees a smooth job transition. In order for this training to have the most beneficial effects, it should be well planned, it should be conducted within the first week of employment (preferably the first day), and it should be somewhat formal. The practice of some companies of combining individual training into group sessions delays and interferes with the advantages of the training. Consider the following case.

> Mark had just been hired as an orderly in a large metropolitan hospital. After arriving at work his first day, he was told by his supervisor that he would soon receive in the mail a card inviting him to an orientation session. He was further informed that at this session he would be given specific details about his benefits, as well as the hospital's policies and procedures. After two weeks, Mark called the personnel department to ask when he could expect his card. In response to Mark's question, the personnel director responded, "Orientation is conducted in groups. As soon as a sufficient number of new workers are hired, a session will be conducted." Mark was fired six months later for violation of a policy of which he was unaware. Three months thereafter, he received a card from the personnel department instructing him to report for orientation training.

Group orientation can be an effective training method. However, when promptness is sacrificed for the sake of cost, both the organization and the employees suffer.

Job instruction training (JIT)

Job Instruction Training, which evolved during World War II, was developed to provide guidelines for furnishing on-the-job skill training to both white- and blue-collar employees and technicians.[7] Basically, JIT is a structured approach to training which requires an orderly progression through a series of steps. Step One involves orienting trainees to the situation by providing them with an overview of the job, a perspective of its purpose within the total process, and a statement of the goals of the training program. This stage should promote motivation and demonstrate the meaningfulness of the material. Step Two involves a demonstration of the entire job by the trainers. In conjunction with physically performing the tasks, trainers typically verbalize each action. In Step Three, trainees perform the job as often as necessary until satisfactory performance is obtained. During this phase, trainers provide continual feedback to the workers regarding their performance. The final phase of JIT involves periodic monitoring of employee performance and the provision of supplementary training, if necessary.[8]

Exhibit 6.3

Sample Company Orientation Checklist for Policies and Procedures

_______ Issued Policy and Procedures Manual

I. Policies and Procedures Explained

Compensation Issues

_______ A. Pay Schedule and Classification System
_______ B. Overtime Pay
_______ C. Bonus Payments
_______ D. Commission Payments (sales personnel only)
_______ E. Pension and Profit Sharing Program
_______ F. Company Stock Plan Option

Insurance Benefits

_______ A. Hospitalization Plan
_______ B. Dental Plan
_______ C. Life Insurance Option
_______ D. Workers' Compensation
_______ E. Disability Insurance
_______ F. Travel and Accident Benefits

Time Off Benefits

_______ A. Holidays
_______ B. Sick Leave
_______ C. Compensatory Time
_______ D. Annual Leave (Vacation Time)
_______ E. Pregnancy Leave
_______ F. Jury Duty
_______ G. Military Service
_______ H. Bereavement

Miscellaneous Benefits

_______ A. Educational Expenses
_______ B. Counseling Services

II. Required Forms Completed

_______ A. W4 Signed and Verified
_______ B. Insurance Forms
_______ C. Personal Information Form
_______ D. Payroll Form
_______ E. Employment Agreement
_______ F. Physical Examination

III. Introductory Activities

_______ A. Plant Tour
_______ B. Safety Program
_______ C. Logistical Map Issued (parking, nurse's office, etc.)

As late as 1970, JIT was still the most popular and most commonly used industrial training program.[9] Tracing the process through the various steps, it is easy to see how the method provides for motivation, instantaneous feedback, repetition and practice, positive transfer, and meaningfulness of material. Like other on-the-job methods, its success relies to a large degree on the skill of the trainer. For this reason, JIT advocates special training sessions for trainers before implementing the program.

Apprenticeship training

One of the oldest forms of on-the-job training is **apprenticeship training.** Commonly found in industries such as metalworking, carpentry, and plumbing, apprentices are trainees who spend a prescribed period of time working with an experienced journeyman. When planned properly, apprenticeship programs allow workers to earn wages while learning both on and off the job.

One disadvantage to apprenticeship programs is the uniform time period placed on the program. People have different abilities and learn at varied rates. Establishing a fixed time period for learning does not allow for these differences. Trainees who learn quickly may leave the occupation out of frustration, while slower learners may require additional training time.[10]

In today's fast-paced, technologically changing environment, apprenticeship programs face new challenges. Trainees who spend years learning specific skills may find, upon completion of their programs, that the job skills they acquired are no longer appropriate. In fact, the occupation itself may have dramatically changed. Apprentices may be outdated before they even obtain their first position. For this reason, effective apprenticeship programs require constant monitoring and updating of training materials in order to keep pace with the changing times.

Job rotation

In **job rotation training** programs, trainees are periodically moved to different jobs within the organization. This system is commonly used for management training programs, and individuals receive the benefit of training in various phases and operations of the organization. Aside from alleviating boredom, job rotation allows workers to build rapport with a wide range of individuals within the organization, facilitating future cooperation among departments. In addition, cross-trained personnel provide a great deal of flexibility for organizations when transfers, promotions, or replacements become necessary.

Even the best planned job rotation programs can present difficulties. The programs create generalists, when sometimes specialists might better serve the company's needs. Trainees do not usually spend long enough in any single phase of the operation to develop a strong degree of expertise. In fact, for slow learners, the program may not allow sufficient opportunities to integrate material adequately. Furthermore, sometimes workers can become confused when they are exposed to rotating managers. Today's manager's instructions may be changed tomorrow by another manager.

Exhibit 6.4

Diplomas Awarded after Successful Completion of an Apprentice Program*

Commonwealth of Virginia

Certificate of Completion of Apprenticeship

Know ye That Roland C. Windmiller has satisfactorily completed an apprenticeship of two years at the trade of Cosmetician on this 1st day of October A.D. 19 80 in accordance with standards approved by the Virginia Apprenticeship Council and is, by virtue of the Statutes of the Commonwealth, awarded this certificate.

In Testimony Whereof the official signatures of the Virginia Apprenticeship Council have been subscribed hereon this 14th day of November A.D. 19 80.

For the Council

Raymon N. Roberts, Chairman

Robert L. Beck Jr., Secretary

*2,000 hours of various course work and practical supervised work experience required.

Coaching and mentoring

Coaching is a one-on-one relationship between trainees and supervisors which offers workers continual guidance and feedback about their performance. **Mentoring** is a particular form of coaching used by experienced executives to groom junior-level managers. Normally, mentoring involves one-on-one coaching for a period of several years until the individual is eventually capable of replacing the mentor.

There is no doubt that coaching provides an excellent opportunity for providing continuous feedback. When used properly, it contributes to learning and increases motivation. On the other hand, coaching, and especially mentoring, may lead to feelings of jealousy on the part of other workers. If mentors or coaches form overly strong bonds with trainees, unwarranted favoritism may result. This can have a demoralizing effect on other workers, and result in work behaviors which are detrimental to the organization.[11]

Off-the-Job Training

Aside from initial orientation and skills training programs, most other industry training probably occurs away from the actual job site. Varying in format from a short lecture to an extensive series of seminars, these programs are taught by in-house staff, professional trainers and consultants, or university faculty.

Off-the-job training adds a degree of flexibility to training which would otherwise be unavailable to many companies. Programs can be creatively designed to meet changing needs without being hampered by the lack of on-site resources. Personnel from several company locations can be combined into one training program, and a variety of trainers can be used for different sessions, thus providing individualized expertise. Finally, off-the-job training fosters an environment for learning. Unlike on-the-job training, where the goals of productivity and training are sometimes misconstrued, the primary objective of off-the-job programs is learning.

Ironically, one of the primary benefits of off-the-job training also contributes to its major weakness. In their attempts to foster learning environments, trainers fail on many occasions to induce positive transfer of material to the workplace. Programs which are designed to train combined groups of employees focus on general material, and many seminar participants cannot transfer this generalized material to their individual environments. Furthermore, for reasons of propriety, many participants are reluctant to discuss specific situations in general training sessions. All too often, trainers forget that the value of the material learned is its applicability to the work environment.

Lectures

Lectures, one of the oldest methods for imparting knowledge both on and off the job, provide information to large numbers of people in a highly cost-efficient manner. A well-prepared lecture provides useful information when audiences are homogenous in nature.

Several limitations of the lecture method require that it be examined carefully prior to its usage. First, the hearing of material in no way guarantees that it has been learned. Second, the lecture is a one-way communication technique which does not provide adequate opportunity for clarification of meanings, reinforcement, feedback, practice, or evaluation of trainee retention. Lastly, it is highly doubtful whether attitudinal and behavioral changes can be promoted through the lecture method.[12]

Vestibule training

Vestibule training involves the creation of an off-site environment similar to the actual workplace. Some companies set off a small area within the plant for this type of training, while other, usually larger organizations, establish vestibule schools. Operating as separate entities, these schools have their own facilities, professional training staffs, and may require a number of months for training.

The advantages of vestibule training are fairly obvious. It literally provides on-the-job training in a well-monitored, controlled environment with professionally trained staff. Motivation is high, learning is promoted, material is meaningful, trainees are provided individualized attention, and transfer of training is readily facilitated. On the negative side, however, is cost. For most organizations, the cost of establishing a duplicate environment solely for training is unjustifiable. Unless a company has a large turnover, is in a rapid growth stage, is sufficiently large that it continually hires large numbers of new employees, or is engaged in an occupation where the ramifications of errors cannot be tolerated (such as training nuclear power plant workers), vestibule programs are usually cost prohibitive.

Programmed Instruction (PI)

Programmed instruction, sometimes referred to as *programmed learning,* is a self-taught, self-paced learning system which eliminates the need for instructors. Material is presented to trainees in written form or by learning machines through a series of steps called *frames.* Each frame consists of factual material to be mastered, which is directly followed by a question. The trainees' responses are immediately verified after each frame. If the replies are correct, the trainees proceed to the next frame. If the responses are incorrect, the frame is repeated.

Programmed instruction offers the advantage of individualized training. Trainees progress at their own pace, receive immediate feedback, and are active, as opposed to passive, learners. A drawback of this method is the expense.[13] In addition, it is highly doubtful if any material other than concrete facts can be taught using this method. Mastering the science of human resource management through programmed instruction is not an absolute guarantee that an individual will be able to apply that knowledge to the art of managing people on a day to day basis.[14]

Exhibit 6.5

Training Techniques and Activities for Which They Are Typically Used

	Orienting new employees, introducing innovations in products and processes	Special skill training	Safety education	Creative, technical, and professional education	Sales, administrative, supervisory, and managerial education
On-the-Job Techniques					
Orientation training	✓				
Job-instruction training	✓	✓			
Apprentice training	✓	✓		✓	✓
Internships and assistantships		✓		✓	✓
Job rotation	✓				✓
Junior board					✓
Coaching		✓	✓	✓	✓
Off-the-Job Techniques					
Vestibule	✓	✓			
Lecture	✓	✓	✓	✓	✓
Special study	✓	✓	✓	✓	✓
Films	✓	✓	✓	✓	✓
Television	✓	✓	✓	✓	✓
Conference or discussion	✓		✓	✓	✓
Case study				✓	✓
Role playing					✓
Simulation	✓	✓		✓	✓
Programmed instruction	✓	✓	✓	✓	✓
Laboratory training				✓	✓

Source: Bernard M. Bass and James A. Vaughan, *Training in Industry: The Management of Learning* (Belmont, CA: Wadsworth Publishing Company, 1966): 132. Reprinted with permission.

Computer-Assisted Instruction (CAI)

The use of written materials or learning machines for self-instruction has been replaced technologically by computers. In essence, **computer-assisted instruction** is a sophisticated form of programmed learning. Unlike conventional programmed instruction, however, CAI offers the capability of analyzing trainees' responses and refining the individualized learning process.

CAI's major advantages are its instruction and reinforcement potential.[15] As computers become more sophisticated, the possibilities offered by CAI appear to be substantial. At present, however, aside from its fad appeal, CAI appears to be an even more expensive version of programmed instruction.

Case study and incident methods

The **case study method,** which is widely used in educational settings and management development seminars, involves analysis and discussion of either true or hypothetical organizational problems. Trainees are presented with written cases which they analyze individually, and subsequently discuss as a group. Theoretically, the learning benefits derived from the case study method are directly related to the ensuing group discussions, rather than individual problem-solving strategies.

The **incident method**[16] is a variation of the case study method and attempts to duplicate more closely the actual managerial decision-making process. Rather than providing the trainees with all the necessary details to analyze the case, they are given only a brief synopsis of the problem. To effectively solve the case, participants must query the trainer for additional facts. The ultimate decision arrived at by the group is a two-fold process. First, they must decide on relevant questions to ask, and second, they must appropriately analyze all the available data.

Criticisms of the case study method focus primarily on the trainer's behavior during the discussion period. Cases are not supposed to have correct answers. Some trainers take positions, indicate preferred solution routes, do not reveal their strategies, and fail to establish trainee independence. In order for the case study method to be effective, trainers should be less dominating, and they should use cases which closely resemble, or are identical to, those of the trainees' actual work environment.[17]

In-basket technique

The **in-basket technique** is another method in which trainees assume managerial roles in order to cultivate their skills. Training goals are accomplished by having trainees respond to a series of written memos within a given time frame. Trainees record their responses in writing, and subsequently discuss the answers with other group members and the trainer.

In-baskets are often used in conjunction with other training materials. They are easy to administer to large groups, relatively inexpensive, and fun to do. Similar to the case method, any benefits derived from using in-baskets depend largely on the skill of the trainer in providing feedback. The major disadvantage of in-baskets is the stress potential on trainees who are unable to complete the exercise within the allotted time period.[18]

Role playing and multiple role playing

Role playing is the portrayal of real work situations in which trainees have the opportunity to experience subordinate and supervisory positions. A typical session consists of one trainee being assigned the role of subordinate and another trainee portraying the supervisor while the remaining trainees and the trainer observe. At the conclusion of the exercise, the trainees discuss the role behaviors, recommend modifications, and replay the roles using the suggestions presented. This procedure is repeated until all trainees have had an opportunity to participate. Sometimes trainees exchange roles in order to understand the situation from a new perspective. The reversal of roles aids in heightening the awareness of the trainee to include both the supervisory and subordinate points of view.

When the size of a training group is too large to allow each trainee an opportunity to role play, **multiple role playing** is used. Trainees are divided into groups of four, five, or six members each, and they role play situations within their groups. After completing their sessions, the groups re-assemble to discuss their findings.[19]

Role playing is rarely used by itself, and is typically employed with other management training methods. While analyzing cases provides opportunities for trainees to refine their cognitive skills, effective management also requires the development of human relations skills. These skills are usually not learned from books, lectures, or discussions. Rather, people skills are acquired by actually relating to people.

Sensitivity training

Sometimes called *T-group* or *laboratory training,* **sensitivity training** is probably the most controversial and extensively researched training method. The goal of sensitivity training, which was developed at the National Training Laboratories in Bethel, Maine, is to enhance trainees' awareness of how they are viewed interpersonally by others. Groups, which usually consist of between eight and twelve participants, meet for several days in an environment away from their actual work site. Participants may be from the same department, division, or company, or they may be combined from different organizations. Exercises are designed to elicit attitudes, values, beliefs, relevant behaviors, and any other factors which would enable participants to learn how they view others and to provide feedback about how others perceive them. The overall goal is to become a more sensitive person.

Sensitivity training has generated both criticism and praise over the past thirty years.[20] There is a long list of advantages, disadvantages, and cautions organizations should be aware of when they contemplate using this method. The lack of trainer skill,[21] the inability of trainees to transfer the material to the work site, and the short-lived results of the training are the most common problems associated with sensitivity training. Nevertheless, because of the inability of cases, games, and other simulation methods to generate interpersonal awareness, sensitivity training, as well as other similar methods, still enjoys popularity among employers.

Management or business games

Most **management games** or business games require that groups of participants (each representing a separate enterprise) make a series of decisions affecting their business. These games are complex in nature, and success requires a knowledge of general managerial principles. Teams compete with each other, simulating the real-world environment, and the outcome is a function of the quality of the decisions made by each group in comparison with the decisions made by the other groups.

Management and business games have several distinct benefits. They compress years of experience into a few days, they are intrinsically interesting, they provide immediate and objective feedback, and they aid in understanding the complex interrelationships among organizational units. On the other hand, there are limitations to these games. Participants become so engrossed in the games that they sometimes overlook their underlying managerial principles. Furthermore, the games themselves may stifle creativity because innovative managers may be penalized during the game for using unorthodox strategies.[22]

Career Development[23]

The knowledge and understanding of career development, the ways in which career decisions and choices are made, and the employee's entry into and departure from organizational life provide a valuable data base for human resource managers. Career information contributes to the understanding of individual differences among employees, their motivations, and the influence of numerous variables on job satisfaction and productivity. Career information also furnishes human resource personnel with knowledge about employees' skills, aptitudes, and abilities which are essential components of selection and training decisions. In addition to benefiting the organization, career knowledge is also useful for meeting employees' developmental needs. One of human resource managers' primary responsibilities is assisting individuals to develop and realize their optimum potential.

Matching and Process Theories

Numerous methods are employed to study the career process. Some theorists define career choices in terms of matching individuals with careers. Matching theorists place primary focus on the compatibility of an individual's interests, self-identity, personality (needs and values), and social background (socioeconomic status) with his or her chosen occupation. Consistent with this orienta-

Exhibit 6.6

Itinerary for a Supervisory Training Seminar

Monday

8:00 AM	Welcome/Orientation	Don Michael Personnel Director
8:45 AM	Coffee Break	
9:00 AM	Introduction to Supervision	Paul Synam Consultant
10:30 AM	Break	
10:45 AM	Introduction to Supervision continued	
12:00 PM	Lunch Break	
1:00 PM	Planning and Organizing	Jane Morrison Director Research and Development
1:45 PM	Break	
2:00 PM	Planning and Organizing continued	
4:00 PM	Adjourn	
7:30–10:30 PM	Social	Suite 487

Tuesday

8:00 AM	Safety and Health Procedures	Sally Clean, R.N. Safety Coordinator
10:00 AM	Break	
10:15 AM	Fair and Equal Treatment of Employees	John Standing EEO Coordinator
12:00 PM	Lunch Break	
1:00 PM	Assessing Employee Performance	JoAnn Synam Consultant
1:45 PM	Break	
2:00 PM	Assessing Employee Performance continued	
3:45 PM	Seminar Evaluation and Certificate of Participation Distribution	
4:30 PM	Adjourn	

tion is the belief that individuals also make decisions about which company to work for based on their personal orientation.

Process theories, which tend to be more dynamic and developmental in nature, highlight the stages of career decision making. Individuals are faced with specific occupational tasks and choices at particular stages in their vocational development (such as play acting occupations as children or selecting a major in college). It is valid to say that the elements of both approaches contribute to our understanding of how and why individuals make particular career choices. Therefore, we will examine a number of variables which are consistent with both theoretical approaches.

Factors Influencing Career Choices

Career development, which is one aspect of total development, is a complex interaction of psychological, social, and economic factors. Psychological factors, such as interests, aptitudes, and self-esteem have a significant influence on career orientations. Individuals often select particular career paths in an attempt to satisfy personal needs. An individual who has a strong need to be with others may not accept a job which requires him to work alone most of the time. Other individuals may gravitate toward a particular career because of a special aptitude or an acquired interest. An individual may be predisposed to enter a medical profession because of a particular aptitude or interest in science.

Social factors, such as socioeconomic status and parents' educational and occupational levels, also affect the aspirational levels and subsequent directions of individuals' careers. These factors in turn interact with and are affected by current economic conditions, employment trends, and the effect of technology on the job market. Today, individual career paths are charted by the current availability of jobs in accounting, data processing, and other business-related fields. These trends may fluctuate in the future and affect educational and career decisions as well.

Career Stages

It is widely recognized that individuals progress through developmental career stages which parallel life stages. Each stage is distinguished by unique needs, motives, and tasks. Childhood is generally characterized by fantasy, role playing, and experimenting with various career avenues. During adolescence, career identity begins to emerge in conjunction with self-identity. The adolescent stage is represented by an exploration of vocational interests in school, leisure, and work. Adulthood is devoted to education and training, career establishment, organizational entry, career stabilization, and eventually retirement. The departure from the workforce presents distinct developmental tasks and challenges for individuals. Retirement is a time when some people disengage from the workforce and others begin new careers.

In addition to typical career stages, some people have unique circumstances which interrupt or postpone the occupational cycle. For example, women who interrupt their careers in order to raise families frequently resume their vocational pursuits later in life. In addition, some individuals change careers in midlife. In both circumstances, an inconsistency between career and life development stages often results. These individuals have unique needs which have direct consequences for human resource personnel.

Organizational entry

Young adulthood is primarily devoted to education and training. When a recruit makes a smooth transition from this preparatory work stage into the mainstream of organizational life, he or she has the potential to become a productive and satisfied worker. However, the initial job experience is often surprisingly frustrating and disappointing for many recruits. It is common for recruits to encounter real contradictions between job expectations and the organization's job demands. The organization, as well, is often disappointed with the performance of recruits. It is fair to concede that the perceptions and practices of both recruits and organizations contribute to this "reality shock" syndrome. Unfortunately for both the employee and employer, the direct consequences of these unmet expectations lead to unused human resource potential and dissatisfaction.

Minimizing reality shock In order to minimize the effects of unrealistic expectations, it is important for recruits to receive accurate job preview information. Organizations may also facilitate a recruit's transitional period by enriching job environments to promote autonomy, responsibility, and growth. In addition, recruits should be provided with ongoing feedback in order to foster organizational goals, reinforce learning, and encourage correction and self-improvement. When organizations effectively use the potential of new recruits by offering these individuals work environments consistent with their developmental needs, the human resource input becomes an investment for the company as well.

The middle career syndrome

During mid-life, individuals reach a career plateau which is often characterized by stress or boredom. A developmental task of this career stage is the reconciliation of earlier goals and aspirations with present circumstances. Individual reactions at this stage are complex and varied. Some individuals respond by accepting, reexamining, and readjusting aspirational levels. Other individuals, plagued with boredom and lack of challenge, look either to new careers or to stimulation outside of work.

Growing old with the company poses both real and imagined problems and threats to employees at mid-life. During this period in the life cycle there is some natural slowing down of physical and mental processes. Individuals often suffer from depression and other health problems, and they carry these feelings and attitudes over into their work lives. Many individuals fear that they will be replaced by brighter and younger employees, and that they will become obsolete and be put out to pasture. This somewhat negative and stressful perspective on the part of the employee influences both satisfaction and productivity levels. If human resource personnel are prepared for these challenges in advance and they can devise training strategies to minimize the consequences of these challenges, the result will be the simultaneous enhancement of both employee and organizational goals.[24]

Approaching retirement

Individuals respond uniquely to their retirement years for a variety of reasons. Even though retirement is characterized as a declining developmental stage, many individuals look forward to this period as a time of freedom from the stresses and regimentation of a lifetime of work. In addition, they also view their work departure as an opportunity to explore interests that a busy work schedule had never previously permitted. Others begin new educational and career paths at this time in their lives. Despite the fact that for many, retirement adds a positive, new, life dimension, for others, it is unfortunately overshadowed by negative feelings. The loss of work identity, which is closely entwined with self-identity, leaves many retirees feeling useless and unproductive. In addition to a late life identity crisis, many people are also burdened with financial problems and adjustments to home and family life as well. The elimination of mandatory retirement ages enlarges the work pool of individuals in this developmental stage. Human resource personnel are once again faced with the challenge of understanding, using, and training human resources in the best interests of both the employee and the organization.

Evaluating the Training Effort

Understanding learning principles, designing programs, and conducting training sessions is only relevant when trainees learn material they can subsequently transfer to their actual jobs. After training has been conducted, it would seem only natural that organizations would expend a significant effort determining how effectively the training goals were met. Interestingly, however, with all the resources devoted toward the training effort, only a fraction is allocated toward the evaluation phase. In fact, some of the most sophisticated, well-designed, and expensive training programs have either rudimentary or non-existent evaluation programs. Evaluations must be conducted to determine if these training sessions accomplished their objectives.

It is quite obvious that the goal of evaluation is to determine which training programs accomplish their mission and which do not. Those programs which fail to reach their goals will be eliminated, and those which succeed will be retained. To simplify the evaluation procedure requires that the evaluation process be broken down into four logical steps. These are: reaction, learning, behavior, and results.[25]

Reaction Reaction is the degree to which trainees enjoyed the program. Most organizations, regardless of whether or not they conduct any other evaluation, measure reaction. The standard procedure is to administer an evaluation form to each participant at the conclusion of the training program. These evaluation forms typically require trainees to rate on a bi-polar scale both the trainer and the material taught. In addition, trainees are given an opportunity to subjectively provide any additional reactions or recommendations.

The value of measuring reaction is undeniable. Little learning takes place if trainees are uninterested or dislike the presentation. The evaluation forms have to be carefully used in evaluating programs. Some companies sum the total of the responses, divide that total by the number of participants, and use the average as an overall rating to determine training effectiveness. Other companies react to one negative comment and cancel a program. Entertaining trainers may score highly, but the test of their effectiveness is the value of the learning experience. The reaction of trainees is only the first phase of the evaluation process, and not the culmination.

Learning Liking and learning are not necessarily correlated. A measurement of whether or not trainees actually learned material at the sessions cannot be accomplished adequately by using trainee evaluation forms. In fact, some practitioners jokingly refer to these evaluation forms as "happy scales" because they seem to correlate with whether the trainees felt they were entertained at the

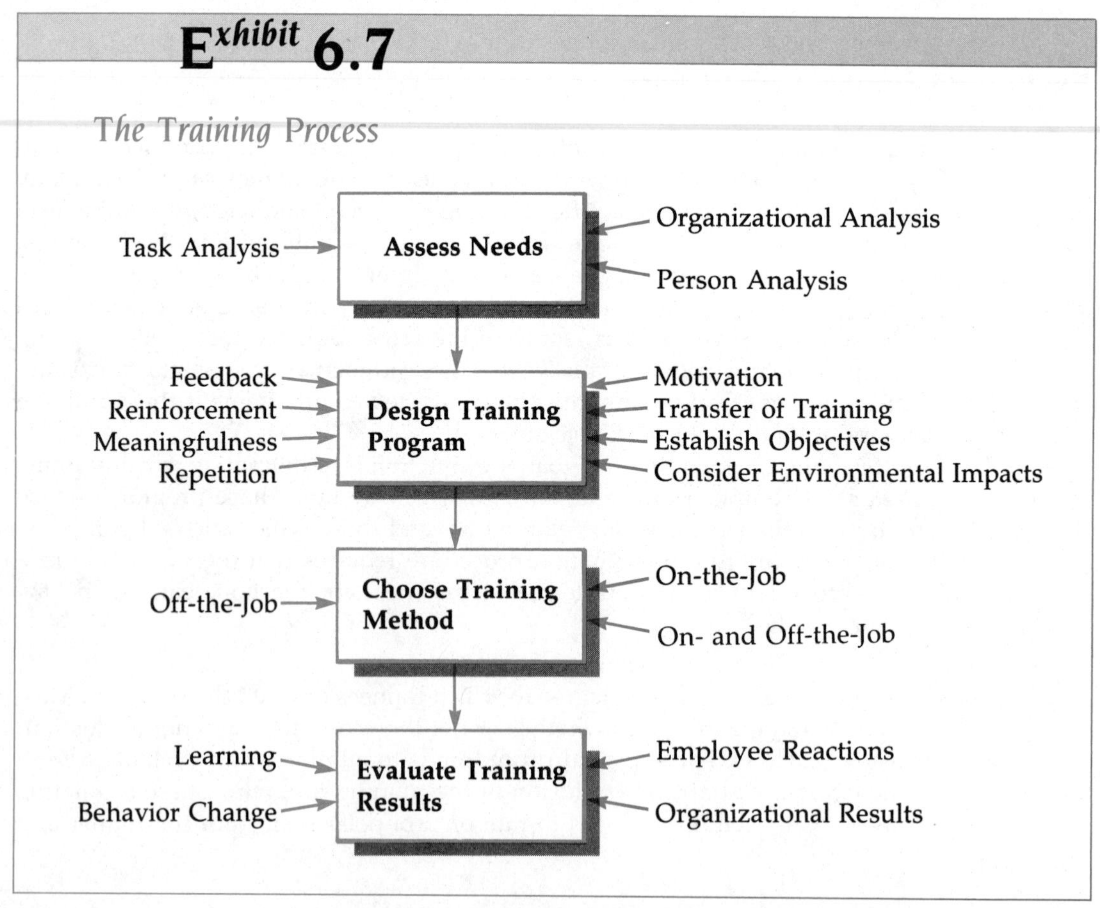

sessions, and not whether they learned. The appropriate measure of learning is dependent on the goals of the training. If the material to be learned can be measured through paper-and-pencil testing, then this type of format should be employed. If, on the other hand, other skills were to be mastered, appropriate ability measures should be developed to assess them.

Behavior Material which has been learned must be transferred into practice in order for training to be effective. Evaluating this phase requires that before and after measures be established. If training had the desired effect, then there should be a significant difference in the work performed before and after training.

Results The final phase of the evaluation process is concerned with the overall impact training has on the organization. Training may have increased individual productivity, but the cost of the total effort may have been excessive. Furthermore, the training may have had significant personal gain for the worker, but little, if any, for the company. The four-step evaluation is an important tool for determining the usefulness of training endeavors. Realistically, however, most companies judge training effectiveness solely on the trainees' evaluations of the programs. Even companies that conduct a more comprehensive evaluation rarely progress beyond the learning stage. Omitting the latter two facets of the evaluation leaves significant doubt as to whether the training program has succeeded in its goal of facilitating positive transfer to the work site.

A Final Note

Although the importance of training is recognized by organizations, individuals' priorities interfere with scheduling the time to attend sessions. Emergencies always seem to coincide with training responsibilities, and excuses not to attend are commonplace. The design of effective programs is unproductive if employees fail to appear for the training. Therefore, when developing training agendas, it is essential to generate not only interest among employees, but also commitment.

Companies employ various strategies in an effort to promote trainee attendance. Some organizations mandate training as a job responsibility, while other companies lure their employees into training by the attraction of a vacation-like atmosphere. Training by coercion causes negativism and diminishes motivation. Vacation-like seminars motivate employees because of the fringe benefits rather than the learning sessions. Furthermore, the frivolous costs of the latter programs make it exceptionally difficult to justify training results.

The answer to this enigma is not to spend excessive amounts of money or to make training a requirement. People will want to attend sessions if several conditions exist. First, participants must believe in the program's goals. Second, they must perceive the trainers as credible. Third, they must see the potential for rewards. Finally, companies must be willing to provide rewards for session attendance, for demonstrated learning, and for improved performance.

Summary

In today's world, large sums of money are devoted to training efforts. Organizations are constantly attempting to provide employees with opportunities to develop their potential, in the interest of improving their work performance. For some workers, this means extensive on-the-job programs designed to improve motor skills, while for other employees, it may involve off-the-job programs, the goal of which may be self-awareness.

The realization of training benefits is contingent on the degree of planning and effort expended on designing, implementing, and evaluating the training programs. The haphazard conduction of training programs results in wasted resources, poorly motivated employees, and no measurable increases in productivity. On the other hand, programs which are designed, conducted, and evaluated properly have innumerable benefits to both the trainee and the organization.

Key Terms to Identify

Training
Principle of potentiality
Organizational analysis
Task analysis
Person analysis
Motivation
Feedback
Reinforcement
Transfer of training
Positive transfer
Negative transfer
No transfer
Behavioral objectives
On-the-job training
Orientation training
Job instruction training (JIT)
Apprenticeship training
Job rotation training
Coaching and mentoring
Off-the-job training
Lectures
Vestibule training
Programmed instruction (PI)
Computer-assisted instruction (CAI)
Case study method
Incident method
In-basket technique
Role playing
Multiple role playing
Sensitivity training
Management games

Questions for Discussion

Do You Know the Facts?

1. Why do companies allocate significant resources for the training and development of human resources?
2. What methods do companies use to assess their training needs?
3. What principles underlie effective training programs?
4. Discuss the advantages and problems associated with the different on-the-job and off-the-job approaches to training.
5. What is the importance of the evaluation phase of training programs?

Can You Apply the Information Learned?

1. What factors may organizations overlook when developing training programs that could undermine the successful results of the programs? What can they do to prevent unsuccessful outcomes?
2. What is the importance of the relationship between behavioral objectives and the evaluation phase of training?
3. Using the information in this chapter, design a training program for the following employees: a human resource manager, a production supervisor, and a fast food counterperson.
4. Design a training program to stress the importance of safety to line workers.

Career Crossroads—A Difficult Choice

Jack Ruffing sat in his office, staring out the window. Until today, life seemed to be in order. He is 28 years old, married with two wonderful children, and the proud owner of a new home. He graduated from Rutgers University with a bachelor's degree in management, and has been pursuing an MBA degree in the evening at New York University. He has been employed by Universal Chemical Corporation, a giant chemical manufacturing firm, for the past seven years since his graduation from Rutgers.

Universal Corporation is the second largest chemical company in the world. It was formed in 1910 and has grown by leaps and bounds through the years to its present size. The firm is stable and solid, it has been consistently profitable, and its future seems secure. When Jack first started with the firm as a management trainee, he felt fortunate to have been selected by such a fine company and he fully anticipated that he might have a long career with them. He progressed well, and after several promotions, he is currently head of a small department in the Distribution Division. He supervises 22 employees and is responsible for all motor carrier operations for the firm. His immediate superior, 44-year-old traffic manager Bob Jolly, has been with the firm for 22 years. He is more like a friend than a boss, constantly praising Jack's performance and assuring him that he has a very bright future with Universal Corporation.

About two months ago, Jack received a telephone call from Carl Sutton, the president of Median Publishing Company. Mr. Sutton explained that they were seeking a successor to their General Manager, Frank Foss, who was retiring. He pointed out that a business associate had recommended Jack for the position, and he encouraged him to apply. Mr. Sutton was quite convincing, and Jack agreed to an interview, even though he seriously doubted he would leave Universal.

Median Publishing Company is a nationally known firm which has been in business for 30 years. It is privately owned by its chairperson, P. K. Loebe, and Mr. Sutton, and is many times smaller than Universal. Median is a medium size firm which publishes several magazines and many books. It has been exceptionally profitable for most of its existence. Currently, the firm is doing well both in terms of total volume and in terms of finances. During the interview, Jack found Mr. Sutton, Ms. Loebe, and the rest of the personnel at Median to be pleasant and likeable. He did observe, however, that the firm's operations appeared to be somewhat shoddy. Mr. Sutton emphasized that the new hiree would be third in command behind the chairperson and himself, and that he would have as much freedom as possible in running the firm's operations. To his own surprise, Jack found himself agreeing to additional interviews to further explore the possibilities of employment with Median.

A second and third series of interviews followed and seemed to go well. Today, Mr. Sutton called Jack and extended an offer of employment at more than twice Jack's current salary. Jack thanked him profusely and requested time to discuss the decision with his family. Mr. Sutton readily agreed and said that he hoped Jack would accept the offer to join their fine company.

Jack was confused. He was making good progress with a major corporation and was happy with his life. Yet, the opportunity to manage a company, even a smaller one, at a substantially higher salary was most inviting. His wife, Janet, said she would support whatever decision he made, as long as he was happy. Seeking guidance, Jack decided to call his father. Jack respected his father, who had recently retired from his job as a life-long assembly line worker for a major automobile manufacturing plant, and was hoping for some concrete advice. When Jack mentioned the offer, his father responded by telling him that he would have to be out of his mind to even consider leaving Universal for a risky venture such as that offered by Median Company. He argued that Jack had the security of seven years with a reputable Fortune 500 firm, a salary that enabled him to pay his bills with no problems, and responsibilities of a home and family. He didn't want to listen to Jack's explanation that this might be the opportunity to show what he could do at a salary which far surpassed his present income. When the conversation ended Jack stared out the window, more confused than ever.

Questions for Discussion

1. What choice would you make if you were Jack? Why?
2. Does Jack really want to leave Universal to take the position at Median? What clues support your answer?
3. What techniques might Jack use to help him make a decision?
4. How much security does Jack really have with Universal?
5. What appears to be the best scenario of the future? The worst?

This case was prepared by O. C. Brenner, of James Madison University.

The Botched Assignments

When the Gibralter Appliance plant changed its finishing processes from hand-spraying in batches to a continuous, semi-automatic spray line, the number of painters was reduced from twenty-three to five. All of the displaced spray-painters were placed by the human resources department in other jobs throughout the plant. One of the displaced painters, Tyrone F., was assigned to the cabinet-forming department to learn the job of a class B spot-welder.

When Tyrone reported to the cabinet department, Sally Olds, his new supervisor, said to him, "I don't know whether your assignment here will be permanent. Work is a little slow right now, and we really don't need another welder. In the meantime, however, I'll see that you have a place to hang your coat and a bench to sit at." So, for the first few days, all Tyrone did was stand around and watch the other welders. Finally, at the end of the week, Sally told Tyrone, "I've got good news for you. Orders are picking up in the plant, and we'll be able to put you to work for real on Monday."

On Monday, Sally assigned Tyrone to a welding machine. It seemed like a relatively simple operation. All the operator needed to know was how to slide a sheet-metal panel into a positioning fixture, clamp it in place with a holding mechanism, and then punch an electric switch. The actual welding was done automatically. When the operation was completed, the welder would release the holding clamp, and an air blast would automatically eject the panel onto a moving belt to carry it on to the next operation.

"Here," said Sally to Tyrone, "Watch this operation. It's as easy as ABC. Even an airhead could do this job after learning these four steps. Sometimes I think a moron would do this job better than a normal person." Sally then demonstrated the four steps very slowly. As she did each step, she explained what was happening. After repeating the demonstration a half dozen times,

Sally got up from the machine and said to Tyrone, "Now you try it." Tyrone performed the operation right the very first time he tried it. With Sally standing by, he welded twenty panels without a mishap. "There," said Sally, "I told you there was nothing to it. In a couple of days, you'll be able to do this job in your sleep." That was the last time Tyrone saw Sally to speak to until Friday.

Between Monday and Friday, however, the following things happened to Tyrone: The air ejection mechanism jammed twice and he had to get a co-worker to show him how to free it. Several panel sheets that looked slightly shorter than the others came to Tyrone, but he welded them anyway and sent them on to the next operation. Unfortunately, these panels could not be assembled, and they had to be discarded. Friday, as Tyrone was sliding a metal sheet into the machine, a sharp edge caught the fleshy part of his thumb and ripped a one-inch gash in it. Tyrone was rushed off to the first-aid station, and that was when Sally found time to talk to Tyrone again.

Questions for Discussion

1. How do you think Tyrone feels about his new job and about his new boss?
2. In what ways were the incidents that occurred between Monday morning and Friday afternoon related to Tyrone's training?
3. What were some of the things that were wrong with the way Sally trained Tyrone to operate the welding machine?
4. If you were Sally, what would you have done to improve Tyrone's learning process?

This case was prepared by Lester R. Bittel, Emeritus Professor of Management, James Madison University.

Endnotes and References

1 Two of the most well-known government-sponsored programs in this area are the Targeted Jobs Tax Credit Program and the Job Partnership Act.

2 Michael L. Moore and Philip Dutton, "Training Needs Analysis: Review and Critique," *The Academy of Management Review,* Vol. 3, No. 3 (1978): 532–545. Also see William McGehee and Paul W. Thayer, *Training in Business and Industry* (New York: McGraw-Hill, 1961).

3 For an excellent discussion on transfer of training, see Irwin L. Goldstein, *Training in Organizations: Needs Assessment, Development, and Evaluation,* 2nd ed. (Monterey, CA: Brooks/Cole Publishing Company, 1986): 88–98.

4 Irwin L. Goldstein, *op. cit.,* 81–83.

5 Planning the Training Program. *Personnel Management: BNA Policy and Practice Series* (Washington, D.C.: The Bureau Of National Affairs, 1975).

6 William McGehee and Paul W. Thayer, *op. cit.*

7 Bernard M. Bass and James A. Vaughan, *Training in Industry: The Management of Learning* (Belmont, CA: Wadsworth Publishing Company, 1966): 88.

8 War Manpower Commission, *The Training Within Industry Report* (Washington, D.C.: U.S. Government Printing Office, 1945).

9 Stuart B. Utgaard and Rene V. Dawis, "The Most Frequently Used Training Techniques," *Training and Development Journal*, Vol. 24 (February 1970): 41.

10 A comprehensive study of apprenticeship programs can be found in *Research in Apprenticeship Training* (Oshkosh, WI: The University of Wisconsin, Center for Vocational and Technical Education, 1967).

11 Mentoring is especially popular for high-level executive replacements. For a comprehensive discussion on the pros and cons of mentoring, see George S. Odiorne, "Mentoring—An American Management Innovation," *Personnel Administrator*, Vol. 30 (May 1985): 63–66 and Donald W. Myers and Neil J. Humphreys, "The Caveats in Mentorship," *Business Horizons*, Vol. 28 (July–August 1985): 9–14.

12 Bernard M. Bass and James A. Vaughan, *op. cit.*, 94–95.

13 R. L. Prather, "Introduction to Management by Teaching Machine," *Personnel Administration*, Vol. 27, No. 3 (1964): 26–31.

14 There are different types of programmed instruction methods available. Among the most common are the autoinstructional method, the branching programming method, and the linear programming method. For a comprehensive discussion of these methods, and programmed instruction in general, see Irwin L. Goldstein, *op. cit.*, 189–199.

15 Irwin L. Goldstein, *op. cit.*, 208.

16 The incident method was originated by P. Pigors and F. Pigors. For more detailed information see: *The Incident Process: Case Studies in Management Development* (Washington, D.C.: The Bureau Of National Affairs, 1955).

17 An interesting and controversial criticism of the case study method was proposed by Chris Argyris. Argyris claims that double-loop learning, whereby the correction of error requires changes in underlying policies, assumptions and goals, is undermined by the case study method. For a discussion of this criticism see: Chris Argyris, "Some Limitations of the Case Method: Experiences in a Management Development Program," *The Academy of Management Review*, Vol. 5, No. 2 (1980): 291–298.

18 Dugan Laird, *Approaches to Training and Development* (Reading, MA: Addison-Wesley Publishing Company, 1983).

19 N. R. F. Maier and L. F. Zerfoss, "MRP: A Technique for Training Large Groups of Supervisors and Its Potential Use in Social Psychology," *Human Relations*, Vol. 5 (1952): 177–186.

20 For a comprehensive summation of the advantages and disadvantages of sensitivity training see Marvin D. Dunnette and John P. Campbell, "Laboratory Education: Impact on People and Organizations," *Industrial Relations*, Vol. 8 (1968): 1–44. See also Cary L. Cooper, "How Psychologically Dangerous are T-Groups and Encounter Groups?" *Human Relations*, Vol. 28 (1975): 249–260.

21 Many researchers have stressed that the major problems which have resulted from sensitivity training are related to the lack of ability of the group leader. For extensive information on the impact of leader behaviors on T-Group participants, see Cary L. Cooper, "Adverse and Growthful Effects of Experiential Learning Groups: The Role of Trainer, Participant, and Group Characteristics," *Human Relations,* Vol. 3 (1977): 1103–1129.

22 Kenneth N. Wexley and Gary P. Latham, *Developing and Training Human Resources in Organizations* (Glenview, IL: Scott, Foresman and Company, 1981): 203.

23 Except where noted the information on career development was drawn primarily from Douglas T. Hall, *Careers in Organizations* (Pacific Palisades, CA: Goodyear Publishing Company, Inc., 1976).

24 For a discussion of the effects of mid-life work changes, see O. C. Brenner and Marc G. Singer, "Career Repotters: To Know Them Could be to Keep Them," *Personnel,* Vol. 65, No. 11 (1988): 54–60.

25 Donald L. Kirkpatrick, "Evaluation of Training." In *Training and Development Handbook,* 2nd ed., edited by Robert L. Craig. (New York, McGraw-Hill Book Company, 1976): 18–1 to 18–27.

Chapter 7

Appraising Performance

Objectives

After reading this chapter you should understand:

1. The reasons why performance appraisals are used.
2. The differences among the three types of performance data.
3. The differences among the various types of rating scales and the advantages and disadvantages of each type.
4. The different rater errors, and how to compensate for them.
5. The advantages and disadvantages of using supervisors, peers, and others to perform ratings.
6. The way performance evaluations are conducted, and the legal ramifications of appraisals.

Informing individuals about their performance and helping them to improve is a process which begins in early childhood. Initially, parents and significant others provide feedback to children by rewarding and punishing their actions. Children quickly learn that performing appropriate behaviors will either result in a reward or avert a negative consequence. Similarly, inappropriate behaviors are likely to result in punishment.

Upon entering school, individuals are exposed to their first formalized evaluation systems—tests and report cards. From this point on, teachers, coaches, peers, and eventually supervisors provide individuals with a continual stream of feedback about their performance. The process of providing information to individuals concerning their work performance is referred to as **performance appraisal.**

> ***Performance appraisal***
>
> *Performance appraisal is a formal process of providing workers with diagnostic feedback (positive and negative knowledge of results) about their job performance.*

Reasons for Using Performance Appraisals

The conduction of performance appraisals, which are also referred to as performance evaluations, performance reviews, employee appraisals, employee reviews, and merit ratings, is one of the most important tasks of a supervisor. As noted in Chapter 6, little learning or improvement of behavior occurs unless individuals are provided with feedback about their performance. Providing knowledge of how effectively the job was performed is crucial to fostering positive behaviors and eliminating inappropriate actions. The principal rationale for using performance appraisals is to maximize productivity by identifying and capitalizing on the strengths of employees.

Aside from providing feedback, performance appraisals serve other functions within organizations. Some of the more common uses of appraisals are for assisting in:

- Determining appropriate salary increases and bonuses for workers based on performance measures.
- Determining promotions or transfers depending on the demonstration of employee strengths and weaknesses.
- Determining which employees to lay off or dismiss based on demonstrated work performance.
- Determining training needs and evaluation techniques by identifying areas of weakness.
- Promoting effective communication within organizations through the interchange of dialogue between superiors and subordinates.
- Complying with government rules and regulations by serving as the criterion measure for validation of employment measures.

As indicated by the preceding list of performance appraisal uses, adequately conducted appraisals have many benefits for organizations. When faced with conducting performance appraisals, however, most supervisors are comfortable with informal procedures and are hesitant about using formal systems. This demonstrated reluctance by supervisors to conduct formal appraisals usually stems from being inadequately trained, particularly in the areas of developing performance criteria and conducting evaluation sessions; being required to use

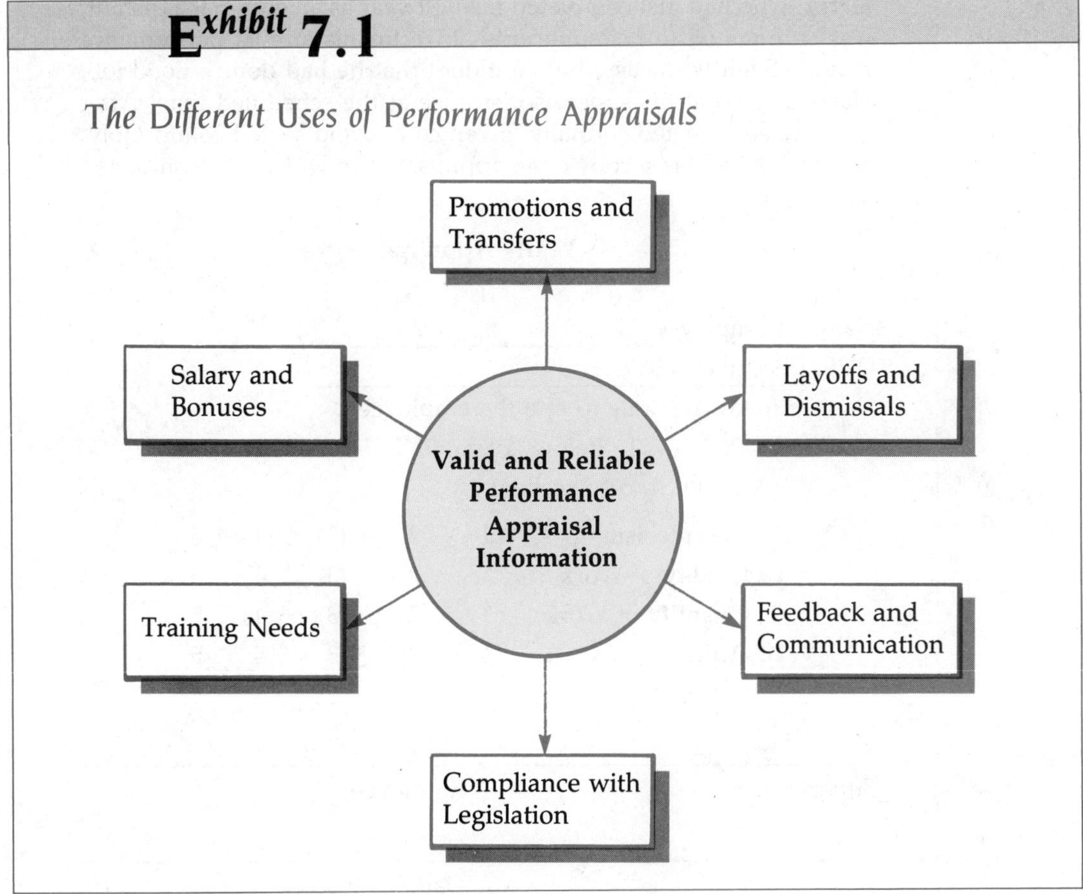

Exhibit 7.1

The Different Uses of Performance Appraisals

poorly developed rating scales; or being placed in the position of having to make subjective evaluations about employees. This chapter focuses on establishing relevant criteria, selecting an appropriate appraisal system, avoiding common rater pitfalls, and conducting evaluation sessions.

Establishing Criteria

In order for performance appraisal systems to be effective, both supervisors and workers must have comprehensive job knowledge. This information should be readily available if the organization has previously conducted job analyses. Too often, however, the absence of these analyses results in appraisals based on subjective evaluations of workers' personality characteristics rather than on their ability or inability to perform job duties. Consider the following case:

Harry, who had just completed his first year as an editorial assistant, was summoned to his superior's office for his annual performance review. Slightly uneasy, but confident that he had done a good job, Harry arrived at his supervisor's office at the scheduled time. After he had been greeted cordially, given coffee, and seated comfortably, Harry was handed a copy of an appraisal form which was completed as follows:

Yearly Appraisal

Name of Employee: Harry

Date: December, 1989

Use the following scale to rate the employee:

1—Poor 2—Below Average 3—Average
4—Good 5—Excellent

A. Absenteeism	1	2	(3)	4	5
B. Quality of Work	1	2	(3)	4	5
C. Quantity of Work	1	2	(3)	4	5
D. Attitude	1	(2)	3	4	5
E. Personality	1	(2)	3	4	5

Supervisor ____________ Employee ____________

Date ____________ Date ____________

Harry was mystified. Why had he never received any negative feedback until now? How are attitude and personality measured? What on earth is an average personality? Seeing his befuddled reaction, Harry's supervisor proceeded to tell him about the politics of organizations, and about how Harry had to learn to become a team player. He also gave him a lecture on the inappropriateness of a correspondence Harry had had with the company's president four months earlier. Speechless and dejected, Harry left the office. To this day, Harry is still not certain what he needs to do in order to improve his performance and obtain higher ratings.

The preceding case demonstrates the effects of conducting performance appraisals without clearly identified criteria. To maximize the use of performance reviews requires that attempts be made to identify and rate job-related behaviors. These behaviors can be measured objectively through the use of production and personnel data, and judgmentally by means of rating techniques.[1]

Production Data

The simplest method for determining worker productivity is to quantify the results of their work using **production data.** Line workers can be judged by how many units they produce, warehouse employees by the amount of units loaded and unloaded, salespersons by the amount of sales volume generated, and typists by the amount of words typed per day. In this method employee productivity is compared to some pre-established standard.

While it is tempting to use production data because of its obvious objectivity, several factors should be considered. First and foremost is the fact that many jobs are not quantifiable. It would be inappropriate to judge the effectiveness of trainers by summing the amount of trainees they teach, or to judge supervisors by how many pieces of paper they push across their desk in a given period of time. Rather, the impact of trainers on learning, and the impact of supervisors on their subordinates are the keys to their effectiveness.

The second problem with production data is the fact that the results obtained may not be solely attributable to worker effort. In individual performance assessments, attempts are made to differentiate one employee from another. Using production units as the sole criterion for judging performance implies that differences in total units produced are attributable to individual differences in either skill or effort. In fact, however, there are other extraneous influences on productivity. Winning a horse race may be a function of the speed of the horse as well as the ability of the jockey. Similarly, a worker who produces a large number of units may have a faster machine or more conducive working conditions. Judging workers purely on the basis of productivity output fails to take into consideration variables which are not under employee control.

Finally, it is foolhardy to merely quantify productivity without taking quality into account. Rapid typists who make many errors may not be as productive as slower, meticulous typists. Production workers who produce large amounts of defective units may cost the company more money in the long run than slower, errorless workers.

By itself, production data is insufficient. Combined with other measures of performance, it provides an additional source of information for use in a total evaluation system.

Personnel Data

Another form of objective data, which is not dependent on the task itself, is **personnel data.** Personnel data is usually maintained in personnel departments, and is valuable for performance appraisals. The data includes employee records concerning attendance, accident frequencies, and seniority.

Job attendance, which is usually measured in terms of absenteeism and tardiness, is the most frequently used measure of personnel data. Most companies maintain the philosophy that employees with good attendance records are more valuable to the company than those who are frequently absent. While there is a strong degree of truth inherent in this statement, absenteeism should not be considered in isolation, but in conjunction with other variables. Legitimately ill workers may be more valuable than employees who are absent less frequently for unexcused reasons. A worker who is absent for two weeks because of pneumonia is less damaging to a company than an employee who fails to appear for work, without prior notice, on seven consecutive Fridays. Organizations would be well advised to concern themselves with the underlying causes of absenteeism and tardiness, rather than the total amount of work time missed.[2]

Frequent accidents are costly to organizations. Lost work time, damaged equipment and materials, higher unemployment and medical premiums, and time spent filing accident reports are but a few of the costs that accidents impose on businesses. Realistically, the use of accident data is dependent on the particular job. Accident data gathered on airplane pilots, chauffeurs, truck drivers, and physicians is obviously a more significant measure of productivity than similar data collected on teachers, computer programmers, and secretaries. In industries and jobs where safety is a significant factor, companies rely heavily on accident data and reward individuals who have a low frequency of accidents.

There is a variety of viewpoints regarding the importance of seniority for appraisals. Arguments in favor of using this variable stress the high costs involved in training replacements. Individuals opposed to using seniority as a variable maintain that length of service is not necessarily indicative of competence. Employees who have been on the job ten years may or may not be more productive than workers employed for seven years. Depending on the particular situation, both arguments appear to have merit. Organizations with many employees in highly skilled positions find longevity an advantage, while companies with less training costs prefer rapid turnover. In general, the role of seniority in performance appraisal should be reserved for decisions between employees who are otherwise equal on all other levels. In these instances, length of service should be used to decide which employees should be promoted, transferred, advanced, or laid off.

Judgmental Data

Whenever possible, using objective measures for evaluation is preferable to using **subjective judgment.** Realistically, however, most jobs do not lend themselves to objective measurements. Often, performance is not quantifiably measurable and personnel data may contribute very little to performance assessment. The resulting evaluations are usually subjective in nature, relying upon judgments made by superiors. In an attempt to control for the inherent biases in subjective ratings, and to improve the validity and reliability of these appraisals, rating techniques are used.

Rating Techniques

Many different procedures are used to evaluate employees. Some techniques are simple to develop and use, while others require extensive developmental efforts coupled with lengthy user training programs. Regardless of the sophistication of the technique, however, they all have the goal of placing workers along some form of continuum of productivity effectiveness. A comprehensive discussion of all the techniques available is obviously beyond the scope of this book, so the present discussion centers on the most frequently used techniques. These include: graphic rating scales, ranking methods, paired comparisons, critical incidents, checklists, forced choice, Management by Objectives (MBO), and Behaviorally Anchored Rating Scales (BARS).

Graphic Rating Scales

Graphic rating scales, which can be traced back to 1922,[3] are one of the oldest and most widely used methods of performance appraisal. The use of these scales requires raters to judge employees on the degree to which they exhibit certain characteristics, such as quantity of work, quality of work, and dependability. Scales typically consist of between ten and fifteen factors, and workers are rated between one (usually denoting poor or worst) and five (denoting excellent or best) for each factor.[4]

> **Graphic rating scales**
>
> *Graphic rating scales require raters to judge employees on the degree to which they demonstrate certain factors deemed to be important in job performance.*

Graphic rating scales are simple to use, and they are readily understandable by both raters and workers. These factors probably account for the scales' wide popularity. Using the scale, however, requires that raters be aware of certain errors they may unwittingly commit. These include the halo error, leniency or strictness errors, and errors of central tendency.

Halo error The halo effect, a problem associated with selection interviewing which was discussed in Chapter 5, is similar to the **halo error.** The halo error involves the assignment of good or bad ratings to individuals based on general overall impressions, rather than true analysis of each factor. As a result, ratings that are given on one factor affect ratings given in unrelated categories. It is important to note that the halo error is not a conscious rating distortion. On the contrary, raters truly believe they are assigning appropriate ratings to individuals. This factor, more than any other, may explain the validity of the statement "more people are advanced, promoted and or fired due to personality reasons rather than ability to perform the job."[5]

> **Halo error**
>
> *The halo error is the tendency of raters to judge employees in favorable or unfavorable terms based on their general overall impressions of the individual rather than on true assessments of the specific rating factors.*

Exhibit 7.2

A Graphic Rating Scale Used by the U.S. Government

ASSESSMENT OF SUPERVISORY POTENTIAL/PERFORMANCE

1. EMPLOYEE'S NAME		2. POSITION *(Title/Series/Grade)*
3. IS THIS A SUPERVISORY POSITION? ☐ YES ☐ NO	4. PRESENT ORGANIZATION	
5. RATING OFFICER	6. RATER'S POSITION TITLE	7. DATE OF APPRAISAL
8. NO. OF MONTHS RATER HAS SUPERVISED EMPLOYEE:	9. PERIOD COVERED BY THIS RATING FROM: TO:	
10. REVIEWING OFFICIAL		11. REVIEWING OFFICIAL'S POSITION TITLE

INSTRUCTIONS

The importance of supervisory personnel in the management system of the agency requires special emphasis in promotion actions. This form is to be used in conjunction with the EPA Form 3115–5,General Performance Appraisal, required for all employees.

If the employee currently occupies a supervisory position, the form must be completed in terms of the employee's performance as a supervisor. If the employee does not currently occupy a supervisory position, the form must be completed in terms of the employee's *potential* to be a supervisor.

Rate the employee on each factor by placing an "X" in the appropriate box. Mark "NA" for those items which do not apply. When the form is completed, and signed, obtain the reviewing official's comments and signature and forward the form to the Personnel Office.

SUPERVISORY ABILITIES AND TRAITS	*TRUE OF HIM	MORE TRUE THAN FALSE	NEITHER TRUE NOR FALSE	MORE FALSE THAN TRUE	FALSE	DON'T KNOW
1. SUPERVISORY ABILITIES-EMPLOYEE DOES/WOULD						
a. DEFINE ASSIGNMENTS OR PROJECTS CLEARLY						
b. PLAN AND CARRY OUT ASSIGNMENTS EFFECTIVELY						
c. DELEGATE AUTHORITY AND RESPONSIBILITY AND WORK WITH AND THROUGH OTHERS EFFECTIVELY						
d. INSTRUCT, GUIDE, AND REVIEW THE WORK OF OTHERS EFFECTIVELY						
e. ESTABLISH AND MAINTAIN HIGH STANDARDS OF QUALITY AND QUANTITY FOR THE WORK PRODUCED						
f. BE FAIR AND OBJECTIVE IN DEALINGS WITH AND JUDGMENTS OF SUBORDINATES						
g. UNDERSTAND THE THEORIES AND TECHNIQUES OF SOUND PERSONNEL MANAGEMENT IN DEALING WITH EMPLOYEES, BOTH INDIVIDUALLY AND IN GROUPS						
h. MOTIVATE, TRAIN, DEVELOP, AND GUIDE EMPLOYEES OF VARIED BACKGROUNDS AND SKILL LEVELS EFFECTIVELY						
2. ORGANIZATION AND MANAGEMENT ABILITIES–EMPLOYEE DOES/WOULD						
a. DEVISE ECONOMICAL AND EFFECTIVE ORGANIZATIONAL OR OPERATIONAL PLANS AND PROCEDURES						
b. ESTABLISH PROGRAM OBJECTIVES OR PERFORMANCE GOALS AND ASSESS PROGRESS TOWARD THEIR ACHIEVEMENT						
c. ADJUST WORK ACTIVITIES AND SCHEDULES TO MEET EMERGENCY CONDITIONS OR UNANTICIPATED REQUIREMENTS						
d. UNDERSTAND, INTERPRET, AND GAIN SUPPORT FOR MANAGEMENT GOALS AND OBJECTIVES						
e. DEVELOP IMPROVEMENTS IN OR DESIGN NEW WORK METHODS AND PROCEDURES						
f. COORDINATE AND INTEGRATE THE WORK OF SUBORDINATE EMPLOYEES OR ORGANIZATIONAL SEGMENTS EFFECTIVELY						
g. RESOLVE ORGANIZATIONAL, MANAGEMENT, PERSONNEL, AND TECHNICAL PROBLEMS						
3. ABILITY TO MAKE RECOMMENDATIONS AND DECISIONS–HE DOES/WOULD						
a. ABSORB NEW FACTS AND CONCEPTS QUICKLY						
b. ANALYZE COMPLEX ISSUES OR PROBLEMS THOROUGHLY AND QUICKLY						
c. KEEP ORGANIZATIONAL OBJECTIVES IN MIND						
d. ASSESS THE ADVANTAGES AND DISADVANTAGES OF ALTERNATIVE PLANS OR COURSES OF ACTION						
e. MAKE SOUND DECISIONS, E.G., BASED ON PAST EXPERIENCE, PRESENT EFFORT, AND FUTURE OUTCOME						
f. ACCEPT RESPONSIBILITY						

EPA Form 3115–6 (3–73) REPLACES FORM HEW–526 WHICH WILL NOT BE USED

CONTINUED ON REVERSE

*Categories can be defined by adjectives or numerical equivalents, such as 1–5 and NA.

Leniency and strictness errors **Leniency and strictness errors** occur when raters demonstrate tendencies to evaluate all ratees either higher or lower than the normal standard. Students are well aware of professors who have histories of giving high grades and those who are notorious for giving low grades. These differences in ratings are usually a function of the deviation in rater standards. The higher the raters' personal standards are, the more likely it is that strict ratings will be imposed. Similarly, those with lower standards tend to rate more leniently.

The problems caused by leniency and strictness errors are more apparent when comparisons across raters are necessary. Suppose, for example, that several employees from different work groups are eligible for a supervisory promotion. To be able to effectively use performance appraisals as a selection criterion requires that all employees be evaluated equally. If the same individual rates all the employees, overly strict or lenient ratings do not distort the comparisons made among workers. The ratings for every employee are based on the same standard. On the other hand, if employees from work groups with different supervisors are being compared, the impact of these errors is more profound. Comparisons across groups may be invalid because of fluctuating standards of measurement.

Leniency and strictness errors

Leniency and strictness errors are the tendencies for raters to judge all ratees either higher or lower than acceptable standards.

Errors of central tendency When raters are reluctant to assign ratings other than average to all employees, **errors of central tendency** occur. These errors occur most often when raters are compelled to evaluate workers for whom they have minimal information. In addition, these errors are also found when the assignment of an exceptionally high or low rating results in raters having to defend their evaluations. Many companies unwittingly foster these errors by assigning new supervisors to work groups shortly before performance evaluations are due. Eager to demonstrate their proficiency, but lacking sufficient information to adequately rate their subordinates, these supervisors play it safe by assigning average scores to all workers.

Central tendency error

Central tendency error is a trend exhibited by raters who assign only average ratings to avoid the evaluation of all employees at the extreme ends of the scale.

Exhibit 7.3

*Forcing a Normal Distribution of Ratings**

Number of Employees Allowed per Category (25 Total)

1 (2%)	3 (14%)	17 (68%)	3 (14%)	1 (2%)
Poor (1)	Below Average (2)	Average (3)	Good (4)	Excellent (5)

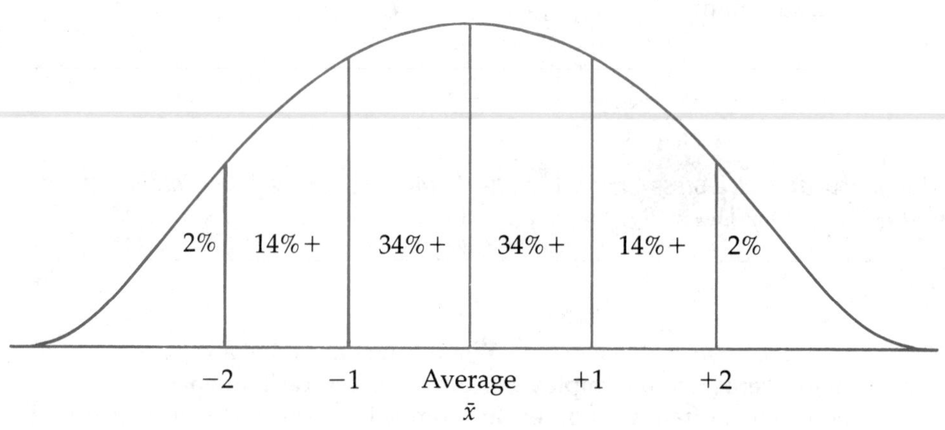

***Note:** The forced distribution may be any number per category chosen by the organization. For example, 5% in the high and low categories, 20% in the middle two categories, and 50% in the middle (average) category.

Ranking Method

One of the simplest rating methods is the rank ordering of employees, by merit, along a continuum from best to worst. The **ranking method** may be utilized in two ways. Workers may be evaluated in terms of total performance (that is, who is number one, two, or three in terms of overall productivity), or rated separately for individual performance factors (that is, who is number one, two, or three for quality of work; who is number one, two, or three for dependability, and so on).[6]

Ranking method

The ranking method involves evaluating and ranking workers along a continuum from best to worst, without regard to how much better or worse each is from the other.

There are three basic problems which may develop when the ranking method is used. First, the technique is highly subjective, and raters can suffer from the halo error. Second, as the number of workers to be evaluated increases, the evaluation procedure becomes increasingly more difficult. While most evaluators can usually identify their best and worst workers, they experience difficulty differentiating among employees in the middle of the continuum. Obviously, the greater the number of employees to be evaluated, the more difficult the discrimination becomes. Finally, the results of the ranking method position workers in terms of performance, but they fail to indicate the degree to which individual workers differ from one another. Thus, the disparity between the number two ranked employee and the number three ranked employee might be minimal, while the difference between the number three ranked employee and the number four ranked employee may be substantial.

Another problem with the ranking method is its comparison base. By their very nature, rankings require that individuals be compared with, and against, other employees. Most appraisal literature recommends that employees be compared to job criteria, not to other workers. Using the ranking method encourages individual comparison.

Without a doubt, ranking is at best a rudimentary method of evaluation. The use of this method should be reserved for situations where:

1. Small numbers of employees are to be rated.
2. The rating concern is only with best or worst, without regard to how much better or worse.
3. The workers will not be compared across groups.
4. Feedback to employees is not a prime purpose of the evaluation procedure.[7]

Paired Comparisons

The **paired comparison** method requires raters to compare each worker to every other worker and to judge who is better. This method is usually used to compare workers on overall performance, and while it can be used to make comparisons on several dimensions, it is rarely used in this manner. The reason for not using the method with large numbers of employees, or to make comparisons on several factors, is the number of evaluations which are necessary. The number of comparisons necessary can be computed by the formula $N(N - 1)/2$, where N is equal to the number of workers to be evaluated. For example, the number of comparisons necessary for a group of twenty (20) people would be 20(20 – 1)/2 or 190. If there were ten different dimensions for which evaluations had to be made, then the rater would be required to make 1900 comparisons (190 times 10). As a result, the method of paired comparisons is reserved for use with groups consisting of small numbers of workers, who are rated on only a few work dimensions. When large numbers of workers are involved, or when several factors are to be rated, the use of this method is unwieldy.

Paired comparisons

The paired comparisons method requires raters to compare each employee within the group to every other employee, and to determine who is the better worker on a specific factor.

Critical Incidents

The **critical incident** technique of performance appraisal[8] requires the supervisor to maintain records of significant occurrences, both positive and negative, which affect performance. Designed to eliminate rater biases associated with subjective evaluations, the critical incident technique requires raters to focus on and document actual job behaviors. Using critical incidents facilitates the feedback process by providing the worker with concrete examples of actual behaviors which should be continued, modified, or eliminated.

Although the critical incident technique appears to overcome many of the subjectivity problems associated with other appraisal systems, it has disadvantages as well. In order to be effective, it requires that supervisors maintain a continual record on workers. Most supervisors, however, become lax in maintaining logs, and they mistakenly rely on their memories to recall significant events. The end result is an appraisal error called the *recency error* (discussed in detail later in this chapter), in which raters tend to remember only those behaviors which occurred recently (usually within the last two weeks). When supervisors do maintain continual logs, other problems often develop. Some workers, knowing that their supervisor is documenting their behaviors, become anxious and hostile. Others tend to hide those behaviors which they feel will adversely affect their reviews. In either case, the end results are distorted performance reviews.

Critical incident technique

The critical incident technique requires the rater to log, identify, and record those behaviors, both positive and negative, which have a significant impact on performance.

Checklists

The **checklist** method requires evaluators to review a list of several behaviors, traits, or job characteristics and to indicate which statements best exemplify employee performance. In the usual case, the list represents previously determined critical incidents. A more sophisticated version of this appraisal technique is the **weighted checklist,** which assigns a relative value to each item on the list. Each behavior is evaluated in terms of its importance for job performance. Those items deemed most important are assigned higher numerical values (weights). Workers' scores on the appraisal are determined by summing the scores of the items checked by the raters.

The advantages of using checklists lie in their simplicity and feedback benefits. Generally, evaluators are required to make simple yes–no or true–false responses on checklists. As a result, time is used economically, and a greater number of items can be included on the checklist. These features provide workers with a large amount of relevant performance feedback. On the other hand, however, checklist users are susceptible to all the errors inherent in subjective evaluations. Raters can readily ascertain which statements represent positive traits, and although they are usually unaware of the assigned point values, they can determine which items are worth more points. As a result, halo errors, leniency and strictness errors, and other biases may enter into the appraisal.[9]

Checklist method

The checklist method requires evaluators to review a list of critical job behaviors, traits, or characteristics and to check those items which the employee demonstrates.

Forced-Choice Method

The **forced-choice method,** which was developed during World War II,[10] attempts to eliminate the raters' knowledge of whether or not they are giving the employee a good overall score. In the simplest form of this method, items are presented in pairs, and the rater must select the item which best describes the worker. The pairs of items are constructed in such a way that raters must choose between two equally attractive or unattractive alternatives. Each item is subsequently paired throughout the scale with other equally desirable or undesirable factors. For example, raters may have to choose between describing the worker as ambitious or dependable, two highly desirable traits. Or, raters may have to choose between describing workers as slovenly or disorderly, two undesirable traits. Based on the ratings assigned, profiles of employee on-the-job behaviors and traits are determined.

The advantage of the forced-choice technique is that it truly minimizes rater bias. Unfortunately, the development of appropriate scales requires professional assistance in creating equally attractive and unattractive items. The result is an exceptionally expensive rating procedure. Furthermore, the use of the technique for providing employee feedback, one of the primary purposes of performance appraisals, is greatly reduced. Because raters are not even certain of whether they are giving good or bad evaluations, they experience extreme difficulty in explaining results to workers.[11]

> **Forced-choice method**
>
> *The forced-choice method requires raters to choose from pairs of equally attractive or unattractive alternatives the one factor which they feel best describes the worker.*

Management by Objectives (MBO)

Management by objectives is a philosophy of management which can be traced back to 1954.[12] When using management by objectives, individuals:

1. Establish and discuss goals and objectives together with their supervisors.
2. Formulate action plans.
3. Review and modify their behavior.
4. Have evaluations based on how well they achieved their planned objectives.

The success of this program depends largely upon the ability of the employees and managers to establish measurable and verifiable objectives of performance. In its ideal form, MBO requires upper-level management to establish their objectives and communicate them to their subordinates. The subordinates follow the same process until all levels of workers in the organization have established objectives and formulated action plans. The end result is a clear set of objectives throughout the company, all of which lead to the accomplishment of the overall organizational objectives.

> **Management by objectives**
>
> *Management by objectives (MBO) is a process in which individual goals and action plans designed to mesh with the overall organizational objectives are implemented and systematically reviewed and revised.*

In addition to ongoing informal assessments, MBO programs incorporate periodic formal evaluations. The major purpose of these reviews is to identify any previously unforeseen problems and to develop methods for eliminating

Exhibit 7.4

An MBO System's Objectives for Bank Executives

Position	Behavioral objective
President and CEO	To gain approval from the Board of Directors by November 15 for the capital expenditures required to establish two new supermarket branches.
Vice President Operations	To establish two new supermarket branches by March 15.
Vice President Marketing	To alert the public of the establishment of two new banking branches through weekly advertising on the radio and in the local newspaper.
Vice President Loans	To train four new loan officers by March 15.
Vice President Personnel	To select and train two branch managers, two assistant branch managers, and eight tellers by March 15.

them. These reviews are typically held one-on-one, but they may also involve group discussions.

The implementation of MBO is facilitated by the use of a series of eight interdependent steps. These steps are:

1. The formulation of long-range organizational goals and plans.
2. The development of key area objectives to be accomplished, as well as the time period in which they are to be completed.
3. The establishment of subobjectives.
4. The establishment of standards of performance.
5. The formulation of action plans designed to meet the objectives.
6. The implementation of corrective action when necessary.
7. The systematic review and evaluation of individual progress toward the attainment of the goals.
8. The appraising, reinforcing, and strengthening of appropriate behaviors through training, rewards, and career planning.[13]

Over the past thirty-five years, the popularity of MBO programs has diminished. Although the benefits from a well-designed program are substantial, few organizations have been able to implement a true MBO process. Viewing MBO as a panacea, companies have overlooked the fact that it is a philosophy of management, rather than an operating tool to be used. In order to reap the benefits of an MBO program, organizations must have well-established communication channels. Regretfully, most organizations are lacking in this crucial area. As a result, MBO is rarely used in its original form, but is constantly modified to fit the existing organizational management philosophy. The end result is usually a system of one-way communication in which workers and lower level managers are required to submit their objectives, but they are not privy to their superiors' goals. Any meshing of individual objectives with overall organizational goals is usually purely coincidental. Furthermore, although most managers begin the process in earnest, their interest diminishes rapidly. As a result, objectives are established, action plans are formulated, but the process of adequate systematic reviews rarely occurs. Without this phase, MBO becomes just another planning procedure.

Behaviorally Anchored Rating Scales (BARS)

One of the major problems inherent in rating scales is that subjective evaluations are required to interpret scale values. Whether an employee is rated as poor, average, or above average for a given behavior is dependent upon the rater's conception of what these terms mean. **Behaviorally anchored rating scales** (BARS) were introduced as an attempt to overcome the ambiguity associated with interpreting rating scale values.[14]

> ***Behaviorally anchored rating scales* (BARS)**
>
> BARS *require evaluators to rate employees on a scale continuum of defined critical behaviors ranging from negative to positive.*

The BARS approach requires the development of scales which incorporate the use of critical incidents to identify scale points. Rather than requiring raters to judge the merit of employee actions, actual behaviors are listed along the continuum. Raters seek out the scale points (critical incidents) which coincide with particular work behavior. For example, a scale for evaluating the performance of a dormitory Resident Advisor may include an item for evaluation such as "Is consistent and assertive in dealing with students who do not follow policies." Instead of requiring raters to evaluate performance on a scale of poor to excellent, behavioral anchors would be developed such as:

1. Deals immediately with individual violations and does so in an educational manner.
2. Deals with individual violations in the same manner all the time, and shows little diversity of action.
3. Vacillates or is arbitrary in dealing with students who do not meet expectations.

Assessment by raters requires the identification of behaviors on the scale which employees frequently demonstrate.

Developing a behaviorally anchored rating scale is a complex, time-consuming task.

Exhibit 7.5

BARS Scale for Resident Advisor Dimension

Position: *Resident Advisor*
Dimension: *Knowledge of Students*

Rating	Points	Behavioral anchor
Excellent	10 points	Knows relevant background information about 85% or more of the students in the unit. Knowledge includes family, campus activities, peer group, and future goals and aspirations.
	9 points	
Good	8 points	Knows relevant background information, present campus activities, peer reference group, and future goals of between 50% and 84% of the students in the unit.
	7 points	
Average	6 points	Knows relevant information, but does not know goals and aspirations of unit members.
	5 points	
	4 points	
Below Average	3 points	Is cognizant of only a small number of unit members' backgrounds, campus activities, peergroupings, and/or goals and aspirations. Makes a demonstrated effort to obtain this information.
	2 points	
	1 point	
Poor	0 points	Is unaware of the backgrounds, activities, or goals of their unit members, and makes no effort to identify this information.

Source: Marc G. Singer and Lynn M. Loeffler, *Rating Resident Advisors* (Harrisonburg, VA: M.C. Press, 1976): 6–13.

1. Groups of employees or supervisors gather together to identify and define all the relevant job characteristics necessary for successful performance.
2. Another group of workers provides examples of behaviors which demonstrate high, medium, and low performance for each job characteristic.
3. A third group is then given the job characteristics and a randomized list of the behavioral examples as determined by the second group. The third group's task is to match the behaviors provided by the second group with the job characteristics determined by the first group. This process is called *retranslation*.
4. The characteristics which survive the retranslation process are forwarded to yet another group which attaches values to each scale item.
5. The scale is given to supervisors for use in rating their subordinates.[15]

Many organizations do not employ BARS because of the length of time and the cost involved in developing a system. When used, however, it does offer several advantages. First, because its development involves large numbers of employees and supervisors, it lends credibility to the evaluation process by requiring critical, in-depth study of the characteristics necessary for successful job performance. Second, it requires evaluators to rate actual, observable worker actions, rather than to make subjective interpretations about employees. Last, by providing all levels of workers with easily understandable behavioral characteristics, BARS appears to enhance the feedback process.[16]

Who Conducts Evaluations?

Once evaluation criteria and instruments have been selected, the next step is to determine who will conduct the evaluations. For most organizations, the appraisal process is a management function of the employee's immediate supervisor. There are, however, alternatives to this procedure. These include the use of self-appraisals, as well as peer, committee, and subordinate evaluations.

Immediate supervisors Most organizations conducting performance reviews use the immediate supervisor as the sole evaluator, or they use supervisory judgments in conjunction with other appraisals.[17] There are several logical reasons for these options. Immediate supervisors know the job requirements of their work units, and they are able to determine how each job interfaces with the total organizational structure. They are in close contact with employees on a continual basis and should be in the best position to evaluate employees' strengths and weaknesses. Finally, because supervisors usually control the rewards and punishments administered to workers, it is more likely that employees will give credibility to their evaluations.

Exhibit 7.6

Advantages and Disadvantages of Using the Various Performance Appraisal Methods[18]

	Graphic	MBO	Ranking	BARS	Paired comparison	Critical incident	Checklist	Forced choice
Cost of development	Fair	Fair	Low	High	Low	Fair	Fair	Low
Cost of use	Low	High	Low	Low	Low	High	Low	Low
Ease of use	Good	Fair	Good	Good	Fair	Poor	Good	Poor
Ability to give feedback	Fair	Good	Poor	Good	Poor	Good	Fair	Poor
Salary and bonuses	Fair	Fair	Good	Good	Good	Good	Fair	Good
Promotions and transfers	Fair	Fair	Good	Good	Good	Good	Fair	Good
Assessing training needs	Fair	Good	Poor	Good	Poor	Good	Good	Poor
Compliance with government regulations	Good	Good	Poor	Good	Poor	Good	Good	Poor

Self-appraisals Self-appraisals involve individuals rating themselves on characteristics which they feel are important for good performance. The value of self-appraisals probably resides in how they are used. When appraisals are used for determining pay and other incentives, it is likely that they will be greatly exaggerated. On the other hand, if the evaluations are used strictly for feedback purposes, employees will tend to reflect their true performance more accurately.

The popularity of self-appraisals has increased largely because of the increased involvement of organizations in individual goal-setting programs. The use of MBO, for example, is dependent to a great extent on individuals being able to establish goals, and subsequently to review and modify their behavior. Individuals demonstrate exceptional capabilities when analyzing their needs, especially in determining training requirements. Furthermore, when used in conjunction with supervisory evaluations, self-appraisals provide excellent feedback vehicles.[19]

Peer evaluations Although they are rarely used as evaluators, peers and co-workers may possibly be the most valid sources of appraisal information. Peers are familiar with the job requirements, they have ample opportunity to observe relevant and critical behaviors, and they provide a large sample of evaluators. Organizations overlook peer evaluations for several reasons. First, many peers are reluctant to evaluate their co-workers.[20] Second, employees view themselves in competition for the finite rewards provided by organizations. Subconsciously, they may protect their own interests by rating co-workers at a lower level. Finally, most workers lack the training and knowledge necessary to conduct adequate ratings.[21]

Committee evaluations In an attempt to eliminate some of the biases found in individual performance ratings, some organizations are turning to rating committees. This technique involves multiple raters, usually managers one level above the employee being rated, who have had contact with the worker. The advantage of this technique is that multiple raters would probably have observed varying behaviors. In addition, when several raters are involved, individual biases are reduced.

On the negative side, committee appraisals require excessive time and scheduling to discuss and rate individuals. Conflicting ratings, which must be negotiated, are more taxing and demand additional time. Furthermore, the use of this technique requires the cooperation of several supervisors who are familiar with the worker's behavior. For most organizations, it is a rarity that more than one supervisor will have ample opportunity to observe a worker's behavior.

Subordinate evaluations The use of immediate subordinate ratings within organizations is limited. Faced with evaluating their superiors, many workers tend to exaggerate the ratings either positively or negatively. Some employees view these ratings as an opportunity to score points, while others use the ratings to get even for past injustices. Furthermore, employees tend to rate supervisors based on their perceived organizational power and authority, rather than on their actual performance.[22]

The major advantage of subordinate ratings is their ability to identify supervisory communication skills, demonstrated interest in workers, and skill in obtaining needed resources. On the other hand, workers usually possess little knowledge regarding the supervisor's overall job duties. This factor, coupled with the previously mentioned biases, tends to minimize the benefits of subordinate ratings.

Conducting the Evaluation

For most supervisors and workers alike, the mention of performance appraisals generates thoughts of a formal process conducted once a year. In actuality, however, the appraisal process should be an informal, ongoing day-to-day practice. It is untenable to imagine a situation where an employee makes errors in January and is not informed of the mistakes until the formal review process in July. Similarly, when a worker demonstrates good performance, positive reinforcement should be accorded swiftly. Unfortunately, most supervisors provide negative feedback almost instantaneously, but seem to wait until the formal review process before providing positive reinforcement. For performance reviews to have the desired effect of improving performance, both positive and negative feedback should be provided continually.

While most performance appraisal researchers stress the importance of daily feedback, few supervisors seem to adhere to these principles. Instead, most of them rely on the formal yearly evaluation sessions for providing feedback. As a result, the manner in which raters prepare for and conduct review sessions is crucial to the appraisal process.

The Planning Stage

The performance appraisal process usually culminates in an evaluation interview. During this session, raters provide workers with a detailed account of their strengths and weaknesses in an effort to improve employee performance. Like employment interviewing, the ultimate success of these sessions depends, to a large extent, on the skill of the interviewer. The amount of prior effort placed on the gathering of information and the techniques employed in the actual session will determine the ultimate success of the process.

In order to effect change in the behavior of individuals, two factors are necessary. First, the individuals must be aware of the negative behavior, and second, they must be willing to change it. A large part of the rater's job is to bring these behaviors to the attention of workers in such a manner that they not only understand them, but also have a desire to adopt more appropriate actions. The successful accomplishment of this task requires raters to gather behavioral data for the entire evaluation period and to present it to employees in a non-threatening, helpful manner.

Gathering data—using behavioral logs Like selection interviewing, a large part of the success of the evaluation interview is dependent on the amount of homework the interviewer performs prior to the actual session. For raters, this involves gathering performance data about each employee and completing the appraisal form or scale. While completing this task, many raters unwittingly commit a performance error known as the **recency error.**

Recency error

The recency error is the tendency to evaluate employees based on their most recent or current actions rather than on their behaviors over the entire evaluation period.

To overcome this error, raters are well advised to keep **behavioral logs** on employees. These logs involve the daily recording in a diary of employees' positive and negative actions. When the time to make evaluations approaches, raters can refer to these logs rather than relying purely on their memories. As a result, workers are evaluated for their performance over the entire period, rather than just the last two weeks.

Behavioral logs

Behavioral logs are daily diaries kept on workers, in which both positive and negative behaviors are recorded.

The appraisal session should not be scheduled until the relevant data has been collected and the appropriate appraisal scale has been completed. It is essential that sufficient time be set aside for conducting the interview. In addition, privacy during the session and a comfortably arranged environment should be provided.

The Interview Stage

The purpose of the appraisal interview is to detail diagnostic feedback to employees so that they can either enhance positive actions or eliminate inappropriate behavior. Viewed in this fashion, appraisal interviews are akin to training sessions. Employees would be expected to approach these sessions with the anticipation of learning. In fact, however, most workers view appraisal sessions as salary reviews, and they approach them with a degree of trepidation. As a result, the initial task of evaluators is to establish a learning climate by reducing anxiety, establishing rapport, and choosing an interview approach which is most appropriate for the particular employee.

Reducing anxiety and establishing rapport The initial task of the evaluator is to create a climate which reduces the defensiveness of the worker. If employees view the sessions as disciplinary meetings designed solely for the purpose of determining salary raises, they will be highly defensive. Workers believe that admitting to having performed inappropriate behaviors is tantamount to reducing their own raises. As a result they refuse to accept negative feedback, and they fail to take corrective action. The superior should place employees at ease by assuring them that the sessions are designed to improve performance and to foster self-development. To aid in accomplishing this goal, it is sometimes advisable to inform the worker of his or her wage increase at the beginning of the session rather than at the end. Once the discussion of wages is concluded, there is a greater tendency to view negative feedback openly rather than defensively.

Another technique which aids in fostering rapport is the use of positive feedback. Whenever possible, raters should begin with positive behaviors, conclude with positive actions, and sandwich negative behaviors in between. The entire discussion should focus on the improvement of future performance, rather than on criticisms of past behaviors.

Exhibit 7.7

Ten Tips to Good Performance Reviews

1. Evaluate performance, not personality characteristics.
2. Base the appraisal on thorough job analyses.
3. Use critical incidents, not trivial acts.
4. Train appraisers in techniques to use and errors to avoid.
5. Keep managers and supervisors appraised of legal issues.
6. Conduct appraisals in writing and have employees sign the form to verify that they have been informed of the rating.
7. Don't use past appraisals as a basis for current evaluations.
8. Make certain that the appraisal form is valid for every purpose for which it is being used.
9. Periodically audit the appraisal and make necessary adjustments.
10. Appraise daily. Formal appraisals are no substitute for providing ongoing feedback.

Choosing an interviewing approach There are three generally accepted approaches from which to choose when conducting evaluation interviews. These include: the tell and sell approach, the tell and listen approach, and the problem-solving approach.[23]

Tell and sell approach The **tell and sell approach** to evaluation interviewing is based on the premise that employees desire to change weaknesses of which they are aware. The rater's role as a superior is to judge the employee and to effect behavioral change through the art of persuasion. The success of this method relies on the degree of linking and respect that the employee has for the supervisor. The more highly respected and liked the superior is, the more likely it is that this method will be successful.

Tell and listen approach The **tell and listen approach** is designed to overcome the defensiveness which many employees bring to the evaluation setting. This method is based on the premise that individuals will change their behavior once their defensive feelings are removed. When employing this technique, evaluators use standard interviewing techniques such as reflecting, probing, and summarizing in an attempt to display an environment of empathy. This method fosters the development of favorable attitudes toward the superior, which heightens the potential for success of the session.

Problem-solving approach The **problem-solving approach** incorporates many of the techniques involved in non-directive interviewing. The goal of this approach to evaluation is for employees to progress beyond releasing their feelings by developing new ideas and interests. When using this method, evaluators become counselors and help employees to realize their own potentials. Without a doubt, the use of this method assures acceptance by the employee, but sometimes the changes which occur may be in directions the superior had not foreseen.

Rater Errors—Some Realism

The effectiveness of performance appraisals depends largely on the ability of raters to evaluate employees as objectively as possible. Throughout this chapter, mention has been made of the errors inherent in performance appraisals. These errors confound the evaluation process by causing evaluators to move from objective behavior evaluations into the realm of subjectivity. Included within this group are errors such as: the halo effect, strictness and leniency errors, the error of central tendency, and the recency effect.

In addition to the inherent errors caused by raters, organizations unwittingly confound the rating process by using unqualified raters to make evaluations, by using poorly designed appraisal instruments, and by requiring raters to defend extreme ratings.

Using unqualified raters Many supervisors who are required to evaluate employees are unqualified to perform ratings. In order to adequately conduct evaluations, supervisors must be well trained in observing and recording behavior, in interviewing skills, and in ways of overcoming the pitfalls involved in performance evaluations. Unfortunately, for many companies, the total amount of effort expended for performance review training consists of a one-day seminar

Exhibit 7.8

Some Performance Appraisal Errors

Central tendency
The tendency to rate all workers toward a mid-point or average.

Different from me
The tendency to assign poorer ratings to workers who demonstrate characteristics or behaviors different from those of the rater.

Halo effect
The tendency to allow the rating of an individual in one category to influence, either positively or negatively, the rating in other categories.

Introductory impression
The tendency to evaluate individuals based on initial impressions, rather than on sustained performance over time.

Leniency error
The tendency to assign favorable ratings to all employees.

Person-to-person
The tendency to compare individuals with other individuals rather than to rate them by established job standards.

Recency error
The tendency to assign ratings based on the most recent behaviors of individuals, rather than on their performance over the entire rating period.

Same-as-me
The tendency to assign higher ratings to individuals who demonstrate traits or behaviors similar to the rater.

Set responses
The tendency to rate individuals similarly on all characteristics instead of attending to all scale items.

Spillover effect
The tendency to rate individuals based on their past evaluations, rather than on their current performance.

Strictness error
The tendency to rate all employees harshly.

Exhibit 7.9

Performance Appraisal Time Again

It's ironic that most employees eagerly look forward to a performance evaluation. Most bosses dread it! Why should that be?

Here's my opinion. As employees, most of us are starved for recognition. We yearn to be told that what we do is important, that we have made a positive contribution, that the company is better off because we're here, and that the people for whom we work really do appreciate us. We feel deprived of performance feedback, and eagerly anticipate that some of these needs will be addressed in a performance evaluation discussion with the boss.

As bosses, a lot of us worry that if we acknowledge to employees that they're really doing a good job, they'll get a "swelled head," demand more money or somehow become less subservient. We're also concerned that we might get into an argument or hurt an employee's feelings when we have to deal with people whose performance doesn't quite measure up. Some insecure bosses fear that their employees will find out there are things about the job the boss doesn't know.

The employee and the boss should collaborate on setting goals at the beginning of the year. They should consult frequently throughout the year as to progress being made, problems encountered, changes that are necessary, ways to improve, etc.

Immediately after the end of the year, all exempt level employees will have a performance evaluation discussion with their bosses as required by corporate policy. Many other employees will undergo the same procedure in accordance with division practice. The purpose of this exercise is to review, wrap up and document the year's activity and to begin planning the next year's objectives.

Here are some tips for bosses to make performance appraisals more pleasant and effective:

1. Evaluate the performance—not the person.
2. Measure the person's performance against an objective, observable standard—not against your subjective feeling about what he/she should have done. Be specific—use examples.
3. Remember—every employee has a right to see his/her performance through the boss' eyes.
4. Remember—no person can improve performance at anything they do unless they get objective, real-world feedback.
5. Let the chips fall where they may. Don't think in terms of good and bad—think in terms of helping employees count how many times they've hit the target and how they might improve their batting averages.

Source: Harold L. Durrett, Vice-President, Human Resources, Rocco Enterprises, "Performance Appraisal Time Again," *Rocco Messenger*, Vol. 3, No. 4 (Winter 1987): 21. Reprinted with permission.

6. Don't look at this as a one-sided conversation. Most employees know more about their own performance than the boss knows, and most will be helpful and objective in the process if you'll give them the opportunity. If the employee doesn't do at least half the talking, you've done something wrong.
7. Be unflinching and nonthreatening. Become the employee's ally in tallying up the score and planning how to improve it. Don't gloss over or ignore low scores, but don't beat people over the head with them either.
8. Don't feel you have to find something wrong with every employee's performance. While no one is perfect, there are a lot of employees who clear all the major hurdles and meet all performance standards. It's okay to help such people plan improvements, but don't make the mistake of raising the performance standard each time until the employee fails to make it.

These are tips when you're on the receiving end of a performance evaluation:

1. Don't be defensive. When you have fallen short of achieving a goal, acknowledge it and enlist the boss' help in figuring out how to reach it next time.
2. Remember, the boss needs help in this process. Participate willingly and enthusiastically.
3. Don't bluff, cover up or deceive. Trying to fool the boss is an employee's most deadly mistake, and it never works over the long haul.
4. Don't make this a gripe session. Your complaints and gripes should be dealt with as they occur, and not saved up for this occasion. They can poison the atmosphere to a point where the objective of performance evaluation is obscured.

Both the employee and the supervisor should look at goal setting and performance evaluation as a joint endeavor designed to maximize the employee's contribution, to help the employee become more valuable to the company, to help the employee develop to the maximum of his/her potential, and to aid the employee in exploiting whatever abilities he/she possesses for personal benefit. Viewed in this context, a performance evaluation discussion can be a pleasant, exciting and positive experience for both.

on appraisals. For the performance review process to have the desired effect, extensive training, including the use of experiential methods, is a necessity. Companies which fail to provide this training are likely to be faced with unqualified raters who unwittingly create anxiety, frustration, and hostility among the employees.

Poorly designed instruments Obviously, a performance appraisal scale which is invalid or unreliable should not be used. However, even valid instruments can sometimes cause rating problems. One of the most common problems with rating scales is that they fail to provide an opportunity for raters to indicate that they do not have sufficient information in order to make an evaluation. Without this category, raters find themselves in the uncomfortable position of having to evaluate employees on behaviors which they have had an inadequate opportunity to observe. When faced with this task, raters usually make evaluations in one of two ways. Either they will assign a rating of *average* to those categories which they have had insufficient opportunity to observe or, if they are influenced by the halo effect, they will assign scores similar to the pattern of ratings the worker has been receiving. To eliminate this potential problem, scales should include a rating category allowing evaluators the opportunity to indicate that they do not have sufficient information to make adequate evaluations.

Defending the extremes Many companies reduce the amount of available rating categories by requiring raters to justify extreme evaluations. Suppose, for example, that an organization requires that any evaluations of either one or six on a six-point scale be accompanied by a letter explaining the rating. All other ratings, however, do not require similar documentation. The likelihood of supervisors using the extremes is nil. Most employees will receive ratings between two and five. In effect, the scale has been reduced from a six-point scale to a four-point scale.

Appraisals and the Law

Performance appraisals are viewed by the courts as tests. In this vein, they are subject to all the legislation applicable to selection instruments. They must be validated and monitored, and their use must not contribute to illegal discriminatory practices.

In order to use performance appraisals within the established guidelines, several prerequisites are necessary. First, appraisals must be based on current and comprehensive job analyses. Second, raters must be trained in rating techniques, including communication principles involved in providing feedback. Third, all information used for personnel decisions must be well documented. Last, constant monitoring and updating of the system should be undertaken to eliminate any potential discriminatory biases.

Summary

Performance appraisal is the process by which managers and supervisors observe worker behavior in order to provide employees with diagnostic feedback concerning their strengths and weaknesses. The logic behind the evaluation process is that work performance will be improved if employees are provided with relevant information concerning both their positive and negative behaviors.

For many organizations, performance evaluations are formalized procedures which are conducted annually or semi-annually. These appraisals consist primarily of the completion by supervisors of rating scales which evaluate the work performance of employees. These scales range in sophistication from simple ranking procedures to highly complex systems involving intricate designs. Regardless of the complexity of the system, however, the basic goal of performance appraisal is to provide feedback to employees about their work effectiveness.

In order to enhance the evaluation process, organizations must embark on rater training programs. This training should include information on methods for observing behavior and proper ways of conducting evaluation interviews, and it should also instill an awareness of the errors inherent in conducting evaluations. In addition, organizations must constantly monitor and update appraisal systems to make certain that they comply with prevailing government rules and regulations.

Key Terms to Identify

Production data
Personnel data
Judgmental data
Graphic rating scales
Halo error
Leniency and strictness errors
Errors of central tendency
Ranking method
Paired comparison
Critical incident technique
Checklist
Weighted checklist
Forced-choice method
Management by objectives (MBO)
Behaviorally anchored rating scales (BARS)
Recency error
Behavioral logs
Tell and sell approach
Tell and listen approach
Problem-solving approach

Questions for Discussion

Do You Know the Facts?

1. What are the advantages and disadvantages of appraising employee performance using objective and judgmental data?
2. Discuss how rating errors subjectively, and often unwittingly, influence the accurate assessment of employee performance.
3. Who are the sources of performance appraisal information? How do each of them contribute to the knowledge of employee performance?
4. Discuss the stages involved in conducting a performance appraisal.

Can You Apply the Information Learned?

1. How does the management of performance appraisal systems contribute to an organization's effective use, or potential misuse, of human resources?
2. How may the human resource department assist the supervisors of other departments in designing and implementing effective performance appraisal programs?
3. What steps can be taken to minimize the subjectivity inherent in appraising employee performance?
4. Discuss how you would decide what performance appraisal scale and/or technique you would use within an organization. How would you train first line supervisors in the important principles of your program?

Appraising the Appraiser

It was almost December. For Sherry Majors, December meant conducting performance evaluations and her first real challenge as a manager. As she searched frantically for her old lecture notes, she recalled how her human resource management instructor kept telling the class how hard and important it was to conduct good performance appraisals. "The main purpose of appraisals is to provide the worker with feedback. Too many managers mess it up. Avoid . . ." Gosh, she just couldn't remember! Like all the other students, Sherry had been too concerned with whether or not the material would be on the examination. A scant six months later, when she needed to use it, it was forgotten.

Finally, she found her notes and began reading. "Keep a behavioral log." How could she have been so foolish? She had forgotten to do it. Now, all she could recall was what her employees had done over the last two weeks. She read on. "Be objective! Subjectivity should be kept to a minimum!" How do you do it? The appraisal forms required her to rate the workers on attitude, initiative, and cooperation. Furthermore, Sherry had to rate each worker as poor, below average, average, good, or excellent on each factor. What's a good attitude? What's average cooperation? "Avoid these common pitfalls." Sherry closed the book. The more she read, the more anxious she became. There had to be a better way. But what?

After what seemed like hours of anxiety, Sherry decided to call her friend Sam. Sam Justice had graduated a year earlier than Sherry, and was employed in a similar position at another plant. Perhaps he had experienced the same problem and had found a solution. When Sherry explained her predicament, Sam began laughing. Just as she had deduced, Sam had experienced the same problem and had found a solution. He had reviewed the employees' past appraisals and scored the new appraisals within the same basic range. If an employee had received an average rating previously, Sam recorded either an average or good. After all, B students usually got Bs all the time, and C students got Cs. Why should workers be any different?

The solution was so simple. Sherry thanked Sam and called personnel for copies of her workers' previous performance reviews. After reviewing the reports, she began to fill out the new forms. It was easy. Obviously, professors really didn't know what happened in the "real world."

The next two weeks were a nightmare. It seemed that none of Sherry's employees were willing to accept her subjective explanations as valid reasons for their ratings.

Questions for Discussion

1. What should Sherry have done to prepare herself for conducting the performance appraisals?
2. What major mistakes did Sherry make?
3. If you were in Sherry's position (with insufficient time to gather appropriate data), how would you have conducted the appraisals?

Endnotes and References

1 Robert M. Guion, *Personnel Testing* (New York: McGraw-Hill Book Company, 1965): 90–112. Also see Paul M. Muchinsky, *Psychology Applied to Work*, 2nd ed. (Chicago, IL: The Dorsey Press, 1987): 306–311.

2 Paul M. Muchinsky, "Employee Absenteeism: A Review of the Literature," *Journal of Vocational Behavior* Vol. 10 (1977): 316–340.

3 Donald G. Patterson, "The Scott Company Graphic Rating Scale," *Journal of Personnel Research* (August 1922): 362–366.

4 Robert L. Taylor and Robert A. Zawacki, "Trends in Performance Appraisals: Guidelines for Managers," *Personnel Administrator* 29 (March 1984): 71–80.

5 For a concise discussion on the halo error, as well as other common rater errors, see Terry R. Lowe, "Eight Ways to Ruin a Performance Review," *Personnel Journal* (January 1986): 60–62.

6 See Frank Landy and James L. Farr, *The Measurement of Work Performance, Methods, Theory, and Applications* (New York: Academic Press, 1983).

7 The discussion of the ranking method and its advantages and disadvantages was drawn from Laurence Siegel and Irving M. Lane, *Personnel and Organizational Psychology*, 2nd ed. (Homewood, IL: Richard D. Irwin, Inc., 1987): 155–156.

8 John C. Flanagan, "The Critical Incident Technique," *Psychological Bulletin*, Vol. 51, No. 4 (July 1954): 327–358.

9 Laurence Siegel and Irving M. Lane, *op. cit.*, 152.

10 D. E. Sisson, "Forced-Choice: The New Army Rating," *Personnel Psychology,* Vol. 1 (1948): 365–381.

11 For discussion of forced-choice rating scale use, see Albert Zavala, "Development of the Forced-Choice Rating Scale Technique," *Psychological Bulletin,* Vol. 63, No. 2 (1965): 117–124.

12 Peter F. Drucker, *The Practice of Management* (New York: Harper & Row, 1954).

13 Anthony P. Raia, *Managing by Objectives* (Glenview, IL: Scott, Foresman and Company, 1974): 18–22.

14 P. C. Smith and L. M. Kendall, "Retranslation of Expectations: An Approach to the Construction of Unambiguous Anchors for Rating Scales," *Journal of Applied Psychology,* Vol. 47, No. 2 (1963): 149–155.

15 Frank J. Landy, *Psychology of Work Behavior,* 3rd ed. (Homewood, IL: The Dorsey Press, 1980): 185–187.

16 See William J. Kearney, "The Value of Behaviorally Based Performance Appraisal," *Business Horizons,* Vol. 19 (June 1976): 75–83.

17 H. John Bernardin and Lawrence A. Klatt, "Managerial Appraisal Systems: Has Practice Caught Up to the State of the Art?" *Personnel Administrator,* Vol. 30 (November 1985): 79–86.

18 Developed from information in H. John Bernardin and Richard W. Beatty, *Performance Appraisal: Assessing Human Behavior at Work* (Boston, MA: PWS-KENT Publishing Company, 1984): 190–191; Richard W. Beatty and Craig Eric Schneier, *Personnel Administration: An Experiential/Skill-Building Approach,* 2nd ed. (Reading, MA: Addison-Wesley Publishing Company, 1981): 106–107; and Richard M. Steers, *Introduction to Organizational Behavior,* 3rd ed. (Glenview, IL: Scott, Foresman and Company, 1988): 261.

19 For discussion, see Herbert H. Meyer, "Self Appraisal of Job Performance," *Personnel Psychology,* Vol. 33 (Summer 1980): 291–295.

20 Harry E. Roadman, "An Industrial Use of Peer Ratings," *Journal of Applied Psychology,* Vol. 48, No. 4 (1964): 211–214.

21 For discussion, see L. L. Cummings and Donald Schwab, "Who evaluates?" in *The Performance Appraisal Sourcebook,* edited by Lloyd Baird, Richard W. Beatty and Craig E. Scheier (Amherst, MA: Human Resource Development Press, 1982): 81–85.

22 Richard Henderson, *Performance Appraisal: Theory to Practice* (Reston, VA: Reston Publishing Company, 1980): 173.

23 Norman R. F. Maier, *Psychology in Industrial Organizations* (Boston, MA: Houghton Mifflin Company, 1973): 558–559.

Chapter 8

Working with Difficult Employees

Objectives

After reading this chapter you should understand:

1. The concept of employee counseling and its role within organizations.
2. The supervisor's role in employee counseling.
3. The various techniques used to counsel employees.
4. The types of employee assistance programs and their role within organizations.
5. The purposes and methods of employee discipline and how discipline should be administered.
6. The concept of employment-at-will, and what is meant by unjust discharge.
7. The way to avoid unjust discharge litigation.

Workers bring a variety of skills, knowledge, and abilities to their jobs. The job of supervisors and managers is to assist employees in managing these various attributes so they can make productive contributions to the workplace. Selection procedures are designed to identify candidates with the most appropriate combination of characteristics for successful job performance. Training and development programs are designed to teach people how to use and improve their talents. In addition, performance appraisals are conducted on an ongoing basis to provide feedback to workers about whether or not they are making full use of their potential.

Along with their various work traits, employees bring a host of unique personal problems to the workplace. Some employees have family difficulties; others may suffer from alcoholism, drug dependency, or a variety of physical or psychological ailments. All these personal difficulties have the potential to interfere with workers' abilities to satisfactorily perform their jobs.

Astute supervisors are cognizant of the various behaviors demonstrated by troubled employees. Productivity declines; absenteeism increases; and company policies, procedures, and rules are ignored or disobeyed. When these signs become apparent, intervention is usually indicated.

Initially, supervisors and managers attempt to aid employees through counseling. Work-related problems are usually dealt with at the supervisory level, and if needed, with the assistance of the human resource department. Problems of a more personal or complex nature should be referred to professionally trained personnel.

If counseling fails to alleviate the problems, supervisors turn to disciplinary procedures. These programs are designed to foster positive behavior through formalized systems consisting of oral and written warnings, suspensions, and ultimately discharge. This chapter focuses on methods used by supervisors and human resource managers to deal with troubled employees. Proper and legal procedures for terminating workers are also discussed.

Counseling Employees

Employee counseling is a major activity in the promotion of employee development. Supervisors and managers engage in formal counseling sessions for the purposes of handling grievances; dealing with discipline matters; improving performance; disseminating information about benefits, policies, and procedures; and helping employees in career development and retirement planning. Human resource managers also frequently find themselves acting as liaisons between employees and management in settling disputes and clarifying communication difficulties.

In addition to formally established sessions, astute managers routinely conduct informal counseling sessions with employees. These sessions are usually a result of spontaneous conversations with employees which develop into discussions of a more serious nature. What appear on the surface to be ordinary problems may, through further scrutiny, emerge as more serious issues. Informal meetings often bring these issues to the forefront. Once this awareness is achieved, employees may deal with the issues themselves, or they may seek additional professional assistance.

The connotation of the word *counseling* is sometimes misleading. Some of the skills and techniques used in employee counseling resemble those used by professional therapists. It is imperative to emphasize, however, that although the techniques are similar, the purposes of the sessions are dramatically different. Employee counseling is reserved for work-related problems. Effective human resource managers recognize their limitations, and they refer employees with other, more serious problems to appropriate professionals. Consequently, a major role of employee counseling is to help employees recognize problems and seek appropriate assistance.

What Is Employee Counseling?

Employee counseling is a process of helping workers solve work-related problems. Through the use of various techniques, counselors aid employees in understanding their problems and in seeking their own solutions. At this point, a clear distinction must be made between solving problems for employees and assisting and encouraging them to solve their problems independently. Included in the counselor's role of helping employees understand and develop their own solutions to problems are: the presentation of information, the provision of alternatives, and the process of listening, reflecting, and clarifying employees' thoughts and feelings. The final decisions rest with the employees.

It is important to realize the fundamental difference between therapeutic and workplace counseling. The major goal of therapy is to make individuals feel good or better about themselves. Workplace counseling is concerned with developing employee competence. Aside from the important fact that most lay counselors are not equipped to handle therapeutic counseling, attempting to make people feel good about themselves is an individualistic goal which often conflicts with employees' roles in organizations. The goal of employee counseling is to develop competence in order to succeed in corporate life. Other counseling, if necessary, is best left to professionals in therapeutic sessions. The best and only real assistance that employee counselors can provide for their counselees is to help them identify and generate valid solutions to their workplace problems.

Exhibit 8.1

Common Workplace Counseling Situations

- Career development
- Discipline
- Employee assistance
- Goal/objective setting
- Grievances
- Interpersonal/co-worker conflicts
- Motivational/pep talks
- Performance appraisals

> **Counseling**
>
> *Counseling is the utilization of skilled techniques for the purpose of assisting people in understanding and developing their own solutions to problems.*

Counseling Techniques[1]

In order to be successful, counselors use various skills and techniques to increase people's awareness of problems and to decide on appropriate actions. The accomplishment of these purposes requires that counselors be active listeners who use their skills to formulate educated guesses and to continually test, reject, or accept these hypotheses. Some of the most effective methods counselors use to achieve these purposes are silence and gestures, reflection, restatement, and open-ended questioning.

Silence and Gestures

Active listening requires that counselors encourage their employees to speak as much as possible. A frequent method used to encourage the flow of speech, especially by non-directive counselors, is the appropriate timing of silence and gestures. When counselors feel that employees have not completed their thoughts, or that the topic requires elaboration, they may choose to remain silent or to use non-verbal communication. A nod of the head, a raised eyebrow, or a facial expression may serve to encourage employees to continue their conversation. In this manner, counselors elicit additional thoughts while remaining in a listening mode.

Reflection

Counseling sessions often involve the release of emotional feelings by employees. This venting of emotions, known as *catharsis,* is a healthy process which counselors encourage by repeating the feelings expressed in different words. This process of **reflection**

1. Enables the counselor to concentrate on emotions rather than on content.
2. Allows the counselor an opportunity to demonstrate to the employee that he or she is empathetic.
3. Gives the employee an opportunity to redefine his or her feelings if the counselor has misinterpreted them.

This technique is particularly useful during the early stages of counseling sessions when employees are typically involved in expressing their feelings. Statements such as "I gather you are rather upset about receiving a below average rating" or "you feel the other workers mistrust you" are examples of reflection.

> **Reflection**
>
> ***Reflection is a technique used by counselors in which they reiterate the employee's expressed feelings using different words or phrases.***

Restatement

Often, statements made by employees during counseling sessions require clarification. Rather than risk misinterpreting what the counselee meant, counselors either restate the employees' exact words or paraphrase their statements, in an attempt to obtain clarification. For example, suppose an employee states "I just can't stand working in that environment any longer without a change." The statement can have many meanings for the counselor. Does the employee wish the environment changed, or does he want a transfer? Rather than interrogating the employee, counselors prefer to use **restatement.** In this case, the reply might be "You feel that you can't work in the environment unless change occurs?" Usually, restatement results in elaboration and clarification by the counselee.

Exhibit 8.2

Some Effective Counseling Tips

- Allow employees to express their feelings freely.
- Remain impartial and open minded.
- Use active listening skills.
- Be empathetic.
- Focus on one problem at a time.
- Be specific.
- Encourage employees to assume responsibility for both positive and negative behaviors.
- Encourage employees to explore alternatives, make decisions, set goals, and solve their own problems.
- Emphasize self-assessment and correction as a means of improving performance.
- Behaviorally document critical behaviors as supportive evidence.
- Realize your own limitations and refer employees to others when appropriate.
- Achieve closure and set action plans.
- Follow up.

> **Restatement**
>
> *Restatement is a clarification technique used by counselors in which the counselee's words are restated by the counselor.*

Open-Ended Questioning

The use of questioning techniques is an integral part of counseling sessions. By selective questioning, counselors lead counselees into appropriate areas for analysis. The type of questions most appropriate for this purpose are **open-ended questions,** which cannot be answered in yes or no fashion. For example, requests such as "Tell me a little more about your past work history" or "What was your home life like?" are examples of open-ended, non-directive questions. In order to answer these types of questions, counselees must elaborate and clarify their statements.

> **Open-ended questions**
>
> *Open-ended questions require elaboration and cannot be answered in a simple yes or no manner.*

The Supervisor's Role in Counseling

It would be foolhardy to expect supervisors to be fully trained as functioning counselors. In fact, many problems are created because supervisors fail to realize their limitations as counselors. They sometimes delve too deeply into non-workplace problems and inadvertently cause more harm than good. The most effective supervisory counselors are those who are trained, usually by human resource professionals, to identify problems, to encourage employee awareness of problems, and to be knowledgeable about the sources of help that are available for referral. One such resource that has gained popularity over the last two decades is Employee Assistance Programs (EAPs).

Employee Assistance Programs (EAPs)

The number of organizations using **employee assistance programs** has increased dramatically since its inception during the 1940s.[2] Originally, employee assistance programs were created to aid workers in overcoming problems associated with alcoholism. Today these programs are multi-faceted, and they offer assistance to workers who are troubled by alcoholism, drug problems, marital and family problems, health-related problems (particularly mental health problems such as depression), and any other issues which have the potential to interfere with job performance.

Employee assistance programs (EAPs)

Employee assistance programs are employer-sponsored counseling programs whose goal is the identification and treatment of employee problems either in-house or through external referrals.

Organizations which use employee assistance programs find that their successful operation depends on adequately identifying troubled employees and determining the most appropriate treatment program.

Identifying Troubled Employees

Most employee assistance program referrals are generated by self-referrals from the troubled employees. In order for EAPs to generate these self-referrals, the EAPs must be promoted by the company, and employees must have confidence in the services offered. Advertisement of EAPs is usually accomplished through meetings, printed literature, and face-to-face communication. Credibility for EAPs is best achieved by maintaining confidentiality or anonymity for the client.

A significant percentage of the self-referrals by troubled employees are the direct result of suggestions made by supervisors. Although the average supervisor is untrained in diagnosing mental or physical problems, he or she is capable of monitoring declining work performance. This in turn may result in suggestions being made to employees to visit the EAP. Often, particularly in the case of alcoholism, the realization by employees that their job may be in jeopardy prompts them to seek help.

Determining the most appropriate treatment

There are many avenues of treatment available to employees. Some organizations employ professionals, such as counselors, in their in-house EAPs, and consequently, they offer in-house treatment programs. Other companies find that the needs of their employees are best served by referrals to community agencies, such as counseling centers and Alcoholics Anonymous. The success of any EAP depends on organizations being able to determine the best available program for their employees. Realistically, this decision is not only based on obtaining the best possible services for employees, but also on the costs associated with the various alternative programs.

Evaluating EAPs

The obvious benefit of EAPs is the savings in productivity which results from lowered absenteeism, turnover, and accidents.[3] These benefits, however, are difficult to measure. To date, very little information is available on the success rates of employee assistance programs. In addition, while the cost of these programs is highly visible, it is difficult to quantify the results of EAPs.

Another problem related to the use of EAPs is the availability of services. Many communities, particularly small ones, do not have the multitude of community services necessary to provide workers with comprehensive treatment. As a result, employees identified as needing help may experience frustration in obtaining qualified assistance. This may serve to exacerbate, rather than alleviate, the problem.

Finally, it must be realized that the success of EAPs is highly dependent on the attitudes of management and workers alike. If troubled employees are not afforded confidentiality or anonymity, if they are not offered clean slates after treatment, or if their job security is in jeopardy, then the program may be bound for failure.

Disciplining Employees

Disciplining employees is an onerous task for most supervisors and managers. As in performance appraisals, the goal of **discipline** is to foster positive employee behaviors that will promote organizational objectives. The manner in which this goal is accomplished, however, differs among individuals and organizations. Performance appraisals rely on the use of constructive feedback mechanisms, whereas traditional discipline procedures usually involve the administration or threat of punishment.

The proper administration of disciplinary procedures necessitates prior planning. The rule infractions for which discipline will be administered, the method by which it will be administered, and the respective punishments must be decided on and communicated to employees prior to taking corrective action. Complaint procedures must be established to allow employees who believe that they were unjustly treated to appeal the disciplinary action. Finally, supervisors and managers must be instructed in the proper administration of these procedures, as well as the legal ramifications surrounding their use.

Approaches to Administering Discipline

There are two basic approaches to administering discipline. The first, the traditional approach, emphasizes punitive measures in an effort to stop undesirable behaviors. The *hot-stove* and *progressive discipline* approaches are the principal traditional approaches.

A more modern approach to administering discipline involves the use of procedures designed to prevent the future occurrence of negative behaviors. The goal is not to eliminate bad performers, but rather to promote productive workers. Discipline procedures which fall into this category are known as *positive discipline* approaches.

The hot-stove approach

The **hot-stove** method of disciplining workers is analogous to approaching and touching a hot stove. Any individual who approaches a hot stove receives a warning in the form of radiating heat. Similarly, all employees are warned of the consequences of negative behaviors prior to their occurrence. Ignoring the heat warning and touching the stove results in an immediate burn, consistently and uniformly administered without prejudice. Likewise, conforming to the hot-stove approach requires that supervisors administer unprejudiced discipline consistently to all employees who violate the pre-established rules.

Hot-stove approach

In hot-stove approach, all employees are pre-warned about which behaviors are punishable, and they are immediately and consistently punished, without prejudice, if they violate the rules.

The advantage of the hot-stove approach is its impersonal and consistent treatment of employees. If it is administered correctly, all employees are treated equally and without favoritism. Unfair discrimination is eliminated, and employees understand and trust the system, regardless of their personal feelings about its fairness.

Ironically, the main feature of the system, its non-discriminatory mode of administration, is the aspect which is most often cited as problematic. Because it fails to discriminate among workers, it does not allow for individual or situational differences. Consequently, new workers are expected to know and obey the rules to the same degree as long-term employees.

The progressive discipline approach

Progressive discipline systems are probably the most commonly used approaches, particularly in manufacturing environments. The use of this technique requires the organization to identify the behaviors which require discipline and to establish a progressive punishment system based on the severity of the infraction and the frequency of its occurrence. The more serious the rule infraction, the harsher the immediate consequence. For example, one incident of unexcused absenteeism may result in an oral warning issued by the supervisor, whereas intoxication on the job may result in a three-day suspension, or even termination.

Progressive discipline

Progressive discipline involves identifying behaviors for which discipline will be applied and establishing a progressive list of punishments to be administered based on the severity of the offense and its frequency of occurrence.

The application of a progressive discipline system usually involves a four-step approach for minimal infractions. For the first offense, a verbal warning is administered by the supervisor. The second occurrence of the behavior results in a written warning. Third infractions are punishable by suspensions without pay, usually for three days. Finally, further occurrences of the behavior results in termination. Of course, the immediacy of the punishment increases as the severity of the offense increases. Thus, termination for insubordination may be established and administered for the second violation.

It is important to note that successful use of the progressive approach requires that rule infractions and their progressive punishments be communicated to employees in written form. Furthermore, rule infractions, and the subsequent administration of discipline, should be behaviorally documented.

The positive discipline approaches

For many organizations, traditional disciplining strategies have worked well. For others, these systems have resulted in the development of adversarial role relationships between supervisors and workers. Vindictive supervisors have attempted to "*get* troublesome employees," and workers have retaliated by pushing the system to its limits in an attempt to see how much they can "get away with." Furthermore, to avoid the potential legal problems of discriminating against one employee in favor of another, overzealous supervisors have exploited the system by punishing even the most minute infractions.

In response to this situation, a new discipline system which emphasizes *discipline without punishment* has evolved.[4] Instead of the progressive punishment steps outlined earlier, this **positive discipline approach** uses oral reminders, written reminders, paid decision-making leave, and ultimately dismissal.

Positive discipline

Positive discipline is an approach designed to foster future positive behaviors by emphasizing positive steps to be taken rather than administering punitive actions.

Initial infractions of organizational rules generate a verbal meeting between the supervisor and the offending worker. Unlike progressive discipline systems, where the worker is given a verbal warning of the consequences of further in-

Exhibit 8.3

A Progressive Discipline System

The purpose of these policies is to define your rights. Because the violation of some policies is more serious than the violation of others, the type of discipline accompanying each policy is stated.

Policy	First offense	Second offense	Third offense
Violating safety rules	Verbal	Written	Dismissal
Committing actions which affect the safety of equipment or other personnel	Verbal	Written	Dismissal
Knowingly punching the time card of another employee, having another employee punch your time card, or unauthorized altering of time cards	Written	3-day layoff	Dismissal
Being late to work	Twice in 30 days	Three times in 30 days	Four times in 30 days
Unexcused absence	Written	3-day layoff	Dismissal
Loafing or goofing off	Written	3-day layoff	Dismissal
Smoking in restricted areas	Written	3-day layoff	Dismissal
Reporting to work intoxicated	Written and sent home	Dismissal	
Disorderly conduct on company property	Written correction to dismissal depending on offense		
Immoral conduct or indecency on company property	Verbal correction to dismissal depending on offense		
Dishonesty or removal of property belonging to the company or to others	Verbal correction to dismissal depending on offense		
Insubordination	Verbal correction to dismissal depending on offense		
Consuming or distributing intoxicants or narcotics on company premises	Dismissal		
Possession of firearms, fireworks, or explosives on company property without company permission	Dismissal		

fractions, oral reminders are designed to elicit worker cooperation in adhering to the corporate rules. No punishments are administered or mentioned. This meeting is usually followed up by a memo detailing the commitment made by the worker. If this fails to correct the negative behavior and a further incident occurs, the supervisor then issues a written reminder reiterating the fact that the employee has failed to abide by his or her commitment.

In the event that both the oral and written reminder fail to eliminate the negative behavior, an employee is given a paid decision-making day off to contemplate his or her future with the company. By paying the employee, management indicates their desire for the employee to remain a productive team member. Upon returning to work, the employee is immediately required to inform the supervisor of his or her decision to change behavior and remain with the organization, or to terminate employment.

The decision-making day off is the most controversial feature of discipline without punishment. Opponents of the system maintain that it promotes hostility toward the system among good workers because it appears to reward negative behavior. Also, poor workers are likely to take advantage of the system by obtaining an undeserved paid holiday. Proponents, however, maintain that these concerns are unfounded. Research appears to indicate that productive employees regard the paid leave as a severe step, and those employees to whom it is issued view it as anything but a vacation.[5]

The future of positive discipline approaches depends largely on its acceptance by supervisors and managers. It is not easy for managers to change their philosophies or behaviors regarding discipline. For many supervisors and managers, positive discipline is in effect no discipline. If they are willing and able to change their traditional modes of administering discipline, and are willing to give the system a chance to work, the approach promises benefits. On the other hand, if they refuse to accept it, it will ultimately fail.

The Appeal Procedure

The effective administration of a discipline system requires that organizations establish procedures for appeal. Just as union environments provide for a grievance procedure to correct injustices, many non-union organizations have established methods for workers to appeal felt inequities. These systems are usually communicated in writing; they involve progressive step processes; and they may include the use of hierarchical systems, open-door policies, peer reviews, or an ombudsman.

Hierarchical systems

Hierarchical appeal systems are probably the most commonly found systems in non-unionized organizations. In this highly formalized procedure, workers' immediate supervisors serve as the sole judges of their actions. Supervisors identify the offense, issue the citation, and then sit in judgment.

Appeal procedures under hierarchical systems usually involve a formal step process beginning with the immediate supervisor and terminating three or four managerial levels higher. If, after appealing to his or her supervisor, a worker still feels that he or she was unjustly treated, a written appeal is sent to the supervisor's superior. After a predetermined time period, usually three to five working days, the superior rules on the employee's petition. If the worker is still unsatisfied, the process can be continued to the next level. This procedure is repeated until it reaches the final ruling authority. Some organizations whose final ruling authority is a corporate board located in another section of the country have even gone so far as to supply transportation and attorneys to workers who felt they were unjustly treated.[6]

Open-door policies

Open-door policies are one of the oldest methods for handling grievances, and they are usually present regardless of whether or not they are formally established by the organization. Simply stated, open-door policies allow all employees with problems to contact any designated supervisor or manager within the organization. Depending on the organization, this may include first-line supervisors all the way up to and including the Chief Executive Officers. Organizations that employ open-door policies usually designate one person, or group of people, as the final decision-making authority.

On the surface, open-door policies seem to afford easy access to managers and a quick, informal method for resolving grievances. However, as many employees are prone to stating, "only fools and relatives" would use the system. Many managers

1. Are unwilling to listen to employee complaints in an open and unhostile manner.
2. Refer employees back to their immediate supervisors for fear of undermining their actions.[7]
3. Fail to provide a system for consistent treatment of all workers.

These shortcomings have resulted in organizations establishing more formalized procedures for dealing with employee appeals.

Peer reviews

Peer reviews consist of committees composed of equal numbers of worker and management representatives who conduct hearings and issue the final ruling on all employee grievances. Employee members are usually elected by their coworkers for a specified period of time. Similarly, management representatives are selected by upper management, and they serve on the committee on a rotating basis for a predetermined duration.

There are some obvious advantages to peer reviews. With the inclusion of workers on the committee, enhanced feelings of justice are promoted among workers. The system resembles the judicial system and trial by one's peers. Also, committee rulings are less likely to suffer from individual bias because the procedure requires discussion and interchange among several people prior to the issuance of the final judgment.[8]

Ombudsmen

Ombudsmen are designated individuals within organizations who serve as party mediators in arriving at mutually acceptable solutions to grievances. These ombudsmen have no authority to issue final settlements, and they employ a variety of problem-solving approaches to help the parties reach mutual consensus.[9]

In the past, the use of ombudsmen has been reserved principally for government agencies, educational institutions, and nonprofit organizations. Ombudsmen have, however, been used successfully in major private organizations, such as Xerox, and as their benefits become more widely known, their use will probably increase in the future.

Discipline and the Law

The legal disciplining of employees requires that all of the procedures be administered in a manner which is consistent and fair to all workers. Disciplinary procedures constitute employment situations, and as such, all of the laws regarding protected class members apply. To safely administer discipline programs, supervisors would be well advised to

1. Determine if the infraction truly justifies the disciplinary measure imposed.
2. Discipline all workers similarly.
3. Behaviorally document and maintain records on all infractions and disciplinary corrections.

The Discharge Process

The final step of discipline usually results in termination. Even in the most justifiable cases, where workers blatantly abuse company rules, the process is costly. Organizations must repeat the selection process, train new hirees, and attempt to compensate during the interim for losses in productivity because of the workforce shortage.

Termination also indicates that something went wrong. Usually, the problem is traceable to an organizational function. Perhaps the recruitment and selection processes are deficient in identifying appropriately skilled candidates. Maybe the training program is not adequately preparing employees for their job duties. It is also possible that problems with organizational feedback, communication, or motivation methods could be occurring independently or in combination with one another. Regardless of the reasons for the failure, organizations must analyze the events in an attempt to prevent future occurrences.

In spite of an organization's awareness of the potential difficulties inherent in poorly conducted discharges, many supervisors are still unprepared to effectively deal with terminations. Instead of discharging employees after thoroughly documenting behaviors and implementing planned procedures, many supervisors react hastily and emotionally. Employees are discharged for a range of reasons which may be unjustified. For example, terminations of employees because of age, personality characteristics, reprisals for filing complaints, or refusals to commit illegal acts are all too frequent. In fact, most researchers and practitioners would probably agree that more workers are terminated for personality conflicts than for the inability to perform their jobs.

Until recently, most discharges went unchallenged. Organizations practiced, and the courts upheld, the "at will" employment doctrine which gives employers the unequivocal power to terminate employees for any or no reason at all. This state of affairs appears to be changing rapidly. Today, more and more workers are contesting unjust discharges.

Employment-at-Will

For the last century, almost every court in the United States has subscribed to the doctrine of **employment-at-will.** This doctrine maintains that in all instances, except those specifically prohibited by Title VII, the NLRA, OSHA, or ADEA, continued employment of workers who have not been hired for an express period of time is a matter to be decided between employers and employees. Just as workers are free to terminate their employment without any justification, so too are employers free to discharge workers for any good reason or for no reason at all.

> **Employment-at-will**
>
> *Employment-at-will is the employment doctrine followed in the United States which allows employers to dismiss any worker who has not been hired for a specific length of time, who is not covered by any contract, or who is not protected by an enumerated law, for any reason they choose.*

Despite the continued complaints of employers about government legislation infringing on their ability to operate their businesses, the employment-at-will doctrine provides private sector employers[10] with wide discretionary powers in the discharge of non-protected workers. Proponents of this principle maintain that the doctrine is justified for several reasons. First, it affords employers the same rights as employees. Workers may terminate their employment for any reason they choose, so employers should also have the right to terminate employees for reasons they choose. Second, free market economics dictate that workers with sufficient skills are free to negotiate a set contract length. Realistically, however, most individual employees lack sufficient bargaining power to negotiate such contracts, so it is not hard to see why unions offering job security attract 20 percent of the workforce. Last, the result of not having a policy of employment-at-will could result in the imposition of an undue

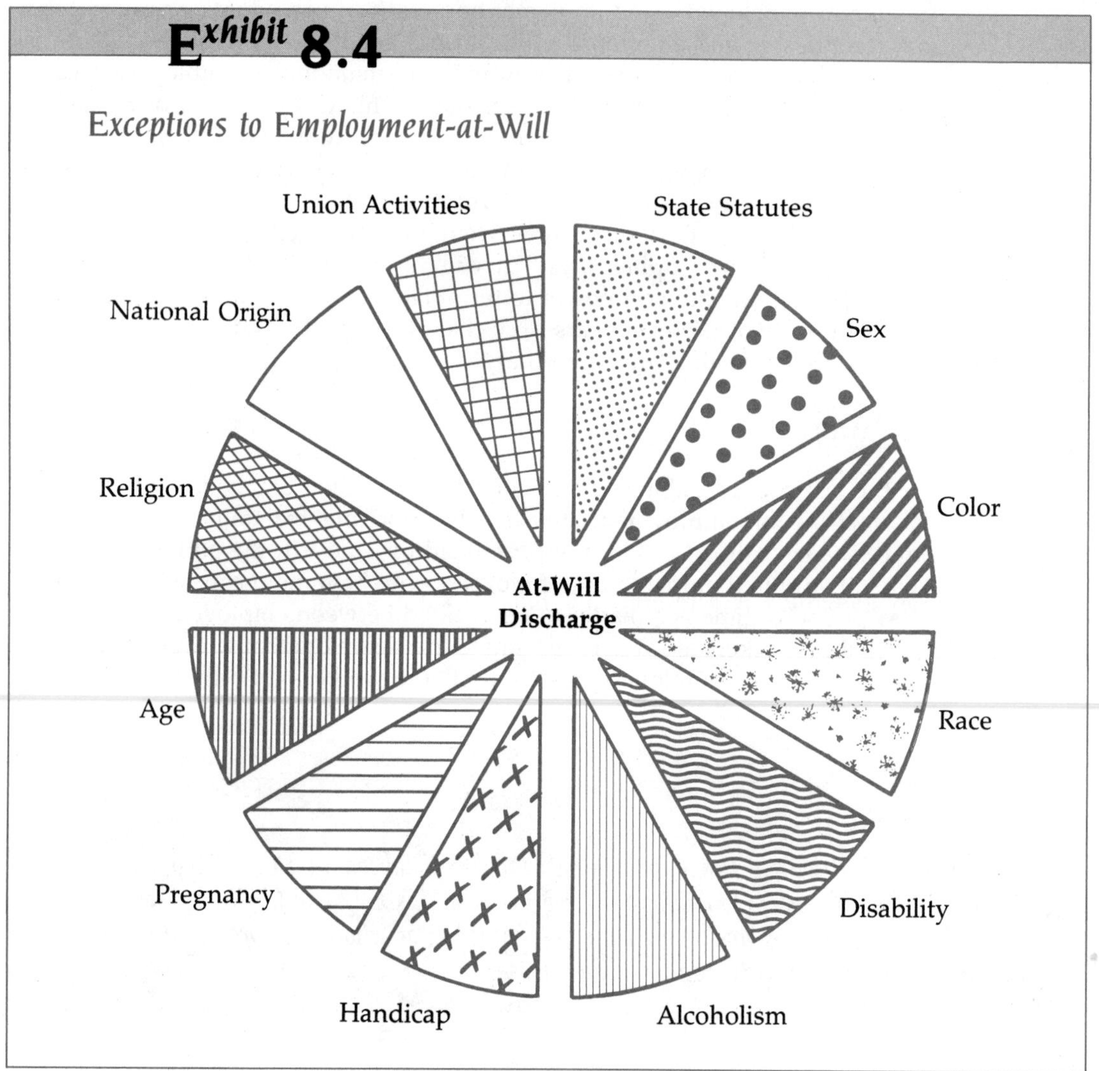

hardship on employers, the courts, and society. Under the present system, termination is allowable for any reason except those prohibited by law. The reverse, requiring enumeration by statute of every possible justifiable cause for termination, would probably result in a continual flow of litigation.

Opponents of employment-at will contend that there are approximately one million workers discharged from their jobs annually. Of these dismissals, it is estimated that about 20 percent, or 200,000 workers a year, are released unjustifiably.[11] Most of these unjustifiable terminations are for reasons most people would find unacceptable. Employers have discharged workers for informing the authorities of wrongdoings (whistleblowing) even if public safety was at stake, they have dismissed people because of their sexual preferences (even if job performance was unhampered), and they have fired employees just because they objected to their opinions.

During the past decade, additional controls have been imposed on employers' freedom to terminate workers at-will. These restrictions have been imposed by individual states and have resulted from common law interpretations in the courts.

Common law interpretations

A growing number of states have imposed limitations on the employment-at-will doctrine. To date, these modifications have varied from state to state and they are primarily seen in the form of laws regulating the use of lie detectors in employment situations, the protection of whistleblowers, and the termination of employees for unjust causes. For example, South Dakota enacted a statute which provides that any employee who is hired at an annual salary is presumed to be employed for a period of one year. To terminate such an employee, the employer would have to demonstrate the employee's "habitual neglect or continued incapacity to perform or wilful breach of duty."[12] Similarly, states such as Michigan and Connecticut have established statutes to protect employees who "whistleblow," and Puerto Rico has a statute which enumerates "just cause" violations and cites penalties based on length of service for unjust employee discharges.

Variation in state exceptions to the doctrine of employment-at-will are likely to continue as long as state courts rule on discharge challenges. Common law, by definition, is not a formally stated statute, but rather an accepted set of principles passed down from judge to judge through written rulings and interpretations. Because discharge cases are tried in state courts, interpretations of the law obviously vary. The **common law interpretations** impacting on employment-at-will are classified into three major categories. These include wrongful discharges based on:

1. Public policy.
2. Express and implied contracts.
3. Commission of workplace torts.

Public policy

The **public policy exception** to employment-at-will is the one which is most widely accepted by the courts, and it maintains that employers are not permitted to discipline or to dismiss workers for exercising their legal rights or duties created under statutes. For example, employees who refuse to violate a law, such as to falsify reports; employees who fail to testify falsely in a legislative hearing;[13] employees who whistleblow; and employees who answer jury calls even though they are expressly forbidden to do so by their employers, are usually protected from discharge under the public policy exception. In addition, employees who are discharged for exercising a statutory right, such as collecting workers' compensation benefits, are usually afforded protection from employment-at-will discharges.[14]

Express and implied contracts

Express contracts, which indicate employment for a specific duration of time, or collective bargaining agreements, which are negotiated by unions, exempt workers from at-will terminations. Other employees who are not covered by these specifically written contracts have attempted to legally demonstrate that an **implied contract** existed. To date, litigants who were able to demonstrate the existence of some implied written contract, such as company-wide written policy and procedure manuals which explicitly enumerate grounds for discharge, have been protected from at-will terminations.

In order for a contract to be implied, it does not always have to be written. Promises of employment duration made to, and relied on, by employees at hiring, or yearly fixed salaries for which employees can prove implied employment for a one-year duration have been interpreted by the courts to be valid contracts.[15] Although it is more difficult to prove and less likely to result in an exception to at-will discharges, supervisors and managers must be aware of the potential for implying employment duration, even in vague references.

Commission of workplace torts

The third common exception to employment-at-will centers around tort theory. A *tort* is a legal term which indicates a civil harm for which the injured party is given some form of compensation. Many state courts have prohibited any dismissal or discipline which causes a wrongful harm. Some of the more commonly committed **workplace torts** include: defamation of character, invasion of privacy, and intentional infliction of emotional distress.[16] Although they are less commonly used by the courts as grounds for setting aside at-will terminations, wrongful discharges which inflict harm are a distinct future reality. As more and more information about people becomes available through advanced technology, such as computers and sophisticated surveillance techniques, the invasion of individual rights of privacy becomes increasingly more likely.

Some advice for human resource managers

The future will undeniably see an upswing in employment at-will litigation. Many states have either already made significant modifications to their at-will doctrines or they appear willing to revise the doctrine under appropriate conditions. With the increasing trend toward protection of individual rights, particularly the rights of privacy, increased legal challenges of unjustifiable dismissals are a certainty. Management prerogatives in disciplining and dismissal, once thoroughly unchallenged, may undergo extreme modification.

For human resource managers, the safest course of action appears to be to establish, to adequately communicate, and to firmly adhere to a written policy on what actions constitute "just cause" discipline and termination. Like other established employment policies, this statement should:

1. Include behaviors which are job related.
2. Be clearly articulated to workers and supervisors before being instituted.

3. Involve an established procedure for determining the validity of the alleged infraction prior to taking action.
4. Be consistently and uniformly enforced throughout the organization.

Constructive Discharge

Employers frequently attempt to minimize the potential costs and litigation risks involved in dismissals by convincing or pressuring workers to resign their positions. They reason that workers who voluntarily quit are not eligible for unemployment compensation benefits and are unlikely to file wrongful discharge suits. This assumption is correct provided that employees are not compelled to terminate because of unreasonable working conditions caused by the employer's acts or negligence to act. In situations where workers are able to demonstrate that their resignation was coerced, courts will rule that it was a **constructive discharge** rather than a voluntary resignation.

Constructive discharge

Constructive discharge exists when an employer deliberately makes working conditions so intolerable that employees are forced to resign.

Originally, the law of constructive discharge was applied in cases involving employer violations of the National Labor Relations Act. Under Section 8(a) of the act, workers are protected from unlawful discharge for engaging in union activity. In an obvious attempt to sidestep this statute, some supervisors attempted to harass workers into voluntarily quitting by creating intolerable working conditions. These actions resulted in litigation in which the courts ruled that the employer's behaviors constituted unlawful motives and constructive discharge.[17]

Recently, the constructive discharge ruling has been applied in cases involving activities other than those protected by the National Labor Relations Act. In these cases, the courts have eliminated the need for evidencing unlawful motives. Usually, the only proof required is a demonstration of a deliberate attempt by employers to create intolerable working conditions.

A determination of the existence of constructive discharge is based on two factors. First, the court attempts to determine whether the behaviors in question were intentionally designed to cause the employee to resign. The key elements in the court's determination of intention is whether or not resignation was foreseeable by the employer,[18] and whether or not employers or their agents were aware of, and did nothing about, the intolerable conditions.

The second factor considered by courts is the concept of "intolerable" conditions. Generally, the accepted standard is the determination of whether any reasonable person would have been expected to quit if placed in the same working environment.[19] In this assessment of the tolerability of the environment, the worker's subjective assessment of the environment is unimportant.

Common practices resulting in wrongful discharge suits

In order to eliminate unlawful discharge litigation, supervisors and human resource managers must be cognizant of which behaviors will probably result in constructive discharge suits. Generally, employee complaints are filed after resignations resulting from transfers, demotions, or disciplinary counseling.

Transfers **Transfers** are lateral moves of workers to different jobs requiring the same basic skills, knowledge, and abilities as the previously held position. Transfers occur for a variety of reasons. Organizations transfer employees to avoid laying them off. Other workers are transferred because their skills are needed elsewhere. Sometimes workers are transferred as a result of work group conflicts. Regardless of the reason, transfers imply movement to a substantially equal work environment. When employers transfer workers to notably different environments and employees subsequently resign, the practice becomes questionable.

Demotions A **demotion** implies a reduction in job rank, duties, and usually salary. Organizations institute demotions after employees who had been assessed as having fundamentally sound and valuable skills are unable to complete their present job assignments. The goal is to place the worker in a position that will foster growth and development. When the procedure is used punitively, with the hope that the employee will quit, the practice may be viewed as a constructive discharge.

In determining the reasonableness of the transfer or demotion, courts will compare the present and former job regarding salary and benefits, working conditions (including frequency of travel), and the impact on the employee's prestige and status. The primary criterion used is wages and benefits; prestige is considered only when the impact is severe and caused by a substantial change in jobs.[20]

Disciplinary counseling Most disciplinary procedures involve counseling. The purpose of counseling is to discover and discuss negative work behaviors and to develop plans for their improvement. Regrettably, many human resource practitioners use these sessions to convince employees that it is in their best interest to resign because they will most likely be fired.

Most employers would be well advised to eliminate the practice of offering workers the option of voluntarily resigning or being fired. Instead, they should terminate the worker directly. If workers contest the resignation for purposes of collecting unemployment compensation and for wrongful discharge suits, the procedure will usually be construed by the courts as constructive discharge. Constructive discharge is harder for employers to defend against than contentions of wrongful discharge.

Avoiding Wrongful Discharge Litigation

Unjust discharge suits can usually be avoided if organizations plan for the inevitability of discharging workers. This planning phase should include the following:

1. Training supervisors and managers in the legal ramifications involved in dismissals, including constructive discharges.
2. Creating a **just-cause policy** that includes provisions for:
   a. Forewarning employees of the disciplinary consequences of their behaviors.
   b. Determining which offenses are deemed job related and of a severe enough nature to justify termination.
   c. Conducting fair and unbiased investigations prior to implementing discharge procedures.
3. Behaviorally documenting all of a worker's negative behaviors, along with the disciplinary procedures instituted prior to initiating the discharge procedure.
4. Conducting "exit" interviews with all terminated employees for the purpose of creating as favorable a company image as possible under the circumstances.
5. Developing a written "at-will" policy statement to be distributed and signed by all employees upon initial hiring.

Exhibit 8.5

Guidelines for Avoiding Unjust Discharge Suits[21]

- Review application forms to avoid any contractual implications.
- Audit the interview process to eliminate any employment promises.
- Remove references to salary in any issued job offer letters.
- Establish and periodically review complaint procedures for effectiveness.
- Regularly review performance appraisals.
- Establish and periodically review just-cause policies.
- Set forth clear policies in a well-written employee handbook.
- Validate the legality of any disclaimers included in employee handbooks.
- Audit employee handbooks on a yearly basis.
- Centralize discharge procedures in the hands of one or two objective members of management.
- Conduct proper and comprehensive investigations of all facts prior to instituting discharge procedures.
- Time discharges carefully.
- Conduct exit interviews.

Summary

An important ingredient of every supervisor's job responsibilities involves helping workers overcome work-related problems. Supervisors, with the support of human resource managers, engage in activities designed to assist employees in identifying problems and developing contingency plans for dealing with these difficulties.

As a result of counseling sessions, supervisors sometimes discover that an employee's difficulties stem from personal, non-work-related causes. Difficulties with marriage and family relations, alcoholism, and drug abuse are becoming increasingly more frequent at the workplace. Astute supervisors recognize their limitations in these areas and appropriately refer employees to professional personnel.

In order to effectively handle the increasing number of employee problems associated with substance abuse, many organizations seek help from Employee Assistance Programs. These corporate programs are designed to confidentially aid workers in overcoming personal problems while simultaneously encouraging them to continue in their roles as productive members of the organization.

When employee counseling fails to resolve problems satisfactorily, employers institute more drastic disciplinary measures. These procedures are designed to promote positive organizational behavior by imposing a pre-set system of punitive measures on those who deviate from the established rules.

In the event that all attempts at intervention are fruitless, discharge procedures are instituted. In an attempt to minimize costs and to guard against wrongful discharge litigation, current human resource practices include training supervisors and managers in proper disciplinary and discharge procedures, developing and communicating just-cause policies, and documenting and maintaining records on disciplinary measures imposed.

Key Terms to Identify

Counseling
Reflection
Restatement
Open-ended questions
Employee assistance program (EAP)
Discipline
Hot-stove approach
Progressive discipline
Positive discipline approach
Hierarchical appeal systems
Open-door policies
Peer reviews
Ombudsmen
Employment-at-will
Common law interpretations
Public policy exception
Express and implied contract exception
Workplace torts
Constructive discharge
Transfers
Demotions
Unjust discharge
Just-cause policy

Questions for Discussion

Do You Know the Facts?

1. Describe three techniques a supervisor might use in counseling employees.
2. What criteria would you use to determine whether an EAP should be implemented in your organization? How would you determine whether to use outside community services in conjunction with an internal program?
3. Compare and contrast traditional discipline systems with positive discipline approaches.
4. What is meant by *constructive discharge*? What supervisory methods of convincing workers to voluntarily quit have recently been the subject of constructive discharge cases?

Can You Apply the Information Learned?

1. What behavioral signs might indicate that workers are abusing alcohol or drugs?
2. How would you approach and convince workers engaging in substance abuse that they need to seek professional help?
3. What arguments would you use to convince long-term supervisors that positive discipline is preferable to traditional methods?
4. What steps would you undertake to insure that your supervisors and managers adhered to just-cause policies?

Mattix Furniture Creates an Employee Assistance Program as a Cost-Effective Benefit

Mattix Furniture Company manufactures high quality furniture for dining and living rooms. For two generations, the company has produced unusual and expensive furnishings, hand-crafted dining suites, and colonial reproductions. The company, located near Buffalo, New York, has an excellent reputation, employs nearly 400 workers, and is headed by Jennings R. (J.R.) Hendon, president and CEO. J.R. is a religious man and is respected by his employees, but he is "tough" and has little tolerance for inappropriate behavior. Nearing his sixtieth birthday, J.R. has been grooming his son Richard to take over the company. Richard, at age 37, holds an MBA from Cornell, but he shares very few of his father's conservative feelings.

This case was prepared by David H. Holt of James Madison University.

In early 1988, J.R. and Richard had a serious disagreement that could have crippled their relationship, but instead, Mattix Furniture made a dramatic change in its approach to leadership which brought father and son closer together. Mattix Furniture recently won a coveted award for furniture design, and the designer, an employee who had been with Mattix since 1963, was honored at a gala dinner in Manhattan. The employee had several drinks that evening and disappeared after dinner, only to be arrested for being drunk and disorderly at a nearby hotel. J.R. fired the man on the spot, refusing to post bail or to talk with him. Richard went behind J.R.'s back to get the employee out of jail and assured the designer that he would be reinstated. This infuriated J.R., who was on the verge of firing his own son for insubordination.

Two days later, J.R. and Richard got into a shouting argument that could be heard throughout the office. J.R., refusing to reinstate the employee, said he had never tolerated "drunks" at Mattix, and that he would not start now, regardless of who was involved. Richard pointed out that the employee was an "alcoholic" who needed help. Moreover, he said, there were other good employees who had drinking problems, but J.R. was too intolerant to realize that many of his employees needed help, not discipline. J.R. defended his point of view, citing incidents where he had fired employees for "inappropriate and immoral" behavior. In many instances, drinking had been the issue—or drinking had led to absenteeism, conflicts at work, or family problems. J.R. would not budge on the issue, but Richard was determined to resolve it.

Several weeks later, Richard confronted his father again, this time armed with information. He had gone over the records of employees who had been fired during the past three years, called several of them, and consulted with several friends in other companies who were members of the American Society for Personnel Administration. What he discovered was that between 3 and 6 percent of the employees in any firm are likely to have alcohol-related problems, and that an additional 5 percent are likely to turn to alcohol or substance abuse, or to display other "maladaptive" behavior because of family stress, monetary pressure, career burnout, or one of many other circumstances. Richard found that Mattix had fired 47 employees during a three-year period for behavior that was probably alcohol related. He also discovered that 62 other employees had been let go for reasons that could be related to stress, career pressure, family problems, and on-the-job anxiety.

The 109 Mattix employees represented about 9 percent of those employed by the company for the three-year period, and Richard estimated that it had cost the company more than $200,000 to replace them. He showed J.R. that for every employee replaced, the company spent about $1,000 recruiting, $500 training, and another $500 for insurance, benefits, and administrative work needed to terminate and replace an employee. Just as important, the company had lost about 600 work-days by replacing employees; in addition, new employees needed about 60 days to become as productive as those they had replaced, resulting in lost productivity that cost the company between $400,000 and $500,000. J.R. was stunned by Richard's figures. This was a half-million-dollar-a-year problem.

Richard proposed an *employee assistance program* that would offer alcohol-abuse and substance-abuse referral; job and career counseling; and in-house seminars for personal development, stress management, and family assistance. The program was estimated to cost $80,000 a year for one full-time staff counselor, a manager assigned to coordinate training, and clerical support. Mattix would not get involved in treatment, but would establish external referral services with agencies such as Alcoholics Anonymous and career consulting firms. The in-house program would focus on personal and job development.

J.R. agreed to the program, but refused to endorse "substance abuse" as something they should deal with. During 1988, the firm spent $93,000 on EAP efforts, reduced terminations to 28 persons (about 4 percent), and saved approximately $170,000. The award-winning designer was reinstated and was the first employee to volunteer for AA counseling.

Questions for Discussion

1. Evaluate the EAP program and discuss other services that Mattix might have included for employees. Would you have included "substance abuse" or would you agree with J.R. that it should be excluded from employee assistance? Explain.
2. From a human resource perspective, should EAPs be adopted by all employers? Are employers responsible for problems beyond the workplace?
3. From a business perspective, do EAPs make sense? What costs and benefits can you identify, and would they apply to any employer? Explain.

Endnotes and References

1 Further discussion of these techniques can be found in almost any counseling book.

2 A large part of the interest in EAPs is caused by the fact that troubled employees cost employers about 5 percent of their salary. See William Wagner, "Assisting Employees with Personal Problems," *Personnel Administrator,* Vol. 27, No. 11 (November 1982): 59–64.

3 Donald W. Meyers, "A Standard Measure of EAPs," *EAP Digest* (September–October 1984): 15–20.

4 David N. Campbell, R. L. Fleming, and Richard C. Grote, "Discipline Without Punishment—At Last," *Harvard Business Review,* Vol. 63, No. 4 (July–August 1985): 162–178.

5 Ibid.

6 This event was related to the author by a plant manager at one of Tenneco's subsidiaries. The episode took place during the late 1970s.

7 This is not meant to imply that referring employees back to their immediate supervisors is always inappropriate. Sometimes, particularly when employees have not

previously discussed their problems with their immediate supervisors, it is a most appropriate solution. The problem occurs when as a general practice managers immediately refer workers to the lowest level in the procedure regardless of the circumstances.

8 A good discussion on this and other appeal procedures can be found in Fabius P. O'Brien and Donald A. Drost, "Non-Union Grievance Procedure: Not Just an Anti-union Strategy," *Personnel,* Vol. 61, No. 5 (1984): 61–69.

9 Alan Balfour, "Five Types of Non-union Grievance Procedures," *Personnel,* Vol. 61, No. 2 (1984): 67–76.

10 Most public sector employees are covered by a wide array of laws not afforded to private sector employees by individual states.

11 P. Weiler, "Promises to Keep: Securing Workers' Rights to Self-Organization Under the NLRA," *Harvard Law Review,* Vol. 96, No. 8 (1983): 1769–1827.

12 S.D. Codified Laws, Sect. 60(1), (3).

13 The most notable case involving dismissal of an employee for refusing to testify falsely in a legislative hearing is probably *Petermann* v. *International Brotherhood of Teamsters,* 344 P.2d 25 (Cal. 1959).

14 For further discussion on employer retaliation against employees claiming workers' compensation benefits, see Theodore A. Olsen, "Wrongful Discharge Claims Raised by At-Will Employees: A New Legal Concern for Employers," *Labor Law Journal,* Vol. 32, No. 5 (May 1981): 265–297.

15 See *Doody* v. *John Sextron Co.,* 411 F2.d 1119 (1st Cir. 1969), and *Lanier* v. *Alenco,* 459 F.2d 689 (5th Cir. 1972).

16 One of the most notable examples of an employer causing intentional distress probably occurred in the case of a restaurant owner who lined waitresses up in alphabetical order and dismissed them one by one when they refused to provide any information regarding the person or persons pilfering food. See *Agis* v. *Howard Johnson Co.,* 355 N.E. 2d 315 (Mass. 1976).

17 One of the precedent setting cases on this topic involved the continual threat of termination against a union activist by his supervisor. Although he was never terminated, the court ruled that the worker's voluntary resignation was constructive discharge. See *NLRB* v. *Tennessee Packers, Inc., Frosty Morn Division,* 339 F.2d 203 (6th Cir. 1964).

18 *Mueller* v. *U.S. Steel,* 509 F.2d 923 (10th Cir. 1975).

19 *Frazer* v. *KFC National Management,* 491 F. Supp. 1099 (M.D. Ga 1980 aff'd 636 F.2d 313 (5th Cir. 1981).

20 A notable case of constructive discharge as the result of a transfer occurred when a university removed a professor from classroom teaching and assigned non-professional responsibilities. See *Lincoln* v. *Board of Regents of the University System of Georgia,* 697 F.2d 928 (11th Cir. 1983).

21 For further elaboration on this, see Kenneth L. Sovereign, *Personnel Law,* 2nd ed. (Englewood Cliffs, NJ: Prentice-Hall, Inc., 1989): 190–205.

Part 4

Compensation, Benefits, and Health and Safety

Chapter 9

The Compensation Function

Objectives

After reading this chapter you should understand:

1. The factors which influence compensation plans.
2. The government regulations affecting compensation.
3. The comparable worth controversy.
4. The purposes of job evaluation.
5. The ranking, classification, factor-comparison, and point methods of job evaluation.

One of the most significant tasks confronting human resource managers is the design and implementation of employee **compensation** systems.[1] These systems, which are designed to serve many purposes, have as their primary goal the deliverance of fair and equitable remuneration to all employees. In addition, the compensation program must be one which provides equity to the workers while allowing the organization to remain competitive in the marketplace. This factor is highly significant, particularly in light of the fact that for many organizations approximately 50 percent, or more, of their costs may be directly attributable to employee compensation.

Compensation

Compensation refers to the intrinsic and extrinsic rewards provided by a company for the fair and equitable remuneration of employee services performed.

In response to the term *compensation*, most people presume a reference is being made to the monetary reward systems established by organizations. In this context, compensation is merely the administration of wage and salary programs. In its broadest sense, however, compensation is an all-encompassing term which incorporates both extrinsic and intrinsic rewards. Extrinsic compensation includes those factors which are monetarily based. Pay and benefits are the most obvious examples of this category. Intrinsic rewards refer to those compensatory factors which are less tangible. Recognition of a job well done, promotional opportunities, and challenging work are all examples of intrinsic compensation. Both this chapter and Chapter 10 focus on the development and implementation of extrinsic compensation programs. These include: wage and salary programs, incentive programs, benefits, and other perquisites. Subsequent chapters, particularly Chapter 15 on motivation, concentrate on those rewards categorized as intrinsic compensation.

Influences on Compensation Plans

No single factor determines a company's entire compensation program. Many interacting forces contribute to an organization's development and subsequent modification of its compensation program. Some of the impacting forces are externally generated, while others are a function of internal conditions. The degree of impact which these forces have on the design of compensation programs is determined both by the objectives of the organization and by the particular role which companies want their compensation systems to play in obtaining these goals.

The Labor Market

Many organizations use compensation to attract workers, particularly good employees, to their companies. For most employees, the primary reason for choosing one position rather than another is the direct compensation offered. As labor markets tighten and the available supply of workers in relation to the demand is diminished, compensation becomes increasingly more important. Those organizations which provide the best overall packages will attract the majority of workers. On the other hand, organizations whose compensation programs are below par, particularly in their wage and salary aspects, will soon find themselves at a competitive disadvantage in attracting good employees.

Once employees are attracted to a company, the company must make a concerted effort to retain them. A major cause of turnover in many organizations is an inadequate compensation system. Although many systems are highly competitive in attracting new employees, these plans fail to keep pace with the market value of their current employees. As a result, in order to attract new employees, the organization may find itself in the unenviable predicament of creating positions in which salaries are higher for new employees than for current workers. This inevitably causes feelings of inequity on the part of the current workforce, which often result in dissatisfaction, lowered morale, decreased productivity, and employee turnover.

Wage Surveys

In order to remain competitive in terms of both attracting and maintaining workers, organizations must constantly monitor the existing wage rates within their geographic area and their occupational field. To accomplish this task, many employers rely on data obtained through **wage surveys.**

> **Wage surveys**
>
> *Wage or pay surveys are studies conducted by organizations, consultants, or other professional groups in order to determine the compensation paid by employers within the same geographic area or occupational grouping.*

Organizations may choose to conduct their own pay surveys,[2] or they may obtain information from data collected by the Bureau of Labor Statistics or other professional associations. Regardless of the method used to gather the data, caution must be exercised prior to implementing programs based on the information. Aside from ascertaining the validity and reliability of the measures used, organizations must determine the similarity between their job classes and the sample used in the wage survey. Jobs may have the same title, but they may be very different in content. In addition, care must be taken to compare the total compensation package and not just the wage figures. One company may be paying more in direct salary, while another organization's indirect costs of benefits may more than offset the additional take home pay.

Cost of Living Adjustments (COLAs)

In addition to gathering information from wage surveys, organizations use data concerning the cost of living when implementing pay programs. *Cost of living* is a term used to refer to the consumer price index (CPI), a figure determined by the Bureau of Labor Statistics which measures changes in the prices of a fixed basket of goods and services. As the CPI increases, wages should increase proportionately to enable workers to maintain their standard of living. Compensation systems which do not allow for increases in employees' pay equal to the cost of living are in effect reducing their workers' compensation. To make up for this factor, many companies have automatic **cost of living adjustments** (COLAs) built into their pay systems. These COLAs adjust wages periodically based on a predetermined formula.[3]

Union Influences

The influence of unions and collective bargaining on compensation plans is undeniable.[4] For unionized firms, this impact is readily observable through the wage and benefit packages labor organizations are able to obtain at the bargaining table. In good economic times, in highly organized firms, unions have been able to obtain strong wage and benefit packages for their constituents. When economic conditions are harsh, unions have agreed to pay cuts in order to insure the future survival of organizations.[5]

Non-unionized employers are also impacted by the wage settlements reached in unionized plants. If non-unionized employers fail to offer comparable wage and benefit packages, they cannot remain competitive in attracting or retaining employees. Furthermore, one of the major reasons employees seek to join unions is that they perceive their wages and benefits to be substandard; thus, lower compensation packages may lead to unionization.[6]

The major difference between union and management approaches to wage and benefit programs probably lies in the area of individual compensation. Employers prefer to establish pay programs to reward workers individually based on productivity and other job-related factors, but labor organizations opt for uniform pay for all workers performing similar jobs. Individual wage determinations are usually of little, if any, concern to unions.

Government Influences

When designing a compensation program, human resource managers must take into account the various pieces of government legislation which regulate wage and salary administration.[7] These laws have been instituted over the years primarily for the purpose of maintaining the social and economic well-being of the nation. By mandating minimum wage rates, overtime pay, and child-labor standards, among others, the government seeks to insure that organizations treat individual employees fairly and equitably, in an open, competitive marketplace. In addition, laws which deal with retirement benefits, equal employment opportunity, and comparable worth attempt to provide for individual security while maintaining the integrity of the country.

Davis-Bacon and Walsh-Healy Acts[8]

The **Davis-Bacon Act** of 1931 was the first federal law enacted to provide for the protection of employees' wages. According to the provisions of the Davis-Bacon Act, any organization which held a federal government contract for $2,000 or more had to pay workers the prevailing wage rate of the locality in which the work was being performed. The **Walsh-Healy Act** of 1936 further extended the provisions of Davis-Bacon by requiring that all contractors holding federal contracts in excess of $10,000 pay the prevailing industry rate rather than the area minimum. In addition, the Walsh-Healy Act established overtime compensation at one and one-half times the hourly pay rate for any hour in excess of eight per day, or forty per week, which an employee worked.

Fair Labor Standards Act

The **Fair Labor Standards Act** of 1938 is the principal law covering the majority of today's workers. The major provisions of this law are:

1. Minimum wage rates—Originally $.25 per hour, the law currently provides for a minimum of $3.35 per hour to be paid to all employees.

2. Overtime pay—All hours in excess of forty in a given week are to be paid at one and one-half times the hourly pay rate.
3. Child-labor standards—This provision prohibits the employment of individuals below the age of 16 in interstate commerce jobs (unless they are employed by a parent in a nonhazardous job and a permit is obtained), and the employment of persons between the ages of 16 and 18 in hazardous jobs (such as meat processing plants).

Exempt from the provisions of the Fair Labor Standards Act are small retail businesses whose gross yearly sales do not exceed $362,000 and certain classes of employees. Employees who are not involved in interstate commerce; who are engaged in seasonal industries; or who are classified as executives, administrators, professionals, or outside salespeople are exempt from the minimum wage rate and overtime provisions of the law. In fact, these groups of employees are categorized legally as *exempt workers*. On the other hand, *nonexempt workers*, who are typically engaged in skilled or semi-skilled blue-collar jobs, are subject to the minimum wage rate and overtime provisions of the law.

Equal employment opportunity laws

There are three laws administered by the Equal Employment Opportunity Commission which prohibit pay discrimination. The **Equal Pay Act** (EPA) of 1963,[9] an amendment to the Fair Labor Standards Act, prohibits wage discrimination among employees on the basis of sex when employees perform similar jobs requiring equivalent skills in comparable circumstances in the same establishment. Pay differentials between jobs falling under the previously mentioned stipulations are only justifiable on the basis of:

1. A bona fide seniority system.
2. A legitimate merit system.
3. A system of pay which is performance based (measuring quality and quantity of output).
4. Any factor other than sex.

The **Civil Rights Act of 1964 (Title VII),** the second law administered by the EEOC, prohibits employment discrimination of all types (including compensation) on the basis of race, color, religion, sex, and national origin. Subsequent amendments to Title VII in 1972 and 1978 strengthened the enforcement powers of the EEOC and expanded its coverage to educational and governmental institutions and private employers of more than fifteen people. In addition, the pregnancy amendment of 1978 prohibits discrimination based on pregnancy or any of its related conditions.

The third law administered by the EEOC is the **Age Discrimination in Employment Act (ADEA)** of 1978. As enacted, the ADEA prohibits employment discrimination, including compensation discrimination, of persons over the age of forty. Specifically related to compensation, the act invalidates compulsory retirement in pension plans until age seventy for the private sector, and it eliminates compulsory retirement at any age in the federal government. Justifiable retirement under the act exists in only three instances. These include:

1. Individuals who demonstrate an inability to do the job.
2. Executives in policy making positions.
3. People whose pension, excluding Social Security, exceeds $44,000 per year.[10]

The Comparable Worth Controversy

Without a doubt, one of the most significant compensation issues during the past decade has been the controversy over **comparable worth.**[11] The focus of the argument has been on whether jobs which are of equal value to a company but are dissimilar in content and job responsibilities should be paid equally. This debate stems from the fact that, traditionally, occupations which primarily

Exhibit 9.1

Government Laws Affecting Compensation[12]

Law	Major provision	Affects
Davis-Bacon Act (1931)	Workers must be paid the prevailing wage rate of the locality where work is being performed.	Government contractors of $2,000 or more.
Walsh-Healy Act (1936)	Workers must be paid the prevailing industry rate rather than the area minimum. Overtime wage is paid at the rate of one and one-half times the hourly rate paid for hours in excess of eight per day or forty per week.	Government contractors of $10,000 or more.
Fair Labor Standards Act (1938)	1. Established minimum wage rates. 2. Established overtime pay in excess of 40 hours per week. 3. Established child labor standards.	All employers involved in interstate commerce with exceptions for certain occupations and retail establishments.
Equal Pay Act (1963)	Prohibits wage discrimination on the basis of sex.	Employers of two or more workers.
Civil Rights Act (1964)	Prohibits wage discrimination because of membership in a protected class.	Employers of fifteen or more workers affecting commerce.
Age Discrimination in Employment Act (1967)	Prohibits wage discrimination on the basis of age.	Employers of twenty or more workers.

employed women tended to be lower paying than occupations performed primarily by men. This disparity in wages approximates 35 percent, and is caused mostly by discrepancies between the sexes in terms of number of years of experience and continuity of service. However, even when length of service, ability to acquire needed skills, and knowledge of job availability are held constant, there is still a 16 percent pay difference between men and women.[13]

In spite of the rhetoric attached to the comparable worth controversy, the issue remains unresolved. Advocates of equal pay maintain that certain occupations, such as nursing and teaching, are undervalued because they are traditionally dominated by women. Opponents maintain that the concept of supply and demand is the major impetus for determining wage rates across occupations, regardless of the gender composition of the workforce. Furthermore, it is estimated that installing a comparable worth program nationwide to correct the inequity between female and male salaries would cost approximately $320 billion. This in turn could create economic disaster by causing an inflation rate of 10 percent and reducing the country's competitiveness in the international marketplace. (Statistics are from the Hay and Associates study.)[14]

To date, the Supreme Court has not been willing to make a definite ruling on the comparable worth issue. This failure to resolve the issue is probably attributable to the problems associated with determining the "true worth" of jobs, and the predicted devastating economic impact which could result from implementing comparable worth nationwide. As a result, the EEOC does not consider comparable worth to be a legitimate argument for determining sex discrimination in establishing compensation. This does not mean that the EEOC fails to consider sex discrimination cases involving compensation plans. Rather, the EEOC continues to vigorously pursue claims of wage discrimination when the evidence indicates that traditional compensation programs are being administered unfairly.[15]

For practitioners, comparable worth is an issue which needs to be monitored closely. The court rulings which have been highly publicized, such as *AFSCME* (American Federation of State, County, and Municipal Employees) v. *State of Washington,* have stressed the importance of the wage determination methods which the employer used in establishing different pay rates.[16] Because most of these systems (discussed later in this chapter) involve some use of subjective evaluations, human resource managers must carefully monitor the development and use of the compensation system. Furthermore, if comparable worth advocates succeed in introducing legislation favoring their position, employers must realize the economic realities of implementing such a plan and competing for needed personnel in a higher cost labor market.

Organizational Considerations

Ultimately, when developing and implementing their compensation programs, organizations must take into account the internal impact of their decisions. Enterprises create programs to reflect their ultimate organizational objectives. Effective compensation programs consider how the program will be administered, its impact on the needs of employees, and the organization's ability to pay.

Program administration

A well-designed compensation system may ultimately fail to achieve its objectives if it is administered in a haphazard fashion. All too often, organizations expend considerable effort and resources on the design of the system itself, and they overlook its implementation. Proper administration, a major function of human resource management, requires the continual monitoring and modifying of the system to assure its continued effectiveness. In today's constantly changing environment, compensation systems cannot remain constant. As with other programs, periodic auditing is necessary to fine tune the process.

Employee needs

One of the most important elements in the design of an effective compensation system is the satisfaction of employee needs.[17] If pay satisfaction is low, then the result is likely to be low job satisfaction.[18] As indicated in the following chapter, there are several compensation programs and combinations of programs available for use. The selection of the programs to be adopted is ultimately based on an organization's long-term goals and the needs of employees. Some organizations may choose to provide most of the compensation directly through wages and salary. Others may find that both individual and organizational goals are best served by providing greater indirect compensation in terms of benefits and incentives. For example, companies which consist primarily of young workers may discover that direct compensation in terms of extra take-home pay is preferable to long-term benefits. On the other hand, older and more highly paid employees may prefer compensation programs which defer taxes into retirement years.

In addition to meeting the long- or short-term monetary needs of their employees, organizations must consider the daily impact compensation has on individual workers. Over the years, theorists have debated about the impact of pay on individual motivation, job satisfaction, and productivity. The results of these arguments have been mixed. Some people assert that money impacts greatly on both motivation and job satisfaction, while others maintain that the effect is minimal. Furthermore, some studies indicate that performance-based pay produces higher motivation, while other researchers have shown that pay for performance may actually reduce motivation and performance on intrinsically task-motivated jobs.[19]

The diverse findings regarding the effect of pay are probably attributable to the simple fact that employees differ significantly in their desires. It would seem only natural to assume that if workers' preferences for the types of benefits desired differed, so too would the impact of these plans on individual motivation and satisfaction. In order to meet these diverse needs, organizations should design their compensation programs with as much flexibility as possible, allowing for individual freedom of choice.

Finally, organizations must consider the effects of their pay plans on worker equity. Compensation systems which reward all workers equally in spite of individual differences in job content and contribution to the organization's objectives are destined to create feelings of inequity. Employers who determine that internal consistency is important to their organization develop intricate systems to support this belief. On the other hand, businesses that feel internal equity is relatively unimportant for meeting organizational goals (that is, businesses which are highly understaffed and must compete economically for a limited supply of labor) may choose to channel all available resources in other directions.

Ability to pay

In order to implement a compensation system, organizations must generate sufficient revenues to cover the costs of the program. For most private sector businesses, profits are a direct result of the sales of goods and services. These sales are directly attributable to competition in the marketplace. When business is good, profits are high, and the organization's ability to pay greater wages is increased. Downturns in the sales of goods and services, however, sharply curtail the organization's capability to provide substantial wage packages.

Exhibit 9.2

Major Influences on Compensation Plans

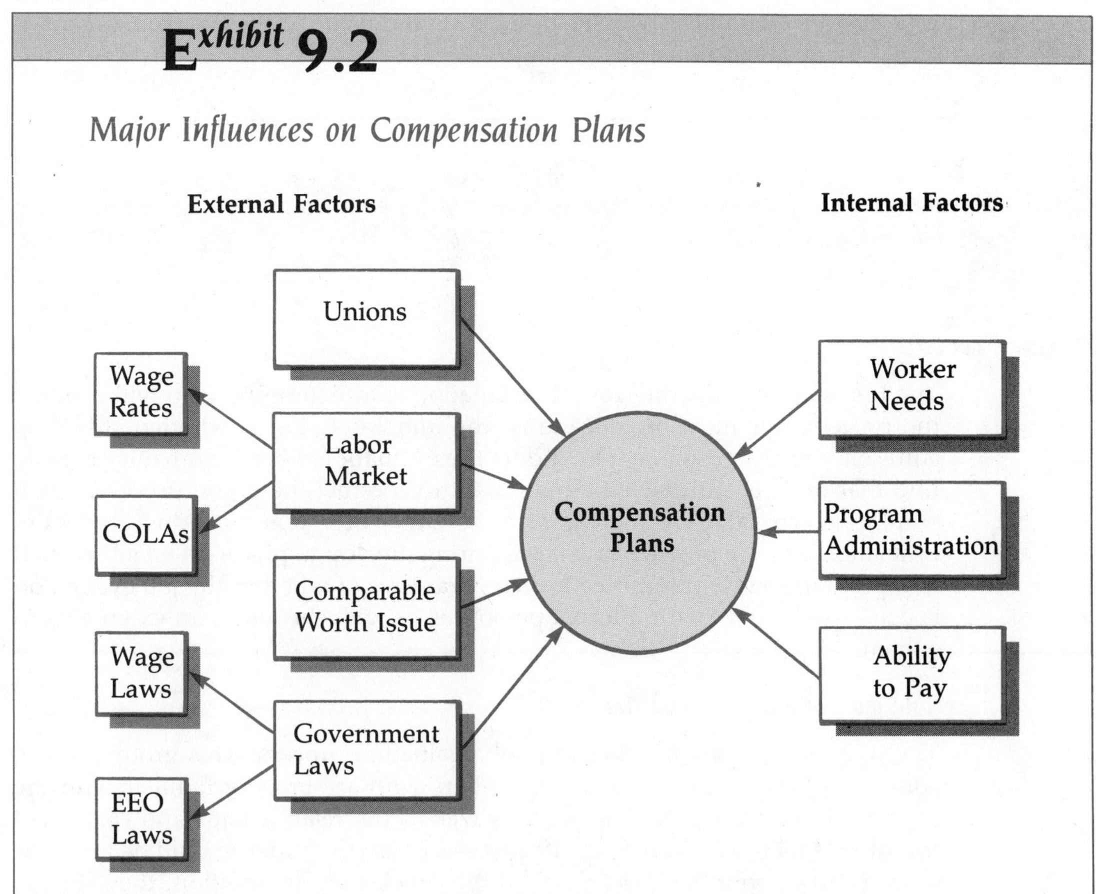

In essence, if organizations overestimate their potential revenues, they may inadvertently create compensation systems which severely tax the company's resources. Regardless of the desire by employers to pay high salaries, market conditions determine the maximum pay level. Exceeding this ceiling leaves the organization with two basic choices. It can either raise prices in order to generate additional working capital or it must allocate a greater percentage of revenues to labor costs.[20] In either case, both actions can result in severe consequences for the organization. If market conditions are extremely competitive, the increase in prices can result in lost revenues. Similarly, re-allocating revenues to cover labor costs can curtail other company activities that are necessary to remain competitive.

Job Evaluation—Determining the Worth of Jobs

In addition to establishing wage scales based on market and internal influences, many organizations use specific procedures to determine the worth of the various jobs in the company. The process undertaken by these organizations is called **job evaluation.**

> ***Job evaluation***
>
> *Job evaluation is a process undertaken to ascertain the relative worth of each and every job within an organization.*

Initial Procedures

The first step in preparing for job evaluation is to determine who will conduct the process. For most organizations, the initial decision is whether there are sufficient internal resources to conduct the evaluation. Large companies usually find that there is sufficient internal talent to conduct the entire process. Small employers typically hire consultants who either design and conduct the entire evaluation, or only provide assistance during the design phase. Most job evaluation programs use a committee format regardless of whether the job evaluation is conducted totally with internal personnel or with the aid of an external consultant.

The job evaluation committee

The committee is the heart of any job evaluation process. This group usually consists of between five and ten members who are broadly familiar with the organization's goals and objectives, as well as the relationships and content of the various jobs. For maximum effectiveness, the committee should be involved in the process from the onset through the conclusion. In addition, they should be trained in identifying job elements, decision making, and following the procedures involved in the particular job evaluation method used.

The members of the job evaluation committee are usually chosen to represent all parties involved. Typically, the committee is composed of at least a management representative, a human resource employee (usually a compensation specialist), a union member, an employee representative (differentiated from a union member because not all workers are necessarily members of the union), and sometimes an external consultant.

The tasks confronting most committees involve selecting the job evaluation plan to be used and ultimately judging the job evaluator's work. Rarely do the committee members conduct the actual evaluation process. Rather, they serve as a board to evaluate the work of the specialists and to make final recommendations.

Collecting data

The next phase of the evaluation process involves obtaining uniform details about each job. This is accomplished by using information from previously completed job analyses, or from those specifically conducted for the job evaluation process. From these analyses, job descriptions (written summaries of the duties and responsibilities) and job specifications (employee qualifications necessary for satisfactory performance) are developed.

Compensable factors

In order for the various jobs within an organization to be compared, similar elements of each job need to be identified. These common elements, termed **compensable factors,** are used to compare the jobs on content area and to eventually aid in determining the compensation paid to each job. Because the results of the entire process hinge on the adequate comparison of jobs on these compensable factors, extreme care must be taken when writing descriptions and specifications which facilitate the job evaluator's comparison of job content.

> **Compensable factors**
>
> ***Compensable factors are the common elements present in all jobs within an organization that serve as the basis for job evaluation comparisons.***

Although some employers develop their own compensable factors, most use previously developed components. These range from factors such as know how, problems solving, and accountability (used predominantly by Hay Consulting), to skill, effort, responsibility, and working conditions (factors identified by the federal government in the Equal Pay Act).

The particular factors an organization chooses are dependent on the types of jobs to be analyzed and the job evaluation method chosen. For example, an analysis of managerial jobs may use planning as a major compensable factor, while an analysis of production jobs may focus on manual dexterity. The final choice of which factors to use is ultimately specific to the organization. There are, however, criteria which may be used for a general overall decision. These are:

1. The compensable factors should be acceptable to management, employees, and the union. If the factors are perceived as irrelevant, the entire system will be viewed as inequitable.
2. The compensable factors must validly distinguish among jobs.
3. The factors must be present to some degree in all jobs.
4. Different jobs must vary regarding the amount of each factor present.
5. Each factor must be measurable, or it will not be useful in determining relative worth.
6. Factors should measure different things. If factors measure the same element, double weight will be added, biasing the evaluation.[21]

Job Evaluation Methods

There are four basic job evaluation methods. They are: the ranking method, the classification method, the factor comparison method, and the point method.[22] Ranking and classification methods use a "whole job" approach and are considered qualitative systems. Factor comparison and point methods require job content to be divided into and evaluated by compensable factors. These latter methods are more specific and involve quantitative measures. In addition, the methods differ regarding the standard used for comparison. Ranking and classification methods require whole jobs to be compared to one another. Factor comparison and point methods rate jobs against a descriptive standard or scale.

The Ranking Method

The **ranking method** is the easiest system for employees to understand and the least expensive to use. Like other ranking procedures, such as performance appraisal, the ranking method requires evaluators to compare different job descriptions and order them along a continuum from most difficult and most important to least difficult and least important.

> **Ranking method**
>
> *A ranking method requires evaluators to compare jobs to one another and to order them along a continuum from the most important job in the organization to the one of least importance.*

Ranking may be accomplished several ways, but two methods appear to be most common. The first technique involves placing job titles and short job descriptions on individual cards or papers (one card or paper for each job to be evaluated). Evaluators review the cards, choosing the job which is most important to the organization. This card is then removed from the deck and placed in a pile. Once again the deck is searched for the most important job remaining. After selection, it is placed directly under the first choice. This procedure is repeated until the total deck is exhausted. The final rankings are then reviewed for accuracy and agreement. Subsequently, each job is assigned a numbered rank for later use in assigning pay.

The second ranking method, which is probably the most commonly used method, is "paired comparisons." Unlike the deck of cards method, where overall global judgments are made, paired comparisons requires that each job be compared with each and every other job, and judged on its importance to the organization. The job receiving the highest amount of "most important" rankings is assigned a value of one, the next job two, and so on. In order to facilitate this approach, most evaluators use a comparison table or matrix.

When more than one evaluator is involved in the ranking procedure, individual rankings are conducted and the results are subsequently averaged. Sometimes broad discrepancies among evaluators occurs. At this point, it is advisable for the evaluators to discuss the rationale underlying their rankings of the jobs in question. These discussions usually aid in obtaining agreement among the evaluators.

Although it is a relatively uncomplicated system to use, the ranking method is not widely recommended. It is a highly subjective method which is open to inherent rater biases, and it fails to provide any concrete reasons for the ultimate rankings obtained. Without this rationale it is difficult, at best, to explain or justify the final rankings to managers and workers.

Another major difficulty encountered in the use of the ranking method is its unwieldiness in later job evaluation stages. Although the ranking method arranges the jobs in a hierarchy in terms of importance, it fails to discriminate among jobs in terms of degree of relevance. This lack of information makes it extremely difficult when the time comes to assign different pay ranges to the jobs.

Finally, use of the ranking method is limited to situations where small numbers of jobs need to be evaluated. As indicated in Chapter 7 on performance appraisal, the formula for determining the number of rankings to be conducted is $N(N - 1)/2$. Ranking 25 jobs means that 300 evaluations have to be made. Furthermore, it is not unreasonable to assume that an inverse relationship exists between number of jobs requiring evaluation and rater knowledge of each specific job. As the number of jobs increases, the evaluator's intricate knowledge of each job decreases. The end result is a system based on scant, rather than comprehensive, information.

The Classification Method

The **classification method** attempts to overcome some of the shortcomings inherent in the ranking method. Instead of comparing jobs to each other, the classification system requires evaluators to establish a hierarchy of class levels for cataloging each job. The system may be compared to a school consisting of various grade levels. For each grade, specific descriptions of the curriculum and knowledge required is established. Just as a child is placed in a certain class or grade based on his or her knowledge and age, so too are jobs classified into grades based on the amount of skill and responsibility inherent in the position.

> **Classification method**
>
> *The classification method requires evaluators to establish and define class levels covering the range of organizational jobs, and subsequently to place each job into the appropriate class.*

The initial task confronting evaluators is to establish the range of grades. There are two major considerations during this phase. First, a sufficient level of grades to cover the entire job spectrum must be established. Second, and probably most bothersome, class descriptions must be written. The more diverse the job families are in the organization, the harder it is to establish and define classes into which each job can readily be placed. For example, writing class descriptions aimed at office personnel may present problems when attempting to classify distribution clerks who have similar, but different, duties and responsibilities.

Probably the best known classification system is the one used by the federal government's Office of Personnel Management. Commonly known as "GS" (General Scale) levels, this system classifies jobs into eighteen grades, each consisting of ten steps or levels. For all practical purposes, the system really consists of sixteen grades because the top three levels (16, 17, and 18) have been collapsed into a "supergrade" grouping consisting of senior level executives. Consequently, most jobs are classified into levels 1 through 15, based on the level of difficulty inherent in each job. The various steps within each grade are used to provide pay increases based on length of service. Thus, a GS 5–3 could be doing the same job as a GS 5–1, but have more time in rank.

The classification system is not without criticism. Writing job descriptions seems deceptively simple, but in reality, it is a cumbersome process. Many administrators have been known to work around the system, rather than through the system, in order to achieve their ends.[23] Creating an effective scale can be both time consuming and costly. As the diversity of jobs increases, the difficulty in writing the job descriptions expands. After the classification phase has been completed, it may be discovered that jobs qualify for insertion into more than one grade level.

Another related disadvantage is the fact that, like the ranking method, the classification method does not provide justifiable explanations for the eventual classifications. As a result, managers and workers tend to feel that job wages can be improved by rewriting job descriptions to fit different class levels.

Exhibit 9.3

General Schedule Pay Scale—January 1989

	Time-in-grade step increases									
	1	2	3	4	5	6	7	8	9	10
GS–1	$10,213	$10,555	$10,894	$11,233	$11,573	$11,773	$12,108	$12,445	$12,461	$12,780
GS–2	11,484	11,757	12,137	12,461	12,601	12,972	13,343	13,714	14,085	14,456
GS–3	12,531	12,949	13,367	13,785	14,203	14,621	15,039	15,457	15,875	16,293
GS–4	14,067	14,536	15,005	15,474	15,943	16,412	16,881	17,350	17,819	18,288
GS–5	15,738	16,263	16,788	17,313	17,838	18,363	18,888	19,413	19,938	20,463
GS–6	17,542	18,127	18,712	19,297	19,882	20,467	21,052	21,637	22,222	22,807
GS–7	19,493	20,143	20,793	21,443	22,093	22,743	23,393	24,043	24,693	25,343
GS–8	21,590	22,310	23,030	23,750	24,470	25,190	25,910	26,630	27,350	28,070
GS–9	23,846	24,641	25,436	26,231	27,026	27,821	28,616	29,411	30,206	31,001
GS–10	26,261	27,136	28,011	28,886	29,761	30,636	31,511	32,386	33,261	34,136
GS–11	28,852	29,814	30,776	31,738	32,700	33,662	34,624	35,586	36,548	37,510
GS–12	34,580	35,733	36,886	38,039	39,192	40,345	41,498	42,651	43,804	44,957
GS–13	41,121	42,492	43,863	45,234	46,605	47,976	49,347	50,718	52,089	53,460
GS–14	48,592	50,212	51,832	53,452	55,072	56,692	58,312	59,932	61,552	63,172
GS–15	57,158	59,063	60,968	62,873	64,778	66,683	68,588	70,493	72,398	74,303
GS–16	67,038	69,273	71,508	73,743	75,473	76,678*	78,869*	81,060*	82,500*	
GS–17	76,990*	79,556*	82,122*	82,500*	83,818*					
GS–18	86,682*									

*Basic rate payable is limited to rate for Executive Schedule, Level V.

The Factor Comparison Method

The **factor comparison method,** which was originated by Eugene Benge in 1926 and later broadened by Burk and Hay, is an expansion of the ranking method. It is more complex than either the ranking or classification systems, and it is used by about 10 percent of the companies which use formal evaluation systems.[24] The method requires that jobs be evaluated based on a universal set of compensable factors, and that they be assigned wages according to "key or benchmark jobs." *Key jobs* are those which the committee feels are representative of the organization from top to bottom and whose current wage rate is considered correct by the evaluation committee. The success or failure of the evaluation process is highly dependent on the proper selection of these key jobs.

Factor comparison method

The factor comparison method requires evaluators to select and evaluate "key or benchmark jobs" according to selected compensable factors, to establish wage scales based on these rankings, and subsequently to compare all remaining jobs to these key jobs.

Steps in the factor comparison method

Step 1 The first step in the factor comparison method is to conduct job analyses based on a set of universal factors. According to Benge, Burk, and Hay, five universal factors should be considered. For hourly workers these would include: mental requirements, skill requirements, physical requirements, responsibilities, and working conditions. For supervisory, technical, and clerical positions, the universal factors would include: mental requirements, skill requirements (experience rather than manual manipulation), physical factors (combining physical requirements and working conditions), supervisory responsibility, and other organizational responsibilities not previously included.[25]

Step 2 After the job analyses have been completed, key jobs are selected. As mentioned earlier, committee members must agree that these jobs are representative of the broad range of jobs to be evaluated and that their existing wage rates are accurate. In addition, key jobs are defined as jobs whose content remains stable over time, jobs which are common to many firms, and jobs which are recognized in the marketplace as wage setting positions.

Step 3 Once the key jobs have been selected, they are ranked independently by the committee members according to each of the five compensable factors. Subsequently, the results are compared, and each key job is given a rank in relation to every factor. Any disagreement among the committee members is usually resolved by open discussions in which the rationales behind the rankings are detailed. Unlike the ranking method, which results in whole jobs being compared to each other, the factor comparison method ranks the job against each factor.

Step 4 The fourth step involves determining how much of the wage rate paid for key jobs is attributable to each factor, ranking these wage rates, and comparing the factor and wage rate rankings. For example, suppose that a drill press operator is being paid $7.48 per hour. The first determination is how much of the $7.48 is assigned for mental requirements, how much is assigned for skill requirements, and so on. Next, the portion of the wage paid for the factor would be ranked in comparison to other key jobs. Thus, if $3.48 of the $7.48 is determined to be attributable to skill requirements, and $3.48 is the highest amount being paid (among the key jobs) for skill, then it is assigned a rank of 1.

Finally, the factor rank assigned and the wage rate assigned are compared. If the compensable factor of skill required is ranked number 1 for a drill press operator and the wage assigned for that factor is ranked number 1, then the process is completed. If inconsistencies occur within the scale, the process must be repeated until agreement is reached.

Step 5 When consistency is reached, the committee constructs a master comparison scale which inserts each key job into a slot corresponding to its dollar value per factor. This scale serves as the basis for cataloging all other non-key

Exhibit 9.4

Some Factors Used by Different Systems in Evaluation[26]

Hay System (Hourly Jobs)	American Association of Industrial Management (formerly the National Metal Trades Association)	Federal Civil Service GS–1 through GS–15 (FES)
Mental requirements	Skill	Knowledge
Skill requirements	Effort	Supervisory controls
Physical requirements	Responsibility	Complexity
Responsibilities	Working conditions	Guidelines
Working conditions	Training required	Scope and effect
	Initiative	Personal contacts
	Supervision	Purpose of contacts
		Physical demands
		Work environment

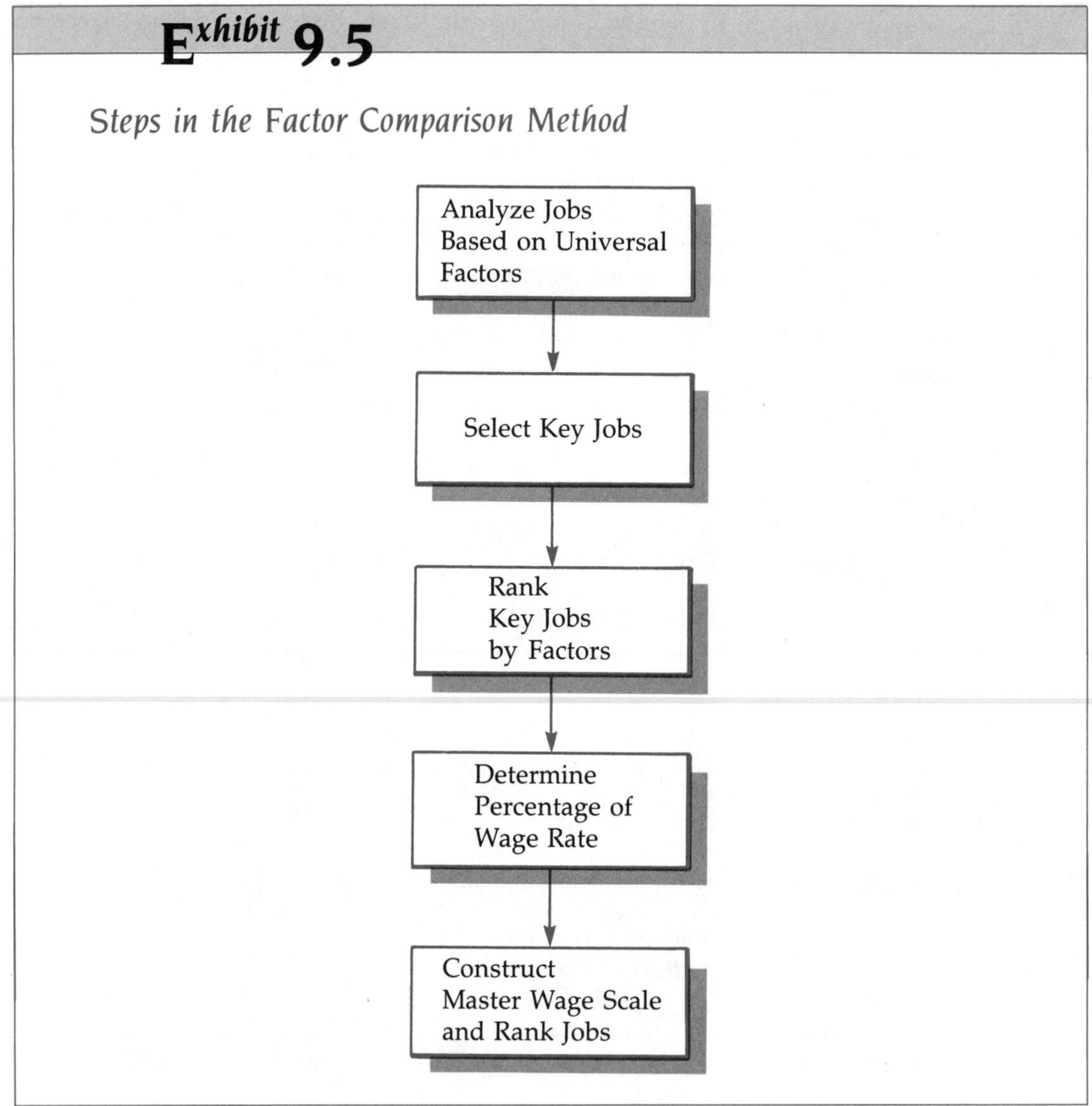

Exhibit 9.5

Steps in the Factor Comparison Method

jobs. Each remaining job is analyzed in terms of how it ranks per factor in comparison to the key jobs, and is assigned a monetary value for each factor. The total of the monetary assignment for the five factors constitutes the pay rate for the job. As each job is compared, it is slotted into the master scale. Subsequent jobs are then compared to the entire scale, including the key and non-key positions. Upon completion, all jobs within the organization will become part of the scale.

The use of the factor comparison method is advantageous in that the end result is a custom-made scale which may be easily used by unskilled individuals.

Unfortunately, although it is usually easy to employ the scale, initially creating the scale is quite tedious. In many instances, it is difficult to select key jobs which are representative of the entire job spectrum. While lower level jobs are common, supervisory and managerial positions are diverse and unique. Furthermore, the method is extremely complex, and explaining it to workers and supervisors is a formidable task.

The Point Method

The **point method** is probably the most widely used job evaluation system. Of the various point methods available for use, the most commonly used is the Hay Plan (Guide-Chart Profile Method).[27] This method requires evaluators to identify, describe, and assign point values to compensable factors, which then serve as the basis for evaluating all other jobs. Unlike the factor comparison method, which compares jobs to key jobs, the point method uses predefined subfactors as measures against which all other positions are evaluated. The end result is a determination of the relative worth of each job; the pay level is then based on the total amount of points assigned.

Point method

The point method requires compensable factors to be identified, described in terms of subfactors, and assigned point values based on their relative worth. Subsequently, each job is evaluated in terms of how many of the factors it possesses; it is assigned the corresponding point values, and it is slotted into a pay scale based on the total amount of points received.

Steps in the point method

Step 1 The first step in the use of the point method is to conduct job analyses and to select appropriate compensable factors. When choosing the factors to be included, committee members should strive to identify factors which are important to the organization and which also have the greatest potential for discriminating among the various jobs. Some guidelines for selecting the factors include:

1. The factors should differentiate among jobs in terms of difficulty, importance, and worth to the organization.
2. Each factor should be common to all jobs in greater and lesser amounts.
3. Each factor must be weighted to reflect its overall worth to the jobs.
4. No factor should measure the same element as another factor.
5. All factors should be acceptable to employees and managers alike in terms of fairness and completeness.

6. The number of factors chosen should provide completeness and simplicity without blurring judgments or limiting flexibility.
7. All factor definitions should be clear enough to assure uniformity of interpretation among different raters.[28]

Step 2 The second step is to define the factors and establish the factor scales. Written statements are usually developed which define, as objectively and behaviorally as possible, the factor in general, and the subcategories within each factor. For example, suppose an organization is using the factor "training and experience." The global definition may be "amount of time individuals must have to satisfactorily complete the job in order to justify continued employment." Within the category, there may be four degrees or levels which include:

Level 1—up to and including three months.

Level 2—three months and one day to six months.

Level 3—six months and one day to twelve months.

Level 4—one year and one day or more.

Organizations have two basic choices when deciding on which factors to use. They can either create and define factors specifically for use in their environment or they can adopt already existing factors from a standard plan. Regardless of the method chosen, however, the factors will invariably need some modification before they are applicable. Custom-made factors must be defined from scratch, and existing commercially available plans usually require adjustments within the subfactors.

Step 3 The factors and factor scales must be assigned points after they have been established. Point assignments may be accomplished subjectively by having committee members allocate 100 percent of the value among the various factors, or through statistical procedures. Regardless of which method is employed, the number of points assigned to the highest degree of a given factor may not exceed proportionately the weight assigned to the factor. For example, suppose it has been determined that 35 percent of the job's worth of a five-factor plan is the result of the factor "skill required." If the maximum points obtainable for all five factors is 250, then the highest degree of "skill required" cannot be evaluated at more than 87.5 points (250 × .35).

Once the points have been agreed on, key jobs are chosen to be compared to each other. After the evaluation has been completed, each job's position in the hierarchy is reviewed. If the committee determines that the hierarchical arrangement is appropriate, they proceed to the final step. If agreement cannot be reached, re-evaluation is undertaken.

Step 4 The final step in the point method is to document the procedure in manual form and to evaluate the jobs. The purpose of creating a manual is to enable the procedure to be replicated by others at a later date. Consequently,

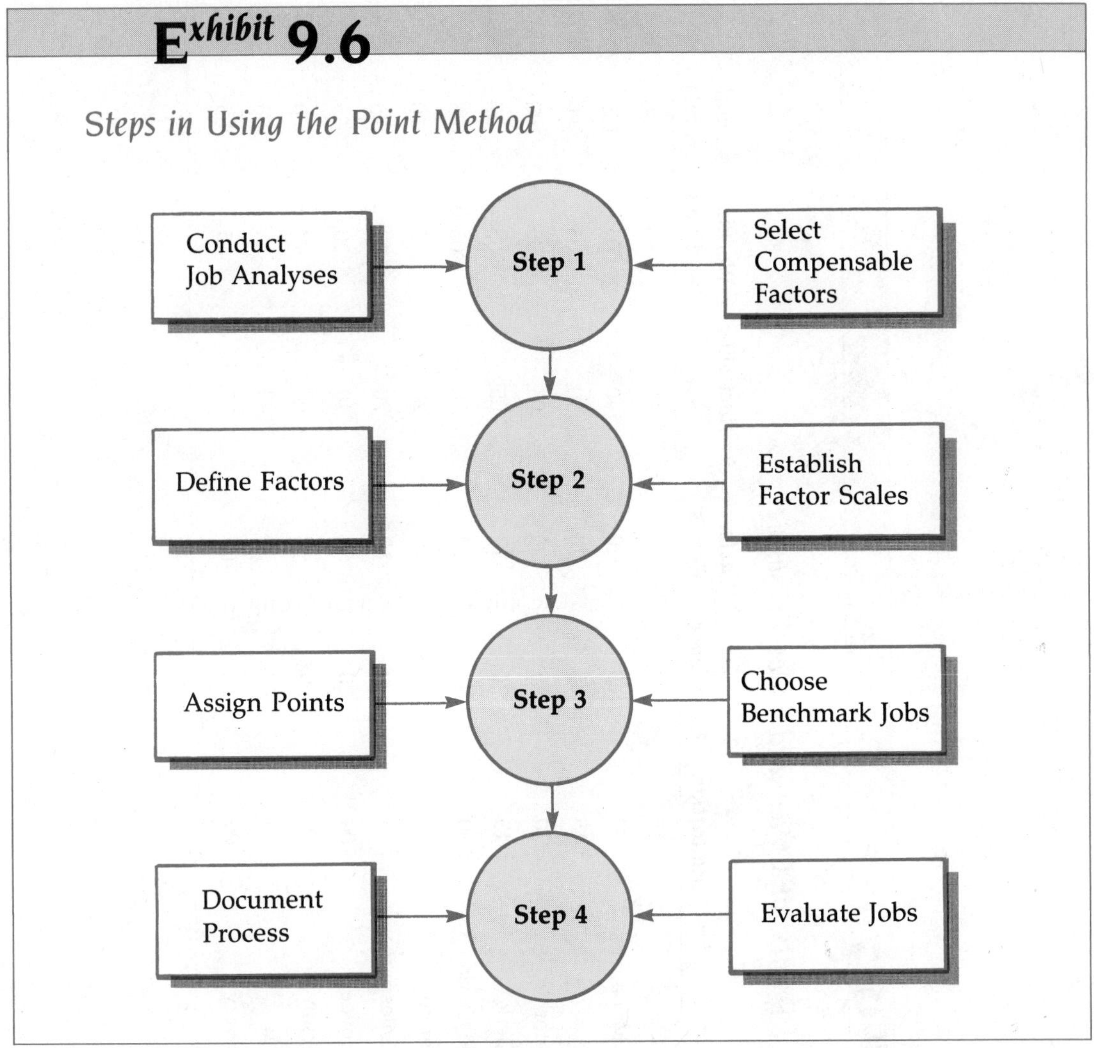

it is advisable for the documentation to include not only the procedural steps undertaken, but also the rationale behind the selection and weighing of the various factors.

The advantages of the point method are obvious. First, once the factors and degrees are defined, there is usually agreement among committee members in the evaluation of job descriptions. Second, barring any drastic change in the organization's purpose, the compensable factors are relatively stable over time. Finally, if documented correctly, the system is easily explained to employees.[29]

Without a doubt, the creation of a point system is a complex process, which is its major weakness. For most organizations, particularly small ones, the ex-

Exhibit 9.7

Assignment of Points for Office and Sales Personnel

Job title	Education	Experience	Factors/ Errors	Contact with others	Working conditions	Total points
Accounting Clerk	15	40	10	10	05	80
Assistant Credit Manager	30	60	20	40	05	155
Billing Clerk	15	40	20	10	05	90
Computer Operator	30	40	20	05	05	100
General Office Clerk	15	20	10	05	05	55
Accounts Payable Clerk	30	40	20	10	05	105
Switchboard Operator	15	20	10	20	05	70
Assistant Route Salesperson	15	20	10	20	10	75
Warehouse Employee	00	20	05	10	20	55
Regional Salesperson	30	60	40	60	10	200
Route Salesperson	15	40	20	40	15	130
Truck Driver/Delivery	00	40	05	05	15	65

pertise necessary to develop a point manual is not present in-house. Outside assistance in the form of consultants is usually necessary. The process can thus be time consuming, and expensive.[30]

Establishing the Pay Structure

Organizations establish pay structures after a job evaluation has been completed. If the organization chooses to use one of the nonquantitative job evaluation methods (ranking or classification), they virtually always group jobs into a grading system. On the other hand, using a quantitative job evaluation method (factor comparison or point) which develops an unlimited continuum allows organizations to either create individual ranges by points or to group jobs with similar point totals together.

Grouping jobs into grades reduces the amount of fine discriminations which need to be made among positions. Jobs whose content areas are substantially the same are grouped into one pay grade and have similar salaries. This allows organizations, particularly those which use job rotation programs, the opportunity to shift workers from job to job without having to make adjustments to their wages. Furthermore, organizations which employ a job posting system have the added benefit of listing the grade level of job openings. This enables potential internal applicants to quickly ascertain whether or not the open position offers them an advancement opportunity.

Once grades have been developed and jobs have been assigned, organizations typically establish ranges within the grades. These ranges are usually listed in step fashion, broken down by minimum and maximum dollar amounts. For example, suppose one grade included all jobs assigned point values between 150–200 points. Within this grade, there may be three steps:

Step 1—$3.75—4.00
Step 2—$4.00—4.25
Step 3—$4.25—4.50

The minimum wage assigned any job evaluated between 150 and 200 points is $3.75 per hour, while the maximum is $4.50 per hour. The fluctuation within the range allows organizations the opportunity to reward workers for merit, seniority, or other individual pay needs (discussed in the next chapter).

The successful institution of a grading system requires that a large enough number of grades be created. If an insufficient amount of levels are developed, then it is inevitable that jobs which have identifiably different content will be grouped together. In addition, jobs which are close in content area may arbitrarily be assigned different pay grades (one on the top of a pay grade and the other at the bottom of the next pay grade). This format has the potential not only for causing internal inequity among workers but also for posing difficulty in the event that an equal employment opportunity suit must be defended. It is

Exhibit 9.8

A Grading System by Points

Grade level	Point range	Steps 1	Steps 2	Steps 3
1	50–80	$3.35–3.75	$3.60–4.00	$3.85–4.30
2	81–105	4.25–4.55	4.40–4.75	4.60–5.00
3	106–135	4.90–5.25	5.15–5.50	5.45–6.00
4	136–160	5.90–6.30	6.25–6.75	6.70–7.50
5	161–200	7.50–8.25	8.15–8.75	8.65–9.25

quite difficult to explain to workers, or to others, why jobs which are so substantially similar in content are assigned different wage levels.

Pay systems should be periodically reviewed and revised for accuracy. Changes in the labor market and inflation rate, among other factors, may necessitate shifts in the minimum and maximum dollar amounts assigned each grade. Organizations which fail to monitor their systems routinely inevitably find themselves with an antiquated pay system. The end result of a poorly monitored system may be a pay structure that has severe repercussions for the company.

Summary

One of the most important tasks confronting organizations is the establishment and administration of compensation systems. Effectively accomplishing this task requires that companies provide wage and salary systems which employees view as fair and equitable. In addition, the system which is implemented must enable the organization to remain competitive.

Compensation systems are impacted by external and internal factors. The labor market, unions, and government rules and regulations are several external factors which affect the development and implementation of wage and salary plans. Furthermore, organizational considerations, such as the impact of the pay plan on worker needs and perceptions of equity, play a pivotal role in determining what type of compensation plan will emerge.

Once market and internal factors have been considered, organizations are ready to design compensation systems. To determine the relative worth of each job, many organizations use one of four common job evaluation procedures. These methods range from those which compare whole jobs to each other (ranking and classification methods) to more sophisticated techniques which compare jobs to a predetermined measure or scale (factor comparison and point methods). Regardless of the method used, the ultimate goal is to establish a pay structure which is easily explained to workers, which serves as a source of motivation, which adheres to government rules and regulations, and which endures over time.

Key Terms to Identify

Compensation
Wage survey
Cost of living adjustment (COLA)
Davis-Bacon Act
Walsh-Healy Act
Fair Labor Standards Act
Equal Pay Act
Civil Rights Act of 1964 (Title VII)
Age Discrimination in Employment Act (ADEA)
Comparable worth
Job evaluation
Compensable factors
Ranking method
Classification method
Factor comparison method
Point method

Questions for Discussion

Do You Know the Facts?

1. Discuss the impact that the labor market has on compensation planning. What methods might a company use to obtain labor market information?
2. What are three major laws which affect compensation plans? How do they impact on the plans?
3. Discuss the pros and cons of the comparable worth issue. Do you think the courts have ruled logically on the issue or in response to lobbying pressures?
4. What are the advantages and disadvantages associated with the four common job evaluation procedures?

Can You Apply the Information Learned?

1. As a manager, how would you explain the laws of supply and demand to workers who are complaining that their wages are substantially lower than those of new employees being hired?
2. What programs would you install in your organization if comparable worth were ruled to be the law of the land?
3. As a human resource manager, what steps would you take in order to prepare your company for job evaluation?
4. What steps would you take if after conducting job evaluation you discovered that 50 percent of your employees were underpaid? Would your answer be the same if your business were highly labor intensive? Capital intensive?

The Kohler Company

Bill Board was hired as a Caster Trainee by the Kohler Company in January. Bill, who quickly got the nickname Road Runner because of his old red Plymouth, received a starting wage of $6.62 per hour. A caster's job was to mold bowls for porcelain bathroom fixtures. The skill required to cast a piece that fires properly takes three months to learn and as much as two years to bring to a consistently high level. Casting is the first step in the production process; it is followed by coating with a glaze and firing, which turns the greenware into fine vitreous porcelain.

When Road Runner was first hired, he was assigned one-to-one with a casting instructor. This trainer showed him how to clean the molds, prepare the slip (the liquid clay used in molding), pour the slip into the molds, remove the hardened greenware, smooth and join the components, and finish the surface of the piece. Road Runner worked with this casting trainer for three weeks.

Next, he was assigned to a foreman who supervised several employees at various stages in their training. While he was a trainee, Road Runner's pay was calculated on the basis of .387 earned hour for each mold he completed. Trainees usually completed about 10 to 12 molds. That rate of production is not sufficient to earn the full hourly rate of $6.62, so the deficiency is made up by the company. Satisfactory completion of the three-month probationary period resulted in an automatic increase of 10¢ per hour. With greater competence, the new employee is allowed to increase the number of molds he is given to cast. After six months of successful work experience, the employee is eligible to bid into other jobs or other floors in the plant which may result in greater earnings.

The Kohler Company's Spartanburg plant was opened in 1958. It has been expanded several times, most recently to accommodate the manufacture of fiberglas tub and shower enclosures. The plant employs well over one hundred casters. The work required of these casters is determined by job analysis and the pay level is determined by job evaluation. The job content and pay system are developed individually at each plant to reflect the demands of the jobs at that particular location. Spartanburg's system was developed about fifteen years ago and has been updated as needed in the interval. Job content factors were identified, and all jobs are measured against them and assigned points. (See Figure 1 for the description and evaluation of the Caster II position.) Jobs are usually re-evaluated on an annual basis or if some substantial activity in the job changes.

The Industrial Engineering department determines the standard rate of output for each position. Setting the rate must take into account the average production output, costs, impact of technology on output, and physical and mental effort required.

This case was prepared by Barbara Hastings of the University of South Carolina at Spartanburg. Reprinted with permission of the Kohler Company.

Figure 1 *Job Description*

TITLE: Caster, Group #2
REPORTS TO: Casting Foreman
BASIC FUNCTION:

Produce A–1 quality greenware in accordance with specifications, instructions and standards, working at a predetermined production rate, and adjusting to varying production conditions.

Daily attendance is required to fulfill casting cycle.

Requires working knowledge of simple equipment, and working to expert knowledge of complicated methods and a variety of materials. Care must be taken to prevent possible damage to molds, gauges, etc., and frequent loss of materials.

Must coordinate with coworker, and take care to avoid injuries from sharp tools or ordinary handling of 31 to 75 lbs. There is exposure to dirt, dust, and dampness, and occasional use of respirator.

Assist fellow workers and train new casters when required.

Job Evaluation

KNOWLEDGE:			EFFORT:		
Education	Some high school	50	Physical	Fairly heavy	90
Experience	4 to 12 months	100	Mental & Visual	Frequent attention	45
Initiative & Ingenuity	Average initiative, some ingenuity	50	Continuity of Effort	30% effort	20
RESPONSIBILITY:			WORKING CONDITIONS:		
Equipment	Some, w/some supervision	20	Working Atmosphere	High degree of undesirability	35
Molds, Material or Product	Fair degree	35	Hazards	Some exposure to injury	35
Safety of Others	Limited	10			
Effect on Others' Work	Limited	10	TOTAL EVALUATION POINTS		500

RATED BY: Crowley, Scoggins, Suits, Frantz, J. R. Brown

Industrial Engineering has determined that each piece produced by a Caster II is worth .387 of an earned hour. Knowing that, Road Runner can quickly calculate what pay he will earn at a specific level of production. For example:

21 pieces
× .387 earned hour
8.127 earned day
× $6.72 hourly rate
$54.61 daily rate

Road Runner knows that the company places an emphasis on quality and that he can earn Quality Premium Rate. The QPR of 10¢ per piece is paid to a caster who produces A–1 quality goods—those of sufficient quality to be sold with no rework. The bonus is calculated for a week's worth of work and is checked at the point of shipment. If a piece is broken or if some other quality problem arises in glazing, firing, or finishing, the caster receives no QPR for it. Products can be traced by an identifying number placed by the caster on the greenware leaving his bench.

To maintain sufficient output and quality levels, the casting supervisor evaluates each caster weekly. If Road Runner falls below standard output of 21 pieces a day or below an acceptable percentage of A–1 quality, molds may be removed from his bench. That will result in lower pay and cause him to concentrate his efforts on his remaining molds. A return to original quality and productivity will cause the molds to be reinstated.

It is now December, and Road Runner is been assigned to his first floor. He has been able on average to cast and finish 25 molds per day.

Questions for Discussion

1. If Road Runner can produce 25 molds a day on his bench with 62 percent average A–1 quality, what will his weekly wages be?
2. What kind of pay plan does Kohler have?
3. In your opinion, is the practice of withholding molds as a quality control measure appropriate? Will it be effective? Why?
4. What other job factors might Kohler include in its job evaluation system?
5. What theories of motivation are incorporated in the QPR plan? Do you think it is fair that the caster gets no QPR bonus if the piece is damaged or misworked after it leaves his bench?

Southeastern State University

Personnel-related problems often evolve out of a series of events which occur over a period of time. The impact is frequently not felt until long after the activities or the individuals which precipitated them have changed.

Such was the situation found in the residence halls' food-service operations at Southeastern State University. After a period of growth and facilities expansion, accompanied by a change in management approaches, several internal in-

This case was prepared by Sally A. Coltrin of the University of North Florida.

equities in both job classifications and wage rates became apparent, causing dissension and dissatisfaction among several groups of employees.

Southeastern's residence halls' operations remained rather stable from the time of its inception through the 1960s. There were three small-to-moderate-sized dining halls serving 600 to 700 students each. Each unit operated under the direction and supervision of a dietitian, an assistant food supervisor, and a chef. The food supervisors and chefs held civil service appointments, while the dietitians had faculty appointments. As an additional part of their compensation, dietitians received free room and board. Small apartments were provided for them in either the dining hall building or in one of the women's dormitories. Of course, meals were provided in the dining rooms and the dietitians were on duty for all three meals. Under these live-in arrangements, being a residence halls dietitian was not just a job, it was a way of life in which time on and off the job tended to blend together. Although the chefs were salaried employees, they worked somewhat more regular hours than dietitians. When overtime was required of chefs, it was strictly accounted for and compensatory time off was later given. Under these circumstances little, if any, consideration was given to the relationship between the job classifications and pay scales of chefs and dietitians. The two types of positions simply were not comparable.

Each food unit was operated on a fairly autonomous basis. Miss Smedley, the senior dietitian in the group, was not only the manager of the largest food unit, Wilson Hall, but also was an assistant-director of residence halls operations. As such she was a member of the top-management policy-making group. Although the other dietitians "officially" reported to their respective unit managers, they looked to Miss Smedley for direction and guidance.

The chefs had equally unique working relationships. Mr. DuBose, the chef working under Miss Smedley in Wilson Hall, was the senior chef in the division. Every new chef joining the organization served an apprenticeship under DuBose, and thus all the chefs looked to him for advice even though their "line reporting relationship" was to the dietitian in their respective unit. These unique relationships did not initially cause any animosity within the organization because all the dietitians acknowledged DuBose's exceptional competence.

DuBose's excellent performance over the years had been recognized and rewarded with regular salary increases and periodic upgrading (reclassifying) of his position. Thus, by the time of his retirement in the early 1970s, his position held a civil service classification of Food Service Manager IV and his salary was in excess of $25,000. (Figure 1 describes the early organizational relationships.)

George Ramsey, the next most senior chef, who was not nearly the overall caliber of DuBose, was chosen to replace DuBose upon the latter's retirement. Ramsey was transferred to Wilson Hall, given the existing position classification of Food Service Manager IV, and initially was expected to assume the "head chef" role which DuBose had held.

Within a few years of Ramsey's promotion, a large number of additional changes began occurring. The division of residence halls entered a period of rapid growth and expansion during which five new food-service units were built. This expansion obviously required the hiring of many new personnel, including additional chefs and dietitians. The subsequent retirement of Miss

Figure 1 *Organization Chart Before Expansion and Management Changes*

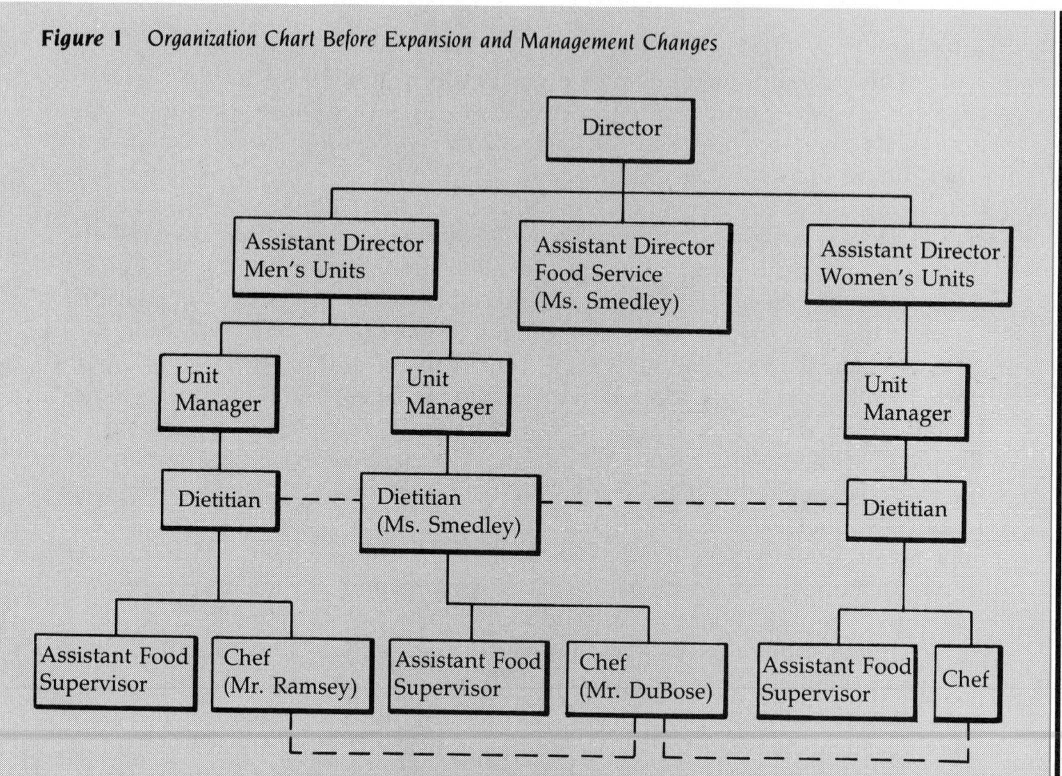

Smedley during this period provided a good opportunity to evaluate the organizational structure and overall food-service management philosophy, and to do some long-range planning. After considerable deliberation, it was decided there was need for greater coordination of the various food-service unit operations to improve and standardize the quality of operations and to insure more uniform personnel policies and practices. To execute the coordination efforts, a new position of director of food services was created. Miss Smedley's replacement then became just a unit dietitian, and she as well as all other newly hired dietitians held civil service classifications, without room and board perks, rather than faculty appointments.

Under the new management philosophy it was also felt that stronger role relationships should be developed between the unit dietitians and their respective assistant supervisors and chefs. To facilitate this the "head chef" connotation of Ramsey's role was gradually phased out, and he became simply the Wilson Hall unit chef. He still retained his Food Service Manager IV classification and corresponding salary, however, in recognition of his years of faithful service to the division, and the fact that his role change was not at his request, but rather was a result of management prerogative.

Figure 2 *Revised Organization Chart*

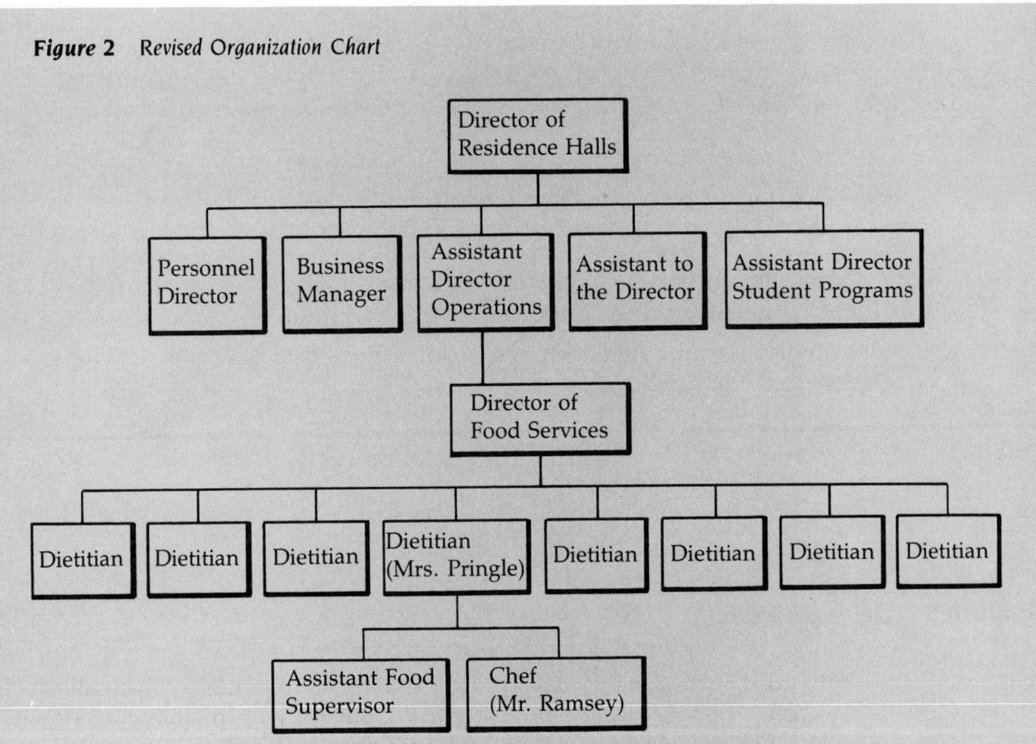

However, Ramsey's classification and salary gradually became a major bone of contention among a number of employees under the new system. Mrs. Pringle, who was hired to replace Miss Smedley as the Wilson Hall Manager, received a classification of Food Service Manager III, which was equal to the highest classification of any other unit dietitian, but still a grade *lower* than her subordinate, Ramsey! While Mrs. Pringle could understand the rationale for this inequity on a theoretical plane, from a practical standpoint it continued to bother her, and in fact adversely affected her performance. The other chefs also began to question the unfairness of the existing inequity between their salaries and Ramsey's. The majority of them felt that Ramsey's technical expertise was no better than their own, and now that he had only unit responsibilities similar to their own, his longevity of service was hardly justification for a classification two steps higher than any of them. (Figure 2 and Table 1 show a revised organization chart and civil service classifications and salary scales.)

Table 1 *Civil Service Classifications and Salary Scales*

Classifications	Salary ranges
Food Service Manager I	$10,000–$15,000
Food Service Manager II	$15,000–$20,000
Food Service Manager III	$20,000–$25,000
Food Service Manager IV	$25,000–$30,000

Thus, the growing resentment of the unit chefs and Mrs. Pringle presented a problem which the new food service director and the division's personnel director felt compelled to face and resolve in some equitable manner for all concerned.

Questions for Discussion

1. What should the university do about Mr. Ramsey's job classification and salary? Identify the advantages and disadvantages of your proposed actions.
2. Is there anything that could have been done along the way which would have prevented this problem from occurring?

Endnotes and References

1 For a good discussion on strategies and planning for instituting compensation plans in organizations, see Robert J. Greene, "Effective Compensation: The How and Why," *Personnel Administrator,* Vol. 32 (February 1987): 112–116.

2 Because comprehensive surveys are unrealistic, companies typically survey only "key" jobs. See Theodore E. Weinberger, "A Way to Audit the Job Matches of Salary Survey Participants," *Compensation Review,* Vol. 16, No. 3 (1984): 47–58.

3 Douglas R. LeRoy, "Scheduled Wage Increases and Cost-of-Living Provisions in 1981," *Monthly Labor Review,* Vol. 104 (January 1981): 9–14.

4 Richard B. Freeman and James L. Medoff, *What Do Unions Do?* (New York: Basic Books, 1984).

5 See the discussion concerning Ford Motor Company and givebacks in Chapter 13.

6 Fred K. Foulkes, *Personnel Policies of Large Non-Union Companies* (Englewood Cliffs, NJ: Prentice-Hall Book Company, 1979): 157–166.

7 The Tax Act of 1986 is causing human resource managers to take a much closer look at their compensation strategies. For a discussion on the short- and long-term effects of this act, see John D. McMillan, "Tax Reform: What it Means," *Personnel Administrator,* Vol. 31 (December 1986): 95–100.

8 Provisions and discussion are from The Davis-Bacon Act (40 USC Sect. 276) and The Walsh-Healy Act (41 USC Sect. 35–45).

9 29 USC Sect. 206 et seq.

10 For added provisions and discussion regarding government influences, see Patrick J. Cihon and James O. Castagnera, *Labor and Employment Law* (Boston, MA: PWS-KENT Publishing Company, 1988) and Kenneth L. Sovereign, *Personnel Law* (Reston, VA: Reston Publishing Company, 1984).

11 Thomas A. Mahoney, Benson Rosen, and Sara Rynes, "Where Do Compensation Specialists Stand on Comparable Worth?" *Compensation Review,* Vol. 16, No. 4 (1984): 27–40.

12 Many states have enacted laws that extend beyond the provisions established by the federal government. A complete discourse of these laws is beyond the scope of this text. Readers would be well advised to familiarize themselves with these laws because they affect the legality of specific payroll deductions.

13 Francine Blau and Marianne A. Ferber, *The Economics of Women, Men, and Work* (Englewood Cliffs, NJ: Prentice-Hall, Inc., 1986).

14 Bruce A. Nelson, Edward M. Opton, Jr., and Thomas E. Wilson, "Wage Discrimination and Title VII in the 1980s: The Case Against 'Comparable Worth'," *Employee Relations Law Journal,* Vol. 6, No. 3 (1980): 380–391.

15 In June of 1984, in a case involving prison matrons in Washington County, Oregon, the Supreme Court ruled that a sex discrimination suit could be brought on charges other than discrimination based on "equal or substantially equal work." For a comprehensive discussion of this case and other comparable worth issues, see Michael F. Carter, "Comparable Worth: An Idea Whose Time Has Come," *Personnel Journal,* Vol. 60, No. 10 (October 1981): 792–794, and Robert Buchele and Mark Aldrich, "How Much Difference Would Comparable Worth Make?" *Industrial Relations,* Vol. 24, No. 2 (Summer 1985): 222–233.

16 After the conclusion of appeal procedures, sizable salary adjustments, back pay, and penalties are likely because the court ruled that the State of Washington was guilty of overt pay discrimination, See E. James Brennan, "Why Laws Have Failed to End Pay Discrimination," *Personnel Journal,* Vol. 63, No.8 (August 1984): 20–22.

17 See R. L. Opsahl and M. D. Dunnette, "The Role of Financial Compensation in Industrial Motivation," *Psychological Bulletin,* Vol. 66 (1966): 94–118.

18 Graef S. Crystal, "Pay for Performance—Even If It's Just Luck," *The Wall Street Journal,* March 2, 1981: 16.

19 Edward L. Deci, "Effects of Externally Mediated Rewards on Intrinsic Motivation," *Journal of Personality and Social Psychology,* Vol. 18 (1971): 105–115.

20 George T. Milkovich and Jerry M. Newman, *Compensation,* 2nd ed. (Plano, TX: Business Publications, Inc., 1987): 208.

21 Frederick S. Hills, *Compensation Decision Making* (Chicago, IL: The Dryden Press, 1987): 172–173.

22 For expanded treatment of the four most commonly used evaluation methods, see Douglas Bartley, *Job Evaluation* (Reading, MA: Addison-Wesley Publishing Company, 1981).

23 J. M. Shafritz, *Position Classification: A Behavioral Analysis for the Public Service* (New York: Praeger Publishers, 1973): 23.

24 Allan N. Nash and Stephen J. Carroll, Jr. *The Management of Compensation* (Belmont, CA: Wadsworth Publishing Company, 1975).

25 Eugene J. Benge, "Specific Job Evaluation Systems: The Factor Method, in *Handbook of Wage and Salary Administration* 2nd ed., edited by Milton L. Rock (New York: McGraw-Hill Book Company, 1984): 12/2.

26 For further elaboration, see Eugene Benge, "Specific Job Evaluation Systems"; Christy Karr and Glenn T. Fischbach, "Specific Job Evaluation Systems: American Association of Industrial Management"; and Paul A. Katz, "Specific Job Evaluation Systems: White Collar Jobs in the Federal Civil Service," in *Handbook of Wage and Salary Administration*, edited by Milton L. Rock (New York: McGraw-Hill Book Company, 1984): 12/2; 13/2,3; 14/7.

27 For a discussion of the Hay Plan (Guide-Chart Profile Method), see Edward N. Hay, "Characteristics of Factor Comparison Job Evaluation," *Personnel*, Vol. 23 (1946): 370–375; E. N. Hay, "Creating Factor Comparison Key Scales by the Percent Method," *Journal of Applied Psychology* Vol. 32 (1948): 456–464; and E. N. Hay and D. Purves, "A New Method of Job Evaluation: The Guide-Chart Profile Method," *Personnel*, Vol. 31, No. 1 (1954): 72–80.

28 Robert J. Kelly, "Job Evaluation and Pay Plans: Office Personnel." In *Handbook of Modern Personnel Administration*, edited by Joseph J. Famularo (New York: McGraw-Hill Book Company, 1972): 28–7, 28–8.

29 Frederick S. Hills, *op. cit.*, 207.

30 Today, the point method is being scrutinized by researchers. See Edward E. Lawler III, "What's Wrong with Point-Factor Job Evaluation?" *Compensation and Benefits Review*, Vol. 18, No. 2, (March–April 1986): 20–28.

Chapter 10

Instituting Incentive Plans

Objectives

After reading this chapter you should understand:

1. The different types of individual, group, and organizational incentive plans available.
2. The different plans available to compensate production, sales, managerial, and executive personnel.
3. The various differences among available pension plans.
4. The advantages and disadvantages of Employee Stock Ownership Plans.
5. The effective administration of compensation plans.
6. The effect of pay systems on the motivation of employees.

The basic wage and salary system within organizations is initially established through job evaluation procedures. After these fundamental wage and salary systems have been developed, many organizations design incentive pay plans for both workers and managerial employees. The purpose of these plans is to provide additional rewards to employees making significant contributions (usually over and above their basic job requirements) to the overall organizational goals and objectives.

Incentive programs are designed to strengthen the relationship between productivity and the reward received for this achievement. As a result, organizations attempt to develop incentive programs which provide encouragement to employees not only to meet but also to exceed organizational objectives. Most of these incentives are monetarily based and are applied at individual, group, or organizational levels.

Initial Considerations for Incentive Programs

The basic principle underlying any incentive plan is that workers will tend to produce more if their reward is a function of their output rather than their time invested.[1] In order to effectuate this type of program, certain conditions must exist. First, there must be a method to objectively measure productivity on either an individual or a group basis. Second, the current productivity level has to be improvable, and workers must believe that they can attain these higher levels. Third, employees must place a high value on money, and must perceive a strong relationship between increased productivity and the attainment of additional monetary rewards. Last, other nonmonetary rewards, such as promotions or advancements, are a possible result based on increased productivity.[2]

After considering the preceding factors, organizations must determine whether to institute individual incentive plans or group incentive plans. If performance is a function of collective rather than individual effort, then the organization would lean toward establishing group incentive plans. On the other hand, when success is a function of individualized effort, and when the organization can readily assess individual versus group performance, the organization can reasonably expect to have success through the use of individual plans.

Individual Incentive Systems

Individual incentive programs vary depending on the employees for whom they are designed. These programs are usually designed for production workers, salespeople, managers, and executives.

Production Employee Incentives

Historically, the first use of incentive plans can probably be traced back to efforts aimed at increasing the productivity of hourly production personnel. Frederick Taylor's development of a piece-rate plan in the late 1800s set forth different pay rates based on employee productivity levels. Similarly, D. W. Merrick formulated a comparable plan, which differed from Taylor's only in regard to the number of pay rates (Taylor had two levels and Merrick's plan used three rates).[3] Current pay plans differ primarily with regard to the amount of pay provided for each additional piece of output. The most common plans are: the piecework plan, the standard-hour plan, and the measured daywork plan.

Piecework plan

Piecework plans are the least complicated and most commonly used incentive plans.[4] Workers are paid a set amount of dollars for each and every unit produced. Usually, time and motion studies are conducted to determine the standard number of units employees can reasonably be expected to produce in a day's time. These production units are then divided into the daily wage rate in order to determine the amount the employee will receive per unit. For example, suppose that workers are being paid $40.00 per day and they produce, on the average, 25 units. The pay for each unit would be $1.60 (40 divided by 25).

Piecework plan

A piecework plan is an incentive payment system which provides workers with a set amount of reward for each unit of output produced.

If used in their purest sense, piecework systems pay in direct proportion to the amount of productivity per worker. While most systems are developed so that normal, experienced workers are capable of earning amounts in excess of that provided under minimum wage laws, care must be taken to insure that trainees, or others, are paid at least minimum wage. For this reason, most piecework plans establish a minimum daily rate of pay earned.

Standard-hour plan

The **standard-hour plan** is similar to the piecework plan with the exception that productivity is measured in terms of time units rather than output units. Under this plan, time and motion studies are conducted to determine the amount of time it takes to complete a particular job. Based on the hourly assignment of wages, each job is then assigned a time allotment, and consequently a dollar amount.[5] For example, suppose that a given job has been determined to require 30 minutes to complete. Employees earning $6.00 an hour would be given $3.00 to complete the job (.50 hour × $6.00) whether it took them longer or shorter than the allotted 30 minutes. Consequently, employees who complete three jobs within the hour would be paid $9.00.

Standard-hour plan

A standard-hour incentive plan is a payment system which provides workers with a set amount of money for jobs based on the average amount of time units required to complete the job.

Usually, the actual time required to complete a job is expressed to workers as a percentage of the standard time. Completing three jobs with a standard time of .50 in an hour would thus be presented as 150 percent [.50 divided by .333 hour (actual time for each job) × 100% = 150%]. Employees can then multiply their percentage of time by their hourly rate and arrive at their wages (150% × $6.00 = $9.00).

Exhibit 10.1

Selected Standard Hourly Labor Rates for Some Automotive Service Bay Operations

Service required	**Chilton time**
Lubricate chassis, change oil and filter Includes: Inspecting and correcting all fluid levels	.6
Wheels, Balance	
One	.3
Each additional	.2
Wheels, Rotate (All)	.5
Aim headlamps	
Two	.4
Four	.6
Clean or renew spark plugs	.6
Reset ignition timing	.4
Compression Test	.7
Engine tune up (Electronic ignition) Includes: Testing battery and cleaning connections; tightening manifold mounting bolts; checking engine compression; cleaning and adjusting or renewing spark plugs; resetting ignition timing; adjusting minimum idle speed; servicing air cleaner; inspecting and adjusting drive belts; checking operation of EGR valve	1.4

Source: *Chilton's 1987 Labor Guide and Parts Manual.* (Radnor, PA: Chilton Book Company, 1986): 548.

The most familiar example of standard-hour plans is the one used by automobile repair shops. Most customers request estimates for repairs prior to the actual service performed. The rate which they are quoted is a combination of the cost of the parts needed plus the standard hourly rate to complete the job in question. If additional parts are needed, the customer is charged extra. The time estimate, however, is usually fixed, regardless of whether it takes more or less time to complete the job.

Measured daywork plan

Under the **measured daywork** plan, the organization determines the formal production standards necessary to complete a job, and then judges employee performance relative to those standards. The main features of the measured daywork plan are the formal standards which are established and the frequency of measurement (evaluation is conducted at least quarterly). It is most applicable in situations where many unstandardized conditions exist, which makes performance judgments crucial.[6]

> **Measured daywork**
>
> ***The measured daywork system requires that formal production standards be developed against which employee performance can be frequently judged.***

Pros and cons of production incentive systems[7]

Production worker incentives have the advantage of being easily understood and accepted by employees. In addition, because workers are paid directly in proportion to their output, they tend to view the plans as fair and equitable, and they are highly motivated to produce.

For the organization, these plans usually result in greater productivity and less cost per unit of output. Overall pay satisfaction is increased, and workers tend to earn higher wages than they would have otherwise.

There are, however, several drawbacks to production incentive plans. The first is the amount of administrative and clerical work necessary in order to make changes in pay rates. As market conditions change and as salaries increase, adjustments must be made in the piecework system. If these conditions occur frequently, the continual determination of base rates becomes an expensive and time-consuming process.

A second problem with these systems occurs when there is a time delay in the payment of the incentive wages. Many companies pay workers a regular base rate and delay the payment of the incentive wage. For example, workers may receive a weekly base wage of $150, but their performance pay may be delayed for several pay periods. This causes confusion among workers and weakens the link which they make between performance and pay.

Another problem which can result concerns perceptions of inequity by those employees who are not involved in the incentive programs. As the limit on workers' pay is only bound by their own efforts, it is conceivable that talented, highly motivated individuals can earn higher wages than employees engaged in higher level positions. In fact, these workers may earn more than their immediate supervisors. This tends to create feelings of inequity among the higher level employees. In order to compensate for this problem, organizations impose maximum ceilings on the amount workers can earn. This reduces the problem, but may dampen the enthusiasm generated by the piecework plan.

Finally, individual incentive plans may create attitudinal problems. Employees may distrust the system and feel that if they produce too highly, either the overall base standards may increase or layoffs may occur. This perceived fear causes workers to operate at, or only slightly above, standard. Also, workers who are not motivated primarily by monetary rewards may feel pressured by, and resist, the increasing production standards. To this end, managers must remember that incentive systems are primarily motivating to those employees who seek monetary rewards. Employees need and value other rewards. Incentive systems are just one of many motivational tools.

Incentives for Salespeople

Sales jobs are unique. These positions, and the people who occupy them, are different from others within the organization. Unlike other positions within companies, there are few, if any, levels or advancement steps to which salespeople aspire. Salespeople work for businesses, but they are really independent operators. The nature of their job does not allow for direct and close supervision, and motivation is primarily self-directed. Realistically, salespeople function as individual entrepreneurs under the umbrella of the organization that employs them.[8] Their need satisfaction is obtained primarily through money and reinforcers, which satisfy needs of recognition, achievement, status, and prestige.

It may not be realistic to consider incentive systems as optional programs for salespeople. Although there are companies which pay salespeople a straight salary, most organizations reserve this form of payment for sales trainees. Instead, pay systems usually involve some variation of three **commission pay plans.** These include: straight commission, draw plus commission, or salary plus commission. In addition, some organizations use a bonus system either in conjunction with or instead of commissions.

Straight commission

Straight commission is a true incentive-based pay plan. Salespeople are paid based on a percentage of their total sales. Their income is a function of their productivity. Those salespeople who produce highly are paid substantially. Those whose productivity, measured in total sales, is low receive less compensation.

Draw plus commission

Draw plus commission is a variation on the straight commission pay plan. Under this program, salespeople are paid a weekly, bi-weekly, or monthly salary which is deducted from their future commissions. The basic premise underlying this form of compensation system is that sales volume usually fluctuates over time. Rather than living under feast or famine conditions, salespeople can equalize their living style over time.

Salary plus commission

Under this form of incentive plan, salespeople are paid a regular salary plus commissions on their sales. The commission rate on sales is generally lower than that found under the other two pay plans because the organization is providing a guaranteed minimum salary.

Bonus plans

Many companies use **bonus pay plans** instead of, or in addition to, commissions. Unlike commissions, which reward salespeople for total sales, bonuses are paid for sales which exceed a predetermined quota. For example, salespeople may be paid a certain salary or commission until they reach a certain dollar figure (usually calculated so as to justify the base salary). After this point, additional compensation is paid based on additional sales. Although bonuses provide a degree of motivation in any situation, their greatest impact is probably on straight salary salespeople.

Pros and cons of sales incentives

As with production employees, the primary reason for using incentives with salespeople is to tie pay to productivity. Sales incentives accomplish this objective. In addition, sales incentives serve as a strong motivator, they provide an objective standard against which to measure performance, and they allow for independence of action on the part of the salesperson.

Sales incentives are not free of problems. Aside from the normal administrative concerns present with any incentive program, sales plans have a unique problem associated with the distribution of territories.[9] Some salespeople are assigned lucrative territories, and with minimal effort, they generate huge sales volumes. Other salespeople, who are assigned more difficult territories, expend considerable effort and realize very little sales. The effect on morale may be devastating. To compensate for this problem, many organizations set quotas based on the sales potential of the territory. Unfortunately, this process is only

Exhibit 10.2

Monthly Wages of Sales Personnel

Straight commission	Draw plus commission	Salary plus commission	Salary plus bonus
.01% of total monthly gross	.01% of total sales less $200 weekly draw	$150/week + .007% of total sales	$200/week + .01% of sales in excess of 80,000 units
.01% × 200000* = $2000/month	$800 (4 × 200) + .01% × 200000* = $800 draw = $2000/month	$600 (4 × 150) + .007% × 200000* = $2000/month	$800 (4 × 200) + .01% × 120000 = $2000/month

*Based on 200000 units at $100 each.

useful in equalizing the wages of those salespeople who operate on a percentage of sales above the quota. Those organizations which pay commissions based on total sales must still compensate for the inequitable feelings generated in those salespeople whose territories are extremely difficult.

Managerial and Executive Incentive Systems

There are three common forms of incentives given to managerial and executive personnel. Some organizations use combinations of these incentives in compensating executives.[10] The incentives include: merit incentives, bonuses, and stock options. In addition, there is generally a wide variety of perquisites (perks) reserved for use at executive levels.

Merit pay

Merit pay is probably the most frequently used method of rewarding managerial performance. At some designated time during each year, organizations adjust the wages of their managerial personnel. This adjustment is usually accomplished through a cost of living raise (COLA) and merit pay. The COLA is frequently a standard percentage of salary or a lump sum which is allocated across the board. Merit pay is based on individual performances as reflected through performance appraisals. Once given, both the COLA and the merit pay become part of an individual's base salary.

> **Merit pay**
>
> *Merit pay is the assignment of money to employees' base pay on the basis of their performance.*

Pros and cons of merit systems

When applied correctly, merit pay certainly links pay to performance. The payment of adequate rewards to those individuals who perform well fosters motivation both among the employees receiving the increase and among those who desire to receive it in the future. In addition, it sends the message to all employees that the organization considers productivity important and is willing to reward the efforts of those who contribute to the organization's goals and objectives.[11]

The use of merit pay is hampered by several problems. The first of these is tied directly with the performance appraisal system. In order to gain employees' acceptance of a merit pay system, the allocation of moneys must be based on objectively administered performance appraisals. All too often, both the appraisal system and the way it is administered are executed haphazardly. Merit pay is assigned based on subjective evaluations, rather than on objective performance data.

Problems develop even when performance appraisal systems are correctly developed and administered. Merit pay attempts to link pay to performance. Many jobs, especially at the managerial and executive levels, are difficult to measure in terms of productivity. Executive productivity is difficult to quantify in terms of the number of memoranda which cross the desk or in the number of decisions made daily. Unless the executives in question are involved in highly visible positions, it is unlikely that their job performance will be noticed by many others. As a result, the link between the amount of merit pay received and performance is not readily apparent. This perceived inequity tends to generate feelings of unfairness in those individuals who believe that their performance deserved greater recognition.

Probably the biggest problem with merit pay lies in the way it is administered. Merit pay usually becomes part of an employee's base salary. Thus, the employee is continually rewarded for past performance in spite of current behavior. This may continue to perpetuate inequitable situations. Consider the following case.

On January 2, 1988, Sally and Mike were both hired to fill supervisory positions. Each was given a yearly salary of $20,000 and assigned similar duties. At the end of the year, Jennifer, their supervisor, conducted performance appraisals for each employee.

During the appraisal session, Sally was told that her performance had been outstanding during the previous year. She was further informed that her salary beginning January 1989 would be increased by $2,500. This was the result of a 10 percent COLA adjustment being given to all employees and a $500 merit increase. Her new salary was $22,500.

Mike's appraisal was not as good. Jennifer informed Mike that, based on his appraisal, his salary for the coming year would be $22,000, reflecting only a COLA raise.

Another year passed, and appraisal time approached. This time, however, things had changed. Unfortunately, Sally had slacked off. When it came time to allocate raises, she was given only the 10 percent COLA adjustment. Her third year's salary was $24,750 ($22,500 + $2,250). Mike, on the other hand, consumed with the desire to earn more money, did an outstanding job. He received the 10 percent COLA increase and the $500 merit pay. His salary was now $24,700 ($22,000 + $2,200 + $500). He was furious! How could this have happened? Both he and Sally had started with the same salary. They both received one year's merit pay. In fact, he had improved, while Sally had let the company down! Why was he making $50 less than Sally? Jennifer's explanations of mathematics and economics were to no avail. Mike resigned the next day!

Exhibit 10.3

Allocating Merit Pay

Employee A		Employee B	
Performance appraisal—*Average*		Performance appraisal—*Good*	
Base salary	$15,000/year	Base salary	$15,000/year
End of year		End of year	
COLA*	(.10 × 15000)	COLA	(.10 × 15000)
	$ 1,500		$ 1,500
Merit raise	$ 500	Merit raise	$ 1,000
New salary	$17,000	New salary	$17,500

*10% COLA Adjustment across the board

The preceding case demonstrates the problems encountered when merit pay is inserted into the base pay of employees. Once it becomes part of the salary, employees are continually rewarded for past performance, regardless of current productivity levels.[12]

Bonuses

After merit pay, bonuses are the most common form of managerial and executive incentives used. For managerial personnel, bonuses typically tie performance to pay over a specified time period, such as one year. Managers who perform above average during the prescribed period are rewarded with a cash bonus based on a predefined percentage of their base salary. This percentage typically ranges from 20 percent of base salary in the case of lower level managers to 80 percent for senior level executives.[13]

Unlike managerial bonuses, which are mostly supplements to income, executive bonuses are an integral part of the executive's total compensation. These bonuses, which may be short or long term (short term being usually one-year in duration; long term implying periods of between three and five years), are designed to link executive performance to company profits, and constitute 50 percent of their total compensation package.[14]

There are several methods of calculating executive bonuses. The most common method for top level executives is the payment of a discretionary bonus based on yearly determined formulas. Lower level executives, such as district and regional sales managers, are usually paid bonuses based solely on permanently established predetermined formulas. These fixed formulas must be monitored periodically to make sure they do not become outdated, causing managers to either have to work more or less to obtain the same results.

Pros and cons of bonus plans

Bonuses have the potential of being highly motivational, especially when they are administered properly. They tie performance directly to pay and foster cooperation among employees, particularly when bonuses are tied to overall company profits.

The administration of successful bonus plans requires careful planning and monitoring. Managers whose compensation is tied closely to profits may manipulate accounting techniques, such as inventory control, accounts receivable, and bad debt collections, in order to maximize short-term profits. Furthermore, short-term bonuses may cause managers and executives to target short-term gains, rather than plan for the future.[15] Finally, the payment of large cash bonuses may cause some small companies to experience cash flow problems.

Stock options

Stock options give executives the right to buy a stated number of shares of company stock for a fixed price at a future date as long as they are still employed by the organization. The price agreed on is usually close to the market price per share at the time the option is issued. At any point during the stated time period, the executive may exercise all, or part, of these options in purchasing stock. Should the market value of the stock appreciate greatly, the executive gains substantially.[16] For example, suppose an executive is given the option to purchase 1000 shares of stock over the next five years at the current market value of $25 per share. If the stock rises in price to $50 three years later, the executive can exercise the option, resulting in a gain of $25,000 ($50,000 present value of 1000 shares less $25,000 cost). Because executives realize financial gains based on future company performance, stock option incentives generate motivation to make sound long-term organizational decisions.

The popularity of stock options has vacillated over the years. During the 1950s, 1960s, and into the 1970s, stock options were an integral part of executive compensation. With the high volatility of the stock market, the drastically changing tax laws (especially the 1987 tax changes), and the fluctuation in interest rates, the popularity of stock options has declined. Stock options were once the principal part of an executive's compensation package, but now many organizations regard them as supplemental incentives.[17]

Group Incentive Systems

The use of incentive systems on the group level is predicated on the same assumption used to justify individual incentive programs. Just as individual systems attempt to tie pay to performance, group incentive systems reward employees when the organization experiences an increase in profits or a decrease in costs. Unlike individual systems, however, the link between individual effort and productivity is not apparent. Individual incentives promote rewards based on one employee's extra effort and work, but group incentives usually result from employees collectively working more effectively.

Organization-Wide Incentives—Gainsharing

Organizations typically choose to use incentives company-wide when the measurement of productivity increases is based on overall corporate profits. This data is accumulated by gathering historical information which compares the cost of labor (inputs) to some standard of production (outputs). Through the use of various plans, most of which involve sharing formulas, all employees participating in the **gainsharing** plan are rewarded for gains in profits as a result of increased productivity (outputs), reduced labor costs (inputs), or both (increased outputs and reduced inputs).

The gainsharing plan which organizations choose is predicated on their goals and objectives. In order to choose the most appropriate plan, organizations must answer the following questions:

1. What is the reinforcement strength of the incentive pay system in relation to base pay?
2. To what extent should the inputs and outputs be included in the formula used?
3. Are the different formulas used within the organization perceived as fair and equitable?
4. Can the gainsharing programs chosen be administered in a smooth, effective manner within the existing procedures of the organization?
5. Does the gainsharing program set sufficiently high targets before rewarding performance?[18]

Gainsharing plans can be divided into three categories. The first group includes plans which are cost reducing or cost saving. The most commonly used plans within this category are the Scanlon, Rucker, and Improshare systems. The second group includes profit-sharing plans, such as the renowned program which operates at Lincoln Electric Company. The third group includes various stock ownership plans which are available to employees.

Cost-reducing Plans

The Scanlon Plan

The **Scanlon Plan,** one of the earliest formal gainsharing plans, was named for its developer, Joseph N. Scanlon. The Scanlon Plan was originally designed in an attempt to promote employment, productivity, and profits during the Depression of the 1930s. Essentially, the plan focuses on determining the ratio of the labor costs involved in production to the sales value of production (SVOP).

The latter figure includes the sales revenues generated and the total value of goods in inventory.[19]

In concept, the operation of the plan is uncomplicated. Historical data of labor costs and the SVOP for a period usually consisting of five to ten years is gathered and analyzed to determine the average costs. Labor costs serve as the equation's numerator, and the SVOP is the denominator. When the fraction is divided, a ratio is produced (the **Scanlon ratio**). For example, suppose a company determines that the average labor costs have been $5,000,000, and the SVOP has averaged $15,000,000. The resulting ratio would be .33 (5,000,000 divided by 15,000,000 = .33). This ratio then becomes the standard above which profits are shared with workers.

In a typical operation of the Scanlon Plan, all employees who satisfy a waiting period (usually between one and three months) are rewarded monthly, based on the cost savings realized by the company. Although originally the entire cost savings was distributed among employees, most organizations using Scanlon plans distribute 25 percent of the savings to the company, 75 percent of the remaining savings to the employees, and the rest to an emergency fund for deficit months. For example, suppose the previously mentioned company, which is operating on a ratio of .33, had a monthly labor cost for March of $400,000 and a monthly SVOP of $1,250,000. The allowable labor cost for the month is $412,500 (.33 times $1,250,000). The savings to the company for the month of March is $12,500, of which $3,125 would be allocated to the company, $7,031.25 would be divided among the employees participating in the plan (75 percent times 12,500 − 3,125 = 7,031.25), and the remaining $2,343.75 would be placed aside in the deficit fund. If the deficit fund is not exhausted by the end of the year, the remaining money is distributed to workers. Consequently, should the ratio be exceeded each and every month, the effective yield to employees is 75 percent of savings.

Scanlon Plan

The Scanlon Plan is a cost-reduction gainsharing plan by which all participants are rewarded, usually monthly, based on a ratio formula of labor costs to sales value of production.

$$\text{Scanlon Ratio} = \frac{\text{Labor costs}}{\text{Sales value of production}}$$

The Rucker Plan (share of production plan)

The **Rucker Plan,** also known as the share of production plan (SOP), was developed by the Eddy-Rucker-Nickels Company,[20] and differs from the Scanlon Plan in regard to the complexity of the formula used to calculate the bonus ratio. The major difference between the two plans is the way in which the labor ratio, referred to as the *economic productivity index* (EPI) in the Rucker Plan, is calculated. The Scanlon Plan uses labor divided by SVOP to arrive at the ratio, and the Rucker formula calculates the economic productivity index by dividing the value added by labor's efforts (SVOP minus costs of materials, supplies, and services) by the labor costs.

Implementation of Scanlon and Rucker Plans Unlike other bonus plans which rely on greater employee effort to generate increased profits, Scanlon and Rucker plans attempt to raise profits by encouraging cost savings. This is accomplished in two ways: the establishment of a productivity norm and the development of effective worker committees.[21]

The establishment of a productivity norm requires that accurate and careful accumulation of baseline data involved in determining the formulas be undertaken. When gathering the information organizations must make certain that the final data is representative of a typical productivity year. Should data be gathered from atypical years, such as extreme recessions, then both the information and the bonus plans will be distorted. Furthermore, as with other incentive plans, the success of the plans relies to a great extent on its acceptance by those employees involved. If the base formula developed is not accepted as fair and equitable, the program will probably not produce its intended results.

The second consideration involves the implementation of employee productivity committees. The purpose of these committees is to elicit and evaluate suggestions from workers and managers concerning methods of increasing productivity or reducing costs. If the suggestions recommended by the groups result in cost savings to the company, these savings are paid to the entire work group. The effect of these productivity groups has been to substantially increase the number of usable suggestions in organizations that have traditional suggestion systems.

Scanlon and Rucker plans are most likely to flourish in organizations that establish psychologically healthy work environments. For successful implementation to occur, a strong working relationship between employees and management is necessary. In organizations where management believes that workers can make mental as well as physical contributions, these plans will flourish. On the other hand, those organizations whose management philosophies do not allow for active participation of workers in the thinking process would be well advised to consider other forms of employee compensation.

Improshare

Improshare (Improved productivity through sharing) is an industrial-engineering productivity and sharing plan which was developed by Mitchell Fein in the 1970s. The plan is based on the use of past production records to establish base performance standards.

In order to implement Improshare, organizations must identify several factors. First, the participating employees are selected. These groups may consist of hourly, salaried, incentive-based employees, or any other workers designated by the organization. Next, the organization establishes a **base period,** a **base period products cost,** and the **base productivity factor** (BPF).[22]

Exhibit 10.4

Comparison of the Scanlon and Rucker Plans

Given: Averages for five-year period

SVOP	15,000,000
Labor costs	5,000,000
Cost of materials, etc.	8,000,000

Ratio Calculations

Scanlon Plan

$$\frac{\text{Labor costs}}{\text{SVOP}} = .33$$

Rucker Plan

$$\frac{\text{Labor costs}}{\text{SVOP} - \text{cost of materials, etc.}} = .06$$

$$\text{Economic productivity index} = \frac{1.00}{.06} = 16.67$$

Bonus Period—Month of March

SVOP	1,250,000
Labor costs	400,000
Cost of materials, etc.	600,000

Scanlon Plan

.33 × 1,250,000 = 412,500 allowable labor cost

400,000 actual labor cost

12,500 savings to be divided

25% to company = 3,125.00

75% of remainder to employees = 7,031.25

Balance to emergency fund = 2,343.75

Rucker Plan

Actual value of production = SVOP − (materials, etc. + labor) = 250,000

Expected value of production = EPI × labor cost = 666,800

Savings = expected value − actual value = 416,800

Employees' share = .06 × 416,800 = $25,008

75% distributed immediately = 18,756

25% placed in Emergency Fund = 6,252

Base period, base period products cost, and base productivity factor

The base period is the time designated to establish productivity standards. The base period product costs are all costs used by management during the base period. They represent the direct labor hours necessary to produce a product by major operations and by total products produced. The base productivity factor is the relationship in the base period between the actual hours worked by employees in the plan and the value of work produced by these employees measured in standard worker hours.

After the relevant productivity data for the base period has been gathered, management calculates the current performance in hours worked and the resulting productivity output. A comparison between this data and the data obtained during the base period yields the *Improshare earned hours* (any hours saved). These Improshare earned hours are used to calculate each worker's share of the gain.

In order to permit changes to be readily made in measurement standards, organizations establish three controls. These are: a ceiling on productivity improvement of 160 percent, cash buy-back of measurement standards, and an 80/20 share of improvements which are the result of capital equipment.[23]

Under Improshare, employees receive monthly increases in their wages based on a percentage of the gain. This is accomplished by a 50/50 split of the gains between the employees and the organization. There is a ceiling of 160 percent, and the extra gains (above 160 percent) are placed into a reserve fund which is reinserted during the next period that productivity gains fall below 160 percent. In the case where productivity gains remain over 160 percent for an extended period, management has the right to buy back the gains by making a one-time annual bonus payment of 50 percent of the fund to the employees. Subsequent to this buy-back, the base period is adjusted for future use to reflect the increased productivity. For example, suppose an employee earns $6.00 an hour and worked 2,000 hours (40 hours per week × 50 weeks) during the past year. If the percentage gain were 190 percent, employees would receive 50 percent of the difference (190 − 160) in a one-time annual bonus. This would result in an additional $1,800 per worker.

(30 percent buy-back) × .50 (gain division) × $6.00 (wage/hour) × 2,000 (hours worked) = $1,800 (buy-back bonus).

As a result, future base periods would be adjusted by 1.19 (1.9/1.6).

Profit Sharing

Profit sharing is one of the oldest forms of incentive compensation. Most researchers trace the origins of profit sharing to Albert Gallatin, who introduced the plan into his glassworks factory in Pennsylvania during the late 1700s, and to Edme-Jean Le Claire (the "father of profit sharing"), who owned a painting and decorating business in France during the 1840s.[24] Le Claire introduced the program to his employees after determining how much they could save the organization by using their time, materials, and tools more efficiently. After discussing these saving plans with the workers, Le Claire offered them a percentage share of the savings resulting from the newly introduced methods. The plan was well received, and it is still one of the most successful examples of profit-sharing plans.

Profit sharing

Profit sharing is any method or procedure which employers use to pay additional wages to employees, over and above their regular pay, based on the profitability of the organization.

There are three commonly used types of profit-sharing plans, which are differentiated on the basis of when the profit shares are distributed. These are: cash or current-distribution plans, deferred plans, and combination plans.[25]

Cash plans

Cash plans provide for the distribution of profit shares at regular intervals as earned. This distribution is made in cash, company stock, or a combination of both, according to a predetermined formula.

Deferred plans

Deferred plans provide for the distribution of profits, which are usually placed into an escrow account, at a future date. Typically, deferred profit-sharing plans serve as the backbone for the company's pension or retirement programs.

Combination plans

Combination plans are profit-sharing plans that utilize features of both cash and deferred plans by distributing part of the profits earned immediately and placing the remainder into the fund reserved for later disbursement.

The effectiveness of profit-sharing plans varies widely. Some companies find that the use of these programs increases worker motivation by fostering a direct link between company profits and individual pay. Individuals who participate in profit-sharing plans identify with the company's goals and profits and tend to increase productivity.[26] Other organizations, however, find that profit-sharing plans soon become just another hygiene factor (see Herzberg's two-factor theory in Chapter 15) and they have little, if any, permanent impact on employee motivation.

For profit sharing to have success, workers must be able to connect their reward directly to their productivity. The best known and most widely publicized example of a profit-sharing plan that accomplishes this goal is the plan used by Lincoln Electric Company of Cleveland, Ohio.

Lincoln Electric's Plan

The Lincoln Plan is an incentive compensation program started in 1914 by James F. Lincoln.[27] Initially, the plan called for a simple piecework system, but over the next twenty years it evolved into a multifaceted program including a year-end bonus plan based on profit-sharing principles. The profit-sharing bonus plan developed in 1934 after Lincoln denied a wage raise of 10 percent because he felt that profits would not sustain such an increase. In response to having their raise request turned down, the employees requested that year-end bonuses be paid if they increased company profits through greater productivity and lowered costs. The plan was accepted by Lincoln, and it is still successfully operating.

The effect of the bonus plan at Lincoln Electric has been to pay workers almost as much in bonuses as in regular earnings. This is especially relevant in

Exhibit 10.5

Types of Incentive Plans

Production	Sales	Management	Group/ Organization
Piecework	Standard comm.	Merit pay	Gainsharing
Standard hour	Draw + commission	Bonuses	Scanlon Plan
Measured daywork	Salary + commission	Stock options	Rucker Plan
			Improshare
			Profit sharing
			ESOP

light of the fact that for several decades after its initiation, Lincoln maintained 1933 prices on most of its products. These pricing policies were held until the 1970s, when inflation caused a shift in pricing philosophy. Furthermore, the firm's return on investment was in excess of 15 percent during the inflationary period of 1975–1982. These facts, coupled with a reputation for offering a highly competitive basic pay and benefits package and having reportedly low rates of turnover and absenteeism (as low as 0.3 percent per month in 1983 for total absenteeism) when compared to the manufacturing industry in general, have caused researchers to conclude that the Lincoln Plan is successful from every point of view.[28]

Employee Stock Ownership Plans (ESOP)

Until the mid-1970s, most stock bonus plans were reserved for upper management and executive personnel. With the passage of the Tax Reduction Act of 1975, organizations expanded their incentives by offering ESOP (employee stock ownership plans) to additional employees. The continued popularity of ESOP programs is evident in its widespread adoption by many organizations.

An employee stock bonus plan, which is governed through a trust fund (ESOT), is established solely for the purpose of administering the ESOP plan. Each worker is assigned an individual account in the trust, and the organization contributes a given amount of cash or shares of stock to the trust fund. Upon termination of employment or retirement, employees are entitled to the amount of shares which have accumulated in their account.

Types of ESOPs

There are two types of ESOPs which may be established. The first is termed an **ordinary ESOP** and requires the company to make annual cash contributions to the trust fund (in some instances the company makes the contribution in shares of stock). These funds are then used by the ESOP trust to buy shares in the company stock which are credited to each employee's account. At retirement or termination, employees receive their accumulated stock.

Ordinary ESOP

In an ordinary ESOP, the company contributes an amount of cash from its profits to the ESOP trust fund, which is used to purchase employee shares in company stock.

A second type of ESOP used by organizations is the **leveraged ESOP.** Under this plan, the employer can use the ESOP as a means to obtain additional capital through borrowing. The ESOT (employee stock ownership trust) borrows money from the bank to purchase the stock, using the company shares as collateral for the loan. The company can then use the funds for whatever it deems necessary (for example, capital expenditures). Each year, the company repays the principal and interest due to the ESOT, which in turn makes payments to the bank until the loan is repaid.[29]

Leveraged ESOP

A leveraged ESOP *allows a company to borrow money against shares of company stock, and to repay the principal and interest each year until the loan is satisfied.*

TRASOPs *and* PAYSOPs

With the passage of the 1975 Tax Reduction Act, employers were allowed tax credits for ESOPs based on a percentage of the company's capital investments, if the company placed the additional credit into an ESOP. These ESOPs were known as **TRASOPs** (Tax Reduction Act Stock Ownership Plans) and were extremely popular among capital-intensive industries such as utilities. Beginning in January 1983, the laws were changed to provide employer credit based on a percentage of the company's payroll costs, rather than its capital investments. These ESOPs were dubbed **PAYSOPs** (deriving their name from the fact that they came from payroll costs), and they required companies to contribute a corresponding amount of cash or stocks to the PAYSOP within 30 days of claiming a deduction on their federal income tax. Today, the distinctions between TRASOPs and PAYSOPs are in name only because subsequent legislation (in 1984 and 1986) repealed the tax credit benefits.[30]

Pros and cons of ESOPs

There are various opinions concerning the effectiveness of ESOPs.[31] As with other bonus and incentive plans, organizations hope that ESOPs will promote greater motivation and links between the employee and the organization. If they are administered correctly and appropriately, ESOPs have the potential for increasing productivity and reducing turnover and absenteeism—hence, their increasing popularity.

On the negative side, ESOPs appear to have less than desired results when they are introduced in an effort to salvage a dying company. In order to successfully save the company, employees must make wage concessions in the hopes of greater gains in the future through bonuses. Frequently, however, the return on investment for the workers is substantially lower than it was initially expected to be. Rather than having the desired effects, the program may backfire and cause severe repercussions for the organization.

Exhibit 10.6

Ordinary and Leveraged ESOP Transactions

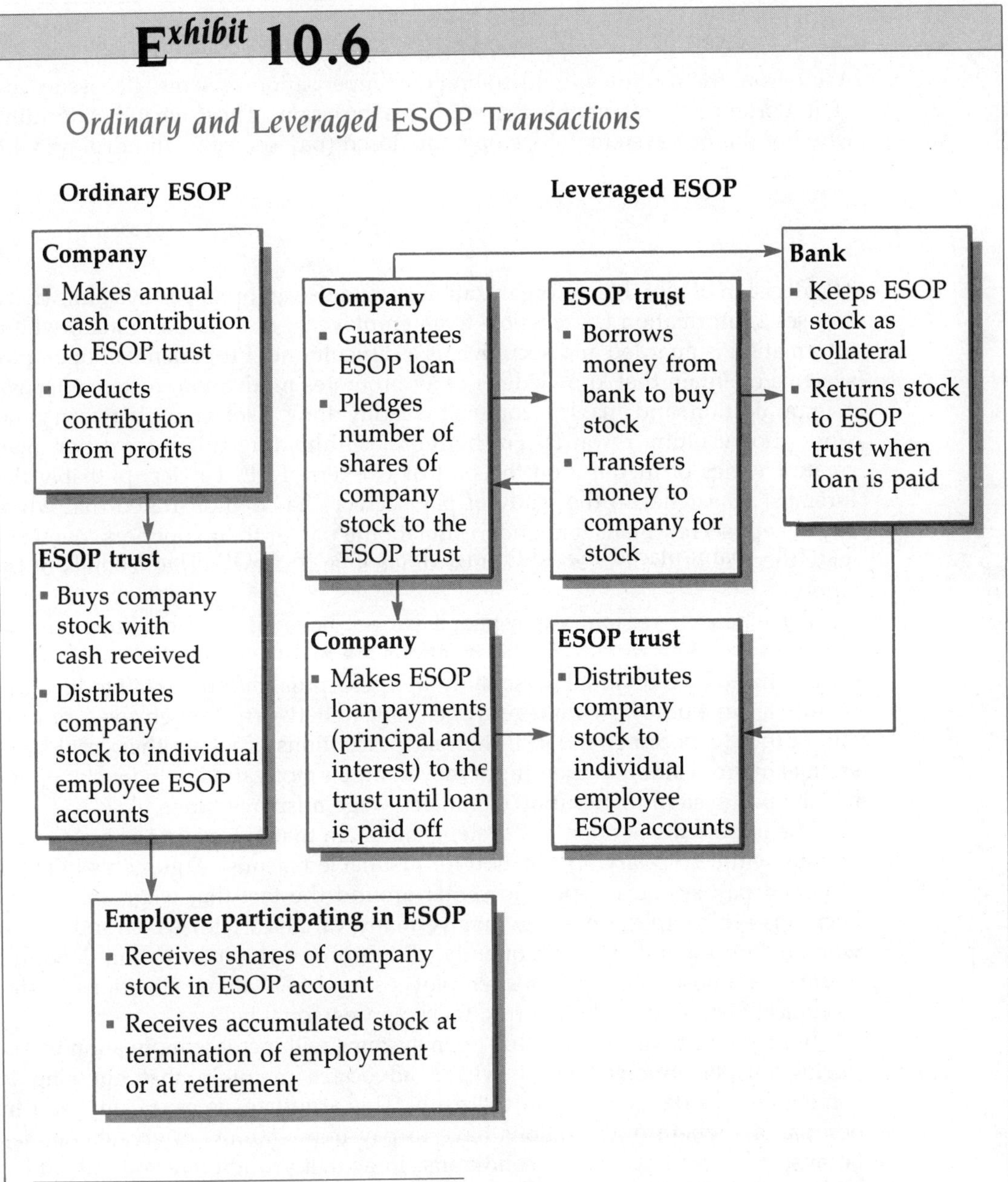

Source: Vida G. Scarpello and James Ledvinka, *Personnel/Human Resource Management* (Boston, MA: PWS-KENT Publishing Company, 1988): 443. Reprinted with permission.

Administering Compensation Plans

Aside from the routine administration of compensation systems, two issues are of importance in maintaining a workable program. These include: deciding whether the pay system will be open or closed (pay secrecy), and dealing with wage compression.

Pay Secrecy

The decision of whether an organization should use an open pay system, where pay scale information is accessible to all employees, or a closed system, where information is guarded and secretive, is a difficult one. Proponents of open pay systems maintain that knowledge of pay promotes motivation, fosters effective communication, and enables workers to readily draw associations between good work and resulting rewards. Furthermore, withholding this information may create feelings of inequity on the part of workers. E. E. Lawler, probably the foremost researcher in the study of pay secrecy, has demonstrated that when pay is kept secret, managers underestimate the pay of their superiors, overestimate the pay of their peers and subordinates, and demonstrate feelings of inequity.[32]

For whatever reason, when people do not have all the facts, they tend to hypothesize. Their unfounded speculations are highly susceptible to distortion errors caused by individual personality and perceptual differences. If motivation is truly a function of the linkage workers make between the perceived reward and output (expectancy theory), then misperceptions of what other employees are making in relation to their input may dampen motivation. Obviously, opening the pay system for scrutiny eliminates wage misperceptions.

The opponents to open pay systems maintain that organizations have traditionally withheld salary information for justifiable reasons. Arguments in favor of closed pay systems appear to center around the fact that wage and salary decisions are complex and they involve many variables with which individual workers are unfamiliar. Consequently, disclosure of the information is bound to create animosity because most employees tend to evaluate situations in stereotypical fashion (mostly favoring their own personal beliefs).

In response to arguments that open systems will increase motivation by reducing misperceptions, closed system advocates maintain that guessing is sometimes less damaging than the truth. This argument is especially valid in occupations where organizations have to pay new employees greater salaries because of prevailing market conditions. In actuality, there are *real* inequities, and openly publishing salaries may perpetuate dissatisfaction among the workforce. Hypothesizing may cause no greater damage to motivation than the actual facts.

To date, the research has shown mixed findings on whether pay systems should be open or closed. For an open system to have the desired results, several factors appear to be necessary. First, the measures of performance currently in use should be objective. Second, the link between pay and performance should be readily apparent to employees. Third, organizations should ascertain, through observation and other communication devices, workers' attitudes about pay secrecy. Finally, there should not be any blatant differences between the wages of employees doing comparable jobs.[33]

Wage Compression

When employees believe they are not receiving adequate compensation for the amount or type of work they contribute, pay inequity exists. One of the most common causes of inequity is wage or pay compression.

> **Wage compression**
>
> *Wage or pay compression is a continual shrinkage between the pay levels of highly valued jobs and those perceived as having less importance in the organization.*

There are three causes of **wage compression.**[34] The first cause is attributable to government intervention. As a result of increases in minimum wage levels, entry-level jobs are paid greater wages. Existing workers, however, usually do not receive comparable percentage raises in pay. The result is a smaller differential between lower and higher level positions.

Union wage negotiations are a second explanation for wage compression. When unions negotiate raises for their constituents, managers and supervisors, who are not represented, are unaffected. If a comparable increase in supervisors' and managers' salaries does not occur, compression results.

The last and most common cause of wage compression is attributable to market conditions. In many instances, the market value for new college graduates, or for personnel changing jobs, is greater than the wages paid to comparable workers with several years experience. Organizations are being forced to pay these higher wages in order to retain their competitive edge. The result is a continual shrinking of the pay differential between upper and lower level employees.

It is difficult to deal with pay compression. The obvious solution is to adjust the salaries of those employees involved. Some companies place a minimum percentage differential which cannot be violated between lower and upper level salaries. For example, the company may decide that supervisors will be paid 10 percent more than the highest paid employee they supervise. Whenever adjustments are made in employee wages, corresponding adjustments are made to supervisors' salaries in order to maintain the 10 percent differential. Other companies pay supervisors overtime salary for hours in excess of forty and for weekend and holiday work.

Realistically, however, most companies, especially those in labor-intensive industries, cannot economically withstand continual upgrading of their wage systems. These organizations attempt to deal with the problem by either offering other non-monetary benefits (such as reserved parking or choice of office), or by attempting to adequately explain the market condition state of affairs to their employees. Unfortunately, both methods are limited in their effectiveness, and motivation and turnover problems still exist. As long as changing technology and market conditions create a scarcity of skilled labor, wage compression is an issue human resource managers will have to deal with.

Summary

Many organizations supplement the basic pay of employees through incentive programs. These programs include individual incentive systems, group programs, and incentives which are designed for organization-wide use.

At the individual level, incentive systems provide a direct link between worker productivity and pay. Piecework systems, commission plans, merit pay, and executive stock options are the most common types of individual programs used.

Group incentive programs, which are predicated on the same belief as individual systems, are used when measures of productivity identify gains from collective employee efforts. As company profits increase, group members are rewarded for their contributions toward increased productivity or reduced costs.

Organization-wide incentive systems, known as gainsharing, are becoming increasingly more common. Traditional cost reduction programs, such as the Scanlon and Rucker plans, are being supplemented by newer systems, such as Improshare. Profit-sharing plans, one of the oldest forms of incentive programs, as well as employee stock ownership plans, continue to flourish.

Key Terms to Identify

- Piecework plans
- Standard-hour plan
- Measured daywork
- Commission pay plans
- Bonus pay plans
- Merit pay
- Stock options
- Gainsharing
- Scanlon Plan
- Scanlon ratio
- Rucker Plan (Share of production plan)
- Improshare
- Improshare base period
- Improshare base period products cost
- Improshare base productivity factor (BPF)
- Profit sharing
- Ordinary ESOP
- Leveraged ESOP
- TRASOPs and PAYSOPs
- Wage compression

Questions for Discussion

Do You Know the Facts?

1. What differences exist among the three types of production worker incentive systems? How are they similar?
2. Discuss why some salespeople are paid straight commission and why others opt for plans such as draw or salary plus commission.
3. Discuss the advantages and disadvantages of merit pay, stock options, and bonus plans for managerial personnel.
4. What are the differences among the Scanlon, Rucker, and Improshare gain-sharing plans? Which provides the greatest reward to workers, and why?

Can You Apply the Information Learned?

1. How would you explain the reason for production incentive systems to supervisors who are complaining about the fact that their line workers make more money than they do each week?
2. What encouragement and advice would you give an energetic salesperson who complains about the miserable territory which he has been assigned to handle? How would you structure territories to try and obtain an equitable balance among your salespeople?
3. How would you sell workers on ESOP programs? Would you use similar tactics if the workers have to initially forego their raises in order to participate in the program?
4. It has been said that executives who are willing to gamble on incentive payments rather than guaranteed salaries have more confidence in their abilities. Do you agree or disagree, and why?

It Takes Money to Make Money

Jeremy was perplexed. He knew that the company was in trouble. Something had to be done, and quickly. But how could he convince the CEO that a new sales incentive system was necessary? Every time he tried, he was reminded of the declining gross profit. If only he could somehow prove the old axiom: "It takes money to make money."

Jeremy Jamison is the Senior Vice-President in charge of sales and marketing for Roll-Em Tire and Rubber Company. The Roll-Em Tire Company was started in 1927 by Harry Penley as a small family-owned retail tire business. Through hard work, a little luck, and foresight, RTC grew to be the largest and most profitable independent manufacturer, wholesaler, and distributor of passenger car tires on the East Coast. Beginning in 1985, however, coinciding with the retirement of Harry Penley Jr. and the sale of the company, RTC experienced a downturn. Long-term customers began to buy their tires from other manufacturers, turnover among sales personnel was at an all-time high, and gross profit was down almost four percentage points.

Ever since its inception, the company had maintained the philosophy that friendly and courteous service was the key to success. As part of that philosophy, Harry Penley established a system of route-sales personnel that required each salesperson to sell, deliver, and service his or her own customers. Other companies used professional sales staffs, separate delivery personnel, and a clerical staff to deal with customer complaints. Harry was convinced, however, that small rural filling stations would respond better to personal treatment. And, in fact, it seemed to work.

The major difficulty with Harry's marketing scheme was finding and retaining qualified personnel who were willing to both sell and deliver tires. In order to motivate these personnel, Harry developed a very generous incentive system. The route sales personnel were paid a salary, were provided with the standard company benefit package, and were given a commission based on a percentage of their monthly sales. In addition, they were provided with a company vehicle, which they were allowed to use for personal use, they were given a liberal expense account, and they were allowed to choose their own hours of work. The only requirement imposed on the sales personnel was that they reached a quarterly quota jointly established by Harry and the sales force.

When Harry Penley Jr. took over the company, he retained the sales incentive system. The company was profitable, sales continually climbed, the customers seemed happy, and sales staff problems were practically nonexistent. In 1985, however, the company was sold. Unlike the Penleys, the new owners believed that costs could be cut and profits increased by using a professional sales staff and separate delivery personnel. Rather than paying compensation of $60,000 plus expenses to route-sales personnel, they reasoned that a driver could be employed for a straight salary of $15,000 and a good salesperson could be employed for a salary of between $18,000 and $22,000 plus commission. The personal automobiles and flexitime were eliminated.

Shortly thereafter, the company instituted the plan. Drivers were hired, and the route-sales people were offered the option of accepting the new position of salesperson at the reduced rate or terminating their employment. Eighty percent of the staff resigned and were replaced. Sales fell almost immediately. However, despite Jeremy's persistence, the new president remains unconvinced that the problem is the fault of the incentive system.

Questions for Discussion

1. Discuss the pros and cons of Harry Penley's original incentive system. How about the new system?
2. Do you think that reinstituting the original incentive system will increase sales? Why or why not?

Endnotes and References

1 Some researchers maintain that tangible rewards, such as money, actually may lower performance rather than improve it. For an interesting discourse on whether monetary rewards and praise reduce the intrinsic motivation of individuals, consequently leading to lower rather than higher performance levels, see Alfie Kohn, "Incentive Can Be Bad for Business," *Inc.* (January 1988): 93–94.

2 David W. Belcher, "Wage and Salary Administration" in *Motivation and Commitment*, edited by Dale Yoder and Herbert G. Heneman, Jr. (Washington, D.C.: Bureau of National Affairs, 1975). See also Richard Kopelman, "Linking Pay to Performance is a Proven Management Tool," *Personnel Administrator*, Vol. 28, No. 10 (October 1983): 60–68.

3 Frederick W. Taylor, "A Piece Rate System," *Transactions of the American Society of Mechanical Engineers*, Vol. 16 (1895): 856–905. Also see D. W. Merrick, "Time Studies as a Basis for Rate Setting," *The Engineering Magazine* (1920).

4 T. H. Patten, *Pay: Employee Compensation and Incentive Plans* (New York: Free Press, 1977).

5 Frederick S. Hills, *Compensation Decision Making* (Chicago, IL: The Dryden Press, 1987): 358. Also see Edward A. Shaw, "Measured Daywork: One Step Toward a Salaried Workforce," in *Payment Systems*, edited by T. Lupton. (Harmondsworth, Middlesex, England: Penguin, 1972): 143–165.

6 David W. Belcher and Thomas J. Atchison, *Compensation Administration*, 2nd ed. (Englewood Cliffs, NJ: Prentice-Hall, Inc. 1987): 288.

7 This discussion is based in part on the treatment in Frederick S. Hills, *op. cit.*, 359–362.

8 Frederick S. Hills, *op. cit.*, 363.

9 Frederick S. Hills, *op. cit.*, 366.

10 Lawrence Wangler, "Simplicity Improves Understanding of Executive Compensation," *Personnel Administrator*, Vol. 28, No. 6 (June 1983): 90–93.

11 For a discussion of the validity of merit pay as a means of improving performance, see Bruce R. Ellig, "What's Ahead in Compensation and Benefits," *Management Review*, Vol. 72, No. 8 (August 1983): 56–61.

12 For a good discussion on how employees view merit pay, see Frederick S. Hills, K. Dow Scott, Steven E. Markham, and Michael J. Vest, "Merit Pay: Just or Unjust Desserts," *Personnel Administrator*, Vol. 32 (September 1987): 53–59.

13 See Graef S. Crystal, *Financial Motivation for Executives* (New York: American Management Association, 1970): 137.

14 William H. Holley and Kenneth M. Jennings, *Personnel/Human Resource Management*, 2nd ed. (Chicago, IL: The Dryden Press, 1987): 383.

15 Pearl Meyer, "Executive Compensation Must Promote Long-Term Commitment," *Personnel Administrator*, Vol. 28, No. 5 (May 1983): 37–42.

16 Frederick S. Hills, *op. cit.*, 369.

17 Stock options, along with other enhanced benefits, are becoming quite common for top executives of large U.S. companies. For more detail on which benefits are most

popular, see "Exploring Executive Benefits in 50 Large Companies," *Spencer Survey, Employee Benefits Plan Review* (November 1987): 54, 56.

18 George T. Milkovich and Jerry M. Newman, *Compensation*, 2nd ed. (Plano, TX: Business Publications, Inc., 1987): 317–318.

19 Frederick G. Lesiur, editor, *The Scanlon Plan* (Cambridge, MA: MIT Press, 1958). Also see Linda S. Tyler and Bob Fisher, "The Scanlon Concept: A Philosophy as Much as a System," *Personnel Administrator*, Vol. 29, No. 7 (July 1983): 33–37.

20 For expanded discussion, see Carl Heyel, editor, *The Encyclopedia of Management*, 2nd ed. (New York: Van Nostrand Reinhold, 1973): 895–900.

21 George T. Milkovich and Jerry M. Mewman, *op. cit.*, 320–321.

22 Mitchell Fein, *An Alternative to Traditional Managing*, (Hillsdale, NJ: Mitchell Fein, 1980): 28–41.

23 Richard I. Henderson, *Compensation Management*, 5th ed. (Englewood Cliffs, NJ: Prentice-Hall, Inc., 1989): 366.

24 Profit-sharing plans in the U.S. were introduced in 1794 by Albert Gallatin in Pennsylvania. Le Claire is credited with being the "father of profit sharing" because his plan was one of the most successful. See Richard Henderson, *op. cit.*, 350.

25 David W. Belcher and Thomas J. Atchison, *op. cit.*, 290–291.

26 "Employee Wrath Hits Profit-Sharing Plans," *Business Week* (July 18, 1977): 25, 28.

27 James F. Lincoln, *Incentive Management* (Cleveland, OH: The Lincoln Electric Company, 1951). Also see *Lincoln's Incentive System and Approach to Manufacturing* (Cleveland, OH: The Lincoln Electric Company, 1972), a collection of articles dealing with Lincoln's systems.

28 Paul S. Greenlaw and John P. Kohl, *Personnel Management* (New York: Harper & Row, Publishers, 1986): 369–370.

29 For discussion of the various ESOP programs, see John J. Miller, "ESOPs, TRASOPs, and PAYSOPs: A Guide for the Perplexed," *Management Review*, Vol. 72, No. 9 (September 1983): 40–43.

30 See Frederick W. Rumack and Robert E. Wallace, "The PAYSOP: A Gift from ERTA," *Personnel Administrator*, Vol. 28 (January 1983): 66–69.

31 See John Hoerr, "ESOPs: Revolution or Ripoff?" *Business Week* (April 15, 1985): 94–98.

32 Edward E. Lawler, "Secrecy about Management Compensation: Are There Hidden Costs?" *Organizational Behavior and Human Performance*, Vol. 2 (1967): 184–185. Also see "Secrecy and the Need to Know" in *Managerial Motivation and Compensation*, edited by Henry L. Tosi, Robert House, and Marvin D. Dunnette (East Lansing, MI: Michigan State University, 1972): 455–496.

33 For a comprehensive treatment on pay and pay secrecy's impacts, see Edward E. Lawler III, *Pay and Organizational Effectiveness: A Psychological View* (New York: McGraw-Hill Book Company, 1971).

34 Mary G. Miner, "Pay Policies: Secret or Open? And Why?" *Personnel Journal*, Vol. 53, No. 2 (1974): 110–115.

Chapter 11

Administering Employee Benefits

Objectives

After reading this chapter you should understand:

1. The reasons why benefits have become an important part of employees' compensation packages.
2. The methods organizations use to determine the most effective benefits to offer employees.
3. The impact of government legislation on benefits.
4. The way different pension plans impact on both organizations and employees.
5. The reasons why organizations decide to offer voluntary benefits in addition to those mandated by law.
6. The importance of specific benefits in improving employee motivation and productivity.

During the past fifty years, the importance of employee benefits has increased tremendously. Prior to the 1950s, benefits were commonly referred to as "fringes" because they were only small supplemental additions to employee paychecks. Today, however, these fringes have expanded into costs ranging from between 18 and 65 percent of payroll.[1]

The dramatic increase in the importance of benefits, along with their related costs, has established benefits as a major component of the compensation package. Unlike wages and incentives, however, benefits are not usually based on performance. Instead, they are universally provided by employers to all workers in an attempt to raise the quality of work life. If these benefits were not provided by the employer, workers would be forced to obtain them with their own after-tax income, usually at substantially higher rates. For many employees, the diverse benefits they receive from their employers would be otherwise financially unobtainable.

> **Benefits**
>
> *Benefits are any legally mandated or voluntary services, other than direct wages, which are provided to workers in whole or in part by employers.*

Reasons for the Growth of Benefits

Prior to the Depression of the 1930s, benefit programs were the exception rather than the rule. Most employers who provided benefits were either paternalistic or were attempting to thwart unionization. There were no mandated programs to afford worker protection, and few businesses saw any advantage to the voluntary expenditure of money for these services. As the nation emerged from the Depression, this state of affairs began to change. Government legislation which mandated social security benefits, wage stabilization programs, and tax incentives combined with a strong labor movement to provide most of the impetus for the tremendous growth in benefit programs over the past fifty years.

The Social Security Act (1935)

The passage of the Social Security Act of 1935 was probably the earliest major legislation affecting benefit programs. Originally designed as a retirement income system covering approximately 60 percent of all workers, social security has been expanded to provide survivor, disability, and health and retirement benefits to about 95 percent of today's workforce. The original employer contribution for each employee was under $50 per year, but today's employer tax approximates $3,000.

Wage Controls

The popularity of benefits increased substantially as a result of the wage stabilization programs implemented by the government during both World War II and the Korean War. Although wages were frozen, the government viewed benefits as fringes and exempted them from pay controls. Relatively little unemployment existed at that time, so employers increased employee benefits as a strategy for attracting and retaining workers.

Tax Incentives

Over the years, tax laws have fostered the establishment of employee benefit programs by allowing generous deductions. Employers were allowed current-year tax deductions, and employees usually obtained the benefits either tax free or tax deferred. As personal income taxes rapidly spiraled upward during the

1970s and early 1980s, benefits became an increasingly popular means of receiving compensation. However, if the trend that began with the passage of the Tax Reform Act of 1986, which reduced personal income taxes and imposed restrictions on employer-sponsored benefit plans, continues, the popularity of benefit programs in lieu of wages may see a decline during the 1990s.

Union Influence

Unions have played a major role in securing increased amounts of benefits for their constituents. Beginning with the passage of the National Labor Relations Act in 1935, and supported by court rulings during the next decades, benefits were determined to be a mandatory bargaining item in the same vein as wages. As a result, benefit programs expanded in both unionized and non-unionized firms. From the simplest pension and retirement programs to more sophisticated plans offering dental coverage, unions have been in the forefront in securing more and greater benefits for their members.

Benefit Planning

Until recently, benefit planning was a nonexistent function within most organizations. Because the relative costs of benefits in proportion to the total costs of compensation were small, organizations did not expend much effort in choosing benefits. For most companies this resulted in a benefit package consisting of inadequate overlapping programs which, at best, satisfied the needs of only a small percentage of employees.

Today the picture has changed. An increase in employer contributions to government-mandated programs; a rapid rise in health care costs; and an increase in benefits, which are no longer viewed as optional by employees, have caused most organizations to carefully plan out their benefit programs.

The planning of benefit programs involves a careful analysis of several diverse factors. Robert McCaffery, a noted benefits specialist, identifies five internal factors and five external factors for consideration when planning benefit programs. The internal factors are: the human resource management philosophy, the business objectives, the total compensation strategy, the wants of the employees, and the cost issues. The external factors are: the legal requirements, taxation, inflation, competition, and benefit innovations.[2]

Internal Factors Affecting Planning

Human resource management philosophy

Whether stated explicitly or implicitly, all employers have a philosophy which influences their behavior toward employees. Organizations which believe that employees need direction and protection will tend to choose benefit packages for their workers. These programs are usually administered uniformly to all workers, they are noncontributory, and they consist primarily of security programs. On the other hand, organizations which perceive workers as individuals who have unique needs may establish benefit plans which provide the opportunity for employees to choose their benefits from among several options.

Business objectives

Depending on both the short- and long-term goals of the organization, different benefit plans may be more or less applicable for employees. Organizations which plan to expand their operations in the near future may consider adding relocation benefits, such as home purchasing, in order to facilitate the transfer of personnel. On the other hand, companies which are considering downsizing may wish to plan for the implementation of early retirement programs, outplacement services, and employee counseling.

Total compensation strategy

Until recently, many organizations divided compensation management and benefit administration into two separate functions. Each program was planned independently of the other. Realistically, however, the functions are intricately tied to one another, and rather than being individual components, they constitute one compensation package. This fact becomes quite obvious when companies realize that many benefit costs are tied directly to wages and salaries. As direct compensation increases, the cost of those benefits which are directly tied to wages, such as pension and retirement programs, also increases.

Expressed wants of employees

As mentioned previously, early benefit programs were slapped together haphazardly, usually meeting the needs of very few workers. Effective benefit administration involves sampling employee wishes and attempting to provide programs which will satisfy the needs of the majority. In many cases, establishing effective programs based on the needs of employees is no more costly, and in many instances is less expensive, than randomly choosing programs.

Cost issues

Aside from government-mandated benefit programs such as social security, organizations have a choice regarding the type of programs they choose to establish. A large variety of insurance programs, with varying costs attached, may be considered. Just as individuals shop for those products which offer the greatest need satisfaction for the price, so too must organizations balance need satisfaction with program cost. Furthermore, decisions must be made regarding how much of the cost will be contributed by the employer and how much will be borne by the employee.

External Factors Affecting Planning

Legal requirements

Government regulation of benefits requires that benefit managers continually stay abreast of current and proposed legislation. Both the mandatory programs, such as social security and workers' compensation, and the government-regulated pension plans, such as ERISA, are constantly changing. This requires benefit managers to periodically monitor and modify their programs to meet the requirements of the law.

Taxation

Tax laws are at best transitory. In the past, employers and employees expanded their benefit coverage because of the favorable tax laws. When these laws changed, however, eliminating the tax relief, shifts occurred in the popularity of certain benefit programs. For example, in 1982, the availability of opening individual retirement accounts (IRA) caused many employees to channel funds into these tax-sheltered programs. After the tax changes of 1986, which eliminated the tax break for employees who had other pension plans, the popularity of IRAs declined substantially.[3]

Inflation

The high inflation rate over the past two decades has caused benefit managers to re-evaluate their programs. Just as wages are subject to fluctuations in the economy, so too are those benefits directly tied to salaries. As wages increase substantially, the cost of these benefits also increases. Even when the benefits are fixed, and not tied to wages, employee pressures for increased benefits during inflationary times necessitates adjustments.

Competition

Attracting and retaining employees in today's labor market is a function of not only wages but also the total compensation package. Potential employees are becoming more sophisticated in their knowledge of available benefits, and organizations are continually introducing new programs. Competitive organizations monitor both the prevailing wage rate in the industry and the standard benefit package being offered.

Benefit innovations

In today's rapidly changing environment, very little remains static. Benefit programs need to be monitored continually to take advantage of cost-saving programs and to determine their appropriateness for the needs of employees. Programs which served the needs of workers five years ago may no longer be appropriate. Successful programs are innovatively planned for the particular organization and are not adapted from some other company.

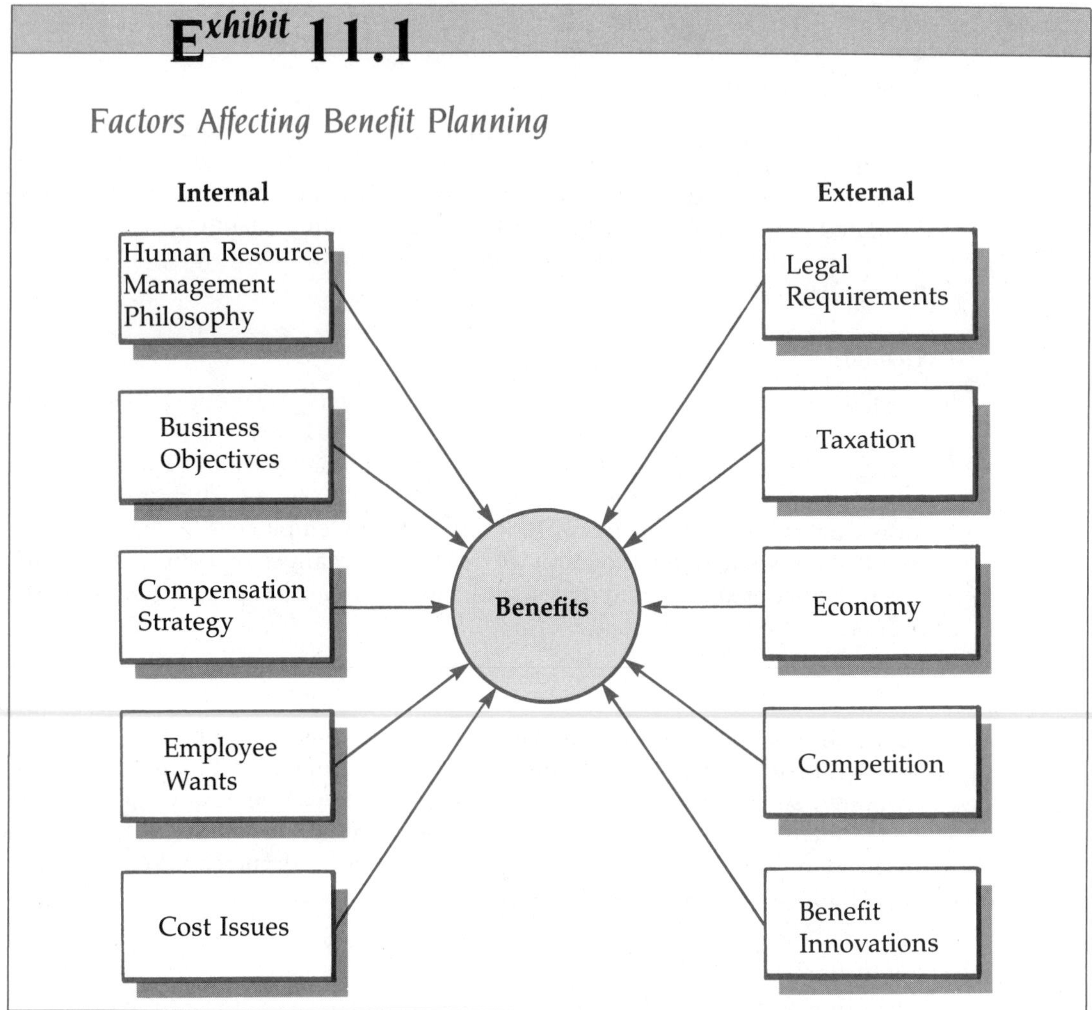

Types of Benefit Programs

Organizations have a variety of employee benefit programs from which to choose. Mandatory programs are created to comply with government regulations. Others are voluntarily chosen by employers in an attempt to satisfy the specific needs of their workers.

Mandatory Benefits[3a]

Government regulations require organizations to provide workers with benefit coverage for retirement, illness, disability, and periods of unemployment. These **mandatory benefits** programs represent a large portion of the total benefits package. In many instances, they are more costly to an organization than the sum total of all other voluntary benefits expenditures. All organizations are required, by law, to provide the following social insurance programs for their employees: social security, unemployment compensation, and workers' compensation.

Social security (OASDHI)

Social security is a term used by individuals to refer to the federal government's old-age, survivors', disability, and health insurance (OASDHI) programs. The act, which was enacted in 1935, and its subsequent amendments are designed to provide members of society with economic security. Although many employers and employees alike complain about the high cost of coverage (in 1988, employers matched employee FICA taxes at a rate of 7.51 percent of earnings up to a total of $45,000 in income), it is reasonable to assume that because employees would probably demand these benefits anyway, the government's programs protect employers from having to assume the complete economic burden of coverage.

Eligibility for coverage Between 90 and 95 percent of all workers in the United States are covered under the social security program. To be insured completely under the law, one of two conditions must be met. The first of these requires that an individual achieve credit for forty quarters of work under social security. A quarter is credited each time social security taxes are paid on $500 in annual earnings, up to a maximum of four quarters per year. Thus any worker who pays social security taxes on $2,000 ($500 × 4) during any year earns the maximum four quarters allowed per year (1989 figures).

The second way in which individuals qualify for coverage is if they have at least six quarters of credit and at least as many quarters of coverage as years elapsed since 1950 (or age twenty-one, whichever is later), before they are disabled, attain the age of sixty-two, or die. For example, a worker who reached her sixty-second birthday in 1989 would need thirty-nine credits of service in order to qualify for full benefits. On the other hand, a worker who turned twenty-one in 1979, and became disabled in 1989, would only need ten quarters of credit to qualify.

The available benefits Three principal benefits are available under social security. These are: retirement benefits, survivors' benefits, and disability benefits.

Retirement benefits Fully insured workers are eligible to receive social security benefits as early as age sixty-two. Electing to receive retirement benefits prior to age sixty-five, however, results in a permanent reduction in the amount received. In addition, the following individuals are eligible to receive benefits:

1. Spouses attaining the age of sixty-two (once again a permanently reduced rate if the benefit is elected prior to age sixty-five.)
2. Any age spouse who is caring for a retiree's child aged sixteen or below or who is disabled.

3. Dependent, unmarried children below the age of eighteen who are enrolled as full-time students.
4. Disabled children of any age, providing they were disabled prior to age twenty-two.

Survivors' benefits Survivors' benefits represent a form of life insurance payable to the deceased's dependents. In order to be entitled to complete benefits, the worker must be fully insured. For those employees who are currently insured, reduced benefits are available to the survivors. Currently insured workers are those who do not meet the requirements for full insurance outlined earlier, but who have credit for at least six quarters of coverage out of the thirteen quarters prior to their death.

Disability benefits Disability benefits are available to workers under age sixty-five who are, or who are expected to be, mentally or physically unable to engage in any form of gainful employment for a period of at least twelve months. Disability benefits are subject to a waiting period of six full months and are only paid to those employees who have worked under social security for at least five out of the ten years prior to becoming disabled. Payments are distributed in the same fashion as retirement benefits, and in fact, they are converted to retirement benefits when the insured reaches age sixty-five.

Unemployment compensation

Prior to 1935, few, if any, employees had any form of coverage for periods during which they were unemployed. After the passage of the act, employers were required to render a payroll tax to finance **unemployment compensation** insurance programs established and administered by the states. Currently, all states provide UCI (Unemployment Compensation Insurance) which covers approximately 95 percent of all workers.

Exhibit 11.2

Weekly High/Low Unemployment Benefits

State	Minimum	Maximum
AL	$22.00	$120.00
AZ	40.00	135.00
AR	36.00	204.00
CA	30.00	166.00
CO	25.00	213.00
DC	26.00	250.00
GA	37.00	155.00
HI	5.00	223.00
ID	44.00	188.00
IL	51.00	176.00
IN	40.00	96.00
IA	26.00	167.00

State	Minimum	Maximum
KS	51.00	204.00
LA	10.00	191.00
ME	28.00	161.00
MD	25.00	195.00
MA	14.00	238.00
MN	38.00	250.00
MS	30.00	130.00
MO	22.00	140.00
NE	20.00	134.00
NV	16.00	177.00
NM	31.00	158.00
NC	16.00	204.00
ND	43.00	179.00
OK	16.00	197.00
PA	35.00	252.00
PR	7.00	110.00
SC	20.00	132.00
SD	28.00	140.00
TN	30.00	145.00
TX	34.00	210.00
UT	13.00	202.00
VA	68.00	167.00
VI	30.00	138.00
WA	55.00	205.00
WY	38.00	198.00
AK	38.00	188.00
DE	20.00	205.00
KY	22.00	151.00
NH	39.00	156.00
OR	62.00	222.00
WV	24.00	225.00
FL	10.00	200.00
MI	58.00	229.00
MT	45.00	181.00
NJ	48.00	241.00
NY	40.00	180.00
OH	42.00	167.00
RI	43.00	225.00
VT	17.00	160.00
WI	38.00	200.00

Source: U.S. Department of Labor, 1988.
Note: The computational formulas listed above are not based totally on an individual's wages. Some states use trust fund accounts, others use quarter of work qualifiers. Individuals should check their own state formulas for exact calculations.

Financing benefits Unemployment insurance is financed solely through employer contributions except in Alabama, Alaska, New Jersey, and Pennsylvania. The required federal payment is 6.2 percent of the first $7,000 of wages for each worker, but this figure is offset by taxes which are paid to state programs. The net result is a federal tax amounting to 0.6 percent, which is used primarily to administer the state programs. The amount individual employers pay to the state is dependent upon their *experience rating*. Those employers who have laid off few, if any, workers in the past will pay a minimal percentage of payroll (usually less than 1 percent). On the other hand, employers with poor experience ratings, characterized by a history of laying off many workers, pay higher figures—up to 10 percent in some states.

Benefits available Workers are eligible for benefits if they:

1. Have previously been employed.
2. Are able and available for work.
3. Are actively seeking employment.
4. Have satisfied the waiting period.
5. Are free of any prescribed disqualifications.

These benefits are usually paid for a period of twenty-six weeks (some states pay slightly longer), and they are determined by a formula based on the worker's past earnings. Each state has a different minimum and maximum rate. In 1988 the lowest minimum weekly allowance was $5.00 in the state of Hawaii; the highest allowable amount was in the state of Rhode Island at $281.00.

Workers' compensation

Prior to the passage of **workers' compensation** laws, employees were unprotected from accidents or illnesses incurred at the workplace. In the event employees were incapacitated as a result of an on-site work-related incident, their only recourse was to sue their employer for damages. For workers, the odds on winning a damage suit was minimal because of three common law defenses available to the employer. First, under the "contributory negligence doctrine," workers are unable to collect if their negligence contributed in any fashion to the accident. Second, under the "fellow-servant doctrine," workers are prohibited from collecting from employers if a co-worker contributed to the injury. Finally, under the "assumption-of-risk" doctrine, workers are unable to collect if they knowingly assumed jobs which have certain inherent risks associated with them.[4]

Unlike unemployment compensation insurance, in which the federal government levies a tax, workers' compensation is a state function. It is noncontributory on the part of workers; the expense is borne solely by the employer. Although most states require compulsory coverage, a few states allow for election of coverage by employers. In the rare instance where employers choose not to participate in the state's program, they are open to employee suits without the benefit of protection under the three previously stated doctrines. Therefore, it is not surprising that most employers in elective states voluntarily choose to participate in workers' compensation programs.

Eligibility for coverage In order to qualify for coverage under the law, employees in covered occupations must be disabled or killed by an accident which is sudden, unexpected, and can be placed in a specific time and place. Self-inflicted injuries, accidents resulting from intoxication, and purposeful accidents are usually excluded from coverage. In addition, coverage is included for diseases which are specifically enumerated by the law.

Available benefits Workers' compensation laws provide benefits which include medical care, disability income, rehabilitative services, and death benefits. There is no waiting period for the receipt of medical benefits, and the small waiting period for disability benefits, which is usually a week, is negated by retroactive payment.

Death benefits include a burial allowance and cash income payments to the spouse and any children under the age of eighteen. The burial allowance is a flat amount which varies from state to state, and the cash income is dependent on the employee's average wages prior to death. Some states make payments until the spouse remarries and the children attain the age of eighteen. Other states make payments for a specific number of years, such as fifteen, or until a maximum amount has been paid, such as $25,000.

Exhibit 11.3

Mandatory Benefits

Plan	Eligibility	Benefit
OASDHI social security	Be credited with 40 quarters of work or at least 6 quarters credit and as many quarters as years elapsed since 1950 (or age 21) before disabled, age 62, or death.	**1.** Retirement **2.** Survivors **3.** Disability
Unemployment compensation	Anyone previously employed, able and available for work, actively seeking employment, who satisfies a waiting period, and is free of any prescribed disqualifications.	Weekly income usually for a period of 26 weeks, based on past earnings.
Workers' compensation	Employees in covered occupations who are disabled or killed by a sudden, unexpected accident in a specific place and time.	**1.** Medical Care **2.** Disability **3.** Rehabilitation Services **4.** Death Benefits

Voluntary Benefits and Services

Aside from the mandatory benefits required by government rules and regulations, employers provide a wide variety of benefits and services to their employees. For convenience, these benefits may be grouped into four categories. These are:

1. Insurance plans.
2. Pension plans.
3. Pay for time off.
4. Other benefits.

Insurance plans

Insurance plans are one of the most common forms of benefits employers provide for their employees. Companies usually provide plans which offer health coverage, life insurance, and disability insurance.

Health coverage The most popular and widely offered employee benefit is health care. The basic benefits include employer-paid group insurance plans which cover employees for hospital and medical expenses. In addition, many companies are offering coverage for dental, optical, and psychiatric care, as well as coverage for prescription drugs.

Although employers can provide and finance employee health benefits in a variety of ways, they usually opt for either Blue Cross/Blue Shield plans, Health Maintenance Organizations (HMOs), or Preferred Provider Organizations (PPOs).

Blue Cross/Blue Shield In most states, **Blue Cross/Blue Shield** associations are considered nonprofit organizations which offer hospitalization (Blue Cross) and medical (Blue Shield) benefits for specifically designated geographic regions. These organizations have negotiated arrangements with hospitals and physicians in their regions to accept specific fixed payments for medical services rendered. When a covered employee or dependent is treated by a participating physician or afforded services in a member hospital, the payment made by Blue Cross/Blue Shield is accepted as payment in full.

Most employers fund the total cost of the employee's Blue Cross/Blue Shield insurance. In addition, employees are usually offered the opportunity to purchase coverage for their dependents. Although the cost of the dependent insurance is borne by the employee, the low rate available through the group plan makes it an exceedingly popular option.

Health maintenance organizations (HMOs) **Health maintenance organizations** (HMOs) were patterned after the prepaid group health insurance plan provided to employees and their families by Henry Kaiser in the late 1930s. The plans are operated by groups representing physicians and health-care professionals who provide a wide array of services to subscribers on a prepaid basis.

HMOs have grown substantially since 1973 because of the passage of the

Health Maintenance Organizations Act. Presently, there are between 350 and 400 HMOs nationwide, with approximately 25 million participants.[5] The HMO act specifies that any employer located within an HMO service area who employs 25 or more employees must make available the option of HMO coverage as an alternative to other coverage. If elected by the employee, the employer must pay the same amount for the HMO coverage as they would have paid for the conventional plan. The difference, if any, is paid by the worker.

There are two common types of HMOs available. The earliest form, **group practice HMOs,** consists of physicians and health-care professionals who are either employed and paid salaries by the HMO or who have contractual arrangements with the HMO to provide services to its subscribers. These plans are often referred to as "closed-panel plans" because subscribers are required to use the personnel employed by, or contracted by, the HMO.

Group practice HMOs

The term group practice HMOs refers to those plans in which the subscriber is required to obtain treatment from physicians and health-care professionals who are either employed by the HMO or who have contractual arrangements to provide services to the HMOs' subscribers.

The second type of HMO plan includes **individual practice association HMOs.** Under this arrangement, the HMO uses physicians who continue to practice individually, but who have agreed to accept payment from the HMO on a fee-for-service basis, according to a specific, fixed rate. Known as "open panel plans," subscribers using this type of HMO may select physicians from a list provided by the HMO. Typically, there is a wider range of physicians to choose from, particularly in medical specialty areas, under individual practice plans.

Individual practice association HMOs

Under individual practice association HMOs, subscribers choose physicians and health-care professionals from a list of private-practice personnel who have agreed to accept a fixed rate of payment on a fee-for-service basis.

Preferred provider organizations (PPOs) **Preferred provider organizations** have developed and grown rapidly in the last decade. In fact, by late 1986, approximately 25 million employees had this health option available to them.[6] Under PPOs, employers contract directly with groups of health-care providers to

Exhibit 11.4

A Comparison of Different Health Care Plans

Benefits	BC/BS Basic Plan	BC/BS KeyCare	BC/BS Cost Awareness	PruCare	Equicor	Kaiser-Permanente	Network
Inpatient Care: Pre-admission Review is required **Hospital Care in Semi-Private Room for Illness (including Surgery), Injury or Pregnancy**	120 days per confinement after $100 deductible	365 days per confinement after $100 deductible	365 days per confinement after $100 deductible	All medically necessary care.	All medically necessary care.	All medically necessary care.	All medically necessary care.
Hospital Care in Semi-Private Room for Mental and Nervous, Alcohol or Drug Abuse	120 days per calendar year after $100 deductible per confinement.	30 days per calendar year after $100 deductible per confinement.	30 days per calendar year after $100 deductible per confinement.	30 days per calendar year. No deductible.	30 days per calendar year. No deductible.	30 days per calendar year. No deductible.	30 days per calendar year. No deductible.
Skilled Nursing Home Care in Semi-Private Room	120 days per confinement, payment limited to $65 per day.	180 days per confinement.	180 days per confinement.	180 days per calendar year.	180 days per calendar year.	180 days per calendar year.	180 days per calendar year.
Inpatient Professional Services for Illness, Surgery, Injury, Pregnancy, Mental Illness and Skilled Nursing Care	120 days per confinement (except up to 45 days for psychiatric and substance abuse).	365 days per hospital and 180 days per skilled nursing home confinement. Psychiatric and substance abuse covered up to 30 days per calendar year.	365 days per hospital and 180 days per skilled nursing home confinement. Psychiatric and substance abuse covered up to 30 days per calendar year.	All medically necessary care, subject to day limits for mental and nervous illness and skilled nursing care.	All medically necessary care, subject to day limits for mental and nervous illness and skilled nursing care.	All medically necessary care, subject to day limits for mental and nervous illness and skilled nursing care.	All medically necessary care, subject to day limits for mental and nervous illness and skilled nursing care.
Outpatient Institutional Care **Hospital Care for Accidental Injuries and Medical Emergencies**	Accidental injuries: Covered at UCR if treated within 72 hours.	Covered after $30 deductible.	Covered after $30 deductible.	Covered if life threatening or approved in advance; $25 copayment per visit if not admitted to hospital.	Covered if life threatening or approved in advance; $25 copayment per visit if not admitted to hospital.	Covered if life threatening or approved in advance; $25 copayment if not admitted to hospital.	Covered if life threatening or approved in advance; $25 copayment per visit if not admitted to hospital.
Home Health Care Visits	Covered at UCR for 90 approved visits per calendar year.	Up to 90 approved visits per calendar year. $10 deductible only for visits by a doctor.	Up to 90 approved visits per calendar year. $10 deductible only for visits by a doctor.	All medically necessary care when approved in advance.	All medically necessary care when approved in advance.	All medically necessary care when approved in advance.	All medically necessary care approved in advance.
Outpatient Physician & Professional Services **Illness or Injury**	Accidents, surgery and diagnostic tests covered at UCR. Other conditions, including medical emergencies, covered at 80 percent UCR after deductible.	$10 deductible per visit and 10 percent copayment for X-rays, lab tests and certain shots.	$10 deductible per visit and 10 percent copayment for X-rays, lab tests and certain shots.	$3 copayment per visit to primary care or specialist physician.	$5 copayment per visit to primary care physician. $10/after 5 p.m. $10/specialist visit.	All medically necessary care.	$5 copayment to primary care physician ($10 after hours).
Preventive Care	Not covered.	Well-baby care through age 5. 100 percent for common immunizations; $10 deductible per office visit and 10 percent copayment for diagnostic tests.	Well-baby care through age 5. 100 percent for common immunizations; $10 deductible per office visit and 10 percent copayment for diagnostic tests.	$3 copayment per visit to primary care physician.	$5 copayment per visit to primary care physician.	100 percent.	$5 copayment to primary care physician.
Dental Care	Not covered.	Diagnostic and preventive services covered in full up to 2 visits annually. Routine at 80 percent. No deductible. $1,000 annual limit.	Diagnostic and preventive services covered in full up to 2 visits annually. Routine at 80 percent. No deductible. $1,000 annual limit.	Diagnostic and preventive services at 80 percent with no deductible. All other services subject to $50 deductible. Basic services at 80 percent, major services at 50 percent. Orthodontic services, if approved in advance, at 50 percent, up to $1,000 maximum lifetime.	Diagnostic, preventive services at 100 percent. Basic services at 70 percent. $25 deductible per individual, $75 per family.	Not covered.	Not covered.
Diagnostic Tests & Laboratory	100 percent UCR.	90 percent.	90 percent.	100 percent.	100 percent.	100 percent.	100 percent.
Outpatient Psychiatric Services	First 50 visits covered at 80 percent UCR after deductible and visits 51-70 covered at 50 percent.	$10 deductible per visit, up to $2,000 in benefits per calendar year.	$10 deductible per visit, up to $2,000 in benefits per calendar year.	Self-referral $5 per session for the first 25 sessions, $15 per session for sessions 26-50.	First visit at 100 percent upon referral from primary care physician. Visits 2-50, $15 copayment per visit.	Upon referral for up to 50 visits. $15 copayment.	Upon referral, $15 copayment per visit up to 50 visits.

1989 Monthly Premiums

		STATEWIDE			RICHMOND		TIDEWATER	N. VIRGINIA	
	ACTIVE EMPLOYEES	BASIC	KEYCARE	COST AW	PRUCARE	EQUICOR	EQUICOR	KAISER-PERMANENTE	NETWORK
EMPLOYEE ONLY	YOU PAY	$ 0.00	$ 3.00	$ 3.00	$ 13.24	$ 12.18	$ 12.18	$ 8.30	$ 6.32
	STATE PAYS	$ 92.00	$ 92.00	$ 92.00	$ 92.00	$ 92.00	$ 92.00	$ 92.00	$ 92.00
	TOTAL PREMIUM	$ 92.00	$ 95.00	$ 95.00	$105.24	$104.18	$104.18	$100.30	$ 98.32
FAMILY COVERAGE	YOU PAY	$ 66.70	$ 74.20	$ 74.20	$103.06	$ 96.84	$ 96.84	$ 87.44	$ 82.50
	STATE PAYS	$163.30	$163.30	$163.30	$163.30	$163.30	$163.30	$163.30	$163.30
	TOTAL PREMIUM	$230.00	$237.50	$237.50	$266.36	$260.14	$260.14	$250.74	$245.80
FAMILY COVERAGE BOTH SPOUSES STATE EMPLOYEES	YOU PAY	$ 46.00	$ 53.50	$ 53.50	$ 82.36	$ 76.14	$ 76.14	$ 66.74	$ 61.80
	STATE PAYS	$184.00	$184.00	$184.00	$184.00	$184.00	$184.00	$184.00	$184.00
	TOTAL PREMIUM	$230.00	$237.50	$237.50	$266.36	$260.14	$260.14	$250.74	$245.80
CARVE OUT EMPLOYEE ONLY	YOU PAY	$ 0.00	$ 1.80	$ 1.80	$ 11.90	$ 10.44	$ 10.44	$ 0.00	$ 3.78
	STATE PAYS	$ 56.98	$ 56.98	$ 56.98	$ 56.98	$ 56.98	$ 56.98	$ 45.18	$ 56.98
	TOTAL PREMIUM	$ 56.98	$ 58.78	$ 58.78	$ 68.88	$ 67.42	$ 67.42	$ 45.18	$ 60.76
EMPLOYEE WITH CARVE OUT & DEPENDENT WITH FULL	YOU PAY	$ 44.34	$ 49.14	$ 49.14	$ 69.48	$ 66.96	$ 66.96	$ 48.34	$ 54.44
	STATE PAYS	$104.64	$104.64	$104.64	$104.64	$104.64	$104.64	$ 97.14	$104.64
	TOTAL PREMIUM	$148.98	$153.78	$153.78	$174.12	$171.60	$171.60	$145.48	$159.08
EMPLOYEE WITH FULL & DEPENDENT WITH CARVE OUT	YOU PAY	$ 27.46	$ 32.26	$ 32.26	$ 52.60	$ 50.08	$ 50.08	$ 23.96	$ 37.56
	STATE PAYS	$121.52	$121.52	$121.52	$121.52	$121.52	$121.52	$121.52	$121.52
	TOTAL PREMIUM	$148.98	$153.78	$153.78	$174.12	$171.60	$171.60	$145.48	$159.08
EMPLOYEE & DEPENDENT BOTH WITH CARVE OUT	YOU PAY	$ 27.46	$ 31.06	$ 31.06	$ 51.26	$ 48.34	$ 48.34	$ 3.86	$ 35.02
	STATE PAYS	$ 86.50	$ 86.50	$ 86.50	$ 86.50	$ 86.50	$ 86.50	$ 86.50	$ 86.50
	TOTAL PREMIUM	$113.96	$117.56	$117.56	$137.76	$134.84	$134.84	$ 90.36	$121.52
	RETIREES								
	RETIREE ONLY, FULL	$ 92.00	$ 95.00	$ 95.00	$105.24	$104.18	$104.18	$100.30	$ 98.32
	RETIREE ONLY, W/MEDICARE	$ 42.31	$ 58.78	$ 58.78	$ 68.88	$ 67.42	$ 67.42	$ 45.18	$ 60.76
	RETIREE & DEPENDENT, ONE FULL & ONE W/MEDICARE	$134.31	$153.78	$153.78	$174.12	$171.60	$171.60	$145.48	$159.08
	RETIREE & DEPENDENT BOTH W/MEDICARE	$ 84.62	$117.52	$117.52	$137.76	$134.85	$134.85	$ 90.36	$121.52
	FAMILY, FULL COVERAGE	$230.00	$237.50	$237.50	$266.36	$260.14	$260.14	$250.74	$245.80

Source: Commonwealth of Virginia, *Personnel Communique* (September, 1988). Reprinted with permission.

provide medical services at a reduced fee. Unlike HMOs, however, benefits are not provided on a prepaid basis. Rather, fixed payments, which are the same for all PPO participants, are made on a fee-for-service basis.

A second difference between PPOs and HMOs lies in the choice of providers to use. HMO subscribers are required to use designated providers, while PPO plans offer incentives to employees to choose PPO providers, but allow employees the choice of using non-PPO personnel. The use of non-PPO practitioners is discouraged by the offering of reduced benefits to employees. For example, full coverage may be available when using a PPO provider, but only 80 percent is available for a non-participating physician.

Pensions

After health plans, pension plans are the most frequently offered employee benefits. The popularity of these plans is attributable to a variety of factors. First, benefits available from the government's social insurance programs do not afford most employees the same standard of living they achieved while they were working. Second, while the law protects individuals over the age of forty from age discrimination, older workers find it difficult to obtain employment and supplement their income. Third, most human beings have a tendency to live for today, at the expense of the future. The average worker finds it difficult, especially in light of rapid inflation, to save enough to insure financial security for later years. Finally, employer-sponsored pension programs are preferred because these programs are generally treated more favorably under the tax laws than individual savings accounts.[7]

Types of pension plans Pension plans are usually characterized by the nature of their funding. **Contributory pension plans** require payments by both employers and employees; **noncontributory pension plans** are funded solely by the employer. Regardless of the funding mechanism, however, pension plans all share a common link. They all place aside a portion of the employee's working life compensation and defer payment until a future date. In essence, pension plans may be viewed as a form of deferred compensation.

> **Contributory and noncontributory plans**
>
> *Contributory pension plans require joint funding of pension plans by both employees and employers. Noncontributory plans are funded solely by the employer.*

Defined-contribution plan Pension plans may also be classified according to the amount of pension benefits paid to employees. Under the **defined-contribution plan,** individual accounts are established for each employee. The plan specifies the exact amount an employer is required to contribute, but it does not guarantee a particular benefit amount for the employee. When employees become eligible to receive benefits, their pensions are based solely on the amount of money, plus any earnings, accumulated in their accounts. Employees covered by this plan bear the total burden for poor investments and reap the benefits of good plan ventures.

Defined-contribution plan

The defined-contribution plan requires employers to contribute a specified amount to individual employee pension accounts. These funds, along with any earnings, will be distributed to employees when they reach eligibility.

Defined-benefit plan Unlike the defined-contribution plan, the **defined-benefit plan** offers employees greater retirement security. Although the plan does not specifically outline the amount to be contributed by the employer, it does promise to pay a specific benefit to each employee. Each year, calculations are made to determine the employer contribution necessary to fund the program. Individual employee accounts are not established, and each employee draws from the entire fund for his or her defined benefit. Usually, the actuarial process adequately determines the yearly contributions necessary to fund the plan. Should there be insufficient funds available, however, the employer is responsible for making up the difference.

Defined-benefit plan

The defined-benefit plan requires employers to periodically contribute specified funds necessary to provide employees with fixed benefits upon eligibility.

Individual Retirement Accounts (IRAs) Originally, **individual retirement plans** were established by Congress to provide pension benefits for those individuals not covered under employer-sponsored programs. These plans were subsequently made available to any individuals with earned income. After the major tax changes of 1986, the tax benefits associated with IRAs were once again reserved primarily for those employees who are not covered by a qualified pension plan.

Basically, the law stipulates that any individual who is not covered by a pension plan at work and who has earned income may make contributions to an IRA account of 100 percent of their earned income or $2,000, whichever is less. In addition, if the individual has a spouse who has no earned income, an additional $250 is allowable. The total of $2250 may then be divided between the two accounts in any fashion, as long as the contribution to either account does not exceed $2,000.

The contributions made to IRA accounts are tax deductible, and the yearly interest is not taxable. Withdrawal of IRA funds may not occur prior to age fifty-nine years and six months (except in the case of death or disability), without incurring a sizable tax penalty. In addition, distribution of funds must begin by age seventy years and six months. These distributions are taxed as ordinary income during the year of receipt, but usually the recipient is in a lower tax bracket.

Salary Reduction Plans 401(k) Plan Under Section 401 (k) of the Internal Revenue Code, employers may establish a retirement savings program which allows employees the opportunity to contribute to the plan through payroll deductions. All employee contributions are in pretax dollars, which lowers their current taxes, and all monies in the plan are tax-free until withdrawal. The contributions made by employees are frequently matched by the employer. In addition, employees are usually provided with the opportunity to decide among different venture options for investment of their funds.

The popularity of **401 (k) plans** and the resulting loss of tax revenues probably contributed to the government's placing limitations on them through the major tax changes of 1986.[8] Beginning in 1987, the maximum permissible annual tax-deferred amount contributed to a 401 (k) plan was substantially reduced, ($7,000 in 1987 indexing up to $7,627 in 1989, and adjusted yearly only by cost-of-living adjustments). Furthermore, greater restrictions were placed on the proportion of highly compensated employees in an organization who were allowed to participate in 401 (k) plans.[9]

Government regulation of pension plans Prior to 1974, many employees found that, upon retirement, their pensions were sharply reduced because of fund mismanagement or that they were ineligible to receive benefits because of complex plan provisions. In order to prevent these abuses and to protect employee interests, Congress passed the **Employee Retirement Income Security Act** (ERISA) of 1974.

The ERISA imposes certain standards of conduct on individuals who control and administer pension funds (fiduciaries), it establishes guidelines for **qualified pension plans** in order to receive preferential tax treatment, and it requires the disclosure of relevant financial information to both employees and the government. ERISA does not require employers to provide pension plans to employees, but if they are established, it may require the program to meet certain minimum standards.[10]

Qualified pension plan

A qualified plan is any pension program which meets ERISA's *standards for tax-preferred treatment.*

Fiduciary responsibilities ERISA requires all pension plans to designate the responsibility and authority of the fund management to one person. This individual is expected to act in the best interest of the plan's participants, and he or she must be bonded for at least 10 percent of the funds (but in no instance less than $1,000 or more than $500,000). In addition, the individual is prohibited from the following: 1) engaging in self-dealing with the plan, 2) receiving any personal consideration from any person dealing with transactions involving the plan's assets, 3) investing more than 10 percent of the fund's assets with securities or property of the employer, and 4) transferring the plan's assets, such as making loans, to a party-in-interest.

Eligibility requirements In order to qualify for preferential tax treatment, the law requires at least 70 percent of the employees to be covered, and at least 80 percent of those employees must participate in the plan. In addition, the employer is prohibited from denying plan participation to any employee over the age of twenty-five (amended to twenty-one years of age by the Retirement Equity Act of 1984), or any employee who completes one year of service (twelve months of employment during which at least one thousand hours were worked). The law allows the one-year service requirement to be extended to three years provided that the employer credits employees with 100 percent of their benefits after the three-year period. Thus, an employee who was hired prior to age twenty-two and who works continuously to age twenty-five must be credited with at least three years service. Pension plans that meet ERISA's minimum requirements or are more lenient in their eligibility requirements qualify for preferential tax treatment. Plans which have more stringent requirements are not eligible for relief.

Vesting When employees are entitled to their accrued benefits, regardless of whether or not they are still employed by the employer at retirement or are currently ineligible to collect them, they are considered **vested.** Any qualified pension plan must comply with minimum vesting rights established by ERISA.

> ***Vesting***
>
> *Employees are vested when they are entitled to their accrued benefits regardless of whether they are currently eligible to collect their pensions or are still employed by the employer when they retire.*

According to the provisions of ERISA, all pension plans must provide full and immediate vesting of employee contributions. Employer contributions, however, are vested under one of three alternatives. The first is the "Ten-Year Service Rule" and requires 100 percent of the employer's contributions to become vested for the employee after ten years of service. The second option is the "Graded Fifteen-Year Service Rule" and provides for incremental percentage vesting over a fifteen-year period. For example, employees are vested 25 percent after five years of service, 40 percent after eight years of service, 80 percent after thirteen years of service, and 100 percent upon the completion of fifteen years of work. Finally, employers may choose to use the "Rule of Forty-Five." Under this vesting option, employees with at least five years of service whose combined age and service equals forty-five (for example, an employee aged thirty-nine with six years of service would receive 50 percent vesting), or employees with ten years of service with the employer, must receive at least 50 percent vesting. From that point onward, 10 percent additional vesting is obtained per year, until 100 percent is achieved.

Under the Tax Reform Act of 1986, ERISA's vesting provisions were modified beginning December 31, 1988. Under the present system, in order to qualify for tax-preferred status, employers must either provide plans offering 100 percent vesting after five years or 20 percent vesting after three years, with an additional 20 percent each year thereafter, until 100 percent vesting is achieved (seven years).

Portability For most employees, **portability,** or the ability to transfer accrued pension benefits from one plan to another, is highly desirable. Although it is not required, ERISA provides employers with the option of allowing vested employees leaving the organization the opportunity to transfer, tax free, any of their accrued funds into an Individual Retirement Account (IRA). Once deposited, these funds are subject to the same rules and regulations governing IRA accounts.

Pay for Time Not Worked

Payment for time off from the job consistently ranks as one of the top benefit costs. The U.S. Chamber of Commerce reports that the average cost of these benefits is 13.6 percent of the payroll.[11] The most common benefit costs are vacations, holidays, and personal and sick leave days.

Vacations

There are two basic reasons underlying paid vacations. First, both the physical and mental health of employees is enhanced if they periodically take time off from their jobs. This in turn leads to a more productive workforce. Second, paid vacations serve as rewards to loyal employees for their dedication and service to the organization. In essence, it is an incentive-based benefit.[12]

Most organizations establish a specified waiting period before vacation time may be earned. This interval varies from organization to organization and is usually longer for lower level employees. For example, a production line worker may earn one week of vacation after one year of work, but an upper level manager may earn two weeks of vacation for a similar amount of service. In addition, the amount of paid vacation increases as the length of service increases. Thus, employees with from one to ten years of service may be entitled to two weeks of paid vacation, while employees with ten or more years of service may receive three weeks of paid vacation.

Many employers require employees to use their accrued vacation time during the year in which it is earned or to forfeit the benefit. The logic underlying this philosophy stems from the aforementioned belief that vacations are necessary for the physical and psychological well-being of the employee. Therefore, employers encourage the use of the accrued time.

Other organizations, particularly those who grant large amounts of paid vacation time, such as a month or more, allow employees to carry over a certain percentage of their vacation time from year to year. The logic underlying this practice is that beyond a certain amount of time the benefits associated with time away from the job are negligible. In fact, some employees find it difficult to schedule so much time away from their jobs and they actually resent being forced to take vacations. By allowing a percentage of time to be saved, employees reap the benefits of time away from the job while maintaining flexibility of scheduling.

Holidays

Most employers pay workers for approximately ten holidays per year. The scheduling of holidays is usually determined by the type of business in which the firm engages. For example, government agencies and banks are controlled by laws which require them to close on certain days. Other businesses, such as retail establishments, try to remain open when the majority of organizations are closed. The logic behind this practice is that people who are not working are potential shoppers, and shoppers cannot make purchases if businesses are closed.

Some organizations, such as hospitals, find it necessary to always remain open throughout the year. These organizations usually establish plans which allow for rotation of traditional holidays, and they offer substitute days to make up the difference. For example, one employee may be off Christmas day, but required to work New Year's day, while another employee may work Christmas and be off on New Year's day. Both of these employees would then be granted an additional holiday day which might or might not correspond to a traditional holiday. For example, they might be allowed to take off on their birthday.

One system of allocating holidays which has gained popularity over the years is the allocation of "floating holidays." Rather than pre-assigning the total amount of days allowed for holidays, organizations are finding it useful to reserve some of these days for later assignment. Thus, employees may be informed that they will receive ten holidays, of which seven are scheduled, including Christmas and Thanksgiving. The remaining three days are assigned at management's discretion. If the organization enters a slow sales period, employees may be instructed to take one, two, or three of their floating holidays. Using holidays in this fashion has allowed some companies to avoid layoffs, while still providing adequate benefits. Of course, should a specific need for the days not develop, employees would still be granted their three holidays prior to the year's end.

Personal and sick leave days

Employers are aware of the fact that, sooner or later, all employees are going to have to be absent from their jobs because of unforeseen and uncontrollable events. Sickness, a death in the family, jury duty, and personal religious observances are some of the more common reasons why people are absent from work. Most organizations make some provisions to compensate employees for legitimate absences which are beyond their control.

The most common way organizations handle these absences is by publishing policies regarding the benefits allowed. For example, individuals may earn one sick day for each month employed, and unused days are either carried over from year to year or are forfeited. It is important to note that in those companies where individuals lose their unused sick days at the end of the year, a large number of sick calls occur just prior to the end of the period. The logic behind this phenomenon is simple. Workers feel that it is their right to take off because they earned the time.

If a death in the family occurs, three days may be allowed with pay. Jury duty may be compensated in total, or the organization may reimburse the difference between the amount received from the court and the worker's normal daily wage. Regardless of the policy established, publishing the procedures avoids conflicts and guarantees uniformity of administration among employees.

Other Employee Benefits

All of the previously mentioned benefits are fairly standard across organizations. In addition to these commonly offered programs, many organizations provide supplementary benefits to employees in the hope that these programs will motivate employees to make greater contributions to the organization. The types of programs offered vary from organization to organization, but all of them originate from the premise that, if employees are afforded benefits, their resulting work efforts will profit the organization. Some of the more common programs offered include: educational benefits, employee assistance programs (EAPs), relocation assistance, and child care.

Educational benefits

Educational benefits are one of the most frequently offered employee services, with approximately 86 percent of full-time employees being offered tuition reimbursement programs.[13] Most educational assistance programs provide either company-sponsored seminars and symposia or tuition allowances for work-related courses. When organizations sponsor specific programs, the total costs are usually borne by the company. On the other hand, educational assistance for external courses, such as vocational or college courses, varies from full to partial reimbursement. For example, some organizations allow workers time off from their jobs with pay to take courses at colleges, and they assume all related fees. Other companies pay only tuition, and employees are responsible for paying book fees, transportation costs, and other related expenses. Regardless of the amount covered, however, most organizations stipulate two conditions employees must satisfy in order to be reimbursed. First, the course taken must be job related. Second, employees must complete the course with an acceptable grade (usually a "C" or better). Failure to meet these conditions usually results in the employee's having to bear the full brunt of the educational expenses.

Employee assistance programs (EAPs)

When **employee assistance programs** (EAPs) were first introduced in the 1940s, they were designed to provide assistance to employees troubled with alcohol-related problems. Today, these programs, which are sponsored by as many as 80 percent of Fortune 500 companies,[14] offer health services, personal counseling (including marital, family, financial, and career counseling), and assistance for any other employee problems. The goal of these programs is to save the organization money by aiding employees in dealing with personal problems which are either currently interfering with or have the future potential to hamper job performance. To this end, organizations either provide in-house EAPs or they participate in referral systems.

Exhibit 11.5

Common Employee Benefits

Mandatory	Voluntary	
Social security	Insurance	Medical Life Cancer Dental Vision
Unemployment compensation	Pensions	Qualified Deferred
Workers' compensation	Paid time off	Jury duty Vacations Sick leave Holidays Personal Family death
	Other benefits	EAPs Relocation Child care Employee discounts Use of organization's equipment Education Credit Union

Relocation assistance

Many organizations, particularly those in tight labor markets, find that policies allowing for relocation expenses provide a competitive edge in recruiting personnel. Companies that offer this type of benefit program usually distinguish between assistance available for new hires and the allowance available for currently employed workers who are being transferred to another company facility. In the case of new hires, assistance is usually provided only for directly related moving expenses. This may include travel expenses, moving company fees, and temporary meals and lodging. On the other hand, expenses for transferred employees can be quite costly and may include, in addition to the costs mentioned for a new hire, costs associated with finding a new residence, costs associated with finding employment for a spouse, and costs associated with the purchase and sale of a principal residence, as well as the interest payment difference required to finance a new residence.

Determining whether or not relocation assistance policies should be implemented requires that cost analyses be undertaken. In the case of new hires, organizations must determine whether or not the local job market has been extensively tapped. Before transferring employees, organizations usually weigh the costs associated with relocation against the costs associated with recruiting, selecting, and training new employees. When all variables have been considered, even extensive relocation costs may sometimes prove to be less costly than other approaches. Part of this reasoning stems from the fact that realistic relocation plans sometimes determine whether chosen applicants accept or reject a job offer.[15]

Child and dependent care

The overwhelming increase of working mothers over the past two decades has brought an unprecedented demand for child-care arrangements. To accommodate this need, many employers are providing various child- and dependent-care programs. For most employers, these programs take the form of actual payments for child care. These payments, which are subject to specified limitations (usually up to $5,000), are excludable from an employee's annual taxable income. Other employers are prescreening child-care facilities and, in effect, serving as a child-care referral center for their employees. Furthermore, a few employers have instituted their own child-care facilities on site. These companies maintain that the high costs associated with the programs are more than offset by the savings associated with the resulting decrease in turnover and absenteeism among their employees.[16]

Choosing Benefit Programs

Until the 1960s, the only choice available to most employees was whether or not they wished to be enrolled in the employer-sponsored benefit plans. Organizations provided a specific, defined set of benefits, and very little latitude was afforded participants to vary from the established programs. Today, flexible benefit plans (**cafeteria benefit plans**) are being offered by an increasing number of employers. These plans give employees greater control and flexibility over the types of benefits they receive.

Flexible or cafeteria benefit plans

Flexible or cafeteria benefit plans are programs which provide employees with the flexibility of selecting the mix of employer-offered benefits which best suits their individual needs.

The implementation of flexible benefit plans is usually accomplished by utilizing one of three (or any combination of the three) approaches. These are:

1. **The core approach.**
2. **The module approach.**
3. **The flexible spending account approach.**[17]

Core spending account approach

The core approach provides all employees with a basic set, or core, of similar benefits and an additional dollar amount from which employees can choose additional benefits to satisfy their own particular needs.

Module spending account approach

The module approach gives employees a choice among several pre-established benefit packages. Each of these packages provides the same degree of compensation, but with a different mix of benefits. For example, some employees may choose between a health package offering dental coverage, but minimal psychiatric coverage, while other employees may sacrifice dental benefits for extended psychiatric benefits.

Flexible spending account approach

The flexible spending account approach provides employees with the greatest flexibility in choosing benefits. Under this option, employees are given a total dollar amount from which they may select benefits. Under this approach employees are free to tailor their entire benefit package to suit their individual needs.

Exhibit 11.6

Three Major Types of Flexible Benefit Plans

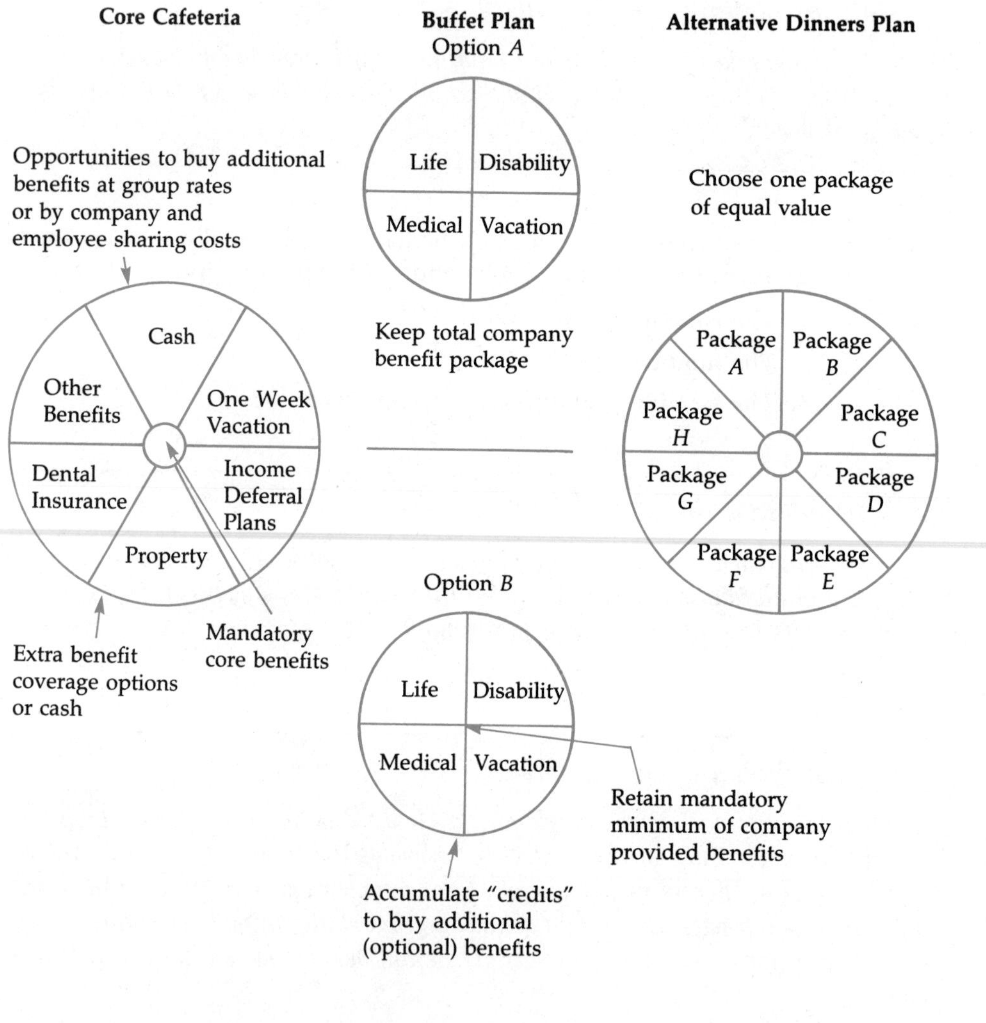

Source: Adapted from Albert Cole, Jr., "Flexible Benefits Are a Key to Better Employee Relations," *Personnel Journal*, Vol. 62, No. 1 (1983): 49–53.

The choice of which options to offer employees is not an easy one. Organizations must consider the cost of administering these programs as well as employee reactions to the plans. Critics of flexible benefits maintain that: these programs represent administrative nightmares, they are difficult and costly to communicate, they are rarely endorsed by labor organizations, and they place important choices in the hands of uneducated workers. In fact, these criticisms are not without merit. However, with the increased use of computers, a little extended effort on the part of human resource departments in communicating available options, and an increasing acceptance of cafeteria plans by unions, flexible benefits are becoming an increasingly attractive option to both employers and employees.

Summary

A significant portion of the total compensation package employees receive is in the form of benefits. The various benefits offered by employers fall into two broad categories: those mandated by the government and those offered voluntarily by employers.

The major impetus for government-mandated benefit programs traces back to the enactment of the old-age, survivors', disability, and health insurance programs (OASDHI) enacted in 1935. This major piece of legislation is responsible for the establishment of the social security program, unemployment compensation, and workers' compensation. Today, more than 90 percent of workers are covered by one or more of these programs.

In addition to mandated benefits, many employers provide voluntary services for their employees. These benefits vary widely from company to company, but are usually classified into four major categories. These include: health care benefits, pension and retirement programs, pay for time not worked, and other employee services. The establishment of an effective benefits program is highly organization-specific, and it requires thorough cost analyses and employee needs assessments.

Key Terms to Identify

Mandatory benefits
Social security
Unemployment compensation
Workers' compensation
Blue Cross/Blue Shield
Health maintenance organizations (HMOs)
Group practice HMOs
Individual Retirement Account (IRA)
Salary Reduction Plan, 401 (k) Plan
Employee Retirement Income Security Act (ERISA)
Qualified pension plan
Fiduciary
Vesting
Portability

Individual practice association HMOs
Preferred provider organizations (PPOs)
Contributory and noncontributory pension plans
Defined-contribution plan
Defined-benefit plan
Employee assistance programs (EAPs)
Cafeteria or flexible benefits plans
Core approach
Module approach
Flexible spending account approach

Questions for Discussion

Do You Know the Facts?

1. What factors account for the rapid growth of benefits in the United States?
2. Discuss how both internal and external factors affect the benefits planning process.
3. What are some of the rules established by the federal government which affect the eligibility of employees for social security, unemployment compensation, and workers' compensation?
4. Discuss how the federal government regulates pension plans. What changes were made in ERISA by the Tax Act of 1986?

Can You Apply the Information Learned?

1. What factors would you consider in determining what benefit packages to offer to your employees?
2. Many people complain about the uselessness of the social security system. Discuss whether or not you feel employees would be better off in the long run if benefits were solely voluntarily administered by employers.
3. Discuss whether or not you feel it is the organization's responsibility to provide EAP, and child-care programs for employees.
4. Discuss how you would defend the implementation of a flexible benefits plan in an organization which has always been highly paternalistic.

Whose Responsibility Is it Anyway?

Adriana Plickford couldn't believe her ears. She had just been informed by the corporate office that the company's attorneys had agreed to settle a lawsuit out of court for one hundred thousand dollars. No matter how she rationalized the decision, however, it seemed wrong. It just was not the company's responsibility!

It had all started one year earlier. Adriana Plickford was the personnel administrator for a local retail outlet of a national grocery chain. One morning she received a call from Jane Jones, the wife of one of the store's employees, informing her that her husband Don had been in an automobile accident and was in the hospital. However, it didn't appear too serious and he would be back at work the next day. Sure enough, Don arrived at work the next morning sporting a full neck brace, which he continued to wear for the next five weeks.

Seven months later, Don suddenly began to experience excruciating neck and back pains which prohibited him from working. He began to draw disability payments and sought medical attention. After a thorough examination process it was determined that Don had to undergo surgery on both his neck and back to repair injuries sustained during the accident. In addition, during the testing process, the doctors discovered that Don had a hereditary heart problem which needed to be repaired, as well as Carpal Tunnel Syndrome. He remained out of work and on disability while awaiting a date for surgery.

After Don's twenty-two weeks had expired, Adriana, according to company policy, informed Don that he was going to be terminated. He responded that the company had no right to fire him because he was recovering from Carpal Tunnel Syndrome and other work-related problems. After thoroughly researching Don's records, Adriana found that the only accidents which had ever been reported were a small finger cut requiring two stitches and a fall off the second rung of a ladder three years earlier. In both cases, only minor medical attention was required. There were no other incidents mentioned. Based on the facts, Adriana made the decision to terminate Don.

Shortly thereafter, the company was informed that Don was claiming benefits under workers' compensation. Furthermore, they were receiving bills related to Don's medical expenses. They refused to pay the bills, and challenged Don's rights to collect compensation benefits. Don sued for benefits, payments of the bills, and future lost income. Now the company wants to settle out of court, and Adriana believes it's not the company's responsibility.

Questions for Discussion

1. Should the company be responsible for Don's bills and compensation? Why or why not?
2. What type of voluntary benefit programs might be established to protect future occurrences of this type?

Endnotes and References

1 U.S. Chamber of Commerce, *Employee Benefits 1985* (Washington, D.C.: U.S. Chamber of Commerce, 1986).

2 Robert M. McCaffery, *Employee Benefit Programs: A Total Compensation Perspective* (Boston, MA: PWS-KENT Publishing Company, 1988): 5–24.

3 For a discussion of the impact of the 1986 Tax Act on benefit programs, see Fredrick I. Schick, "Tax Reform's Impact on Benefit Programs," *Personnel Administrator,* Vol. 32 (January 1987): 80–88.

3a. The discussion of the mandatory benefits is derived from the treatment of this subject in Burton T. Beam, Jr. and John J. McFadden, *Employee Benefits* (Homewood, IL: Richard D. Irwin, Inc., 1988): 15–45.

4 Burton T. Beam, Jr. and John J. McFadden, *op. cit.*, 41.

5 Glenn Kramon, "Overpayments on H.M.O.s," *New York Times* (October 20, 1987): D2.

6 Paul Susca, "Preferred Provider Organizations: The Alternative Approach," *CFO (The Magazine for Chief Financial Officers),* Vol. 2, No. 10 (October 1986): 87.

7 The discussion of pension plans through defined-benefit plan is from Burton T. Beam, Jr. and John J. McFadden, *op. cit.*, 255.

8 For a discussion of the impact of the 1986 Tax Reform Act on pension plans, see Dick Raskin and Jay Peters, "Tax Reform's Effect on Qualified Plans," *Personnel Administrator,* Vol. 31 (November 1986): 70–74.

9 Jack H. Schechter, "The Tax Reform Act of 1986: Its Impact on Compensation and Benefits, Part 1 and Part 2," *Personnel,* Vol. 63, No. 12 (1986): 61–67, and Vol. 64, No. 1 (1987): 72–75.

10 Patrick J. Cihon and James O. Castagnera, *Labor and Employment Law* (Boston, MA: PWS-KENT Publishing Company, 1988): 490–491.

11 U.S. Chamber of Commerce, *Employee Benefits 1986* (Washington, D.C.: U.S. Chamber of Commerce, 1987).

12 Robert M. McCaffery, *op. cit.*, 134.

13 U.S. Department of Labor, Bureau of Labor Statistics, *Employee Benefits in Medium and Large Firms, 1985* (Washington, D.C.: U.S. Government Printing Office, July 1986), 82.

14 *ACA News,* Vol. 30, No. 3 (April 1987): 14.

15 Howard G. MacMillan Jr., "Your Relocation Policy as a Recruiting Tool," *Mobility* (November–December 1980): 19–22.

16 See Robert M. McCaffery, *op. cit.*, 153–155.

17 Robert C. Wender and Ronald L. Sladky, "Flexible Benefit Opportunities for the Small Employer," *Personnel Administrator,* Vol. 29, No. 12 (December, 1984): 111–118.

Chapter 12

Health and Safety

Objectives

After reading this chapter you should understand:

1. The causes of accidents and ways to prevent them.
2. The way the federal and state governments regulate health and safety within organizations.
3. The record-keeping requirements for organizations.
4. The ways safety programs are fostered within companies.
5. The impact of substance abuse on the workforce.
6. The definition of stress, the impact of stress on employees, and ways to deal with the negative consequences of stress.

Employee safety and health is a growing organizational concern. Employers are increasingly investing concern and resources to support the well-being of their employees. Each year workplace accidents kill thousands of employees and disable millions more. The effect of these misfortunes on productivity is staggering. Accident costs are continually spiraling upward. In 1984 workplace accidents were estimated by one researcher to cost the United States approximately \$33 billion;[1] other estimates placed the cost at one million productive people-years and approximately \$51 billion in lost wages, medical expenses, property damage, and insurance costs. The impact of these injuries on the U.S. economy is tantamount to shutting down the entire country's industrial activities for a full week's period. Industrial accidents are responsible for more deaths since 1900 than war and all other natural catastrophes combined.[2]

These alarming statistics have not gone unnoticed. Incidents such as the 1984 toxic gas leak in Bhopal, India, which claimed the lives of over 2,500 people and injured approximately 200,000 more,[3] cause industry to take a hard look at the safety of work environments. Furthermore, various state and federal laws provide for the welfare of workers by setting forth health and safety standards with which employers are required to comply.

The creation of a healthy and safe work climate requires the joint cooperation of employers and employees. Most accidents are caused by people, not by equipment. Employer-provided safety equipment, such as eye goggles, will not prevent accidents if employees fail to wear them.

The provision of healthy and safe work environments is a two-fold process. First, government-mandated standards must be understood, implemented, and monitored. Second, employers and employees must cooperate in designing, establishing, and administering health and safety programs on a continual basis. This chapter discusses the causes of accidents, the government's role in establishing a safe working environment, and the various programs companies institute in an attempt to insure the health and safety of their employees.

The Causes of Accidents

Accidents are the result of either unsafe conditions or unsafe acts. Unsafe conditions include poorly designed equipment; environmental hazards, such as spilled water on the floor; or old and deteriorated equipment. Unsafe acts are employee generated and usually result from improper use of equipment and tools, such as using a screwdriver in lieu of a chisel, or horsing around. It is important to note that all unsafe acts do not necessarily result in accidents, and all accidents do not result in injuries. However, in order to avoid potential future mishaps, the consequences of which may be even more severe, effective safety programs should include an examination of the causes of all accidents.

Many safety investigators believe that the majority of accidents result from human error. Of course, some accidents are caused by faulty equipment or unsafe work environments. In the majority of cases, however, the benefits of safe equipment and environments are negated by employees who are unwilling to heed, or who are negligent about, safety precautions. Consider the following case:

> Pete, a metal stamping worker, was paid based on a piecework system. In compliance with government standards, the stamping machine Pete operated had a safety feature installed. To operate the stamper, Pete had to place a piece of metal under the stamper, remove both hands, and simultaneously press two large buttons that were approximately ten inches apart. The two-button system was installed after repeated injuries had resulted from workers attempting to feed the metal with one hand and to engage the stamper with the other hand. The new design slowed productivity, but it reduced accidents significantly.
>
> Pete, who desired to increase his productivity, and consequently his pay, found the two-button system highly inconvenient. One day, he arrived at the perfect solution. By taping one button, he was able to feed the metal through the machine with one hand and to engage

> the stamper with the other. The perfect solution! In fact, to this day, Pete still tapes one button closed. He feeds the metal with his right hand (an occupational injury crushed his left hand), and then engages the stamper.

Although people are concerned about safety, the desire to conserve effort, time, and money often overshadows this concern. Coupled with the feeling that "accidents only happen to other people," this view of safety equipment as inconvenient may cause employees to become lax in their attitudes concerning safety.

Accident Proneness

The theory of **accident proneness** maintains that certain people have specific characteristics which make them more likely to have accidents, regardless of the environmental conditions present. Individuals who accept this theory maintain that the elimination of accidents requires a simple three-step process. First, characteristics of accident proneness are identified. Second, all employees are tested for these characteristics. Last, high-risk jobs are reserved for employees who test low for accident proneness and low-risk jobs are assigned to employees demonstrating a high propensity for accidents.

The simplicity of the solutions to safety offered by the accident proneness theory makes it highly attractive to many individuals. Realistically, however, many researchers conclude that accident-prone people simply do not exist. In order to prove the existence of accident proneness, investigators would have to demonstrate that the same people repeatedly have accidents because of factors other than chance. In fact, those people who have repeated accidents from year to year represent only a small percentage of the total yearly accident rate.[4] Aside from characteristics such as alcoholism, drug addiction, inexperience, and poor psychomotor skills, little, if any, evidence has emerged to link accidents with individual characteristics. Nevertheless, despite the lack of evidence, there are still ardent supporters of the accident proneness theory.

Federal Regulation of Employee Health and Safety

In 1970, after many years of intense lobbying efforts by employee groups, unions, and the National Safety Council, Congress passed the **Occupational Safety and Health Act** (OSHA). This act requires all employers who deal in businesses "affecting commerce" to provide working environments that are "free" from hazards which cause, or which are likely to cause, death or serious physical harm. However, OSHA does not provide coverage for miners (who are covered under the Federal Mine Safety and Health Act), federal, state, and local employees (who are covered under different laws), domestic servants, and self-employed persons.

Three federal agencies have been established to advance OSHA's purposes.

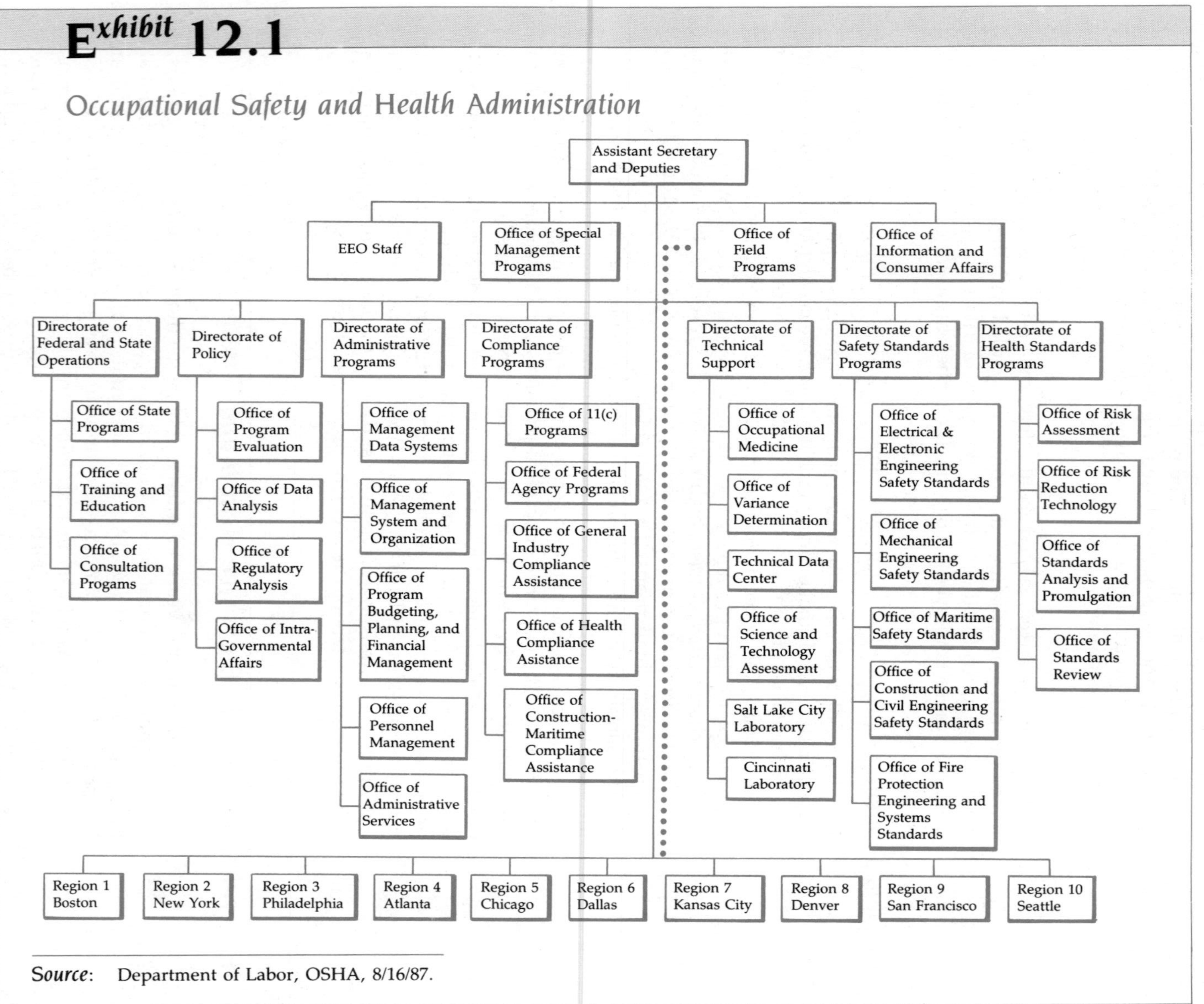

Source: Department of Labor, OSHA, 8/16/87.

The Occupational Safety and Health Administration (OSHA) is the major agency responsible for executing and enforcing the act. OSHA, which is headed by an assistant secretary of labor, sets regulations for health and safety and conducts inspections to insure compliance with these standards. OSHA is empowered to issue citations and to assess penalties against any and all employers who fail to comply with the act's provisions.

The second agency created by the Occupational Safety and Health Act is the **Occupational Safety and Health Review Commission** (OSHRC). OSHRC is an independent, quasi-judicial review board consisting of three members appointed by the president of the United States. This board is responsible for the adjudication of disputes among employers, employees, and the secretary of labor concerning OSHA's citations and penalty assessments.

The third agency, the National Institute for Occupational Safety and Health (NIOSH), is located in the Department of Health, Education and Welfare. Through its main function of conducting research, NIOSH develops and recommends occupational health and safety standards.

There are many responsibilities assigned to these three agencies by the Occupational Safety and Health Act. Of primary concern to employers, however, are those which deal with

1. Meeting established safety standards.
2. Dealing with inspections, violations, and citations.
3. Keeping appropriate records.

OSHA *Safety Standards*

The Occupational Safety and Health Act charged OSHA with the responsibility for developing and enforcing three types of safety standards: interim standards, permanent standards, and emergency standards. Standards are subject to review and modification by the secretary of labor based on research conducted by NIOSH and petitions received from interested groups. Management's responsibility is to continually keep abreast of these standards and to modify working conditions to comply with the regulations.

Interim, permanent, and emergency standards

Interim standards are standards which the secretary of labor was empowered to issue for two years after the effective date of the act. These provisions were based on existing industry standards prior to the passage of the act. Permanent standards are new and revised interim standards usually based on NIOSH *research or suggestions made by interested parties, such as employers, employees, or union groups. Emergency standards are temporary standards issued by the secretary of labor when it is determined that employees are being exposed to agents which may be toxic or physically harmful.*[5]

For the average manager, compliance with OSHA's standards is described, at best, as a nightmare. The original standards are all inclusive and contain information ranging from specifications for the design of toilet seats (round or horseshoe shaped) to warnings on appropriate behaviors to be taken when dealing with manure. It would probably be reasonable to assume that most organizations are not in compliance with the law at any given time and that those who are in compliance today may not be tomorrow.

OSHA's response to its critics has been to eliminate many standards judged as trivial[6] and to attempt to clarify the ambiguity in the remaining standards. Nevertheless, the interpretation and implementation of OSHA's standards remain a formidable task. Employers would be well advised to assign the responsibility for this job to individuals who have both sufficient technical knowledge to understand OSHA standards and sufficient knowledge of the company's operation to determine which OSHA standards are applicable to it.

OSHA Inspections

OSHA determines whether or not organizations are in compliance with its standards by conducting on-site inspections. These work site inspections are performed by trained OSHA personnel called *compliance officers.* By law, these inspectors must arrive unannounced, present their credentials, and conduct an opening conference. During this meeting, inspectors usually discuss the reasons for their visit (such as an employee complaint), answer any questions, and solicit information concerning company safety. Prior to 1978, compliance officers had blanket authority to enter and inspect any and all workplaces. In the case of

Exhibit 12.2

Some of OSHA's Most Frequently Cited Violations

- Poorly maintained equipment
- Inaccessible or poorly maintained fire equipment
- Lack of rails around pits, and drops of 4 feet
- Unmarked exitways
- Failure to wear eye and hearing protective devices
- Failure to wear hardhats
- Clogged aisleways
- Missing safety guards on machinery and tools
- Forklifts left running and unattended
- No markings of aisles for forklifts
- Missing rungs on ladders
- Failure to provide clean washplace

Marshall, Secretary of Labor, et al. v. *Barlow's Inc.*, however, the Supreme Court tempered OSHA's authority by allowing employers the right to demand a search warrant before allowing access to their facilities.[7]

After the initial meeting, inspectors usually conduct "walk-around inspections," accompanied by both an employer and an employee representative. In the absence of an employee representative, OSHA inspectors usually confer with randomly selected workers, either openly or in private.[8]

At the conclusion of the OSHA inspection a second meeting is held with the employer. During this meeting compliance officers advise the employer of any conditions and practices noted which may constitute safety and health violations. The inspector is not required to provide or to suggest solutions to these violations, nor does he or she issue citations at this time. The inspector may, however, inform the employer that citations and penalties may be forthcoming. OSHA inspectors do not have the authority to shut down a facility without a court order.

OSHA *Violations and Citations*

If an OSHA standard has been violated, the area director issues a written citation to the company. This citation describes the specific standard violated, any penalty assessed, and a proposed time period for abatement. Should employers feel that the citation is unwarranted or that the time period for abatement is unreasonable, they have fifteen days to lodge a complaint with OSHRC. If no challenge is filed during the fifteen-day period, the decision becomes final.

Fines levied against employers may be as much as $10,000 per penalty for repeated or willful violations.[9] In practice, however, the average penalty for serious willful or repeat violations in 1979 was $367, and the average penalty for non-serious violations was $98.[10] In determining the amount, OSHA considers both the type of violation committed and the intention of the employer. The types of violations enumerated by law are:

1. **Imminent danger violation** An **imminent danger** is a condition or practice which could reasonably be expected to result in death or serious illness before it can be remedied through the enforcement procedures outlined under the act. If such a condition exists, compliance officers attempt to have the condition immediately rectified through voluntary employer compliance. If this fails, OSHA usually goes to the courts for legal action.
2. **Serious violation** If inspectors determine that there is a substantial probability that death or serious injury could result from a violation, and that the employer knew of, or should have been expected to know of, the danger, a **serious violation** exists.
3. **Non-serious violation** If the violation present would likely result in some consequence other than death or serious injury, or the employer was unaware of the potential hazard, then a **non-serious violation** exists.
4. **De minimis violation** In lieu of a citation, violations enumerated in the act which have no direct relationship to health or safety are issued no-

Exhibit 12.3

Sample OSHA Citation Form

U.S. Department of Labor
Occupational Safety and Health Administration

Citation and Notification of Penalty

3. Issuance Date	4. Inspection Number
5. Reporting ID	6. CSHO ID
7. Optional Report No.	8. Page No. of

1. Type of Violation(s)	2. Citation Number

The violation(s) described in this Citation are alleged to have occurred on or about the day the inspection was made unless otherwise indicated within the description given below.

10. Inspection Date(s):

11. Inspection Site:

9. To:

Penalties Are Due Within 15 Days of Receipt of This Notification Unless Contested

(See enclosed Booklet)

This Section May Be Detached Before Posting

THE LAW REQUIRES that a copy of this Citation be posted immediately in a prominent place at or near the location of the violation(s) cited below. The Citation must remain posted until the violations cited below have been abated, or for 3 working days (excluding weekends and Federal holidays), whichever is longer.

This Citation describes violations of the Occupational Safety and Health Act of 1970. The penalty(ies) listed below are based on these violations. You must abate the violations referred to in this Citation by the dates listed below and pay the penalties proposed, unless within 15 working days (excluding weekends and Federal holidays) from your receipt of this Citation and penalty you mail a notice of contest to the U.S. Department of Labor Area Office at the address shown above. (See the enclosed booklet which outlines your rights and responsibilities and should be read in conjunction with this form.) You are further notified that unless you inform the Area Director in writing that you intend to contest the Citation or proposed penalties within 15 working days after receipt, this Citation and the proposed penalties will become a final order of the Occupational Safety and Health Review Commission and may not be reviewed by any court or agency. Issuance of this Citation does not constitute a finding that a violation of the Act has occurred unless there is a failure to contest as provided for in the Act or, if contested, unless the Citation is affirmed by the Review Commission.

12. Item Number / 13. Standard, Regulation or Section of the Act Violated	14. Description	15. Date by Which Violation Must Be Abated	16. Penalty

17. Area Director

18.

Total Penalty for This Citation

Make Check or Money Order Payable to: "DOL-OSHA"

Indicate Inspection Number on Remittance

NOTICE TO EMPLOYEES — The law gives an employee or his representative the opportunity to object to any abatement date set for a violation if he believes the date to be unreasonable. The contest must be mailed to the U.S. Department of Labor Area Office at the address shown above within 15 working days (excluding weekends and Federal holidays) of the receipt by the employer of this Citation and penalty.

EMPLOYER DISCRIMINATION UNLAWFUL — The law prohibits discrimination by an employer against an employee for filing a complaint or for exercising any rights under this Act. An employee who believes that he has been discriminated against may file a complaint no later than 30 days after the discrimination with the U.S. Department of Labor Area Office at the address shown above.

EMPLOYER RIGHTS AND RESPONSIBILITIES — The enclosed booklet outlines employer rights and responsibilities and should be read in conjunction with this notification.

ORIGINAL

CITATION AND NOTIFICATION OF PENALTY

OSHA-2 (Rev. 1/84)

tices. Unlike citations, employers are not required to post **de minimis violation** notices at or near the site where the violation occurred, and no monetary penalty is assessed.

5. **Willful violation** A **willful violation** exists when employers knowingly commit violations or do not make reasonable efforts to correct hazardous conditions.
6. **Repeated violation** A **repeated violation** exists when a second citation is issued for a previously abated violation.

OSHA Record-Keeping Requirements

Every employer with seven or more employees is required to keep occupational health and safety records for each employee. These records include logs, supplementary records, and summaries of occupational injuries and illnesses. All records are maintained for five years following the last year to which they relate, and they must be presented to OSHA representatives on request.

Injuries and illnesses which must be recorded are those which result in deaths, cause employees to miss work, or require medical treatment other than minor first aid. Unlike other OSHA materials, record-keeping forms are straightforward and appear relatively easy to understand. Still, managers criticize OSHA's record-keeping procedures as another example of unnecessary bureaucratic red tape. To this end, employers attempt to avoid the reporting procedure by classifying as many injuries as possible under the heading of "minor injuries."

Employee Rights Under OSHA

Along with granting the obvious right of an environment free from health and safety hazards, OSHA offers retaliation protection for employees who exercise their rights under the act. In addition to protecting employees from discharge or discrimination because of a filed complaint or testimony, OSHA prevents employers from disciplining employees who refuse to work under conditions which they reasonably assume to be dangerous. Employees may exercise the right to refuse to work when they are exposed to a dangerous condition and there is insufficient time to remedy the situation under the normal statutory procedures.

The Occupational Safety and Health Act encourages each state to adopt and administer its own health and safety programs. One law which some states have adopted is an **employee right-to-know law.**[11] These laws grant employees the right to know if there are hazardous or toxic materials present at the workplace and the privilege to be trained in the proper handling of these materials. Furthermore, the company is required to inform the employees' physicians of the chemical components in the substance in order to facilitate diagnosis and treatment of illnesses.[12]

> ***Employee right-to-know laws***
>
> *Employee right-to-know laws are state laws which require employers to inform workers if toxic chemicals are being used at the workplace, to label such containers, to train employees in the proper handling of these materials, and to divulge the chemical composition of the substances to employees' physicians.*

The Impact of OSHA

To date, there is little evidence to support the effectiveness or ineffectiveness of OSHA. Some critics maintain that OSHA is ineffective, and in fact, that it hampers businesses.[13] On the other hand, there are researchers who assert that statistics have definitely shown a significant decrease in accidents since OSHA's inception.[14] They blame the reason for OSHA's overall ineffectiveness on its inability to impose harsh enough punishments on violators.[15] Regardless of the view taken, there is one certainty. As long as OSHA remains in existence, human resource managers must be ever-cognizant of OSHA regulations.

Developing Safety Programs

In addition to complying with government standards imposed by OSHA, organizations initiate many safety actions on their own. These programs are designed to involve employees as well as supervisory personnel. Some of the more prevalent approaches used by organizations include safety research, safety committees, and training and motivational programs.

Safety Research

Safety research, which is usually conducted by the company's safety engineer, attempts to discover the causes of accidents, injuries, and illnesses and to determine the methods which may be used to prevent their future occurrence.

Most research begins with the investigation and identification of safety weaknesses in the workplace. After a comprehensive study has been completed, safety engineers may recommend a course of action to improve employee safety. This action may include such changes as redesigning equipment, color-coding danger zones and traffic patterns, and introducing or enforcing the use of protective equipment. Many experts are currently turning to the applied science of **ergonomics** for practical assistance.

> ***Ergonomics***
>
> *Ergonomics is the applied science of designing environments, equipment, tools, and tasks to be compatible with the diverse characteristics, behaviors, and needs of individuals.*

Exhibit 12.4

A Self-Inventory Checklist for Safety

1. Is there an organizational policy on safety? Is it written?
2. Are all managerial and supervisory staff fully aware of their safety obligations?
3. Are employees being fully involved in safety programs? Are there safety committees? Training programs?
4. Are there written guidelines regarding safety? Are they being consistently and uniformly enforced?
5. Who is ultimately accountable for safety? Are departments charged for accidents?
6. Are safety inspection procedures clearly formulated and enforced?
7. Are all employees indoctrinated regarding proper safety procedures?
8. Are there programs in place to provide on-going motivation to avoid accidents? Has their effectiveness been evaluated?
9. Are complete and accurate record-keeping procedures in order? Have they recently been internally audited?
10. Are first-aid and medical facilities available to all personnel at all times? Are all employees aware of the procedures involved in obtaining help?

Often, the study of accidents is facilitated by computing a company's accident rate. OSHA provides organizations with several formulas which enable them to compare their own accident frequencies with industry and national figures. The easiest approach recommended by OSHA is to report accidents in terms of the number of injuries per 100 full-time employees per year. This formula is:

$$\frac{\text{Number of illnesses and injuries}}{\text{Total work hours of all employees}} \times 200{,}000$$

(200,000 is used as the multiplier so that incidence rate is expressed as the number per 100 employees).

Safety Committees

Many organizations use safety committees consisting of management and hourly employees. The purpose of these committees is to uncover the causes of accidents and to recommend action to prohibit their recurrence. Depending on the nature of individual committees, the recommendations may be successful or fruitless. Successful committees find that workers are usually more familiar with the intricacies of their jobs and they frequently discover safety hazards of which managers are unaware. Second, employees are more willing to listen, accept, and abide by safety recommendations made by their peers. Last, safety committees demonstrate to workers that the organization is committed to fostering employee health and safety.[16]

The success of safety committees depends to a large degree on management's commitment to listening to and implementing the committee's recommendations.[17] Employers who scoff at or delay implementing the recommendations of their safety committees, particularly because of the expense involved, soon find themselves in a controversial position.[18] Placing a dollar value on the health and safety of employees is a conflict employers seldom win.

Training and Motivational Programs

Proper communication and training programs are essential to promoting safety. Usually, safety training is an integral part of the orientation program for new employees. This training involves speeches on safety, movies or slide presentations, and the issuance of written material in the form of manuals and pamphlets. In order to be effective, this form of safety training should be continually reinforced by supervisors in the workplace.

In addition to safety training, some companies have attempted to reduce accidents by providing employees with incentives for maintaining good safety records. For example, some companies offer employees their choice of a prize if all workers maintain an accident-free environment for a specified length of

Exhibit 12.5

A Factory's Posted Safety Rules

1. Always use the safety buttons when working on machinery, even if you will be finished in just one second.
2. Wear safety goggles or glasses when using the grinding equipment.
3. Wear short sleeves or button long sleeves tightly. Loose clothes get caught in equipment.
4. Clean up liquid spills immediately.
5. Lift heavy loads with your legs, not your back.
6. Do not run in the plant.
7. Refrain from horseplay.
8. Use tools for their intended purpose. A screwdriver is not a chisel!
9. Do not block exits, aisles, or fire lanes at any time.
10. Inform your supervisor of any injuries, regardless of how small or insignificant you may think they are.

time. Other organizations establish contests between groups of employees for lowering the accident rate or for suggesting safety measures. To date, the results of these contests appear mixed. Some organizations find that safety is enhanced; others find that the contests fail to reduce accidents, but rather they increase the likelihood that employees will fail to report them.[19]

Promoting Employee Health

The health of employees is becoming increasingly more important to organizations. Each year, millions of dollars in lost productivity is attributable to employee health problems. Some of these lost dollars are the result of expected absenteeism because of normal illnesses such as the flu. Other illnesses, which are referred to as "occupational diseases," are job-induced and manifest themselves as either physical or mental disturbances in normal body functioning. These illnesses are usually the result of exposure to hazards in the workplace, and include, for example, the effects of inhaling of harmful gases, impaired hearing because of sustained noise exposure, skin diseases, and the long-term effects of handling carcinogenic agents.

Unfortunately, occupational diseases are not the sole health concern of organizations. Substance abuse, job stress, and mental illness are costing companies billions of dollars yearly. Estimates place the yearly cost of drug abuse and alcoholism at $60 billion,[20] excessive job stress at approximately $100 billion, and mental illness at between $15 and $20 million.[21] As a result, more and more companies are instituting programs at the workplace to aid employees in dealing with these various problems.

Substance Abuse

The impact of **substance abuse** on society is devastating. Each year, alcoholism alone is a contributing factor in about 10 percent of all deaths, approximately 43 percent of traffic fatalities, and almost 670,000 injury-producing accidents in the United States. Estimates place the economic costs of alcoholism to employers and employees at almost $51 billion, and drug abuse costs at an additional $26 billion.[22] Substance abuse exists among blue-collar workers, white-collar workers, males, females, teenagers, and children; it cuts across all racial and ethnic lines. It presents a significant problem for employers, the judicial system, and society as a whole.

> **Substance abuse**
>
> *Substance abuse is the continued use of alcohol or drugs without sufficient medical grounds, resulting in a psychological and/or physical dependency and socially unacceptable behavior.*

Alcoholism and drug abuse

Alcoholism is a formidable problem facing employers.[23] Alcoholic employees demonstrate poor performance, increased absenteeism and tardiness, and an increased accident rate.[24] Despite this fact, most organizations have insufficient established policies to deal with the problem. There are several reasons why employers are reluctant to formalize procedures to treat alcoholism. First, according to the law, alcoholism is a disease and it is treated as a handicap. Second, many supervisors are incapable of identifying alcoholics unless they demonstrate severe symptoms. Last, intervention is difficult because research has failed to uncover, with any certainty, the causes of alcoholism.

The use of drugs by employees at the workplace appears to be on the increase. It is estimated that about 10 to 23 percent of all workers in the United States use dangerous drugs in the workplace.[25] Not only are illegal drugs, such as marijuana, heroin, and cocaine, being used but also employees appear to be abusing amphetamines, barbiturates, and tranquilizers. Unfortunately, the impact of employees using illegal drugs is not confined solely to economic losses at the workplace. An incident such as the Amtrak train accident which killed in excess of 60 innocent people in 1987, and in which the engineer had been using marijuana, gives a clear indicator of the problems caused by drug abuse.

The treatment of alcoholism and drug abuse is probably best left to professionals. Supervisors should routinely behaviorally document employee job performance. This documentation may result in the identification of declining performance among certain employees. In the normal course of performance reviews, supervisors should apprise employees of their declining performance. No mention of suspected substance abuse need take place. Employees have the option, as with other health problems, of seeking assistance from company EAPs or other available service. If they choose not to seek assistance and their productivity continues to decline, the supervisor is free to discipline them for poor job performance.[26]

Testing for substance abuse

In an attempt to combat the significant occurrence of substance abuse among employees, employers and other concerned groups have lobbied for the legalization of drug testing. In the case of *Davis* v. *Bucher*,[27] the court ruled that drug abuse and alcoholism are "physical or mental impairments" which are afforded protection under the Rehabilitation Act. Subsequent to this ruling, Congress amended the definition of *handicap* to exclude coverage for alcoholics or drug addicts whose current use of the substance prohibits the effective completion of their job or whose presence represents a threat to the health and safety of others.

Based on the definition of handicap under the amended Rehabilitation Act, employers may legally test, and refuse to hire, individuals who test positively for alcohol or drugs provided it can be demonstrated that current substance abuse interferes with job performance or poses a threat to others. Similarly, current employees demonstrating erratic behavior may be tested for drugs and discharged if they pose a threat to the well-being of others. Applicants and employees who are not currently using drugs or alcohol, but whose past history reveals substance abuse, are afforded handicapped status under the law.

Smoking at the Workplace

Smoking at the workplace and in public places has long been a topic of heated debate. Smokers maintain that they have a constitutional right to smoke.[28] Non-smokers contend that smokers infringe on their rights by subjecting them to the dangers associated with inhaling "passive smoke."[29] Furthermore, the economic impact of smoking is large. Smoking accounted for as many as 81 million lost work days per year during 1980 at a cost to employers and employees of approximately $37 billion. Part of the reason for this economic loss is the fact that male smokers are absent from work approximately 40 percent more, and female smokers are absent approximately 25 percent more, than their non-smoking counterparts.[30]

The response by organizations to the smoking controversy has been mixed. Some employers establish programs to help their employees quit smoking. Other companies designate special areas where smokers can go without impacting adversely on non-smokers. Some organizations have adopted policies of "no smoking allowed," and have refused to hire any applicants who smoke.[31]

To date, employers have legally been able to establish whatever smoking policies they deem necessary. However, it appears that until such time as smoking policies are tested by a Supreme Court case, the controversy over the rights of smokers versus the rights and health of non-smokers will persist.

Stress Management

The importance of stress management

There are various definitions of the term *stress*. For many people, stress engenders negative feelings of tension, anxiety, nervousness, and discomfort. It is viewed as the negative consequence of physiological pressures placed on the individual's internal system by external stimuli called **stressors.** For example, divorce, the failure of an important examination, or the death of a family member are all stressful situations which may cause feelings of discomfort for individuals. Other individuals picture stress in a positive manner. Receiving a large raise or promotion, getting married, or having a baby may also result in stress arousal for an individual. Unlike the negative feelings associated with stress, however, these joyful emotions are welcome circumstances.

Stress

Stress encompasses the physiological and psychological reactions which people exhibit in response to environmental events called stressors.

Regardless of whether aroused emotions are the result of positive or negative stressors, people are confronted with having to adjust to changes in their systems. Metabolically, their blood pressure may rise, their heart rate may increase, and other sympathetic and endocrinologic system functions may be activated as well. Sometimes stress causes individuals to mobilize and respond in a manner which leads to increased performance and benefits for the organization. This healthy adaptive process is known as **eustress.** All people, however, do not respond to stress in a healthy fashion. Rather, the response may be one of **distress,** whereby the individual responds in a manner which is detrimental to both the organization and the individual.[32]

Eustress and distress

Eustress is the healthy, adaptive response made by an individual to a stressful situation. Distress occurs when an individual responds to stress in an unhealthy manner, resulting in behaviors which are detrimental to both the organization and the individual.

Researchers and theorists are primarily concerned with how stress is generated and the manner in which people physiologically and psychologically respond to stressful situations. Once these factors are identified, organizations may be able to control those stressors which cause strain and anxiety and result in damage to the overall company objectives. In addition, properly identifying and controlling stress may lead to increased productivity, morale, and employee satisfaction.

Sources of stress

There are three major categories of stressors which impact on people. The first category, "organizational stressors," are directly related to the work environment and are a direct function of the job. The second category, "life events," are not organizationally induced, and they vary widely from marital problems to anxiety experienced over planning for future retirement. Finally, "individual stressors," such as specific unique personality characteristics, cause people to view their environments in distinctly different fashions.[33]

Although stress may be generated by the factors in any of the preceding three categories, it is more likely that simultaneous pressures are exerted by a combination of events from different categories. For example, the need to work overtime on the job may conflict with family demands to attend a ball game or a recital. Individual events may be insufficient to create stress; when combined, however, competing pressures for limited time serve to increase the potential for a stressful situation.

Organizational stressors Stressors that adversely affect one person may have little, if any, impact on other individuals. In spite of the fact that stressors are often specific or unique, there are definite job characteristics which, by their very nature, have the potential to generate stress across the working population at large.

Although occupational stress may vary from job to job, certain professions are noted for being highly stressful. For example, air traffic controllers, physicians, and managers are more likely to exhibit stress symptoms than college professors or teachers. It seems safe to assume that certain factors, such as responsibility for others, meeting deadlines, and decision-making frequency, appear to be common to all stressful positions.

Non-stressful jobs have the potential to generate distress when stressors are uncontrolled. Work overload, in which workers have too many tasks to accomplish in too short a time period, is a common stressor across occupations. In addition, feelings of insecurity or boredom, or a sense of being treated unfairly, are also frequent causes of stress.

In the process of performing their job responsibilities, employees are influenced by the expectations inherent in their positions. These expectations, which are imposed by others within the organization, are known as *roles*. Workers who are unable to fulfill their roles because of uncertainty about expected behaviors, or because of conflicting demands are likely to experience distress. The first of these problems is termed **role ambiguity** and the latter is **role conflict.**[34]

> **Role ambiguity and role conflict**
>
> *Role ambiguity exists whenever job incumbents experience confusion about the behaviors expected of them on the job. Role conflict occurs whenever job incumbents are confronted with two or more conflicting job roles.*

Role ambiguity is most often attributable to poor supervisory communication concerning job tasks. Lacking proper information, workers guess about the tasks required, and they may become anxious about the possibility that they have interpreted their duties incorrectly.

Role conflict occurs when workers are given task orders which conflict with previously established task roles. Stress is a direct result of the dissonance between the conflicting expectations.

Life event stressors In many instances, the severity of perceived individual stress is a function of life events. Holmes and Rahe, noted stress researchers, maintain that certain life events contribute to the severity of stress individuals experience. Based on their research, they developed the Social Readjustment Rating Scale (SRRS), which determines the likelihood of people developing stress-related diseases within the near future. People who score high on the scale are more likely to react adversely to stressful situations, whereas those scoring lower on the SRRS tend to have a higher tolerance to stress-producing events.[35]

Exhibit 12.6

The Social Readjustment Rating Scale

Rank	Life event	Mean value
1	Death of spouse	100
2	Divorce	73
3	Marital separation	65
4	Jail term	63
5	Death of close family member	63
6	Personal injury or illness	53
7	Marriage	50
8	Fired at work	47
9	Marital reconciliation	45
10	Retirement	45
11	Change in health of family member	44
12	Pregnancy	40
13	Sex difficulties	39
14	Gain of new family member	39
15	Business readjustment	39
16	Change in financial state	38
17	Death of close friend	37
18	Change to different line of work	36
19	Change in number of arguments with spouse	35
20	Mortgage over $10,000	31
21	Foreclosure of mortgage or loan	30
22	Change in responsibilities at work	29
23	Son or daughter leaving home	29
24	Trouble with in-laws	29
25	Outstanding personal achievement	28
26	Wife begin or stop work	26
27	Begin or end school	26
28	Change in living conditions	25
29	Revision of personal habits	24
30	Trouble with boss	23
31	Change in work hours or conditions	20
32	Change in residence	20
33	Change in schools	20
34	Change in recreation	19
35	Change in church activities	19
36	Change in social activities	18
37	Mortgage or loan less than $10,000	17

Source: Thomas H. Holmes and Richard H. Rahe, "The Social Readjustment Rating Scale," *Journal of Psychosomatic Research*, Vol. 11, No. 2 (New York: Pergamon Press, Ltd., 1967): 216. Reprinted with permission.

Rank	Life event	Mean value
38	Change in sleeping habits	16
39	Change in number of family get-togethers	15
40	Change in eating habits	15
41	Vacation	13
42	Christmas	12
43	Minor violations of the law	11

The preceding scale was developed by Holmes and Rahe in order to measure the likelihood of an individual developing serious illnesses such as ulcers, heart attacks, colitis, and other serious diseases. By scoring responses for events occurring over the past twelve months, the researchers demonstrated a correlation between high scores and probability of illness occurring. A score of 300 or more has been correlated with 80 percent of patients with serious illnesses. A score between 150 and 300 increases the likelihood of sickness by approximately 50 percent. People who score below 150 have small probabilities of becoming ill during the next few years.

Individual stressors The unique traits and characteristics of individuals cause them to react differently to stress-producing events. Age, sex, health status, exercise pattern, and diet have all been studied in relation to incidence of stress. The most well-known individual characteristics, however, are the Type A and Type B **personality types** identified in the 1950s by Friedman and Rosenman.[36]

Type A and Type B personalities Type A individuals are typically impatient, hard driving, competitive, and constantly under time constraints. According to Friedman and Rosenman, Type A people are characterized as "action-emotion complex individuals . . . aggressively involved in a chronic, incessant struggle to achieve more and more in less and less time, and if required to do so, against the opposing efforts of other things or other persons." Type A personalities are dependent on environmental stimuli for catalysts. In the absence of stressors, Type A behaviors do not occur.

Type B personalities are direct complements to Type A patterns. Unlike Type A personalities, they are unhurried and not unduly pressured by time restraints, and they are less competitive. They are equally as intelligent, ambitious, and concerned with their positions, but they approach situations in a more logical, calm manner.

Over the years, Type A behavior patterns have been linked to higher levels of stress and greater incidence of heart attacks and coronary disease than their Type B counterparts.[37] It is probably incorrect to assume that the personality type itself contributes to these phenomena. Rather, it appears that Type A personalities are more vulnerable because they expose themselves to situations where the likelihood of being stressed is significant. For example, they tend to overwork themselves, they take on many projects simultaneously, and they attempt it all within unreasonable time frames.

Consequences of severe stress

Severe stress manifests itself in undesirable consequences for both the individual and the organization. Psychologically, stress may affect people's behavior by causing them to engage in heavy smoking, to overuse alcohol and drugs, or to become violent or depressed. Physiologically, stress is linked to backaches, heart attacks, coronary diseases, ulcers, ileitis, colitis, and headaches.

The natural result of these individual stress reactions for organizations is decreased productivity. Stressed workers exhibit higher turnover, absenteeism, and tardiness rates. Their productivity declines in both quantity and quality. The number of grievances and accidents increase. Inevitably, these workers suffer low morale, low motivation, and poorer job satisfaction. In short, employees experience **burnout,** losing the previously existing enthusiasm they once felt for their jobs and careers.

Burnout

Burnout is a form of organizational distress akin to psychological depression, in which previously enthusiastic individuals lose their desire and vitality for their job or career.

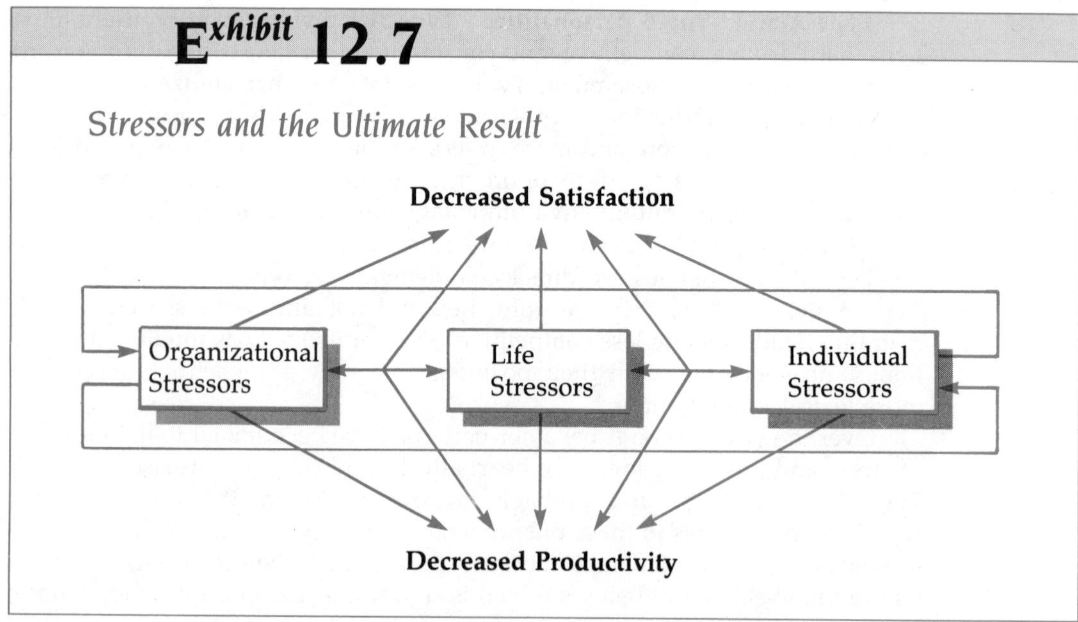

Preventing stress

Organizations realize that the simplest and surest method for overcoming stress is to prevent its occurrence. Preventive programs have two major goals. First, corporate programs are designed to promote and maintain the present and future health of employees. Corporate training programs designed to teach individuals to cope with stress, company-sponsored exercise classes, and financial encouragement for workers to enroll in health and wellness centers are a few of the more common methods used by companies to reduce the negative impact of stress.

The second goal of preventive programs is the reduction of organizational stressors present on the job. Once identified, stressors should be reduced or eliminated. This may entail, among other things, the elimination of extraneous tasks through job redesign, the rescheduling of workflows, the clarification of roles, and the introduction of job enrichment programs.

Stress management requires the active participation of both individual employees and the organization. Distress must be recognized and rejected. Too many individuals readily accept distress as a natural part of corporate jobs. While a certain amount of stress is beneficial, excessive amounts, resulting in distress, are harmful. Organizations which take an active approach in training employees in stress management and in identifying and eliminating unnecessary stressors will discover that they are able to optimize the potential of their human resources.

Exhibit 12.8

Hints for Reducing Stress on the Job

1. Rate your tasks in order of importance and complete the most important ones first.
2. Whenever you can, delegate!
3. Set realistic deadlines and establish a schedule. Then, stick to it!
4. Plan ahead for future events. Good supervisors are not only determined by the quality of their decision but also by the contingency plan they created in the event the decision is wrong.
5. Stop and take breathers during the work day. Everyone fatigues sooner or later, and fatigue usually results in lowered productivity.
6. Don't procrastinate on making decisions. Worrying about them is sometimes more damaging than the negative consequences of making a bad decision.
7. Determine whether or not you can control the outcome. It serves no purpose to worry about something you can't control anyway.
8. Eat sensibly; avoid indulging in alcohol, tobacco, and drugs; get adequate rest; and exercise regularly.

Summary

The health and safety of workers is becoming increasingly more important to employers. Workplace accidents are responsible for thousands of deaths and millions of disabilities each year. These overwhelming accident statistics account for billions of dollars in lost productivity. The result is an increased interest in providing healthy and safe environments for workers.

The task of creating safe workplaces is shared jointly by government and private sector employers. Lobbying efforts on behalf of several interest groups caused Congress to pass the Occupational Safety and Health Act of 1970. This act requires that all employers create and regularly monitor workplaces which insure hazard-free, safe, and protective environments for their workers. To accomplish this purpose, several government agencies were established to conduct research, audit workplace environments, cite violations, and impose fines.

In addition to abiding by the federal regulations imposed, many employers voluntarily institute health and safety programs. These programs, which are designed to aid workers in dealing with personal issues, such as substance abuse, marital problems, and financial matters, are gaining widespread popularity. Furthermore, many organizations are realizing the impact that stress has on their workforce, and they are establishing programs to help workers cope with the everyday trials and tribulations of their jobs.

Key Terms to Identify

Accident proneness

Occupational Safety and Health Act (OSHA)

Occupational Safety and Health Review Commission (OSHRC)

National Institute for Occupational Safety and Health (NIOSH)

Interim standards

Permanent standards

Emergency standards

Imminent danger violation

Serious violation

Non-serious violation

De minimis violation

Willful violation

Repeated violation

Right-to-know laws

Ergonomics

Substance abuse

Stressors

Eustress

Distress

Role ambiguity

Role conflict

Personality types

Burnout

Questions for Discussion

Do You Know the Facts?

1. What are the major causes of accidents in industry? Can most of these accidents be attributable to accident-prone people?
2. What is the function of OSHA and its associated agencies? How do OSHA investigators operate?
3. Discuss the various impacts which stress has on the overall productivity of organizations.

Can You Apply the Information Learned?

1. If you were a safety inspector, under what conditions would you allow an OSHA investigator to enter your premises?
2. What organizational stressors appear to be most common across organizations? How would you control for them?
3. Design the strategies you would employ to cost-justify to the company's board of directors a comprehensive health and safety program, including financial co-sponsoring of employee memberships in a wellness center.

Avtex Fibers—"When the Doors Close for Good"

When the American Viscose Corporation opened its new rayon manufacturing plant in the small town of Front Royal, Virginia, it was a symbol of a bright new future. The year was 1940 and the $20 million plant was a sign of a new era of prosperity. For nearly fifty years the plant employed a major portion of the workforce in this northern valley area. It was the backbone of the economy.

Twelve years ago Avtex Fibers Corporation of Valley Forge, Pennsylvania, acquired the plant. Avtex's chairman, John Gregg, responded to critics of this leveraged buyout by saying, "We were not supposed to make it a year." Recently Mr. Gregg responded to local leaders that although the company had faced difficult times, they were "not in serious trouble." Now this major employer faces the prospect of closing its doors once and for all.

Avtex Fibers Incorporated is the northern Shenandoah Valley's biggest em-

This case was prepared by W. Lee WanVeer, Management and Professional Development, Virginia Power Company.

ployer and the world's largest producer of rayon. The fibers produced at this plant are used in rocket boosters for both the NASA space shuttle and the Department of Defense's missile systems. The raw fibers are woven by other contractors and treated for heat resistance before going to Morton-Thiokol and the space shuttle. Avtex has a sister plant in Lewistown, Pennsylvania. There are 1,300 employees in the Virginia plant who live in five surrounding counties. Many of the employees have served in this plant for well over twenty years. The annual payroll is $25 million, with annual county taxes of $263,000 and town taxes of $80,000. Ninety percent of the stock in the company is owned by the Gregg family. The average salary for an Avtex worker is $370 per week, $67 a week higher than the county's average.

Avtex has two main competitors in carbonized rayon production: BASF Fibers of Germany and Courtaulds Fibers, Inc. of Britain, which are seen by Gregg as using unfair trade practices. Courtaulds has been importing pulp from a plant owned by one of its business partners in South Africa at a price $160 less per ton than what Avtex can obtain domestically. Courtaulds's plant in Mobile, Alabama makes the cut rate pulp available to BASF, which operates a plant in Enka, North Carolina. Both companies are accused of using this low-priced pulp to cut the price of rayon and undermine Avtex's position.

In addition to the eroding of Avtex's competitive position, the company has experienced environmental, health, safety, and financial problems. The Water Control Board has reported violations of the company's water discharge permit for a period of ten years, and finally it had to refer the matter to the state attorney general's office. After three separate deaths within a period of two months, the State Department of Labor and Industry conducted comprehensive safety and health inspections of the plant. This resulted in 1,921 major and minor citations leading to the demand for extensive plant repairs. Many of the repairs have still not been made and further action has been referred to the attorney general's office. The Environmental Protection Agency is requiring modifications because of chemicals found in the ground water near the plant. These modifications should cost around $9 million. The Natural Resources Defense Council served notice that it would sue Avtex over discharged permit violations.

The Amalgamated Clothing and Textile Workers Union filed a complaint with the National Labor Relations Board accusing Avtex of bypassing the union in dealing with workers. Several years earlier the workers had voted to give up $1.35 per hour in order to keep the plant open.

The combination of higher raw material costs, the undermining of Avtex's competitive position, and the long list of federal and state health and safety violations led to the decision to close the plant.

On October 31, 1988, the chairman of Avtex Fibers, John Gregg, announced that the Front Royal, Virginia, fiber-producing plant would close as of Thursday, November 3. Thirteen hundred employees lost their jobs. There was no mention of severance pay. The Pension Benefit Guaranty Corporation, a federal agency, had been asked to allow the company to terminate its defined benefit pension plan because it had been underfunded. NASA officials were caught by surprise and felt the plant closing would jeopardize the space program. Avtex owes

$79,827 in personal property and real estate taxes to the town of Front Royal, $105,413 in county real estate taxes, and $158,130 in personal property taxes to the county. An additional $43,000 in real estate taxes is still owed from the previous year. Continued benefits for sick leave and vacation have not been supplied to employees and were in negotiation at the time of the plant closing. Relocation and reemployment opportunities became the responsibility of state and local agencies.

Questions for Discussion

1. Who are the affected parties in the plant closing and what are their interests?
2. What is Avtex's obligation to its employees?
3. How should these obligations be fulfilled?
4. What obligation does Avtex have to the community?
5. How is the community likely to react?
6. How will employees at the Lancaster, Pennsylvania plant react?

Endnotes and References

1 Robert L. Simison, "Safety Last: Job Deaths and Injuries Seem to be Increasing after Years of Decline," *The Wall Street Journal* (March 18, 1986): 1.

2 Paul M. Muchinsky, *Psychology Applied to Work*, 2nd ed. (Chicago, IL: The Dorsey Press, 1987): 679–680.

3 Richard I. Kirkland, Jr., "Union Carbide, Coping with Catastrophe," *Fortune* (January 7, 1985): 50, 52–53.

4 Leo DeBobes, "The Psychological Factors in Accident Prevention," *Personnel Journal*, Vol. 65 (January 1986): 34, 36–38.

5 Patrick J. Cihon and James O. Castagnera, *Labor and Employment Law* (Boston, MA: PWS-KENT Publishing Company, 1988): 469–470.

6 In the late 1970s OSHA removed approximately 1,000 so-called trivial standards. See Walter S. Mossberg, "Safety Agency will Tighten Regulations on Health Hazards, Drop Trivial Rules," *The Wall Street Journal* (May 19, 1977): 48.

7 *Marshall, Secretary of Labor, et al.* v. *Barlow's Inc.*, May 23, 1978, Docket No. 76-1143. Also see Daniel L. Reynolds, "OSHA and the Fourth Amendment," *Human Resource Management*, Vol. 17 (Fall 1978): 17–24. It is estimated that, in spite of this ruling, only about 2 percent of safety inspectors require OSHA to produce a warrant before admission. See Mark A. Rothstein, "OSHA Inspections After *Marshall* v. *Barlow's Inc.*," *Duke Law Journal* (February 1979): 63–103.

8 In the past, these walk-arounds required that the employee be paid by the employer for the time spent with OSHA. This provision became a bone of contention with

employers, and OSHA subsequently relented. Presently, walk-around pay has been eliminated. See "The Door at OSHA Opens up to Industry," *Business Week* (April 6, 1981): 32.

9 There is debate about whether or not the fining system is severe enough to discourage offenders. See Frederick D. Braid, "OSHA and NLRA: New Wrinkles on Old Issues," *Labor Law Journal*, Vol. 29 (December 1978): 755–770.

10 Benjamin W. Mintz, *OSHA, History, Law and Policy* (Washington, D.C.: Bureau of National Affairs, 1984): 338–339.

11 In 1984, right-to-know laws were adopted by: Alaska, California, Connecticut, Illinois, Maine, Maryland, Massachusetts, Michigan, Minnesota, New Hampshire, New Jersey, New York, Oregon, Rhode Island, Washington, West Virginia, and Wisconsin.

12 For more information on right-to-know laws, see Matthew M. Carmel and Michael F. Dolan, "An Introduction to Employee Right-to-Know Laws," *Personnel Administrator*, Vol. 29, No. 9 (September 1984): 117–121.

13 See James J. Cicchetti, "Does OSHA Help or Hinder Loss Control?" *Risk Management*, Vol. 27 (December 1980): 38–40.

14 See Barbara Gray Gricar and H. Donald Hopkins, "How Does Your Company Respond to OSHA?" *Personnel Administrator*, Vol. 28 (April 1983): 53–57; Lawrence P. Ettkin and J. Brad Chapman, "Is OSHA Effective in Reducing Industrial Injuries?" *Labor Law Journal*, Vol. 26 (April 1975): 236–242; and Mary Hayes, "What Can You Do When OSHA Calls?" *Personnel Administrator*, Vol. 27 (November 1982): 65–66.

15 See Garth L. Mangum, "Warning! This Job May be Hazardous to Your Life," *Personnel Administrator*, Vol. 32 (November 1987): 76–80, 82–83.

16 William H. Holley and Kenneth M. Jennings, *Personnel/Human Resource Management*, 2nd ed. (Chicago, IL: The Dryden Press, 1987): 451.

17 It has been demonstrated that, similar to the Hawthorne Effect, when managers give workers the impression that safety is important, safety programs are successful. See Roger Dunbar, "Managers' Influence on Subordinates' Thinking about Safety," *Academy of Management Journal*, Vol. 18 (June 1975): 364–369.

18 There is some evidence which demonstrates that some workers feel safety committees are a waste of time and money because management fails to listen to or to implement any of their suggestions. See John Zalusky, "The Worker Views the Enforcement of Safety Laws," *Labor Law Journal*, Vol. 26 (April 1975): 224–235.

19 Robert McKelvey, Trygg Engen, and Marjorie Peck, "Performance Efficiency and Injury Avoidance as a Function of Positive and Negative Incentives," *Journal of Safety Research*, Vol. 5, No. 2 (June 1973): 90–96.

20 Janice Castro, "Battling the Enemy Within," *Time* (March 17, 1986): 52–55, 57–59, 61.

21 See *BNA Policy and Practice Series—Personnel Management* (Washington, D.C.: Bureau of National Affairs, 1984): 245:121; Peter R. Bensinger, "Drugs in the Workplace," *Harvard Business Review*, Vol. 82 (November–December 1982): 48–50, 54–60; and William S. Cohen, "Health Promotion in the Workplace," *American Psychologist*, Vol. 40, No. 2 (1985): 213–216.

22 Kenneth R. Williams, "Linking Risk Avoidance and Insurance Coverage," *Personnel Administrator*, Vol. 31, No. 12 (December, 1986): 68–76.

23 Estimates place the percentage of alcoholics at 25 percent white collar, 30 percent blue collar, and 45 percent managerial and professional employees. See Christine A. Filipowicz, "The Troubled Employee: Whose Responsibility?" *Personnel Administrator,* Vol. 24 (June 1979): 17–22, 33.

24 Frank E. Kuzmits and Henry E. Hammons II, "Rehabilitating the Troubled Employee," *Personnel Journal,* Vol. 58 (April 1979): 238–242, 250.

25 Janice Castro, *op. cit.,* 53.

26 For an excellent discussion on dealing with substance abuse at the workplace, see Jerry Kinard, John Tanner, and Peter Wright, "Controlling Substance Abuse in the Workplace," *Business* (October–December 1987): 25–29.

27 *Davis* v. *Bucher,* 451 F. Supp. 791, E.D.Pa., 1978.

28 Some people maintain that smoking bans are discriminatory. See Lewis C. Solomon, "The Other Side of the Smoking Worker Controversy," *Personnel Administrator,* Vol. 28 (March 1983): 72–73, 101.

29 For a discourse on the medical effects of smoking on employee health and productivity, see William L. Weis, "Can You Afford to Hire Smokers?" *Personnel Administrator,* Vol. 26 (May 1981): 71–78.

30 H. J. Harwood, D. M. Napolitano, P. L. Kristiansen and J. J. Collins, *Economic Costs to Society of Alcohol and Drug Abuse and Mental Illness* (Research Triangle Park, NC: Research Triangle Institute, 1984) and *Vital and Health Statistics: Disability Days* (Washington, D.C.: Department of Health and Human Services, Series 10, No. 143).

31 See William L. Weis, *op. cit.,* 71–78.

32 Hans Selye, *Stress Without Distress* (Philadelphia, PA: J. B. Lippincott, 1974). See also Hans Selye as interviewed by Laurence Cherry, "On the Real Benefits of Eustress," *Psychology Today* (March 1978): 60–70.

33 For a good discourse on stress, see Hans Selye, *The Stress of Life* (New York: McGraw-Hill Book Company, 1976) and K. Albrecht, *Stress and the Manager* (Englewood Cliffs, NJ: Prentice-Hall Publishing Company, 1979).

34 R. L. Kahn, "Role Conflict and Ambiguity in Organizations," *Personnel Administrator,* Vol. 9 (1964): 8–13.

35 Thomas H. Holmes and Richard H. Rahe, "The Social Readjustment Rating Scale," *Journal of Psychosomatic Research,* Vol. 11, No. 4 (1967): 213–218.

36 Meyer Friedman and Ray Rosenman, *Type A Behavior and Your Heart* (New York: Alfred A. Knopf, Inc., 1974).

37 Ray Rosenman, Meyer Friedman, Reuben Straus, C. David Jenkins, Stephen Zyzanski, Moses Wurm, "Coronary Heart Disease in the Western Collaborative Group Study: A Follow-up Experience of $4\frac{1}{2}$ Years," *Journal of Chronic Disease,* Vol. 23 (1970): 173–190.

Part 5

The Dynamics of Industrial Relations

Chapter 13

Labor Relations: Legal Ramifications, Structure, and Organizing

Objectives

After reading this chapter you should understand:

1. The significant laws affecting labor–management relations.
2. The concept of unfair labor practices and the implications of these practices for both unions and employers.
3. The reasons why employees want to be represented by labor organizations.
4. The structure of unions on local, national, and international levels.
5. The way union organizing campaigns are conducted, and the employer's response to the effort.
6. The union election, and the National Labor Relations Board's role in labor–management relations.
7. The decertification process.

The mere mention of the word *union* generates strong emotions in many individuals. From its very onset, the labor movement in the United States has been characterized by fierce struggles between workers and management over issues crucial to the workplace. Beginning in 1794, with the formation of the Federal Society of Journeymen Cordwainers (shoemakers), and continuing through the first two decades of the twentieth century, unions fought an uphill battle. Initially, they were not viewed by employers as legitimate organizations, they were enjoined and punished by courts who rejected the collective activity, and they were undermined by competition from an increasingly large amount of cheap immigrant labor. Despite these many hardships, however, collective activity still flourished, particularly among skilled workers.

With the passage of the Clayton Act in 1914, organized labor appeared to receive its first truly beneficial piece of legislation. Until this point in time, legislation had overwhelmingly favored employers. The Clayton Act, particularly Sections 6 and 20, which removed labor from the jurisdiction of the Sherman Antitrust Act and limited the use of federal injunctions, seemed to balance the scales. However, the enthusiasm generated by this act was short lived. The courts continually interpreted the ambiguous wording of the act in favor of employers.

In the 1930s, new organizing philosophies arose. During this era, union membership began to increase because of a more favorably disposed governmental hierarchy, the Depression, new labor–management legislation, and new union leadership. In addition, public policy toward unions shifted. Major legislation in the form of the Wagner Act (National Labor Relations Act, 1935), set the stage for present-day labor–management relations. In fact, this act, along with the Taft–Hartley Act (1947) and the Landrum–Griffin Act (1959), determines to a large extent the union–management environment which presently exists.

In spite of attempts by the government to balance the power between labor organizations and employers, the struggle for control of the work environment still persists. The legislation concerning unionization, the reasons workers join unions, the types and structure of unions, and the way organizing takes place are the focus of this chapter. The following chapter concentrates on the collective bargaining process, the development and administration of contracts, and the issues involved in discipline and grievance handling.

Significant Legislation

The Wagner Act (1935)

The passage of the **Wagner Act** (National Labor Relations Act, 1935) marked the beginning of a new era in labor–management relations. Prior to the enactment of the act, the federal government retained a laissez-faire attitude toward labor disputes. This stance allowed employers to fight labor organizations in any legal fashion they chose. In opposition to management's tactics, unions responded with whatever meager economic resources they could muster. The enactment of the Wagner Act changed this state of affairs drastically. It indicated that the federal government was committed to directly regulating labor relations by aiding workers in obtaining organizing and collective bargaining rights.

Sections 7 and 8 are the heart of the Wagner Act. Section 7 states:

> Employees shall have the right to self-organization, to form, join, or assist labor organizations, to bargain collectively through representatives of their own choosing, and to engage in concerted activities, for the purpose of collective bargaining or other mutual aid or protection.[1]

Basically, the Wagner Act provides coverage for "protected concerted activities." This involves two or more employees engaged in activities concerning either "wages, hours or working conditions." If employers interfere with these rights, or if they refuse to bargain collectively with representatives of their employees, they are in violation of the law. These violations are spelled out in Section 8 and are referred to as *unfair labor practices* (ULP). They include:

1. To interfere with, restrain or coerce employees in the exercise of their rights guaranteed in Section 7.
2. To dominate or interfere with the formation or administration of any labor organization or contribute financial or other support to it.
3. By discrimination in regard to hire or tenure of employment or condition of employment to encourage or discourage membership in any labor organization.
4. To discharge or otherwise discriminate against an employee because he has filed charges or given testimony under this act.
5. To refuse to bargain collectively with the representatives of his employees, subject to the provisions of section 9 (a).[2]

To oversee the administration, interpretation, and enforcement of labor policy, the Wagner Act also established the **National Labor Relations Board** (NLRB). This agency consists of five members (the original board consisted of three members, but was increased to five by the Taft–Hartley Act of 1947), appointed by the president and confirmed by the Senate, who have wide latitude in the enactment of labor policies. The NLRB has the primary responsibility of preventing unfair labor practices and deciding issues concerning representation.

The Taft–Hartley Act (1947)

There is no question that the Wagner Act was successful in increasing union membership, promoting collective bargaining, and, as a result, reducing the number of strikes. Unfortunately, the Wagner Act also provided an environment in which unions were protected at the expense of the rights of employers, individual employees, and the general public. The **Taft–Hartley Act** (Labor Management Relations Act–LMRA, 1947) was enacted to remedy these injustices and to restore the balance of power in bargaining.

The objective of the Taft–Hartley Act was to amend the Wagner Act in order to balance the power between unions and employers. The Wagner Act was concerned solely with the rights of employees, and the Taft–Hartley Act established provisions which protected other factions of society. The main features of Taft–Hartley are: the banning of closed shops, the enacting of right-to-work provisions, the establishing of certain employer rights, the enacting of the national emergency impasse procedure, and the enumerating of unfair labor practices for unions.

The banning of closed shops

Until this point in time, unions were allowed to establish closed shops.

> **Closed shop**
>
> *A closed shop is a union security clause in a contract which requires union membership of all employees as a condition of hiring as well as of continued employment.*

After the passage of Taft–Hartley, unions were limited to security clause provisions within contracts that provided only for **union shops** or **agency shops.**

> **Union and agency shop**
>
> *A union shop provision does not require union membership prior to initial hiring, but does require membership after a specified time period, usually thirty days, for continued employment. An agency shop provision does not require union membership, but it requires employees to pay that portion of the union dues which are attributable to collective bargaining.*

Right-to-work provisions

Section 14(b) of the Taft–Hartley Act grants states the power to enact more restrictive labor policies regarding employees' rights to refrain from union activity if they so desire. With the consent of the general populace, states can pass laws outlawing any contract provision requiring union membership as a condition of employment. These **right-to-work laws** currently exist in twenty-one states, and they allow only the establishment of open shops within the work environment.

> **Open shop**
>
> *An open shop is a union contract provision, or absence of union contract coverage, in which employees can choose whether or not they want to join a union and/or pay union dues.*

> **Right-to-work laws**
>
> *Right-to-work laws are statutes passed by states that outlaw any contract provision requiring union membership as a condition of employment.*

Section 14(b) of the Taft–Hartley Act has generated heated debate since its enactment. Unions contend that right-to-work laws encourage "free riders" because any contract provisions which are negotiated must include all covered employees regardless of whether or not they belong to the union. On the other hand, proponents of the law maintain that requiring union membership of all workers relegates them to the role of "captive passengers," having to pay for services which they did not request. Regardless of the strength of the convictions on both sides, right-to-work laws appear to be more symbolic than substantive. In fact, it seems that the controversy is primarily an emotional one, because the average employee is either uninformed or misinformed concerning his or her rights under the law.[3]

Employer rights

After the passage of the Wagner Act, it was assumed that any discussion between employers and workers concerning union organizing constituted an unfair labor practice. Employers were required to remain neutral during union organizing attempts. The Taft–Hartley Act recognized employers' rights to assume positions on this issue provided that the actions taken did not constitute a threat of reprisal or a promise of any benefit not to join the union. In general, unfair labor practices for employers can be summarized as:

1. Threats of reprisal for engaging in union activity.
2. Promises of benefits for not engaging in union activity.
3. Surveillance of union activity.
4. Interrogation of employees concerning union activity.
5. Visitation of homes to urge employees to refrain from union activity.
6. Conversations with employees about union activity or affairs which are exercised from a position of management authority.

The national emergency impasse procedure

During strike activity, costs are typically incurred by unions, employers, and the general public. These costs are usually insignificant in terms other than dollars. Occasionally, however, work stoppages may result in significant dangers to the national health and security of the general public. For example, a strike in a steel factory during wartime could endanger the safety of the country. To protect the general public, the Taft–Hartley Act established a set of procedures whereby the government can intervene in labor disputes when it determines that national health and safety is at stake.

Unfair labor practices for unions

The Wagner Act established unfair labor practices for employers which were reiterated by the Taft–Hartley Act. In addition, Taft–Hartley set forth **unfair labor practices** for unions by adding provisions to Section 8 of the Wagner Act. These provisions include:

Exhibit 13.1

The Geography of the Right-to-Work Laws

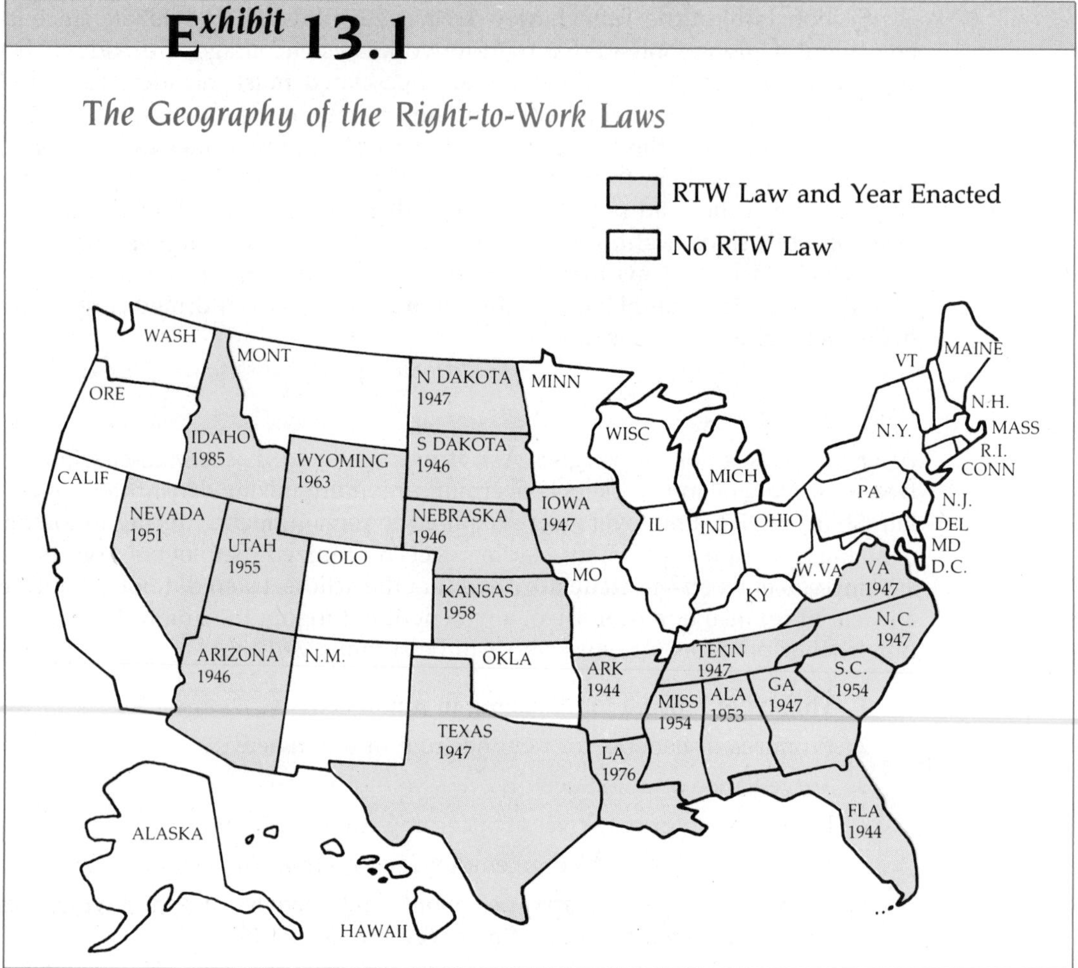

1. The restraint or coercion of workers in the exercising of their rights as guaranteed by the Wagner Act.
2. The restraint or coercion of employers in the selection of the parties they wish to bargain on their behalf.
3. The persuasion of employers to discriminate against any of their employees.
4. The refusal by a union to bargain collectively with an employer.
5. The participation by unions in secondary boycotts and jurisdictional disputes. (Secondary boycotts involve the union's ceasing to deal with another employer who is entirely neutral in the battle.)
6. The attempt by unions to force recognition from an employer when another union is already the certified bargaining agent.

7. The imposition by unions of excessive initiation fees.
8. The requirement of payment from employers for services not performed. This practice is referred to as **featherbedding.**[4]

> **Featherbedding**
>
> *Featherbedding is the practice by unions of requiring employers to pay for services which are currently not being performed.*

Supporters of the Taft–Hartley Act praised it as accomplishing its goal of equalizing bargaining power. Not surprisingly, unions immediately criticized the act as tantamount to reinstating "slave labor," and they lobbied earnestly through the 1970s for its repeal or amendment. Favorable public sentiment, however, coupled with the belief by unions that an even more unfavorable piece of legislation might result, has caused unions to retreat from their initial stance.

The Landrum–Griffin Act (1959)

In spite of the criticisms by unions of unfair treatment, Congress was still not satisfied that the existing labor legislation fully protected public rights. In the 1950s, a series of Senate investigations referred to as the *McClelland Hearings* uncovered abuses of power, unethical conduct, and corrupt practices in some labor organizations (such as the alleged misuse of Teamster pension funds).[5] Although these practices were not widespread, the severity of the incidences led Congress to believe that legislation was warranted. As a result, the **Landrum–Griffin Act** (Labor–Management Reporting and Disclosure Act) was passed in 1959.

The Landrum–Griffin provisions greatly extended the Taft–Hartley Act by establishing detailed regulations of internal union affairs. Specifically, the major provisions of the Landrum–Griffin Act include: writing a bill of rights of labor organization members, submitting reports by labor organizations and employers, creating trusteeships, and requiring union elections.

The bill of rights of labor organization members

Each member of a labor organization is guaranteed the right to have freedom of speech and assembly, the right to nominate candidates and vote in union elections, the right to attend union meetings, and the right to participate in union business. In addition, the manner by which dues are structured and set, the rights of employees to sue the labor organization, and the rights of individuals to obtain copies of the collective bargaining agreements are set forth.

Reporting by labor organizations and employers

The act requires that the bylaws and constitutions of unions be submitted to the secretary of labor and be available for public scrutiny. In addition, an annual financial report must be submitted to the secretary and it must be made available to all of the union's members.

Trusteeships

Trusteeships previously had been created by some unions as a method of suppressing rank and file workers. The act's provisions eliminate national and international unions' practice of placing their subordinate bodies under trusteeships merely for political expedience. Instead, specific guidelines were established to detail the conditions under which trusteeships could be created.

Union elections

Once every five years, national and international unions are required to elect officers either by secret ballot or by delegates chosen through secret balloting. Local unions must elect their officers every three years. Each union member in good standing is entitled to one vote. The ballots and other pertinent records

Exhibit 13.2

Significant Labor Laws

The Railway Labor Act (1926)

Purpose To provide for the prompt disposition of disputes between carriers and their employees, and for other purposes.

Major provisions

1. Established rights of employees to choose their own collective bargaining representative.
2. Established dispute settlement procedures, such as mediation, arbitration, and emergency boards.

Norris–LaGuardia Act (1932)

Purpose To amend the judicial code and to define and limit the jurisdiction of courts sitting in equity.

Major provisions

1. Prohibited courts from granting injunctions for nonviolent union activities, such as strikes.
2. Outlawed yellow dog contracts.

Wagner Act (NLRA, 1935)

Purpose To diminish the causes of labor disputes burdening or obstructing interstate and foreign commerce, and to create a National Labor Relations Board.

Major provisions

1. Established National Labor Relations Board.
2. Outlined unfair labor practices for employers.
3. Established the duty to bargain collectively through chosen representatives.

Taft–Hartley Act (LMRA, 1947)

Purpose To amend the NLRA, to provide additional facilities for the mediation of labor disputes affecting commerce, and to equalize legal responsibilities of labor organizations and employers.

Major provisions

1. Banned closed shops.
2. Outlined unfair labor practices for unions.
3. Provided states with the power to enact right-to-work laws.
4. Established national emergency impasse procedures.
5. Outlawed featherbedding.

Landrum–Griffin Act (1959)

Purpose To protect employees' rights to organize, choose bargaining representatives, and protect the free flow of commerce by requiring labor organizations, employers, and their officials to follow ethical standards of conduct when administering their organizations.

Major provisions

1. Established bill of rights for union members.
2. Established union election guidelines.
3. Outlawed hot-cargo agreements.
4. Established reporting and disclosure procedures for unions and employers.
5. Established guidelines for trusteeships.

Civil Service Reform Act (1978)

Purpose To protect all non-uniformed, non-managerial federal service employees and agencies.

Major provisions

1. Allowed employees the right to choose their own bargaining agent.
2. Established the right to bargain on non-economic and non-staffing issues.
3. Required that unresolved grievances be arbitrated.

must be retained for a period of not less than one year, and every candidate is allowed an observer at both the election polls and the ballot counting site.

In addition to setting forth guidelines concerning the internal affairs of unions, Landrum–Griffin also sought to close up some loopholes in the Taft–Hartley Act. First, it allows the NLRB to relinquish to states jurisdiction over cases involving small employers engaged in interstate commerce. This enables the NLRB to concentrate its resources on cases having substantial impact on the general public. Second, it closes loopholes which developed in the prohibition of secondary boycotts (the practice of unions boycotting neutral employers for the purpose of having them refrain from doing business with the targeted organization). Third, it outlaws "hot-cargo" arrangements, in which employers agree not to deal with or handle products of another employer involved in a labor dispute. Last, it rules recognition and organization picketing as unfair labor practices if:

1. The employer is lawfully recognizing another union.
2. No election petition has been filed with the NLRB within thirty days after the picketing began.
3. There is an election bar in effect.[6]

Why Employees Join Unions[7]

Contrary to popular belief, most employees do not seek union membership solely for economic reasons. Many union organizational drives arise from employers' errors in supervision and in the administration of pay and benefits. When workers lose confidence in their employers or feel helpless in controlling their own destinies, they seek outside assistance. In essence, employees join unions to gain satisfaction of important needs which they feel cannot be satisfied any other way.[8] This help is readily available in the form of unions.

Probably the most common reason that workers join unions is the existence of a union shop clause. As previously stated, this security clause requires workers to join unions in order to continue their employment. In essence, unionism is forced if the worker wishes to remain employed. Aside from union shop clauses, however, workers are seldom motivated to seek union representation solely on the basis of one factor. Rather, unionization is usually a response by workers to a combination of poor benefits, inadequate communication, unfair treatment, and poor supervision. Rarely, if ever, do workers vote for unions. Rather, they cast votes against management.[9]

When employees become sufficiently frustrated in their individual attempts to gain equitable treatment, they respond by banning together. The most prevalent causes of this behavior are combinations of the following: feelings of job insecurity, the inconsistent enforcement of policies, the lack of a valid grievance procedure, inadequate pay and benefits, and poor working environments.

Feelings of Job Insecurity

This factor is usually fostered by inadequate employer communication regarding the health, goals, and achievements of the business. When people are faced with uncertainty about the continued satisfaction of their basic needs, they become anxious and fearful. They see union membership as a means of obtaining security.

The Inconsistent Enforcement of Policies

Company policies, rules, and regulations should apply equally to all members of an organization. When these procedures are inconsistently enforced from department to department, when supervisors play favorites, or when organizational decisions affecting workers are made hastily and emotionally, employees feel helpless to control their own destinies. This factor leads workers to feel stymied concerning promotion, advancement, pay raises, and future opportunities. At this time, union membership is viewed as an attractive vehicle for obtaining consistent and equitable treatment.

The Lack of a Valid Grievance Procedure

A common reason for unionization is the lack of acceptable channels for airing employee grievances. When employees' gripes and complaints are ignored, they feel powerless and become frustrated. Union contracts invariably establish detailed grievance procedures for protecting the rights of workers.

Inadequate Pay and Benefits

When workers perceive their pay and benefits as substandard, they seek to join unions. Increasing workers' job duties without adjusting pay levels, requesting an increased share of contributions for insurance and other benefits, or giving small yearly increases, all contribute to this perception on the part of workers. The original purpose of collective activity was to sustain existing wage levels, and today's unions continue this tradition of concern for their members' pay and benefits.

Poor Working Environments

Employers who fail to provide safe and healthy working environments usually find themselves in the midst of a union organizing effort. Today, unsafe working conditions appear to be less of an impetus for unionization than during the nineteenth century and early part of the twentieth century. This factor is probably attributable to a combination of past union pressures coupled with extensive

Exhibit 13.3

Typical Non-Union Grievance Procedure

Grievance procedure

Sometimes during the course of employment, certain questions, problems, and personal troubles may develop that can affect your performance. In order to aid you through this troublesome period, the company has established the following procedure:

Step 1 Discuss the problem verbally with your immediate supervisor.

Step 2 When a satisfactory solution has not been reached through Step 1, employees should notify (in writing) their department head within (3) three working days. A meeting between the employee and the department head will then be scheduled within (5) five working days.

Step 3 If the solution in Step 2 is still not satisfactory, then a meeting between the CAO or CEO will be scheduled within (5) five working days. At this stage, a final decision will be rendered regarding the grievance.

We believe that this system will insure that your problem gets thoroughly reviewed. In case of "emergency" situations, every effort will be made to speed up the time periods involved between the steps.

We also realize that some problems are of such a personal nature that you prefer not to discuss them with your immediate supervisor. If this situation should arise, please feel free to either discuss the matter with the personnel department or any other supervisor of your choice. Above all, remember that we cannot solve problems of which we are unaware. This procedure is your "hot line" to management—USE IT.

government regulation of the working environment. Nevertheless, poor working conditions still serve as a primary motive for joining unions.

It appears obvious from the preceding discussion that the primary reason workers join unions is because of poor management. In fact, labor relations consultants have been known to say that "any company that gets a union probably deserves it." In essence, it is implied that conditions are so intolerable that workers are induced to pay a third party to intervene on their behalf. The establishment of a safe, healthy workplace, with open communication channels, in an environment which provides adequate rewards and which remains free of prejudice and bias, will negate the necessity for a union. If management fails to recognize or satisfy these basic worker needs, unions will flourish.[10]

Types of Unions

Originally, unions were differentiated solely by the nature of the bargaining units they represented. Unions which organized and represented only skilled groups of employees, such as carpenters and plumbers, were known as **craft unions.** On the other hand, unions which organized and represented entire plants, regardless of skill level, were known as **industrial unions.**

> ***Craft and industrial unions***
>
> *Craft unions are labor organizations that represent only skilled employees. Industrial unions represent all employees within a specific bargaining unit, regardless of skill level.*

These distinctions in unions existed until the early part of the 1960s when a phenomenon known as **union raiding** occurred. Spurred by a desire to increase their financial base, many unions sought to enlarge their membership by enticing other union members to change their collective bargaining representative. As a result of union raiding, the lines of distinction between types of unions became clouded. Many traditional craft unions now represent industrial units, and many industrial unions represent skilled crafts.

> ***Union raiding***
>
> *Union raiding is the practice in which one union entices members of another union to join its ranks and to allow it to negotiate collective bargaining agreements on their behalf.*

Aside from the types of skills represented, craft and industrial unions may be distinguished by their purposes. Craft unions attempt to restrict their membership in the hope that they can increase their wages through the law of supply and demand. Allowing less skilled members in the union creates an environment in which each member can command higher pay. Industrial unions, on the other hand, seek strength in numbers. Because they organize and represent entire workforces, industrial unions' power lies in the potentially devastating effect of a strike.

Structure of Unions

The structure of organized labor is complex. Basically there are three formal components of the labor movement in the United States. These include the *local* unions, which usually are chartered by *national* unions, who may opt for affiliation with the *federation* (AFL–CIO). In addition, there are independent local unions which are not chartered by nationals and major unions (such as The United Mine Workers) which are not affiliated with the federation.

The Local Union

Usually, local unions arise as a direct result of an organizing effort. After they have obtained bargaining rights, local unions typically apply for national charters and elect officers. These local officers are elected democratically by direct participation of all members, and they serve without pay. Even in the relatively large shops, where officers conduct union business full-time and receive compensation, it is usually an amount similar to what they would otherwise receive from the employer.

To the average worker, the local union is the most important labor body. Through the local union, employees deal with employers on a daily basis. The primary functions of the local union are to represent employees in the collective bargaining process and to negotiate grievances. To facilitate these functions, most locals utilize *business representatives* and *stewards* who function as administrators of the labor agreement and representatives of the constituents.

Business representatives are usually dominant local union officials. Their job is to negotiate and administrate the labor agreement. They are typically responsible for collecting dues, recruiting new members, arranging meetings, and coordinating social activities.

For the average employee, the union steward is the primary liaison with the supervisor and management. These stewards, who are usually elected for a one-year period,[11] have the responsibility of representing the interests of their members in the interpretation and administration of contract disputes. The regulation and handling of these grievances are more crucial to employees than the benefits secured in the collective bargaining agreement. As a result, the way in which grievances are handled has a significant impact on the attitudes of workers toward their local union and its officers.

The National Union

The national union's role is to provide representative services for its locals. The predominant services provided are financial support during strikes, administration of pension plans and other fringe benefits, officer training, and governmental lobbying for support of union activities.

In exchange for these services, many national unions usually exert strong control over their respective locals. Permission must be granted for strikes. Locally negotiated collective bargaining agreements must have national approval before being implemented, and other general local housekeeping policies, such

Exhibit 13.4

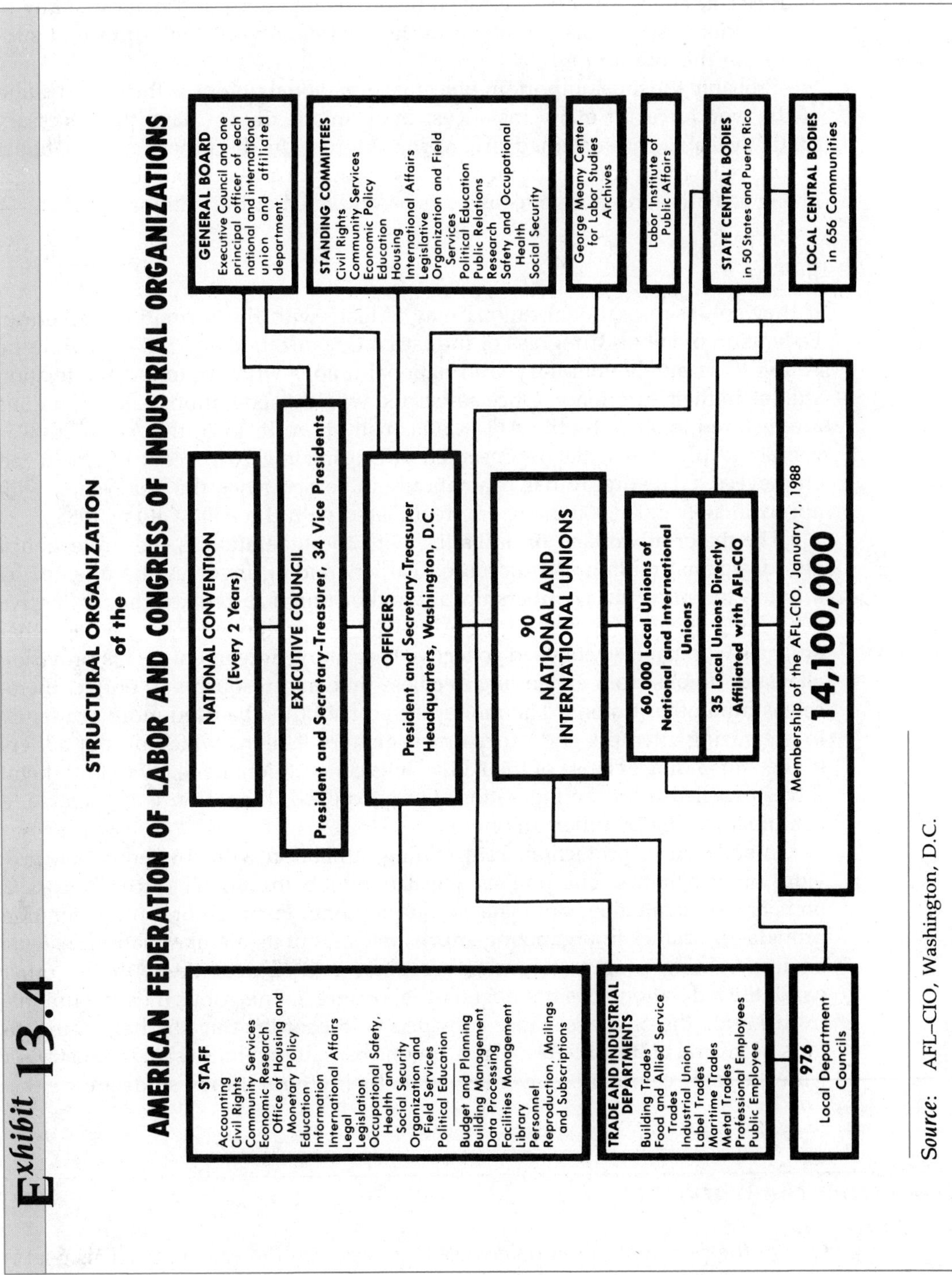

Source: AFL–CIO, Washington, D.C.

as dues collection, must be approved before being effected. Violation of any of these national standards can result in the national union's withdrawal of support from the local union.

Probably the most important objective of national unions is the organization of the workforce. In many instances, local unions do not have the necessary funds available for sustained organizing efforts. On the other hand, national unions have the resources of many locals at their disposal. Consequently, organizing activities are more effective when conducted at the national level.

The Federation

If they so desire, national unions may affiliate with the federation (American Federation of Labor–Congress of Industrial Organizations). Affiliation with the AFL–CIO is purely voluntary, and national unions who opt for such affiliation still retain their autonomy. Once associated with the federation, national unions are required to abide by the AFL–CIO constitution. In 1985, the AFL–CIO was composed of unions that represented approximately 70 percent of unionized employees.[12] This figure has dramatically increased since the Teamsters, with approximately 2,000,000 members, reaffiliated with the AFL–CIO in 1988.

The major advantage of affiliating with the federation is the protection it affords against raiding. As discussed earlier, raiding involves the attempt by a union to entice the membership of another union to replace their collective bargaining agent. Members of the AFL–CIO are prohibited from raiding other affiliates who have established collective bargaining agreements. This provision alleviates unions from expending needless time and resources to protect themselves from other unions. The money saved may then be used more prudently in organizing attempts and other union matters. Unions which do not adhere to the "no raiding" clause of the AFL–CIO's constitution are likely to find themselves expelled from the federation. Once expelled, the union is vulnerable to continual raiding by other unions.

In addition to protection from raiding, affiliation with the federation provides other benefits. The political legislative lobbying power of the AFL–CIO on behalf of its member unions is second to none. Furthermore, the federation provides assistance in organizing efforts, mergers of its member nationals, legal advice, training programs, and other union-related activities. On the other hand, the federation does not negotiate labor agreements for its member unions. In this area, the only assistance provided is in coordinating the bargaining efforts of several of its affiliates. Thus, unions bargaining in the same industry, or with the same company, may consolidate their efforts if they so desire.

Organizing the Workforce

One of the principal union objectives is to organize the workforce. This goal is not an easy task to accomplish. Today's employers are highly sophisticated in their approaches to resisting organizing efforts, and in many cases, they will expend considerable amounts of money to thwart unionization. In order to be successful, unions expend large amounts of resources on organizing campaigns. The way these campaigns are conducted, and either won or lost, is the subject of this section.

Choosing Targets

The most frequent reason for union interest in particular organizations is solicitation by employees. Disgruntled employees either contact unions directly or they may request assistance through third parties. These third parties are usually friends or relatives employed in union environments who happen to hear employees complaining. They, in turn, inform their shop steward, who relays the information to the union. Consider the following case.

> The "U" Deposit Bank and Trust had decided to expand its services by opening mini-branches within grocery stores. After negotiating for space with a local food store, the bank hired two tellers and opened its first branch. For several months, everything proceeded as planned. Customers seemed to like the facility, and business grew steadily. Shortly thereafter, the bank decided to expand the mini-bank's hours of operation. Despite the complaints of the tellers, bank hours were expanded to include Saturday mornings and Wednesday evenings. The tellers, who were extremely unhappy, griped constantly to the grocery clerks about the fact that they were ignored and overlooked. Feeling sorry for the tellers, one of the clerks asked the local shop steward if there was anything that could be done to help those poor people. Three weeks later, the bank found itself in the midst of an organizing campaign.

All organizational campaigns are not generated through employee inquiries. Reasons other than worker queries can initiate union interest in an organization. One such factor is geographic location. If a plant chooses to locate in an area of the country which consists primarily of union shops, the likelihood of it being the subject of a union organizational drive is high. If, on the other hand, organizations choose sites which are unfriendly to unions, the chances of being unionized are diminished. For this reason, organizations motivated to remain non-union may attempt to locate plants in one of the twenty-one right-to-work states (predominantly in the southern and sun-belt states), which have a reputation for being inhospitable to unions.[13]

It is important to note, at this point, that the preceding reasons represent the major ways organizing interest is created. They are, however, not exhaustive. Other factors, such as plant acquisitions and the percentage of organized workforce within a particular industry, may precipitate union attention. Regardless of the reason, however, one fact remains quite clear. Unions choose targets predominantly on a cost-effectiveness basis. Like companies which fail to use their resources wisely, unions which do not employ rational organizational decision making based on costs may find themselves so severely weakened economically that they are unable to survive.

The Employers' Perspective

As previously mentioned, today's employers expend large amounts of resources attempting to thwart unionization. An earlier discussion centered on the reasons why employees seek unionization, so it seems prudent at this time to discuss the reasons why employers so vigorously oppose efforts to organize the workforce.

The reasons most employers attempt to remain nonunion can be summarized in two major categories. These include:

1. Costs.
2. The loss of management control.

Costs

Undeniably, the cost of unionization varies from industry to industry. Generally, however, it has been estimated that the cost of operating a union shop is between 25 and 35 percent greater than the cost of operating a non-union environment.[14] Some of the costs include:

1. Work stoppages.
2. Additional personnel.
3. Administrative costs.
4. The adequacy of the workforce.

Work stoppages Strikes cost money. When unions and employers fail to agree on a contract, the likely result is a work stoppage and a union boycott of the employer's product. The union's goal is to have a significant economic impact on employers in order to force them to return to the bargaining table. If successful, work stoppages cause organizations to lose income in direct sales to consumers, and in sales to other companies whom they supply with products.

Additional personnel Having a unionized workforce requires the employment of additional personnel who have the responsibility for the labor relations function. Large companies which are unionized usually employ a labor relations specialist as part of the human resources department. This individual's responsibility is devoted solely to serving as a liaison between the company and the union for the purpose of maintaining the collective bargaining agreement. In addition, large unionized companies employ labor attorneys and other personnel whose expertise is needed for negotiating and administering the collective bargaining agreement.

Administrative costs This general category encompasses any costs which are associated with union activity. Examples of some typical costs include: the costs of contract negotiations, grievance handling, and clerical costs incurred in deducting dues from workers' payroll checks.

Adequacy of the workforce Many employers complain that unions protect inadequate workers. The logic behind this assumption is based on the fact that union contracts traditionally opt for uniform wages across workers. Regardless of the effort expended or the level of productivity, all workers performing the same job receive the same rate of pay. As a result, employers contend that good employees suffer from feelings of inequity and leave for better paying positions. The remaining workforce is, at best, mediocre.

The loss of management control

When an organization is unionized, employees lose the ability to negotiate individually with management on matters relating to wages, hours, and working conditions. Typically, any and all matters relating to any of these facets is detailed in the collective bargaining agreement. In addition, the contract usually specifies the action to be taken by managers and supervisors in dealing with these areas. As a result, management forfeits its prerogative in dealing with employees and the workplace. For many managers this is tantamount to removing their supervisory duties and relegating them to the role of "contract monitor" and "enforcer."

Gaining Recognition

The goal of an organizing effort is for a union to be recognized as the employees' exclusive bargaining representative. Unions can accomplish this task in a number of ways. For example, the employer may voluntarily recognize the union after it has proven that it represents a majority of the bargaining unit employees. In order to prove that they represent a majority of employees, unions attempt to have employees sign **authorization cards** or petitions on which they state that they want the union to represent them for the purpose of collective bargaining.

> **Authorization cards**
>
> *Authorization cards are documents which employees sign on which they indicate that they want the union to represent them for the purpose of collective bargaining and/or they authorize the union to seek an* NLRB *election.*

The second and most common method by which unions gain recognition is through an NLRB-conducted election. For this procedure to occur, unions must

Exhibit 13.5

Facsimile of Union Authorization Card

AUTHORIZATION TO SAS

Date ______________________ 19___

I, ______________________ authorize SAS to represent me for the purpose of collective bargaining.
Print Name

____
Address City Zip Phone No.

____
Class of Work Hourly Rate Clock No. Dept. No. Shift

Employed by ______________________________________
Company Address

____
Signature of Employee

demonstrate to the NLRB a "showing of interest" on the part of workers. This is accomplished by petitioning the NLRB after signatures on authorization cards or petitions from at least 30 percent of the bargaining unit employees have been collected. Realistically, most unions do not petition for elections until they have collected signatures from 60 to 65 percent of the bargaining unit employees.

A third method by which unions become the exclusive collective bargaining agent is by the NLRB issuing a **bargaining order.** If the union can demonstrate that it held a majority status at some point prior to the election and that the employer committed unfair labor practices which resulted in the union's losing the election, the NLRB may order the company to bargain with the union. The logic behind this practice is that by committing serious unfair labor practices, employers may have contaminated the environment so severely that employees are not able to vote freely.

Bargaining order

A *bargaining order is an order issued by the* National Labor Relations Board (NLRB) *instructing an employer to undertake collective bargaining with the soliciting union.*

Exhibit 13.6

FORM NLRB-502
(5-85)

FORM EXEMPT UNDER 44 U S C 3512

UNITED STATES GOVERNMENT
NATIONAL LABOR RELATIONS BOARD
PETITION

DO NOT WRITE IN THIS SPACE	
Case No.	Date Filed

INSTRUCTIONS: Submit an original and 4 copies of this Petition to the NLRB Regional Office in the Region in which the employer concerned is located. If more space is required for any one item, attach additional sheets, numbering item accordingly.

The Petitioner alleges that the following circumstances exist and requests that the National Labor Relations Board proceed under its proper authority pursuant to Section 9 of the National Labor Relations Act.

1 PURPOSE OF THIS PETITION *(If box RC, RM, or RD is checked and a charge under Section 8(b)(7) of the Act has been filed involving the Employer named herein, the statement following the description of the type of petition shall not be deemed made.)* **(Check One)**

☐ **RC-CERTIFICATION OF REPRESENTATIVE** - A substantial number of employees wish to be represented for purposes of collective bargaining by Petitioner and Petitioner desires to be certified as representative of the employees.

☐ **RM-REPRESENTATION (EMPLOYER PETITION)** - One or more individuals or labor organizations have presented a claim to Petitioner to be recognized as the representative of employees of Petitioner.

☐ **RD-DECERTIFICATION** - A substantial number of employees assert that the certified or currently recognized bargaining representative is no longer their representative.

☐ **UD-WITHDRAWAL OF UNION SHOP AUTHORITY** - Thirty percent (30%) or more of employees in a bargaining unit covered by an agreement between their employer and a labor organization desire that such authority be rescinded.

☐ **UC-UNIT CLARIFICATION** - A labor organization is currently recognized by Employer, but Petitioner seeks clarification of placement of certain employees: *(Check one)* ☐ In unit not previously certified. ☐ In unit previously certified in Case No. ________.

☐ **AC-AMENDMENT OF CERTIFICATION** - Petitioner seeks amendment of certification issued in Case No. ________
Attach statement describing the specific amendment sought.

2. Name of Employer	Employer Representative to contact	Telephone Number

3. Address*(es)* of Establishment*(s)* involved *(Street and number, city, State, ZIP code)*

4a. Type of Establishment *(Factory, mine, wholesaler, etc.)*	4b. Identify principal product or service

5. Unit Involved *(In UC petition, describe* **present** *bargaining unit and attach description of proposed clarification.)*	6a. Number of Employees in Unit:
Included	Present
	Proposed *(By UC/AC)*
Excluded	6b. Is this petition supported by 30% or more of the employees in the unit? * ___ Yes ___No *Not applicable in RM, UC, and AC
(If you have checked box RC in 1 above, check and complete EITHER item 7a or 7b, whichever is applicable)	

7a.☐ Request for recognition as Bargaining Representative was made on *(Date)* ________ and Employer declined recognition on or about *(Date)* ________ *(If no reply received, so state).*

7b.☐ Petitioner is currently recognized as Bargaining Representative and desires certification under the Act.

8. Name of Recognized or Certified Bargaining Agent *(If none, so state)*	Affiliation
Address and Telephone Number	Date of Recognition or Certification

9. Expiration Date of Current Contract, If any *(Month, Day, Year)*	10. If you have checked box UD in 1 above, show here the date of execution of agreement granting union shop *(Month, Day, and Year)*
11a. Is there now a strike or picketing at the Employer's establishment*(s)* Involved? Yes ____ No ____	11b. If so, approximately how many employees are participating?

11c. The Employer has been picketed by or on behalf of *(Insert Name)* ________, a labor organization, of *(Insert Address)* ________ Since *(Month, Day, Year)* ________

12. Organizations or individuals other than Petitioner *(and other than those named in items 8 and 11c)*, which have claimed recognition as representatives and other organizations and individuals known to have a representative interest in any employees in unit described in item 5 above. *(If none, so state)*

Name	Affilation	Address	Date of Claim *(Required only if Petition is filed by Employer)*

I declare that I have read the above petition and that the statements are true to the best of my knowledge and belief.

____
(Name of Petitioner and Affilation, if any)

By ________ ________
(Signature of Representative or person filing petition) *(Title, if any)*

Address ________ ________
(Street and number, city, State, and ZIP Code *(Telephone Number)*

WILLFUL FALSE STATEMENTS ON THIS PETITION CAN BE PUNISHED BY FINE AND IMPRISONMENT (U. S. CODE, TITLE 18, SECTION 1001)

Exhibit 13.7

NOTICE TO EMPLOYEES

FROM THE

National Labor Relations Board

A PETITION has been filed with this Federal agency seeking an election to determine whether certain employees want to be represented by a union.

The case is being investigated and NO DETERMINATION HAS BEEN MADE AT THIS TIME by the National Labor Relations Board. IF an election is held Notices of Election will be posted giving complete details for voting.

It was suggested that your employer post this notice so the National Labor Relations Board could inform you of your basic rights under the National Labor Relations Act.

YOU HAVE THE RIGHT under Federal Law

- **To self-organization**
- **To form, join, or assist labor organizations**
- **To bargain collectively through representatives of your own choosing**
- **To act together for the purposes of collective bargaining or other mutual aid or protection**
- **To refuse to do any or all of these things unless the union and employer, in a state where such agreements are permitted, enter into a lawful union security clause requiring employees to join the union.**

It is possible that some of you will be voting in an employee representation election as a result of the request for an election having been filed. While NO DETERMINATION HAS BEEN MADE AT THIS TIME, in the event an election is held, the NATIONAL LABOR RELATIONS BOARD wants all eligible voters to be familiar with their rights under the law IF it holds an election.

The Board applies rules which are intended to keep its elections fair and honest and which result in a free choice. If agents of either Unions or Employers act in such a way as to interfere with your right to a free election, the election can be set aside by the Board. Where appropriate the Board provides other remedies, such as reinstatement for employees fired for exercising their rights, including backpay from the party responsible for their discharge.

NOTE:

The following are examples of conduct which interfere with the rights of employees and may result in the setting aside of the election.

- **Threatening loss of jobs or benefits by an Employer or a Union**
- **Promising or granting promotions, pay raises, or other benefits, to influence an employee's vote by a party capable of carrying out such promises**
- **An Employer firing employees to discourage or encourage union activity or a Union causing them to be fired to encourage union activity**
- **Making campaign speeches to assembled groups of employees on company time within the 24-hour period before the election**
- **Incitement by either an Employer or a Union of racial or religious prejudice by inflammatory appeals**
- **Threatening physical force or violence to employees by a Union or an Employer to influence their votes**

Please be assured that IF AN ELECTION IS HELD every effort will be made to protect your right to a free choice under the law. Improper conduct will not be permitted. All parties are expected to cooperate fully with this agency in maintaining basic principles of a fair election as required by law. The National Labor Relations Board as an agency of the United States Government does not endorse any choice in the election.

NATIONAL LABOR RELATIONS BOARD

an agency of the

UNITED STATES GOVERNMENT

THIS IS AN OFFICIAL GOVERNMENT NOTICE AND MUST NOT BE DEFACED BY ANYONE

FORM NLRB-666 (8-83) ★U.S.GPO:1987-0-181-574/62752

There are other methods by which unions can gain recognition, such as recognition strikes, unit-clarification procedures, and bluffing. These methods, however, are not the norm, and they rarely result in unions being sanctioned as the collective bargaining agent. The present discussion will concentrate on the organizing tactics used in the majority of instances—those resulting in an NLRB election.

The Organizing Campaign

The initial goal of union organizers is to obtain bargaining unit employees' signatures on authorization cards. To accomplish this task, they rely on several organizing tactics. These include the recruitment of internal employee organizers, leafleting, meetings, home visiting and telephoning, and media campaigns.

Recruiting internal organizers

The most effective organizing is conducted inside the organization by employees. In fact, it is ludicrous to envision outside organizers having any success without inside assistance. By law, the rights associated with the ownership of private property are protected. Except in rare cases where access to workers is otherwise impossible union organizers do not have the legal right to enter and conduct organizing campaigns on company premises. Employees, however, can solicit on non-work time in non-work areas. In order to conduct an effective campaign, the first task of organizers is to recruit internal personnel for assistance in the organizing effort.

Leafleting

By the time leafleting occurs, unions have usually obtained considerable employee support. Rarely, if ever, do organizing efforts start with leafleting, as this tactic obviously has high visibility. Unions prefer to operate as inconspicuously as possible, accomplishing their goal before employers are aware of their presence. The goal of leafleting is to reach a larger group of employees, who may otherwise be inaccessible, and to convince them to join the ranks. In addition, it enables unions to disseminate information uniformly.

Meetings

The organizing meeting is designed to be a social affair for the purpose of transmitting information and impressions to uncommitted workers. At the same time, organizers reinforce the loyalty and dedication of those already committed employees.[15] Unlike management, unions do not have the legal right to hold meetings on company time or on company premises. These mass meetings must be conducted on the employees' own time. In order to bolster attendance, organizers not only select convenient meeting schedules and locations but also provide other inducements as well.

Home visits and telephoning

On occasion, union organizers visit the homes of employees for the purpose of urging them to vote for the union. The advantage of this technique is the involvement the organizer can have with the family. Many workers discuss the decision to sign authorization cards with family members prior to actually committing to it. Home visits allow the organizer to answer questions posed by family members and to stress the benefits of unionization. As a result of these home visits, organizers may gain the support of family members, who in turn may apply pressure on the employee.

The obvious disadvantage to home visits is the cost involved in both time and resources. As a result, many organizers use telephone solicitation to reach a greater number of employees in a shorter period of time. Aside from the cost benefit associated with telephoning, this tactic allows organizers to quickly gauge the strength of their support. This information aids unions in timing their election requests or continuing with their organizing campaign.

Media campaigns

Media campaigns which manipulate public opinion can be an effective means of influencing workers. People are swayed by others, especially when emotional issues are involved. By appropriately using mass media through news releases, organizers can disseminate information which may impact on either the employees themselves or on those who have an impact on their decision making.

The Employers' Response

After the passage of the Wagner Act, employers were prohibited from actively involving themselves in union organizing efforts. Unionization was considered a worker activity, and any involvement by employers was considered an unfair labor practice. Recognizing the fact that management had an inherent legitimate interest in whether or not the workforce was organized, Congress amended this provision via the Taft–Hartley Act to allow employers to take an active role in the organizing campaign. Today, employers who so desire may actively campaign against unionization provided their actions do not violate any of the enumerated unfair labor practices.

Generally, most employers resist attempts to unionize their workers. To accomplish this objective they usually seek help from outsiders. These experts, who usually are labor attorneys and consultants, provide assistance by conducting training programs and by designing and implementing campaign strategies.[16]

Although the tactics used and the information provided vary from company to company, several issues are universal. Most employers stress the economic hardships of strikes, the fact that the union is an outsider, and the benefits currently enjoyed by the workers. In addition, employers will attempt to respond to any and all allegations of which they feel the union has falsely accused them.

These tactics, coupled with plant closings and layoffs, have been a major impetus in the membership downslide unions have experienced during the last decade.[17]

The Election

If the union is successful in getting at least 30 percent of the bargaining unit employees to sign authorization cards, they may petition the NLRB to conduct a representation election. After verifying the legitimacy of the union's claim and meeting with both parties, the NLRB will set an election date. The election is usually held on the employer's premises, it is conducted by an NLRB official, and both the union and the employer are allowed to have a designated number of observers. All eligible bargaining unit employees cast one vote, in secrecy, to either be represented or not represented by the union.

At the conclusion of the voting procedure, the NLRB tallies the ballots. For unions to be certified as the recognized bargaining representative, they must obtain a majority of the votes cast (at least 50 percent plus one vote). It is important to note that only the actual votes cast count and not the total number of employees in the bargaining unit. For example, suppose a bargaining unit consists of thirty employees. If only twelve workers vote in the election, the union only needs seven votes (50 percent plus one) to win. All thirty employees would then be represented by the union. Mathematically, an abstention is in fact a vote for the union. In reality, however, this rarely occurs because a high percentage of the eligible bargaining unit members vote.

After the election, both parties have five working days to file any objections they may have regarding the conduction of the election. If an objection is sustained, the election is rerun. More commonly, however, the final procedural step for most elections is certification. If the union fails to prevail, the NLRB issues a **certification of results** and places an **election bar** into effect. This means that the NLRB will not honor a petition for another election within a one-year period. In essence, if the company wins, they are union-free for at least one year. On the other hand, should the union prevail, the NLRB will issue a **certification of representation,** indicating that the employer has a legal duty to recognize and bargain with the union as the exclusive representative of the bargaining unit employees.

Election bar

An election bar is an administrative rule of the NLRB in which they will refuse to honor a petition for an election for one year from the time that a previous election was certified in the particular bargaining unit.

Exhibit 13.8

UNITED STATES OF AMERICA ★ N

NOTICE O

PURPOSE OF THIS ELECTION This election is to determine the representative, if any, desired by the eligible employees for purposes of collective bargaining with their Employer. (See VOTING UNIT in this Notice of Election, for description of eligible employees.) A majority of the valid ballots cast will determine the results of the election.

SECRET BALLOT The election will be by SECRET ballot under the supervision of the Regional Director of the National Labor Relations Board. Voters will be allowed to vote without interference, restraint, or coercion. Electioneering will not be permitted at or near the polling place. Violations of these rules should be reported immediately to the Regional Director or the agent in charge of the election. Your attention is called to Section 12 of the National Labor Relations Act:

ANY PERSON WHO SHALL WILLFULLY RESIST, PREVENT, IMPEDE, OR INTERFERE WITH ANY MEMBER OF THE BOARD OR ANY OF ITS AGENTS OR AGENCIES IN THE PERFORMANCE OF DUTIES PURSUANT TO THIS ACT SHALL BE PUNISHED BY A FINE OF NOT MORE THAN $5,000 OR BY IMPRISONMENT FOR NOT MORE THAN ONE YEAR, OR BOTH.

An agent of the Board will hand a ballot to each eligible voter at the voting place. Mark your ballot in secret in the voting booth provided. DO NOT SIGN YOUR BALLOT. Fold the ballot before leaving the voting booth, then personally deposit it in a ballot box under the supervision of an agent of the Board.

A sample of the official ballot is shown at the center of this Notice.

ELIGIBILITY RULES Employees eligible to vote are those described under VOTING UNIT in this Notice of Election, including employees who did not work during the designated payroll period because they were ill or on vacation or temporarily laid off, and also including employees in the military service of the United States who appear in person at the polls. Employees who have quit or been discharged for cause since the designated payroll period and who have not been rehired or reinstated prior to the date of this election are not eligible to vote.

CHALLENGE OF VOTERS An agent of the Board or an authorized observer may question the eligibility of a voter. Such challenge MUST be made before the voter's ballot has been placed in the ballot box.

AUTHORIZED OBSERVERS Each of the interested parties may designate an equal number of observers, this number to be determined by the Regional Director or agent in charge of the election. These observers (a) act as checkers at the voting place and at the counting of ballots, (b) assist in the identification of voters, (c) challenge voters and ballots, and (d) otherwise assist the Regional Director or agent.

INFORMATION CONCERNING ELECTION The Act provides that only one valid representation election may be held in a 12-month period. Any employee who desires to obtain any further information concerning the terms and conditions under which this election is to be held or who desires to raise any question concerning the holding of an election, the voting unit, or eligibility rules may do so by communicating with the Regional Director or agent in charge of the election.

VO
For Ce
ABC

THOSE ELIGIBLE TO VOTE:
All Physical Plant employees emp
at 111 Anywhere Place and 222 Ma
ending Sunday, May 30, 1990.

THOSE NOT ELIGIBLE TO VOTE:
All service workers, groundskeepe
guards and supervisors as defined

DATE, H
DATE: W

8:00 a.m. to 8:3
7:30 a.m. to 8:00 a.m.

BALLOTS WILL BE CO-MINGLED AND COU

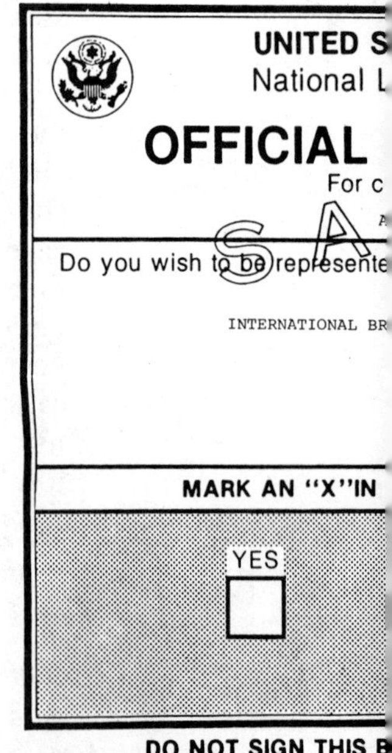
UNITED S
National L
OFFICIAL
For c
SA
Do you wish to be represente
INTERNATIONAL BR
MARK AN "X" IN
YES

DO NOT SIGN THIS B
If you spoil this ballot re

WARNING: THIS IS THE ONLY OFFICIAL NOTICE OF T

Form NLRB-707 (1-77)

ONAL LABOR RELATIONS BOARD

ELECTION

of

ployer at its two locations
the bi-weekly payroll period

port personnel, professionals,

S OF ELECTION
18, 1990
ES
nce room at 111 Anywhere Pl.
om at 222 Main Way

RE PLACE POLLING PLACE AT APPROX. 8:45 a.m.

F AMERICA
tions Board

ET BALLOT
yees of

es of collective bargaining by

STUDENT WORKERS LOCAL 00-00Z

E OF YOUR CHOICE

d and drop in ballot box.
Board Agent for a new one.

RIGHTS OF EMPLOYEES

Under the National Labor Relations Act, employees have the right:

- To self-organization
- To form, join, or assist labor organizations
- To bargain collectively through representatives of their own choosing
- To act together for the purposes of collective bargaining or other mutual aid or protection
- To refuse to do any or all of these things unless the Union and Employer, in a State where such agreements are permitted, enter into a lawful union security clause requiring employees to join the Union.

It is the responsibility of the National Labor Relations Board to protect employees in the exercise of these rights.

The Board wants all eligible voters to be fully informed about their rights under Federal law and wants both Employers and Unions to know what is expected of them when it holds an election.

If agents of either Unions or Employers interfere with your right to a free, fair, and honest election, the election can be set aside by the Board. Where appropriate the Board provides other remedies, such as reinstatement for employees fired for exercising their rights, including backpay from the party responsible for their discharge.

The following are examples of conduct which interferes with the rights of employees and may result in the setting aside of the election:

- Threatening loss of jobs or benefits by an Employer or a Union
- Misstating important facts by a Union or an Employer where the other party does not have a fair chance to reply
- Promising or granting promotions, pay raises, or other benefits to influence an employee's vote by a party capable of carrying out such promises
- An Employer firing employees to discourage or encourage union activity or a Union causing them to be fired to encourage union activity
- Making campaign speeches to assembled groups of employees on company time within the 24-hour period before the election
- Incitement by either an Employer or a Union of racial or religious prejudice by inflammatory appeals
- Threatening physical force or violence to employees by a Union or an Employer to influence their votes.

The National Labor Relations Board protects your right to a free choice

Improper conduct will not be permitted. All parties are expected to cooperate fully with this agency in maintaining basic principles of a fair election as required by law. The National Labor Relations Board as an agency of the United States Government does not endorse any choice in the election.

NATIONAL LABOR RELATIONS BOARD
an agency of the
UNITED STATES GOVERNMENT

LECTION AND MUST NOT BE DEFACED BY ANYONE

U.S. GOVERNMENT PRINTING OFFICE: 1980-625-416

Exhibit 13.9

GPO : 1984 O - 435-440

FORM NLRB-501 (8-83)

FORM EXEMPT UNDER 44 U.S.C. 3512

UNITED STATES OF AMERICA
NATIONAL LABOR RELATIONS BOARD
CHARGE AGAINST EMPLOYER

DO NOT WRITE IN THIS SPACE	
Case	Date Filed

INSTRUCTIONS: File an original and 4 copies of this charge with NLRB Regional Director for the region in which the alleged unfair labor practice occurred or is occurring.

1. EMPLOYER AGAINST WHOM CHARGE IS BROUGHT

a. Name of Employer		b. Number of workers employed
c. Address *(street, city, state, ZIP code)*	d. Employer Representative	e. Telephone No.
f. Type of Establishment *(factory, mine, wholesaler, etc.)*	g. Identify principal product or service	

h. The above-named employer has engaged in and is engaging in unfair labor practices within the meaning of section 8(a), subsections (1) and *(list subsections)* ________________ of the National Labor Relations Act, and these unfair labor practices are unfair practices affecting commerce within the meaning of the Act.

2. Basis of the Charge *(be specific as to facts, names, addresses, plants involved, dates, places, etc.)*

By the above and other acts, the above-named employer has interfered with, restrained, and coerced employees in the exercise of the rights guaranteed in Section 7 of the Act

3. Full name of party filing charge *(if labor organization, give full name, including local name and number)*

4a. Address *(street and number, city, state, and ZIP code)*	4b. Telephone No.

5. Full name of national or international labor organization of which it is an affiliate or constituent unit *(to be filled in when charge is filed by a labor organization)*

6. DECLARATION

I declare that I have read the above charge and that the statements are true to the best of my knowledge and belief.

By ________________ *(signature of representative or person making charge)* ________________ *(title if any)*

Address ________________ ________________ *(Telephone No.)* ________________ *(date)*

WILLFUL FALSE STATEMENTS ON THIS CHARGE CAN BE PUNISHED BY FINE AND IMPRISONMENT (U. S. CODE, TITLE 18, SECTION 1001)

Exhibit 13.10

GPO : 1985 O - 468-533

FORM EXEMPT UNDER 44 U.S.C. 3512

FORM NLRB-508 (8-83)

UNITED STATES OF AMERICA
NATIONAL LABOR RELATIONS BOARD
CHARGE AGAINST LABOR ORGANIZATION OR ITS AGENTS

DO NOT WRITE IN THIS SPACE	
Case	Date Filed

INSTRUCTIONS: File an original and 3 copies of this charge and an additional copy for each organization, each local, and each individual named in item 1 with the NLRB Regional Director of the region in which the alleged unfair labor practice occurred or is occurring.

1. LABOR ORGANIZATION OR ITS AGENTS AGAINST WHICH CHARGE IS BROUGHT

a. Name

b. Union Representative to contact

c. Telephone No.

d. Address *(street, city, state and ZIP code)*

e. The above-named organization(s) or its agents has *(have)* engaged in and is *(are)* engaging in unfair labor practices within the meaning of section 8(b), subsection(s) *(list subsections)* ______________ of the National Labor Relations Act, and these unfair labor practices are unfair practices affecting commerce within the meaning of the Act.

2. Basis of the Charge *(be specific as to facts, names, addresses, plants involved, dates, places, etc.)*

3. Name of Employer

4. Telephone No.

5. Location of plant involved *(street, city, state and ZIP code)*

6. Employer representative to contact

7. Type of establishment *(factory, mine, wholesaler, etc.)*

8. Identify principal product or service

9. Number of workers employed

10. Full name of party filing charge

11. Address of party filing charge *(street, city, state and ZIP code)*

12. Telephone No.

13. DECLARATION

I declare that I have read the above charge and that the statements therein are true to the best of my knowledge and belief.

By ______________ *(signature of representative or person making charge)* ______________ *(title or office, if any)*

Address ______________ ______________ *(Telephone No.)* ______________ *(date)*

WILLFUL FALSE STATEMENTS ON THIS CHARGE CAN BE PUNISHED BY FINE AND IMPRISONMENT (U. S. CODE, TITLE 18, SECTION 1001)

Certification of election

Certification is the formal means by which the NLRB reports the results of an election. It is either the certification of a union as the collective bargaining agent or merely the certification of the results, if a union does not prevail.

After the Election

The representation election culminates the organizing effort. If the employer prevails, the bargaining unit remains non-union. Should the union win, however, the process of bargaining begins. Negotiating and administering labor agreements, grievance and discipline handling, and the general area of industrial relations are the subject of the next chapter.

A Final Note

As with other organizations, the possibility of unions outliving their usefulness is a distinct reality. When labor organizations fail to meet and satisfy the needs of their members, they are subject to being ousted. This process of removing a certified representative is called **decertification.** During the past decade, 75 percent of decertification elections have resulted in the ousting of the union as the collective bargaining agent.[18]

Decertification

Decertification is the process undertaken by bargaining unit employees to prohibit the certified collective bargaining agent from further representing them.

The procedures involved in a decertification effort are, in essence, a reversal of the events undertaken by unions during organizing campaigns. Workers are required to demonstrate to the NLRB an interest in having the union removed as the certified collective bargaining agent. This claim can be substantiated through cards, petitions, or any other documentation by which employees indicate that they do not wish to be represented by the current collective bargaining agent. When a sufficient amount of signatures from bargaining unit employees is gathered (30 percent), the employees may petition the NLRB to hold an election.

During recent years, employees have succeeded in decertifying unions without conducting elections. They have accomplished this task by collecting signatures from a majority of bargaining unit employees (over 50 percent) and by subsequently demanding that management refrain from any further bargaining with current representatives. If the documentation is valid, employers are indeed required to withdraw recognition.

Unlike organizing campaigns where employers may actively participate against unions, management is required to remain neutral during a decertification. Any actual or attempted aid of employees during this effort may constitute an unfair labor practice. If the charges are upheld, the decertification will be voided.[19]

Summary

The labor movement in the United States has had a long and arduous history. Initially, organized labor was scoffed at by both government and businesses alike. Legislation was one-sided, with laws seemingly protecting only employers. Still, collective activity persisted, with early unions fighting mainly to resist wage cuts.

This trend in labor–management relations persisted until the mid-1930s with the passage of the Wagner Act. This major piece of labor legislation established unfair labor practices for employers, created the National Labor Relations Board, and recognized the legitimacy of organized labor. Spurred by this major law, as well as by favorable public opinion, unionization began an upswing.

For twelve years, unions flourished. In 1947, Congress enacted the Taft–Hartley Act, which enumerated unfair labor practices for unions, gave states the power to enact right-to-work laws, outlawed the closed shop, and provided for other major labor provisions. As a result, the balance of power between labor and management was restored.

Today, as in the past, a major objective of unions is organizing. This costly process enables unions to increase their membership while retaining their existing constituency. It is not an easy task, as employers strongly resist attempts at organizing their workforces. For organizers to be successful, they must demonstrate a sufficient showing of interest on the part of workers in having the union serve as the exclusive collective bargaining representative. Once this interest has been demonstrated, the NLRB conducts elections to determine the will of the majority. Should the union prevail, it becomes the designated representative of the bargaining unit employees.

Key Terms to Identify

Wagner Act
National Labor Relations Board (NLRB)
Taft–Hartley Act
Closed shop
Union shop
Landrum–Griffin Act
Craft unions
Industrial unions
Union raiding
Authorization cards
Bargaining order

Agency shop
Right-to-work laws
Unfair labor practice
Featherbedding
Certification of results
Election bar
Certification of representation
Decertification

Questions for Discussion

Do You Know the Facts?

1. Trace the history of organized labor in this country. How did government legislation hamper and aid the labor movement?
2. Discuss the main features of the Wagner Act. What significant amendments did Taft–Hartley make to the Wagner Act?
3. What constitutes unfair labor practices for employers?
4. How did the Landrum–Griffin Act serve to protect the public from unscrupulous union behavior?
5. Discuss the reasons why employees join unions.
6. How do union organizers gain success within companies?

Can You Apply the Information Learned?

1. What would be the impact on management–employee relations if the Taft–Hartley Act were not in existence today?
2. How would you combat a union organizing effort in your company?
3. Do you feel that large, independent unions, which are capable of resisting raiding efforts, have anything to gain by affiliating with the AFL–CIO?
4. What policies and procedures would you implement in your company after successfully defeating a union in an election?
5. Defend or criticize the statement, "Companies that get unions probably deserve them!"

The Questionable Address

Steven Rogers, personnel director for Wonder Whistle, Inc., had a decision to make. For the past several months the United Whistle Workers of America (UWWA) had been conducting an organizing campaign at the main plant. Having secured a sufficient amount of authorization card signatures, the UWWA petitioned for and granted the right to conduct a representation election by the National Labor Relations Board. After conducting a hearing, the NLRB determined that the bargaining unit would consist of all production and maintenance employees, excluding supervisors and office clerical personnel. In addition, a representation election was scheduled for Friday, March 24, from 3:00 PM to 6:00 PM in the main plant cafeteria. This date was chosen because it was determined that conducting an election on Friday, a payday, would assure maximum voter turnout. Also, because shift change occurred at 4:30 PM, the voting time period chosen appeared to be the most convenient for both day and evening shift workers.

In anticipation of the upcoming election, Wendy Wonder, the company's president, had requested that Steven review and comment on the contents of a speech she was preparing to give to both the day and evening shift workers on the afternoon of Thursday, March 23. Wendy had explained to Steven that this time period was chosen so that both shifts would be easily accessible and so that the contents of the speech would be fresh in their minds when they went to the polls on Friday. The text includes the following passages:

> In going to the polls tomorrow, I want you all to understand that I know that no company is perfect, including ours. However, I also think it is in the best interests of us to work things out together, without the intervention of a third party like the UWWA. In my experience, unions exist to collect dues, call strikes, make promises they usually cannot keep, and create a lot of confusion among employees. What I am asking for is a chance to continue trying to make your experience at Wonder Whistle a better one by working with you directly and not through an outside entity.
>
> Now I recognize that some of you felt it was necessary to seek the assistance of an outsider to represent you, and I know that some mistakes have been made in the past. But, at the same time, our management team is sincerely interested in improving things. We already have in place programs to improve scheduling, to increase training opportunities, and to update our machinery. We have also begun to undertake a full-scale wage and benefit review, and we have been looking into establishing a grievance procedure so that you can bring your complaints or job-related concerns to our attention in a way that will ensure full and fair consideration.
>
> You should also keep in mind that even if you vote for the union tomorrow, there are no guarantees about what might happen. Bargaining is a two-way street. We have the same rights as the union to present proposals and counterproposals that we think are in the company's, as well as the employees', best interests. The law does not require us to agree to any specific proposal put forth by the union, be it wages, benefits, or anything else. Bear in mind that bargaining can be a risky venture. It may actually happen that you could lose some of the benefits you currently enjoy in the process of give-and-take at the bargaining table. And don't forget, strikes are always possible in the event that negotiations break down.
>
> Remember, the whistle industry is an extremely competitive one right now. I believe that at Wonder Whistle we have been able to remain competitive because of the efficiency of operating in an environment free of outside influences distracting us from the work at hand. If the UWWA comes onto the scene, however, there is no telling what effect it will have on our ability to maintain our present production and profit levels, to hold onto our share of the whistle market, or to stay in business at all!

I hope you bear some of these things in mind when you go to the polls tomorrow.

Questions for Discussion

1. What advice would you give Wendy Wonder about the legality of her remarks?
2. Aside from the legal issues involved, what are the practical management implications of the work promises made in the speech?
3. Do you believe that Wendy's speech would sway voter opinion? Why or why not?

This case was prepared by Larry Rothman, National Labor Relations Board, Washington, D.C.

Endnotes and References

1 From *The Wagner Act (National Labor Relations Act)*, Approved July 5, 1935, 49 Stat. 449, Section 7.

2 From *The Wagner Act (National Labor Relations Act)*, Approved July 5, 1935, 49 Stat. 449, Section 8.

3 Marc G. Singer, "Comprehension of Right-to-Work Laws Among Residents of the Right-to-Work States," *Journal of Collective Negotiations in the Public Sector*, Vol. 16, No. 4 (1987): 309–323.

4 From *Labor Management Relations Act, 1947 (Taft–Hartley)*, June 23, 1947, 61 Stat. 136, as amended by Act of September 14, 1959, 73 Stat. 519, Sec. 8 (b).

5 "Dissidents in the Teamsters are Gaining Clout." *Business Week* (November 13, 1978): 136–139.

6 From *Labor–Management Reporting and Disclosure Act of 1959 (The Landrum–Griffin Act)*, 73 Stat. 519.

7 For a comprehensive discussion of why employees join unions, see Thomas Kochan, *Collective Bargaining and Industrial Relations* (Homewood, IL: Richard D. Irwin, Inc., 1980).

8 Donna Sockell, "Toward a Theory of the Union's Role in an Enterprise." In *Advances in Industrial and Labor Relations*, edited by David B. Liskey and Joel M. Douglas. (Greenwich, CT: JAI Press, 1983): 221–232.

9 An excellent discussion on why employees join unions can be found in Jack Fiorito, Daniel G. Gallagher, and Charles Greer, "Determinants of Unionism: A Review of the Literature," in *Research in Personnel and Human Resources Management*, Vol. 4, edited by Kendrith M. Rowland and Gerald R. Ferris (Greenwich, CT: JAI Press, 1986): 269–306.

10 For a discussion of why workers do not join unions, see James E. Martin, "Employee Characteristics and Representation Election Outcomes," *Industrial and Labor Relations Review,* Vol. 38, No. 3 (April 1985): 365–376. Also see Robert L. Aronson, "Unionism Among Professional Employees in the Private Sector," *Industrial and Labor Relations Review,* Vol. 38, No. 3 (April 1985): 352–364.

11 Alex Kotlowitz, "Job of Shop Steward Has New Frustrations in Era of Payroll Cuts," *The Wall Street Journal* (April 1, 1987): 1, 23.

12 Richard B. Freeman and James L. Medoff, *What Do Unions Do?* (New York: Basic Books, Inc., 1984): 37. Also see *Statistical Abstract of the United States 1984,* 104th edition (Washington, D.C.: U.S. Department of Commerce, 1984): 440.

13 Right-to-work states include: Alabama, Arizona, Arkansas, Florida, Georgia, Idaho, Iowa, Kansas, Louisiana, Mississippi, Nebraska, Nevada, North Carolina, North Dakota, South Carolina, South Dakota, Tennessee, Texas, Utah, Virginia, and Wyoming.

14 Thomas M. Rohan, "Would a Union Look Good to Your Workers?" *Industrial World* (January 26, 1976): 36.

15 John G. Kilgour, *Preventive Labor Relations* (New York: Amacom, 1981).

16 See John J. Lawler and Robin West, "Impact of Union Avoidance Strategy in Representation Elections," *Industrial Relations,* Vol. 24, No. 3 (Fall 1985): 406–420.

17 See Seymour M. Lipset and William Schneider, "Organized Labor and the Public: A Troubled Union," *Public Opinion* (August–September 1981): 52–56; and Leonard M. Apcar, "Unions Forced to Retrench More, Fear Their Clout May Not Return," *The Wall Street Journal* (May 20, 1983): 33. Also, the Gallup Poll conducted in 1981 (*Gallup Report,* 1981, 6–8), indicates that over the past forty-five years, public opinion favoring unions has steadily declined.

18 Francis T. Coleman, "Once a Union Not Always a Union," *Personnel Journal,* Vol. 64 (March 1985): 42–45.

19 For a discussion on decertification behaviors, see Ellen R. Peirce and Richard Blackburn, "The Union Decertification Process: Employer Do's and Don'ts," *Employee Relations Law Journal,* Vol. 12, No. 2 (1986): 205–220. Also see John Kilgour, "Decertifying a Union: A Matter of Choice," *Personnel Administrator,* Vol. 32 (July 1987): 42–51.

Chapter 14

Collective Bargaining and Contract Administration

Objectives

After reading this chapter you should understand:

1. The meaning of the phrase "the duty to bargain" and how to prepare for the bargaining process.
2. The different types of bargaining strategies and tactics.
3. The subject matter of bargaining and the issues involved.
4. The types and effects of various work stoppages.
5. The mediation and arbitration process.
6. The problems encountered in administering a labor agreement.
7. The grievance procedure and its implementation.

The success of unions in representation elections marks the beginning of new relationships between employers and employees. Before unions enter the environment, employers are free to deal with individual workers as they see fit, within the confinements of the law. Wages, hours, and working conditions are established by management either with or without the advice of employees. In addition, workers may negotiate individually with their supervisors or management on any matter they choose. The issuance of a certification of representation and ultimate bargaining order drastically changes this state of affairs. At that point employers are required by law to bargain collectively in good faith with the chosen representative of the employees. The manner in which employers and unions prepare for negotiating sessions, the methods of bargaining used, the rules and regulations surrounding the sessions, and the contract and its ultimate administration constitute the subject matter of this chapter.

The Duty to Bargain in Good Faith

By law, the duty to bargain in good faith is one of central principles of labor–management relations. As stated in the Taft–Hartley Act:

> . . . to bargain collectively is the performance of the mutual obligation of the employer and the representative of the employees to meet at reasonable times and confer in good faith with respect to wages, hours and other terms and conditions of employment. . . . but such obligation does not compel either party to agree to a proposal or require the making of a concession.[1]

Nothing in the act mandates that either the union or the employer concede issues in order to reach agreement. In fact, the only stipulation is that both parties bargain in good faith. This means that both the union and the employer make an earnest effort to reconcile their differences in order to arrive at a mutually acceptable contract. **Collective bargaining** involves both parties using whatever legal tactics are at their disposal to gain favorable provisions for the constituents they represent.

> ***Collective bargaining***
>
> *Collective bargaining is a process in which representatives meet and use whatever legal tactics are at their disposal to effect the best possible employment agreement for the parties whom they represent.*

Over the years, unions and employers have employed a variety of maneuvers to achieve their purposes. Because bargaining often places individuals in adversarial relationships, many collective bargaining sessions in the past were characterized by the use of irrational techniques. Bluffing, cajoling, threatening, and wheeler-dealing were some of the more common phrases used to describe the typical bargaining session. Today, however, unions and employers are more sophisticated in the manner in which they approach the collective bargaining session. The table pounding, rowdy negotiating techniques of old have been replaced by rational discussions centering on factual matters. Success at the bargaining table depends on the efforts of advance preparation, the skill of the negotiators, and the bargaining strategies and tactics used.

Preparation for Bargaining

Bargaining can be viewed as a cyclical, never-ending process. Some parties begin preparing for the next collective bargaining session as soon as a contract is signed. Others start several months to a year before the current contract expires.

Regardless of the time period allotted to this prenegotiation process, adequate preparation is necessary to minimize the occurrence of errors at the bargaining table. If mistakes are made by either unions or employers both parties will have to live with the consequences for the duration of the contract period.

When preparing for negotiations, both unions and employers attempt to anticipate the demands of the other party. Bargaining usually results in a give-and-take situation where both parties make concessions in order to achieve their objectives. The successful anticipation of the other party's requests enables unions and employers to make adequate counterproposals. This preparation should include the items desired, the discussion items necessary to avoid a strike, and those items deemed unacceptable for discussion.[2]

What to Prepare

The preparation process can be broken down into three major areas. These include:

1. Gathering information.
2. Choosing the negotiating team.
3. Mapping the strategy and tactics to be used.

Gathering information

Employers and unions draw on various sources of information. Of major interest to both sides is data concerning economics, problems encountered with administering previous contract clauses, and general demographics of the workforce. This data is usually gathered both from within the particular organization and from information available concerning negotiations which have taken place between unions and other companies.[3]

Economics Both unions and employers typically accumulate economic data. A crucial subject at any negotiation session is wages. Unions and employers alike must keep abreast of the predominant wage rate being paid in similar industries within the particular company's geographic region. It is usually fruitless for unions to attempt to get large wage increases in companies with decreased sales or in businesses located in areas where the overall wage rate is low. Similarly, employers who are not versed in current wage data and the cost of various benefit programs may find themselves competitively at an economic disadvantage.

Information concerning economics is available from several sources. Government publications, including those distributed by the Bureau of Labor Statistics, national publications, and wage surveys completed by the local Chamber of Commerce and manufacturing associations are invaluable sources of data. In addition, companies can accumulate information by conducting their own wage surveys among local businesses.

Past contract administration Most negotiating teams maintain a copy of the current agreement and previous contracts in a **clause book.** This ledger is usually arranged in loose-leaf fashion, with a separate page allotted for each contract clause. Along with the contract provisions are statements detailing the difficulties or ease experienced in administering the provision. This document serves as a basis for discussing ways by which the agreement can be modified to alleviate problems.

Clause book

A clause book is a ledger, usually arranged in loose-leaf fashion, in which each previous labor contract clause, and the experiences in its administration, is recorded.

The information contained in a clause book is amassed from several sources. The results of past grievances, arbitration awards, and other formal procedures provide information about which clauses have been difficult to administer. Furthermore, discussions with supervisors and managers regarding their experiences and recommendations produce invaluable information for determining bargaining objectives.

General workforce demographics Information concerning the composition of the workforce with regard to sex, race, age, years of employment, and job classification are necessary in order to determine the costs associated with a new agreement. In addition, any data which is available concerning time lost because of layoffs, breaks, and other union activities impacts on the overall agreement.

Choosing the negotiating team

Both unions and employers use a team approach to select their negotiating representatives. The union team typically consists of business agents, shop stewards, the local union president, and any other individuals who may add strength to the union cause. The team from the employer usually consists of someone from the human resource or industrial relations departments, an executive with company-wide knowledge, a labor attorney, and an individual with expertise in economics.

Two factors are of paramount importance in determining who should serve on the bargaining team. First and foremost is the knowledge and skill which the individuals possess. Individuals with a limited understanding of the issues involved and the manner in which bargaining takes place will weaken their side's bargaining position. On the other hand, people who have a good understanding of these factors will lend strength to the bargaining process.

The second factor which must be considered in choosing bargaining agents is individual temperament. Negotiating sessions can be stressful situations marked by long-lasting debates, strife, anxiety, tension, and uneasiness. Emotional people do not think well, and consequently they bargain poorly. In fact, to gain an advantage at bargaining, many tactitioners advocate the use of strategies designed to raise the emotional level of the opponents. Generally, people who are knowledgeable, verbal, hard to excite, and intuitive make good bargaining team members.[4]

Preparing strategy and tactics

The result of the collective bargaining session is an agreement which both parties must live with for an extended period of time. How successful either side is in obtaining its objectives depends largely on the strategies and tactics employed. Strategy involves the designing of an overall plan which includes the goals to be pursued at the bargaining table. Tactics are the specific techniques

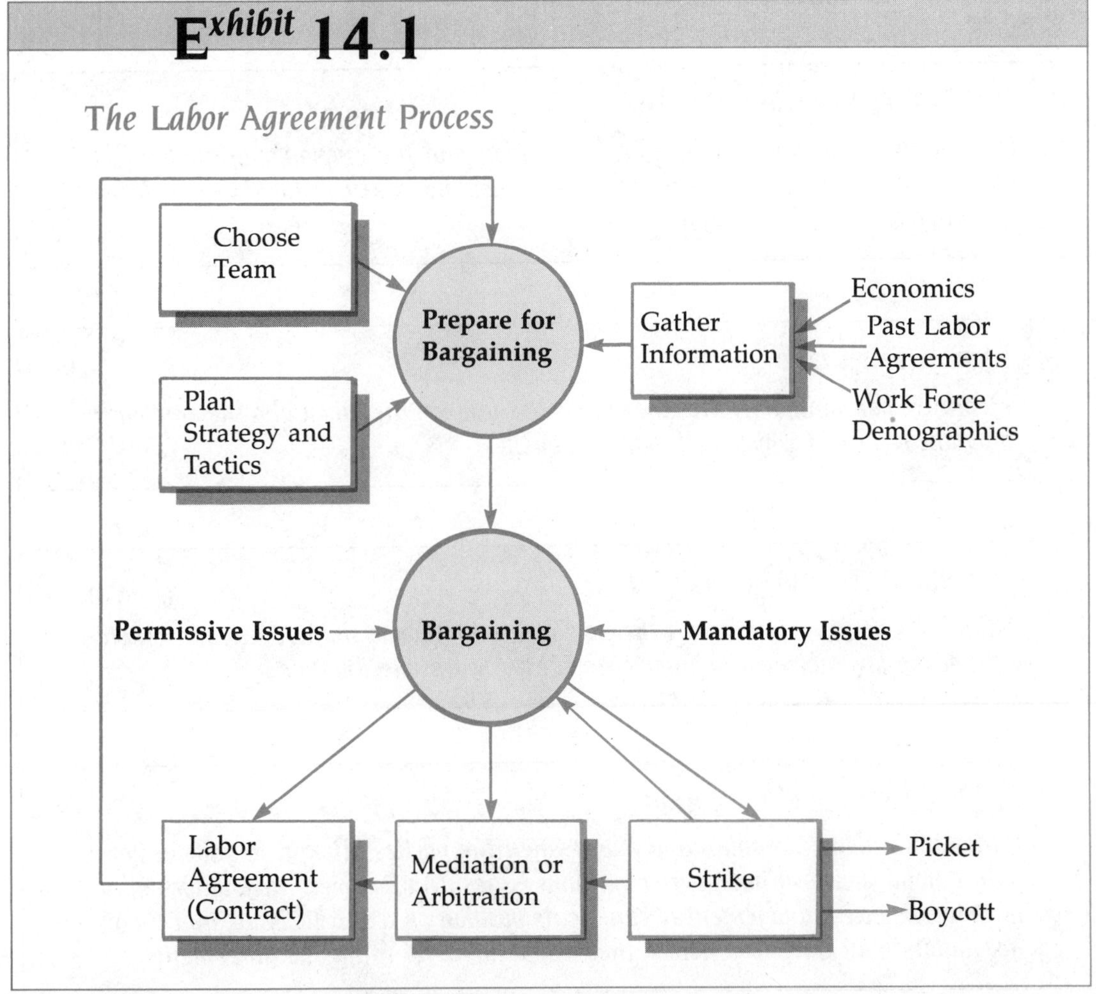

Exhibit 14.1

The Labor Agreement Process

and actions which will be undertaken to achieve the objectives. If unions have been less forceful in recent negotiations, especially the particular union in question, then employers may choose a strategy which relies on hard-line tactics. On the other hand, if unions have become more militant, the employer may decide to soften the bargaining strategy and the resulting tactics. Regardless of the strategy or tactics, however, negotiators must remember that most negotiations are conducted in an atmosphere of mutual respect and honesty.[5]

The strategies and tactics used by both unions and employers vary depending on the specific bargaining situation. In general, during negotiations four types of bargaining may occur which impact on the overall strategy and tactics selected for use. These are:

1. **Distributive bargaining.**
2. **Integrative bargaining.**
3. **Attitudinal structuring.**
4. **Intraorganizational bargaining.**[6]

Distributive bargaining

Distributive bargaining occurs when the union and the employer are in conflict over an issue and resolving the issue will cause one party to have a gain while the other party suffers a loss.

Integrative bargaining

Integrative bargaining involves the joint cooperation of the union and the employer to obtain results in which both parties benefit.

Attitudinal structuring bargaining

Attitudinal structuring involves the parties attempting to manipulate and create attitudes of favorableness or unfavorableness toward one another.

Intraorganizational bargaining

Intraorganizational bargaining develops when the parties attempt to gain uniformity among their own members regarding issues. Management negotiators may have to convince management to change its position on a specific issue, and union negotiators may have to convince their constituents to ratify the agreement.

Of all the available tactics which have been used, none has received more attention than the tactic used by General Electric during the 1960s. Named after Lemuel Boulware, who was GE's vice president of public and employee relations, this tactic, called **Boulwarism,** involves the development by management of a final offer early in the negotiations and their subsequent refusal to vary from it.

Boulwarism was first used as a tactic following an attitude survey which GE administered to a sample of workers. Based on the results of the questionnaires, a bargaining plan was developed and presented to the union. By using this tactic, GE had its proposal accepted by the IBEW (International Brotherhood of Electrical Workers). Union leaders subsequently filed unfair labor charges on the grounds that Boulwarism constituted a refusal to bargain. Ruling on behalf of the union, the NLRB substantiated the claim by the union that Boulwarism demonstrated a failure on the part of management to bargain in good faith.[7] GE appealed the decision and won in the lower courts, but it was subsequently informed by the Supreme Court that it had to permit the union to obtain benefits and save face with its membership.

Boulwarism

Boulwarism is the practice by management of presenting a final offer early in the negotiation process and then refusing to vary from the offer.

Today, Boulwarism does not have the impact it once had. Unions have become stronger and better prepared to deal with this tactic. The use of Boulwarism now results in long, costly negotiations during which gains usually cannot be made. Furthermore, because the Supreme Court upheld the NLRB ruling, even General Electric, the founder of the technique, has suspended its use.

The Subject Matter of Bargaining

The Taft–Hartley Act of 1947 delineates three distinct categories of issues which constitute the subject matter of bargaining. These are: mandatory issues, permissive or voluntary issues, and prohibited or illegal issues.

Mandatory Issues

Employers and unions must meet for the purpose of discussing wages, hours, and employment conditions. Topics relating to these factors are classified as **mandatory issues.** Examples of these items include bargaining issues concerning: salary and wage rates, paid holidays, paid sick days, agency shop clauses, and grievance procedures. To ascertain whether or not an item is mandatory requires that a determination be made as to how quickly and directly the union members' jobs will be affected. Those issues which impact on the nature of the workers' jobs or the compensation for the work are mandatory and must be included in collective bargaining if either side wishes to negotiate them. Thus, a proposal to close or relocate a plant or plans to subcontract work would qualify as mandatory issues.

> **Mandatory bargaining issues**
>
> *Mandatory bargaining issues are those items for which the law requires employers and unions to collectively bargain in good faith. They include all issues related to wages, hours, and conditions of work.*

Permissive or Voluntary Issues

Permissive or voluntary issues may be discussed if both parties agree to do so, but it is not required by law. Usually, these issues are the subject of bargaining when the items brought to the table are of mutual interest to the union and the employer. Examples of permissive items include: company pricing policies, union label agreements, and product design. It is important to note, at this point, that employers and unions cannot refuse to reach an agreement on a contract because of a permissive or voluntary issue.

> **Permissive or voluntary bargaining issues**
>
> *Permissive or voluntary issues are those items raised for bargaining which neither party is obligated by law to consider.*

Prohibited or Illegal Issues

Prohibited or illegal issues are those issues which are outlawed statutorily. Closed shop agreements, featherbedding, hot-cargo agreements, and discussion of union or agency shops in right-to-work states are all examples of prohibited or illegal items. Employers and unions are prohibited from collectively bargaining on these issues.

> **Prohibited or illegal bargaining issues**
>
> *Prohibited or illegal issues are those items for which employers and unions are forbidden to collectively bargain.*

Exhibit 14.2

Examples of Mandatory, Permissive, and Illegal Bargaining Issues[8]

Mandatory bargaining issues	Permissive bargaining issues	Illegal bargaining issues
Wages	Prices firms charge for products	Closed shop agreements
Benefits, such as insurance, vacation, time off	Fining of union members for crossing picket lines	Featherbedding
Overtime premiums	Determination of union voting rights	Union or agency shop clauses in right-to-work states
Stock options, pension plans, profit sharing	Pensions and benefit rights of retired personnel	Hot-cargo agreements
Grievance procedure	Supervisory compensation	Hiring clauses that violate Equal Employment Opportunity Laws
Superseniority for union officials	Supervisory discipline	
Management prerogative clauses	Safety rules	
Agency shop, union shop clauses		
No-strike clauses		
Workloads		
Subcontracting		
Job assignment transfers		
Layoffs and recalls		
Promotions and demotions		
Job posting		
Plant relocation and/or closings		

The heart of the collective bargaining process is negotiations concerning mandatory issues. Failure to reach agreement over these mandatory issues creates situations which lead to conflicts between employers and unions. When these situations become so severe that negotiations break down, both parties may resort to harsh methods. The ultimate union response is to strike; the ultimate employer response is a lockout.[9]

Strikes

In an effort to force employers to either return to the bargaining table or to concede to the union's demands, labor organizations may resort to a strike.

Strike

A strike is the stoppage of work by employees.

This frequently used union threat is undertaken after careful consideration of several factors. First, the legality of the strike is considered. During a legally executed strike, workers are protected from reprisals by employers. On the other hand, employers are free to dismiss, and on occasion take legal action against, workers engaged in illegal strikes.

Second, unions consider the willingness of the membership to endure the many hardships which may result from an extended strike. If workers are unable to maintain the strike effort, then the union's power is drastically reduced. Usually, union members will endorse a strike when they see the attainment of their needs being frustrated.[10]

Last, unions consider the ability of the employer to endure a strike. The effectiveness of strikes rests on the economic hardships which are imposed on employers. If the employer can continue to operate satisfactorily in the face of a strike, then the union's likelihood of gaining acceptance of its demands is minimized. One factor which greatly impacts the ability of employers to withstand a strike is the unemployment level existing in the company's geographic region. Consider the following case:

> The "Wee Tot" pajama company, which was located in a small southern town with an unemployment rate of 9.8 percent, was undergoing contract negotiations with the PSA (Pajama Stitchers of America). After much heated debate, a bargaining impasse occurred. The union struck the next morning. That afternoon, the Wee Tot company began advertising for replacements to work during the strike. As the new applicants began to arrive in droves, panic set in among the strikers. Dropping their picket signs, they began returning to their jobs. Shortly thereafter, the employees ousted the union.

The preceding case demonstrates how economic conditions contribute greatly to the impact of a strike. If employers can readily replace workers because of high unemployment, then the effect of the strike will be minimal. In fact, some employers even resort to a tactic called a **lockout** whereby they refuse to allow employees to work. If, on the other hand, employers cannot replace workers, the strike will have a greater impact.

Several types of strikes may occur. The differences among these strikes lie in the legality of the actions and the extent of protection afforded employees.

The Various Types of Strikes

Economic strike

An **economic strike** is a strike that is undertaken for the purpose of obtaining better wages, hours, or working conditions. During economic strikes, employers may hire permanent replacements. In the event that economic strikers have been permanently replaced, the NLRB cannot order their reinstatement as long as the permanent replacement remains in the job.

Unfair labor practice strike

An **unfair labor practice strike** involves a work stoppage designed to protest employer actions which have been determined to be in violation of the National Labor Relations Act. Examples of this type of strike are those protesting the employer's refusal to bargain collectively, its interference of organizing rights, and its denial of union recognition. Unlike economic strikes, workers engaged in unfair labor practice strikes have the right to immediate reinstatement of their position. Any replacements must be dismissed, and failure to do so is construed as a violation of the Labor Act.

Wildcat strike

A **wildcat strike** is a work stoppage instigated by a group of workers that is not sanctioned by the union. Workers who engage in wildcat strikes are unprotected by law and they may be discharged. In fact, unless there is a previous agreement of *nonsuability* between the employer and the union, the employer may sue the union for damages incurred as a result of a wildcat strike.

Jurisdictional strike

A **jurisdictional strike** is a work stoppage caused by a dispute between two or more unions over which group has the right to perform the work. These types of conflicts have been particularly prevalent in the building trades because many of the tasks involved in the different jobs overlap. Jurisdictional strikes are illegal under the Taft–Hartley Act.

Strikes are usually accompanied by other actions designed to publicize the union's plight while causing economic hardship on the employer. During strikes it is common practice to see union members **picketing** the employer.

Picketing

When picketing, union members walk around the employer's place of business, usually carrying printed signs, in the hopes of stopping others from entering the organization.

It is important to note that picketing is used for different purposes. Sometimes picketing is used to gain recognition as the employees' bargaining representative, sometimes it is used to advertise a difference of opinion between the union and the employer, and on other occasions it is used to persuade the public to buy products elsewhere. Picketing is a legal activity, but any violence accompanying the picketing is illegal.

Another frequent tactic used by unions is a **boycott.**

> **Boycott**
>
> *A boycott is an abstention by union members and others from purchasing or using the products produced by an employer engaged in a dispute with a labor organization.*

Along with picketing and strikes, boycotts serve the purpose of causing economic hardship on employers in the hopes of driving them back to the bargaining table.

Strikes are usually harsh on employers and employees alike, with the average strike affecting 350 workers and lasting 35 days.[11] Economically, employers lose revenues and employees lose wages. Even more important, however, is the emotional strife which is generated by long-lasting work stoppages. Friends and relatives become permanently divided over ideological issues resulting from strikes. Some strikes involve violence, resulting in damage to people and property. Unfortunately, the inevitable division of a workforce because of a strike persists even after the parties eventually reach agreement.

In addition to adversely affecting employers and employees, strikes have negative impacts on the general public as well. In many cases they halt the delivery of vital goods and services, which ultimately impacts on the economy. In other instances, such as strikes levied against hospitals, the potential exists for dire consequences to occur. To reduce the trauma of strikes and to aid in reaching a contract settlement, the parties often turn to mediation or arbitration.

Mediation and Arbitration

Sometimes, employers and unions require assistance in order to reach final agreement. This assistance is available to the parties through either **mediation** or arbitration.

> **Mediation**
>
> *Mediation is a process in which a neutral third party provides recommendations and suggestions to aid the parties in voluntarily reaching an agreement.*

For mediators to be successful, they must gain the trust and respect of both the union and the employer. Because mediators have no power to enact a final remedy, they must convince the parties that they have the necessary expertise and that they will be fair and equitable in their proposed solutions. If desired, mediators may be obtained through the Federal Mediation and Conciliation Service of the United States.

Arbitration

Arbitration is a process in which a neutral third party or panel listens to both sides, evaluates the evidence, and makes binding recommendations on what should be included in the final contract.

The use of **arbitration** for solving contract impasses is infrequent, especially when compared to its use in resolving grievances (discussed later in this chapter). This is especially true of contract arbitration, which is frequently used in the public sector because public employees are legally prohibited from striking, and seldom, if ever, used in the private sector.[12] The reasons for contract arbitration's (sometimes referred to as *interest arbitration*) lack of use can be traced to several factors. First, the use of arbitrators creates delays and extra costs. Second, the arbitration process appears to have a chilling effect on negotiations, causing parties to delay in the hopes of obtaining a better deal through arbitration. Third, contract arbitrators appear to demonstrate inconsistency from case to case. Fourth, because the judgment rendered often involves "splitting the differences," contract arbitration appears to cause the parties to take extreme positions. Finally, contract arbitration appears to have a narcotic effect. This manifests itself in a greater reliance on contract arbitration rather than the negotiation process to solve differences.[13]

The Labor Agreement

The result of the collective bargaining process is a legal contract endorsed by both parties. Normally, these contracts are enacted for periods from one to five years. However, as with any other provisions, contract durations are subject to negotiations. Varying in length from a few pages to more than fifty pages, labor agreements include numerous provisions which impact on daily management–labor relations. Large organizations whose workforces have been unionized for some time tend to have extensive labor agreements. On the other hand, recently unionized companies with small numbers of bargaining unit members are likely to have relatively short contracts.

Typical Contract Provisions

In addition to length and duration, contracts differ regarding subject matter. The variation is easily understandable because of the legal stipulation allowing both parties to discuss any mutually agreeable permissive issues. These items tend to be based on the characteristics of the particular workplace and the individual needs of the parties involved. For example, workplaces where the jobs involve extremely hazardous conditions (such as coal mines) are more likely to have extra provisions covering safety, hours of work, and insurance benefits. On the other hand, teachers' unions are more likely to include clauses regarding professional development opportunities, class preparation time, and tenure.

Although there are variations among specific contract clauses, certain issues are included in all labor agreements. These may be classified into wage and economic issues and nonwage issues.

Wage and economic issues

Employee salaries, health benefits, and other economic supplements are the most difficult issues confronting negotiators. These mandatory issues center on establishing current wage scales, determining paid time off from work (holidays, sick days, vacations, and rest periods), and providing employee benefits (insurance and pension plans).

It is unlikely that any other bargaining issue generates as much discussion as wages. Not only must unions and management agree on a current wage rate but also they must build future wage increases into the contract. In order to arrive at a settlement, both parties must consider the comparative wage rates within the industry and the company's ability to pay them.

The determination of wage norms requires that employers and unions consider the wages paid to other unionized firms within the industry. Negotiators logically assume that the wages paid to bargaining unit members in one firm should be comparable to those paid to members doing the same work in another company. Unfortunately, this logic is flawed. Other factors, such as geographic location, supplemental benefit plans, and job content, may vary from company to company. These factors, coupled with the profitability of the particular firm, play a major role in determining wage scales. For example, it may seem logical to assume that all police officers have the same job, and consequently they should receive the same rate of pay. Realistically, however, the job duties vary greatly depending upon where the police officers are employed. Urban areas with greater percentages of violent crimes present different hazards than small rural communities. Unions representing the urban police officers would invariably attempt to procure higher wages based on the considerable risks involved.

An organization's ability to disburse wages must also be taken into account. Historically, unions reasoned that profits were a direct result of employee contributions. Organizations experiencing large profits can and should be generous in dispensing wage increases to workers. Other firms with only modest profitability can only grant modest increases. Realistically, however, profit is only one factor in determining an organization's ability to pay.[14]

The use of profit as the sole determinant of an organization's ability to pay overlooks several important factors. First, consideration must be given to whether the company is labor or capital intensive. Those organizations which are highly capital intensive can afford larger raises during profitable times because labor is a small part of their overall productivity costs. A labor-intensive firm, however, could find itself severely jeopardized in the future if wages were overextended. Second, the success of an organization depends on its appropriate use of profits. Without a return on investments, stockholders will cease to invest in the firm. If the firm does not retain some earnings, it will find itself facing future disaster in the event of a recession. Finally, depending upon the industry, firms may need to divert larger amounts of profit into research and development in order to remain competitive. In industries such as those involving high technology, diverting money away from research and development is likely to be detrimental to the company in the long term.

It is important to note, at this point, that unions also consider other factors, aside from profit, when negotiating wages. When the United Auto Workers (UAW) was negotiating with Ford Motor Company during the early 1980s, company profits were not the union's sole concern. During the early 1980s, Ford's profits were exceptionally high. In fact, proportionately, Ford's profits exceeded those of the other major companies within the auto industry. If the UAW had attempted to extract large wage concessions from Ford, negotiations with the rest of the industry, which did not have similar profits, would have been a nightmare. Union representatives would not have had an adequate explanation for GM's workers, who were doing the same work in the same geographic region (Detroit, Michigan) for substantially less money! In order to avoid this problem and to develop a pattern of bargaining, the UAW adopted a bargaining strategy called **pattern bargaining** which enabled them to obtain a reasonable settlement across the industry.[15]

> **Pattern bargaining**
>
> ***Pattern bargaining occurs when a union which represents the majority of workers in a particular industry attempts to establish a contract model through negotiations with a target company.***

Nonwage issues

Nonwage issues can be divided into several basic categories. These are issues dealing with managerial prerogatives, clauses which constitute union security items, provisions regarding personnel, and matters concerning the work environment.

Managerial prerogatives Prior to the existence of unions, or in shops where contractual arrangements did not exist, managers were free to run their operations as they saw fit. Today, many employers still adhere to this *reserved rights doctrine,* which maintains that management can exercise its own discretion in dealing with issues not specifically covered in the contract.

Unfortunately, particularly for management, the reserved rights doctrine cannot be applied universally because of three factors. First, there are legal obligations to negotiate mandatory items. Second, arbitrators' decisions often conflict with management interpretations of contract language. Last, the tendency by some arbitrators, management, and union officials to view the contract as a living document causes them to view the labor agreement in flexible terms.[16]

In an attempt to overcome the problems associated with reliance on the reserved rights doctrine, employers usually negotiate either long or short **managerial prerogatives clauses.** In its short form, the clause is an all-encompassing statement allowing management the right to operate its business in all affairs otherwise not governed by the contract. This blanket provision, preferred by many employers, sometimes causes an excessive amount of grievances to be filed. Arbitrators must then determine whether the action taken is in the realm of managerial prerogative, or is covered by the contract.

Managerial prerogative clauses

Managerial prerogative clauses are negotiated provisions giving management the right to exercise their discretion in dealing with any work situation not specifically enumerated in the contract.

In order to avoid needless and costly grievances, employers have leaned toward the negotiation of long-term managerial prerogative clauses. Basically, the long form includes an all-encompassing statement and an enumerated list of the specific rights reserved. Even in the long form, however, incidents occur which are not included, necessitating arbitration.

Union security **Union security clauses** are negotiated contract provisions which strengthen the union by making it easier to enroll and retain members. The most common forms of union security provisions include the negotiation of shop clauses and dues checkoff.

Shop clauses were discussed in the previous chapter and include contract provisions calling for either union shop or agency shop environments. A **dues checkoff** clause allows union members to have dues withdrawn from their paychecks and forwarded directly to the union. Although a dues checkoff is not strictly a security clause in the sense that it enrolls or retains members, it does allow the union to have an uninterrupted cash flow. If this provision did not exist, unions would be spending excessive amounts of resources attempting to individually collect dues from their memberships.

Exhibit 14.3

A Managerial Prerogative Clause

Section 2—Management Function It is herewith recognized that all management functions shall be retained by the company. These functions include, but are not limited to, the full, complete, and exclusive control of direction of the workforce, scheduling of production, operation of the plant, acquisition of materials, production of products, the location of such production, and the methods of sale and distribution of its products; the right to change or establish job classifications and descriptions; the right to introduce new or improved procedures; the right to abolish any job or department; the right to make and enforce reasonable shop rules; and the right to hire, fire, suspend, train, discipline, discharge, advance, transfer, lay off, and recall employees. These rights shall all be the function of management unless expressly stated otherwise within this agreement.

Source: Union contract.

Dues checkoff

Dues checkoff is a process in which the employer withholds union dues from employees' paychecks and forwards the money directly to the union.

Personnel This general category includes all negotiated contract clauses that impact directly on employees. Examples of items which may be covered in the contract include:

- **Job Security**—Clauses which protect the individual employee's job.
- **Subcontracting**—The manner in which work is delegated outside the company.
- **Promotions and Transfers**—The methods by which new job opportunities are announced and the methods for selecting employees for promotions or transfers.
- **Seniority**—The methods for determining seniority and layoffs.
- **Training and Development**—The selection and development of trainees to be involved in developmental programs.
- **Work Scheduling**—How shifts are determined and how overtime is assigned.

Exhibit 14.4

Example of a Dues Checkoff Contract Clause

Section 8—Dues Checkoff The company agrees to deduct from the pay of all union members the regular union dues payable by the employee and remit same promptly to the Union. Such deductions shall be made twice monthly, on the regular payday. The Union agrees to furnish the company with proper checkoff authorization cards duly signed by the employee, authorizing said deductions. The wording of the dues deduction shall be as follows: I __________ , the undersigned employee of Company ABC, having become a member in good standing of XYZ Union, hereby authorize ABC Company to deduct from my wages twice monthly my regular dues, until such time as I may revoke, in writing, this authorization.

Source: Union contract.

The work environment The predominant issues negotiated in this category are concerned with how technology and health and safety have impacted on workers.

During recent years, technological advances and changes have caused unions to take a hard look at the security of their workers. Increasing technology may enable workers to be removed from hazardous, unnecessary repetitive environments and to be placed into safer, more productive jobs. On the other hand, as a result of their lack of training in the new technology, employees can be removed from the employment situation entirely. The first instance is viewed as a blessing by managers, union officials, and workers alike. The second case is obviously construed as a threat to worker and union security. In environments where jobs are at risk, there is a strong tendency to negotiate clauses which will protect rank and file members through seniority rules, compensation clauses, or control over the times during which technological change is scheduled.

Health and safety provisions are frequently found in labor agreements. Most of the provisions are a direct result or extensions of the legislation imposed by the Occupational Safety and Health Act (OSHA).

The predominant issues raised recently under safety and health provisions are concerned with the rights of employees to refuse to work under hazardous conditions, to examine on-the-job medical records, and to know the toxic nature of substances to which they are exposed. These issues, among others, have caused unions to take a strong position on negotiating general statements of safety and health responsibility and, in some instances, establishing specific guidelines.

Administering the Contract

After the collective bargaining process has been completed, both the union and the employer are bound by the contract provisions for the duration of the agreement. This period is characterized by various interpretations of contract clauses on which the parties usually differ. The true test of a labor agreement is not determined by the negotiation process, but rather by the ways in which the parties handle the inevitable disagreements which occur. In fact, contract administration consists primarily of settling the various grievances which arise during the span of the contract.

Grievances

In the broadest sense of the term, **grievances** include any complaint, concern, or gripe which employees have against the employer, or which the employer has against the labor organization. In accordance with this definition, the only charge excluded from consideration would be one whose resolution requires the alteration of an existing contract provision. A more narrow definition of grievances, applied more universally, restricts grievances to employee complaints which are specifically related to contract provisions.

> **Grievances**
>
> ***Grievances are employee complaints or concerns about alleged violations of a contract provision which are submitted for resolution through a formally established procedure.***

The preceding definition is limited in scope, implying that grievances are formally defined and handled through provisions established during the collective bargaining process. What constitutes a grievance, and how grievances are resolved, are issues which unions and employers negotiate. Consequently, any concerns employees have regarding items not covered by the contract or items specifically excluded from the grievance procedure constitute complaints, not grievances.

Causes of Grievances

Employees file grievances for various reasons. Regardless of the specific cause, however, all grievances have the underlying purpose of serving the specific interests of the complainant. For the sake of convenience, grievances can be classified into three categories, defined by the cause and type of self-interest they serve. These are:

1. Those caused by misunderstanding.
2. Those generated by intentional contract violations.
3. Those which are symptomatic of problems not specifically related to contract provisions.[17]

Misunderstanding

When contract negotiations occur, both parties are concerned with obtaining agreement on significant issues. Rarely, if ever, do negotiators slave over each word in the agreement, particularly in dealing with clauses which have generated little or no controversy in the past. In addition, some contracts are written with a degree of legalese which may be fully understood by the negotiating teams, but is foreign to the average employee and supervisor. These factors all contribute to interpretation problems on the part of the constituents. Unclear and ambiguously written contracts consistently generate excessive amounts of grievances.

Even well-written contracts produce grievances if the parties fail to read them. Supervisors and workers are not rewarded for contract administration or grievance prevention. Rather, both are rewarded for effective productivity. Employees tend to rely on their stewards for contract administration, and supervisors depend on human resource personnel. Consequently, contracts are ignored by those who are most directly affected by them. The end result is the filing of needless and avoidable grievances.

Intentional contract violations

The negotiation and signing of a contract do not automatically guarantee that both parties will abide by its provisions. Untrained, unskilled, or incompetent managers and supervisors constantly demonstrate poor management skills. Unfortunately, these violations of contract provisions are sometimes minor infractions compared to some of the other atrocities committed. Poor supervisors or managers ignore contract provisions, assuming that their knowledge of how to deal with particular problems is superior to any negotiated provision. Furthermore, they violate clauses on purpose, doing just what they wish, under the assumption that workers will allow the inappropriate behavior to slip by. When these infractions occur, grievances are commonplace.

Intentional contract violations are not only the result of poor management. Sometimes, the violation of a specific contract clause is viewed by management as economically necessary for the company and of insignificant substantive importance to workers. In fact, many companies justify these violations as being the result of negotiations that were conducted years earlier without full knowledge of future conditions. They rationalize that if current facts had been known in the past, even the union would have negotiated a different agreement.

Symptomatic grievances

In many instances, the grievance presented does not represent the true problem. Rather, the grievance is the surface indication of another concern. These symptomatic grievances stem from employees' personal problems, union politics and showmanship, or problems inherent in the contract language.

A wide array of personal problems cause employees to file grievances. Most of these grievances are a direct result of employee frustration. Medical problems, family difficulties, job dissatisfaction, boredom, and ostracism by the work group are only a few of the underlying reasons behind employee gripes. In most of these instances, the complaint itself is merely a manifestation of the true problem.

Grievances filed because of union politics are difficult for supervisors to understand. Unions, like other organizations, have their own internal politics. The winning of a local office by one political faction within the union may cause the opposing side to file grievances which cannot be won. This has the effect of discrediting the newly elected leadership in the eyes of the employees.

Some employers claim that a large amount of grievances are caused by union showmanship. In an attempt to demonstrate to their members the necessity of union affiliation, unions periodically flex their muscles. As with any other service, people begin to question the value of unions when they consistently pay dues, but see no tangible action. For example, people who rarely have to claim insurance benefits periodically question the premium payments. When they have an accident, however, they remark about how glad they are that they have insurance. Similarly, when workers pay dues monthly without seeing concrete evidence of union activity, they begin to question the union's merit. Filing grievances is a concrete way to continuously remind its membership of the union's significance in the workplace.

The final underlying cause of grievances is contract language. As mentioned previously, one of the major considerations in negotiating new contract clauses is the types of experiences previously encountered in administering the past contract. A favorite bargaining tactic of unions is to file an excessive amount of grievances highlighting a specific issue in the hopes of gaining a bargaining advantage. Clever employers will recognize these grievances for what they are and negotiate their resolution at the bargaining table, not at the grievance hearings.

The Grievance Procedure

Most labor agreements specify a formal grievance procedure.[18] In some organizations, the grievance procedure involves as many as eight or nine steps, while in others it may consist of only one. Regardless of the number of stages involved, the goals of all grievance procedures are to resolve the grievance as swiftly and as efficiently as possible, and to insure employee protection against arbitrary management action.[19]

The following grievance procedure is representative of those found in most labor agreements.

Step 1 The first step in most grievance procedures involves the aggrieved employee attempting to adjust the matter with his or her immediate supervisor. In some contracts the employee confronts the supervisor directly, while in other agreements the grievance is presented by the job steward. In either case, if the grievance is not settled to the satisfaction of the employee within a specified time period, the employee proceeds to have the grievance adjusted by the next level supervisor on the organizational hierarchy.

Step 2 About 75 percent of grievances are settled after Step 1.[20] If the grievance has not been adjusted to the satisfaction of the employee, if the union is not satisfied, or if the employee claims that an unfair labor practice has been committed by the employer, the grievance is set forth in writing. This written statement is usually submitted within a specified time period either to the plant's industrial relations manager or to another designated individual (usually the department manager). Upon receipt of the written complaint, the industrial relations manager typically schedules a hearing for the employee. At the conclusion of this hearing, a written decision regarding the grievance is issued.

Step 3 If the actions undertaken during Step 2 still fail to satisfy the employee or the union, the grievance is presented to the company president. The previously filed written grievance is submitted within a specified time period and the president renders a written decision within a specified time frame.

Step 4 If the grievance appealed to the company president is concerned with the commission of an unfair labor practice or if the grievance raises a question regarding the meaning of a contract provision and the union and employer cannot adjust the matter to their mutual satisfaction, the grievance may be presented for arbitration by either party. Arbitration involves the introduction of a neutral third party to hear the case and make a ruling.

Grievance Arbitration

The vast majority of grievances are solved through the first three stages of the grievance procedure. Sometimes there are some grievances which, for one reason or another, cannot be solved in this manner. This usually occurs when there is a difference as to the meaning of the contract language and each of the parties involved believes that its position is correct. In addition, failure to reach satisfaction occurs when there is disagreement as to the facts of the case. When this state of affairs exists, Step 4 is enacted, and the grievance is submitted to arbitration.

Unlike contract arbitration (discussed earlier), grievance arbitration is common (about 90 to 95 percent of all labor agreements seem to have provisions for this form of arbitration). Contracts stipulate the processes which determine how the disputes go to arbitration and the procedures involved in selecting arbitrators.

Selecting arbitrators

The choice of arbitrators initially involves making a decision about the type of arbitration hearing to be used. Some hearings rely on a single impartial arbitrator who hears the facts of the case and renders a decision. Other hearings utilize a tripartite board consisting of company and union representatives and a neutral chairperson.

The procedures by which arbitrators are chosen are usually stated in the labor agreement. Some organizations, particularly those in which long-term bargaining relationships have existed, use permanent arbitrators. These permanent arbitrators remain in their position until one of the parties feels that their performance is unsatisfactory.

The advantage of using permanent arbitrators rests in the fact that they are familiar with both the labor agreement and the parties involved. On the other hand, permanent arbitrators may have a tendency to split awards over time. However, the permanence of these arbitrators is, at best, tenuous. Most permanent arbitrators are highly vulnerable in situations where militant unions which bring large amounts of nuisance grievances are present. In these situations, arbitrators are likely to frequently rule for management, causing the union to rate their performance as unsatisfactory.[21]

A more frequently used method of selecting arbitrators is to use the ad hoc method. Using this procedure, arbitrators are appointed on a case by case method, with neither party being obligated to use the arbitrator for future cases. Generally, these referees are selected from lists of arbitrators supplied by either party or from organizations such as the American Arbitration Association and the Federal Mediation and Conciliation Service. The umpires on these lists are either attorneys who work primarily as labor arbitrators or other professionals, such as academics who teach labor law, labor relations, human resource management, and labor economics.

The arbitration process

In many respects the process of arbitration is similar to a liberally conducted court case. Arbitrators have the prerogative either to rule on written evidence or to conduct an actual hearing. If the arbitrator decides it is necessary to hear witnesses and examine evidence, an actual presentation of facts takes place.

Both the union and the employer are represented by parties that they choose. Attorneys do not have to be employed, and in fact, they are rarely used in cases involving small companies. Rather, the case presentation is usually handled by local union officials and industrial relations or human resource personnel.

Barring discipline and discharge cases, the union assumes the role of the plaintiff. In this capacity, the union has the responsibility to present evidence, including calling witnesses, to prove its contentions. Upon the conclusion of the union's case, the employer presents its arguments in a similar manner. Both parties have the option of objecting to evidence, cross-examining witnesses, and, should they choose, presenting closing arguments. Following the hearing, additional material in the form of briefs may be submitted as additional support.[22]

The Arbitration Award

The preparation of **arbitration awards** requires arbitrators to consider several factors. Initially, decisions are made on the basis of whether or not the grievance truly involves a breach in the contract. In many instances, the determination of this factor relies on the arbitrator's interpretation of the contract language. As mentioned earlier, most labor agreements include provisions which define true grievances. If the arbitrator determines that the particular grievance filed does not entail a violation of the contract, then the hearing may be terminated.

> **Arbitration award**
>
> *The award represents the arbitrator's decision in the case and includes: a summation of the evidence presented, the rationale underlying the arbitrator's decision, and, if necessary, the action required to correct any injustices.*

As soon as the grievance is judged arbitrable, the arbitrator examines the evidence. In deciding the award, major consideration is given to the legitimacy of the employer's actions against the grievant and whether or not the employee was accorded "due process" under the terms of the contract. Most labor agreements stipulate that employers must have "just cause" for any disciplinary or punitive action taken against employees. In order for the employer to prevail, the evidence must demonstrate that the actions taken were indeed justified.

If the arbitrator finds that due process was accorded the employee and the employer's actions were justifiable, an award is usually made. Arbitrators have wide latitude in determining penalties (non-punitive), and unlike courts, they are not bound to rule or assess penalties based on past precedents. Each case is unique, and therefore judged solely on its own merits. Penalties imposed by arbitrators may vary in leniency and stringency from case to case. This incongruence is evident in cases which are similar in nature.

Most awards are adhered to by both parties. In fact, most labor agreements state that the decision of arbitrators is final and binding on the parties. If, however, either party still feels that it was treated unjustly, it is free to seek legal action through the court system. This course of action is rarely taken, and the courts are generally reluctant to overturn arbitration rulings. The one exception to this rule is when the arbitrator's pronouncement is clearly a decision based on his or her concept of industrial justice, rather than on a strict interpretation of the labor agreement.

Criticisms of Arbitration

There are two major criticisms of the arbitration process. First, arbitration has been cited as being unduly costly. Second, the time lag involved between the filing of a grievance and the eventual issuance of an award is usually excessive.

Cost involved

Arbitration can be an expensive procedure. Arbitrators' per diem fees range from a daily norm of about $300 to in excess of $600 for special cases. These fees, which are usually shared by employers and unions, along with the travel expenses and study time of the arbitrator (paid on a daily fee basis), attorneys' fees (which typically exceed the fees paid to the arbitrator), wages paid to employee witnesses, and the costs associated with lost productivity during the arbitration hearings all contribute to making the arbitration process an expensive proposition.

In addition to the usual expenses associated with arbitration, unions and employers tend to substantially increase the costs by other actions. They insist that arbitrators spend time reviewing unnecessary materials and that they hear testimonies from witnesses who lend no credible bearing to the case. Furthermore, they have a tendency to expend needless dollars on excessive frills, such as lavish hotel suites, in an attempt to use a neutral arbitration site. Unfortunately, these actions serve to increase the costs associated with arbitration without materially affecting the ultimate quality of the decision.[23]

Time lag

Aside from the excessive costs involved in the arbitration process, the time involved from the filing of the grievance to the ultimate presentation of the award is, on the average, between 200 and 263 days.[24] For the most part, these delays are caused by the backlog of cases which the relatively limited supply of experienced and popular arbitrators have on their calendars, as well as the excessive amount of evidence presented by both unions and management that requires review.

Expedited or Mini Arbitration

In an attempt to reduce the costs and time element associated with arbitration, some employers and unions use **expedited or mini arbitration procedures.** These methods, which were first used by the steel industry in the early 1970s, involve the use of relatively inexperienced arbitrators who are chosen from lists and who serve on a rotating basis. All arbitration hearings are scheduled within ten days after they are requested, and the award must be made within forty-eight hours after the hearing. Rather than using expensive professionals and inundating the arbitrators with needless materials, cases are presented by local union representatives and management personnel, and they are prohibited from using transcripts and briefs.

Expedited arbitration

Expedited arbitration involves the use of inexperienced arbitrators who hear grievances within ten days after their filing and provide the parties with short, precise awards within forty-eight hours of the hearing.

Expedited arbitration is obviously not a panacea. Using inexperienced arbitrators limits the grievances presented through this process to those complaints which are simple and routine in nature. Cases of greater complexity, which represent significant meaning to the parties, are still reserved for the standard arbitration process and experienced arbitrators. Expedited arbitration does, however, serve to reduce costs and time delays. More importantly, it serves as a needed training ground for new and inexperienced arbitrators.

A *Final* Note

It would be unfair to leave this section with the impression that arbitration has more negative than positive facets. In fact, one of the major criticisms of arbitration, cost, is one of its major benefits. Without arbitration, there would probably be many more strikes and court-litigated cases. The amount of expense involved in these procedures, coupled with the negative impacts which strikes have on society, make arbitration a most viable alternative to solving grievances.

Summary

Collective bargaining involves an attempt by unions and employers to negotiate a mutually acceptable labor agreement. This process is conducted by teams of negotiators who spend considerable resources preparing information and developing strategies and tactics.

The bargaining sessions are characterized by individual parties attempting to obtain advantageous contract provisions for their constituents. Negotiable items include wages, hours, and working conditions (mandatory issues), and they may also include other mutually agreeable topics (permissive issues). Under no circumstances may any discussion occur regarding those items which have been outlawed statutorily (illegal issues).

Collective bargaining sessions culminate with both parties ratifying the labor agreement. Thereafter, the attention of employers and unions is focused on the administration of the contract. This period is characterized by differing interpretations of contract clauses which are brought to the forefront through the filing of grievances by employees.

Most labor agreements have negotiated provisions for handling grievances. Although these procedures vary from organization to organization, they all include arbitration as the final resolution stage. This process involves the presentation of the grievance to a neutral third party who renders a decision. This decree, known as an award, is usually adhered to by both parties.

Key Terms to Identify

Collective bargaining
Clause book
Distributive bargaining
Integrative bargaining
Attitudinal structuring bargaining
Intraorganizational bargaining
Boulwarism
Mandatory issues
Permissive or voluntary issues
Prohibited or illegal issues
Lockout
Economic strike
Unfair labor practice strike
Wildcat strike
Jurisdictional strike
Picketing
Boycott
Mediation
Arbitration
Pattern bargaining
Managerial prerogatives clauses
Union security clauses
Dues checkoff
Grievances
Arbitration award
Expedited or mini arbitration procedures

Questions for Discussion

Do You Know the Facts?

1. What information do unions and employers attempt to gather in preparation for collective bargaining?
2. What strategy and tactics might bargaining teams employ during the negotiating sessions?
3. Discuss the different types of strikes in which unions engage.
4. What contract provisions are most likely to be found in the majority of labor agreements?
5. List the major reasons grievances are filed.
6. All grievances eventually culminate in arbitration. Discuss the arbitration process, including the selection of arbitrators and the award.

Can You Apply the Information Learned?

1. Discuss how you would continually collect data for use in collective bargaining.
2. If you were involved in negotiations with a hostile union, what strategy and tactics might you employ? Why?

3. How would you deal with a union that wanted to negotiate permissive items for which your company was uninterested in negotiating?
4. What actions would you take to halt the filing of grievances that were initiated because of internal union politics?

It Certainly Was Different

Jesse Storm sat at the conference table mulling over the past month's events. "This year certainly was different," he thought. "They didn't stick us between a rock and a hard place, or did they?"

It all started fifteen years ago when Jesse had just been hired by Magellan Poultry Plant as the Industrial Relations Coordinator. Magellan had had a long history of labor strife and had recently undergone a long and costly organizing campaign with the local poultry worker's union. In the end, the union had prevailed and a contract had been negotiated. Jesse, an industrial relations major, was hired into the personnel department immediately after the contract had been signed.

The initial contract term was for a period of three years. As the time for new contract negotiations neared, Jesse received a telephone call from Frank Bando, Magellan's president and CEO. During the conversation Frank instructed Jesse to make a bargain with the union as quickly as possible. "Give them what they want, as long as it doesn't cost me much money," Frank had said. "We spent enough money on the campaign, and we can't afford long, drawn out contract negotiations." Reluctantly, Jesse negotiated a quick deal that extended the union security items, but minimized the immediate economic impact on the company.

Subsequent negotiation sessions were no different. Prior to every negotiation session Jesse received a call from Frank instructing him to "bargain gently." Jesse felt that each succeeding contract was strengthening the union's position in the company while weakening the authority of management. If the present trend continued, Jesse felt certain that the employees and the company would eventually suffer.

However, the state of affairs did change. Two years into the present contract, Magellan was bought out by a large, non-unionized firm. The new owners had a totally different philosophy regarding how to negotiate. Jesse was instructed to take a "hard stand" on permissive issues and to "soften up" on the economic issues.

Jesse bargained hard. He conceded on economic conditions, but refused to grant the union's requests that workers be prohibited from withdrawing from the union except during a two-week period in March, and he challenged the shop steward's super-seniority clause. The union countered by claiming that the working conditions at the plant were abominable and that the company's tactics were designed purely to "bust" the union. Neither side would give in. Finally, two weeks before Thanksgiving, the union struck the plant!

This year it certainly was different.

Questions for Discussion

1. What is your opinion of Frank's approach to negotiations? Do you think it is typical or atypical of most company approaches?
2. Do you think the new owner's negotiation approach was designed to bust the union?
3. What do you think the eventual outcome of the strike will be?

Endnotes and References

1 *The Labor Management Relations Act of 1947* (Taft–Hartley), June 23, 1947, 61 Stat. 136, as amended by Act of September 14, 1959, 73 Stat. 519. Section 8, paragraph 7(d).

2 Reed C. Richardon, "Positive Collective Bargaining," in *ASPA Handbook of Personnel and Industrial Relations*, edited by Dale Yoder and Herbert G. H. Heneman, Jr. (Washington, D.C.: Bureau of National Affairs, 1979): 7/115–7/130.

3 Some negotiators, in preparation for negotiations, have been known to read union national convention minutes. See Ronald L. Miller, "Preparations for Negotiations," *Personnel Journal*, Vol. 57 (January 1978): 36–39, 44.

4 Collective bargaining sessions are influenced by many variables. For a discussion of these variables, see George E. Constantino, Jr. "The Negotiator in Collective Bargaining," *Personnel Journal*, Vol. 54 (August 1975): 445–447.

5 Paul Diesing, "Bargaining Strategy and Union–Management Relationships," *Journal of Conflict Resolution*, Vol. 5 (December 1961): 369–378.

6 Richard E. Walton and Robert B. McKersie, *A Behavioral Theory of Labor Negotiations* (New York: McGraw-Hill, 1965).

7 Herbert R. Northrup, *Boulwarism* (Ann Arbor, MI: Bureau of Industrial Relations, University of Michigan, 1964).

8 For further understanding of mandatory, permissive, and illegal bargaining issues, see Robert A. Gorman, *Basic Text on Labor Law Unionization and Collective Bargaining* (St. Paul, MN: West Publishing Company, 1976): 496–539.

9 An understanding of how to bargain successfully is required in order to avoid the negative consequences of bargaining. A good discussion on how to bargain successfully can be found in "Labor Contract Negotiations: Behind the Scenes, A Conversation Held with Fritz Ihrig," *Personnel Administrator*, Vol. 31 (April 1986): 55–56, 58–60.

10 Woodruff Imberman, "Who Strikes—And Why?" *Harvard Business Review*, Vol. 61 (November–December 1983): 18–28.

11 Richard B. Freeman and James L. Medoff, *What Do Unions Do?* (New York: Basic Books, 1984): Chapter 14.

12 Richard Johnson, "Interest Arbitration Examined," *Personnel Administrator*, Vol. 28 (January 1983): 54, 56–57.

13 William H. Holley and Kenneth M. Jennings, *The Labor Relations Process*, 3rd ed. (Chicago, IL: The Dryden Press, 1988): 246.

14 When profit is used, it is the variability of profitability, not the level, which affects strike activity. See Joseph S. Tracy, "An Investigation in the Determinants of U.S. Strike Activity," *The American Economic Review* (June 1986): 423–436.

15 Part of this discussion comes from remarks made by Ernest J. Savoie, Director Employee Development Office, Employee Relations Staff, Ford Motor Company, during guest lectures at James Madison University in November 1987. For more information on the concessions at Ford and other givebacks during the last decade, see Robert L. Simison, "Ford Workers Vote Concessions by Wide Margin," *The Wall Street Journal* (March 1, 1982): 3; and Leland B. Cross, Jr., "1982 and 1983: The Concession Bargaining Years," *Personnel Administrator*, Vol. 29 (November 1984): 27–32, 35.

16 William H. Holley and Kenneth M. Jennings, *op. cit.*, 394–395.

17 This discussion is based on the treatment in David A. Dilts and Clarence R. Deitsch, *Labor Relations* (New York: Macmillan Publishing Company, 1983): 223–231.

18 There are several purposes and types of grievance procedures. For discussion of these, see Alan Balfour, "Five Types of Non-Union Grievance Systems," *Personnel* Vol. 61 (March–April 1984): 69–76; and Dale Yoder and Paul D. Staudohar, "Auditing the Labor Relations Function," *Personnel*, Vol. 60 (May–June 1983): 36–43.

19 T. A. Kochan, *Collective Bargaining and Industrial Relations* (Homewood, IL: Richard D. Irwin, Inc., 1980).

20 Dan R. Dalton and William D. Todor, "Antecedents of Grievance Filing Behavior: Attitude/Behavioral Consistency and the Union Steward," *Academy of Management Journal*, Vol. 25, No. 1 (1982): 158–169.

21 Robben W. Fleming, *The Labor Arbitration Process* (Urbana, IL: University of Illinois Press, 1965): 219–220.

22 John A. Fossum, *Labor Relations*, 3rd ed. Plano, TX: Business Publications, Inc., 1985: 412–414.

23 Samuel H. Jaffee, "It's Your Money! Cutting the Costs of Labor Arbitration," *Arbitration Journal*, Vol. 26 (1971): 161–178.

24 "Labor Arbitration Seen in Need of Improvement," *Daily Labor Report* (May 14, 1983): 1; and John Zalusky, "Arbitration: Updating a Vital Process," *American Federationist*, Vol. 83 (November 1976): 6.

Part 6

Effective Utilization of Human Resources

Chapter 15

Motivation of Employees

Objectives

After reading this chapter you should understand:

1. The motivational process.
2. The various content, process, and reinforcement theories of motivation, including:
   a. need hierarchy theory
   b. ERG theory
   c. two-factor theory
   d. acquired needs theory
   e. equity theory
   f. VIE theory
   g. goal setting theory
   h. behavior modification and OB mod
3. The practical implications of the various motivation theories.
4. The importance for supervisors of establishing motivating work environments.

Motivation is probably one of the most frequently and extensively studied psychological concepts. The utility of motivation theories has been incorporated into other areas, such as learning, personality, employee behavior, and job satisfaction. In these situations, motivation has advanced beyond theory to become a useful managerial resource for shaping behavior.

The theoretical framework of motivation focuses on understanding and predicting the rationale underlying human behavior. The applied aspect of motivation emphasizes active intervention for the purpose of changing, improving, and developing desired behavioral responses. Parents and teachers continually expend great energy searching for means to motivate children, while managers use motivation theory and research as a resource to improve the quantity and quality of worker productivity and job satisfaction.

Of the many difficulties motivational theorists encounter, the vast differences in human behavior are likely to be the most problematic. At this point in time, a universal theory of motivation, which is acceptable and applicable to all individuals in all situations, remains to be developed. It is highly improbable that one theory will ever be sufficiently adequate to fully encompass the atypical nature of motivation. However, there are currently many well-researched, documented theories which make bona fide contributions to understanding human behavior. When applied thoughtfully and selectively, these theories are greatly beneficial to management and employees alike.

The Motivational Process

Motivation is a complex process composed of physical, psychological, social, and cultural needs which operate both individually and interactively to energize human behavior. Needs activate the motivation process to direct the action of the behavior, to determine the strength of the response, and to sustain the duration of the effort involved. When individuals must decide between alternative actions, motivational forces determine their responses. When drives are aroused, motivated individuals not only direct their behavior toward a particular goal, but also expend considerable energy in achieving it. Truly motivated individuals sustain their efforts over an extended period of time, but non-motivated people lose interest and energy rapidly.

Motivation

Motivation is a multi-faceted psychological process which energizes individuals' behaviors toward a desired goal or objective.

Managers have the unwieldy task of learning the individual needs of their employees and translating this information into the management of their work behavior. Motivation is primarily an internal, personal process; thus it is incumbent upon supervisors to create a work environment in which individuals can satisfy or fulfill their individual needs. The positive outcome of the effective application of motivational theory to the workplace is efficient productivity and worker satisfaction. The mismanagement or lack of interest in worker motivation results in unhappy, unproductive workers who do not fully use their potential.

Motivation Theories

Motivation theories are classified according to the aspects of human behavior they reflect and emphasize. **Content theories** are primarily concerned with individual needs; **process theories** include both cognitive and perceptual elements; and **reinforcement theories** apply learning principles to the work setting.

Content Theories

Content theories of motivation emphasize physical and psychological needs as the primary forces activating individual behavior. They identify needs and illustrate the behavioral responses necessary for gratification of these needs.

The complexity and uniqueness of individuals is an important consideration when applying content theories. Distinctive needs, values, attitudes, and beliefs are the very attributes which set people apart from one another. What one individual desires and devotes boundless energy to achieve may be regarded as a worthless activity by another person. For example, while some workers may relish the opportunity to work overtime in anticipation of extra pay, other employees may be resentful about having to sacrifice time with their families.

Another consideration in applying content theories is the unstable nature of needs. What motivates individuals one day or even one hour ago may have no effect, or perhaps a different effect, on their behavior on another occasion. For example, everyone has had the experience of being exceptionally hungry prior to entering a restaurant for lunch. At that moment, behavior is directed toward satisfying the hunger need. After gorging oneself on the all-you-can-eat buffet bar, however, one's hunger need is quickly appeased. At least for the present time, behavior is no longer likely to be generated by rewards promising satisfaction of the hunger need.

Several content theories have evolved because of the diversity of thinking regarding the psychological impact and role of needs on motivation. Some of these theories address universal needs, while others focus on the unique needs of individuals. The present discussion will examine four major theories. They are: Maslow's Hierarchy of Needs, Alderfer's ERG Theory, Herzberg's Two-Factor Theory, and McClelland's Acquired Needs Theory.

Maslow's need hierarchy theory

One of the most widely accepted theories of motivation is Abraham Maslow's **hierarchy of needs theory,** which was developed in the early 1940s.[1] The theory postulates that all human needs are classified into five levels ranging from the most essential needs common to all people to higher order needs which only a few individuals are motivated to satisfy. The needs, listed from lowest level to highest level, are represented as a hierarchy.

1. **Physiological needs** These are the most basic needs, such as food, water, air, and sex.

2. **Safety needs** These needs, also referred to as *security needs*, include the desire for both physiological and psychological freedom from stress and protection from existing and future environmental threats.
3. **Social needs** This category, sometimes referred to as *belongingness* or *love needs*, includes the needs for developing friendships, love, peer acceptance, and a general sense of belonging and acceptance in a social environment.
4. **Esteem needs** These needs not only focus on self-esteem, but also highlight the individual's drive toward acquiring respect, prestige, and attention from others based on personal achievement.
5. **Self-actualization needs** This category incorporates those needs which enable individuals to reach their fullest developmental potential. Basically, it can be viewed as the individual's motive for complete self-fulfillment. This is the highest level on the need hierarchy.

Exhibit 15.1

Maslow's Hierarchy of Needs

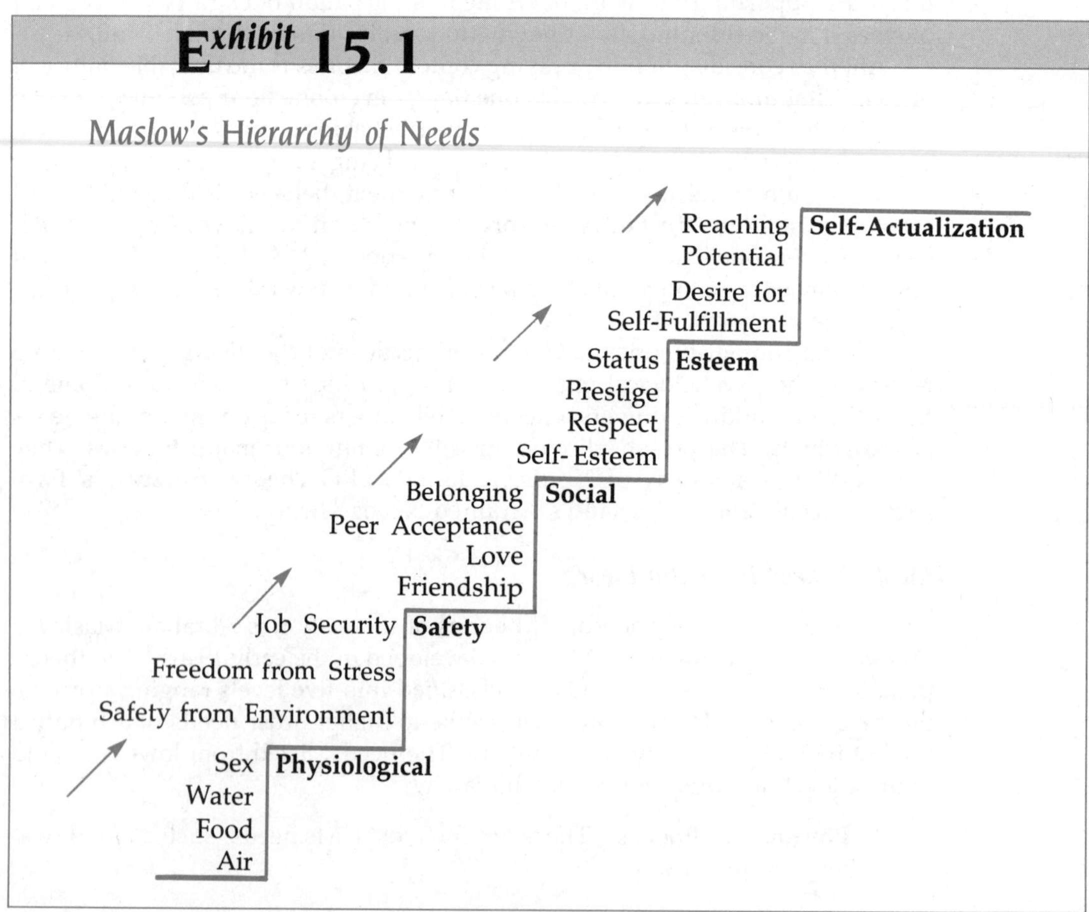

Maslow hypothesized that human beings are creatures of desire who crave satisfaction of certain needs and who pursue the paths essential to their procurement. The manner in which they prioritize need gratification is predetermined in a set, predictable fashion and is universal across populations. Once a need becomes satisfied, and as long as it remains satisfied, people's behavioral priority shifts to the next highest need level. If individuals fail to achieve gratification, or if fulfillment is withdrawn, they experience tension and anxiety. These psychological forces result in motivated behaviors designed to reduce the stress and restore internal equilibrium.

Suppose, for example, that an individual is attempting to satisfy the need for social interaction (social needs on the need hierarchy). For this state of affairs to exist, the first two need levels (physiological and safety needs) would be in a state of satisfaction. All motivated behavior would center on the gratification of the social need. Should the individual suddenly lose his job, causing the gratification of the physiological and safety need levels to be in jeopardy, the individual would redirect his priorities toward satisfying these lower level needs.

Implications for management In order to effectively utilize the principles of the need hierarchy theory, management is required to determine which needs employees are presently attempting to satisfy. Subsequently, managers have the responsibility for creating environments which allow workers the opportunity to gratify these needs. When needs are correctly identified, motivated behavior is a likely consequence. Failure to accurately identify employee needs may result in behaviors which satisfy the needs of the individual, but are inappropriate for meeting the goals of the organization. Consider the following case.

> Gertrude, a housewife for the past twenty years, decided to seek employment. Her main motivation for returning to the workplace was her desire to interact with people. Her children were grown, all of her friends worked, and she was thoroughly bored at home. Within a short time, Gertrude obtained a position as a drill press operator in a local metal shop. After several weeks on the job, Gertrude's supervisor requested a conference with the company's consultant. It seemed that Gertrude's behavior was disruptive to her work group. Instead of working at her machine, she was constantly visiting and chatting with her co-workers. Regardless of the promises of performance bonuses, promotions, and advancements, her inappropriate behavior persisted. The supervisor was dumbfounded. All of the other workers had always responded positively to these rewards. Was the only option to dismiss her?
>
> After reviewing the situation, the consultant determined that the problem was simply a result of the fact that Gertrude's job rewards did not offer satisfaction of her current needs. Economically, Gertrude did not need to work. She was working only to satisfy her social needs. Operating a machine, isolated in a factory corner, certainly did not provide gratification of these needs. On the other hand, her

inappropriate chatting behavior provided her with the social fulfillment she needed. The solution was simple. Today, the company has the most effective receptionist/switchboard operator of its fifty-year history.

Realistically ascertaining worker needs and providing adequate reward systems is quite complicated. Sometimes the theory cannot be readily applied to the real work situation. Many needs are unconscious, and individuals are unaware of their existence. In some cases, identifying individual needs is fruitless. Supervisors have a limited repertoire of rewards at their disposal, and if none can provide need satisfaction, then all efforts at motivation may still fail. This fact, however, should not preclude supervisors from attempting to use the theory. Most job environments can be structured to allow individuals to find need satisfaction through appropriately motivated behavior. It requires a willingness by management to expend the effort necessary to identify individual needs and to be creative in designing and providing new reward systems.

Alderfer's ERG *theory*

ERG theory, which was formulated by Clayton Alderfer (1969, 1972),[2] is a modified version of Maslow's need hierarchy theory. Alderfer's ERG theory classifies human needs into three distinct groupings, as opposed to Maslow's five categories. The three groupings are:

1. **Existence needs** These are the most basic needs required for human existence and include those which can be satisfied by environmental factors. This category includes the needs for food, water, pay, pleasant working conditions, and good benefits.
2. **Relatedness needs** This need category centers on social relationships with co-workers, superiors, subordinates, friends, and family.
3. **Growth needs** This level includes the need for personal development and the need to maximize one's potential to its fullest.

Aside from synthesizing need categories from five into three, a number of other significant differences separate ERG and need hierarchy theory. According to Maslow, as satisfaction of lower needs occurs, individuals progress upward on the hierarchy in an orderly fashion. On the other hand, Alderfer views need levels as being arranged along a continuum, with individuals moving back and forth across the levels.

Both theories accept the concept of *fulfillment–progression,* which is defined as moving toward fulfillment of the next highest level need. However, the proposals about how individuals accomplish this goal are what set apart the two theories. Maslow believed that individuals only move upward on the scale after they satisfy the lower level need. According to Alderfer, however, people move along in either a fulfillment–progression or a frustration–progression process. ERG theory, unlike Maslow's theory, proposes that if individuals are stymied in their attempts to satisfy one level of needs (such as growth), they may revert their attention to another lower level of needs (such as relatedness), in spite of its existing state of satisfaction.

Another difference between the theories concerns the impact unsatisfied needs have on an individual's behavior. According to Maslow, motivation is at its highest level when individuals have needs which remain unsatisfied. For example, the more esteem needs are thwarted, the more effort individuals will expend in satisfying them. On the other hand, ERG theory postulates that raising an individual's frustration level causes him to revert his attention to a lower level need. Thus, the inability to satisfy growth needs will cause more effort to be focused on relatedness needs.

Implications for management ERG theory adds a new dimension to practitioners of need theory. The use of Maslow's theory requires that supervisors identify the particular needs employees are seeking to gratify and offer appropriate rewards. When gratification of these needs is obstructed, however, or when suitable rewards are unavailable, the supervisor may be powerless. Using Alderfer's model allows for the diversion of energy into other need levels, and it provides supervisors with additional motivational channels.

Herzberg's two-factor theory

In 1959, Frederick Herzberg and his associates developed a widely popular and practical theory of motivation known as **two-factor, or motivator–hygiene theory.**[3] As with need theory, Herzberg maintained that individuals have certain needs which they seek to gratify. These needs, however, are not divided into five or three categories; they fall into two distinct sets: motivators and hygiene factors.

Motivators **Motivators,** which are sometimes referred to as **satisfiers,** are upper level needs and correspond to the esteem and self-actualization needs of Maslow. They are intrinsic to the job content, and they are somehow related to innate drives that cause people to seek challenge, autonomy, and self-fulfillment. In addition, motivators are directly related to job satisfaction and performance, and they serve as the primary impetus for causing employees to work hard. When present in the work environment, these factors have the potential to produce job satisfaction. When absent from the workplace, however, they do not result in dissatisfaction, but merely a feeling of neutrality. Included within this category are the needs for achievement, responsibility, and advancement.

Hygiene factors The **hygiene factors,** known also as **dissatisfiers,** are lower level, maintenance-type needs, and they include the social, safety, and physiological need levels of the need hierarchy. These needs are directly related to the physical work environment, and they are concerned with those environmental conditions which provide pleasant working surroundings. Unlike motivators, the presence of hygiene factors will not create motivation or job satisfaction. They merely reduce the level of dissatisfaction. In their absence, however, dis-

Exhibit 15.2

Herzberg's Motivators and Hygiene Factors

Motivators (intrinsic)	Hygiene factors (extrinsic)
Achievement	Company policy
Recognition	Supervision
Control over work itself	Interpersonal relationships
Responsibility	Working conditions
Growth and advancement	Pay and salary
	Job security
	Status

satisfaction is a distinct possibility. Furthermore, hygiene factors must be satisfied and must remain in a state of satisfaction before individuals can progress to the motivator needs. Examples of these needs include: pay, job security, supervision, relationships with co-workers, and general working conditions.

Implications for management The implications of two-factor theory for practitioners is readily apparent. In order to create motivated employees, supervisors must create an environment that allows individuals an opportunity to obtain higher level need satisfaction. Offering employees only hygiene factor incentives results in a workforce which rarely performs more than adequately. Nevertheless, these hygiene factors must not be overlooked. Without their presence, individuals may become dissatisfied and may seek employment elsewhere. Consequently, hygiene factors are a necessity. They must always be present in the environment before individuals will attend to motivators.

Herzberg contends that motivation is best accomplished through a process of job enrichment in which jobs are augmented to provide workers with interesting and meaningful work. Supervisors must make every effort to continually enhance workers' jobs so that they can achieve self-fulfillment from their daily activities.

McClelland's acquired needs theory

Up to this point, the theories discussed classify needs into a distinct number of categories. Motivation is achieved by satisfying one set of needs at a particular level, and then moving on to a different set. David McClelland (1961, 1962) digressed from this notion of set levels and hypothesized that motivation is chiefly a function of three specific needs: the need for achievement (nAch), the need for power (nPower), and the need for affiliation (nAff).[4]

According to McClelland's theory, motives are acquired through learning processes. The needs develop in varying degrees and orientations from early experiences. If an individual has achieved success early in his/her life, and has enjoyed pleasurable experiences as a result of these successes, he/she is likely to demonstrate high achievement motivation. On the other hand, if an individual's early attempts at achievement were frustrated, resulting in unpleasurable experiences, then another need may dominate his/her motivational force.

In conjunction with the **need for achievement (nAch)** motive, McClelland developed the *motive to avoid failure*. Individuals who are governed by this motive seek situations which minimize pain. They accomplish this goal principally by avoiding the task. The individual cannot fail if the task is not undertaken. In order to understand how this motive develops, consider the following case.

> One evening, Jimmy, a ten-year-old, happened to notice that the kitchen garbage pail was overflowing. Although emptying the trash was not his chore, Jimmy, eager to please, proceeded to dispose of the garbage. Shortly thereafter, Jimmy's father entered the kitchen to remove the trash. Noticing the empty pail, he asked Jimmy if he knew who had disposed of the garbage. With a large smile, in anticipation of a reward, Jimmy proudly announced that he had emptied the trash. At that announcement, Jimmy's father mumbled "Oh" and returned to the other room. The next day, Jimmy tried it again. This time, however, the garbage bag tore and trash was spewed all over the floor. At that moment Jimmy's father entered the room, noticed the mess, and exclaimed "Why did you touch the garbage? It's not your chore. Go to your room!" Jimmy never touched the trash again.

The preceding case demonstrates how the fear of failure motive can be developed. If Jimmy had never touched the garbage on any occasion, he would not have been either rewarded or punished. His successful completion of the task resulted in neither reward nor punishment, but his bungled attempt resulted in admonishment. Therefore, there was everything to lose and nothing to gain by performing the task. Jimmy's future behavior is thus likely to be directed at avoiding pain.

Implications for management The preceding example can realistically be applied to workers. Often employees will perform tasks which are not in their job description, in the hope of being rewarded. Unfortunately, for many, this extra work goes unnoticed and unrewarded. Bungling the job, however, quickly brings a reprimand and a lecture on "sticking to one's job description and the business at hand." However, these same supervisors wonder why their workers are not motivated to take the initiative.

To date, researchers have concentrated on attempting to identify characteristics of high need achievers, and to discern how this motive governs behavior. Individuals whose achievement need is high tend to set moderate goals and to take moderate risks. On the opposite extreme, people with low achievement needs tend to be high risk takers. In addition, high achievers tend to work independently and to delegate infrequently. They crave immediate diagnostic feedback and are preoccupied with their work. Finally, they tend to exhibit high stress levels, particularly when they must abandon projects prior to their conclusion.

More recently, the **need for power (nPower)** and the need for affiliation (nAff) have come to the forefront in human resource thinking. The need for power is characterized by an individual's need to control, dominate, or impact upon others. This need can be manifested in one of two ways. *Personalized power* exists when individuals desire power for power's sake. They are not concerned with what can be accomplished, but rather with the emotional feelings derived from exercising control over others. In contrast, those people who demonstrate the *socialized power* need exercise their influence to accomplish objectives for the betterment of all. Obviously, it is this latter power motive which is prevalent among successful managers.[5]

The last need, the **need for affiliation (nAff)**, appears to have an inverse relationship with effective management. People with a high need for achievement have a great desire to establish strong and supportive interpersonal relationships. Effective management requires that decisions be made irrespective of emotional feelings. Sometimes the ability to make sound judgments is hampered by the concern managers have about being liked by their work group. Consequently, effective managers have been found to be high on the need for power and achievement and low on the need for affiliation.[6]

Process Theories

Process theories of motivation are cognitive in nature. The basic assumption underlying these theories is that human beings make conscious decisions regarding their behavior. Rather than being solely reactive to environmental stimuli, people are proactive as well. Predicting and motivating behavior is a process of understanding individual choices and how and why they are made. Content theories identify the needs which motivate behavior, while process theories examine the cognitive aspects of motivation and the processes by which these behaviors are carried out. The present discussion will concentrate on three process theories. These are: Adams' equity theory, Vroom's VIE (expectancy) theory, and Locke's goal setting theory.

Adams' equity theory

Equity theory, which was first proposed by J. Stacy Adams in 1963,[7] is based on the assumption that all individuals have a desire to be treated fairly. In order to determine whether or not they are being treated adequately, workers compare the rewards they receive for their efforts with those of their co-workers in similar work situations. Equity exists when employees perceive the ratio of their efforts to rewards as comparable with that of their peers. On the other hand, inequity occurs when workers view the ratio of effort to rewards as either more or less than their co-workers.

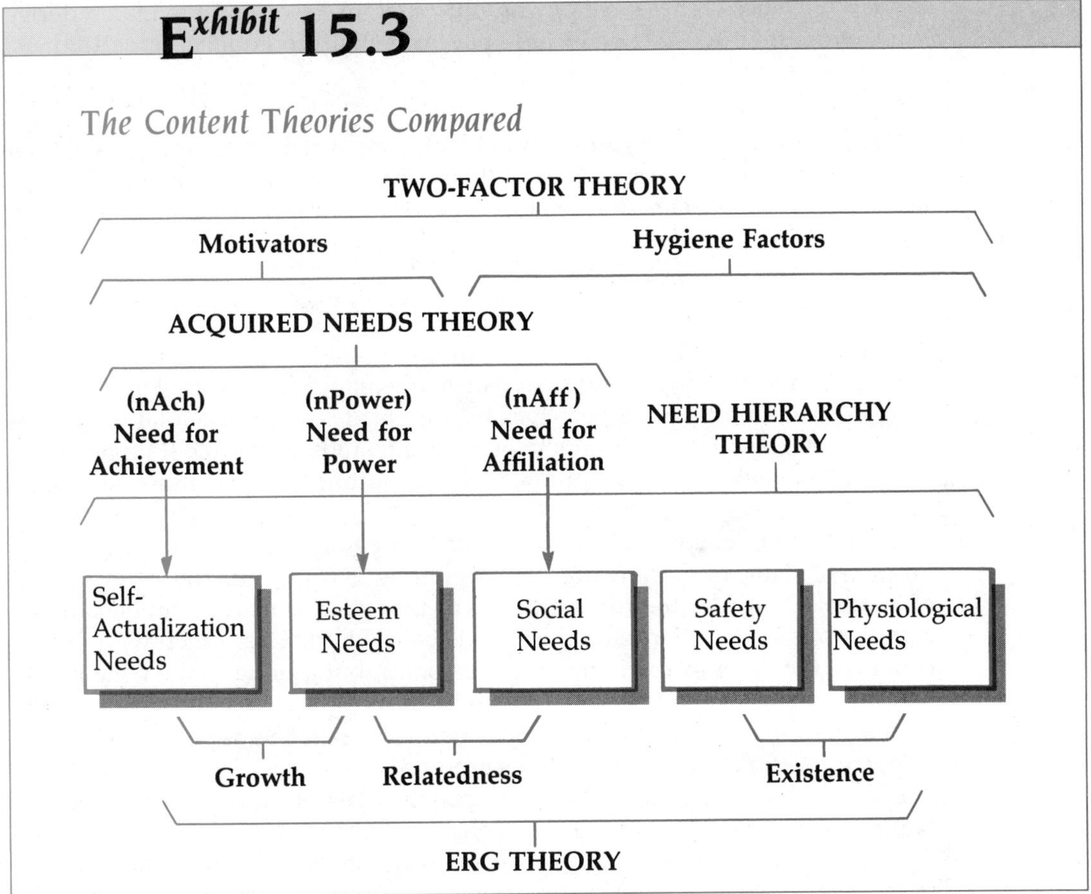

Exhibit 15.3

The Content Theories Compared

Equity

Equity is a feeling of fairness experienced by individuals when they view the relationship of their efforts and organizational rewards as equivalent to the efforts and corresponding rewards of their co-workers.

According to Adams, there are four major components of equity theory.

1. **Person**—These are the people who perceive themselves in relation to other people.
2. **Other**—These are the people that are the basis of the comparisons made.
3. **Inputs**—These are the total of the individual's assets brought to the work environment. They include educational level, work experience, seniority, skills, and talents.

4. **Outcomes**—These are all the outcomes or rewards individuals derive from their jobs. They include pay, benefits, promotional opportunities, and status.

Equity theory maintains that individuals form a ratio of their inputs to their outcomes, and then compare them to their perception of the input/outcome relationships of others. This relationship is expressed in formula fashion as:

$$\frac{\text{person outcomes}}{\text{person inputs}} = \frac{\text{other outcomes}}{\text{other inputs}}$$

Adams assumes that individuals can apply quantitative determinations to the inputs and outcomes and arrive at mathematical formulas. For example, suppose that an individual perceives his inputs at 100 and the total of his outcomes as 100. His ratio of inputs to outcomes would be 100/100. If he perceives the other as having an equal ratio, such as inputting 25 units and receiving 25 units of outcomes (25/25) or inputting 150 units and receiving 150 units of outcomes (150/150), equity will exist. In a state of equity, motivation remains in a position of status quo. Individuals will continue to contribute the same amount of inputs as long as either the outcomes or the other's ratio does not change. It is important to note that only the ratio is considered. Consequently, a person could see the other as receiving more outcomes, but as long as the person feels that the other is contributing more, equity exists.

On the other hand, if the ratio between the person's inputs to outcomes compared with the ratio of the other's inputs and outcomes is unequal, inequity will be felt. Inequity creates tension in people. They, in turn, are motivated to reduce the tension. The greater the perceived inequity, the more severely the tension is felt, and the stronger the motivational force is to reduce it. The method individuals choose in an attempt to regain equity is determined by the factor in the formula which is out of balance and the relative control, or lack of control, they have over situational conditions. Adams suggests six methods used most frequently. These are:

1. **Changing the person's inputs**—Individuals will either contribute more or less effort to the job in an attempt to equalize the ratio. For example, a ratio of 100/100 compared to 50/25 would cause the individual to reduce his inputs to arrive at 100/50, and equity.
2. **Changing the person's outcomes**—This method involves the person's attempt at changing the outcomes received. Probably the most common example of this method is asking for a pay increase.
3. **Perceptual distortion**—This is a complex process that involves the reevaluation of the comparison formula. People may alter the value which they originally placed on their inputs and outputs, or they may rationalize that they misperceived either the other's inputs or outcomes.
4. **Changing the source of comparison**—Rather than comparing himself to the original source, the person may conclude that the original reference source, because of uncontrollable reasons, is atypical. Perhaps the source

has a highly unique skill or is the owner's nephew. Consequently, the person will find other co-workers to serve as a reference point.

5. **Manipulating the other**—This could take the form of persuading the other to apply more effort to his/her job, having the other take on added responsibilities, or in extreme conditions, harassing the other into quitting.
6. **Leaving the situation**—The most extreme response to feelings of inequity is to quit or transfer from the situation. This alternative is usually chosen when all other attempts at equity are fruitless.

Implications for management For practitioners, the application of equity theory centers on the perceptions workers have regarding inputs and outcomes. Managers must be aware of the perceived value workers place on the rewards they receive in comparison to the rewards given to others doing similar jobs. Relative values may have more motivational power than absolute values. Effective supervisors will realize that equity comparisons are likely to be made, especially when rewards are openly visible, such as promotions and pay. Regardless of whether or not management views rewards as fair, workers may perceive them in an entirely different manner. It is these perceptions of equity made by employees which are important, not the judgments of fairness assumed by management.

Vroom's VIE Theory (expectancy theory)

Historically, VIE theory's roots can probably be traced back to the works of psychologists such as Watson, Tolman, and Hull (1920s and 1930s). It was Victor Vroom's work in 1964, however, which popularized the theory.[8] According to Vroom, a person's motivational force is basically a function of three factors. These are: valence, expectancy, and instrumentality.

Valence The first premise underlying expectancy theory is that individuals have a preference for certain outcomes or rewards over others. Vroom termed this concept **valence.** Those outcomes which individuals desire, and which they feel by their obtainment will provide satisfaction, are said to have positive valence. On the other hand, those outcomes which individuals prefer not to have are said to have negative valence. Valence can be determined by having individuals rate, on a scale from −10 to +10, how much they value certain outcomes. Positive valence is indicated in varying degrees between 1 and 10, and negative valence is judged between −1 and −10. Those items which are neutral, neither preferred nor disliked, are scored zero.

Valence

Valence is the position or negative value individuals place on work outcomes based on preferences they believe will provide them with either satisfaction or dissatisfaction.

Expectancy Valuing an outcome by itself does not produce motivation. If something is desired, it does not necessarily mean that the individual is willing to put forth the required effort to obtain it. Before individuals decide to direct their behavior toward accomplishing a task, even one for which the rewards are valued highly, they determine the probability of their efforts resulting in increased performance. In some instances, they may perceive that more effort placed in the task will yield greater performance. Sometimes, however, individuals may conclude that even extreme effort may be to no avail, and favorable outcomes are not likely to occur. For example, studying all night for a geometry test when one does not understand the concepts may not afford any different results than not studying.

Expectancy

Expectancy is the individual's perceived determination of the likelihood of increased performance occurring as a result of the effort expended.

Expectancy is quantifiable along a scale ranging in value from 0 to 1. A score of 0 indicates that the individual sees no probability that increased effort will lead to the desired outcome, while a score of 1 indicates that the individual views increased effort as always leading to the desired outcome.

Instrumentality The third concept of Vroom's motivational theory refers to the subjective probability which individuals perceive of performance leading to other outcomes. For example, individuals determine whether or not they are likely to be rewarded with a merit pay raise for increased performance. High instrumentality indicates that the probability of receiving the reward is great, while low instrumentality would indicate that in spite of the increased performance, the raise will not follow.

Instrumentality

Instrumentality is the probability, either perceived or actual, that a particular level of performance will lead to some outcomes.

Instrumentality is scored on a scale ranging from −1 to +1. A score of +1 indicates that an individual views a given performance level as always leading to a given outcome, while a score of −1 indicates that the individual sees a given performance level as never leading to a given outcome. Similarly, different probabilities (either positive or negative) are possible by assigning scores between the extremes.

Vroom translated an individual's motivational force into a mathematical formula that includes valence, instrumentality, and expectancy. This formula in its simplest form is:

$$F = E \times I \times V$$

where F = Individual's motivational force
E = Expectancy
I = Instrumentality
V = Valence

The larger the numerical value, the greater the individual's motivational force. Thus, the importance of expectancy theory lies in the relationship of the three variables to each other. The probabilities individuals cognitively compute of succeeding at their task and being rewarded for their efforts, along with the values they place on these outcomes, collectively combine to determine motivation. For example, suppose that a manager attempts to motivate a worker by the promise of a promotion if productivity is outstanding. If the worker places little value on being promoted, sees little probability of achieving the performance level, or believes that the likelihood of the promotion occurring is slim, then he or she will probably not be motivated to earn the promotion. Obviously, because the formula is multiplicative in nature, any time a zero occurs on the right side of the equation, motivation will be non-existent.

Implications for management Expectancy theory has valuable implications for the practitioner. Managers would be well advised to assign challenging tasks that allow workers greater productivity as a result of increased effort. The assignment of jobs to workers who see no potential of completion regardless of their effort will probably result in a lack of motivation. Second, rewards should be established which are visibly related to performance levels. Greater effort and higher performance should result in larger rewards. If employees view hard work as leading to increased job performance and equitable rewards, they will be motivated to produce highly. On the other hand, if they perceive the task to

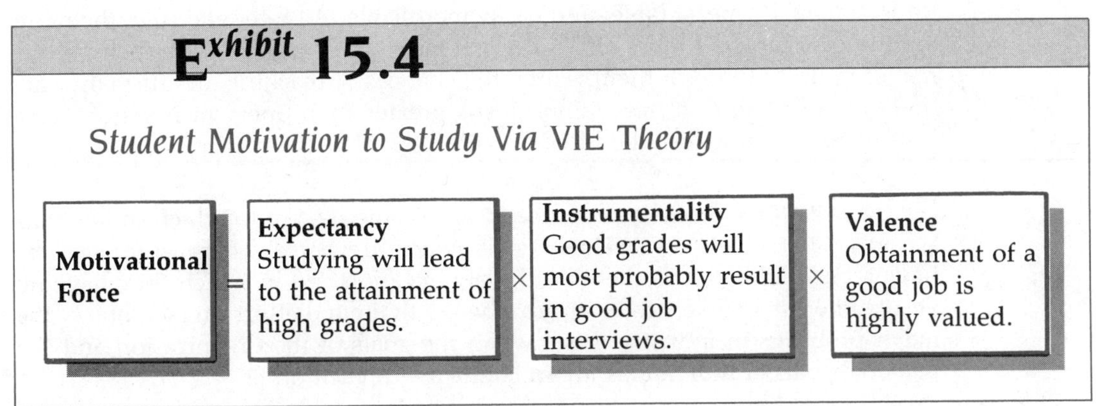

be unfeasible, regardless of their efforts, or if they see only a small likelihood that their efforts will be rewarded, they will probably experience dissatisfaction and decreased motivation. Expectancy theory, as well as equity theory, emphasizes the employee's perception of value and probabilities in determining work motivation.[9]

Locke's goal setting theory

Goal setting theory, which was formulated in 1968 by Edwin Locke,[10] assumes that motivation is a result of rational and intentional behavior. The direction of the behavior is a function of the goals individuals set and their efforts toward achieving these goals. To fully understand motivation requires a thorough analysis of the processes people undergo in setting and achieving their goals.

Originally, Locke formulated goal setting theory based on two principles: goal difficulty and goal specificity. More recently, the model has been expanded to incorporate goal acceptance and goal commitment.[11]

Goal difficulty **Goal difficulty** is the degree to which goals are viewed by individuals as challenging. According to the theory, providing individuals with difficult goals does not necessarily mean that they will perceive the goals as unattainable. In fact, individuals will be likely to expend more, rather than less, effort to reach the more difficult goals. This proposition is especially valid if people have been rewarded for mastering difficult tasks in the past. Those individuals who have been reinforced adequately in the past will probably undertake additional challenging goals when confronted with them at a future date. On the other hand, those people whose previous satisfactory performance has not been rewarded are unlikely to be motivated by challenging tasks in the future.

Goal specificity **Goal specificity** refers to whether or not the goal has been stated in general terms (such as to be an excellent human resource management student), or in highly specific terms (to get an A on the mid-term examination). Specificity is enhanced by setting goals into quantifiable terms. These goals are understandable, measurable, and easily modifiable. As a general rule, the more specific goals are, the more likely it is that individuals will enhance their performance in order to reach them. Thus, the chances of reaching an affirmative action goal of hiring ten new minorities is greater than one which states "This year more minorities will be hired."

Goal acceptance **Goal acceptance** is simply the degree to which individuals accept goals as their own. Those goals which are perceived by employees as having been imposed on them by the organization and in which they have no vested interest are likely to be approached with limited effort. In fact, one of the major problems in industry exists when the goals of the organization and the personal goals of individuals are in conflict with each other.

Goal commitment **Goal commitment** is the dedication which individuals extend toward reaching the set objective. Those organizational goals to which individuals commit will most likely receive the majority of effort and resources, On the other hand, individualized goals, such as the pet project of some executive, are inclined to be ignored by employees.

Implications for management Goal setting theory appears to be one of the most easily understood motivation theories discussed thus far. It does not rely on inherent needs, perceptual differences, or complex constructs such as instrumentality. Rather, the theory maintains that relevant and challenging goals which are applicable to individuals' capabilities should be developed. The task confronting supervisors becomes one of guiding employees in the development and attainment of goals which will provide satisfaction to both the employee and the organization. This process is facilitated by the involvement of workers in organizational goal setting, the setting of challenging and specific individual goals, the provision of continual performance feedback, and the establishment and implementation of adequate rewards for appropriate performance.

Reinforcement Theory

Content and process theories describe motivation in terms of underlying psychological concepts and perceptual processes. Motivational behavior is interpreted by reinforcement theory as a function of both positive and negative associations which individuals learn through environmental consequences. The primary focus of this theory is explained in terms of reactions and responses to environmental stimuli. Those actions which result in positive rewards will be repeated. Behaviors resulting in negative consequences will either be eliminated or be sharply decreased.

Advocates of reinforcement theory acknowledge the importance of the psychological processes underlying behavior. It is their contention, however, that an examination of the "whys" of motivation does not address itself to the most important issue at hand, which involves actually managing, controlling, and adapting individual behavior in order to meet the objectives of the organization. In addition to having a strong theoretical base, reinforcement theory has practical applications for motivation which may be implemented easily into the organizational environment.

Operant conditioning and organizational behavior modification (OB Mod)

The most widely cited research in reinforcement theory is that of the psychologist B. F. Skinner.[12] The theory of **operant conditioning** maintains that behavior may be controlled with the appropriate use and timing of reinforcements. All current and future behaviors are learned reactions based on a system of rewards and punishments. Applying these principles to the controlling of behavior is called **behavior modification.** Its use in businesses has been dubbed **organizational behavior modification** (OB Mod).

Organizational behavior modification

Organizational behavior modification is the conscious application of operant learning principles in organizations for the purpose of controlling behavior.

In order to effectively use organizational behavior modification, principles of reinforcement must be understood and implemented. According to reinforcement theory, behavior is controllable by using one or a combination of four techniques. These are: positive reinforcement, negative reinforcement, punishment, and extinction.

Positive reinforcement Positive reinforcers are those rewards whose attainment is contingent upon individuals' performing appropriately. Pay bonuses and recognition are examples of positive reinforcers. Reinforcement theory contends that the appropriate use of **positive reinforcement** is the major impetus in motivating individuals. People will expend considerable energy in attempts to gain positive rewards which they desire. Of course, for positive reinforcement to have the desired impact, feedback must be consistent and frequent.

Negative reinforcement Sometimes termed *avoidance learning,* negative reinforcers compel individuals to perform appropriately in order to avoid undesirable consequences. Satisfactory performance does not offer gains for individuals, except in the sense that they avert a negative consequence. For example, the threat of losing one's job if performance is not improved is an example of **negative reinforcement.** Performing satisfactorily merely maintains the status quo. Inappropriate actions, however, result in dire consequences. Using negative reinforcement fosters appropriate responses. However, the appropriate behavior is not as quickly elicited, nor does it endure as long, as the responses initiated through positive reinforcers.

Punishment Unlike positive or negative reinforcement, **punishment** does not foster appropriate behavior. Rather, punishment eliminates inappropriate actions. Its use in reinforcement theory is probably best limited to those situations in which the goal is merely the elimination of undesirable actions.

Extinction **Extinction** is the process of withdrawing all reinforcement, both positive and negative, in an effort to eliminate inappropriate behavior. Sometimes even negative consequences are viewed by the recipient as need satisfying. For example, reprimanding a child for misbehavior may seem like a negative consequence to many parents. For the child hungering for attention, however, the reprimand may be rewarding. Ignoring the child's behavior entirely may result in the behavior being eliminated.

Exhibit 15.5

Some Commonly Used Positive and Negative Reinforcers

Positive reinforcers	Negative reinforcers
Money	Avoidance of reprimands
Praise and recognition	Threat of being fired
Job with added responsibility	Threat of demotion
Time off with pay	Threat of suspension
Commendations, such as plaques, tie tacks, letters	Threat of a transfer to a non-desirable job
Promise of a raise	Threat of poor performance appraisal
Company-sponsored social activities, such as picnics or a Christmas dance	
Preferred working environment, such as a larger office or an office with a window	

The primary difference between reinforcement (positive and negative) and punishment is that if a response is reinforced, the probability that the response will occur again in the future is increased. On the other hand, if a response is punished, the probability that it will occur again in the future is decreased.

The scheduling of rewards and punishments also contributes to the effectiveness of behavior modification. Reinforcement schedules can be established by intervals (time between responses) and ratio (the number of responses made). In addition, schedules can be fixed (remain the same), or variable. Supporters of reinforcement theory contend that the manner in which these various schedules are manipulated can have a dramatic impact on an individual's motivational force.

Implications for management The shaping and controlling of employee behavior is accomplished through the systematic and uniform use of specific behavior modification principles. First, supervisors must concentrate on observable behavioral events, not internal feelings and emotional reactions. Second, behaviors should be charted and counted in terms of frequency of occurrence. Third, if behavior is truly a function of its consequences, employees must have a clear understanding of the relationship between their acts and the subsequent rewards.[13]

It is incumbent on practitioners to monitor their employees' behavior patterns and to identify both those appropriate for the work environment and those hampering productivity. The behaviors which are appropriate should be fostered through a program of positive reinforcement. Those which are deemed inappropriate should be eliminated through a systematic process of reducing the occurrence of the negative behaviors. Perhaps the best example of the results of an OB Mod program is the landmark research conducted at Emery Air Freight during the early 1970s.[14] Applying OB Mod over a three-year period saved the

Exhibit 15.6

Comparison of the Motivation Theories

Theory	Basic tenet	Implication for supervisors
Need hierarchy	Needs are classified into five distinct levels arranged along a hierarchy. Gratification of lower order needs is necessary to progress upward.	Identification of employee need allows for the creation of an environment in which the worker can gratify these needs.
ERG	Needs are classified into three categories arranged along a continuum. Individuals move back and forth between levels.	Reliance on succinct needs is unnecessary. Allows for added motivational channels.
Two-factor	Needs are classified into two categories: motivators (satisfiers), and hygiene factors (dissatisfiers).	Environment must be created that allows satisfaction of motivator needs.
Acquired needs	Motivation is a function of three learned needs: nPower, nAffiliation, and nAchievement. Also introduced motivational force involving the need to avoid failure.	Establish environment that allows people to satisfy their need for achievement, affiliation, and/or power. Provide tasks which are readily accomplished for avoidance of failure.
Equity	Motivation is a function of the relationship people perceive between their inputs/outputs and other people's inputs/outputs.	Understand the perceived view of rewards and effort that workers have and establish equitable systems.
VIE	Motivation is a function of the expectancy of reward for action, the probability of reward, and the value placed on the reward.	Tasks having high probability of success and visible rewards associated with success should be available.
Goal setting	Motivation is a result of rational and intentional behavior toward the achievement of a goal.	Relevant and challenging goals need to be developed.
OB Mod	Behavior is a function of the reinforcements received.	Positively rewarding behavioral events leads to task accomplishment.

company in excess of $2 million, and at the same time, improved performance significantly.

Before leaving OB Mod, it appears prudent to put its usefulness into perspective. Regardless of the OB Mod laboratory research supporting positive reinforcement, many managers have difficulty applying positive reinforcement principles. For many supervisors, the idea of offering rewards to unproductive workers in the hope that their performance will improve seems to border on lunacy. The prevailing logic is that workers are hired to do jobs and that they should not have to be enticed to perform the work for which they are already being paid. Besides, negative reinforcement and punishment are simpler and more natural to apply.

These arguments against OB Mod are not without merit. In fact, in spite of the success stories, there are many instances where OB Mod fails. Many times supervisors do not have sufficient rewards with which they can entice workers. Furthermore, the repeated use of rewards reduces their novelty and they lose their reinforcement impact. Once again, as with other theories of motivation, it must be remembered that OB Mod is only a theory, which when applied cautiously, selectively, and appropriately can provide benefits in certain situations.

Summary

This chapter focused on the various theories developed to explain the motivational process. The theories are categorized as:

1. Content theories—those that emphasize individual needs.
2. Process theories—those whose principles are based on cognitive and perceptual processes.
3. Reinforcement theory—whose major emphasis is the application of learning principles to the work environment.

Each of the theories discussed has its avid supporters. There are those theorists and practitioners who would undeniably maintain that the particular theory they advocate is the panacea. Unfortunately, this does not appear to be reality. Research indicates that each of the theories, when used properly, fosters motivation. The theories also have their individual shortcomings.

Experienced managers realize that employees differ greatly both in terms of their individual needs and in their perceptual interpretations. Attempting to motivate individual workers is a futile task. Instead, supervisors must create environments in which workers can motivate themselves. To accomplish this task, supervisors must have both an understanding of individual differences and a comprehensive knowledge of the various motivation theories. Then, an eclectic approach can be utilized in which the various theoretical frameworks are employed at different times for different workers.

Key Terms to Identify

Motivation
Content theories
Process theories
Reinforcement theories
Maslow's hierarchy of needs theory
ERG theory
Two-factor theory
Motivators
Satisfiers
Hygiene factors
Dissatisfiers
Need for achievement (nAch)
Need for power (nPower)
Need for affiliation (nAff)
Equity theory
Valence
Expectancy
Instrumentality
Goal setting theory
Goal difficulty
Goal specificity
Goal acceptance
Goal commitment
Operant conditioning
Behavior modification
Organizational Behavior modification (OB Mod)
Positive reinforcement
Negative reinforcement
Punishment
Extinction

Questions for Discussion

Do You Know the Facts?

1. Explain the difference in orientation among the content, process, and reinforcement theories of motivation.
2. How does movement along the need hierarchy by fulfillment–progression differ from ERG theory's frustration–progression?
3. Why are Herzberg's motivators considered satisfiers, and hygiene factors considered dissatisfiers?
4. What combination of achievement, power, and affiliation needs does McClelland consider best for supervisors? Why?
5. List the various ways inequity can be created.
6. Discuss the different types of reinforcers and their impact on behavior.

Can You Apply the Information Learned?

1. What methods would you use to ascertain the need levels of your employees?
2. Would you employ different motivation theories based on the level of workers supervised? Why or why not?

3. Some practitioners maintain that two-factor theory is only useful for satisfying supervisory positions and higher. Do you agree or disagree, and why?
4. How would you employ McClelland's nAch theory to motivate salespeople?

The Unmotivated Clerical

Erin O'Reilly sat alone in her office staring at the wall, trying to figure out what to do. She had just finished what she thought of as a "counseling session" with Jean, her clerical assistant, and it hadn't gone at all as she had hoped it would. Now, it wasn't clear to her what steps she should take next.

After graduating from college over a year ago, Erin had accepted a job with Wernett's Department Store. Wernett's, headquartered in Houston, was one of the largest department stores in the country, with branch stores in most of Texas's large cities and annual sales exceeding $6 billion. The buyer training program at Wernett's was nationally recognized as one of the very best, and Erin had been quite pleased to be one of the dozen college graduates selected to enroll in the program last year. At the end of the program, she was placed in the china and crystal department as an assistant buyer.

Erin's boss was Ted Goodman, an energetic workaholic in his early thirties. Ted had already made a name for himself at Wernett's as a buyer with impeccable tastes whose annual sales increases and profit margins were among the top in the company. Among Ted's talents was the ability to develop assistant buyers. Erin was bright, quick to learn, and highly motivated, and she felt fortunate indeed to have been assigned to Ted's department. Ted was very pleased with Erin's job performance and delegated increasing amounts of responsibility to her.

Each department at Wernett's was assigned a "clerical," who maintained all departmental records and handled the correspondence of the buyer and assistant buyers. Most of the clericals at Wernett's were young women who were recently out of high school. The starting wage for the position was somewhat above the minimum wage, but was still relatively low. Each clerical received small, but regular, increases in her hourly wage at the end of each six-month period. Each of them also received a 20 percent discount off the price of all clothing purchased at Wernett's and 10 percent off all other merchandise. Job turnover among clericals was relatively high; about half of them left Wernett's each year.

Jean Kroll, the clerical in Ted's department, had been with the department since she graduated from high school eighteen months ago. She was a quiet individual who worked at a slow, but generally steady pace. Her work occasionally contained errors, but in general, it was done accurately and on time.

This case was prepared by Professor Charles Pringle of James Madison University.

Jean's slow manner of speaking and working contrasted sharply with the rushed styles of the Type A dynamos who composed the buying team in the department. She never seemed to be in a rush, no matter how urgent the situation. This slowness was a frequent source of irritation to Ted, Erin, or the other assistant buyers who often needed something done *now*!

Jean usually went on her morning and afternoon coffee breaks alone. Although many clericals spent these breaks together in the employees' cafeteria or in one of the restaurants in the huge downtown store where all the buying offices were located, Jean usually sat by herself, sipping a soft drink.

Although Jean had never placed punctuality high on her priority list, her work attendance had been fairly reliable. Lately, however, even that had become somewhat erratic. To Erin, it seemed that Jean was intent on making certain that she used every "sick day" that was available to her.

Jean's absence last Monday had created a significant problem for the department. A number of reports had to be compiled prior to Ted's departure that afternoon for a trade show in Paris. Jean was supposed to be at work by 9:00 AM, but when she hadn't shown up by 9:15, no one was particularly worried because her arrival time had always been somewhat unpredictable. It wasn't until 9:40, however, that Jean called in to say that she was sick and would be unable to work that day. Erin immediately called Personnel to request a "temporary" for the day, but was told that all of them had been allocated by 9:30. Erin then spent the remainder of the morning and her lunch hour compiling the reports that Ted needed. During that time, she was unable to attend to her own duties and failed to initiate some shipments of china from warehouses to some of the branch stores that had had successful weekend sales.

Ted was disappointed with Erin's mismanagement of the situation, but became even more irate when two of the group sales managers at the branch stores called to ask where their china shipments were. Before he left on his trip, he told Erin to resolve "the Jean matter" by the time he returned.

Erin called Jean into her office on Tuesday morning. She told her that, although the department had been fairly pleased with her overall job performance, Jean's unpredictable arrival times and attendance were placing the department in a bind. She detailed the problems that Jean's absence and late call had created on Monday. Erin concluded by indicating that, if this behavior occurred again, she would have to place a formal written reprimand in Jean's personnel file. Erin then allowed Jean to respond to her appraisal. Jean sat quietly for several moments, then looked at Erin, shrugged her shoulders, and returned to her work.

Questions for Discussion

1. Can Jean be motivated? Explain how by referring to:
   a. Herzberg's two-factor theory.
   b. Vroom's VIE (expectancy) theory.
   c. organizational behavior modification theory.

Endnotes and References

1 Abraham H. Maslow, "A Theory of Human Motivation," *Psychological Review,* Vol. 50 (1943): 370–396.

2 Clayton P. Alderfer, "An Empirical Test of a New Theory of Human Needs," *Organizational Behavior and Human Performance,* Vol. 4 (1969): 142–175. Also see Clayton P. Alderfer, *Existence, Relatedness, and Growth: Human Needs in Organizational Settings* (New York: The Free Press, 1972).

3 Frederick Herzberg, Bernard Mausner, and Barbara S. Snyderman, *The Motivation to Work* (New York: John Wiley & Sons, 1959). Also see Frederick Herzberg, "One More Time: How Do You Motivate Employees?" *Harvard Business Review* (January–February 1968): 53–62.

4 David C. McClelland, *The Achieving Society* (Princeton, NJ: Van Nostrand, 1961); David C. McClelland, "Business Drive and National Achievement," *Harvard Business Review,* Vol. 40, No. 4 (1962): 99–112; and David C. McClelland and David H. Burnham, "Power is the Great Motivator," *Harvard Business Review,* Vol. 54, No. 2 (1976): 100–110.

5 See Richard M. Steers, *Introduction to Organizational Behavior,* 3rd ed. (Glenview, IL: Scott, Foresman & Company, 1988): 171.

6 See David C. McClelland and R. E. Boyatzis, "Leadership Motive Pattern and Long-term Success in Management," *Journal of Applied Psychology,* Vol. 67 (1982): 737–743.

7 J. Stacy Adams, "Toward an Understanding of Inequity," *Journal of Abnormal and Social Psychology,* Vol. 67, No. 5 (November 1963): 422–436. Also see Robert D. Pritchard, "Equity Theory: A Review and Critique," *Organizational Behavior and Human Performance,* Vol. 4 (1969): 176–211.

8 Victor H. Vroom, *Work and Motivation* (New York: John Wiley & Sons, Inc., 1964).

9 For a discussion of the practicality of expectancy theory in industry, see O. C. Brenner and Marc G. Singer, "Expectancy Theory Revisited: For the Manager or the Academician," *Management Quarterly,* Vol. 25, No. 2 (1984): 14–24.

10 Edwin Locke, "Toward a Theory of Task Motivation and Incentives," *Organizational Behavior and Human Performance,* Vol. 3 (1968): 157–189.

11 Gary P. Latham and Edwin A. Locke, "Goal Setting—A Motivational Technique that Works, *Organizational Dynamics,* Vol. 8 (Autumn 1979): 68–80.

12 B. F. Skinner, *Science and Human Behavior* (New York: Macmillan Publishing Company, 1953).

13 Fred Luthans and Robert Kreitner, *Organizational Behavior Modification and Beyond* (Glenview, IL: Scott, Foresman & Company, 1985).

14 W. F. Dowling, "At Emery Air Freight: Positive Reinforcement Boosts Performance," *Organizational Dynamics,* Vol. 2, No. 1 (1973): 41–50.

Chapter 16

Fostering Communication

Objectives

After reading this chapter you should understand:

1. The communication process.
2. The way communications flow within organizations.
3. The different methods of communication and their use in organizations.
4. The barriers to effective communication.
5. The way to improve communication.
6. The different communication styles people use to transmit messages.
7. The different organizational communication philosophies, and their impact on the delivery of messages.

With the possible exception of motivation, it is unlikely that another subject area in business receives more attention and emphasis than communication. Research designed to examine the communication process is continually being conducted. In training programs and classrooms, professionals and teachers employ countless hours attempting to improve their students' written and oral communication skills. The reasons for these efforts are readily apparent. Whether it is person to person, organization to organization, or nation to nation, communication continues to be an essential component of cooperative effort and coordinated activity.

The significance of organizational communication is undeniable. Its primary purpose is to facilitate and enhance all phases of the work process. Supervisors and employees alike require a continual flow of information in order to effectively complete their assigned tasks. If satisfactory communication is absent from the workplace, the potential for workers and supervisors to make decisions based on insufficient or misperceived data is heightened. When decisions are made as a result of distorted communication, the ensuing outcomes are often a function of chance, and they are more likely to be motivated by a desire to satisfy individual rather than organizational goals. On the other hand, effective communication leads to coordinated activity, resulting in the fulfillment of both company and individual objectives.

In addition to work-related information, employees require broader, more extensive knowledge about the organization's economic health, present and future goals, and personnel policies. Employees have a vested interest in how these issues will affect them now, as well as in the future. This knowledge further functions to reinforce and strengthen individual goals so that they can be consistent with those of the organization.

Communication is not the sole criterion for competent performance, successful management–employee relations, and employee satisfaction. It is conceivable for organizations to convey their goals and objectives well, but to not recognize the fact that their plans may be inappropriate and ineffectual. Similarly, supervisors who convey an inadequate message clearly may be effective communicators, but ineffective managers. Communication is a means by which good management practices are instituted. Effective communication alone does not guarantee a problem-free work environment. Its absence, however, inevitably contributes to and often produces unnecessary complications and disruptions in the workplace.

Adequate communication skills are a necessary prerequisite for satisfactory performance in all supervisory positions. It is estimated that managers and supervisors spend in excess of 50 percent of their time in verbal communications.[1] Individuals possess varying degrees of communication skills as a result of their experiences, training, and personality orientations. A primary concern of management is to develop and improve communication on all organizational levels for the purpose of creating a favorable working environment. This chapter focuses on the communication process, the causes of communication breakdowns, the ways of overcoming barriers to effective communication, and the techniques used within organizations to foster productive communication.

The Communication Process

Communication is a two-way process. Simply stated, communication occurs when one person transmits a message to another. When communication is successful, the message sent and the message received are the same. Breakdowns occur, however, when the information sent differs from what is received. In order to minimize the problems inherent in communication and to facilitate effective transmission of information, an understanding of the various elements composing the process is required. These include: the sender or source of the message, encoding, the medium, decoding, the receiver or responder, and the feedback process.[2]

The Source

Within organizations, the source is usually an employee, a company representative, or a group of individuals. The source determines the need for the communication, who receives the message, and the most effective method by which the information is disseminated.

> **Source**
>
> *The source, sender, or communicator originates the message.*

Encoding

Encoding can consist of verbal presentations, such as speeches or conversations, written formats, such as letters and reports, pictorial presentations, such as graphs and charts, or any other symbol the sender determines is appropriate for conveying the message. The crucial consideration in determining the encoding symbol is the likelihood of the receiver misinterpreting the message. If ambiguous symbols are selected, especially those which have diverse meanings, the likelihood of a communication breakdown is enhanced. Even when using a common language, care must be taken because words mean different things to different people. Effective communication necessitates adequate thought prior to transmission; thus, encoding is the critical element.[3]

> **Encoding**
>
> *Encoding is the process by which senders translate their thoughts and ideas into systematic symbols which can be transmitted.*

The Medium

Once the message has been encoded, the receiver must decide on the most effective channel for sending the information. The manner in which encoded messages are transmitted can have a significant impact on how they are received. For example, a verbally encoded message may be delivered face to face, by telephone, or through a recording. Each of these transmission media has different features. Face-to-face communication allows for additional information to be transmitted in the form of nonverbal communication. Telephones enable the message to be transmitted instantaneously, but provide no additional information. Recordings allow the message to be repeated in its entirety at other times and for other people. Each of these media has benefits as well as shortcomings.

Choosing the appropriate channel fosters communication, but making an inappropriate choice may impede the process.

> **Medium**
>
> *The medium is the channel or communication vehicle chosen for the transmission of the message.*

Decoding

When individuals decode messages, they rely to a great extent on experiences and knowledge from their past. If the sender and the receiver attach the same meaning to the message symbols, the **decoding** will be successful. If, however, there is variance between the symbol interpretation of the sender and receiver, the information will probably be misinterpreted.

> **Decoding**
>
> *Decoding is the process by which the receiver interprets and attaches meaning to the message.*

The Receiver

The manner in which receivers interpret or decode messages is dependent on their unique traits, characteristics, and past experiences. Senders have the opportunity to take into account the appropriateness of the message when encoding and transmitting information. Receivers choose whether or not to decode the message, place effort in interpreting it, and take any subsequent action. For example, the author of this text encoded the material for students, but not all students will expend the effort necessary to decode and integrate the material.

> **Receiver**
>
> *The receiver, or responder, is the individual or group to whom the message is directed.*

Feedback

Effective communication usually requires knowledge of results. Of course, the receiver may still fully understand the message even if the sender does not receive feedback. For most communications, however, adhering to this procedure

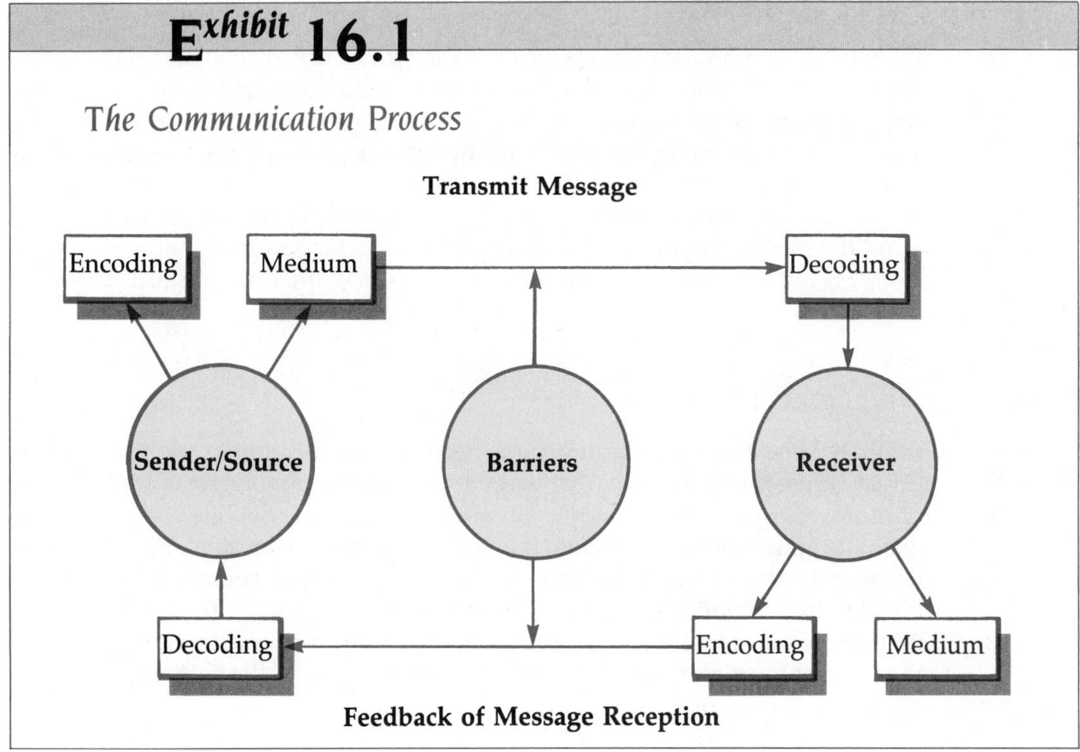

Exhibit 16.1

The Communication Process

is at best risky. Usually some part of a communication, particularly task directions, requires explanation, further elaboration, or clarification. Senders should seek to verify whether or not the message has been received and fully understood. Viewed in this fashion, the communication process is circular. After sending the message, the source receives feedback and may re-start the cycle if the receiver needs clarification of the initial information.

Communications Feedback

Communications feedback is knowledge the sender obtains which indicates whether or not the receiver has correctly interpreted the message.

Directions of Communication

Within organizations communications flow in four distinct directions. These directions are: downward, upward, horizontally, or diagonally.

Downward Communication

Downward communication exemplifies the typical organizational chain of command in which information flows from superior to subordinate. As information moves downward along the organizational hierarchy, the message grows in dimension. For example, the source of the message may be the president of the company, who indicates that he expects the next quarter's profits to expand by 10 percent. The recipients of the message, the vice-presidents, may further expand the message to include goals and objectives for accomplishing this expansion. Eventually, the message reaches employees in the form of specific job procedures.

Upward Communication

In order to be effective, organizations need upward communication as much as downward communication. **Upward communication** involves the transmission of messages from subordinates to superiors. Interestingly, while communication expands in the downward mode, it usually involves censoring, editing, and condensing in the upward channel. In order for upward communication to be a viable tool within organizations, management must view the sources of the messages, the employees, as having credibility. If workers are viewed as nonthinking entities and their communications are sloughed off, then eventually a valuable source of information will be curtailed.

Horizontal Communication

Horizontal communication involves the lateral flow of information from colleague to colleague or department to department. While often overlooked, this communication channel may sometimes have a more significant impact on the organization than the vertical channels discussed previously. The major impact of this type of communication channel can be seen when coordinated activity is necessary in order to achieve common corporate objectives. In addition, horizontal communication fosters social interaction, group cohesiveness, and its resulting need satisfaction.

Diagonal Communication

Used less frequently than other communication channels, **diagonal communication** occurs when the source of a message cannot effectively reach the receiver through other existing channels. For example, a salesperson may require information from shipping in order to determine the possibility of meeting a major customer's time schedule for delivery. Rather than approach his/her manager, who in turn will contact the shipping supervisor, he/she may communicate directly with the shipping scheduler. This communication network can save needed time, and potentially lost sales.[4]

Exhibit 16.2

Organizational Communication Channels

Downward	Upward	Horizontal
Job instructions	Attitude surveys	Meetings
Telephone	Telephone	Telephone
Grapevine	Grapevine	Grapevine
Training programs	Social affairs	Social affairs
Memorandum	Memorandum	Memorandum
Handbooks/ manuals	Grievances	Handbooks/manuals
Newsletter	Suggestion boxes	Newsletter
Union meetings	Union representatives	Union activities
Performance review	Performance review	Lunch meetings

Methods of Communication

There are three methods of communication used within organizations. These are: written, verbal, and nonverbal communication.[5]

Written Communications

Written communications take many forms within organizations. Some methods, such as memoranda, reports, manuals, and employee handbooks, are most suitable for internal organizational purposes. Other modes, such as letters and printed forms (for example, application blanks), are used more frequently for external communication purposes. Much of this type of communication is downward in nature, for the primary purpose of disseminating company information to employees.

There are three major advantages to using written communications. First, they enable the sender to carefully consider messages prior to sending them, which enhances the clarity of the communication. Second, the sender does not need to be present in order to effectively communicate the message. Much time and money can be saved by sending a letter through the mail, particularly when mass communication is necessary. Finally, written communications provide documentation of facts. This factor becomes increasingly more important in complying with legal guidelines.

Ironically, the second advantage of written communications also serves as its major shortcoming. Without being present, the sender receives little, if any, feedback as to whether or not the receiver interprets the message correctly. This missing feedback can also include nonverbal cues, which can function as either a hindrance or a benefit. With the ever-increasing popularity of computers, this drawback is minimized. Now, almost instantaneous feedback is possible through the use of electronic mail.[6]

Verbal Communications

Verbal communications allow for two-way interaction and immediate feedback as to how the message has been received. These communications take many forms and include one-on-one daily conversations, committee and staff meetings, speeches and lectures, and telephone transmissions.

The major disadvantages of verbal communications are two-fold. First, they do not serve to document important messages. Often, controversy arises at a future date as to what had been agreed upon earlier. In addition, the communication is instantaneous and does not allow for advanced planning of messages. This factor has the potential for causing problems, particularly when the interchange involves controversial issues. Without the benefit of time, people are prone to speak emotionally, rather than rationally, and to convey messages they may later regret.

Nonverbal Communications

Nonverbal communications include any and all communications which do not involve the use of words either in verbal or in written form. Approximately 60 to 90 percent of all the messages sent are nonverbal in nature.[7] Probably the most popularized and researched nonverbal communication method is *body language.* People's facial expressions and gestures serve to send messages to others. Receiving a frown in response to a request for a raise is probably a signal that it should not be expected in the near future. On the other hand, a smile and a wink would probably indicate that the request is viewed favorably.

Aside from body language, nonverbal messages are sent through environmental stimuli. Colors can be used to convey emotional meanings. Red carpet may convey harshness, while blue may communicate warmth and sensitivity. Supervisors who sit behind the desk when communicating with employees may be perceived as formal and distant. Depending on the intent of the message, senders would be well advised to consider the effects of their nonverbal communications. When confronted with verbal messages whose meaning conflicts with the nonverbal message sent, receivers invariably choose the meaning attached to the nonverbal message.[8]

Barriers to Effective Communication

It would probably not be an overstatement to say that every day, in every organization, at least one breakdown in communication occurs. A communication breakdown results if the message sent and the message received differ in meaning. Some of these mishaps are of considerable magnitude and involve large numbers of employees. Other communication failures are minor in nature, and may merely involve a mix-up between people regarding which restaurant they were to meet at for lunch. Regardless of the number of people involved, however, the causes of these breakdowns can usually be traced to barriers erected by either the sender, the receiver, or both. Identifying and understanding how these various barriers affect the process is the initial step in improving communications.

Most of the problems associated with communication breakdowns result from the manner in which senders and receivers relay and interpret messages. These characteristics are usually innate, and they are a result of cultural heritage, environmental influences, and previous experiences. In addition, there are organizational variables, mostly a function of organizational structure, which impact on communications. Taken together, these personal and organizational variables contribute to the way messages are sent and subsequently interpreted. This section discusses the different problems which contribute to the majority of message distortions.[9]

Perceptual Impacts

People's reality is based on their individual, unique interpretation and perception of real events. Therefore, what one person views as beneficial may be seen as detrimental by another. In addition, one individual may perceive a communication as favorable, while another person may view it as undesirable. Consider the following case.

> Three supervisors, Alice, Joan, and Pete, were leaving a weekly staff meeting. Upon entering the plant, the three supervisors noticed a group of employees, including some of their own workers, chatting and laughing in a corner of the plant. Alice, a renowned democratic manager, thought to herself, "How wonderful. The talk I gave my workers on coordinating with other departments has succeeded. I must remember to praise my workers for their immediate response." Joan, who was highly authoritarian, with a theory X philosophy, thought, "There they are goofing off again. Not only are they not working, they are also distracting others. I'll get them." Pete, now he's a little different. He knows just why they are laughing. They are obviously laughing at him! He is going to really fix them.

The preceding case demonstrates the problems that can result from differing perceptual interpretations. All the supervisors saw the same event, at the same point in time, in the same environment, yet each interpreted the message differently. As a result, the actions taken will vary greatly. At best, because the interpretations of the communications are so diverse, only one of the supervisors ascertained its correct meaning. In fact, it is quite conceivable that there is a fourth interpretation and that none of the supervisors really interpreted the situation accurately at all.

Past Experiences

Senders encode and receivers decode information largely based on their past experiences. If common experiences are not shared by both the sender and the receiver, then the symbols used in transmitting the message are not interpreted similarly. Suppose, for example, that workers have been informed by their manager that the company has had a substantial third-quarter drop in sales. In the past, a drop has indicated low wage increases in the next year. What the workers heard was that they could expect to see small, if any, salary increases. Management is then befuddled by the hard stance the union takes at the bargaining table to thwart the wage reductions they had no intentions of imposing.

Semantics

People attribute different meanings to words, even when they speak the same language. For example, a consultant once experienced a communication breakdown on an assignment in a Middle Eastern country. Responding to a worker's inquiry as to the nature of some American leisure time activities, the consultant responded that "Many people enjoy shooting pool." To this day, the worker cannot fathom why Americans take delight in firing a gun into a swimming pool.

Semantics

Semantics is the study of meaning in language.

Of course, it is easy to see how **semantics** can interfere with communication when dealing with people whose native tongues are dissimilar.[10] But does it really interfere with workers who share common language? The answer is yes. Different educational levels, peer groupings, cultures, and regional variations all help to diversify the meaning attached to words of the same language.

Jargon

Anyone who has had experience with computer terminology was probably initially befuddled by the use of common English words in a totally different context. Terms such as APL juice, Microfiche, card punch, numeric punch, zone punch, and card or paper jam do not refer to food. This use of specialized terminology or **jargon** is a common barrier, particularly in light of the fact that most users of jargon take it for granted that everyone understands their terminology. Consider the following example.

> Pamela was recently employed as the administrative assistant for a senior vice-president of a bank's data processing division. On her third day of employment her boss requested that she "Check the fiche for his DDA balance as he was going to a YBA meeting that evening." Pamela did nothing. She knew what a fish was, but was not sure why a trip to the supermarket was necessary. Furthermore, what were a DDA (demand deposit account, a bankers' term for a checking account) and a YBA (Young Bankers Association)? She was also afraid to ask, not wanting to look incompetent in an area she thought she might have been supposed to know. The end result was a communication breakdown, an irate boss, and a frustrated employee.

Jargon

Jargon is specialized or technical language within a trade, profession, or cultural group.

Evaluative Judgments

Many communication breakdowns occur because of the value judgments receivers make about the message. People have a tendency to hear what they expect or want to hear. They receive and retain information that meets their personal needs.[11] If a message coincides with already existing beliefs, receivers tend to

Exhibit 16.3

Using Computer Jargon[12]

It is very easy to describe a full meal as we sit at the table. Breakfast consists of your choice of serial, LIOCS and bagels, or a stack of pancakes and sausage links. Buffered toast with either card jam or paper jam is served with every meal. The drink available with your breakfast is APL juice.

For lunch, one might begin with nested loop soup and then choose from such delicacies as microfiche under glass or shared segments of beef.

It is no wonder that with all this food around, we have to worry about de-bugs. The health department would never shut us down though, since everything is washed in a hot data stream after each use.

pay close attention to the message and to accept its content. On the other hand, a message which contradicts already established beliefs will probably be rejected or discounted. For example, if a sales manager for a tire manufacturer has predicted a strong season for snow tire sales, then meteorological information predicting a mild winter may be ignored.

Status Differences

Within organizations, status levels affect the transmission and receipt of information. People with higher status expect to control communications. This is accomplished by either dominating the communication verbally or sending nonverbal signals through the use of body language. In these exchanges, the person with lower status is usually expected to demonstrate a certain degree of respect and to censor any contradictory communications. In addition, the communications which arise from the lower status person, particularly in a subordinate–superior relationship, are designed to foster liking rather than information exchange. Lower status individuals will communicate what they feel is in their best interest, including information they feel the supervisor wants to hear.[13] Consequently, achievements are frequently communicated upward, while mistakes and errors are withheld.

Organizational status levels also affect the emotional states of the parties involved in the communication. The person of lower status is prone to be anxious and fearful, particularly during stressful scenarios, such as disciplinary sessions. As a result, the communications are more likely to be received from a defensive, rather than objective, frame of reference.

Source Credibility

More often than not, people are influenced by sender characteristics when judging the significance of a message. If the communicator has high credibility, the message is perceived as truthful and significant. On the other hand, if the sender is negatively evaluated, the message is likely to be disregarded. Accepting messages based on **source credibility** is not an entirely inappropriate procedure. Naturally, one would be wise to adhere to a sender's advice when seeking information in the communicator's field of expertise. For example, requesting medical information from a doctor and giving credence to the message based on the sender's credentials is probably appropriate. Seeking legal advice from this same doctor, however, and taking it as the truth because of the overall esteem afforded this person would be foolhardy. Similarly, college students, who accept as fact everything written in textbooks and everything expounded by their professors, would be well advised to examine if what they are accepting is the source or the facts.

One of the overwhelming reasons individuals ignore information from certain sources is because of a tendency to *stereotype*. Stereotyping is a form of prejudging individuals or groups using incomplete, distorted, and often biased generalizations. For example, the stereotypical view of the Chinese being dominated by Russia (along with the knowledge that Russia did not want a war with the U.S.) caused the United States to ignore the warning communications which eventually led to the Korean war.

Emotional Impacts

A major source of communication breakdowns is the effect emotions have on both senders and receivers. Perception and judgment are both hampered by extreme emotions. Feelings, particularly stressful ones, affect thought patterns and the way in which communications are sent and received. During periods of insecurity, such as economic recessions, a normal occurrence, such as the rearranging of office furniture, may be viewed by workers as a sign that their jobs are in jeopardy. In times of prosperity, this same action may be interpreted as a favorable improvement in the work environment.

Information Screening or Filtering

In many instances, sources intentionally withhold or censor information from receivers. Sometimes this is done because the sender believes additional information is unnecessary and will only serve to confuse the receiver. Other times, the organization determines that additional information should be withheld for proprietary reasons. In either case, there is an inherent danger that **information screening** may cause the message to be misunderstood or interpreted inaccurately, and that the ensuing breakdown will not be able to be repaired later.[14]

Information Overload

With the increasing use of computers, **information overload** is becoming commonplace. The abundance of computer reports, coupled with all other communications, is making it virtually impossible for receivers to decode all available information. As a result, receivers selectively choose to interpret the messages they deem most important. This selective attention causes decisions to be made based on partial data.

Time Pressures

Most managers and supervisors operate under time constraints. There never seems to be ample time to complete all necessary work tasks. One area which suffers immediately is communications. Supervisors do not have sufficient time to communicate frequently with each employee. Communications are abbreviated, and often workers are passed over in the dissemination process. Furthermore, time constraints may not allow sufficient opportunity for proper encoding or decoding of messages by senders and receivers. This may result in the confounding of otherwise simple messages.

Noise

A common, but often overlooked, barrier to communication is noise. Noise can be defined as any unwanted sound. Particularly in factory settings, the presence of noise in the environment can serve to distort communications or to prevent them from being received. In addition, rumors, which can be classified as unwanted sounds or noise, may hamper relevant communications by preoccupying people's attention. A fueled rumor of a plant shutdown may cause workers to ignore management's communication in favor of a union organizer's promises.

The Absence of Feedback[15]

Perhaps the most important barrier to communication is the omission of feedback within the communication process. Feedback serves to verify that the message the sender encoded and the one the receiver decoded were the same. Without this final step, the sender cannot be certain that the message was received and understood.

The omission of feedback causes at least two major problems. First, the sender may have more information to detail, depending upon the receiver's response to the initial message. Without feedback, the source does not know whether to proceed or to reissue the first message. Second, without verification, receivers may act upon misunderstood messages. The result may be inappropriate behaviors.[16]

Improving Communications

Communication may undergo interference when messages are sent and received. Overcoming these barriers requires both senders and receivers to improve the encoding and decoding processes. Supervisors desiring to improve their communication skills must endeavor to improve the encoding of their messages, as well as the decoding of the communications they receive. In order to successfully accomplish this task, the first requirement is to make a conscious effort to identify the communication problems that exist. Once breakdowns are identified, various techniques can be used to improve the interchanges.

The Communications Audit

Most organizations routinely audit systems to determine if they are functioning properly. Financial statements are reviewed periodically, machinery is regularly checked, and job procedures are continually monitored for efficiency.[17] In the same manner, the organization's communication channels and networks should be periodically reviewed in order to improve their efficiency. Techniques, such as surveys, questionnaires, or interviews, may be designed to elicit information about communication problems which have been encountered. These instruments should be administered to all personnel levels, and the results can be analyzed for common and frequent problems in the communication network. Once this has been accomplished, appropriate techniques can be employed to overcome the various barriers that have been detected.

Overcoming the Barriers

Use Feedback

Probably the single most effective method for improving the communication process is through the use of feedback. Face-to-face interchanges probably provide the greatest opportunity to gather feedback, and the use of this exchange medium is recommended whenever possible. Within organizations, however, face-to-face communications are not always possible. This is especially true for downward communications designed to reach large numbers of employees. Memoranda concerning important policies may have been distributed, but there is no guarantee that they were read or understood. In these instances, the improvement of the communication process necessitates that the source actively seek verification of the message. Upward communication methods, such as group meetings, suggestion boxes, birthday luncheons, and open forums, are examples of programs organizations use to improve the feedback process.

Be Empathetic

Everyone has probably heard the phrase "Put yourself in the other person's shoes." Being empathetic requires that the sender become receiver oriented. Prior to sending the message, particularly those which are emotional or controversial, the sender would be well advised to analyze how the receiver is likely to interpret the information. In many instances, prior diagnoses of the receiver's background and experiences may cause the sender to modify or change the symbols used to encode the message, as well as the medium used for its transmission. This extra effort may alleviate misinterpretation of the message content by the receiver.

Time Messages Carefully

Proper timing of messages can foster effective communications, while poor timing often promotes misinterpretations. The time of day, people's emotions, and task involvement all have the potential to interfere with the encoding and decoding processes. Early in the morning, before workers are inundated with voluminous amounts of communications, may be the most appropriate time to send important messages. Later in the day, receivers may not have ample time available to properly decode all the information they receive. Similarly, people involved in emotional issues or tasks requiring a high degree of attention and concentration interpret communications differently than under normal circumstances. Senders would be well advised to consider these factors when issuing their messages. In fact, the accurate timing of messages is a key factor in overcoming resistance to change, a major problem in many organizations.

Use Simple Vocabulary

Differences in language have been identified as another major source of breakdowns in communication. Aside from the use of semantics and jargon, breakdowns occur because of differences in vocabulary levels. Professors, attorneys, and government agencies, among others, have been criticized for their ability to transform simple facts into complex enigmas by their use of technical, intricate, and often unnecessary language. Supervisors and managers must make concerted efforts to ascertain their workers' vocabulary levels before issuing messages. People are reluctant to inform others that they do not understand their vocabulary (How many students raise their hands to inform professors of this fact?), because they are afraid to appear ignorant. Instead, they guess at the meaning of words, which often results in a misinterpreted message. Rather than attempting to impress people with sophisticated vocabulary, senders should use simple, direct language.

Use Several Media for Reiteration

Repetition is a key factor in both learning and verifying of information. Isolating the important components of a message and reiterating them to the receiver through another medium enhances the probability of the message being decoded correctly. Many people make verbal commitments and subsequently verify, confirm, or remind the other party of the obligation by letter or phone. This practice, used frequently to confirm appointments, eliminates many communication mishaps. The use of many channels to highlight important facts may have the most benefit when the receiver is being sent messages containing new facts or procedures which differ from established practice.

Learn to Listen

Most people listen poorly. Listening skills are one of the weakest points demonstrated by managers involved in verbal communications. In fact, most managers listen with only about 25 percent efficiency.[18] This is especially true when they are involved in communications with people on lower levels of the organizational hierarchy.[19] In spite of this fact, education and training resources are predominantly devoted to reading, writing, and speaking.

Improving communications necessitates that individuals develop their listening skills. For human beings, this is not an easy task. People prefer to talk rather than listen. Listening does not appear to be a natural phenomenon. Rather, it requires a conscious effort and a willingness on the part of people to actively engage in this activity.[20] In addition, good listening requires that messages be heard fully (not judged prematurely), analyzed carefully, and interpret-

Exhibit 16.4

Ten Guides for Effective Listening

1. **Stop talking!**
   You cannot listen if you are talking.
   Polonius (*Hamlet*): "Give every man thine ear, but few thy voice."
2. **Put the talker at ease.**
   Help a person feel free to talk.
   This is often called a permissive environment.
3. **Show a talker that you want to listen.**
   Look and act interested. Do not read your mail while someone talks.
   Listen to understand rather than to oppose.
4. **Remove distractions.**
   Don't doodle, tap, or shuffle papers.
   Will it be quieter if you shut the door?
5. **Empathize with talkers.**
   Try to help yourself see the other person's point of view.
6. **Be patient.**
   Allow plenty of time. Do not interrupt a talker.
   Don't start for the door or walk away.
7. **Hold your temper.**
   An angry person takes the wrong meaning from words.
8. **Go easy on argument and criticism.**
   This puts people on the defensive, and they may "clam up" or become angry.
   Do not argue: Even if you win, you lose.
9. **Ask questions.**
   This encourages a talker and shows that you are listening.
   It helps to develop points further.
10. **Stop talking!**
    This is first and last, because all other guides depend on it.
    You cannot do an effective listening job while you are talking.
    - Nature gave people two ears but only one tongue, which is a gentle hint that they should listen more than they talk.
    - Listening requires two ears, one for meaning and one for feeling.
    - Decision makers who do not listen have less information for making sound decisions.

Source: Keith Davis, *Human Behavior at Work: Organizational Behavior*, 6th ed. (New York: McGraw-Hill Book Company, 1981): 413. Reprinted with permission.

ed without the imposition of subjective bias. In order to achieve proficiency in the skill of listening, extensive practice is required.

Managerial Communication Styles

Managers and supervisors exhibit varying styles when communicating with others. The effectiveness of the particular style depends on the situational variables and the particular characteristics of the communicator. These styles have been identified as: controlling, dynamic, equalitarian, relinquishing, structuring, and withdrawal.[21]

1. **Controlling style** Used primarily to send one-way messages. Unless the purposes of the sender are served, feedback is totally omitted. This style is most effective when the sender has unequivocal control or is viewed as an expert.
2. **Dynamic style** Characterized as "pep talk" style. It is a one-way communication technique designed to boost morale. **Dynamic communication** is most effective when the group members have the skills and abilities to accomplish the tasks.
3. **Equalitarian style** Characteristic of democratic leaders, this style epitomizes two-way communication. The goal of this style is the promotion of interpersonal relations and productivity. **Equalitarian communication** is most effective in complex decision-making situations.
4. **Relinquishing style** Characterized by the sender's willingness to allow others to play dominant roles in the communication process. The goal of this style is to promote cohesive, independent groups. **Relinquishing communication** is most effective when the sender is highly experienced and is dealing with knowledgeable receivers who are willing to accept responsibility.
5. **Structuring style** Characterized by the use of verbal interchanges to detail already established policies and procedures. The primary goal of this style is the clarification, elaboration, and confirmation of existing messages. **Structuring communication** is effectively used by human resource managers in explaining complex tasks, newly developed programs, and handbooks and manuals.
6. **Withdrawal style** Characterized by an absence of communication. The primary goal of the sender is to eliminate communication. The continual use of **withdrawal communication** has serious repercussions for organizations.

In analyzing the six communication styles, it appears that the use of the equalitarian style provides the greatest benefits for organizations. Coupled with the occasional and tactful use of the dynamic, structuring, and relinquishing techniques, supervisors can effectively send messages and expect to receive

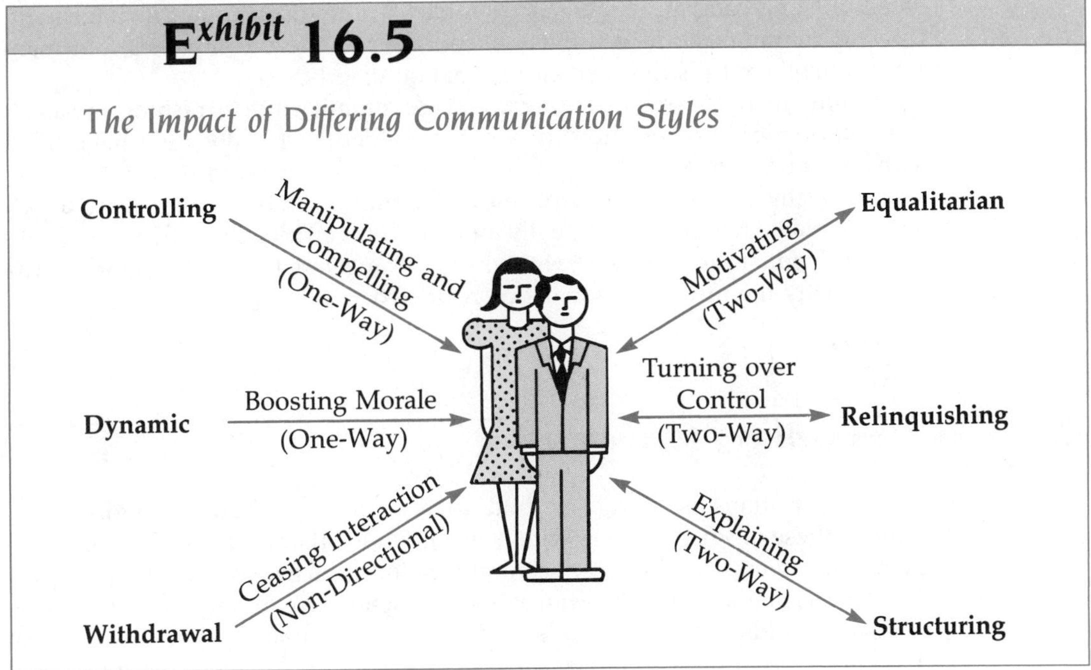

feedback and compliance to work-related instructions. Regretfully, the use of the controlling and withdrawal styles of communication is commonplace in organizations. Supervisors find the controlling style all too easy to use, and they inadvertently create environments which foster withdrawal in workers. Eventually, the only organizational channel remaining is downward communications. As a result, workers become frustrated, alienated, and demotivated.

Organizational Communication Philosophies

The communication delivery mechanisms organizations install depend largely on the organizations' beliefs about what information employees should have. The most common philosophy is probably the belief that workers should be given only enough information to enable them to satisfactorily perform their jobs. All other information is restricted or withheld. These companies are most likely to use only downward communication channels. A second philosophy maintains that workers should receive the information necessary to perform their jobs, and any non-proprietary information will be disseminated, provided company time and resources do not have to be expended. These enterprises allow for upward communication, but do not actively encourage it. A third belief held by organizations is that employees should be provided with all necessary job-related information, and non-proprietary information should be disseminated utilizing company time and resources, at the discretion of management. Upward communication is actively encouraged in these companies, but management still controls the type of information distributed.

Finally, there are organizations which are committed to furnishing any available information workers need or want, provided that it does not have to be withheld for legitimate business reasons. Company time and resources are reserved for this purpose, and sophisticated communication networks are developed, implemented, and continually monitored for efficiency. In these organizations, individuals are provided with either the answers to their questions or the reasons why the information must be restricted.

Communication Delivery Mechanisms

Most organizations use formal methods to facilitate the exchange of information. Some of these mechanisms are widely used, while others are specific to individual organizations. The variety of communication vehicles available for organizational use is limitless. As communication problems arise, enterprises can choose to develop additional methods, specific to their companies, which will assist them in overcoming future obstacles. In fact, some companies continually expand their communication delivery mechanisms based on just such a procedure. When a communication breakdown occurs, organizational members analyze the cause of the malfunction. If the analysis reveals that the current vehicles are

Exhibit 16.6

Four Communication Philosophies

Level 1 Only information necessary for the performance of their jobs will be detailed to employees.

Level 2 Information necessary for job performance will be disseminated. Any additional information will be provided as long as company time and resources are not used.

Level 3 Information necessary for job performance will be disseminated. Company time and resources may be expended for other non-proprietary information, at the discretion of management.

Level 4 Optimum Any information employees want is disseminated, provided it does not have to be withheld for legitimate business or personal reasons. In the event that information must be withheld, management is committed to explaining the reasons for the action.

inadequate for handling the problem, a new delivery mechanism is created to arrest future mishaps.

The particular networks and channels companies choose to use are founded on the company's communication philosophy. Those organizations desiring to disseminate only work-related information employ transmission vehicles designed for downward communication. On the other hand, organizations committed to the philosophy that workers should have all the available information they desire, develop and implement unique vehicles to foster upward communication.

Some Unique Communication Vehicles

There are certain basic communication channels which are used by all organizations. Casual conversations, interviews, committee meetings, attitude surveys, and policy and procedure handbooks and manuals can usually be found within the communication structure of most companies. Some organizations, however, particularly those adhering to the latter two communication philosophies mentioned earlier, have developed simple, but unique modes of transmitting messages and eliciting comments. A look at some of these specialized systems demonstrates how specific communication vehicles can be designed to solve individual organizational needs.

Birthday or anniversary meals

A popular communication vehicle for many companies is monthly luncheons or dinners. These meetings are usually held away from the work environment, and they are attended by the workers whose birthdays or work anniversaries fall during that month, a representative from the human resource department, and a senior executive. Immediate supervisors and managers are intentionally excluded from the meetings, so as not to stifle discussion. During these meetings workers are encouraged to voice their opinions and concerns about relevant matters. Messages are either immediately addressed by the executive present or researched and responded to at a later date.

It is apparent that the use of birthday or anniversary meals requires a willingness and commitment by the organization to share information with its workers. On-the-spot questions can sometimes pose embarrassing moments for upper management, particularly when they have been uninformed or misinformed concerning workplace events.

Question and answer reports

Many organizations use a suggestion box system as a means of promoting upward communication from their workers. In its simplest form, boxes are strategically placed in various locations around the organization. At their convenience, workers place suggestions for improvement of the work environment into the boxes. Subsequently, upper management, at their discretion, responds or does not respond to the suggestions.

A more sophisticated approach to suggestion boxes involves the use of **question and answer reports.** Like the suggestion box system, boxes are placed strategically around the workplace. It is at this point that the similarity ends. Rather than filling the boxes with suggestions for improvement, workers have the freedom to place questions in these boxes. At the end of each month, upper management responds to each and every question, in written tabloid form, regardless of the nature of the question posed. Each question, complete with any spelling or grammatical errors, is printed exactly as it was submitted, and is followed by its answer. Only expletives and individual names are censored and replaced with asterisks. The bulletin is then distributed to all employees or posted on company bulletin boards.

In order to effectively use this technique, a company must be committed to a communication philosophy that believes in freedom of information for workers. Under these circumstances, a reasonable explanation is given to workers regarding the exclusion of certain classified information which must remain unavailable to them. Unless the company maintains an open communication philosophy, it will be unable to respond to each and every question posed.

Exhibit 16.7

Excerpts from a Question and Answer Bulletin

Questions and Answers Bulletin

Question #6: My foreman makes me wear safety glasses to and from breaks to "protect me" but 2nd shift employees enter the department and hang around prior to the start of 2nd shift and they don't wear their safety glasses. This isn't fair.

Answer #6: As you know, we do not require employees reporting for and leaving from work to wear safety glasses if traveling in a designated aisle. Neither are glasses required when going to and coming from breaks while traveling in designated aisles. They are required of everyone in departments that are operating. Your complaint has been reviewed with appropriate personnel and any necessary action will be taken.

Question #7: Why is the time interval between postings of questions and answers so lengthy?

Answer #7: At times, it is due to the lack of questions. Most recently, it was due to procrastination on the part of the Personnel Manager. He has promised to exhibit dramatic improvement in this area in the future.

Question #8: Mr. Edwards, Why don't the B men and set-up operators on 2nd shift have the same privileges as the ones on 1st shift? On 1st shift they are allowed to go in

Source: *Q & A Bulletin* written by Harold Durrett. Reprinted with permission.

the tool crib and get what they need for the set-up job, which they know better than the tool crib man. This saves time for the set-up operator and also the tool crib operator if he's busy on another job.

Answer #8: First of all, set-up operators and set-up men on 1st shift are not allowed to enter the crib at will. Only when prescribed tooling will not produce an acceptable pipe can they enter the crib to help locate substitute tooling.

An S.D.I. covering the Procedure for Controlling Pipe Production Tooling has recently been completed and will be issued shortly. It states in part that "the tool crib attendant can permit set-up men to enter for the purpose of selection of alternate tooling."

Question #9: I know this won't be answered on paper, but I wanted you to know that shortcomings are obvious to the girls in the office. Why is it that there are several men in the office that earn alot of money for 1) carrying a camera around; 2) talking about ballgames for 8 hours; 3) asking everyone in sight for little jobs to do; and 4) carrying blank clipboards?

It's been apparent for some time that there was an excess of male employees, and the solution seems to have been to employ more each day. It's the opinion of several people that there are people being paid just to sit here with their degrees and try to look smart. Isn't it about time they earned their pay or divided it up among the girls that do their work for them?

Answer #9: There may have been occasions when not every employee was performing in an exemplary manner at all times, but from my observations loafing, idle talking, and "goofing off" are by no means exclusive traits of male employees.

It should be noted also that it isn't always possible to judge the value of what an employee is doing by casual observation. The person you think is daydreaming may be mentally solving a technical problem, or the employee "carrying a camera around" may be on assignment to take pictures of defective goods received to substantiate a claim. People should be evaluated only by the results they achieve, and not by outward appearances.

I thought the situation you described in the Production Control department had been resolved some time ago. If it is reoccurring, it will be dealt with.

Trouble shooters

Sometimes organizations find themselves in a communication vacuum because of messages that never reach the intended recipient. Workers may complain to their supervisors, who in turn either send the message upward in a censored fashion or withhold it entirely. Employees who do not realize that the message was never received by the intended recipient may interpret the lack of action as a sign of disinterest in their thoughts, feelings, and opinions.

In an effort to overcome this communication barrier, some organizations have instituted procedures called **trouble shooters.** Trouble shooters are written complaint documents initiated by workers when all other attempts at reconciling a difficulty have failed. Once launched, the document proceeds through the steps of the chain of command until it reaches the uppermost organizational

Exhibit 16.8

A Trouble Shooter

Complaint Form

Date ____________________
Filed by ____________________ Employee # ________
Department ____________________ Shift ________
Date Alleged Incident Occurred ____________________
State the problem below as clearly as possible:
____
____
____
____

Signature ____________________

Immediate Supervisor
State below any and all action taken and any response to above complaint:
____
____
____

Signature ____________________
Date ____________________

Area Director
State below any and all action taken and any response to above complaint:
____
____
____

Signature ____________________
Date ____________________

ALL COMPLAINT FORMS MUST BE COMPLETELY FILLED OUT AND SENT TO THE PLANT MANAGER WITHIN SEVEN WORKING DAYS FROM THE DATE OF INITIATION.

echelon. At each step, the receiver is required to write a response to the initial complaint. This can be either a response to the charge or a statement of action to be taken. Once trouble shooters are initiated, they may not be stopped. Regardless of the actions or responses taken along the way, the written documentation must arrive at the final destination. Ironically, the mere fact that the procedure exists diminishes its use. In an attempt to avoid the use of trouble shooters, supervisors and managers expend extra effort making certain that existing communication channels work efficiently.

Summary

The ability to effectively communicate is one of the most important skills necessary for managing people. Successful communication occurs when an individual receives and interprets a message in a manner identical to the one in which it was transmitted. In order to effectively accomplish this process, senders expend effort encoding messages and choosing appropriate media for their transmission.

There are four basic ways information flows in organizations. Messages can be sent downward from superiors to subordinates, upward from subordinates to superiors, horizontally between colleagues, or diagonally across normal communication channels. The communications sent along these channels use written, verbal, nonverbal, or a combination of these methods to convey the intended messages.

Sometimes communications break down. The causes of these malfunctions are attributable to different communication barriers found in senders, transmission media, and receivers. People's perceptions, experiences, language, idiosyncrasies, and emotions are some of the most common causes of communication distortions.

Improving the communication process within organizations is limited only by the creativity of its members. Many organizations have devised unique, but simple methods to improve feedback mechanisms and to foster two-way communication. Opening various channels for information exchange, using different methods of transmission, and being aware of the characteristics unique to the particular recipient have resulted in increased communication effectiveness in many companies. This in turn leads to a more involved workforce, greater employee satisfaction, and increased productivity.

Key Terms to Identify

Encoding
Decoding
Downward communication
Upward communication
Horizontal communication
Diagonal communication
Semantics
Information screening
Information overload
Dynamic communication
Equalitarian communication
Relinquishing communication
Structuring communication
Withdrawal communication

Jargon
Source credibility
Question and answer reports
Trouble shooters

Questions for Discussion

Do You Know the Facts?

1. What is meant by the communication process, and how does it work?
2. Explain the four directions of organizational communication.
3. How do written, verbal, and nonverbal communications differ with regard to their impact on message reception?
4. What are the major barriers to communication, and how can they be overcome?
5. Discuss the effectiveness of the various communication styles managers can use to relay their messages.

Can You Apply the Information Learned?

1. What traits and personality characteristics of receivers should senders consider before sending messages? Why?
2. What methods of communication would you recommend to transmit information regarding safety procedures? How would you determine if the message had achieved the desired results?
3. What information would you include in a supervisory training program on "Improving Communications"?
4. Discuss how you would change the communication philosophies of a company which presently believes that workers should only be provided with information necessary to satisfactorily perform their jobs (the lowest level).

The Empty Sleeper

Fuzzy Inc., a manufacturer of teddy bears, had always used for-hire transportation. With the onset of the Motor Carrier Deregulation Act of 1980, the executive management team at Fuzzy Inc. decided to experiment with its own fleet in hopes of cutting costs. With this concept in mind, the approval was given to purchase a tractor and trailer and to hire two drivers.

This case was prepared by Marc G. Singer of James Madison University. It is reprinted with permission from Charles D. Pringle, Daniel F. Jennings, and Justin G. Longenecker, *Managing Organizations Functions and Behavior* (Columbus, OH: Merrill Publishing Company, 1988): 427–428.

After several weeks, a "rig" was purchased, and two drivers were employed. Because the initial trip involved a delivery to a customer who was approximately fourteen hours away, it was decided that the trip should begin at night so that arrival would be during regular working hours. Everyone gathered around the truck, the champagne bottle was smashed against the bumper, the drivers climbed aboard (one in the driver's seat, and the other in the sleeper), and they departed on their maiden voyage.

As he headed down the highway, Adam, the driver, realized that they had overlooked a minor detail. In all the excitement, nobody had thought of placing a CB unit in the cab. He made a mental note of the fact and turned on the radio to ease the loneliness.

After approximately four hours of driving, Adam decided to stop at a rest area. He climbed down from the cab and was about to knock on the sleeper to awaken his partner, Dudley, when he thought, "Let him sleep. I'll wake him at the next stop when it's his turn to drive." With that in mind, Adam went to the rest room. Afterwards, he looked for a phone booth, because company policy dictated that the customer be called at each stop to inform him of the estimated time of arrival.

While Adam was seeking a phone booth, Dudley awoke, realized he was at a rest stop, and decided to go to the rest room. A few minutes later, he emerged from the rest room just in time to see Adam and the rig leaving the rest area. Dudley thought for a moment, and immediately decided to call the Traffic Manager for a decision. Upon hearing what had happened, Sigmund, the Traffic Manager, advised Dudley to try to catch Adam further along the route (feeling certain Adam would call when he discovered the mishap). With this advice, Dudley hitched a ride with another truck driver.

After three hours had passed, Adam decided it was Dudley's turn to drive. He turned into a rest area, climbed down and knocked on the door of the sleeper. Getting no answer, he opened the door to find the sleeper empty. Without a bit of hesitation he immediately called Paul, the Assistant Traffic Manager, for a decision. Paul instructed Adam to return immediately and find Dudley. Adam complied.

Can you imagine the thoughts racing through Dudley's mind as he watched Adam speeding along in the other direction? Can you imagine Dudley's feeling when the driver from whom he hitched a ride requested fifty dollars for the lift? The mishap cost the company approximately fifteen hundred dollars and an irate customer. Adam and Dudley endure ribbing to this day. But the company did develop a new slogan. Every truck at Fuzzy Inc. has a sign prominently mounted on its dashboard which reads "IS YOUR BUDDY WITH YOU?"

Questions for Discussion

1. Discuss the communication breakdowns which occurred.
2. What policies could the company institute to prevent similar problems from happening in the future?
3. Could what happened at Fuzzy Inc. really have been prevented?

Endnotes and References

1 William Whitely, "An Exploratory Study of Managers' Reactions to Properties of Verbal Communication," *Personnel Psychology,* Vol. 37 (1984): 41–59.

2 Today's most popular views on the communication elements stem from the works of Claude Shannon, Warren Weaver, and Wilbur Schramm. See Claude Shannon and Warren Weaver, *The Mathematical Theory of Communication* (Urbana, IL: University of Illinois Press, 1948) and Wilbur Schramm, "How Communication Works," in *The Process and Effects of Mass Communication,* edited by Wilbur Schramm (Urbana, IL: University of Illinois Press, 1953): 3–26.

3 John F. Budd Jr., "Is the Focus of Communication on Target?" *Sloan Management Review,* Vol. 24 (1982): 51–53.

4 For an expanded and excellent discussion on the directions of communication, see Daniel Katz and Robert L. Kahn, *The Social Psychology of Organizations,* 2nd ed. (New York: John Wiley and Sons, 1978): Chapter 14.

5 Additional information on these three forms of communication can be found in William J. Seiler, E. Scott Baudhuin, and L. David Shuelke, *Communications in Business and Professional Organizations* (Reading, MA: Addison-Wesley, 1982).

6 Discussion of this topic is derived from the treatment in W. Alan Randolph, *Understanding and Managing Organizational Behavior* (Homewood, IL: Richard D. Irwin, Inc., 1985): 348–350.

7 Albert Mehrabian, "Communication Without Words," *Psychology Today,* Vol. 2 (1968): 53–55.

8 M. A. Hayes, "Nonverbal Communication: Expression Without Words," in *Readings in Interpersonal and Organizational Communication,* edited by R. C. Huseman, C. M. Logue, and D. L. Freshley (Boston, MA: Holbrook Press, 1973). Also see R. G. Harper, A. N. Wiens, and J. D. Matarzzo, *Nonverbal Communication: The State of the Art* (New York: John Wiley and Sons, 1978) and Albert Mehrabian, *Silent Messages* (Belmont, CA: Wadsworth Publishing Company, 1971).

9 For expanded discussion of the various barriers to communication, see David S. Brown, "Barriers to Successful Communication: Part I, Macrobarriers," *Management Review,* Vol. 64 (December 1975): 24–29 and "Part II, Microbarriers," *Management Review,* Vol. 65 (January 1976): 15–21.

10 In Silicon Valley, California, 60 to 90 percent of some firms employ workers whose native tongue is not English. See Cheryl L. McKenzie and Carol J. Qazi, "Communication Barriers in the Workplace," *Business Horizons,* Vol. 26 (March–April 1983): 70–72.

11 Marie Adele Humphreys, "Uncertainty and Communication Strategy Formation," *Journal of Business Research,* Vol. 11 (1983): 187–199.

12 Charles Bilbrey, Donald Musselman, and Marc Singer, "Eating Your Buzzwords," *Datamation,* Vol. 27, No. 4 (1981): 286.

13 Lyle Sussman, "Perceived Message Distortion, or You Can Fool Some of the Supervisors Some of the Time," *Personnel Journal,* Vol. 53, No. 9 (1974): 679–682, 688.

14 Losana E. Boyd, "Why Talking it Out Almost Never Works Out," *Nation's Business* (November 1984): 53–54.

15 For a comprehensive discussion on feedback, see David M. Herold and Martin M. Greller, "Feedback: The Definition of a Construct," *Academy of Management Journal,* Vol. 20, No. 1 (1977): 142–147.

16 Gregory Moorhead and Ricky W. Griffin, *Organizational Behavior,* 2nd ed. (Boston, MA: Houghton Mifflin Company, 1989).

17 R. N. Mara, "A Changing Role of Internal Communications," *Public Relations Quarterly,* Vol. 27 (1982): 25–27.

18 Thomas H. Inman and Barry Van Hook, "Barriers to Organizational Communication," *Management World,* Vol. 10 (1981): 34–35.

19 Keith Davis, *Human Behavior at Work* (New York: McGraw-Hill, 1977): 386.

20 Active listening is promoted by C. R. Rogers and R. E. Farson, "Active Listening," in *Organizational Psychology: A Book of Readings,* 3rd ed., edited by D. A. Kolb, I. M. Rubin, and J. M. McIntyre (Englewood Cliffs, NJ: Prentice-Hall Book Company, 1979): 168–179.

21 For expanded coverage of these communication styles, see the discussions in J. C. Wofford, E. Gerloff, and R. Cummins, *Organizational Communication: The Keystone to Managerial Effectiveness* (New York: McGraw-Hill Book Company, 1977): 147–168 and Jerry W. Koehler, Karl W. E. Anatol, and Ronald L. Applbaum, *Organizational Communication: Behavioral Perspectives,* 2nd ed. (New York: Holt, Rinehart and Winston, 1981): 47–52.

Chapter 17

Towards the Future: Selected Topics

Objectives

After reading this chapter you should understand:

1. The future impact that drug testing is likely to have on organizations.
2. The impact of AIDS on the workplace.
3. The changing demographics of the workforce, including the role of:
   a. illiteracy
   b. younger and older workers
   c. minorities
   d. women
4. The effects of downsizing.
5. The way global business is affecting organizations.
6. The status of unions over the next decade.
7. The purpose of human resource auditing functions.

Predicting future events is, at best, a risky endeavor. Researchers, academicians, and practitioners have varying views regarding which issues will be most important to human resource managers during the 1990s. Some believe that legal issues will dominate the human resource manager's role in the workforce. These theorists maintain that drug testing, AIDS in the workplace, and employee rights to privacy will be the central issues during the next decade. Others believe that the changing demographics of the workforce will dictate the direction taken by human resource managers. A demographic emphasis would include some of the following concerns: recruitment and maintenance of nontraditional workers, such as older workers, women, the handicapped, and immigrant labor; training and re-training of employees; and accommodating dual-career couples. Finally, there are those who contend that future planning would be incomplete without addressing such issues as downsizing, international management, and the role of unions in the workplace.

It is quite apparent that all of the previously mentioned matters will play significant roles in human resource management during the next decade. Some will obviously have a greater impact than others. However, rather than venturing guesses about the emerging dominant topics of the 1990s, this chapter will consider the potential impact each issue is likely to have on human resource managers.

Government Rules and Regulations

Since the 1970s, government employment legislation has significantly impacted human resource management operations. Equal Employment Opportunity laws, Occupational Safety and Health Administration rules, and other important statutes have all served to notably alter the way people and work environments are managed. This trend, which began with the Civil Rights Act of 1964, is likely to continue into the next decade. The rights of individual employees to be judged on the basis of work performance rather than on other non-work-related criteria, and their constitutional rights to privacy are the central concerns being litigated in the courts. Of these issues, the ones most likely to set precedents and to have serious consequences for employers are those involving drug testing and AIDS in the workplace.

Drug Testing and Privacy Rights

The issue of drug testing at the workplace is tied closely to individual privacy rights. Undeniably, substance abuse costs employers billions of dollars each year. The most effective method of curbing substance abuse on the job appears to be to screen out job applicants who have a history of drug use.

The use of drug tests to screen job applicants is legally permissible. In 1985, an estimated 25 percent of all Fortune 500 companies used drug screening procedures for new applicants or for current employees who exhibited signs of illegal drug use.[1] Furthermore, in 1987, an American Management Association survey of 1000 companies demonstrated that 34 percent of the companies had instituted a drug testing policy. Few, if any, lawsuits have been filed in connection with drug testing of either new hires or current employees for whom there is a substantial reason to screen. The predominant cause of litigation is the controversial practice of random drug testing of current employees without reasonable cause.

The main dispute regarding substance abuse testing is not the legitimacy of the drug testing itself. Instead, controversy centers on whether or not individuals' rights to privacy are being unduly invaded. It is important to note at this point that the invasion of privacy claims are not solely isolated to drug testing. Lawsuits have been filed for invasion of privacy by AIDS sufferers who claim breach of confidentiality when employers leak information concerning their condition; opponents of polygraph testing; and others who claim that sophisticated surveillance equipment is being used to probe into private, non-work-related areas.

The arguments against drug testing center on three issues. First, opponents contend that the use of drug tests violates individual rights against illegal search and seizure guaranteed by the Fourth Amendment. Second, the reliability of the test results are questionable because of problems which have developed in the handling and storage of the samples.[2] Finally, critics claim that positive results may indicate traces of drugs administered weeks earlier, which do not currently impair work performance.

To the future

Unfortunately, substance abuse does not appear to be declining. Until such time as the courts disseminate clear-cut policies on how drug testing should be carried out, human resource managers[3] would be well advised to follow certain guidelines. First, clear substance abuse and testing policies should be developed and articulated to all employees. Care should be taken to insure that these policies include provisions for the potential of reasonable searches, even if they are unannounced. Second, whenever possible, consent should be obtained from employees prior to testing. Last, similar to the procedures for copying personnel records, individuals should be allowed to have witnesses present to insure that their samples are handled correctly and that they have not been diluted.[4]

AIDS in the Workplace

No subject has dominated public interest more during the past decade than the issue of Acquired Immune Deficiency Syndrome (AIDS). In 1986, the Center for Disease Control reported that between 1981 and 1986 16,458 cases of AIDS had been reported. Of these cases, over 50 percent of the patients died.[5] Even more frightening than these statistics are the estimates of the future consequences of the disease. In 1991, it is predicted that approximately 145,000 Americans will be afflicted with AIDS, and 54,000 will die from it.[6]

The potential impact of AIDS on business is catastrophic. In 1987, the Supreme Court ruled that persons afflicted with the AIDS virus are considered "handicapped," and are afforded protection under the Vocational Rehabilitation Act of 1973. This means that AIDS victims are protected from discrimination by all federal contractors, and they must be afforded "reasonable accommodation" in the workplace. In addition, several states have enacted legislation to protect AIDS victims from discrimination,[7] and it appears that many other states will follow suit.

Employers' and employees' reactions to AIDS

Much of the controversy about how to handle AIDS victims at the workplace stems from a basic lack of knowledge about the disease. Present research has concluded that the AIDS virus is spread in only three distinct ways. These include:

1. Sexual contact.
2. Exposure to infected blood or blood products (usually as a result of drug users sharing infected syringes).
3. Transmission from an infected mother to her unborn child.

Despite attempts at making the general public aware of these facts, the average worker is still uninformed, misinformed, or skeptical about the information.

The result of this widespread misbelief is fear. Employees refuse to share restroom facilities, to eat at the same cafeteria tables, to use the same telephone,

Exhibit 17.1

Suggestions for Dealing with Drug Abuse and AIDS

Recommendation	Drug abuse	AIDS
Establish a specific and uniform policy	**Yes** 1. Define *prohibited substance.* 2. Define *intoxication.* 3. Define what is meant by *possession.*	**No** In lieu of policy, educate the workforce and managers about AIDS, how it is transmitted, and the fact that it is considered a disability.
Test employees	**Yes** 1. Institute a uniform testing policy. 2. Obtain written permission before testing. 3. Eliminate current drug users, *not* rehabilitated ones. 4. Test before hiring, or after work-related accident or other justifiable cause.	**No**
Institute discipline	Institute progressive discipline for abuse.	All employment decisions should be based on the ability or inability of the employee to do the job, not on their having the disease.
Privacy rights	Maintain strict confidentiality of all information.	Maintain strict confidentiality of all information.

or even to work in close proximity with infected co-workers. In many instances the organization's reaction has been to dismiss the infected employee. This has ultimately resulted in the filing of lawsuits, and in many cases, reaffirmation by states that victims of AIDS are entitled to be granted handicap status.

To the future

For human resource managers, AIDS presents many future challenges. The first priority is the education of workforces about AIDS. Not only must employees learn that their fears about contracting the illness from casual contact with infected people are unsubstantiated, but also they must be educated on the proper employment procedures to be applied in dealing with AIDS victims. Unfounded "AIDS panic" has the potential to cause great economic damage to many organizations.

In dealing with AIDS, supervisors and managers must realize that, as in their dealings with other handicapped employees, the crucial criterion for employment decisions is job performance. Unless job performance will be negatively impacted by the AIDS virus, such as health jobs that require the administration of injections, screening interviewers must avoid asking candidates if they have AIDS or if they have ever been tested for the AIDS virus. Similarly, dismissals, transfers, or the disciplining of AIDS victims solely on the basis of their having the disease should be avoided. Of course, as with other handicaps, the inability to perform the job as a result of the handicap is an acceptable reason for termination.

Finally, human resource managers must be prepared to deal with the economic impacts associated with AIDS. Presently, insurance companies are treating AIDS in the same way that other diseases are being handled. In fact, AIDS is presently less costly, in total, than cancer or heart disease. With the anticipated spreading of the disease, however, this scenario could be drastically altered over the next decade. The economic impact on benefit administration costs, including health insurance, life insurance, and pensions, could skyrocket.[8] Added to the lost productivity hours of the AIDS victims, the cost of this disease to businesses is potentially devastating.

Changing Workforce Demographics

The demographic composition of the workforce of the 1990s and beyond will present new and formidable challenges for human resource managers. During the 1980s employers saw a steady decline in the number of capable young people entering the workforce. This decline, estimated at about a half million people per year, is expected to continue until 1995.[9] In addition, by the year 2000, 80 percent of all new entrants into the labor force will consist of women, minority group members, and immigrants.[10]

The decline in the number of new workforce entries has not been unanticipated. The birth rate in the United States has decreased steadily since the "baby boom" immediately following World War II, partly because of new advances in birth control methods and partly because of the increasing number of women in the workforce. What is surprising, however, is that a significant number of the people entering the job market are leaving school early, ill prepared for entry into the workforce. The impact of a reduced number of total potential workforce participants, coupled with an increased illiteracy rate, is forcing organizations to develop new strategies and tactics for the recruitment, development, and retention of employees.

Recruiting and Retention Problems

Recruiting strategies and tactics, which were once aimed at attracting and retaining young promising recruits, are undergoing modification. Large and small organizations alike are having difficulty filling entry-level, minimum wage positions. In an effort to staff these positions, human resource personnel are turning to segments of the population that were previously overlooked. Older workers (especially retired people), young mothers, workers with disabilities, and immigrants are now being actively sought to fill positions once staffed exclusively by young and inexperienced workers. This trend is most apparent in service industries, such as hotels and restaurants, where the Bureau of Labor Statistics estimates that 90 percent of future worker shortages will occur.

In addition to the difficulty faced in recruiting young workers, organizations are likely to discover that retaining these employees is even more difficult. As a result of the ADEA and the elimination of mandatory retirement, greater numbers of workers are staying on the job longer. Entry-level jobs, which held the promise of fast promotion tracks, are quickly becoming a thing of the past. Young ambitious workers are unwilling to remain with organizations when the promise of promotional opportunities is frequently postponed or deferred to a future time. Consequently, the prospect of workers shifting from company to company appears to be an impending reality.

Training and Development of Personnel

Fluctuating demographics also bring new challenges to training and development departments. Organizations can no longer afford to place their total training resources in job skill training. Many organizations are discovering that the effect of a shrinking labor market is manifesting itself in a growing percentage of their workforce being uneducated. Some estimates place the total number of students who drop out of high school at about 25 percent, with the total number of minority group members somewhere between 40 and 50 percent. In addition, a randomly conducted research study of twenty-year-olds indicated that three out of five of those sampled could not total a simple lunch bill.[11] In today's dynamically changing environment, organizations with uneducated workers cannot remain competitive. Consequently, companies are making concentrated efforts to develop their human resources by providing in-house programs designed to combine basic reading and mathematical skills programs with skills training.

The change in workforce demographics is not the only problem faced by training and development departments. Over the past decade, technology has changed so rapidly that most of the jobs which existed during recent decades have either been totally eliminated or modified extensively. If this trend continues at its current pace, and most experts contend that it will, it is quite conceivable that organizations will have to either re-train or replace their entire workforce every decade. The average worker can be expected to work forty to fifty years, so training and development departments must be prepared to re-train workers at least four times during their careers.[12]

To the future

During the next decade, the divergence among work group entrants will present different challenges for human resource management. The successful management of organizations will require that programs be developed that deal with the unique characteristics of each work group. For convenience, these programs will be divided into those designed for younger workers, older workers, minorities, and women.

Younger Workers

There is a variety of tasks facing human resource managers who deal with young, inexperienced workers. A scarcity of capable young workers will require new recruiting efforts to attract young people to organizations. As more students enter and complete college, the number of young people willing to accept low-level entry jobs will shrink. Ironically, however, the demand for these college-trained individuals will also diminish as more older workers remain employed. Competition for the fewer upper echelon students will invariably increase.

In order to successfully attract the available young people, organizations will have to upgrade their wage and benefit packages, particularly for low-level jobs. This is especially true in service industries experiencing large worker shortages, in large metropolitan ares where competition for workers is great, and in rural communities with low unemployment. In addition, as companies dip deeper into the labor force than ever before, they will find that a larger percentage of their workforce is uneducated. Ultimately, remaining competitive will require them to embark on training programs designed to teach these workers basic educational skills.

In addition to attracting workers, human resource managers must also provide challenging and motivating job opportunities. The large portion of the labor force consisting of baby boomers between the ages of thirty and fifty-five, the ADEA, and the legislation eliminating mandatory retirement ages all contribute to the curtailment of rapid career advancement for the next working generation. With no clear-cut future opportunity in sight, many talented young workers will probably leave companies in the hope of advancement elsewhere.

Competitive organizations will probably find the answer to their turnover dilemma in the creation of new positions. A large percentage of the jobs that existed in the last decade have either been eliminated or replaced. At the current rate of technology change in the environment, organizations will have to either create new jobs or retrain their workforce to keep up with the changes. These new and changing jobs may provide the answers concerning how organizations can increase the job challenges and opportunities for young workers while retaining older employees.

Older Workers

The passage of the ADEA and the elimination of mandatory retirement ages present a major dilemma for organizations. As the workforce ages and employees attain greater seniority, their wages and benefits increase proportionately. This results in higher labor costs with no additional productivity. Although proponents contend that older workers are stable and less likely to turn over, and that they have fewer accidents, it is doubtful whether the savings associated with these factors is sufficient to offset the increased costs of wages and benefits.

Of course, the disadvantages of employing older workers must be placed in perspective. For the most part, these disadvantages concern long-term employees who are in higher level positions. With the reality of the future shortage of workers, the proper utilization of older workers, especially retired employees, in entry-level and part-time positions is both cost effective and productive. Corporations, such as McDonald's, have found that older workers are stable, are eager, have exceptional customer relations skills, and seem to reap benefits other than money from their employment.[13]

Minorities

The effective recruitment and employment of minority workers usually requires organizations to redesign their traditional staffing and training procedures. The employment of handicapped workers may require companies to re-analyze many of their jobs to determine if the handicapped workers can successfully satisfy job requirements. In many instances, organizations find that, with slight modifications, jobs can be redesigned to accommodate disabled workers. These individuals usually demonstrate high motivation and above-average performance.

Effectively recruiting and employing minorities will require organizations to employ previously unused hiring tactics. Because a large majority of unemployed people are inner-city minority workers, organizations, particularly those located in the suburbs, will face difficulties in initially locating these candidates and in transporting them to worksites once they are hired. Success in this area will require that recruiting efforts be extended to those agencies which typically promote minority employment opportunities.

Women

Over the past two decades, women have entered the labor force in great numbers. Currently 51 percent of all adult women work outside the home, and the government predicts that 90 percent of women will work outside their homes sometime during adulthood.[14] This trend is likely to continue well into the twenty-first century. Obviously, women have and will continue to have a distinct economic impact on organizations.

For human resource managers, the major challenges posed by working women appear to be handling child-care arrangements and dealing with the problems of dual-career couples. For many organizations, the answer to the first issue may be either the establishment of in-house child care facilities or the creation of flexible working hour programs. In fact, companies which have instituted these types of programs maintain that the costs of such plans have more than been offset by the increased productivity derived from less turnover and greater job motivation.

Exhibit 17.2

Tomorrow's Workers[15]

Who will they be?

Women and minorities	over 90% of the new workforce
Women	60% of the net increase
Blacks, Hispanics, Asians, and other races	57% of the total labor force growth
Hispanics	29% of the total labor force growth
Immigrants	23% of the change in the labor force
Native white males	15% of all entrants

By the year 2000, women will account for 47% of the total labor force.

Workforce age

Average age of worker	39 years old
Largest share of labor force	between 35 and 54 years old

Fastest growing jobs

Technicians, service workers, professionals, salesworkers, executives, and managers

Major workforce problems

Illiteracy, attracting and retaining employees, training and developing personnel

The major problem of dual-career couples, which will have to be addressed in the future, is relocation.[16] In recent years, companies have experienced an extreme reluctance on the part of employees to relocate to other areas. Much of this resistance has been traced to dual-career couples in which women are becoming more influential in the decision-making process. Unlike couples who have dual "jobs," those with dual careers find that when one spouse relocates, the other may have difficulty finding employment which affords them the opportunity to utilize their skills. This problem, coupled with financial concerns, results in their reluctance to move.

Dealing with the problem of dual careers is not an easy matter. Some companies have eliminated nepotism rules and offered employment to the relocated spouse. Other organizations have responded by taking the role of an employment agency, actually helping to prepare resumes and lining up job interviews. Regardless of their efforts, however, many companies, especially those with facilities in small rural settings, are finding it increasingly difficult to relocate dual-career couples. Because dual-career couples appear to be the trend of the future, human resource managers are going to have to devise new and creative solutions to handling the problems associated with relocating employees.

Downsizing

Most organizations, both large and small, have goals and objectives designed to promote growth. Few, if any, are prepared for the prospect of having to cut back. However, that is just what many organizations had to do during the 1980s. Precipitated by mergers, acquisitions, and increasing competitiveness in both national and international markets, many companies have been forced to downsize.

The objective underlying downsizing, or shrinking the organization, is simple. By trimming the organization to minimum costs, the bottom line is improved, and so is its ability to remain competitive. Often, this pruning begins by terminating employees.[17] While this appears to be a simple and prudent method for accomplishing the goal, unprepared organizations may find that there are emotional issues involved which have the potential to undermine the operation.

Dismissing a worker is never an easy task. Even in the most justifiable situations, where a worker is performing unsatisfactorily, termination is an emotional experience for the supervisor as well as for the employee. In downsizing situations, where supervisors are forced to dismiss qualified, productive employees, the trauma is enhanced. Consequently, it is usually done poorly.[18]

Several organizational repercussions may arise as a result of poorly planned downsizing. The presence of sentiments in decision making tends to hamper objectivity. In the hope that somehow the decree will be changed, managers tend to delay the termination process. Sometimes, particularly when haste is of the utmost importance, this procrastination can have severe impacts on the organization's ability to remain competitive.

More importantly, however, is the irreparable damage done to the organization's credibility. The workers who were dismissed summarily return to the community with a feeling of bitterness toward the company. This manifests itself in a negative public relations image for the organization.

Employees who are fortunate enough to keep their jobs experience feelings of mistrust and insecurity. Any previously held beliefs regarding job security are destroyed. When workers feel insecure, a host of other problems are likely to develop.

To the future

With the advent of large numbers of mergers, takeovers, and acquisitions, as well as predictions of increased international trade competition for the future, the potential for organizations to have to downsize in the coming decade is a distinct reality. While there is never an easy solution to this problem, the effects of this action on employees can be minimized with proper planning.

Planning for downsizing must occur well in advance. Just as organizations plan for growth, so too must they plan for shrinkage. This process should include determining how far in advance workers will be notified, establishing outplacement services, and deciding on the types and amount of benefits the organization will extend to each displaced worker.

Well-planned downsizing efforts are not free from emotion. They do, however, minimize the traumatic impact of job loss. In fact, many workers, particularly those fortunate enough to be part of a well-prepared out-placement program, obtain better positions. These programs, which are established prior to notifying workers of impending dismissals, are designed to assist employees in resumé and cover letter design, skill analysis (frequently through the use of standardized testing programs), and effective interviewing. It is important to remember that for many long-term employees, job search skills have long been forgotten.

For organizations which are unable to execute downsizing planning on their own, help is readily available. In the 1980s, several consulting groups which specialize in organizational downsizing emerged. With adequate notice, these groups can assist organizations in achieving their shrinkage goals while minimizing the negative impacts on the workforce.

International Management

Over the last two decades, businesses have dramatically increased their involvement in foreign markets. This interest in international trade has developed for several reasons. First, competition for markets and resources is increasing. In order to expand and grow, companies are required to search for consumers outside of the United States. Second, just as the competition for markets and resources is expanding, so too is the competition for labor. As both direct and indirect labor costs in the United States continue to rise, organizations seek to reduce costs by locating facilities and employing cheaper labor in other countries.

In addition to the reasons specified here, there is another, more pressing motivation for organizations in the United States to expand globally. Economically, not only has the United States lost its previously held competitive edge in international competition, but also it recently had trade deficits in excess of $150 billion. The United States has become the largest debtor nation in the world. Countries such as Japan and Korea, which were once regarded as the junk merchants of the world, have produced and continue to produce high-quality, high-demand products. Companies such as Toyota and Nissan are rapidly gaining in market share on GM and Ford. Nippon Steel has overtaken USX (formerly U.S. Steel), and Korean companies such as Samsung, Hyundai, and Goldstar are becoming formidable global competitors.

Attempts to Regain a Competitive Edge

Over the past two decades, organizations in the United States have sought solutions to the problem of regaining their previously held competitive edge in the international marketplace. Initially, corporations determined that perhaps emulating the corporate philosophies and modes of operation of countries such as Japan would increase the quality of their products and their ability to compete. Programs such as *Quality Circles* became the fads of the decade, and were widely instituted. Workers were trained and programs were implemented. Regardless of these efforts, however, foreign competitors continued to capture greater and greater market share.

The inherent shortcomings of attempting to imitate foreign business philosophies are well enumerated throughout the literature. Business philosophies and programs such as Quality Circles appear to work in other countries because of their inherent cultural values. However, the social value system of the United States does not seem to readily accommodate these programs.

Currently, more and more United States companies are deciding that future international success is best accomplished through joint international ventures. These cooperative arrangements increase market access, they enable risks to be shared, and most importantly, they avoid government-imposed protectionist prohibitions. During the 1980s companies such as General Motors and Toyota formed New United Motor Manufacturing Inc. (NUM) to produce cars in California, and General Electric combined with SNECMA of France to manufacture jet engines in Ohio. These ventures are occurring with great frequency, and they appear to be the mode of the future.

To the future

Researchers, theorists, academicians, and practitioners all agree that global competitiveness will increase dramatically during the next decade. For most organizations the answer to international competition appears to be engaging in joint ventures with foreign companies, establishing facilities in foreign locales, and employing foreign workers. All of these actions present challenging situations for human resource managers.

Individual nations have their own distinct business and social cultures. When blended together, unusual and diverse reactions occur. Communication barriers exist, cultural values on motivation and reward systems differ dramatically, and codes of conduct vary from one country to another. Cooperation among internationals requires understanding, appreciation, and acceptance of each other's cultures. Failure to consider these differences inevitably results in conflict.

In the past, solving the language barrier among international businesspeople was accomplished by the use of interpreters. Anyone who has witnessed a conversation between two people who are relying on an interpreter can readily appreciate the problems inherent in this method. The standard cues used by people to send and receive messages are virtually eliminated. Countless transmission and reception errors are introduced, leaving both the sender and the receiver uncomfortable during the communication process. Many communications end in confusion and misunderstanding.

As communication contacts between internationals become more prevalent, the need for bilingual employees is becoming increasingly more important. Direct discussion between individuals fosters more efficient communication, eliminating many third-party errors inherent in the use of interpreters. A selection criterion for future workers may well include assessment of their foreign language capabilities. In fact, for Korean corporations, the most desired college graduate is a student who majored in English.

Speaking a foreign language is certainly not the only, or most important, criterion for determining success in international business. Without a doubt, more people in this country are hired, promoted, transferred, and fired for reasons other than their ability to perform their jobs. Similarly, many international business deals have failed because United States businesspeople have not realized the importance of social customs in negotiating foreign business agreements. The primary determinant used by some countries for selecting business associates has more to do with the personal qualities exhibited by the executives and managers than it does with the probable success or failure of the endeavor.

It should come as no surprise to students of human resource management that successful management of foreign workers relies heavily on understanding their cultural values. All people are motivated to satisfy needs. These needs vary among individuals, and they are based in part on learned values. Therefore, the learned secondary needs of foreign workers will differ from those of U.S. citizens. Effectively maximizing both U.S. and foreign employee potential necessitates the creation of environments in which all employees can obtain need gratification.

For human resource managers, employee training is a necessity for survival in the 1990s. Colleges and universities have recognized this need and have begun to train their students to be successful in international business arenas. These graduates offer a promise of hope for the future, but not an immediate solution. Although they are trained in international affairs, they still lack the upper and middle managerial skills which are obtained through experience. Inevitably, successful companies must embark on managerial and supervisory training programs which will enable their current employees to function in a vastly changing world.

The Status of Unions

For almost thirty years, union membership in the United States has been steadily declining. Currently, it is less than one-half of what the total membership was during the mid-1950s. Between 1980 and 1985, non-union industrial sector jobs increased by over 1 million, while there was an over 2 million job decrease among unionized positions.[19]

By all accounts, the union movement in the United States appears to be in trouble. Analysts maintain that there are many reasons for its decline. Globalization has caused many traditionally union-organized industries to decline or to be eliminated. The easing of deregulation controls has allowed new non-union competition to enter and successfully compete in traditionally union-dominated industries. Some observers insist that a rash of anti-union consultants has entered the scene, causing excessive decertifications. However, the primary reason for union descent appears to be an enlightened management. Wages and benefits have increased dramatically in non-union shops, and employees are being treated with more consideration than ever before.

At the onset, unions entered the workplace in an attempt to equalize the power balance which existed between workers and employers. Their initial goal was to increase wages and benefits, improve working conditions, and obtain job security for their members. From the beginning, and continuing through today, they obtained their goals by employing an adversarial relationship with management. In fact, many people contend that through this mode of operation, unions were probably the most instrumental force in achieving today's safer working environments, increased wages and benefits, and laws which protect employee rights.

A Change in Tactics

With the rapidly occurring workplace changes, it is questionable whether existing union-organizing tactics and modes of operation are appropriate for the future.[20] There are divergent opinions regarding these methods depending on whether one consults with union or management representatives. Unions believe that a large part of their future survival depends on developing new organization targets and techniques to accomplish their goals. On the other hand, management and management theorists maintain that union survival will entail changes in the antagonistic relationship which has existed. They see a new spirit of cooperation as the key to the future. In essence, labor–

management cooperation will have to improve in order for organizations to be successful.

To the future

For human resource managers, the future of labor relations will be highly dependent on the nature of their organization. In the past, unions have concentrated their organizing efforts on blue-collar environments. This will change over the next decade. Service industries, such as financial institutions; clerical workers; white-collar supervisors; and mid-level managers are likely organization targets.

Company size will probably also be a factor in organizing efforts. Unlike past drives, however, organizational size will not necessarily determine whether a company is targeted. Large and small businesses alike can expect equal attention. Instead, the size of the organization will be used as the deciding factor in determining the strategies and tactics unions will employ during the organizing campaign. Traditional techniques will be used in organizing small organizations, but corporate campaigns, such as the one first successfully used in 1980 by the Amalgamated Clothing and Textile Workers (ACT) at J. P. Stevens and Company, will be used to deal with large companies.

Corporate campaigns pose unique problems for human resource managers. The essence of the strategy is to attempt to influence the opinions of the company's creditors, stockholders, and directors, as well as the public at large. By reaching groups traditionally outside the normal organizing process, unions attempt to neutralize management's retaliation efforts quickly and succinctly.

The success or failure of corporate campaigns depends largely on the union's ability to identify and attack the company's vulnerable areas. These include any financial weaknesses the company has and any negative characteristics existing in the backgrounds of its officers and directors. For human resource managers to effectively combat this strategy, several actions are recommended. First, through the use of appropriate corporate personnel, such as accounting and finance departments, they must assess corporate vulnerability and attempt to eliminate it. Second, adequate background investigations must be conducted on all proposed officers or directors before they are appointed. Last, adequate communication channels must be developed with the targeted constituencies to assure the rapid and accurate dissemination of information.

Organizations which are unsuccessful in their endeavors to defeat unionization efforts and organizations in which unions currently exist must plan for increased cooperation with unions. The adversarial relationship which once existed between unions and management needs to be mended, and future cooperation should be encouraged. Just as union members harbor an antagonistic view of employers, so too do supervisors and managers hold resentment toward unions. The success of U.S. businesses in the twenty-first century will require that both parties make efforts to work with each other. In order for this relationship to work, supervisors and managers will have to become more familiar with labor relations, relying less and less on specialists. To this end, human resource managers can contribute most through their training and development efforts.

Exhibit 17.3

Human Resource Management Issues of the 1980s and 1990s

Employee rights

1980s (beginning)	1990s (continuing)
Employment-at-will	Employment-at-will
Plant closing notification	Plant closing notification
Hiring illegal aliens	Right to manage issues
Paternity leaves	Paternity leaves
Right-to-know laws	Right-to-know laws
Privacy issues (testing)	Privacy issues (testing)
Comparable worth	Comparable worth
Eliminating mandatory retirement age	Hiring the aged
Whistleblowing protection	Whistleblowing

Health, safety, and benefit administration

1980s (beginning)	1990s (continuing)
Increasing costs	Increasing costs
Wellness programs	Wellness programs
Increase in OSHA fines	OSHA legislation
Tracking of chemicals	Right-to-know suits
AIDS in the workplace	AIDS legislation
Smoking controversies	Smoking legislation
Employee assistance programs	Increase in overall employee benefit concerns, such as retirement health benefits funding
Cafeteria plans	Increase in companies using cafeteria plans
Drug testing	Drug testing and legislation
Increase in social security	Elderly care and social security legislation

Staffing, training, and development

1980s (beginning)	1990s (continuing)
Hiring elderly and hard core workers	Hiring atypical workforce
International management	Language and culture training
Illiteracy	Basic skills training
Flexible staffing programs	Alternative work plans
Dual-career couples	Dual-career couples
Relocation assistance	Relocation assistance
Downsizing	Downsizing
Out-placement training	Out-placement training
Career development training	Career development training
Management development	Management development
	Retraining for technology
	New employee incentives

Auditing the Human Resource Management Function

Human resource managers periodically and systematically evaluate programs in order to determine their overall effectiveness. The purpose of these audits is to determine the cost effectiveness of human resource management functions and to decide whether they are satisfactorily meeting their planned objectives.

There are differing opinions concerning human resource management audit methods and what information should be collected.[21] Some managerial personnel believe both objective and subjective criteria data should be compiled formally. Others feel that formalized evaluations are unnecessary.[22] The ultimate methods decided upon are usually company-specific and depend largely on the nature of human resource management programs currently in existence. A discussion of all the viable methods employed to audit the human resource management function is beyond the scope of this book; thus, the present discussion will center on some of the most widely used methods. These include analyses of:

1. Turnover rates.
2. Absenteeism rates.
3. Employee relations.

Turnover

Turnover refers to the voluntary movement of employees in and out of organizations. Most organizations calculate yearly turnover rates as a barometer of organizational effectiveness. High turnover rates are often indicative of internal organizational problems. Research has demonstrated that employees leave their current positions because their needs cannot be satisfied in their present work environments.[23]

In most instances, excessive turnover is costly to organizations. Whenever workers leave, replacements must be recruited, selected, and trained. In addition, productivity also declines as a result of turnover. Lowered levels of morale and motivation of exiting workers are often exhibited prior to the employees' actual departure.

Traditional calculations of turnover rates are accomplished by the use of statistical formulas. For example, the U.S. Department of Labor recommends that:

$$\text{Turnover} = \frac{\text{The number of separations during the month}}{\text{Total number of employees at midmonth}} \times 100$$

Consequently, if there were 35 terminations during the month, and the total number of workers at midmonth was 400, the turnover rate would be:

$$\frac{35}{400} \times 100 = 8.75\%$$

Although the preceding formula is widely used, it fails to consider terminations that are either preferred or beyond the control of the organization. Sometimes high turnover rates are desired and even beneficial.[24] Resignations from poor or troublesome employees are usually welcomed by organizations. In order to factor in these desired or unavoidable terminations, human resource managers use the following different turnover formula:

$$T = \frac{\text{(Number of total separations)} - \text{(unavoidable separations)}}{\text{Total number of employees at midmonth}} \times 100$$

Absenteeism Rates

The absentee rate is another statistical procedure widely used to determine inherent organizational problems. Excessive worker absences which are not attributable to legitimate causes, such as sickness, accidents, or other justifiable personal reasons, usually indicate internal problems in the work environment.

As with turnover, high absenteeism rates are costly. Productivity, employee benefit costs, and general operational costs usually escalate. Unfortunately, most absences occur with little, if any, advance warning. In instances where workers' jobs are interdependent, employers are forced to hire temporary personnel or pay overtime wages.

There are various statistical formulas used to calculate absenteeism rates. The most commonly used formulas are:[25]

$$\frac{\text{Number of Work Days During the Period Lost to Absences}^{26}}{\text{Average Number of Employees} \times \text{Number of Workdays}} \times 100$$

or

$$\frac{\text{Total hours of absence}}{\text{Total hours scheduled to work}} \times 100$$

Consequently, if there were 200 workdays lost during a month of 20 workdays in a company that employs 350 workers, the absenteeism rate would be:

$$\frac{200}{350 \times 20} \times 100 = 2.86\%$$

Employee Relations

A major component of a human resource manager's responsibility is the promotion of good employee relations. Increasing the morale, motivation, and job satisfaction of workers provides tangible benefits to organizations in terms of increased productivity. On the other hand, job dissatisfaction, poor morale, and low motivation result in a variety of negative ramifications for businesses.

Assessing employee job satisfaction is usually accomplished by analyzing worker complaints and grievances or by the use of employee attitude surveys.

Complaints and grievances

There are several steps involved in auditing complaints and grievances. Because all complaints and grievances do not indicate a human resource management problem (for example, a technical problem with a piece of equipment), the first task in the evaluation process is for complaints and grievances to be categorized. Next, the frequency of grievances is calculated and compared to the company's historical record. An increase in the number of complaints and grievances over past years may indicate the existence of problem areas. Likewise, a decrease in the frequency of filings may indicate successful program implementation. Finally, the severity of the issues raised is considered. It is quite possible that even if the total number of filed complaints and grievances diminished, the severity of the concerns may indicate that corrective action needs to be taken.

Workplace problems are often not apparent from an evaluation of employee complaints and grievances. Many dissatisfied employees harbor negative feelings toward management and their work environment, but they choose not to formally file complaints or grievances. These feelings, however, impact on job satisfaction, morale, motivation, and productivity. In order to uncover these employee feelings, human resource managers often use attitude or opinion surveys.

Attitude or opinion surveys

Attitude surveys are frequently used by organizations as a barometer of employee feelings. These instruments are designed by in-house personnel or external consultants, they are tested for validity and reliability, and then they are administered to workers. The results of these current surveys are tabulated and the data is compared to any previously administered survey results. The findings are subsequently considered by management, and objectives are developed to remedy any problems uncovered. The conclusions and the proposed actions are subsequently disseminated to all employees.

Attitude surveys are conducted through written questionnaires, interviews, or combinations of both. The success of these techniques relies heavily on advance preparation of questions and a conscientious commitment to worker confidentiality. Information obtained in interviews and surveys, as well as the subsequent evaluation and use of this information, must be guarded in order to secure, protect, and encourage the trust and confidence workers place in the procedure.

It is difficult to design written attitude surveys. As with other questionnaires, they suffer from a wide variety of inherent design problems. Extreme care must be taken to insure that the questions posed on the survey do not restrict the respondents' answers. Very few, if any, workers provide information other than what is requested. Consequently, if the survey questions do not tap appropriate areas of concern, the results may be missing essential elements.

In order to avoid omitting crucial information, many organizations employ interviews in conjunction with written instruments.[27] Participants are usually chosen randomly and are guaranteed confidentiality and anonymity. Structured interviewing formats are usually employed, but any interviewing format is appropriate if it is administered uniformly.

The success of attitude surveying depends primarily on the trust and confidence workers place in the procedure. If surveys are administered and little, if any, corrective action is taken by management, future surveying efforts will

Exhibit 17.4

Sample Attitude Survey

INSTRUCTIONS: Please place a check mark in the column which indicates whether you agree or disagree with the statement. ALL RESPONSES ARE STRICTLY CONFIDENTIAL!

	Agree	Disagree	No opinion
Management takes an active interest in each department.			
Company policies are adequately explained to all employees.			
Any changes in policies are effectively communicated to employees in a timely fashion.			
Management is concerned about the opinions and suggestions of employees.			
Employees are encouraged to offer suggestions for improvement.			
The company offers adequate promotion opportunities for employees.			
Management treatment of employees is fair and consistent.			
Employees are encouraged to discuss problems with their supervisors.			
New employees are oriented and trained well.			
On the whole, employee–supervisor relationships are satisfactory.			
Cooperation between departments is friendly and helpful.			
Supervisors give advice and criticism in constructive manners.			
Employees are recognized and praised for good work performance.			

prove futile. If, on the other hand, employees believe that management is truly making a concerted effort to improve the areas of weaknesses that were uncovered, attitude surveying will prove to be a valuable communication technique.

A Final Note

The environment confronting human resource managers is rapidly undergoing change. Retaining a competitive position in the market will require that programs be monitored and updated continually. In order to effectively accomplish this task, human resource managers must be in constant touch with the vast changes occurring in the legal arena and on the national and international scenes. Not only should their programs be current, but also audits must be performed to assess the skills, knowledge, and abilities of the human resource managers. Human resource managers who fail to take current inventories of their own capabilities and to upgrade their competencies will ultimately fail to achieve their objectives.

Summary

The 1990s promise new and exciting challenges for human resource managers. Changes in government regulations, workforce demographics, and labor–management relations will require that organizations modify their traditional methods of operations in order to remain viable competitors.

It appears that although many issues will dominate the next decade, none are likely to have a greater impact than those concerning worker rights. Increased legislation governing the use of drug testing; the right to individual privacy; and the rights of AIDS victims, women, and the aged is imminent. Once enacted, these laws will significantly impact traditional management styles and philosophies.

National issues are not the only concerns facing human resource managers. Expanding world-wide competition for labor and product markets is encouraging many organizations to enter the international arena. The capacity to successfully compete in this new environment will require human resource managers to develop new methods for recruiting, selecting, and training personnel.

The future survival of unions appears to be based on their willingness and ability to alter their traditional philosophies for organizing and dealing with employers. Previously successful adversarial strategies and tactics must be replaced by cooperative labor–management relationships.

Finally, astute human resource managers will realize that a rapidly changing environment requires that both human resource management programs and their own individual abilities be monitored frequently to safeguard continued effectiveness. Failure to conduct these routine audits is likely to rapidly negate the positive impacts of any instituted programs.

Questions for Discussion

Do You Know the Facts?

1. What are the implications of individual privacy rights with regard to drug testing and AIDS at the workplace?
2. Why is the demographic composition of the workforce changing? What implications does it hold for human resource managers?
3. What roles will unions play in the future? Do management theorists and union leaders agree on the strategies unions will have to take in order to survive?
4. Discuss the major statistical methods used in order to audit the human resource management function.

Can You Apply the Information Learned?

1. What type of training programs would you establish in order to effectively educate your workers about AIDS?
2. Discuss how you would recruit and train current employees for transfer to a new Asian facility your company has just built.
3. What benefits would you recommend that your organization institute in order to attract and retain workforces for the twenty-first century?
4. What steps would you take to insure that your knowledge, skills, and abilities are always current during your career?

Endnotes and References

1 Thomas F. O'Boyle, "More Firms Require Employee Drug Test," *The Wall Street Journal* (August 8, 1985): 6.

2 The most commonly used drug test is EMIT (Enzyme Multiplied Immunoassay Test) manufactured by the Syva Company. Syva claims that the test is 97 to 99 percent accurate. Experts, however, claim that because there are no set standards for the handling and storage of these samples other than for labs used by the federal government, the error rate for urinalysis tests may be as high as 40 percent. See "Privacy, Testing for Drug Use: Handle with Care," *Business Week* (March 28, 1988): 61–65, 68.

3 The recommendations provided are for non-union employers. Because drug testing and substance abuse are working environment issues, they are subject to contract negotiations. For unionized companies, any substance abuse policies must be clearly negotiated between the parties.

4 See R. H. Schwartz and R. Hawks, "Laboratory Detection of Marijuana Use," *Journal of the American Medical Association*, Vol. 254 (1985): 788–792.

5 Center for Disease Control, 1981–1986. *Morbidity and Mortality Weekly Report* (Washington, D.C.: Department of Health and Human Services, 1986).

6 Statistics are from the Third International Conference on AIDS held in Washington, D.C., in June 1986. For a detailed resource list on where additional information on AIDS may be obtained, see Ira D. Singer, "AIDS in the Workplace," *Nation's Business* (August 1987): 36–39.

7 Florida, Maine, Massachusetts, New Jersey, New York, California, Wisconsin, and several other states have passed legislation protecting AIDS victims from employment discrimination. See David L. Wing, "AIDS: The Legal Debate," *Personnel Journal*, Vol. 65, No. 8 (August 1986): 114–119.

8 Estimates on the cost of employers' share of treating AIDS patients, including medical insurance, disability payments, life insurance, and retirement benefits are based on the individual employee's salary. Using standard formulas these figures could probably range from just under $100,000 (for someone earning approximately $25,000 a year) to $500,000 (in the case of high-level executives in the six-figure income bracket), assuming that AIDS victims continue to live only three to five years after diagnosis.

9 According to a survey by the American Society for Personnel Administration, the shortages between 1990–1995 are estimated to rise from 20 to 40 percent for office help in the West, 62 to 70 percent for Northeast skilled craftsmen, and 21 to 27 percent for unskilled Midwest workers. See "Labor Letter," *The Wall Street Journal* (February 7, 1989): A1.

10 Harry Bacas, "Desperately Seeking Workers," *Nation's Business* (February 1988): 16–17, 20–23.

11 Ibid.

12 According to noted business consultant Jeffrey Hallett, 50 percent of the jobs being performed in 1987 did not even exist in 1967. Furthermore, Hallett estimates that because of the emergence of the information economy, the year 2007 will see workers doing essentially new jobs. For more information on this phenomenon, see Jeffrey Hallett, *Worklife Visions* (Washington, D.C.: The American Society for Personnel Administration, 1988).

13 McDonald's McMasters program aimed at increasing the number of older workers has been cited as the most successful program to date, with the percentage of older workers exceeding 13 percent of the chain's labor force. See Frederick J. DeMicco and Robert D. Reid, "A Hiring Resource for the Hospitality Industry," *The Cornell H.R.A. Quarterly*, Vol. 29, No. 1 (May 1988): 56–61.

14 Leonard H. Chusmir and Douglas E. Durand, "The Female Factor," *Training and Development Journal*, Vol. 41, No. 8 (August 1987): 32–37.

15 Abstracted from Martha I. Finney, "Planning Today for the Future's Changing Shape," *Personnel Administrator*, Vol. 34, No. 1 (1989): 44–45.

16 An excellent source of information on the problems associated with, as well as proposed solutions for, the relocation of dual-career couples, see Maria Helene Sekas, "Dual-Career Couples—a Corporate Challenge," *Personnel Administrator*, Vol. 29 (April 1984): 36–38, 40, 42, 44, 46.

17 Employee terminations because of downsizing are not restricted to blue-collar employees. During the 1980s, approximately one million mid- and upper-level manag-

ers with three or more years experience were laid off. See "You're Fired," *U.S. News & World Report* (March 23, 1987): 50–54.

18 For an extended discussion of the difficulties in terminating employees, and some steps to insure that organizations are prepared properly, see Perry Pascarella, "When Change Means Saying 'You're Fired'," *Industry Week* (July 7, 1986): 47–49, 51.

19 Kirkland Ropp, "State of the Unions," *Personnel Administrator*, Vol. 32 (December 1987): 50–59.

20 An excellent source treatise on the traditional role unions played and the changes which they will have to make to survive in the future can be found in Edward E. Lawler III and Susan A. Mohrman, "Unions and the New Management," *The Academy of Management Executives*, Vol. 1, No. 3 (1987): 293–300.

21 Terry Hercus and Diane Oades, "The Human Resource Audit: An Instrument for Change," *Human Resource Planning*, Vol. 5, No. 1 (1982): 43–49.

22 Jac Fitz-Enz, "Quantifying the Human Resources Function," *Personnel*, Vol. 57 (March–April 1980): 41–52.

23 A discussion of why employees tend to leave organizations can be found in William Mobley, "Intermediate Linkages in the Relationship Between Job Satisfaction and Employee Turnover," *Journal of Applied Psychology*, Vol. 62 (April 1977): 237–240.

24 Some organizations place too much emphasis on the ramifications of high turnover rates. The rates are confounded by many variables. People leave for health reasons, promotional opportunities, or other factors unrelated to the work environment. For a discourse on this subject, see D. R. Dalton, "Turnover and Absenteeism: Measures of Personnel Effectiveness," in *Applied Readings in Personnel and Human Resource Management*, edited by R. J. Schuler, J. M. McFillen, and D. R. Dalton (St. Paul, MN: West Publishing Company, 1981). Also see Michael A. Abelson and Barry D. Baysinger, "Optimal and Dysfunctional Turnover: Toward an Organizational Level Model," *Academy of Management Review*, Vol. 9, No. 2 (1984): 331–341.

25 This formula is recommended for use by the U.S. Department of Labor.

26 For calculation purposes, absences are any avoidable or unavoidable truancy from the job when employees are scheduled to work. Thus, planned vacations, holidays, or other authorized leaves of absences are not considered.

27 Approximately 66 percent of all organizations using attitude surveys use just written questionnaires, 25 percent use a combination of both, and the remainder use just interviews. See David R. York, "Attitude Surveying," *Personnel Journal*, Vol. 64 (May 1985): 70–73.

Glossary

Ability tests (Ch. 5) standardized, objective, paper-and-pencil inventories designed to assess learning potential by measuring existing abilities and aptitudes.

Accident proneness (Ch. 12) a theory that maintains that certain people have specific characteristics which make them more likely to have accidents, regardless of the environmental conditions present.

Affirmative action (Ch. 2) involves an employer's engagement in positive, results-oriented methods designed to overcome past discriminatory practices by actively seeking to hire and promote women, minorities, handicapped persons, and other protected class members.

Agency shop (Ch. 13) a labor contract provision that does not require union membership, but it requires employees to pay that portion of the union dues which are attributable to collective bargaining.

Application blanks (Ch. 5) written forms completed by job candidates detailing their educational background, previous work history, past references, and certain personal data.

Arbitration (Ch. 14) a process in which a neutral third party or panel listens to both sides, evaluates the evidence, and makes binding recommendations on what should be included in the final labor contract.

Arbitration award (Ch. 14) the award represents the arbitrator's decision in the case and includes: a summation of the evidence presented, the rationale underlying the arbitrator's decision, and, if necessary, the action required to correct any injustices.

Attitude surveys (Ch. 17) a method used by organizations to measure employee feelings toward various organizational factors. Usually organizations employ questionnaires, interviews, or combinations of both in an attempt to gain relevant information.

Attitudinal structuring bargaining (Ch. 14) involves the parties attempting to manipulate and create attitudes of favorableness or unfavorableness toward one another.

Authority (Ch. 1) the legitimate use of power by individuals to make decisions concerning the resources affecting the organization's ultimate goals and objectives.

Authorization cards (Ch. 13) documents which employees sign on which they indicate that they want the union to represent them for the purpose of collective bargaining, and/or they authorize the union to seek an NLRB election.

Bargaining order (Ch. 13) an order issued by the National Labor Relations Board (NLRB) instructing an employer to undertake collective bargaining with the soliciting union.

Base period, base period products cost, and base productivity factor (Ch. 10) the base period is the time designated to establish productivity standards. The base period product costs are all costs used by management during the base period. They represent the direct labor hours necessary to produce a product by major operations and by total products produced. The base productivity factor is the relationship in the base period between the actual hours worked by employees in the plan and the value of work produced by these employees measured in standard worker hours.

Behavioral logs (Ch. 7) daily diaries kept on workers, in which both positive and negative behaviors are recorded.

Behaviorally anchored rating scales (BARS) (Ch. 7) rating technique which requires evaluators to rate employees on a scale continuum of defined critical behaviors ranging from negative to positive.

Behavioral sciences (Ch. 1) a discipline which combines the social and biological sciences in an effort to understand human behavior.

Benefits (Ch. 11) any legally mandated or voluntary services, other than direct wages, which are provided to workers in whole or in part by employers.

Biographical information blanks (BIB) (Ch. 5) extensive multiple-choice forms which elicit information from applicants regarding factual material, attitudes, early life experiences, and social values.

Board interview (Ch. 5) See *Panel interview.*

Bona Fide Occupational Qualification—(Section 703 (*e*) of Title VII) (Ch. 2) allows employers to discriminate on the basis of religion, sex, or national origin in those cases where it can be demonstrated that there is a bona fide occupational qualification reasonably necessary to the normal operation of that particular business or enterprise.

Boulwarism (Ch. 14) the practice by management of presenting a final offer early in the negotiation process and then refusing to vary from the offer.

Boycott (Ch. 14) an abstention by union members and others from purchasing or using the products produced by an employer engaged in a dispute with a labor organization.

Burnout (Ch. 12) a form of organizational distress, akin to psychological depression, in which previously enthusiastic individuals lose their desire and vitality for their job or career.

Cafeteria plan (Ch. 11) programs which provide employees with the flexibility of selecting the mix of employer-offered benefits which best suits their individual needs.

Case study method (Ch. 6) a method which involves analysis and discussion of either true or hypothetical organizational problems.

Cash plans (Ch. 10) profit sharing plans which provide for the distribution of profit shares at regular intervals as earned. This distribution is made in cash, company stock, or a combination of both, according to a predetermined formula.

Central tendency error (Ch. 7) a trend exhibited by raters who assign only average ratings to avoid the evaluation of all employees at the extreme ends of the scale.

Certification of election (Ch. 13) the formal means by which the NLRB reports the results of an election. It is either the certification of a union as the collective bargaining agent or merely the certification of the results, if a union does not prevail.

Checklist method (Ch. 7) a rating technique that requires evaluators to review a list of critical job behaviors, traits, or characteristics and to check those items which the employee demonstrates.

Classification method (Ch. 9) an evaluation technique that requires evaluators to establish and define class levels covering the range of organizational jobs, and to subsequently place each job into the appropriate class.

Clause book (Ch. 14) a ledger, usually arranged in loose-leaf fashion, in which each previous labor contract clause, and the experiences in its administration, is recorded.

Closed shop (Ch. 13) a union security clause in a contract which requires union membership of all employees as a condition of hiring as well as of continued employment.

Coaching (Ch. 6) a one-on-one relationship between trainees and supervisors which offers workers continual guidance and feedback about their performance.

Collective bargaining (Ch. 14) a process in which representatives meet and use whatever legal tactics are at their disposal to effect the best possible employment agreement for the parties whom they represent.

Combination plans (Ch. 10) a profit-sharing plan that utilizes features of both cash and deferred plans by distributing part of the profits earned immediately and placing the remainder into the fund reserved for later disbursement.

Communications feedback (Ch. 16) knowledge the sender obtains which indicates whether or not the receiver has correctly interpreted the message.

Comparable worth (Ch. 9) the compensation issue over whether jobs which are of equal value to a company, but dissimilar in job content and responsibilities, should be paid equally.

Compensable factors (Ch. 9) the common elements present in all jobs within an organization that serve as the basis for job evaluation comparisons.

Compensation (Ch. 9) the intrinsic and extrinsic rewards provided by a company for the fair and equitable remuneration of employee services performed.

Compensatory strategy Ch. 5) a selection approach which allows all applicants to proceed through the entire selection process before being rejected or hired.

Compressed workweek (Ch. 3) requires employees to complete a full week's work in less than five days.

Computer-assisted instruction (CPI) (Ch. 6) a self-taught, self-paced computerized learning system which uses programmed instruction techniques.

Concurrent validity (Ch. 5) a type of criterion-related validity in which both predictor and criterion data are gathered at the same point in time.

Constructive discharge (Ch. 8) exists when an employer deliberately makes working conditions so intolerable that employees are forced to resign.

Construct validity (Ch. 5) a validation technique used to determine if a predictor measures the underlying characteristic or trait responsible for the behavior.

Content validity (Ch. 5) a validation strategy used to determine if a measure assesses an entire content area.

Contributory plans (Ch. 11) pension plans requiring joint funding by both employees and employers.

Core spending account approach (Ch. 11) the core approach provides all employees with a basic set, or core, of similar benefits and an additional dollar amount from which employees can choose additional benefits to satisfy their own particular needs.

Cost of living adjustment (COLA) (Ch. 9) an adjustment made to an employee's wages based on the consumer price index.

Counseling (Ch. 8) the utilization of skilled techniques for the purpose of assisting people in understanding and developing their own solutions to problems.

Craft unions (Ch. 13) labor organizations which represent only skilled employees.

Criterion (Ch. 5) a standard to be accomplished (average or satisfactory job performance).

Criterion-related validity (Ch. 5) a statistical measure which examines and draws inferences about the relationship between a predictor and a criterion.

Critical incidents method (Ch. 7) a rating method that requires the rater to log, identify, and record those behaviors, both positive and negative, which have a significant impact on performance.

Cut-off scores (Ch. 5) minimal acceptable performance levels for predictors which candidates must obtain before being considered further.

Decertification (Ch. 13) the process undertaken by bargaining unit employees to prohibit the certified collective bargaining agent from further representing them.

Decoding (Ch. 16) the process by which the receiver interprets and attaches meaning to the message.

Deferred plans (Ch. 10) plans that provide for the distribution of profits, which are usually placed into an escrow account, at a future date. Typically, deferred profit-sharing plans serve as the backbone for the company's pension or retirement programs.

Defined-benefit plan (Ch. 11) requires employers to periodically contribute specified funds necessary to provide employees with fixed benefits upon eligibility.

Defined-contribution plan (Ch. 11) requires employers to contribute a specified amount to individual employee pension accounts. These funds, along with any earnings, will be distributed to employees when they reach eligibility.

De minimis violation (Ch. 12) the minimum violation enumerated by OSHA, which is usually housekeeping in nature and has no direct relationship to health and safety. De minimis violations are not assessed monetary penalties.

Disparate impact (Ch. 2) discrimination existing when it is demonstrated that an ostensibly neutral employment practice does in fact adversely affect one of the five protected classes under Title VII.

Disparate treatment (Ch. 2) discrimination existing when it is demonstrated that an employer based an employment decision on race, color, religion, sex, or national origin.

Distress (Ch. 12) occurs when an individual responds to stress in an unhealthy manner, resulting in behaviors which are detrimental to both the organization and the individual.

Distributive bargaining (Ch. 14) occurs when the union and the employer are in conflict over an issue and resolving the issue will cause one party to have a gain while the other party suffers a loss.

Downsizing (Ch. 17) the process of shrinking the organization in an effort to trim the bottom line and remain competitive.

Downward communication (Ch. 16) an organizational communication channel in which messages are sent one way from superior to subordinate.

Dues checkoff (Ch. 14) a process in which the employer withholds union dues from employees' paychecks and forwards the money directly to the union.

Economic strike (Ch. 14) a strike which is undertaken for the purpose of obtaining better wages, hours, or working conditions.

Election bar (Ch. 13) an administrative rule of the NLRB in which they will refuse to honor a petition for an election for one year from the time that a previous election was certified in the particular bargaining unit.

Emergency standards (Ch. 12) temporary standards issued by the secretary of labor when it is determined that employees are being exposed to agents which may be toxic or physically harmful.

Employee assistance programs (EAPs) (Ch. 8) employer-sponsored counseling programs whose goal is the identification and treatment of employee problems either in-house or through external referrals.

Employee right-to-know laws (Ch. 12) state laws which require employers to inform workers if toxic chemicals are being used at the workplace, to label such containers, to train employees in the proper handling of these materials, and to divulge the chemical composition of the substances to employees' physicians.

Employment-at-will (Ch. 8) the employment doctrine followed in the United States which allows employers to dismiss any worker who has not been hired for a specific length of time, who is not covered by any contract, or who is not protected by an enumerated law, for any reason they choose.

Employment interviewing (Ch. 5) a verbal exchange between an employer and a prospective employee for the purpose of obtaining information about the applicant's job capabilities, and providing the applicant with knowledge about the organization.

Employment tests (Ch. 5) objective and standardized measures designed to obtain information from individuals concerning the specific characteristics, interests, knowledge, abilities, or behaviors they possess.

Encoding (Ch. 16) the process by which senders translate their thoughts and ideas into systematic symbols which can be transmitted.

Equity (Ch. 15) a feeling of fairness experienced by individuals when they view the relationship of their efforts and organizational rewards as equivalent to the efforts and corresponding rewards of their co-workers.

Ergonomics (Ch. 12) the applied science of designing environments, equipment, tools, and tasks to be compatible with the diverse characteristics, behaviors, and needs of individuals.

Eustress (Ch. 12) the healthy, adaptive response made by an individual to a stressful situation.

Expectancy (Ch. 15) the individual's perceived determination of the likelihood of increased performance occurring as a result of the effort expended.

Expedited arbitration (Ch. 14) involves the use of inexperienced arbitrators who hear grievances within ten days after their filing and provide the parties with short, precise awards within forty-eight hours of the hearing.

Factor comparison method (Ch. 9) requires evaluators to select and evaluate "key or benchmark jobs" according to selected compensable factors, to establish wage scales based on these rankings, and subsequently to compare all remaining jobs to these key jobs.

Featherbedding (Ch. 13) the practice by unions of requiring employers to pay for services which are currently not being performed.

Flexible plan (Ch. 11) See *Cafeteria plan.*

Flexible spending account approach (Ch. 11) provides employees with the greatest flexibility in choosing benefits. Under this option, employees are given a total dollar amount from which they may select benefits. Under this approach employees are free to tailor their entire benefit package to suit their individual needs.

Flexiplace (Ch. 3) allows workers to work part of the time outside of the workplace, such as at home.

Flexitime (Ch. 3) an alternative work scheduling procedure which allows workers the freedom to choose their own working schedules provided that they work a fixed number of hours.

Flexitour (Ch. 3) is a situation where workers chose starting and stopping times, which must be adhered to for a set period of time, from among lists provided by the organization.

Forced-choice method (Ch. 7) a rating technique requiring raters to choose from pairs of equally attractive or unattractive alternatives the one factor which they feel best describes the worker.

Four-fifths rule (Ch. 2) the ratio identified in the Uniform Guidelines on Employee Selection Procedures to be used in determining whether or not adverse impact exists.

Functional job analysis (Ch. 3) a job analysis procedure developed by the U.S. Department of Labor which provides standardization for rating and comparing different jobs. It concentrates on the work performed and worker traits.

Gainsharing (Ch. 10) the use of company-wide incentives when the measurement of productivity increases is based on overall corporate profits.

Gliding time (Ch. 3) exists when workers may vary their starting and finishing times daily, but must work a set number of hours per day.

Graphic rating scales (Ch. 7) rating techniques that require raters to judge employees on the degree to which they demonstrate certain factors deemed to be important in job performance.

Grievances (Ch. 14) employee complaints or concerns about alleged violations of a contract provision which are submitted for resolution through a formally established procedure.

Group practice HMOs (Ch. 11) health plans in which the subscriber is required to obtain treatment from physicians and health-care professionals who are either employed by the HMO or who have contractual arrangements to provide services to the HMOs' subscribers.

Halo effect (Ch. 5) the tendency to make a total assessment of an individual based on observing only one favorable or unfavorable trait.

Halo error (Ch. 7) the tendency of raters to judge employees in favorable or unfavorable terms based on their general overall impressions of the individual rather than true assessments of the rating-specific factors.

Health maintenance organizations (HMOs) (Ch. 11) benefit plans operated by groups representing physicians and health-care professionals who provide an array of services to subscribers on a prepaid basis.

Horizontal communication (Ch. 16) an organizational communication channel which involves the lateral flow of communication from colleague to colleague or department to department.

Hot-stove approach (Ch. 8) a discipline approach in which all employees are pre-warned about which behaviors are punishable, and they are immediately and consistently punished, without prejudice, if they violate the rules.

Human resource management (Ch. 1) a specialty field which attempts to develop programs, policies, and activities to promote the satisfaction of both individual and organizational needs, goals, and objectives.

Hygiene factors (Ch. 15) one of the factors which composes the two factors of Herzberg's theory of motivation. Hygiene factors are organizational elements which satisfy individual needs on any of the bottom three levels of Maslow's need hierarchy.

Imminent danger (Ch. 12) a condition or practice which could reasonably be expected to result in death or serious illness before it could be remedied through the enforcement procedures outlined under OSHA.

Improshare (Ch. 10) an incentive plan based on the use of past production records to establish base performance standards.

In-basket technique (Ch. 6) a training technique in which trainees record their responses to a series of written memos within a given timeframe and subsequently discuss the answers with the trainer and other group members.

***Individual practice association* HMOs** (Ch. 11) a plan in which subscribers choose physicians and health-care professionals from a list of private-practice personnel who have agreed to accept a fixed rate of payment on a fee-for-service basis.

Industrial unions (Ch. 13) unions that represent all employees within a specific bargaining unit, regardless of skill level.

Instrumentality (Ch. 15) the probability, either perceived or actual, that a particular level of performance will lead to some outcomes.

Integrative bargaining (Ch. 14) involves the joint cooperation of the union and the employer to obtain results in which both parties benefit.

Interim standards (Ch. 12) OSHA standards which the secretary of labor was empowered to issue for two years after the effective date of the act. These provisions were based on existing industry standards prior to the passage of the act.

Inter-item reliability (Ch. 5) considers each question as a separate test.

Internal consistency reliability (Ch. 5) involves subdividing a test and treating each part as a separate test.

Intraorganizational bargaining (Ch. 14) develops when the parties attempt to gain uniformity among their own members regarding issues. Management negotiators may have to convince management to change its position on a specific issue, and union negotiators may have to convince their constituents to ratify the agreement.

Jargon (Ch. 16) a specialized or technical language within a trade, profession, or cultural group.

Job analysis (Ch. 3) a process undertaken to determine which characteristics are necessary for satisfactory job performance, and to analyze the environmental conditions in which the job is performed.

Job analyst (Ch. 3) the individual, designated by the organization, who is responsible for collecting the job information. This individual is usually an outside consultant, a current worker, or a supervisor.

Job bidding (Ch. 4) occurs when employees sign a list to indicate their interest in being considered as a candidate for an announced position.

Job characteristics theory (Ch. 3) stresses the intrinsic aspects of jobs and maintains that workers will be satisfied if they view their jobs as meaningful, if they are given adequate responsibility, and if they receive feedback regarding their performance.

Job descriptions (Ch. 3) consist of information extracted from analyses which contain the tasks, behaviors, responsibilities, and activities necessary for the completion of the job.

Job design (Ch. 3) involves the integration of significant job components and worker characteristics to create positions which lead to the need fulfillment of both workers and employers.

Job enlargement (Ch. 3) involves the addition to or expansion of worker tasks until the job becomes an entire meaningful operation.

Job enrichment (Ch. 3) involves the vertical expansion of jobs by increasing the amount of worker responsibilities associated with the positions.

Job evaluation (Ch. 3, Ch. 9) the process of ascertaining how much each job is worth to the organization, comparing the jobs to one another, and then assigning each job a monetary value.

Job instruction training (JIT) (Ch. 6) a structured approach to training which requires an orderly progression through a series of specific steps including a job overview, trainer demonstration, actual job performance by employees, and feedback sessions.

Job posting (Ch. 4) involves the dissemination of information about available position vacancies by posting the listing on bulletin boards or in employee newsletters.

Job rotation (Ch. 3) involves the switching of workers on designated dates among several different simplified jobs.

Job sharing (Ch. 3) occurs when two or more workers are employed to fill the position of a full-time worker.

Job simplification (Ch. 3) a design method whereby jobs are divided into smaller components and subsequently assigned to workers as whole jobs.

Job specifications (Ch. 3) the part of a job analysis generally used for selection purposes. They summarize the human characteristics, such as knowledge, skills, training, and experiences necessary for satisfactory job completion.

Jurisdictional strike (Ch. 14) a work stoppage caused by a dispute between two or more unions over which group has the right to perform the work.

Leniency error (Ch. 7) the tendency for raters to judge all ratees higher than acceptable standards.

Leveraged ESOP (Ch. 10) a plan which allows a company to borrow money against shares of company stock, and to repay the principal and interest each year until the loan is satisfied.

Line managers (Ch. 1) managers who have the final decision-making authority over a phase of operations.

Lockout (Ch. 14) the refusal by employers to allow employees to work.

Management by objectives (MBO) (Ch. 7) a process in which individual goals and action plans designed to mesh with the overall organizational objectives are implemented and systematically reviewed and revised.

Management games (Ch. 6) a complex training situation simulating the real-world environment where trainee participants compete with one another using general managerial principles to make decisions affecting their businesses.

Management inventories (Ch. 4) skills inventories for managerial personnel which also include data concerning the employee's past successes and failures, his or her strengths and weaknesses, and his or her potential for advancement.

Managerial prerogative clauses (Ch. 14) negotiated provisions giving management the right to exercise their discretion in dealing with any work situation not specifically enumerated in the contract.

Mandatory bargaining issues (Ch. 14) those items for which the law requires employers and unions to collectively bargain in good faith. They include all issues related to wages, hours, and conditions of work.

Mandatory benefits (Ch. 11) government regulations requiring organizations to provide workers with benefit coverage for retirement, illness, disability, and periods of unemployment.

Maxiflex (Ch. 3) allows workers the freedom to vary their hours daily irrespective of core times. Maxiflex is similar to a compressed work week.

Measured daywork (Ch. 10) a system which requires that formal production standards be developed against which employee performance can be frequently judged.

Mediation (Ch. 14) a process in which a neutral third party provides recommendations and suggestions to aid the parties in voluntarily reaching an agreement.

Medium (Ch. 16) the channel or communication vehicle chosen for the transmission of the message.

Mentoring (Ch. 6) See *Coaching.*

Merit pay (Ch. 10) the assignment of money to employees' base pay on the basis of their performance.

Mixed interview (Ch. 5) See *Semi-structured interview.*

Mixed strategy (Ch. 5) a selection strategy that automatically rejects every applicant who does not meet a prerequisite requirement; candidates who meet the requirement are not automatically employed, but are required to demonstrate additional skills by continuing through other selection steps.

Module spending account approach (Ch. 11) gives employees a choice among several pre-established benefit packages. Each of these packages provides the same degree of compensation, but with a different mix of benefits.

Motivation (Ch. 15) a multi-faceted psychological process which energizes individuals' behaviors toward a desired goal or objective.

Motivators (Ch. 15) one of the factors in Herzberg's two-factor theory. Motivators are any organizational elements which satisfy needs on the upper two levels of Maslow's Need Hierarchy.

Multiple hurdles approach (Ch. 5) a selection approach which rejects applicants if they fail to satisfactorily complete any stage of the selection process.

Negative reinforcement (Ch. 15) the use of contingencies which compel individuals to perform appropriately in order to avoid undesirable consequences.

Negative transfer of training (Ch. 6) a state of affairs existing when the material learned in training sessions interferes with job performance.

Noncontributory plans (Ch. 11) pension plans that are funded solely by the employer.

Non-directive interview (Ch. 5) See *Unstructured interview.*

Non-serious violation (Ch. 12) an OSHA violation in which the employer was unaware of the potential hazard and which would likely result in some consequence other than death or serious injury.

Ombudsmen (Ch. 8) designated individuals in organizations who serve as party mediators in arriving at mutually acceptable solutions to grievances.

Open-door policies (Ch. 8) are one of the older forms for handling grievances and allow all employees with problems to contact any designated supervisor or manager in the organization.

Open-ended questions (Ch. 8) questions which require elaboration and cannot be answered in a simple yes or no manner.

Open shop (Ch. 13) a union contract provision, or absence of union contract coverage, in which employees can choose whether or not they want to join a union and/or pay union dues.

Ordinary ESOP (Ch. 10) a plan in which the company contributes an amount of cash from its profits to the ESOP trust fund, which is used to purchase employee shares in company stock.

Organizational analysis (Ch. 6) a continuous process of gathering and reviewing information to determine training needs.

Organizational behavior modification (OB Mod) (Ch. 15) the conscious application of operant learning principles in organizations for the purpose of controlling behavior.

Paired comparisons (Ch. 7) a rating method that requires raters to compare each employee within the group to every other employee, and to determine who is the better worker on a specific factor.

Panel interview (Ch. 5) an interview which is conducted by a panel, board, or group of interviewers using a patterned or structured format.

Parallel or equivalent forms reliability (Ch. 5) involves the administration of two comparable tests to the same group of people, and subsequently comparing their scores.

Pattern bargaining (Ch. 14) occurs when a union, which represents the majority of workers in a particular industry, attempts to establish a contract model through negotiations with a target company.

Patterned interview (Ch. 5) See *Structured interview.*

Peer reviews (Ch. 8) a method of handling grievances using committees composed of equal numbers of worker and management representatives who conduct hearings and issue the final ruling on all employee grievances.

Performance appraisal (Ch. 7) the formal process of providing workers with diagnostic feedback (positive and negative knowledge of results) about their job performance.

Permanent standards (Ch. 12) new and revised interim standards usually based on NIOSH research or suggestions made by interested parties, such as employers, employees, or union groups.

Permissive bargaining issues (Ch. 14) those items raised for bargaining which neither party is obligated by law to consider.

Per se violation (Ch. 2) occurs when an employer uses an employment practice which overtly discriminates against one of the protected groupings.

Personality tests (Ch. 5) measures which assess the underlying psychological constructs which determine how individuals will behaviorally respond to social situations.

Person analysis (Ch. 6) concentrates on identifying the strengths and weaknesses specific to individual workers.

Personnel generalists (Ch. 1) human resource professionals who have a broad-based knowledge of all personnel activities and some detailed knowledge of certain human resource areas.

Personnel specialists (Ch. 1) human resource professionals who are narrowly focused and have in-depth expertise in a particular area of personnel administration.

Picketing (Ch. 14) union members walk around the employer's place of business, usually carrying printed signs, in the hopes of stopping others from entering the organization.

Piecework plan (Ch. 10) an incentive payment system which provides workers with a set amount of reward for each unit of output produced.

Point method (Ch. 9) a job evaluation method which requires compensable factors to be identified, described in terms of subfactors, and assigned point values based on their relative worth. Subsequently, each job is evaluated in terms of how many of the factors it possesses; it is assigned the corresponding point values; and it is slotted into a pay scale based on the total amount of points received.

Portability (Ch. 11) the ability of employers to transfer accrued pension benefits from one plan to another.

Position analysis questionnaire (PAQ) (Ch. 3) a structured questionnaire, consisting of 194 items, which quantitatively samples worker-oriented job elements. The job elements include: information input, mental processes, work output, relationships with other persons, job context, and other job characteristics.

Positive discipline (Ch. 8) a discipline approach designed to foster future positive behaviors by emphasizing positive steps to be taken rather than by administering punitive actions.

Positive reinforcement (Ch. 15) the use of desirable rewards to motivate individuals to perform appropriately.

Positive transfer of training (Ch. 6) a state of affairs which exists when the material learned in the training session is directly applicable to the work environment.

Power test (Ch. 5) a test designed so that correct answers are solely dependent on knowledge and ability irrespective of the amount of time allotted.

Predicted validity (Ch. 5) a criterion-related validity in which the predictor and criterion data are collected during different time periods.

Predictor (Ch. 5) a measure, such as a test or an interview.

Preferred provider organizations (PPOs) (Ch. 11) benefit plans contracted directly by employers and health-care providers for medical services at a reduced fee that is not prepaid.

Prejudging (Ch. 5) the tendency to draw conclusions concerning candidates before all the available information has been collected.

Prima facie violation (Ch. 2) a discrimination violation that occurs when it is demonstrated that ostensibly neutral employment practices have the effect of adversely impacting a protected class.

Private information (Ch. 5) consists of personal knowledge which individuals chose to keep secret from others.

Profit sharing (Ch. 10) any method or procedure which employers use to pay additional wages to employees, over and above their regular pay, based on the profitability of the organization.

Programmed instruction (PI) (Ch. 6) a self-taught, self-paced learning system in which material is presented to trainees via a series of graduated steps in written form or by learning machines.

Progressive discipline (Ch. 8) a discipline approach that involves identifying behaviors for which discipline will be applied and establishing a progressive list of punishments to be administered based on the severity of the offense and its frequency of occurrence.

Prohibited bargaining issues (Ch. 14) those items for which employers and unions are forbidden to collectively bargain.

Protected class (Ch. 2) those categories of individuals identified by Title VII and its subsequent amendments as being entitled to protection from discrimination. They include people of minority races, women, the aged, and those with physical disabilities.

Public information (Ch. 5) consists of facts about individuals which can readily be obtained by anyone.

Punishment (Ch. 15) the administration of aversive stimuli in order to eliminate inappropriate behavior.

Qualified pension plan (Ch. 11) any pension program which meets the ERISA's standards for tax-preferred treatment.

Qualitative forecasting (Ch. 4) relies heavily on the subjective judgments of individuals regarded as experts—usually the unit managers.

Quantitative forecasting (Ch. 4) involves the use of mathematical and statistical techniques to forecast human resource needs.

Ranking method (Ch. 7, Ch. 9) a rating method which involves evaluating and ranking workers along a continuum from best to worst, without regard to how much better or worse each is from the other.

Receiver (Ch. 16) the individual or group to whom the message is directed.

Recency error (Ch. 7) the tendency to evaluate employees based on their most recent or current actions rather than on their behaviors over the entire evaluation period.

Recruitment (Ch. 4) the process of actively identifying potentially qualified employees and encouraging them to apply for positions in the organization.

Reference checks (Ch. 5) a process undertaken to gather information about an applicant's past work history, educational background, and social behaviors, from people with whom the applicant has previously been associated.

Reflection (Ch. 8) a technique used by counselors in which they reiterate the employee's expressed feelings using different words or phrases.

Reliability (Ch. 5) refers to the degree to which instruments consistently measure what they intend to measure.

Repeated violation (Ch. 12) exists when a second citation is issued by OSHA for a previously abated violation.

Replacement charts (Ch. 4) visual displays of the positions in an organization, the incumbents, and their potential replacements.

Restatement (Ch. 8) a clarification technique used by counselors in which the counselee's words are restated by the counselor.

Right-to-work laws (Ch. 13) statutes passed by states that outlaw any contract provision requiring union membership as a condition of employment.

Role ambiguity (Ch. 12) exists whenever job incumbents experience confusion about the behaviors expected of them on the job.

Role conflict (Ch. 12) occurs whenever job incumbents are confronted with two or more conflicting job roles.

Role playing (Ch. 6) a method of training portraying real work situations in which trainees have the opportunity to analyze a situation or problem from the supervisory and subordinate positions.

Rucker plan (Ch. 10) an incentive plan which calculates the economic productivity index by dividing the value added by labor's efforts (SVOP minus costs of materials, supplies, and services) by the labor costs.

Salary reduction plan—401(k) plan (Ch. 11) a retirement savings program which allows employees the opportunity to contribute to the plan through payroll deductions.

Scanlon plan (Ch. 10) a cost-reduction gainsharing plan by which all participants are rewarded, usually monthly, based on a ratio formula of labor costs to sales value of production.

Selection (Ch. 5) a process that identifies and matches job applicant qualifications to position requirements in order to choose the most competent candidate.

Selection ratio (Ch. 5) the proportion of candidates who are hired in relation to the amount of candidates in the available applicant pool.

Semantics (Ch. 16) the study of meaning in language.

Semi-structured interview (Ch. 5) an interview characterized by the use of prepared standard interview questions combined with unprepared questions asked at the interviewer's discretion.

Sensitivity training (Ch. 6) a training program in which trainees meet for several days in an off-site environment and engage in group exercises designed to help them understand their perceptions of one another.

Serious violation (Ch. 12) an OSHA violation in which substantial probability exists that death or serious injury could result from the violation and that the employer knew or should have been aware of the infraction.

Sexual harassment (Ch. 2) unwelcome sexual advances, requests for sexual favors, and other verbal or physical conduct of a sexual nature constitute sexual harassment when (1) submission to such conduct is made either explicitly or implicitly a term or condition of an individual's employment; (2) submission to or rejection of such conduct by an individual is used as the basis for employment decisions affecting that individual; or (3) such conduct has the purpose or effect of unreasonably interfering with an individual's work performance or creating an intimidating, hostile, or offensive working environment.

Skills inventories (Ch. 4) current listings of such employee's skills, abilities, capabilities, qualifications, talents, educational level, and training.

Social secretaries (Ch. 1) See *Welfare secretaries.*

Source (Ch. 16) sender or communicator who originates the message.

Speed test (Ch. 5) a test purposely constructed with an abundance of easy items and a time limit which prohibits anyone from completing the entire test.

Split-half reliability (Ch. 5) involves dividing the test into two halves and treating each half as a separate test.

Staff managers (Ch. 1) managers who are authorized to assist and counsel line managers in obtaining the organization's objectives.

Standard-hour plan (Ch. 10) a payment system which provides workers with a set amount of money for jobs based on the average amount of time units required to complete the job.

Strategic planning (Ch. 4) the process of developing long-term organizational objectives and deciding on the methods and processes by which these goals will be reached.

Stress (Ch. 12) the physiological and psychological reactions which people exhibit in response to environmental events called *stressors*.

Stress interview (Ch. 5) is characterized by belittling and chastising interviewees for the sole purpose of observing their behavior under stressful conditions.

Strictness error (Ch. 7) the tendency for raters to judge all ratees lower than acceptable standards.

Strike (Ch. 14) the stoppage of work by employees.

Structured interview (Ch. 5) the use of standard predeveloped questions and a prepared interview format for questioning candidates.

Substance abuse (Ch. 12) the continued use of alcohol or drugs without sufficient medical grounds, resulting in a psychological and/or physical dependency and socially unacceptable behavior.

Synthetic validity (Ch. 5) involves identifying jobs with common elements and validating selection tools for these common dimensions.

Task analysis (Ch. 6) a process undertaken to determine the knowledge, skills, and abilities (KSAs) necessary to complete the various tasks involved in a total job.

Test-retest reliability (Ch. 5) involves administering a single instrument to the same group of people on separate occasions and comparing the scores.

Time and motion studies (Ch. 3) determine the best way to accomplish a job by observing the tasks involved and the amount of time necessary to complete each task.

Tort (Ch. 8) a civil harm for which the injured party is given some form of compensation.

Training (Ch. 6) entails the use of prepared programs which reinforce employees' existing competencies or facilitate the acquisition of new knowledge, skills, and abilities in the interest of improving job performance.

Transfer of training (Ch. 6) refers to the degree of information learned in the training sessions that is directly used in the work environment. This may result in positive, negative, or no transfer.

Trouble shooters (Ch. 16) written complaint instruments initiated by workers after all other attempts at alleviating problems have failed.

Turnover (Ch. 17) the voluntary movement of workers in and out of organizations.

Type A personality (Ch. 12) a personality type characterized by behaviors such as impatience and competitiveness. Highly dependent on environmental stimuli for catalysts.

Type B personality (Ch. 12) a personality type characterized by behaviors such as calmness and logical analysis of problems.

Unfair labor practice strike (Ch. 14) a work stoppage designed to protest employer actions which have been determined to be in violation of the National Labor Relations Act.

Union raiding (Ch. 13) the practice in which one union entices members of another union to join its ranks and to allow it to negotiate collective bargaining agreements on their behalf.

Union shop (Ch. 13) a labor contract provision that does not require union membership prior to initial hiring, but does require membership after a specified time period, usually thirty days, for continued employment.

Unstructured interview (Ch. 5) the use of nonprepared questions, formulated during the course of the interview at the discretion of the interviewer, to probe relevant areas.

Upward communication (Ch. 16) an organizational communication channel involving the transmission of messages from subordinate to superior.

Valence (Ch. 15) the positive or negative value individuals place on work outcomes based on preferences they believe will provide them with either satisfaction or dissatisfaction.

Validity (Ch. 5) the degree to which an evaluation technique truly measures what it is supposed to measure.

Variable working hours (Ch. 3) exist when workers are free to choose hours irrespective of core time, provided they contract a set number of hours with their supervisors.

Vestibule school (Ch. 6) an off-site environment used for training which approximates the actual workplace.

Vesting (Ch. 11) employees are vested when they are entitled to their accrued benefits regardless of whether they are currently eligible to collect their pensions or are still employed by the employer when they retire.

Voluntary benefits (Ch. 11) benefits provided by employers in addition to those required by government regulations.

Wage compression (Ch. 10) a continual shrinkage between the pay levels of highly valued jobs and those perceived as having less importance in the organization.

Wage surveys (Ch. 9) studies conducted by organizations, consultants, or other professional groups in order to determine the compensation paid by employers within the same geographic area or occupational grouping.

Weighted application blanks (Ch. 5) written forms completed by candidates in which each item is weighted and scored based on its importance as a determinant of job success.

Welfare secretaries (Ch. 1) individuals employed by organizations during the early part of the twentieth century for the purpose of assisting workers in improving their work environment and personal lives.

Wildcat strike (Ch. 14) a work stoppage instigated by a group of workers which is not sanctioned by the union.

Willful violation (Ch. 12) an OSHA violation made knowingly by employers, or because of a lack of reasonable effort to correct hazardous conditions.

Work sample tests (Ch. 5) measures designed to sample existing job skills by requiring the completion of actual job tasks.

Subject Index

Y

Name Index

Supplementary References

Arvey, Richard D. and Robert H. Faley, *Fairness in Selecting Employees* (Reading, Mass: Addison-Wesley Publishing Company, 1988): 71–79. (Demonstrating Disparate Impact)

Dilts, David A. and Clarence R. Deitsch, *Labor Relations* (NY: Macmillan Publishing Company, Inc., 1983): 93–102. (Union Structure)

Hall, Francine S. and Maryann H. Albrecht, *The Management of Affirmative Action* (Santa Monica, CA: Goodyear Publishing Company, Inc., 1979): 27–28. (Affirmative Action)

Henderson, Richard, *Performance Appraisal: Theory to Practice* (Reston, VA: Reston Publishing Company, 1980): 172–173. (Committee and Immediate Supervisory Appraisers)

Holley, William H. and Kenneth M. Jennings, *Personnel/Human Resource Management: Contributions and Activities*, Second Edition (Chicago, IL: The Dryden Press, 1987): 176–186, 347–348. (Recruiting; Job Posting and Bidding; Private Employment Agencies; College Recruiting; Comparable Worth)

Ivancevich, John M. and William F. Glueck, *Foundations of Personnel/Human Resource Management*, Third Edition (Plano, TX: Business Publications, Inc., 1986): 698. (Type A and Type B Personalities)

Ivancevich, John M. and Michael T. Matteson, *Stress and Work: A Managerial Perspective* (Glenview, IL: Scott, Foresman & Company, 1980). (Stress Management)

Peterson, Dan, *The OSHA Compliance Manual* (NY: McGraw-Hill, Inc., 1979). (OSHA)

Scarpello, Vida G. and James Ledvinka, *Personnel/Human Resource Management: Environments and Functions* (Boston, Mass: PWS-KENT Publishing Company, Inc., 1988): 1–16, 197–207, 212–249, 689–691. (Introduction; Work Scheduling; Forecasting; Positive Discipline; Job Design Approaches)

Sherman, Arthur W., Jr., George W. Bohlander and Herbert J. Chruden, *Managing Human Resources*, Eighth Edition (Cincinnati, OH: Southwestern Publishing Company, 1988): 460–461. (Open-Door, Peer, and Ombudsman Appeal Systems)

Sovereign, Kenneth L., *Personnel Law*, Second Edition (Englewood Cliffs, NJ: Prentice-Hall, Inc., 1989): 168–205. (Employment-at-Will; Constructive Discharge; Unjust Discharge)